# The Lord's Work

# The Lord's Work

A History of the Catholic Apostolic Church

TIM GRASS

☙PICKWICK *Publications* · Eugene, Oregon

THE LORD'S WORK
A History of the Catholic Apostolic Church

Copyright © 2017 Tim Grass. All rights reserved. Except for brief quotations in critical publications or reviews, no part of this book may be reproduced in any manner without prior written permission from the publisher. Write: Permissions, Wipf and Stock Publishers, 199 W. 8th Ave., Suite 3, Eugene, OR 97401.

Pickwick Publications
An Imprint of Wipf and Stock Publishers
199 W. 8th Ave., Suite 3
Eugene, OR 97401

www.wipfandstock.com

PAPERBACK ISBN: 978-1-4982-9399-0
HARDCOVER ISBN: 978-1-4982-9401-0
EBOOK ISBN: 978-1-4982-9400-3

*Cataloguing-in-Publication data:*

Names: Grass, Tim.

Title: The Lord's work : a history of the Catholic Apostolic Church / Tim Grass.

Description: Eugene, OR: Pickwick Publications, 2017 | Includes bibliographical references and index.

Identifiers: ISBN 978-1-4982-9399-0 (paperback) | ISBN 978-1-4982-9401-0 (hardcover) | ISBN 978-1-4982-9400-3 (ebook)

Subjects: LCSH: Catholic Apostolic Church—History | Catholic Apostolic Church—Great Britain—History | Catholic Apostolic Church—Doctrines | Catholic Apostolic Church—Biography | Catholic Apostolic Church—Clergy | Irving, Edward, 1792–1834

Classification: BX6565 G73 2017 (paperback) | BX6565 (ebook)

Manufactured in the U.S.A. 10/16/17

# Contents

*Tables and Diagrams* | ix
*Acknowledgements* | xi
*Abbreviations* | xiii

**1** Introduction | 1
  Scope | 2
  Sources | 4
  Studies | 8

### Part I: 1830–35: The Church before Apostles

**2** A New Movement Emerges | 13
  Edward Irving and the Restoration of the Charismata | 14
  Albury and London: Two Charismatic Church Orders | 20
  The Movement Spreads | 28
  The Appearance of the Twelve Apostles | 31
  The Council of Zion | 35
  A Parting of the Ways | 39

### Part II: 1835–1901: The Church under Apostles

**3** The New Church Takes Shape (1835–39) | 43
  A Year's Retreat | 43
  The Testimonies | 45
  Gathering Gold | 50

**4** A Succession of Challenges (1840–54) | 56
  Assertion of Apostolic Authority | 56
  The Introduction of Liturgy and Vestments | 61
  A Sense of Lassitude | 65
  Renewed Growth | 69
  Attempts to Reclaim Dalton and Mackenzie | 70

**5** Division and Recovery (1855–68) | 73

**6** Expansion I: Survey | 83
   The Overall Picture | 84
   The Tribes | 88

**7** Expansion II: Strategy | 117
   Catholic Apostolics and the Wider Church | 117
   Outreach Strategies | 122
   Membership | 132
   Pastoral Care | 137
   The Care of Children | 145
   Withdrawal of the Apostles | 149

**8** Catholic Apostolic Polity | 153
   What Made a Church a Church? | 153
   The Church's Ministry | 155
   Financial Arrangements | 186

**9** Catholic Apostolic Liturgical Development | 191
   The Historical Development of the Liturgy | 191
   The Pattern of Worship | 200
   What Had Happened to the Charismata? | 208

## Part III: 1901 Onwards: The Church after Apostles

**10** The Church under Coadjutors (1901–29) | 217
   Prophetic Forewarning of What Would Happen | 219
   The Work of the Coadjutors | 221
   The Cessation of Ordinations | 226
   A Time of Silence | 228
   A Time of Humiliation | 235
   Liturgical Change | 238
   Catholic Apostolics and the Wider Church | 242

**11** The Church under Angels (1929–60) | 248
   The 'Covering of the Altar' | 248
   The Cessation of Prophecy | 251
   Closure of Churches and Disposal of Buildings | 251
   Maintaining a Sense of Identity | 261

**12** Catholic Apostolics and Anglicans after 1901 | 263
   Developing Contacts in Britain | 264
   Catholic Apostolics and Anglican Chaplaincies Abroad | 275
   Perplexity in the Parish | 284

**13** The Church under Priests (1960–71)  |  287

**14** The Church Contracts  |  295
    The Overall Picture  |  295
    Catholic Apostolic Internationalism and Two World Wars  |  298
    The Tribes  |  304

**15** Vestiges of a Church (1971 onwards)  |  315
    The Catholic Apostolic Church Today  |  315
    Rediscovery of the Catholic Apostolic Church  |  321
    Conclusion  |  322

*Appendix: Leading Ministers in the Church*  |  327

*Select Bibliography*  |  331

*Index*  |  359

# Tables and Diagrams

Table 6.1: Ratio of Sealings to Ministers | 85

Table 6.2a: Numbers of Congregations, Europe | 86

Table 6.2b: Numbers of Congregations, English-speaking World | 87

Table 6.3: Numbers of Congregations founded in Britain, by Decade | 87

Table 6.4: The Seven Churches | 89

Table 7.1: Membership Statistics for West Yorkshire Churches | 143

Diagram 8.1 The Local Congregation | 154

Table 8.1 The Fourfold Ministry | 156

Diagram 8.2 The Universal Church | 158

Table 14.1a: Numbers of Congregations, Europe | 296

Table 14.1b: Numbers of Congregations, English-speaking World | 296

# Acknowledgements

WITH GRATITUDE, I wish to acknowledge the help received from many sources. Friends inside and outside the Catholic Apostolic Church have kindly given hospitality and allowed me to consult material in their hands. Some would not wish to be named, and therefore all are anonymous; of course, statements for which personal information is the source (and which therefore lack footnote references) should be treated with the caution appropriate to all oral history. The Drummond Family Papers held in the archives at Alnwick Castle are cited by kind permission of His Grace the Duke of Northumberland. I would also like to express thanks to express thanks to the staff at the British Orthodox Church, the Borthwick Institute for Archives, the Cadbury Research Library, Lambeth Palace Library, West Yorkshire Archives Service, and all the other archives from which material appears in the bibliography, for their assistance and for facilitating access to archive material.

Edwin Diersmann and Manfred Henke kindly read drafts of some chapters and offered valuable comment. Some material in chapters 2 to 6 first appeared in my PhD thesis, but is now much modified and extended.

Finally, my thanks to Abba Seraphim of the British Orthodox Church for permission to reproduce George F. Nye's painting of a Catholic Apostolic liturgy as the cover illustration, and to the photographer, Colin Crisford, for such a superb reproduction. It depicts the Edinburgh congregation at worship in 1875, the liturgy having reached the point at which the celebrant prays, 'Brethren, pray that our sacrifice may be acceptable to God the Father Almighty, through our Lord Jesus Christ.'

# Abbreviations

| | |
|---|---|
| AC | Albury Circulars[1] |
| AD | 'Apostles' Determinations'[2] |
| AR | 'Apostles' Reports' (to 1878) / 'Annual Reports' (from 1879, except 1882, 'Apostle's Record')[3] |
| BIA | Borthwick Institute for Archives, University of York |
| BL | British Library, London |
| BM | Bishops' Meetings |
| BOC | British Orthodox Church, London |
| CAC | Catholic Apostolic Church |
| CRL | Cadbury Research Library, University of Birmingham |
| CUL | Cambridge University Library |
| DEA | Department of Ecumenical Affairs, Lambeth Palace |
| DFP | Drummond Family Papers, in the Archives of the Duke of Northumberland, Alnwick Castle |
| *fl.* | *floruit* (active) |
| *JEH* | *Journal of Ecclesiastical History* |
| LPL | Lambeth Palace Library, London |
| MC | Minutes of Conference[4] |
| *MW* | *Morning Watch* |
| NAK | Neuapostolische Kirche |
| NAS | National Archive of Scotland, Edinburgh |

1. WYAS, 53D95/5/7 (1901–10); others in the Archiv der NAK; some also in the Cadbury Research Library.
2. WYAS, 53D95/5/2.
3. WYAS, 53D95/4/1–3 (1875–1900); BOC (1853, 1870, 1874).
4. Archiv der NAK (1854–73); WYAS, 53D95/3/3, 5 (1874–1912).

*Abbreviations*

NLS    National Library of Scotland, Edinburgh
NC     Notes of Conference[5]
ODNB   *Oxford Dictionary of National Biography*
PM     *Pastorale Mitteilungen*[6]
Record *Angels' Record*[7]
TNA    The National Archives, Kew
WYAS   West Yorkshire Archives Service, Bradford

---

5. Archiv der NAK (1850–54).
6. Archiv der NAK.
7. WYAS, 53D95/1/1–26; some issues in the Cadbury Research Library.

# 1

# Introduction

THE CATHOLIC APOSTOLIC CHURCH has fascinated many who have encountered it, whether by worshipping in or visiting one of its buildings, by reading the works of its ministers, or by meeting former members. Its reserve makes its attraction more compelling, and for some there is the thrill of acquiring hidden knowledge as they learn about a movement which made breath-taking claims concerning its place in the divine purposes of salvation and yet was content to die out without making attempts to perpetuate itself. The Church repeatedly defies attempts to categorize it. Whilst not to be confused with Roman Catholicism, and indeed critiquing that Church for its perceived sectarianism, it is hard to view it in the same light as Protestant dissent. In England it has enriched Anglicanism in various ways, but it was often strongly critical of the Church of England. Believing strongly in the establishment of the Christian religion, it nevertheless relied on the disciplined and voluntary commitment of its members in terms of everything from money to ministry, and received nothing from the state, whether in Britain or anywhere else.

Not surprisingly, it has often been misunderstood, and written off as a fringe sect. To do so says more about the critic than it does about the Church. If belief in the imminence of the Second Advent is seen as odd or 'weird,' then let us remember that studying biblical prophecy was a mainstream intellectual pursuit at the time this movement appeared. If its liturgy is seen as eccentric, we need only point out that the Church was the formative milieu for one of the foremost English-speaking liturgical scholars, Bishop Kenneth Stevenson (1949–2011), who had a family background within the movement's Edinburgh church and relatives in its Danish congregations.[1] Perhaps the most difficult aspect of its faith and practice for non-members to accept is, as it has always been, the claim that God had restored apostles to the Christian

---

1. After his death, his extensive collection of Catholic Apostolic material was deposited at Lambeth Palace Library; see the guide at: http://www.lambethpalacelibrary.org/catholicapostolic. The painting reproduced on the cover of this book (now in private hands) was also his.

Church. Yet plenty of groups attracting serious scholarly attention have made stranger claims, and the Catholic Apostolic Church has always been scrupulously orthodox in upholding the three ancient creeds affirmed by other Western Churches.

What, in a nutshell, was its message? It claimed (i) that the Second Coming of Christ was imminent; (ii) that the Christian Church was woefully ill-prepared for the events believed to be associated with that great day and ripe (along with the nations of Christendom) for divine judgment; and (iii) that God in his mercy had restored the office of apostle to the Church, giving twelve apostles to perfect it at the end of the age as he had given twelve to found it at the beginning. On the strength of these convictions, the Catholic Apostolic Church, led by its apostles, bore witness to the heads of Church and state, to clergy, and to all Christian people, calling on them to accept its message as the answer to the shortcomings of contemporary Churches of which many were partly aware, and as the only way to safety in the face of impending judgment and tribulation.

## SCOPE

This book seeks to offer a connected history of the movement from its origins to the present day. As such, it focuses on the narrative itself rather than any particular interpretation of it, although it will doubtless provide grist to the interpreters' mills. All the same, there are recurrent themes that have emerged. One concerns its national character, another its social class, and a third the development and then dismantling of the Church's leadership structures. Let me comment briefly on each of these in turn.

The Catholic Apostolic Church has usually been seen as essentially a British movement, because the apostles who led it were British; but by the end of the nineteenth century it was almost as much a German movement. English-language writers have not shown sufficient awareness of this. I suggest that it might more accurately be described as 'Anglo-German.' Some of the movement's best theological writing came from the German-speaking world; many of the ministers at higher levels came from Germany; and in recent decades the German congregations have frequently chosen to continue their separate existence whereas British churches have virtually all closed. The movement's headquarters may have been in the Surrey village of Albury, but its center of gravity shifted towards North Germany. Interestingly, prophecy during the early twentieth century indicated that this was becoming the case.[2]

Sometimes regarded as an upper-class movement, the Catholic Apostolic Church proved surprisingly appealing to the poor and working classes. Even the congregation at Gordon Square in London, which numbered many aristocrats and gentry among its adherents and which has therefore skewed perceptions of the movement as a whole, had plenty of the poorer classes within its orbit. The movement did not engage in

---

2. Davson, *Sermons*, 92, saw the center as located after 1901 in Germany, Holland, and Denmark.

the sustained social outreach of the Salvation Army or the city missions, but its message proved attractive to industrial working-class converts in 1830s Scotland, 1850s Germany, and 1880s England, if not always for the same reasons. Social unrest, which made its offer of a place of refuge in the face of coming judgments the more appealing, was present in some contexts, but not all. The opportunity of 'bettering oneself' in becoming a recognized minister was a factor in some cases, but this was not much of an issue earlier in its history.

Works on the Catholic Apostolic Church often give the impression that its structures emerged, if not fully formed, yet much more formed than was the case. There was a degree of fluidity about how things were done, and significant changes to ministerial structures, which have not always been noted. Internal histories would admit this to some extent, but the details have to be pieced together from a range of sources, and it is impossible to offer a comprehensive account of this process. As for the dismantling of those structures after the last apostle's death in 1901, that has received more adequate discussion, but I want to highlight the paradox that, for a movement which placed such emphasis on ordinances (men in office) as channels of divine blessing and on observance of due order, the Catholic Apostolic Church since 1971 has been a lay Church,[3] led by men with no official title beyond that of underdeacon or lay assistant, and facing the challenge of reconciling this reality with its belief in the necessity of the ministrations in word and sacrament of the ordained.

Inevitably my primary focus is on work in Britain. This is partly because the apostles and many of their ministers resided in England, but also because it has not been possible to visit archives in various countries which hold relevant material. Without the assistance of Edwin Diersmann and Manfred Henke, it would not have been possible to draw on as many German sources as have been used. However, this limitation is not quite the problem that it might be for other denominations, since the Catholic Apostolic Church sought to achieve a high degree of homogeneity in its worship and polity.

The narrative follows a chronological approach, but several thematic chapters focus on the period from 1868 to 1901. This is because the Church reached the apogee of its development at that period, and because a coherent discussion was felt desirable of such themes as outreach, pastoral care, liturgy and worship, and response to contemporary religious and intellectual developments. It tries to go beyond the précis of internal narratives (valuable though they are) which has often been the basis of previous histories, giving full weight to a range of manuscript and online sources now accessible and alert to the possibility that internal works sometimes glossed over some of the problems which arose. Lack of space has, however, precluded coverage of the movement's distinctive theology and in particular its eschatology, its social thought, its handling of gender issues, its reaction to contemporary intellectual challenges

---

3. Schröter, *Die Katholisch-apostolischen Gemeinden*, 196.

(especially during the mid-nineteenth century), and its response to the assessments and allegations of its critics.

My presentation should not be treated as definitive for four reasons. The first is the sheer volume of material now known to be accessible to researchers (as can be seen from the bibliography), not all of which I have been able to read. The second, paradoxically, is that there remain significant lacunae in this material; as a result, the chapters dealing with the twentieth century are sometimes more anecdotal than might be wished. The third is that there are various ways of telling this story: for instance, one might approach the Church's history through the lens of its developing eschatological understanding. The fourth, as noted above, is that I have not been able to research developments outside the United Kingdom to the same extent. What follows, then, is selective, and does not replace older works, but it may indicate where future research could profitably focus.

## SOURCES

In his short biography of Edward Irving, H. C. Whitley (who grew up in the Edinburgh church) commented: 'there are many papers and documents in the possession of the various churches which still have to be examined by the student and historian. Only when these have been fully and carefully examined can the full story of the Catholic Apostolic Church be told.'[4] However, most such material is inaccessible. Whilst members have often complained that those writing about the movement tend to give opinions rather than facts, the difficulty of obtaining literature has made this almost inevitable. The Catholic Apostolic Church is known for its reserve towards outsiders wishing to undertake historical investigation.[5] This is not due to a disparagement of historiography per se (from the beginning members were producing historiographical literature, most for the edification of members but some for outsiders), but to disapproval of its history being written by persons who cannot be expected to grasp the movement's significance as 'the Lord's work' (a preferred descriptive phrase for the movement). Members believe that insofar as the Catholic Apostolic Church represents a work of God that is *sui generis*, it is incomprehensible to those who do not accept its divine origin, and to study it may even be dangerous for them by placing them in the position of rejecting God's message through it. Since Christendom is itself under divine judgment, it is in no position to pass judgment upon a divine work.[6] During the 1870s, the high Anglican cleric and critic Edward Miller, researching for his *History and Doctrines of Irvingism*, took to heart the apostle J. B. Cardale's expressed regret that certain critics had not made the requisite inquiries before going

---

4. Whitley, *Blinded Eagle*, 85.

5. For two accounts of this by writers with roots in the movement, see Newman-Norton, *Time of Silence*, iii; Flegg, 'Gathered under Apostles,' 27–28.

6. Davenport, *Albury Apostles*, 183.

into print, and was referred by him to an angel-evangelist. The latter sought to convince Miller of the Church's standpoint, but 'answers to questions upon which I then required information were persistently refused, on the ground that it was presumptuous in any outsider, not to say an opponent, to undertake such work. . . . Warnings in a Christian spirit were given that I should commit the dreadful sin against the Holy Ghost if I continued the work.'[7] Furthermore, the belief that the movement is being divinely dismantled, an action which is a spiritual matter not subject to the normal canons and criteria of scholarly investigation, reinforces the objection to academic research.[8]

Among the records that are thus inaccessible to researchers are, of course, church registers. Those from England (and probably also Scotland and Ireland) are kept at the Church's offices in Gordon Square, apart from some significant exceptions noted below. Those from North America, Australia, and New Zealand are also likely to have been sent there. Scandinavian churches appear to have deposited their records in Copenhagen, and those from Dutch congregations may also be kept centrally. Some German congregations, however, have retained their records (a number continue to meet regularly).[9] Other records from Germany and Austria may be held at the main church in Berlin. I have no information about the fate of records from Belgium, France, Poland, Switzerland, or the Baltic republics, and those from Russian congregations may well have been destroyed.

Other categories of material are also inaccessible at present. There were records of 'remarkable events' in the life of the congregation kept by some, perhaps most churches.[10] We also lack the full records of the apostles' deliberations, personal records of ministers, correspondence between ministers (apart from some frank exchanges between Cardale and Henry Drummond in the Northumberland papers, and some early letters in the Perceval papers), and the quarterly reports and statistical returns required to be submitted by angels of English congregations, which presumably had their counterpart in other countries. It is therefore difficult to gauge the extent of internal debate, something which the Church played down because of its belief in its divine origin. Where such debate was referred to by internal writers, it seems to have been in order to highlight the remarkable way in which this was resolved and steps forward taken, as in the mid-1840s.

Yet the lack of available source material should not be overstated, certainly as far as England is concerned. I have tried to examine all holdings in the country's institutional and public repositories, and these include some records from individual congregations. And a large cache of family correspondence between the historian

---

7. Miller, *Irvingism*, 1:viii–ix.

8. Flegg, 'Gathered under Apostles,' 27–28, 95.

9. Edwin Diersmann to the author, 6 February 2016.

10. Pitcairn, *Pastoral Letter, 1 March 1864*, 9 n. (referring to such a record kept in the church vestry). An early record of events in the life of the Southampton church is in private hands.

Samuel Rawson Gardiner and his wife (Edward Irving's daughter Isabella) and her brother Martin and his wife Mary, as well as other family members, has brought to life the picture one gains from official reports and other internal works. Finally, material in Lambeth Palace Library sheds light on attempts to bring the Catholic Apostolic flocks into the Anglican fold. I have covered these fairly extensively, since the story of such negotiations has not yet been told fully.[11] Where no source is given for statements made, information has usually come through personal contact with members of the churches gathered under apostles.

We must briefly outline here the various genres of Catholic Apostolic literature (further detail is given in chapter 8). It is not possible to establish which works enjoyed any formal approval apart from those authorized for use in worship and church ordering, but as a general rule, the higher the ministerial rank of the author, the more representative and therefore authoritative their presentation of the Church is likely to be. Similarly, works often referred to by other members may be considered reliable presentations of the Church's thought. However, this does not mean that they are necessarily to be considered accurate as historical works.

The relative scarcity of official documents means that a major source has been the sermons, pastoral letters, and instructions disseminating official teaching to the rank and file. Much of this material is, like other documents, held at Gordon Square, but a number of bound volumes collecting the output of certain prominent congregations (such as the Central Church, Bishopsgate, Paddington, Liverpool, Manchester, and Edinburgh) are in the library of the British Orthodox Church. What is accessible is, I believe, a representative fraction, since evidence from it correlates extremely well with that gleaned from official circulars and personal contacts.

A major means of disseminating policy decisions was the stream of circulars to ministers and reports of councils and conferences held at Albury. Much of this material has been inaccessible: official papers belonging to ministers were, when they died, to be forwarded to the apostles.[12] But in the mid-1990s a collection was acquired by Birmingham University Library which appears to have belonged to Philip Peck (1845–1940), sometime angel at Uxbridge and also at Paddington. These circulars cover the period 1901–18. A small number of post-1901 circulars are also in the Bodleian Library; since these were purchased from Norman Priddle in 1972, they must have been deemed suitable for public consumption. The largest body of these circulars, however, forms part of a deposit of material made during the 1990s with the West Yorkshire Archives Service at Bradford: this includes a bound volume of them for the early twentieth century,[13] as well as several volumes of Notes and Minutes of Conferences of the apostle for England with his ministers or with the angels of his churches.

---

11. Part of it is outlined by Gretason in the epilogue to his MPhil thesis: 'Idea of a Church.'
12. Anon., *Book of Regulations*, §757.
13. WYAS, 53D95/5/7; index 53D95/5/8.

Expositions of Catholic Apostolic teaching for non-members appeared in the form of Testimonies or shorter addresses. There were also a large number of evangelistic tracts, along the lines of those produced by other denominations but focusing on the two areas of what might be called 'church teaching' and eschatological expectations. As for historical works, the emphasis was on the provision of narratives for the faithful, demonstrating how God had been at work in every phase of the movement's development. This tendency is evident in accounts of particular congregations, but also in works dealing with the movement as a whole, examples being E. A. Rossteuscher, *Der Aufbau der Kirche Christi auf den ursprünglichen Grundlagen* (1871; 2nd ed. 1886)[14] and F. V. Woodhouse, *Narrative of Events* (1847; 2nd ed. 1885). Woodhouse's work became the standard insider history, perhaps because of its apostolic origin, and was translated into German. However, it does not reveal the identities of the human agents mentioned. By contrast, Rossteuscher's work was not published in English. Around 1970 the Catholic Apostolic trustees considered doing so, but decided against it:

> It describes in some detail some of the early manifestations of the Holy Spirit and makes extensive quotations from words of prophecy. Many intimate details of the early days of the Lord's Work are also given as well as some of the difficulties arising from human weakness amongst members.
>
> It is considered that many of these passages are unsuitable for inclusion in a new publication and might be misunderstood if the book got into the wrong hands.[15]

Few works by members have dealt with the movement's history after the early years, apart from H. B. Copinger's invaluable unpublished chronicle 'Annals: The Lord's Work in the Nineteenth and Twentieth Centuries.'[16] Copinger, as bookseller and librarian at Gordon Square, had access to much internal material, but his coverage is by no means complete and it has not proved possible to identify all the sources to which he refers. In Danish, there is an uncompleted five-volume work by the professional librarian J. Aarsbo of Copenhagen, *Komme dit Rige* (1930–43), valuable for its coverage of the Church's establishment in Denmark before 1877. In German, a useful privately circulated typescript is W. H., *Katholisch-apostolische Gemeinden*.

---

14. I have used an unpublished English translation held by the British Library: Rossteuscher, 'Rebuilding.'

15. CRL, H. B. Evans Collection, Box 451, D. P. S. Nye to N. C. Priddle, 26 June 1970.

16. Copinger continued to update this until his death. I have used a photocopy of the version held by the Archiv der NAK Nord- und Ostdeutschland in Hamburg, which is probably the earliest and bears Copinger's address stamp. Other copies are held by the CRL, the Bodleian Library, and the BOC; the last was transcribed, edited, and further updated by Seraphim Newman-Norton (a few references for the post-1951 period are to this version). Although the foliation of the various versions differs, references should be traceable under the date of the event referenced.

*Lexikalische Sammlung von Daten und Begriffen* (1979–84). Other works provide valuable biographical information about ministers.[17]

Publications by ministers intended for internal consumption were supposed to be anonymous, although on occasion an author's name did appear on the title page, probably because the work was aimed at outsiders. This seems to have been particularly the case with works by American ministers such as W. W. Andrews and J. S. Davenport. However, the identity of the author is often known: it may be indicated by the bibliographies and catalogues compiled by Clement Boase, H. B. Copinger, and others, pencilled on the title page of a particular library copy, or given on the duplicated transcriptions circulated by Gordon Square from the 1950s. To simplify presentation, therefore, I have not followed the usual practice of using square brackets, and I have treated the privately circulated copies as published works.

## STUDIES

The last half-century has witnessed a remarkable increase of interest in Edward Irving and in the Catholic Apostolic Church, but those interested in one have rarely shown much interest in the other.[18] Irving was in effect the movement's John the Baptist, and his popularity owes much to the way in which charismatic theologians have become conscious of the need for a more solid theological undergirding to the movement and have sought precedents in Church history. The pioneer of such works was C. G. Strachan, *The Pentecostal Theology of Edward Irving* (1973). More recent research has focused on specific aspects of his theology, such as his Christology, pneumatology, and eschatology. Rarely has a serious overview been attempted, which was one reason why I wrote a biography of him, *The Lord's Watchman*.[19]

As for the Catholic Apostolic Church, there have been several academic theses on aspects of the movement, usually focusing on the period before 1901. They include those by Roberts (on initiation), and Stevenson and Mast (on the eucharist).[20] Lively has compared the Church with the Latter-Day Saints, while Lancaster has produced an in-depth study of the thought of the apostle J. B. Cardale.[21] The Anglican Rowland A. Davenport wrote *Albury Apostles* in the 1950s, although it was not published until

---

17. BL, X203/482, Newman-Norton, 'Biographical Index'; Schröter, *Bilder*; Schröter, *Die Katholisch-apostolischen Gemeinden*; Sgotzai, *Verzeichnis von Personen*; Abel, *Das Werk des Herrn* (two of many documents available for download from a website maintained by the Netzwerk Apostolische Geschichte).

18. For fuller literature surveys, including works published during the nineteenth century, see Flegg, 'Gathered under Apostles,' 1–6; Grass, 'Church's Ruin and Restoration,' 12–13; Schröter, *Die Katholisch-apostolischen Gemeinden*, 7–23.

19. For a survey of recent works on Irving, see Grass, *Lord's Watchman*, 106–7 n. 1.

20. Roberts, 'Pattern of Initiation'; Stevenson, 'Catholic Apostolic Eucharist,' and several published articles; Mast, *Eucharistic Service*.

21. Lively, 'Catholic Apostolic Church'; Lancaster, 'John Bate Cardale.'

1970; it includes a fair amount of historical material but quotations are unreferenced and the account does not go too deep. However, Davenport's work was considered by members to be the best account by an outsider.[22]

For various reasons, such as difficulty of access to sources (many of which have only come to light since 1990), little has appeared on the Church's twentieth-century history. Shaw avoided saying much out of consideration for his informants: his argument was that outsiders cannot know what has happened since 1901 unless they 'trespass on the good will or the confidence' of members.[23] The passing of time and the volume of material now in the public domain have changed the situation, but Shaw's delicacy is understandable given that his research was undertaken during the early 1930s, when memories were still quite fresh. The only work by an outsider specifically on this period, Seraphim Newman-Norton's brief *The Time of Silence: A History of the Catholic Apostolic Church 1901–1971* (1974; slightly revised 2005), has not enjoyed wide circulation, but is a valuable piece of research grounded in family roots within the movement. Two theses by Mark Gretason also carry forward their coverage into the twentieth century.[24] Perhaps the fullest twentieth-century coverage is in Johannes Albrecht Schröter's two works, *Die Katholisch-apostolischen Gemeinden in Deutschland und der 'Fall Geyer'* (2nd ed. 1998), which although it focuses on the period up to 1863 includes briefer discussion of the Church's history in Germany thereafter, and *Bilder zur Geschichte der Katholisch-apostolischen Gemeinden / Images of the History of the Catholic Apostolic Church* (2001), the first part of which offers a useful bilingual historical summary.

The most significant academic discussion of Catholic Apostolic thought, however, is that by Flegg, because of his background in the movement and his attempt to provide a balanced coverage of all the main aspects of Catholic Apostolic teaching, as well as a detailed exposition of its liturgical and theological debt to Orthodox sources (a focus which skews his presentation somewhat).[25] He concentrates on theology and has little on its history since 1901. This appears to have been deliberate, since as a member he would have had access to at least some of the material in the library at Gordon Square: in a duplicated information request circulated around 1980, he stated his intent only to quote from documents accessible to non-members.[26] This policy seems to have been followed in the published version of his research, although he also expressed gracious disagreement with the Church's policy of reserve in such matters.[27] His emphasis as an Orthodox priest on the commonality of Catholic Apostolic and

22. Flegg, 'Gathered under Apostles,' 4.
23. Shaw, *Catholic Apostolic Church*, 2; this was the published version of his 1935 Edinburgh PhD thesis.
24. Gretason, 'Authority, Provisionality and Process'; Gretason, 'Idea of the Church.'
25. Flegg, 'Catholic Apostolic Church,' published as 'Gathered under Apostles.'
26. Cardale family papers.
27. Flegg, 'Gathered under Apostles,' 28.

Orthodox thinking has not found universal favour among members: although some have joined Orthodox churches, many prefer to see 'the Lord's Work' as *sui generis*.

The Lutheran charismatic Larry Christenson undertook a sabbatical study of the Catholic Apostolic Church, the result being his book *A Message to the Charismatic Movement*, published in 1972 and translated into German in 1974. This contends that the Catholic Apostolic Church offers a historical perspective for evaluating the charismatic movement and, conversely, that the charismatic movement offers a new perspective for evaluating the Catholic Apostolic Church.[28] Christenson's book was one of the most theologically weighty to emerge from the early charismatic renewal, but it was largely neglected. Apart from the likelihood that some charismatic leaders would have been conditioned by their theological training to write off Irving and the Catholic Apostolic Church as an aberration, it was probably too much to expect that a movement owing much to late 1960s counter-culture, with its emphasis on personal self-fulfilment, should be attracted to the study of a Church characterized by an exceptionally finely developed sense of ecclesiastical order.

A perceptive if unsympathetic unpublished study, documenting contemporary contacts with the Church of England, came from the Anglican clergyman and spiritual director Reginald Somerset Ward, 'The Death of a Church and the Problems arising therefrom.'[29] Ward made extensive use of manuscript material and books entrusted by the duchess of Northumberland after the death of the eighth duke to the rector of Albury, Philip Gray, who had previously been Ward's curate at nearby Chiddingfold.[30] These documents included a now lost manuscript volume containing copies of ninety letters by Drummond from 1833 to 1839, as well as transcripts of early words of prophecy.

This book, the latest addition to those discussed above, has been twenty-five years in the making; it could have been as many more, but it is time to commit myself to print. I trust that it will prove a serviceable and thought-provoking introduction to the life of an often misunderstood Christian body.

---

28. Christenson, *Message*, 15–16.
29. Ward, 'Death of a Church.'
30. Morgan, *Reginald Somerset Ward*, 33.

# PART I

1830–35: The Church before Apostles

# 2

# A New Movement Emerges

THE LATE 1820S AND early 1830s were a turbulent period for Church, state, and society in Britain. Following the end of war with France in 1815, there had been economic depression and social unrest, and a conservative reaction set in. Nevertheless, pressure for change continued to mount, evident in areas as diverse as the abolition of slavery, the reform of parliament and the extension of the franchise, the emancipation of Roman Catholics, and the repeal of the Test and Corporation Acts. The established Church of England and Ireland seems to have been caught on the back foot, and tried in vain to stem the tide of reform. By contrast, within an increasingly fractured Evangelical movement a radical wing grew up, radical in theology and ecclesiology, but explicitly opposed to radicalism in politics. In such troubled times, biblical prophecy concerning the end of all things seemed immediately relevant, and a series of conference took place at Albury, Surrey, from 1826–30 to study its application to current events. Among those who gathered were some who would later figure prominently in the development of the Catholic Apostolic Church, most notably the host, Henry Drummond (1786–1860), a wealthy banker and erstwhile MP, and the Presbyterian cleric Edward Irving (1792–1834). These conferences rejected mainstream interpretations of prophecy which saw human history in terms of gradual progress and increasing dissemination of the gospel culminating in a millennium of earthly prosperity and the return of Christ. Instead, they espoused a pessimistic outlook which foretold the apostasy of the Gentile Church and the earth's subjugation under the Antichrist, from which the faithful would be rescued by Christ's return. The Albury conferees and many others were drawn to the emphasis of an Anglican clergyman, James Haldane Stewart, on prayer for the outpouring of the Holy Spirit, which was seen as the Church's only hope. Such an outlook reflected the contemporary impact of Romantic thought, with its love of the mysterious and its heightened sense of the supernatural or supra-rational.[1] A renewed emphasis on the third person of the Trinity was one factor

1. Elliott, *Edward Irving*.

driving a challenge mounted in Scotland to the theology of the Westminster Confession: several ministers who sought instead to stress the love of God and the possibility of enjoying a conscious assurance of salvation. John McLeod Campbell (1800–72) was condemned for what became known as the 'Row heresy' (he ministered in the parish of Row or Rhu, near Helensburgh in the west of Scotland), which proclaimed that God loved all sinners and not the elect alone.[2] This became fatefully conjoined with the expectation that the charismatic gifts of miracles, healings, tongues, and prophecy were to be restored to the Church. Irving would take up Campbell's ideas with enthusiasm; both men were to be deposed from the ministry of the Church of Scotland.

## EDWARD IRVING AND THE RESTORATION OF THE CHARISMATA

Edward Irving was born in Annan on 4 August 1792. Graduating from the University of Edinburgh in 1809, he became a schoolteacher, at the same time studying divinity in order to be licensed as a preacher, the first step towards ordination in the Church of Scotland. Although he found it difficult to secure a post, he served as assistant to Thomas Chalmers at St John's, Glasgow, from 1819–22, when he accepted a call to the Caledonian Chapel, Hatton Garden, London. His ministry proved popular: the chapel was crammed with eager hearers, and a larger building was opened in Regent Square in 1827.

By this time Irving was already becoming known (and suspect) for his pessimistic eschatology, and shortly after this also for his assertion that Christ at his incarnation took fallen human nature. In 1828 A. J. Scott (1805–66) came to London as Irving's assistant. Scott added a potent ingredient to Irving's theology with his claim that the spiritual gifts mentioned in 1 Corinthians 12 and Ephesians 4 had not been permanently withdrawn from the Church in this age. However, Irving was not moved to seek them until he received news in 1830 that the charismatic gifts were being manifested in and around Campbell's parish in Scotland.[3] Scott had preached from 1 Corinthians 12 on the subject of spiritual gifts in Greenock during 1829–30 and some, already influenced by Campbell's preaching on assurance and the universality of the atonement, began praying for the gifts to be restored. Among them was one Mary Campbell (no relation).[4] She reasoned that 'if Jesus as a man in my nature thus spake and thus performed mighty works by the Holy Ghost, which he even promiseth to me, then ought I in the same nature, by the same Spirit, to do likewise "the works which he did, and greater works than these"'.[5] In March 1830, she was the first to speak in tongues.[6]

---

2. Horrocks, *Laws of the Spiritual Order*; Stevenson, *God in Our Nature*.
3. Irving, 'Facts,' 756.
4. Ibid., 755.
5. Ibid., 757.
6. Ibid., 759.

Two of Scott's hearers in Greenock had been the brothers James and George Macdonald. They had come to an assurance of salvation, and found that Campbell's ministry agreed with their own understanding of assurance, the universal scope of redemption, Christ's real humanity, the premillennial Second Advent, and (later on) the intended continuance of miraculous gifts in the Church. They began prayer meetings in their home, and on being forced out of the Church of Scotland they took a chapel for gospel preaching. Regarding existing ordination as something merely human and external, they saw it as their duty to wait and pray until God should give something better.[7] Prophesying became a frequent feature of their meetings, but since the brothers refused to place any restrictions on what they regarded as the voice of God, disorder was inevitable.[8] When they were urged to go to London, where they would have been provided for, they refused, not feeling called by God to do so.[9]

The curious and the critical flocked to the area, as did those who longed for the restoration of the Church's primitive endowments. Among the visitors were John Bate Cardale (1802–77), his wife, and his sister Emily. Cardale was a London lawyer with impeccable Evangelical credentials, and he published his observations in the organ of the Albury conferees, the *Morning Watch*.[10] Emily recalled being 'struck to hear these people, when in mighty power, praying to God to have pity upon His weary heritage (His poor Church scattered and divided), utter this petition: "O Lord, send Apostles, in Thy compassion; none else can heal the schisms of Thy Church," and like expressions, and . . . "we used to say 'Apostles! what can it mean?'"'[11] Cardale and others testified in London to what they had seen, and home meetings were formed to pray for the gifts.[12] Cardale's recollection was that Irving had expressed his satisfaction as to the reality of the gifts when the party returned to London in October 1830.[13] The first manifestations in London occurred in April 1831, when Mrs. Cardale spoke in power: 'The Lord will speak to His people! The Lord hastens His coming! He comes, He comes.'[14] When their minister preached against the gifts, the Cardales sought shelter in Irving's church, becoming members in August 1832.[15]

---

7. Norton, *Memoirs*; Boase, *Supplementary Narrative*, 772.

8. Copinger, 'Annals,' 31.

9. Norton, *Memoirs*, 198; Miller, *Irvingism*, 1:58.

10. Cardale, 'Extraordinary Manifestations,' 869–73; cf. Thompson, *Brief Account*.

11. Trimen, *Rise and Progress*, 17. Trimen was in charge of the Church's records and thus had a unique degree of access to source material: Newman-Norton, 'Biographical Index,' 111.

12. Trimen, *Rise and Progress*, 19.

13. Cardale family papers, J. B. Cardale to Thomas Dowglass, 10 May 1852. This important source contains extensive historical notes and corrections to a draft by Dowglass of his *Chronicle*; although cited throughout under this date for ease of identification, it appears to be more than one letter, written on various dates, and the present arrangement of the papers (which appear incomplete) may not reflect the original(s).

14. Trimen, *Rise and Progress*, 19.

15. Ibid., 24.

Irving was now convinced that the gifts had been restored to the Church, but the Presbytery of London's investigation of his Christological writings preoccupied him until May 1831. With his theology coming under increasingly hostile scrutiny by the Church of Scotland, he agreed to the commencement of prayer meetings for its approaching General Assembly, although these came to focus on prayer for the charismatic gifts. On trial before the presbytery the following year, he recalled: 'We cried unto the Lord for apostles, prophets, evangelists, pastors and teachers, anointed with the Holy Ghost the gift of Jesus, because we saw it written in God's word that these are the appointed ordinances for the edifying of the body of Jesus.'[16]

The gifts first appeared in the Sunday services at Regent Square on 16 October 1831.[17] Uproar ensued, partly because Irving (like the Macdonalds in Scotland) believed that the gifts should not be restrained.[18] Eventually the church's trustees appealed to the presbytery, before whom Irving went on trial from 26 April 1832. While he considered the question one of doctrine—were the gifts from God?—the trustees considered it one of discipline—did such utterances contravene the trust deed's stipulation that worship was only to be conducted by those authorized by the Church of Scotland?[19] In spite of Irving's contention that such things were allowed for in the Church's First and Second Books of Discipline, judgment was given against him and his congregation were forced to find alternative accommodation.

One of those whose exercise of charismatic gifts had caused so much commotion was Robert Baxter, an Evangelical Anglican lawyer from Doncaster who was in occasional contact with Irving and his church between October 1831 and April 1832. Baxter was recognized as a greatly gifted prophet by Irving, who took up themes from Baxter's prophetic utterances as sermon subjects.[20] In Irving's opinion, '[t]he Lord hath anointed Baxter of Doncaster after another kind [i.e., in a manner unlike what had previously been seen], I think one apostolical.'[21] Baxter likewise believed that he was called to be an apostle, expecting that after forty days' waiting God would manifest his call by endowing him with the power to perform signs and wonders.[22] Irving, he prophesied, was rejected from the apostolic office on account of the Church of Scotland's rejection of bishops as 'the standing sign of the apostolic office'; instead, he was to be a prophet to his native land.[23] Baxter also prophesied that the 'spiritual apostles whom the Lord would now send forth' would be more mightily gifted than

---

16. Harding, *Trial before London Presbytery*, 24.
17. Baxter, *Irvingism*, 16–17; Trimen, *Rise and Progress*, 21.
18. NLS, Acc. 12489/1, James Simpson, Journal 9 March 1806–2 July 1832, 28 October 1831. Simpson had been an elder in Irving's congregation, and his wife Jane spoke in tongues and prophesied.
19. For details, see Harding, *Trial before London Presbytery*.
20. Baxter, *Irvingism*, 19–20.
21. Irving to M. N. Macdonald, 24 January 1832, in Oliphant, *Life*, 2:234.
22. Baxter, *Narrative*, 66, 72.
23. Baxter, *Irvingism*, 69.

even the twelve whom Jesus called.[24] But when the promised endowments did not materialize, Baxter was assailed by doubts which culminated in his recantation.[25] His defection, which he explained to Irving on the first morning of the latter's trial, caused a sensation which took years to die down; most critics drew heavily on his works, which recorded his inner experiences in detail. For their part, later Catholic Apostolic authors would devote considerable effort to rebutting some of Baxter's charges and attempting to correct what they saw as the misconceptions to which his works had given rise. Yet at the same time a number of Baxter's key themes were taken up by the nascent Church: the bestowal of a new and 'spiritual' order of ministry superseding existing ordinations, the significance of 14 July 1835 in God's purposes, the disapproval of religious societies, the denunciation of those who rejected episcopacy, the abasement of Irving, and the emergence of a new order of apostles.[26]

Another prophet, Edward O. Taplin (1800–62), played a significant role in the emergence of the new Church. He was by profession a schoolmaster, and was involved in the call of a number of the twelve restored apostles—according to Cardale, the last six to be called.[27] Moreover, as one reviewer explained, on the basis of a major internal source:

> The *Records of the Council* show that nearly all of the important developments, both of doctrine and discipline, in the Church, and very much of the mystical exposition of the Old Testament Scriptures, were due to his utterances. So influential was his position that it was allowed by a great authority, 'If there is anything wrong with Taplin, all is wrong.'[28]

Alongside Taplin were several women who spoke in tongues and prophesied, including Mary Campbell (in March 1831 she had married a young evangelist in Irving's congregation, William R. Caird, and they were awaiting prophetic direction as to where they should go abroad as missionaries)[29] and Cardale's wife and sister. One eyewitness recalled that the 'gifted persons,' as they were known, displayed a variety of styles of speech when speaking 'in the power':

> [Miss Cardale's utterances displayed] always much distress & oppression & withal excitement before she spoke, perhaps for a long time, ½ an hour or more: the first sound was generally a cry of great distress, loud & piercing & a convulsive sob, & then a few words of Scripture said rapidly in a very powerful strong voice & often repeated over & over again, or words of reproach, or intreaty or command. . . . There was something unnatural in the strength

---

24. Baxter, *Narrative*, 69–70.
25. Baxter, *Irvingism*, 46.
26. Shaw, *Catholic Apostolic Church*, 41–45.
27. Cardale to Dowglass, 10 May 1852.
28. Anon., 'History and Doctrines of Irvingism,' 34–65, at 48.
29. Caird, *Letter to Story*, 15.

> of voice for a woman. Mr. Taplin always or almost always began in a tongue, which was a succession of sounds uttered in y$^e$ <u>most rapid manner</u>. There was something peculiarly unpleasant in his manner & excitement. Mr. Drummonds daughters were said to be gifted also, & one other lady.... Mr. Cardale ... always taught like a clever well educated man; his language & manner were good. When he spoke in power as it was called, it was generally in the course of some exposition & unless I had been told before I sh$^d$ hardly have known any difference from his ordinary manner.[30]

According to Thomas Carlyle, an Edinburgh advocate who would shortly be called as an apostle, women could speak 'in the power'; this was deemed not to contravene the Pauline injunctions regarding their silence in worship, presumably because it was the Holy Ghost speaking through them.[31]

The need to discern between true and counterfeit manifestations soon became painfully pressing. One claimant to the gifts who later recanted was George Pilkington, who told his story in *The Unknown Tongues discovered to be English, Spanish, and Latin; and the Rev. Edw. Irving proved to be erroneous in attributing their Utterance to the Influence of the Holy Spirit* (1831). Around this time, Miss Hall, a governess to the children of the future apostle Spencer Perceval (MP and son of the assassinated prime minister), began to speak 'in the power'—or so it appeared. But in March 1832 it was reported to Baxter, shortly before his own defection, that:

> It has pleased the Lord in His great faithfulness completely to discover the heart of poor Mary Hall (who was during your last visit & still is remaining in my house) through a very powerful testimony from Mrs Caird & Miss Emily Cardale that the whole work of utterance in her has been entirely of the flesh. ... It is remarkable that the first utterance in public at the Morning Prayer Meeting in Mr Irving's Church was by a Miss Dixon who it has since appeared has spoken only in the flesh, & the first utterance in the public Sunday Service was by poor Mary Hall, who now tells me that her own conscience shewed her at that very time that it was but the flesh. Even when Mr Irving had all the gifted persons together, & by the command of the Spirit from Miss E. Cardale tried them all, the flesh was sufficient to enable Mary Hall to confess equally with them as she herself now acknowledges.[32]

In a written statement, Miss Hall confessed that she 'felt no nearness to God nor that peace and joy that the others describe,' but 'at meetings I have frequently begun the speaking which has been followed up by the others in a way to make Mr Irving

---

30. Pusey House, M. H., 'Narrative,' n. AA. This manuscript, which was used by the Tractarian theologian E. B. Pusey in a series of critical articles about Irvingism in *The Old Church Porch* (1854-55), is largely a condensation of the first part of Woodhouse's *Narrative of Events*, with notes added to correct what the author saw as Woodhouse's misstatements.

31. Carlyle, *Church of Christ*, 117-19.

32. Banner of Truth Trust, Baxter letters, John Tizard to Baxter, 26 March 1832.

remark how clearly it was one Spirit_ had I only followed the others I might have thought it was the flesh_ but their doing so contributed to making me think I had a gift.'[33] She was subsequently censured in front of the congregation and restored to communion, but it is not clear whether she remained a faithful member[34] or left and 'adopted a different course of life.'[35] By this time Irving was using Mary Caird and Emily Cardale to test the other 'gifted persons.'[36]

Outside London, other emerging congregations faced similar problems. In the villages around Oxford, the erstwhile Baptist minister James Hinton (brother of the Baptist leader John Howard Hinton) struggled to deal with those claiming prophetic gifts. The test usually applied—whether the spirit in an apparently gifted person was prepared to confess Jesus Christ as God manifest in flesh (1 John 4:1)—clearly was not sufficient, for he had one woman calling herself an apostle and claiming that another gifted woman was speaking by evil spirits and must be silenced. Moreover, Cardale had asserted that it was possible for an evil spirit to make the correct verbal confession.[37] In Gloucestershire, the Revd E. C. Probyn was won over to Irving's views, but the real impact in his village was produced by his twin children Julian and Juliana, who for some weeks spoke 'in the power,' their words being given the most reverent attention by their parents and others.[38] Their utterances were very negative towards existing churches: 'Be not Churchy. "The image of the Beast is the Church" we are told by the Spirit.'[39] But the utterances then took an unacceptable turn: 'At last the spirit in Julian began to shew dishonesty desiring a Servant not to pay his debts, forbidding to marry, & ordering others to do strange things, putting the servants on a level with their superiors &c. that we began to doubt & began to talk of trying the Spirits, & during prayer, the Spirit cried out "I will not be tried, if you try me you shall be chastised."'[40]

Related to this was the problem of discerning which of two incompatible individuals claiming to speak in prophecy should be deemed to be speaking from God. The 'gifted persons' had come to be regarded as a distinct group, and possessed the capability of freezing out any claimants whose utterances did not tally with their own, or who were deemed in some way unacceptable. Jane Simpson was one such. She and her husband James were active members of Irving's congregation, and she soon

33. Baxter letters, enclosed in A. G. Perceval to Baxter, 14 April 1832.

34. Archives of the Duke of Northumberland, DFP: C/13/2, undated note.

35. DFP: C/13/3, undated note.

36. Baxter, *Narrative*, 103–8, Irving to Baxter, 21 April 1832.

37. DFP: C/9/19, Irving to Drummond, 20 June 1833, reproduced in Waddington, *Diary and Letters*, 362–63; BL, Add. MS 49192, fols 4–6, James Hinton to Spencer Perceval, 10 August 1833. For more detail, see Grass, 'Restoration,' 283–97; Grass, '"Walking together",' 147–70.

38. See Stunt, '"Trying the Spirits" (1831),' 95–105; Stunt, 'Trying the Spirits,' 400–409. Both have been reprinted in Stunt, *Elusive Quest*, 69–79, 80–88.

39. LPL, Dodsworth-Drummond papers, MS 4727, 12, letter from the Hon. J. J. Strutt, [November 1831].

40. Ibid., 13, Strutt to William Dodsworth (copy), 10 November 1831.

began to speak in tongues and prophesy, encouraged by Mary Caird.[41] However, from the first Emily Cardale seems to have been suspicious of her (or so Jane recollected), and eventually they fell out. The issue of contention with the gifted persons and with Irving was that of discernment of spirits, and in particular how prophecy or prophets should be tested.[42] Jane felt she had a direct testimony from God regarding the genuineness of her gift, and hence saw no reason to submit its exercise to Irving as her minister or to the other gifted persons. Taplin's efforts to find a solution were unavailing, and Irving's threat to exercise his ministerial authority against her left her unmoved. Finally, in July 1832 she decided to visit the Macdonalds in Scotland and explain the situation.[43] Her husband provided an account (dated 4 August) of what transpired: her gift was deemed to be of God, and a prophetic utterance included a prayer that Irving would be brought down to the dust.[44] That December, Irving withdrew their membership of his church.[45] A later critic reported having come to know three families which included members who had exercised charismatic gifts in Irving's church. He claimed that their gifts had been recognized, but that their testimony against Irving's 'ruling spirit' had been rejected, and so the movement had become an exclusive sect.[46] Resolution of such problems (which the Catholic Apostolic Church itself would readily acknowledge marred the earliest days) came as the apostles began to be called, and to give the necessary leadership to unite the movement. The cost was the subordination of the prophetic gift to that leadership.

## ALBURY AND LONDON: TWO CHARISMATIC CHURCH ORDERS

From the beginning the churches were condemned in prophetic utterances as 'Babylon.'[47] Henry Drummond explained what was meant by this: 'The whole Church and all its parts, a mass of contradictions in faiths, forms, ceremonies, doctrines and hopes, is blasphemously called the one "Body of Christ" which is the dwelling of the Third Person of the Holy Trinity, while the Word of God calls the whole, Babylon, Sodom, and Egypt, calling upon us to flee out of it and to rejoice in its destruction.'[48] A Canadian writer alleged that Catholic Apostolic evangelists were proclaiming that

---

41. Acc. 12489/10, Jane Simpson, Diary for 1831, 80–83.

42. Acc. 12489/4, James Simpson, Diary for 1832–38, 25, Jane Simpson to Irving, 31 May 1832; Acc. 12489/14, John H. Simpson, Typescript work on the Simpsons, 91. For a full account of the episode, see Strachan, 'Carlyle, Irving, and the "Hysterical Women",' 17–32.

43. James Simpson, Diary for 1832–38, 4–51.

44. Acc. 12489/11, 'A Brief Account of Mr & Mrs Simpson's Visit to Portglasgow in 1832'; John H. Simpson, Typescript work on the Simpsons, 102.

45. NLS, MS 1676, 232, Irving to the Simpsons, 6 December 1832 (Wadddington, *Letters and Diary*, 325–26).

46. Innes, *Catholic and Apostolic Sect*, 17.

47. James Simpson, Journal 1806–32, 14 September 1831.

48. Drummond, letter book, fol. 10, quoted in Ward, 'Death of a Church,' 76.

*'all the Protestant Churches are Anti-Christ, and together form the mystical Babylon.'*[49] As the Church of Ireland clergyman, Protestant controversialist, and future apostle Nicholas Armstrong (1801–79) summed up, 'Babylon is a church where the Spirit of the Lord is not,' one which therefore resorted to human devices in order to maintain itself; in his view dissenters were even more deserving of the epithet than the established Church.[50] An English observer contrasted attitudes towards the Churches then with those evident later. 'The great burden of the preaching was, that the churches of the land were Babylon, idol temples, their altars the altars of false gods. The command was to come out of them & to be separate.' Until the end of 1838, none who had belonged to the Church of England were allowed to communicate in it any longer and the gifted persons used to denounce those who did so. 'Now, it is to be regretted, the case is different. Whenever separated from their own congregation, they communicate at our altar, and many indiscriminately at either.'[51]

## 'a spiritual plantation': Drummond establishes a Congregation in Albury

Opposition came from the rector of Albury, Hugh M'Neile, to Drummond's attempts to set up home prayer meetings in Albury and nearby Guildford for the restoration of the gifts, apparently because Drummond allowed laymen to pray at these meetings. M'Neile, who had preached in favour of the perpetuity of the gifts and at the final Albury Conference had proposed investigating the Scottish manifestations, then preached against the gifts: witnessing them at Irving's house, he still refused to recognize them as genuine. Drummond therefore withdrew from his parish church in July 1832, and about twenty people began meeting with him and his family.[52] In a letter to the Scottish theologian Thomas Chalmers the following month, he contrasted his experience of the Holy Spirit with the unspiritual state of the existing churches:

> God has certainly returned once more into His Church; he is about to build a spiritual temple for Himself now that He has begun to destroy the outward churches which are all apostate by having set up human standards above His word, & rejected the voice of His Spirit; all He wants is for His creatures to be clay in His hands, & let Him use them, & no longer resist the entrance of His Spirit into their hearts.[53]

---

49. Vero Catholicus, *Address*, 17.

50. Irving and Armstrong, *Expositions and Sermons*, 10. On Armstrong, see Wolffe, *Protestant Crusade*, 54 n. 103, 57–59.

51. M. H., 'Narrative,' n. F.

52. Drummond, *Narrative of Circumstances*, 5–6; Ward, 'Death of a Church,' 30. Drummond's work may have been written in response to M'Neile's condemnation.

53. New College Libary, Chalmers collection, 4.178.25, Drummond to Thomas Chalmers, 23 August 1832.

Part of the stable block at Albury Park was fitted up and registered as a place of worship.[54] The services used the Book of Common Prayer, supplemented by extempore prayer where necessary, and began with confession of the irregular status of such gatherings, meeting as they did without an ordained president.[55] Initially the group hoped that one of the deposed Scottish ministers, or the Anglican Armstrong, could become their pastor, but became convinced that instead God was preparing to raise up a 'spiritual' order of ministry. Drummond was called in prophecy as their pastor, but a prophetic utterance declared that without ordination he could not administer the sacraments. The situation was resolved on 26 December 1832, when Cardale (the first apostle to be called) ordained him as angel, thus setting up the first 'spiritual church.'[56] Cardale had apparently done nothing for two months following his call as an apostle, but seems to have been galvanized into action by the need for ministers at Albury.[57]

After Drummond's ordination, the congregation in Albury began to develop along different lines from Irving's in London.[58] Irving believed that each represented the prototype of a different facet of God's work—Albury of the new type of spiritual congregation being created from nothing, and Newman Street of the renewal of existing churches. As he wrote to Drummond early in 1833, 'Yours is a spiritual plantation, ours is a transmutation from the sensual to the spiritual form of the heavenly life.'[59] Drummond's reading of this was that the London group had first to be purged since it was not starting from nothing but was made up of believers coming out of the Babylon of apostate Christendom.[60] On 25 September 1833, Drummond became the second apostle to be called.[61]

## Irving's deposition and the setting up of the Church in London

After a summer spent worshipping in the North London Horse Bazaar in Grays Inn Road and in the open air on Britannia Fields, a more permanent location was found in Newman Street, off Oxford Street. The new building opened on 19 October 1832. Unusually for the time, all seats were free, there being no pew-rents, and so considerable

---

54. The carpenter who undertook the work alleged that 'common people [were] not allowed': Surrey Local History Centre, Zg/16, Browne, 'Albury Park and Village.'
55. Drummond, *Narrative of Circumstances*, 6.
56. Ibid., 7–9; Rossteuscher, 'Rebuilding,' 381; Trimen, *Rise and Progress*, 29–31.
57. Ward, 'Death of a Church,' 36.
58. Ibid., 37.
59. DFP: C/9/12, Irving to Drummond, 3 February 1833 (Waddington, *Diary and Letters*, 333).
60. Drummond, *Narrative of Circumstances*, 11.
61. Trimen, *Rise and Progress*, 39.

numbers of curious spectators attended the services, and at first it was deemed necessary to hold further private services for the flock, though these soon ceased.[62]

Since Babylon was doomed to destruction, it was necessary by whatever means to warn the baptized to flee from her, in line with the approach adopted by Lewis Way in his sermon to the Continental Society in 1822.[63] Irving exhorted his hearers to 'leave those houses of iniquity, the churches.'[64] Accordingly, from the summer of 1832 thirty or forty young men were sent out to preach in the open air, something which was commanded in one of Baxter's prophetic utterances. They sought conversions, but also testified to their belief in a coming spiritual ministry, which they contrasted with the spiritless ministry of the existing churches. Most of the future apostles and higher ministers engaged in this preaching.[65] However, their belligerence, coupled with a refusal to co-operate with the authorities when asked to cease causing an obstruction in the thoroughfare, brought them before the courts on a number of occasions, where they appear to have caused the magistrates some perplexity. Irving, by contrast, was never impeded, even though he drew much larger crowds; one writer suggests that this was because he was ordained and had high-class followers.[66]

Irving, however, seems to have been somewhat less hot-headed than his followers, counselling them against throwing away their liberty by persisting in preaching in the public thoroughfare.[67] He even tried (unsuccessfully) to secure permission for this preaching from the Prime Minister, Lord Melbourne, arguing that it had been expressly commanded by Christ.[68] And in April 1833 he stated that '[t]he Lord hath shown yesterday [in a prophetic utterance from Cardale] that the witness in the streets shall be no longer but by those whom He shall send forth.' He thanked those who had been preaching for their efforts but directed them to cease and called on the congregation to '[p]ray that God would speedily name the evangelists & send them forth.'[69] Within a week the first evangelists were called through prophecy and ordained, and some of them returned to this work. One was Archibald Campbell Barclay, who in October 1833 was imprisoned for refusing to stop preaching; his activity was seen as acceptable for Bethnal Green in London's East End, but not in the more respectable West End![70] Whilst open-air preaching would feature in later Catholic Apostolic outreach, it played only a minor role. In any case, in some countries it would have

62. Irving, *Exposition and Sermon, October 24, 1832*, 7–8; cf. Irving, *Exposition and Sermon, October 21, 1832*; Baxter, *Narrative*, 47.

63. Way, *Flight out of Babylon*.

64. Irving, *Scripture Reading and Exposition, 12th January 1834*, 29.

65. Baxter, *Narrative*, 37–38; Rossteuscher, 'Rebuilding,' 375–80; Trimen, *Rise and Progress*, 24.

66. Jennings, 'Archibald Campbell Barclay,' 14; cf. *The Times*, 13 April 1832, 8 May 1832.

67. Irving, *Discipline of the Church*, 7.

68. Greville, *Greville Memoirs*, 3:79, 5 September 1834.

69. St Andrews Special Collections, Flegg Collection, MS 38594, Andrew Bonar, ms notes, 25 April 1833.

70. Jennings, 'Barclay,' 13–14.

attracted unwelcome police attention. The Church's mission was to be to the religious, not to the irreligious.[71]

In spite of the setback caused by Baxter's defection, it was not long before the first apostles were called. On 28 September 1832, after Irving had preached on the Ephesians 4 ministries of apostle, prophet, evangelist, and pastor/teacher, prophecy had challenged the congregation, 'know ye not the Lord is waiting to bestow, but your unbelief hindereth.' Irving applied this to Baxter's defection:

> When the dear brother for whom we prayed, and of whom the Lord hath said that we were the cause of his stumbling through our unbelief,—when he came amongst us I felt no manner of doubt, and do not at this moment feel any doubt, that he came commissioned of the Lord with an apostolic commission, and that he would have had the power of laying on of hands like an apostle. It was our unbelief that hindered, or the Lord long ere this, would have raised up apostles, prophets, evangelists, pastors, and teachers.[72]

The generally accepted narrative within the movement has been that at a private prayer meeting on 31 October, Drummond prophesied to Cardale: 'Convey the Holy Ghost for art thou not an Apostle?' Taplin prophesied in similar vein a week later at Irving's house.[73] Any account of the Catholic Apostolic Church has to do justice to the determinative influence exercised by Cardale.[74] 'Although he would repudiate the statement, it could almost be said that the Catholic Apostolic Church was Cardale's church.'[75] To Cardale it owed much of the development of its liturgy and ministry; he was responsible for the shift of emphasis from prophetic to apostolic leadership, and the movement's consequent transformation from an early disordered state into one of the most disciplined Christian communities, expressed in such diverse ways as the personal spirituality of its membership and the legal precision of two works governing its polity and practice, *General Rubrics* (1852) and *The Book of Regulations* (1878). Arguably it was his contribution which ensured that the movement developed an Anglican rather than a Presbyterian ethos. A successful lawyer, by 1830 he was attending an Evangelical proprietary chapel, St John's, Bedford Row, in London. After his minister (Baptist W. Noel) preached against the gifts, he and his family settled among Irving's congregation. We saw that on 26 December Cardale conducted an

---

71. Drummond, *Narrative of Circumstances*, 14.

72. Irving, 'Exposition and Sermon, 28th September 1832,' 2, in Irving and Armstrong, *Expositions and Sermons*.

73. Copinger, 'Annals,' 29. Trimen, *Rise and Progress*, 28, dates it a week later. Irving had written to Baxter: 'We . . . much desire your reappearing in the midst of us with the full power of an apostle to minister the Spirit unto us by the laying on of hands': Baxter letters, Irving to Baxter, postmarked 2 March 1832, in Baxter, *Irvingism*, 22; Waddington, *Diary and Letters*, 294. For a full discussion of Cardale's call, see Henke, '175 Years ago.'

74. For a somewhat fuller account of Cardale's ministry, see Grass, 'Cardale.'

75. Lancaster, 'Cardale,' 44.

ordination at Albury in his capacity as apostle, but at this stage the understanding of what apostles actually did was still developing, and Irving in particular did not find their emergence easy to cope with.

Irving's tempestuous relationship with the Church of Scotland now culminated in his trial for heresy concerning the person of Christ before the Presbytery of Annan on 13 March 1833. When the sentence of deposition from the ministry was pronounced, Irving's friend David Dow prophesied against the court before being silenced. Irving rose to follow him out with the words, 'As many as will obey the Holy Ghost, let them depart!'—words which symbolized the way his ecclesiology had developed.[76] From strong advocacy of the role of the established Church in a nation in covenant with God, Irving had moved to the position that faithful believers must withdraw from the Babylon which was apostate Christendom.[77]

Returning to London, Irving was temporarily inhibited by prophecy from exercising ministerial functions such as administering the sacraments, in recognition of the Church of Scotland's action in deposing him, until he should receive apostolic ordination. We should not take this as indicative of anything beyond the fact that ordination was generally seen as a prerequisite for these acts; there need be no suggestion that the apostles were trying to put Irving in his place, and the fact that he was speedily re-ordained should be taken as a mark of the honor accorded to him. In response to Taplin's prophetic command that Cardale ordain Irving, he was ordained as angel (bishop over a church rather than a diocese) on 5 April, prophecy indicating that as man had taken away fleshly ordinances God would give spiritual ones.[78] Irving's ordination was a crucial moment for the movement: no longer was it a network of individual congregations, but a unified body under the leadership of 'universal' ministries—the apostles; this was the first use of apostolic authority to regulate the actions of a subordinate.[79] The same day, Taplin announced that God 'purposed giving the mystery of the candlestick in the Holy Place': a new pattern for local church order was about to be revealed.[80] On 1 May, his prophecy was fulfilled when Cardale dictated 'in the power' a letter setting this out, *The Mystery of the Golden Candlestick*.[81] This expressed a fundamental principle shaping Catholic Apostolic ecclesiology, that the regulations regarding the construction of the Mosaic Tabernacle and its furnishings typified the way in which Christian churches were to be structured. It was, in Trimen's words, 'the key which unlocked the whole of the types and services of the Law given

---

76. Harding, *Trial before Annan Presbytery*, 26.

77. Irving, *Judgment*.

78. Drummond, *Narrative of Circumstances*, 11, from a letter of Irving to David Dow, April 1833 (Waddington, *Diary and Letters*, 337–38); Woodhouse, *Narrative*, 20; cf. Andrews, *Irving*, 143.

79. Lancaster, 'Cardale,' 55.

80. Copinger, 'Annals,' 33.

81. Ibid., 35.

## Part I—1830-35: The Church before Apostles

by God to Moses.'[82] Utterances often occurred during the reading of the relevant portions of the Pentateuch. Irving shared in laying the groundwork for this, although it appears at least some of the time that he was doing so under the inspiration (or even perplexity) of the moment: 'During y^e reading of the xxi chapt. of Ex. Mr. Irving was so continually interrupted by y^e running exposition of the prophet Mr. Taplin upon it that at last he seemed to me to close the book under a feeling of knowing not how to go on. The most wonderful thing tho' was, the way in which he <u>did</u> take up & use what was so spoken, y^e words themselves scarcely conveying any ideas to the mind.'[83]

With a new church order developing, Irving had to work hard to adapt to the appearance of apostles and prophets. He continued to welcome the exercise of prophetic gifts: Rossteuscher described him as 'always full of confidence whenever he could rest upon a word of prophecy,'[84] while Baxter commented that 'all the changes which took place in Mr. Irving's views and church arrangements, were in subservience and strict obedience to these utterances.'[85] Reliance on prophetic direction proved problematic, however, and things would have been worse without Irving's strong leadership, although he was often hindered from exercising this, either by his own submission to the 'gifted persons' or by their putting him down. As one observer suggested later, 'what one prophet said, was immediately acted upon & then the next day, something else having been spoken, things were all put back again as before. . . . Mr. Irving rose one day & raising his hand said "the spirits of the prophets are subject to the prophets" to restore calmness, & prevent two trying to speak at ye same time.'[86]

Taplin proved something of a handful in this respect. In 1833, Irving wrote to Drummond: 'poor Mr Taplin seems doing every thing to provoke God to supersede him, and to cast him off. He baffles all dealings, and makes void all prayers. I am almost in despair of him. No one knows how my heart has been broken with that man.'[87] Early in 1834, while Cardale and Drummond were in Scotland, a prophecy through Taplin led to sixty evangelists being chosen, each with a 'help' or assistant. Cardale wrote to rebuke Irving and Taplin for their precipitate action, ordering them to countermand these ordinations. Irving complied, but Taplin left the church temporarily.[88] For some months in 1834-35, Taplin was at odds with the London leaders, apparently rebelling against the apostles' gradually strengthening direction of affairs.[89]

---

82. Trimen, *Rise and Progress*, 37.
83. M. H., 'Narrative,' n. C.
84. Rossteuscher, 'Rebuilding,' 508.
85. Baxter, *Irvingism*, 10.
86. M. H., 'Narrative,' n. D.
87. DFP: C/9/22, Irving to Drummond, 16 September 1833 (Waddington, *Diary and Letters*, 367-68).
88. Miller, *Irvingism*, 1:141-42.
89. DFP: C/9/50, Woodhouse to Drummond, 14 December 1834 (Waddington, *Diary and Letters*, 425).

Not until February 1835 was he restored, and that after confessing his error before the church.[90]

Irving's submission to the prophets contrasts with his uneasy relationship with the apostles. Their appearance and the consequent changes in his church's structure caught him off-balance, and one Catholic Apostolic writer described him as being surprised and distressed on learning of Cardale's call.[91] Concerning his relationship with Cardale, he wrote: 'So receive I, through an apostle, my instructions; and having received them, the apostle himself is the first man that must bow to them, and I will take good care that he doth so.'[92] In his last two letters to his flock, Irving confessed to having been impatient with apostolic government.[93] Part of the problem was that the apostles moved away from the initial belief that they could only act as such when under conscious divine inspiration. Irving told Drummond that an apostle should not act or speak in that capacity unless moved by the Spirit to do so, and it was for angels and elders to teach and see fulfilled the words of prophecy concerning offices and ordinances.[94] As he wrote to David Dow, 'Surely this is the mystery of the angel to be the rule and discerner of whatever is said and done in the flock by pastor, evangelist, prophet, or apostle.'[95] Thus, according to Rossteuscher, he found it difficult once Cardale began to perform apostolic functions without waiting for inspiration.[96]

We saw that Baxter had declared that Irving was rejected as an apostle in token of the Church of Scotland's rejection of apostolic government; instead he was to be a mighty prophet to his native land.[97] This expectation may have influenced his decision, even though seriously ill, to return to Scotland and preach. After a lengthy journey, during which his condition continued to worsen, he reached Glasgow, where in the autumn of 1834 he was speaking each Sunday to a small group in the Lyceum Rooms, where McLeod Campbell had been preaching since the beginning of the previous year.[98] Irving continued to decline, and on 7 December 1834 'he sent for Mr. W. saying that he wished to confess his sin in resisting the bringing out of the apostleship, & his jealousy of those who were his children, lest they should lead the flock astray. Having received absolution he almost immediately passed away!'[99] A few days later,

90. Rossteuscher, 'Rebuilding,' 545. One critic claimed that as Taplin had given up his school, he was driven back by economic necessity: Shillingford, *Appendix*, 25.

91. Hewett, *Story*, 68.

92. Irving to Alan Ker, 30 April 1833 (Oliphant, *Life*, 2:334).

93. Irving, *To the Church of God in London* (Waddington, *Diary and Letters*, 426–31).

94. DFP, C/9/27, Irving to Drummond, 21 October 1833 (Waddington, *Diary and Letters*, 373).

95. Irving to David Dow, April 1833 (Drummond, *Narrative of Circumstances*, 16; Waddington, *Diary and Letters*, 345).

96. Rossteuscher, 'Rebuilding,' 488.

97. Baxter, *Narrative*, 67, 69.

98. Arnot, *Life of Hamilton*, 65–66, James Hamilton to his sister, 28 November 1834; Campbell, ed., *Memorials*, 1:102.

99. Copinger, 'Annals,' 44; cf. Woodhouse to Drummond, 29 November 1834 (Waddington, *Diary*

Woodhouse referred in a letter to Irving's jealousy lest apostles should go beyond the borders of their office.[100] He accompanied Isabella on the first stage of her return to London, and then lectured in Edinburgh on the office of apostleship, setting out the main lines of the Church's thinking.

## THE MOVEMENT SPREADS

Other congregations began to emerge in London too. The first was at Bishopsgate: some years earlier an Independent minister, J. L. Miller, began to lay increasing stress in his sermons on biblical prophecy; opposition led to his withdrawal, together with most of his congregation, in October 1829. They began meeting in Salem Chapel in Spitalfields, formerly used by French Protestants. Armstrong (who had lost his licence to officiate as an Anglican clergyman in December 1831) joined them and helped to introduce the charismatic gifts, which were first manifested in June 1832.[101] Irving seems initially to have thought that other emerging congregations would be subject to Newman Street, but Miller took care to avoid countenancing that impression. Once he was ordained as angel by Cardale in May 1833, his position was secure.[102]

The first purpose-built Catholic Apostolic place of worship opened for another new congregation at Islington in 1834, being enlarged soon afterwards.[103] In Southwark, Armstrong gathered a congregation from August 1832; although he used Anglican forms of worship, the congregation was drawn from several denominations.[104] Like Drummond at Albury, he began the services with a confession of their irregular nature.[105] Whilst at first Armstrong thought Irving should exercise oversight of this congregation as well as Newman Street, prophecy directed Armstrong to assume this responsibility himself.[106] In Chelsea, the minister of the Anglican Park Chapel, H. J. Owen, was forced to resign after house meetings under his leadership culminated in prophecy interrupting the services in September 1833. As his licence had not yet been withdrawn by the bishop of London he began conducting services elsewhere, later linking up with the churches under apostles.[107]

Outside London, groups began to spring up in various locations, forced out of existing churches because of their belief in the gifts. Sometimes, it was claimed,

---

*and Letteers*, 418).

100. DFP, C/9/50, Woodhouse to Drummond, 14 December 1834 (Waddington, *Diary and Letteers*, 425).

101. Rossteuscher, 'Rebuilding,' 305–13; Miller, *Irvingism*, 1:134–35; Trimen, *Rise and Progress*, 25.

102. Rossteuscher, 'Rebuilding,' 316, 491, 493.

103. Copinger, 'Annals,' 44. Meetings had been held since 1832.

104. Rossteuscher, 'Rebuilding,' 317; Hewett, *Story*, 35.

105. Hewett, *Story*, 37.

106. Trimen, *Rise and Progress*, 26.

107. Rossteuscher, 'Rebuilding,' 317–18; Hewett, *Story*, 38, 40; Trimen, *Rise and Progress*, 39.

groups sprang up apparently spontaneously, with apostles only later visiting them and ordaining ministers.[108] As with the religious world's rejection of the conclusions of the Albury Conferences, the formation of separate congregations was not what those involved had initially hoped for, although the action of two squires and future apostles, Drummond and Francis Sitwell, in setting up their own congregations and registering buildings for dissenting worship, says much about their attitude towards the established order.[109] The time was one of flux, later seen as one of disorder, with erroneous interpretations of prophecies, feigned manifestations, and human thoughts being mistaken for divine words.[110]

Nevertheless, the movement grew. Drummond reported in 1834 that there were then ten churches, and another seventeen assemblies awaiting God's ordinances (ministers duly set in office).[111] By July 1835, there were congregations in Bishopsgate, Chelsea, Islington, Newman Street, Paddington, Southwark, and Westminster, in London; Bath, Birmingham, Bridgnorth, Brighton, Bristol, Cambridge, Chatham, Chelmsford, Falmouth, Frome, Liverpool, Lowick, Lymington, Melksham, Norwich, Oxford, Newport (Isle of Wight), Plymouth, Southampton, Ware, Wells, and Wolverhampton in England; Chepstow in Wales; Dunfermline, Edinburgh, Greenock, Kirkcudbright, Paisley, and Perth in Scotland; and Dublin in Ireland.[112] As yet no churches had been founded on the continent or in North America, although outreach to both had begun. Prophecy exhorted ministers to travel as far as America and India, since the sealed were to be gathered from all tribes of the spiritual Israel, and all Christian Churches.[113]

A man named Holmes was called by prophecy in September 1833 to go to America, but nothing further is heard of this.[114] Then, at Christmas 1833, a Mr Huott called on Irving. He claimed to be 'Pastor of a small flock in Upper Canada, among whom a testimony for the truth of our Lord's humanity had been lifted, & some persecution had followed in consequence, and having further stated that a spiritual work of some kind had been manifested among his people in regard to which he desired the help & counsel of the Church in London, he was desired to abide for a season & a promise made that the Lord would send help to His scattered sheep in that land by witnesses of His own preparing.'[115] Irving's wife Isabella mentioned in a letter of March 1834 that there had been encouraging accounts from churches in America where a similar

---

108. Davenport, *Albury Apostles*, 88.
109. See Sitwell, *Copy of a Letter*, 15, 20.
110. Dowglass, *Chronicle*, 6–7.
111. Drummond, *No. I*, 1.
112. Cardale to Dowglass, 10 May 1852; Copinger, 'Annals', 47, 52a.
113. Rossteuscher, 'Rebuilding', 532.
114. DFP, C/9/26, Irving to Drummond, 26 September 1833 (Waddington, *Diary and Letters*, 368).
115. NLS, Acc. 8813(i), Caird and Ryerson, 'Journal', 1–2.

work was going on.[116] According to Baxter, Huott claimed that the gifts had appeared among his flock, and that he had been sent to seek spiritual ministers. He preached at Newman Street on several occasions, and Taplin in prophecy declared him to be an angel and a prophet who was to gather and build up God's people, and prophecy directed the church to send two emissaries, the evangelist W. R. Caird and a converted Canadian Wesleyan minister, George Ryerson, to ascertain the facts behind the reports, informing them of the work in England and promising that the Lord would shortly send them an apostle.[117] According to Rossteuscher, 'the church was warned that now that the Lord had Himself built up His Ark of refuge no one might receive any instructions or directions emanating from spirits and Prophets working outside of His ordinances. They [Caird and Ryerson] were bidden to return at once to England and make their report.'[118]

It was with difficulty that Caird and Ryerson had located the congregation whose existence had been reported to them; it had been cold-shouldered by other churches as 'neither moral nor correct.'[119] On doing so they discovered that Huott had been passing himself off to the congregation as Irving's nephew and had been turned out. Nor did they find Huott or one [?Joseph] Smith, concluding: 'We have been betrayed and this by one calling himself a brother. The Lord look upon him and judge.' But they did find openings for their message at Kingston (now in Ontario), especially among Wesleyans, thanks to Ryerson's background and his family's prominence in the denomination.[120] They also encountered the preachers of another movement laying claim to restored apostles, the Latter-Day Saints or Mormons. Huott had remained in London, but around the time that news reached the church from Caird and Ryerson, he disappeared.[121]

Elsewhere in North America, a John Hewitt (could it be the same person?) made contact with the Mormons, bearing a purported letter of commendation dated 21 April 1835 from one Thomas Shaw on behalf of the apostolic church at Barnsley. It stated that Hewitt had formerly been a pastor of an Independent church in the town and a professor at the Independent seminary at Rotherham, but had been excommunicated for his belief in the restoration of apostles. The Mormons initially welcomed him, but were puzzled when, soon after, he disappeared.[122] Catholic Apostolics regarded the letter of commendation as a forgery, there being no church under apostles

---

116. Martin letters, Isabella Irving to Mrs Martin, 5 March 1834.
117. Baxter, *Narrative*, 27–28.
118. Rossteuscher, 'Rebuilding,' 533–34.
119. Baxter, *Narrative*, 28.
120. Caird and Ryerson, 'Journal.'
121. Baxter, *Narrative*, 27–28; Copinger, 'Annals,' opp. 38.
122. LDS Church History Library, MS 22503. Independents became known as Congregationalists, but Hewitt / Huott is not in the comprehensive Surman Index at Dr Williams's Library.

in that town at that point.¹²³ Such contacts ensured that Catholic Apostolics would regard Mormons with grave suspicion, even before the American movement's distinctive doctrines and claims became widely known.

In Bavaria, however, a movement developed which would later coalesce with the Catholic Apostolic Church; again, Caird would play a key role. It seems to have formed part of a wider Pietistic awakening within continental Catholicism, and was centered on the isolated village of Karlshuld, on the Donaumoos. A new settlement, it lacked adequate religious provision, and the priest, J. E. G. Lutz, had Catholics, Lutherans, Reformed, and Mennonites in his congregation. Lutz had been influenced by the renewal movement, and his preaching resulted in a local revival, with hundreds professing concern about the state of their souls. At the end of February 1828, the first prophetic utterances were heard. 'Know ye not that before the Lord comes He will give again apostles, prophets, evangelists, and pastors, and churches as at the beginning?' Within a year, the utterances died down, and in 1831 Lutz seceded, although the rationalistic theology he found in Protestant circles caused him to rejoin the Roman Catholic Church the following year. Not until 1842 did Caird happen to visit Lutz, and it is difficult to say who was more surprised to hear what the other had to say, Caird on discovering this work which predated that in his native Scotland, or Lutz on hearing of what looked to be the fulfillment of his long-cherished hopes. Lutz was directed to remain in the Roman Catholic Church as a witness, but was finally expelled for his views in 1856.¹²⁴ Other localized movements were also regarded by Catholic Apostolics as precedents for their own work, but the links forged with the Church facilitated fuller documentation, although it may be significant that no Catholic Apostolic publications referred to it until after 1880.

## THE APPEARANCE OF THE TWELVE APOSTLES

Irving believed that both Cardale and Drummond experienced doubts about their calling as apostles.¹²⁵ That would not be surprising, given that there was as yet no established understanding of what an apostle was and did. However, four others were called at intervals, and prophecy in June 1835 directed Cardale and Taplin to visit the churches seeking six more.¹²⁶ Ward comments that the apostles were middle-aged and secure, and that the nascent Church took its character from them, being marked by caution, sobriety, system, and authority.¹²⁷ That may be true of the Catholic Apostolic

---

123. Tarbet, *Edward Irving*, 7–8.

124. Hamilton, *Short History*; Scholler, *Chapter*, 31; Trimen, *Rise and Progress*, 8.

125. DFP, C/9/40, Irving to Drummond, 28 June 1834 (Waddington, *Diary and Letters*, 400).

126. Boase, *Supplementary Narrative*, 814; Woodhouse, *Address on the Death of Cardale*, 2; Woodhouse, *Narrative*, 39. For details of the apostles and their calls, see the Appendix.

127. Ward, 'Death of a Church,' 23–24.

Church from the late 1840s onwards, but as an assessment of the ethos of the new movement during its earliest years it is open to question.

There were other calls to apostleship which were not recognized by the Church. Baxter had early indicated M'Neile as an apostle.[128] At Oxford a woman claimed to have been called as an apostle, as we saw earlier. And in Miller's congregation two prophets were suspended for calling an elder and a prophet as apostles.[129] One whose call was recognized by the Church nevertheless did not accept it himself. David Dow, a Church of Scotland minister, had set himself up as an apostle in 1832–33, causing havoc in Edinburgh and southern Scotland before concluding that he had been mistaken. Rossteuscher hints at a divergence between the congregations in England and those in Scotland: 'the Apostles and other chief ministers in London had already received the knowledge that the Lord really revealed himself to this man and had chosen him to be an Apostle. It was because he had misused the power of the spirit for his own exaltation, taking an unauthorized place in a congregation and that not in fellowship with but rather in antagonism to the churches in England because he hastily went before the Lord, he had fallen under the power of the adversary.'[130] When visited by the apostles, Dow was said to have complained against the Lord 'because he had not been allowed to carry out his Apostolic mission in his own way.'[131]

Accounts of the structure of the Church and the activity of the apostles usually have little if anything to say about the way things worked before the apostles were separated on 14 July 1835; this did not necessarily correspond with the movement's developed structures and ways of doing things. Evidence for their activity during this period is fragmentary, and what follows is incomplete.[132]

Whereas the apostles were later assigned areas of jurisdiction within Christendom (their 'tribes'), initially all were active within the British Isles, apparently with particular spheres of influence, and this continued immediately after their separation. Prophecy directed their activity, as when Perceval was directed in the council of the churches on 1 October 1834 to go to Wells, Melksham, Trowbridge, and elsewhere, to visit, strengthen, and counsel the flocks. The same word sent Cardale to Birmingham.[133] Perceval seems to have been active in the West Country, Dalton in the West Midlands, William Dow at Nottingham, Armstrong in East Anglia, Tudor at Brighton, Woodhouse in the South-West, and Carlyle in Scotland. In the absence of any record of this as a formal division of labor, we may conjecture that the various apostles regarded themselves as responsible for the churches to which their own ministry had

---

128. M'Neile, *Letter to a Friend*, 11.

129. Marks, *Narrative*, 124.

130. Rossteuscher, 'Rebuilding,' 483.

131. Ibid., 559.

132. The main sources are the Perceval papers (BL, Add. MS 49192); Rossteuscher, 'Rebuilding'; Copinger, 'Annals'; and some histories of individual churches.

133. Add. MS 49192, 13, word of prophecy in the council of the churches, 1 October 1834.

given rise. Cardale, however, seems to have remained in London for much of the time, overseeing everything and acting as a final court of appeal whenever apostles encountered problems which they were unable to resolve themselves.

Certain churches were designated as regional centres, foreshadowing the later designation of some metropolitan churches as archangels' seats. Birmingham was 'a sort of central point for the work in the western counties,' Dalton as angel (before his call as apostle) being directed to 'spread his wings' over the outlying congregations in Wolverhampton, Dudley, and Bridgnorth.[134] Glasgow was marked out as 'the West Central church' for Scotland, with responsibility for Perth and Dunfermline.[135]

Taplin always accompanied Cardale on visits to new congregations, calling ministers in prophecy, who were then ordained. Early congregations were often led by a clergyman.[136] But some leaders lacked confidence to act, and looked to the apostles for detailed guidance. At Oxford, for example, the ex-Baptist James Hinton seems to have been unsure of himself: 'On Lord's Day week, the period for the Lord's Supper returns, & I feel very reluctant to pass it by a second time; & yet I feel still more reluctant to celebrate it any more according to the fleshly ordinance, greatly desiring the ordinance from heaven. O thou Watchman, enquire of the Lord for me by his Holy Apostle, what He would have me do.'[137]

The apostles also had to establish their position *vis-à-vis* that of the prophets. Armstrong passed on a prophecy to Perceval in 1834 commanding that the prophets be put in their place: 'The Lord has just spoken the following words _ "There is evil in the city—the Apostles do not rule—the Angels do not rule . . . they have been warned to rule the prophets, to set them in their places—bid them see to it—that the prophets keep in their places".'[138] Taplin, as we saw, found it difficult to submit to the apostles. Rossteuscher commented that the prophet 'felt himself shackled, and was afraid that the freedom of the revelations and utterances might be unduly circumscribed.'[139]

The following year, Tudor set out his understanding of the place of prophets in the new church order in a manner which reflected contemporary social distinctions:

> I believe the Prophets (the most precious gift to the church as the means of opening all the rest) most of all need both counsel & rule, & least of all are able to bear it. The very circumstance of their being set for bringing in ordinances & for regulating ordinances always lays them open to the temptation of thinking themselves above all ordinances. And as the prophets have been frequently taken from the humbler walks of life (to spoil the pride of man)

---

134. Rossteuscher, 'Rebuilding,' 536.
135. Ibid., 537.
136. Stevenson, 'Catholic Apostolic Eucharist,' 16.
137. Add. MS 49192, 2–3, James Hinton to Spencer Perceval, postmarked 23 July 1833. On the early history of the Eynsham and Oxford churches, see Grass, 'Restoration of a Congregation.'
138. Add. MS 49192, 11, Nicholas Armstrong to Spencer Perceval, 2 April 1834.
139. Rossteuscher, 'Rebuilding,' 488.

these have the further temptation of despising the distinctions of rank as well as the ordinances of the church. Moreover in all the prophets whom I have known there has been a stiffness & pugnacity combined with ambition in their natural character, which is probably needed for the special work of a prophet; 'to pluck up & to destroy'; but requiring discipline to be exercised with a very patient & loving spirit towards them.[140]

Recommending a particular prophet (Martin, from Brighton) to Perceval, Tudor counselled the latter not to allow him to eat at his own table, nor with the servants—an ambiguity of position reminiscent of that of the Georgian domestic chaplain. Tudor assured Perceval that the prophet concerned now saw the need to observe conventional social distinctions. This implies that hitherto he had not done so, something evident in other radical movements of the time, such as the Brethren. An eye-witness, H. J. Marks, commented that the gifted women were mostly from the servant class.[141] This is probably an exaggeration, but one with more than a grain of truth in it, especially if we take into account the male prophets as well. The apostles' position in relation to the prophets was strengthened when, early in 1835, Armstrong and Woodhouse were commanded by prophecy independently to ordain ministers in their respective spheres of work without waiting for a supernatural impulse.[142]

The twelve were 'separated' to (or freed to undertake) their work at Newman Street on 14 July 1835.[143] This was the climax of a week of meetings which were full of prophecy and high drama as final attempts were made to secure Dow's acceptance of his call. On the last day, a replacement was chosen, a chemist from Islington named Duncan Mackenzie, although we shall see that he later defected. Ironically, the other man presented before the Lord for calling as Dow's replacement, Dr John Thompson, proved far more reliable, and would exercise a long ministry in the Church. Once the twelve were complete, the seven angels of the seven churches in London (a number already seen as symbolic, for reasons to be explained later), laid hands on each apostle, separating them from their existing ministerial responsibilities in local congregations so that they might be free to minister to the whole Christian Church.[144] As a later writer explained, it 'separated them from all that bound them to particular churches, to do a catholic work and to bear testimony to the whole Church of Christ on earth to which the Lord had sent them, and for the sake of which He had raised them up.'[145]

140. Add. MS 49192, 15, J. O. Tudor to Spencer Perceval, 26 March 1835.
141. Marks, *Narrative*, 127.
142. Rupert M. Heath, *Lecture, 9 November 1954*, 7.
143. Baxter had prophesied concerning a period of 1,260 days to terminate on this date, which he interpreted as referring to the translation of believers to heaven before the Great Tribulation and the Second Coming: Baxter, *Irvingism*, 19–20, 23; Shaw, *Catholic Apostolic Church*, 41.
144. Woodhouse, *Address on the Death of Cardale*, 3. Fuller details of that week, taken from the official record of events and including many prophetic utterances spoken, are given in Trimen, *Rise and Progress*, 55–68.
145. Anon., *Ministries delivered in Newcastle-upon-Tyne*, 5.

Accordingly, in June a number of men were called and ordained to fill the offices which would be left vacant by the apostles. With the apparent exception of Drummond, who remained angel of the congregation at Albury for a year or so longer, the twelve laid down their responsibilities as angels, elders, or evangelists in order to give themselves to this ministry (cf. Acts 13).[146] A further stage in their ministry, that of sending forth, lay in the future, at which point they would assume leadership over the whole of Christendom.[147]

## THE COUNCIL OF ZION

At the heart of the young Church's polity was a council of ministers. This had its origins in a weekly meeting of those in office at Newman Street (itself a descendant of Irving's kirk session), at Irving's house and under his chairmanship. Prophecy in July 1833 had directed the angels to meet each week in council, bringing the prophets with them.[148] In 1852 Cardale recounted the genesis of what later became known as the Council of Zion.

> From the time of the ordin<sup>n</sup>. of Mr Irving he had been in the habit of calling together the Elders & Deacons of the Church with those speaking in the Spirit to a weekly council. To this the other Angels as they were ordained were gradually united—with the priests & deacons as they were ordained[,] Mr Irving assembling his own council separately.
>
> In this general Council in January 1834 the Apostles then called were bidden to <u>preside</u>—which was in fact the first overt act of <u>will</u> which they exercised. And they met weekly—until July 1835—the Apostles presiding[,] the Angels sitting in front of them, the priests & Deacons around the Angels.
>
> In June 1835, the word of prophecy came giving light as to the order in which the several Ministers were to be seated. And in July 1835, on the 14th, the day appointed for the meeting of all the Apostles & Angels[,] the Council took their seats in the prescribed order for the first time, & thenceforth met every 4th Tuesday until suspension of Meetings.[149]

As the apostles were called, and their call recognized by the council, they were added to it.[150]

An unpublished lecture, which from internal evidence appears to have been given at the Central Church in London, referred to a list of the council written by

---

146. Rossteuscher, 'Rebuilding,' 547.
147. Carlyle, *Short History*, 16.
148. Trimen, *Rise and Progress*, 38; Copinger, 'Annals,' 34, 37.
149. Cardale to Dowglass, 10 May 1852; Trimen, *Rise and Progress*, 50, 52. According to Rossteuscher, the council had in fact met after this order on 17 June: 'Rebuilding,' 580.
150. Rossteuscher, 'Rebuilding,' 544; Trimen, *Rise and Progress*, 29, 42.

Tudor in 1841/42, diagrammatically arranged.[151] This is probably to be identified with an undated plan of the council which lists around 230 names.[152] But who were they? In an authoritative retrospective by Woodhouse on the Church's development, he explained that before the twelve were separated, the seven churches in London needed to be organized on the pattern of the Tabernacle. This required the completion of the number of priests and deacons, and the call of sixty evangelists to the city, and sixty to the nations, so that the seven churches could be a model of the universal Church. 'Brethren it was a very original & novel idea when the Lord taught us in these last days not only in theory but in practice that the Tabernacle was a model of the X$^{tn}$ Church & that it should be seen in living men, & when in Newman Street in 1835 the model of the council of Zion in living men was manifested for a brief space perhaps in its perfection only once.'[153]

Prophecy through Cardale on 14 July 1835 also enjoined the holding of an assembly of the seven churches in London. These were to take place every four weeks, thirteen meetings a year.[154] On 22 July, therefore, Drummond summoned their angels to gather with their flocks at Newman Street every fourth Tuesday from 11 August for worship in the morning and evening, the council taking place after the morning service.[155] Until 12 February 1839 members of the Council of Zion met for morning and evening services; then the apostles determined that the seven churches in London were to meet at noon.[156]

The council was initially regarded as the Church's ultimate decision-making body. As such, women were excluded.[157] Six months after his call as apostle, Drummond had written to a correspondent seeking his advice: 'With respect to all the questions you put to me I dare not answer them . . . I have no hesitation in saying in the same spirit that you must take no direction from a private and unauthorised letter of Mr. Irving or of any one else to alter anything in God's house. You must put all such questions to the Council in London.'[158]

---

151. Flegg collection, Anon., 'Lecture. On the Sixty Pillars of the Court of the Tabernacle,' c.23 August 1882.

152. Cardale family papers, in Cardale's annotated Old Testament; cf. Anon., *Table of the Council of Zion*. However, Copinger quotes the official record of events for 2 January 1836 as having subjoined to it a list of the ministers comprising the council first drawn up by a William Bagley, a deacon at Chelsea: 'Annals,' 57. The pattern is also detailed in Norton, *Restoration*, 140–44.

153. Woodhouse, *Address on the Death of Cardale*, 4, 6. Once the apostles began their travels (see ch. 3), the council could not continue to meet as such, and so if any apostles were absent, Cardale alone would attend: Boase, *Supplementary Narrative*, 815–16; Davenport, *Albury Apostles*, 106.

154. For a table of the dates of each meeting, including the years 1840–47 (when it was suspended), as far as 1916, see LPL, MS 4942, Notebook by W. R. Stevenson, 309. By 1916 the meetings had reached no. 1063; presumably they were numbered from the first one on 14 July 1835.

155. Copinger, 'Annals,' 53.

156. AC, Isaac Capadose and Edward Heath, 'Albury, 4 December 1906,' 5–6.

157. Trimen, *Rise and Progress*, 39 (24 December 1833).

158. Drummond, letter book, 40, quoted in Ward, 'Death of a Church,' 81; on page 45, an almost

The *modus operandi* was that the five apostles ranking after Cardale laid down the principles governing the case; the five pillar evangelists (whose responsibility in ministry was to prepare for membership those gathered by the work of the evangelists, the title referring to the pillars at the entrance of the Tabernacle) opened the particular case and showed how these principles were applicable to it; the elders gave counsel, which was summed up by the angels of the Seven Churches; liberty was then given for the seven prophets of the universal Church to prophesy; and finally the apostles offered their judgment through Cardale (which might be deferred until a subsequent occasion).[159] In this way, the fourfold ministry (apostle/elder, prophet, evangelist, and pastor), which became a major aspect of Catholic Apostolic ecclesiology, was operative.

An official record was kept by scribes of proceedings in the council, which was probably the main source for the *Angel's Record*. There is a reference to 'the record of proceedings and occurrences from the 7th to the 14th July 1835' being read in council as late as 1891.[160] We have seen that Trimen included it (possibly somewhat condensed), and it is probable that Woodhouse would have drawn on it when writing his *Narrative of Events*. The record was evidently a full one, having reached page 829 by April 1837; the review in which the quoted reference appeared was the only published writing by a non-member to have drawn on it, and referred to it as the 'Records of the Council of the Churches.'[161] Whilst secrecy had been enjoined upon members of the council by prophecy on 12 July 1835, the anonymous author, who was ostensibly reviewing Miller's *History and Doctrines of Irvingism*, evidently enjoyed a measure of access to the Church's archives which later researchers can only dream of:

> We have before us the records of the 'Council of the Churches', authenticated, in many cases, by the signatures of Mr. Drummond and Mr. Cardale. In these there are not only full minutes of the proceedings of the Council, and of the 'word from the Lord' spoken there, but there are also the words of prophecy uttered in the different Churches throughout the land and sent up by their respective Angels. We have studied these minutes very carefully, we have read very many of the 'ministries' of the Apostles and 'words' of the Prophets . . .

The picture which these records present to us of the inner life of the Church is a very curious and interesting one, well worthy of study. All kinds of questions, touching doctrine, discipline, ritual, finance, come before the Council. Some are dealt with in a sufficiently practical way—as when professors are engaged to translate the Testimony

---

identical remark about not taking direction from Irving is dated to the spring of 1834, following Cardale's rebuke of Irving and Taplin. According to Trimen, on Christmas Day 1833 the angels were told to bring matters to the apostles in council rather than doing so privately: *Rise and Progress*, 40.

159. Miller, *Irvingism*, 1:172–73; cf. Drummond, *Discourses*, 107–8; Norton, *Restoration*, 141–42.

160. AD, January 1891, 4; cf. Trimen, *Rise and Progress*, 39.

161. See Anon., 'History and Doctrines of Irvingism,' 59. The earliest quotation in this article is dated 10 June 1835, and the latest 4 August 1840.

(see the next chapter) into German, Italian, and other languages, or a distinguished classical scholar is requested to revise the translation into Latin, but no allusion is made, as we might have expected, to the gift of tongues.

> Sometimes we might fancy ourselves present at a meeting of the Ritual Commission, or Committee of Convocation on Rubrics, except that the voices of the Prophets break in from time to time, much after the manner of the chorus in a Greek play, and with something of their obscurity. Questions of finance, or trust deeds, are dealt with much as by ordinary mortals, even though the decisions are couched in Scriptural language.[162]

By this time, records were also being kept of prophecy given in the various churches, which were then sent to the apostles for comment and potential wider dissemination.[163] Rossteuscher explained how the process worked:

> The words of prophecy spoken in all the churches were to be written and gathered up, and sent to the Apostles and the Prophets with them, and having been by them tested and sifted, and then put together and connected, they were to be given back to the Angels through the Pillar of Pastors, and to be used by them for the instruction, the admonition and the comfort of their respective flocks. They were not to be considered as possessing any permanent authority like the bible, but they were as the Manna which fell daily, and if kept beyond the day bred worms and became unusuable [sic]. So the records of the ever-flowing words of prophecy were, after having been used, to be either locked up or destroyed, in order to prevent their becoming either a cause of stumbling block [sic] to the believers, or a handle to the enemies whereby they might rob God, and materials with which they might build up a structure of lies.[164]

Some angels seem to have sent much fuller records than others, and the apostles seem to have felt on occasion that this was being overdone. William Dow commented on the record of one woman's utterances at Nottingham in 1836: 'Margaret Williams seems to occupy a great deal of time in vain repetitions.'[165] The apostles were now acting as arbiters of prophecy, something which had precipitated the movement's first internal division, to which we now turn.

---

162. Ibid., 54–55; cf. Trimen, *Rise and Progress*, 59.

163. A number of these documents for 1835–37, mostly from the church at Oxford, are preserved in Add. MS 49192.

164. Rossteuscher, 'Rebuilding,' 546; cf. Trimen, *Rise and Progress*, 60.

165. Add. MS 49192, 113, record of words of prophecy at Nottingham, 31 July 1836.

## A PARTING OF THE WAYS

The estrangement of the Greenock congregation from the London apostles in 1834 was the first of several significant divisions which would affect the Church.[166] Subsequent divergences would result in a declaration regarding the nature of the relationship between apostles and other ministers and the withdrawal of one of the apostles (1840), the loss of some members and ministers after the introduction of a liturgy and vestments (1842), and the formation of a splinter group which would become known as the New Apostolic Church (1863).

At the root of this first division was the disagreement about whether final authority lay with prophets or apostles. The disagreement was fuelled by existing differences of opinion regarding the status of certain gifted persons, and the measures to be taken to control the utterances in public worship. In 1839 Robert Norton, a doctor who married Margaret Macdonald in 1832, expressed the opinion that it was the introduction of apostleship and the subordination of prophecy to it which were the main points at issue between the groups:

> That, however, which, above all other things, appears to have quenched and grieved away the Spirit of prophecy from the Irvingite church, was the rising up among the other members of the church, of men assuming the apostleship, and, by making the voice of the prophets subordinate to their superior office, gradually suppressing it. In this way the church gradually became remodelled upon quite another basis, and with quite another constitution; so that in reality it is not, and has scarcely even the least appearance of being, the same church, as it was originally.[167]

Such opposition to the London group's developing emphasis on structures and authority reflected the thinking of A. J. Scott, who considered internal life more important than external structures.[168] Whilst the Port Glasgow group had prayed for apostles, George Macdonald concluded that apostleship as it took visible form was a snare of Satan.[169] Prophecy among them supported this, as the Scottish theologian Thomas Erskine recorded: 'I have since heard from James Macdonald, Port-Glasgow, that the spirit amongst them had testified against the London mission, saying that "they were deceitful workers, transforming themselves into the apostles of Christ".'[170] The Macdonalds therefore rejected the apostolic ordinations (which would include that of a pastor for the apostolic congregation at Greenock early in 1834), and argued

---

166. For fuller coverage, see Grass, 'Taming of the Prophets'; Grass, 'Catholic Apostolic Church in Scotland.'

167. Norton, *Neglected and Controverted Scripture Truths*, 376. Norton joined the Catholic Apostolic Church in 1854.

168. Scott, 'Answer,' 640; cf. Newell, 'A. J. Scott,' 170.

169. Norton, *Memoirs*, 211.

170. Erskine to Miss Rachel Erskine, 11 April 1834, in Hanna, ed., *Letters of Thomas Erskine*, 160.

that true apostles would perform signs or give tokens to confirm their ministry.[171] The Macdonald brothers both died in 1835, and their congregation did not long outlive them.

For their part, the apostles' estimate of the Port Glasgow group was that: 'They prophesied of the ordinances which God has since revived; and because these ordinances appeared first in London, and did not spring up among themselves, and did not assume the form they had imagined, they rejected them. They would interpret their own words; they understood them in an uncatholic, hasty, and literal manner. They measured the depths of God by the reason of man; and so they missed the mark.'[172] It was also alleged that they rejected the subjection of gifted persons to rulers in the Church.[173] According to Irving, they sought to possess the Spirit as individuals instead of as members of a body, placing too much confidence in their own discernment, 'every man his own Church, which is every man usurping to be Head of the Church.'[174] Not surprisingly, the apostolic congregation at Greenock seems to have been liable to the same outlook, and in the summer of 1834 Drummond found it necessary to warn its elders:

> You constitute the ordinance by which God will direct his Church and though He permits prophets to be present they are not set for counsel, and least of all women. Thus, it is greatly tempting the Lord to set aside the eldership as the ordinance for counsel, which we are all tempted to do, and lean upon prophets. Now we must not idolize prophets or their utterances.[175]

The tension between the individual's walk with God and the Church's role in regulating gifts would surface again in the crises of the 1840s, but before that we shall examine how the new Church was shaped by the apostles' year in retreat after their separation.

---

171. Norton, *Memoirs*, 211, 215; BL, MSS Eur F206/106, John McLeod Campbell to James Macnabb, 28 March 1834.

172. Carlyle, *Short History*, 10.

173. Boase, *Supplementary Narrative*, 772.

174. DFP, C/9/36, Irving to Drummond, 2 April 1834 (Waddington, *Diary and Letters*, 391).

175. Drummond, letter book, 56, quoted in Ward, 'Death of a Church,' 48.

# PART II

1835–1901: The Church under Apostles

# 3

# The New Church Takes Shape (1835–39)

## A YEAR'S RETREAT

Immediately following their separation, the twelve apostles, along with the seven prophets of the universal Church, withdrew to Albury, in obedience to prophecy urging them to 'be caught away to the first spiritual church in Albury,' where they were to prepare to set up the 'perfect pattern' of church order and worship.[1] The prophets—all from churches in London and southern England—were Taplin (a schoolmaster), John Bayford (a proctor in Doctor's Commons), John Bligh (a coppersmith), William Martin (a tradesman), Jonathan Smith (a shopkeeper), John Hester (a butler), and Robert Horsnail (a farmer).[2] Their occupations place them in a lower social band than most of the apostles, and we have already noted that this affected relationships in ministry.

The apostles were directed to spend a year in retreat, leaving only for the meetings of the seven churches in London, for 'works of necessity and mercy,' or when their presence was essential for the sake of the gathered flocks.[3] Each Sunday an apostle and a prophet would instruct the faithful at one of the seven churches in London.[4] Every fourth Tuesday, there was the meeting of the Council of Zion. Further afield, most of the apostles (the exceptions being King, Mackenzie, and Sitwell) visited the churches

---

1. LPL, H6572.34.11, F. V. Woodhouse, 'Apostle's Teaching on the Tabernacle. Mr Woodhouse 1887' (n.d.), 1; Trimen, *Rise and Progress*, 53.

2. This list is taken from Boase, *Supplementary Narrative*, 819, which is followed by Copinger, 'Annals,' 53. According to Miller, however, the seven prophets at the council meetings had been Taplin, Drummond and his wife, Cardale, his wife and sister, and Bayford: *Irvingism*, 1:172 n; cf. Baxter, *Irvingism*, 12.

3. Rossteuscher, 'Rebuilding,' 575. In fact, they spent nearly two years: Drummond, *Brief Account*, 22.

4. Miller, *Irvingism*, 1:177.

in the areas assigned to their care.[5] Dalton was deprived of his office as curate of St Leonard's, Bridgnorth, on 28 July 1835, after two years of complaints regarding his preaching un-Anglican doctrine and allowing charismatic manifestations during Anglican worship, but the process seems to have made no impact on the apostles.[6]

The apostles' primary objective was to study the Scriptures; they had planned to begin with Genesis, but prophecy through Taplin on 5 October 1835 directed them to begin with Exodus 25, where the pattern of Tabernacle worship was set out.[7] They proceeded in a similar way to the earlier Albury conferences, but with space for prophetic utterances after each apostle had given his thoughts on the passage of Scripture under review.[8] They concluded that the whole order of the Christian Church had been foreshadowed in the Mosaic law, 'and can only be rightly apprehended by reference thereto.'[9] At the end of a year's study, therefore, their first action, according to Rossteuscher, was to complete the model of a properly constituted church, which had been left in abeyance since their separation.[10] Accordingly, the eucharist, which had been celebrated weekly by the apostles at Albury from 19 August 1835, began to be celebrated weekly in the seven churches in London from 26 June 1836.[11] Drummond was also finally relieved of his responsibilities as angel of the church at Albury and as pillar of pastors.[12]

The apostles' horizons were not bounded by Albury and London. Prophecy on 10 July 1835 had expressed the Lord's longing to see Woodhouse in America, Carlyle in Germany, Sitwell in Spain, Tudor in India, and also ministers in France, to gather angels to lead the churches.[13] At a meeting of the Council of Zion in June 1836, Drummond prophesied that the apostles as princes of the spiritual Israel were to divide Christendom (their mission-field) into twelve tribes, from which the first-fruits of the elect were to be gathered.[14] This was undertaken on 30 September 1836, on the basis of certain spiritual characteristics supposed to reside in each tribe.[15] 'No official pronouncement was ever made by the Apostles as to the application of the names of the twelve tribes to the divisions of Christendom, except in the case of Judah to England.'[16] The assignment of tribes to apostles, in order of their call, followed that of Revelation

5. Their travels can be traced from references in Copinger, 'Annals.'
6. Miller, *Irvingism*, 1:154.
7. Woodhouse, 'Apostle's Teaching,' 3; Hollick, *Church in Liverpool*, 16–17.
8. Irving, *Preliminary Discourse*, 201–2; Rossteuscher, 'Rebuilding,' 576; Albrecht, *Work*, 10–11.
9. Woodhouse, 'Apostle's Teaching,' 6.
10. Rossteuscher, 'Rebuilding,' 589–90.
11. Copinger, 'Annals,' 54, 62.
12. Rossteuscher, 'Rebuilding,' 590–91. Rossteuscher believed that Drummond's having 'a country seat of his own' was a major reason why he continued to hold a plurality of offices.
13. Trimen, *Rise and Progress*, 58.
14. Boase, *Supplementary Narrative*, 826; Rossteuscher, 'Rebuilding,' 590.
15. Copinger, 'Annals,' 66.
16. Rupert M. Heath, *Twelve Tribes*, 6.

7:5–8. As for the equation of the tribes with particular countries, this seems to have been done according to perceived national characteristics and their match with those of the twelve tribes in Genesis 49 and Deuteronomy 33.[17] Cardale and Drummond as the first to be called were charged with overall supervision of the apostles, who were divided into two bands. Those under Cardale were responsible for the mainly Protestant countries of Northern Europe and Russia, and those under Drummond for the largely Catholic remainder.[18] This reflected Drummond's long-standing interest in evangelistic work and Bible translation and distribution in Switzerland, Italy, and elsewhere. All the apostles, however, resided at Albury.[19]

The focus on Europe was said to be because it was 'especially the throne of the great King'; America and 'the Christian colonies' elsewhere were designated 'suburbs,' under the jurisdiction of the heads of the European tribes.[20] One might have expected them all to be placed under Cardale as the apostle for England, but initially at least Woodhouse took responsibility for North America, and Tudor for India and Australia. Non-European Christian communities seem not to have been included in this apportionment, although Armstrong's jurisdiction was later expanded from Ireland and Greece to include 'the East.'

## THE TESTIMONIES

The Testimonies, an important genre in Catholic Apostolic literature, may have originated in Baxter's desire to deliver a prophetic testimony to William IV and the queen,[21] or in a petition of Irving and his church to the king in 1832.[22] They were documents in which the Church set out its stall, and reflected a hierarchical concept of social order, being sent to the rulers in Church and state throughout Christendom on the principle that God dealt 'with the heads through the heads'; rulers were held responsible before God for their subjects' condition.[23] All Testimonies followed a similar pattern: extensive consideration of contemporary evils in Church and state, exposition of biblical teaching concerning God's purpose for humanity and the Church, assertion that through the events culminating in the restoration of apostles God's purpose was being realized, and an urgent appeal to accept the work and so find shelter from coming judgment. Four of the apostles were legally trained (Cardale,

---

17. Norton, *Restoration*, 156; Woodhouse, *Narrative*, 58 n.; Davenport, *Albury Apostles*, 110–11; Flegg, 'Gathered under Apostles,' 70. A different set of identifications was given by Taplin, however, in a letter of 1840 to Drummond: Taplin, *Prophetic Light*.
18. Aarsbo, *Komme Dit Rige*, 4:75.
19. Burne, *Albury*, 2.
20. Rossteuscher, 'Rebuilding,' 591.
21. Rossteuscher, 'Rebuilding,' 353.
22. See Grass, *Lord's Watchman*, 222.
23. Woodhouse, *Narrative*, 61; cf. Cardale, *Notes of Lectures* (1861), 44.

Carlyle, Perceval, and Woodhouse), and the delivery of the Testimonies is reminiscent of the serving of legal documents; once they had been so delivered, it was the responsibility of the recipient to act upon them.[24]

The first to be produced was addressed to the bishops and clergy of the Church of England. In obedience to a prophetic word during September 1835, each apostle wrote down his burden concerning the state of Church, state, and nation, and Cardale harmonized them.[25] The resulting document was read to the seven churches in London on Christmas Day 1835, and then delivered to the archbishops, bishops, and over 150 London clergy, as well as many others in the country.[26] Delivery to the bishops was undertaken by Drummond and Woodhouse.[27]

One of the earliest references to the compilation and delivery of a Testimony was in a letter from Drummond to Perceval in June 1835. A prophecy by Cardale had urged the need for such a witness to rulers, with Perceval to be 'a state prophet' to speak to statesmen in their language. The former MP Drummond agreed with this: 'I have long been grieved at seeing the downfall of every thing, & no testimony gone forth to our rulers, our priests, our princes, & our judges: it is useless testifying to the old women at Albury & Chepstow.'[28] Accordingly, another Testimony, based on the first, was prepared by Perceval for presentation to William IV and the Privy Council.[29] He read it to the king in a private interview at Brighton on 18 January 1836.[30] According to Copinger, the king was 'said to have been moved to tears.'[31] It was also delivered to the members of the Privy Council. At least one politician was appreciative, Perceval's uncle Lord Arden commenting that the exposition of the lack of any fear of God in many politicians and public figures hit the mark.[32] Meanwhile, Drummond went to inform the archbishop of York that 'the end of the world was approaching, and that it was owing to the neglect of himself and his brethren that the nation was in its present awful state.'[33]

---

24. Cf. Miller, *Irvingism*, 1:178. The Mormons adopted a similar approach, an emissary taking an open letter to Queen Victoria detailing the signs of the times and the political destiny of the world, and calling all to join them as God's restored Church: Oliver, *Prophets and Millenialists*, 233–34.

25. Woodhouse, *Address, 14th August 1877*, 7.

26. Boase, *Supplementary Narrative*, 821–22; Shaw, *Catholic Apostolic Church*, 93, following Dowglass, *Chronicle*, 25.

27. Woodhouse, *Address, 14th August 1877*, 7; Copinger, 'Annals,' 57.

28. BL, Perceval papers, Add. MS 49192, 17–18, Drummond to Perceval, 2 June 1835.

29. Rossteuscher, 'Rebuilding,' 586; Copinger, 'Annals,' 59. Some drafts are preserved in Add. MS 49192, 28–76, with drafts of the covering letter to the king.

30. Add. MS 49192, 79, unknown correspondent to Perceval, 17 January 1836; Cardale family papers, Cardale to Dowglass, 10 May 1852.

31. Copinger, 'Annals,' 59.

32. Add. MS 49192, 87, Lord Arden to Perceval, 20 January 1836.

33. Greville, *Greville Memoirs*, 3:340–41 (3 February 1836).

How were the visitors received? The bishops, it was stated in 1861, had all received it courteously and respectfully, and their silence was taken as implying that they found nothing contrary to Christian faith and doctrine.[34] However, contemporary accounts offer a somewhat different picture. A Dublin clergyman recorded a visit from two ex-Anglican clergy, who informed him that the Holy Spirit long prayed for had been poured out, his gifts manifested, and a people gathered; 'they had this proof also of being guided by the Spirit, that while there was a general spirit of insubordination in the world, they distinguished themselves by respect towards those in authority.' He rejected them as they worked no miracles in confirmation of their message, arguing that they had no more proof of the validity of their message than the Quakers had, who likewise believed in their own inspiration.[35] In May 1836, Dalton called on his successor at Bridgnorth, George Bellett, stating that he brought a message from God. Bellett refused to hear him, and later noted the contradiction between the apostles' initial rejection of Anglican ordination and their appeal to clergy when delivering the Testimony on the basis of recognition of Anglican ministerial orders.[36] Another account comes from the political diarist Fulke Greville. According to Lord Howick, Secretary at War in Lord Melbourne's administration, Perceval began his call by announcing: 'You are aware that God has been pleased in these latter times to make especial communications of His will to certain chosen instruments, in a language not intelligible to those who hear it, nor always to those by whom it is uttered. I am one of those instruments, and I am come to declare to you, &c.' The Testimony delivered by Perceval listed the main items of legislation of the preceding five years as evidence of falling away from God or as causes of God's anger. Reactions to Perceval's declaration varied: Howick 'listened to him with patient civility,' Melbourne 'argued with and cross-questioned him,' and Edward Stanley (Patronage Secretary to the Treasury) 'turned him out at once.'[37]

The apostles were conscious that their mission extended to the whole of Christendom, not just to Great Britain, and the first prophetic word about sending a Catholic Testimony came in their Council on 23 February 1836. On 9 June they resolved that 'it should be prepared as on the former occasion[,] each taking the two English Testimonies as a basis.'[38] Before settling down to this, nine of the apostles visited the churches and set them in order so that they could be free to concentrate on the task in hand. Cardale remained in Albury and also took charge of the seven churches in London, which were not deemed to belong to any one tribe; he was assisted by Arm-

---

34. Place, 'Twenty-five years ago,' 3.

35. Anon., *Conversation*, 3.

36. Bellett, *Reasons for Refusing*, 3–4, 26–27. Bellett's brother was the Dublin Brethren leader J. G. Bellett.

37. Greville, *Greville Memoirs*, 3:338 (1 February 1836); cf. Torrens, *Memoirs of Melbourne*, 2:175–76.

38. Cardale to Dowglass, 10 May 1852; cf. Woodhouse, *Address, 14th August 1877*, 8.

strong and Tudor, who kept in touch with their colleagues. Cardale bore the main burden of writing what became known as the Great Testimony, drawing on the two previous Testimonies.[39] It was addressed 'To the Patriarchs, Archbishops, Bishops and others in Places of chief Rule over the Church of Christ throughout the Earth, and to the Emperors, Kings, Sovereign Princes, and chief Governors over the Nations of the Baptized,' and functioned as a yardstick according to which those sent forth to Christendom were to speak.[40] A convenient analysis of the Great Testimony (as it became known) may be offered at this point:

§§1–2 The Church and Christendom described:

> The Church of Christ is the company of all who are baptized in the name of the Father, and of the Son, and of the Holy Ghost, without distinction of age or country, and separated by their baptism from all other men. . . .
>
> As the Church is the aggregate of the baptized, so Christendom is the community of those nations which, as national bodies, profess the faith of Christ's Church . . . . Christendom is one corporate body;—separated from all other nations of the earth, in that they recognise the doctrines of Jesus Christ as the basis of their international law, and of their dealings one with another;—distinguishable from all other nations, in that, by their legitimate organs, they have been brought as nations into covenant with God . . . .[41]

§§3–6 The history of God's dealings with humanity

§§7–17 The state of Christendom, the present crisis, and the offer of a place of refuge

§§18–22 God's purpose in humanity and the Church through Jesus Christ (a recapitulation of salvation history)

§23 The means of effecting it:

§§24–28 (i) The sacraments of baptism and the eucharist, which require an authorized ministry for their celebration

§§29–40 (ii) The four ministries of apostle, prophet, evangelist, and pastor

§§41–42 The uniqueness of apostles as a universal ministry

§§43–51 The Church comprises all the baptized and is one, holy, catholic, and apostolic

§§52–61 The failure of the baptized, leading to the loss of the ministries of apostle and prophet and the idea of bishops as replacements for apostles

---

39. Rossteuscher, 'Rebuilding,' 597–98.

40. Boase, *Supplementary Narrative*, 829; Drummond, *Discourses*, 137.

41. Anon., *To the Patriarchs, Archbishops, Bishops*, 1–2 (§§1–2). The section numbers were added in later editions and are included here as they were often used for reference purposes. An abridged version of the Great Testimony appears in Miller, *Irvingism*, 1:347–437.

§§62–65 The consequences: (i) a lower measure of grace in ministries and sacraments

§§66–67 (ii) the corruption of doctrine; state interference in ecclesiastical life

§§68–74 The true relation of Church and state

§§75–80 The external condition of the Church after the loss of apostles

§§81–88 Protestantism (life) and Catholicism (unity) separated instead of together

§§89–94 The progress of evil principles: abolition of tithe, doctrinal latitudinarianism, and indifferentism regarding the establishment of religion

§§ 95–97 Consequences to the state of the decline of religion, seen in the French Revolution

§§98–100 Events are moving towards the revelation of Antichrist and the Second Coming

§§101–2 The Church's need to be prepared for the coming of the Lord

§§103–14 The work of preparation has begun; its effects

§§115–16 Signs and evidences of God's work

§§117–24 Concluding appeal to rulers and people in Church and state to accept the work

Apostolic blessing

Albrecht spoke for the movement in describing this as 'the most important document that has appeared in the Church since the close of the New Testament Canon.'[42] Before delivery, it was circulated to the angels of the churches,[43] and 'sanctified' by prayer in the assembly of the seven churches in London.[44] According to Copinger, it was read in the assembly on 21 February 1837.[45]

The Testimony's primary recipients were to be the pope, the Austrian emperor, and the French king, as representatives of the three forms of government which usurped, perverted, or misrepresented the authority of Christ: theocracy, autocracy, and democracy.[46] It was therefore delivered to Cardinal Acton for Pope Gregory XVI in May 1838, by Drummond and Perceval. In September it was delivered by Drummond and Woodhouse to Prince Metternich for the Austrian emperor.[47] Shortly afterwards it was to be placed before the French king, Louis Philippe, but, as Albrecht recorded, 'circumstances prevented this. In a book which I found in the library at Albury some

---

42. Albrecht, *Work*, 12; cf. Rossteuscher, 'Rebuilding,' 598.
43. Copinger, 'Annals,' 72.
44. Cardale, *Notes of Lectures* (1861), 23.
45. Copinger, 'Annals,' 69.
46. Boase, *Supplementary Narrative*, 828; Bramley-Moore, *Church's forgotten Hope*, 265.
47. Copinger, 'Annals,' 72–73.

years ago there is a note by Mr Woodhouse stating that Mr Drummond went to Paris to deliver the testimony to the King, but could not be received, as the Court was in mourning at that time. It is believed to have been laid before him subsequently.'[48] Thereafter it was delivered to other monarchs and bishops as access was possible.

Translations were made into Latin, French, German (probably after 1848), and Danish, although in Germany at least, the apostles and their ministers would issue Testimonies written specifically for that setting, as also happened in Scotland and North America. Boase referred to 'getting it properly translated into Latin, as the language common to all Christendom,' which implies the use of outside experts.[49] In 1843 Cardale issued a version intended for members, which omitted parts of the Testimony which were most particularly intended for the wider public: *A Manual or Summary of the special Objects of Faith and Hope in the present Times: For the Use of the Catholic Churches in England*.

## GATHERING GOLD

While still in retreat the apostles had received further light regarding their commission, which was said to involve 'gathering gold' as well as delivering the Testimony. They were to visit the nations of Christendom as private observers, 'to ascertain the state of religion in the countries which they visited; to observe their various customs and practices; to learn how far and in what way it was practicable to convey to them the truths which they themselves had been taught; to seek by intercourse with them to obtain a proper estimate of the value and importance of such forms of worship, and such doctrines and rites as obtained among them; and lastly, to gather gold from all parts of Christendom.'[50]

The last expression refers to their belief that 'in all parts of the Church there is a remnant of truth often hidden and buried under the rubbish of human doctrines and traditions, like pure gold in the bowels of the earth.' They were to examine the doctrines, worship, and customs of Christendom's divisions. The good was to be combined to produce a truly catholic way of worship, ensuring that everything of value escaped the coming judgment upon the apostate Church. Though each Church had but a partial understanding of the truth (which made reconciliation between them impossible), each had something to contribute to a restored and united body, whether in doctrinal understanding or liturgical practice. On reconvening, the apostles would

---

48. Albrecht, *Work*, 13. Woodhouse contradicted himself on this question. Copinger, 'Annals,' 73, stated: 'Mr W. adds "so far as I know the Testimony was never delivered to the French ruler". According to Miller, *Irvingism*, 1:191–92, it was not known whether the Testimony was delivered to Louis Philippe, but a note by Woodhouse asserted: 'It was delivered': Miller, *Miller's Notes*, 2(2). This last source included notes by Woodhouse and was circulated by the Church. For a discussion concluding that the Testimony was probably never delivered, see Anon., '"The Great Testimony"' (Part 1), 3 n. 9.

49. Boase, *Supplementary Narrative*, 829.

50. Woodhouse, *Narrative*, 58–59; cf. Miller, *Irvingism*, 1:185–88.

sift all this, so that 'every thing good in all Christendom might find its proper place in the worship and service of the House of God.'⁵¹ One discovery concerned the use of liturgical vestments, the story being that ministers seeing a Catholic priest vested for mass at Rouen were given a prophetic utterance indicating that this was how the Lord wished his ministers to appear before him.⁵²

From late 1836, some of them had visited their respective tribes, returning during 1837: Armstrong to Ireland, Carlyle to Prussia, Dalton to France, Drummond to Switzerland, King to Holland, and Woodhouse to Canada.⁵³ The apostles set out again from the spring of 1838, each accompanied by a few chosen ministers (a prophet, an evangelist, and a pastor). Cardale and Tudor stayed behind on this occasion, Cardale's area of jurisdiction being England and Tudor assisting him with the oversight of the home churches.⁵⁴ But a small notebook recording the total expenditure for each apostle on this mission, and for the delivery of the Testimony, has no income or expenditure recorded for Tudor (Poland and India) or Sitwell (Spain and Portugal), so it may be that Sitwell did not visit his tribe either.⁵⁵ When Rossteuscher wrote, there were 'still in existence some records kept by individual apostles of that time, some in print for private circulation, others only in manuscript'; we might wish to know more!⁵⁶

Close study together had already begun to rub away the sectarian rough edges of some of the apostles,⁵⁷ and this process was vastly accelerated (for some at least) by the experience of encounter with different Christian traditions. Such contact appears to have made a significant impact on the arch-Protestant Drummond. On his return, he was recorded as testifying to the council of apostles:

> Every part of the ceremony of the Mass is replete with meaning to those who are well instructed, and therefore greatly conducive to devotional feelings.
>
> On a comparison of those who are seeking to serve God in the Papacy with those who are doing the same among the Evangelical sects, the result is vastly favourable to the former, especially in uprightness, moral integrity, absence of cant and boasting. Persons are to be found in France and Italy of

---

51. Woodhouse, *Narrative*, 59.

52. Miller, *Irvingism*, 1:198–99.

53. Copinger, 'Annals,' 61, 67–71.

54. Rossteuscher, 'Rebuilding,' 597; Miller, *Irvingism*, 1:183; Copinger, 'Annals,' 72–73 (drawing on an address given by Cardale in the autumn of 1846), 82.

55. Archiv der NAK, 'The Tribes 1838,' 84–85, 107–8. These countries are also omitted from Copinger's list of the tribes visited: 'Annals,' 72. However, Sitwell does appear to have visited Italy (see below).

56. Rossteuscher, 'Rebuilding,' 613. For further information on the visits to France and Holland respectively, see de Caux, *Early Days*; Ouwerkerk, 'Fragmenten,' 12–13, 28. Carlyle drew on his experiences in *Moral Phenomena*. For brief accounts of the development of the work in each tribe, see chs 6 and 14 below.

57. Boase, *Supplementary Narrative*, 824.

the highest merit, whilst it would be difficult to point out any such amongst the Evangelical Protestants of France and Switzerland.[58]

It was real people, not ideas or books, who made such an impression on him. Writing to Woodhouse in April 1839, Drummond was clear that the journeys were for the purpose of studying people at worship and prayer, not books:

> I wrote to Mr Cardale lately that I was quite sure we were wrong in thinking that 'gold in the earth' meant truth in books and formularies for, if it were so, these could have been much better studied in Albury and more cheaply also, and that it meant the form in which the truth has in the minds of different living men. I was led to this from hearing S[itwell] trying to knock into the head of a poor Italian, a very spiritually minded man, a Calvinist formula about 'standing in the blood,' and if we do not learn to know a gold coin when we see it, whether it has the stamp of Queen Victoria, Louis Philippe, or Joseph, we shall never be able to teach our evangelists to do so either.[59]

He was therefore unimpressed with what he had seen at Tübingen during his travels:

> The university men of Tübingen are just like university men everywhere, and all are men of books and not of action, dealing with mankind as with propositions about eternal purposes etc. Formulas make formal people . . . their whole conversation and out going being with formulas they are useless to living souls; they have never had a broken-hearted formula to bind up nor a forward one to repress. I verily believe a bookman can never make a good minister of a church.[60]

As he wrote to an early evangelist, the objective in speaking to men was not to win an argument but to win souls.[61] It is impossible to avoid the suspicion that Drummond considered Cardale just such a 'bookman,' and we shall see them clashing during the 1840s over liturgical matters. Cardale, of course, had remained in Albury, and so been deprived of the learning experience provided by these journeys.

One aspect of the apostles' message which began to change, at least in the way it was expressed, concerned their estimate of existing Churches. Initially, their negativity towards the Churches and the rejection of their message fed off each other. John Ryerson wrote to his brother, the Canadian Wesleyan leader Egerton: 'I am told that most of their performances are truly disgusting & that thinking people are turning from them with feelings of the warmest disapprobation: this is maddening the Irvinites [sic]

---

58. Anon., 'History and Doctrines of Irvingism,' 63.
59. Drummond, letter book, 100, quoted in Ward, 'Death of a Church,' 55–56.
60. Drummond, letter book, 101, quoted in Ward, 'Death of a Church,' 56.
61. Drummond, letter book, 97, quoted in Ward, 'Death of a Church,' 87.

& with no sparing hand they are dealing damnation round the land upon the heads of all who *dare* to call in question *their Apostolical authority*.'[62]

But Drummond was soon writing with what looks like a degree of self-criticism regarding the intolerance of English evangelists toward foreigners, perhaps in Switzerland: 'I can only weep in spirit before the Lord and deplore the dishonour done to His holy Name by English selfishness, pride, want of respect and deference for the feelings and standing of others; everyone now will have their backs up against me, and all attempts to win them by degrees will be vain.'[63]

The mission undoubtedly reinforced the increased sense of catholicity evident in the Great Testimony. We shall see that within a few years, the apostles were forced by circumstances to encourage those who received their message to remain in, or return to, the existing Churches, and that even after the crisis of the 1840s had passed, they often urged converts to practise a kind of dual membership.

The apostles' self-understanding is evident in their rejection of any kind of designation for the movement which would set them apart from the rest of the Christian Church. Although it has been asserted that the Catholic Apostolic Church received its name as the result of a householder's reply to an official during the 1851 census,[64] it appears that they were using the label '(Holy) Catholic Apostolic Church' from the earliest days. Evidence for this comes from the responses of the congregations in Scotland to a survey conducted during 1836–38 by the Commissioners for Religious Instruction.[65] Some early English baptismal registers, which had to be surrendered to the government in 1840 in connection with the introduction of civil registration of births, marriages, and deaths, use a similar designation: Newman Street described itself as belonging to the 'Holy Catholic Apostolic' denomination (Paddington and Ware using similar terms), and Chelsea as 'One, Holy, Catholic, Apostolical' (Bridgnorth and Westminster similarly).[66] In 1853, the Notes of Conference recorded that the designation had been given by the apostles over fifteen years previously.[67] The name 'Catholic Apostolic Church' was formally adopted for use on the outside of buildings on 10 January 1849.[68] In line with this, the church was careful to insist that it was not 'the Catholic Apostolic Church' in an exclusive sense, but a network of congregations which were both catholic and apostolic. The apostles did not reject the right of other Churches so to describe themselves, but (following the ancient creeds) believed this was the way in which the Christian Church should be designated and that they saw no need for any further elaboration or qualification, regarding other names as sectarian.

62. Sissons, *Ryerson*, 1:360, letter dated 25 September 1836.
63. Drummond, letter book, 129, quoted in Ward, 'Death of a Church,' 87.
64. Shaw, *Catholic Apostolic Church*, 3 n. 1.
65. See Grass, 'Catholic Apostolic Church in Scotland.'
66. TNA, RG4/4249, 4337, 2424, 4294, 3194, 4170 respectively.
67. NC, 2 March 1853.
68. Copinger, 'Annals,' 87; Schröter, *Bilder*, 17.

Moreover, they saw the work as being for the blessing of the whole Church, recalling it to what God intended it to be.[69] As Robert Norton would later explain, 'It has become our distinctive name, simply because we alone are satisfied with it.'[70] Of course, this was no guarantee of a truly non-sectarian outlook, but an 'ecumenical' strand to Catholic Apostolic ecclesiology did develop.

Prophecy had instructed the apostles to assemble after 1,260 days from their separation, on 25 December 1838. Accordingly, they returned briefly to England.[71] They established the outlines of the Church's distinctive fourfold ministry of apostle, prophet, evangelist, and pastor found in Ephesians 4:11. This had its roots in prophetic interpretation of biblical typology, especially in the mystery of the four cherubim in Ezekiel 1. On 22 January 1839, the fourfold ministry was set up in the seven churches in London.[72]

During these deliberations, the apostles were able to use the first part of the Albury church to be built, the adjacent octagonal council chamber. Apart from full meetings of the apostles with ministers of the universal Church, the apostles used to deal with administrative matters there after the Sunday eucharist. The church itself was opened on 4 September 1840. Often known as the Chapel of the Great King, its interior layout differed somewhat from that of other Catholic Apostolic churches, since it was not primarily the meeting place of a local congregation, but the visible focus of the worship offered by the universal Church, in which the apostles played a leading role. One significant difference was the lack of an angel's seat, Christ being regarded as the angel of the universal Church.[73]

However, it appears from notes among Perceval's papers that the apostles were still working out their relation to the rest of the Church, in structural terms at any rate. On 27 November 1838, Woodhouse had warned of the danger of their becoming a fresh papacy, and on 25 December Perceval noted concerning Cardale: 'how can he do things in name of all—as we are told He shall.' Cardale appears to have been acting in the name of the band of six apostles whom he headed up,[74] and we shall see later that he would be accused of acting unilaterally in the name of the twelve. The early insistence of prophecy that the apostles should act unanimously in all matters of

---

69. Woodhouse, *Census*, 15; Davenport, *Albury Apostles*, 214–15. Similarly, in German the title adopted was 'Die katholisch-apostolische Gemeinden' (congregations), not 'Die katholisch-apostolische Kirche': W. H., *Katholisch-apostolische Gemeinden*, 132.

70. Norton, *Restoration*, 160. Norton claimed that the name had been adopted in response to prophecy forbidding any other. If a distinctive name was necessary, however, it was acceptable to use 'churches gathered under apostles': ibid., 159–60.

71. Boase, *Supplementary Narrative*, 832.

72. Carlyle, *Short History*, 15; Woodhouse, *Narrative*, 66–77; Albrecht, *Work*, 15, 19.

73. Edward Heath, *Extract*, 1; Anon., *Albury: Extract*, 2; Davenport, *Albury Apostles*, 99–100. For an explanation of the differences in layout, see Burne, *Albury*.

74. Add. MS 49192, 153, ms notes.

significance was being tested.[75] In the next chapter we shall see it being placed under severe strain and breaking.

75. Rossteuscher, 'Rebuilding,' 554–55.

# 4

# A Succession of Challenges (1840–54)

THE PERIOD AROUND 1840 has perhaps been neglected in studies of the Catholic Apostolic Church, but it was during this unsettled time that significant change occurred as it moved in a high church direction under Cardale's firm leadership. This resulted in some defections, but it is also likely that the Church's survival through this decade owed a great deal to his combination of firmness with tact, even though not all among the apostles, let alone the other ministers, were always happy with the way in which he exercised authority.[1]

The apostles experienced a series of crises affecting their leadership, each resulting in a strengthening of their control of the movement. The first had involved their securing acceptance as genuine apostles and gaining acceptance as leaders of the work in Scotland as well as England. The second, during 1840, settled the nature of their relationship with the prophets and the other ministries. The third, resolved with the introduction of the rite of sealing in 1847, concerned the nature of the spiritual grace conveyed through apostles. The fourth, from 1855, was precipitated by the prophets, and ensured that no replacements would be appointed for apostles who had died, thus securing the movement's eschatological orientation and provisional nature. Each crisis except the third resulted in official teaching being circulated concerning the nature, place, and limits of prophecy, although tensions continued to be felt. This chapter examines the second and third of these episodes; the next examines the fourth.

## ASSERTION OF APOSTOLIC AUTHORITY

Before the Apostles could minister to Christendom's schisms, they had to face a crisis in their own movement. Continuing lack of clarity concerning the role of apostles, as well as their lengthy absence from the young Church which hindered business from

---

1. Ward, 'Death of a Church,' 11.

being dealt with, precipitated a crisis centered on the nature of apostolic rule, and in particular the relation of apostles to the other ministries.[2] Were the apostles merely the executors of the will of the Council of Zion which had separated them (as some ministers appear to have believed), or did they possess independent authority? Were they its agents or its heads? Who was the final interpreter of prophecy?[3] And in the local congregation, who was the ruler—the apostle or the local pastor?[4] One internal writer has suggested that some began to think that the council was the primary agency by which God would guide the Church, with apostles as its instruments.[5]

The emerging Church owed a doctrinal debt to the prophets; before 1832 prophecy had spoken of God's universal love, assurance as of the essence of faith, the need for personal holiness, Christ's personal return and the millennium, Christendom's identification as Babylon, the outpouring of the Spirit in preparation for the Second Coming, the restoration of charismatic gifts, the Tabernacle as foreshadowing the body of Christ, and the need for rebuilding the Church.[6] But after their period in retreat, it might appear almost as if the apostles recognized the prophets as an order of ministry whose utterances legitimated their own position, and which they could not disown because they believed it to be God-given, but whose unpredictable manifestations could be unwelcome unless strictly domesticated. We noted earlier that difference in social class was a factor in their strained relationships with the prophets.[7] More significantly, apostles no longer waited for a sense of the Spirit's leading through prophecy before fulfilling the duties of their office. Now they believed that their gift, while involving spontaneous Spirit-led action, was activated by the intelligence, in contrast to the impulse which activated the prophetic gift.[8]

The apostles had been throughout Europe, 'gathering gold,' and that had proved fruitful, but the earlier attempts to deliver the Great Testimony had not had the anticipated impact. There is some evidence, too, that they were scaling down their claim to authority to apply it to the body they led, 'by way of sample or specimen of what shall be,' rather than the whole of Christendom.[9] But while expectations concerning the success of the apostles' missions had not been realized, the prophets were a potent force in the movement's life, and the idea of government by council had

---

2. Woodhouse, *Narrative*, 83; Boase, *Supplementary Narrative*, 832.

3. Flegg, 'Gathered under Apostles,' 77.

4. Davenport, *Albury Apostles*, 117.

5. Boase, *Supplementary Narrative*, 832. The gatherings of the Seven Churches continued in the absence of the apostles, but for worship only; the Council of Zion did not meet, thus removing a forum in which potentially contentious issues could be discussed and resolved: Woodhouse, *Address on the Death of Cardale*, 3.

6. Boase, *Supplementary Narrative*, 789–90.

7. Cf. Tierney, 'Catholic Apostolic Church,' 300.

8. Woodhouse, *Narrative*, 34–35.

9. Drummond, letter book, 136 (October 1838), quoted in Ward, 'Death of a Church,' 59–60.

ample historical precedent.[10] Some in the council appeared to have 'hoped for quicker results,' although prophecy through Taplin had indicated that their sending forth would not be until twenty-one years from their separation, and that the intervening period would be one of weakness for them.[11] Discontent may have been expressed in the council, and it seems that the apostles were failing to give the leadership necessary: whereas their concerns lay primarily with the universal Church because that was the nature of their ministry, angels were more concerned with the affairs and problems of particular churches.[12]

A useful overview of the crisis was provided by Cardale in his letter of 1852, which I shall quote at length because of the authority with which he wrote as pillar of apostles and the information which he provided. In his opinion, the fundamental problem, made worse by the absence of most apostles abroad, was the mismatch between the apostles' understanding of their role and that held by many of their ministers.

> In 1838/9 the apostles had in the light of prophecy & after several references to the Council in London arranged several most important matters & had announced that in consequence of lack of counsel they were unable to arrange others as they w$^d$. have desired to do.
>
> The fact was that there existed in the minds of the Ministers in London troubles & differences not . . . on the subject of Liturgies & forms, but on the subject of the rule & place of 'apostles'. And a morbid feeling existed that the apostles were acting upon principle without light of prophecy & without having sufficient recourse to the Council. No doubt (as was afterw$^{ds}$ discovered[)] there were misapprehensions on both sides.
>
> Still there was beyond doubt a great ignorance on the part of the Ministers as to the place of the apostles, & an idea that as 'called apostles' they 'took too much upon them'. Notwithstanding, there was so great a desire on the part of certain apostles to go abroad for their work there, that they perhaps did not take all the steps they ought to have done for instructing their brethren on these points, and they left Mr C. in charge under circumstances which could not well lead to a satisfactory result.
>
> The consequence was, that without intentional excess in the exercise of authority, & without intentional resistance to its due exercise, a breach was inevitable sooner or later. This became more & more apparently impending. When a circumstance happened not connected with the state of things just described but with one in particular of the ministers which, added to the unsettled state of mind as respected rule & obed$^{ce}$, compelled the apostles at Albury in March 1840 to summon their brethren forthwith, & they accordingly were summoned & the whole number met on the 29. June following.

10. Miller, *Irvingism*, 1: 207–8; Ward, 'Death of a Church,' 57.
11. Anon., 'Changing Uses,' 2.
12. Stevenson, 'Catholic Apostolic Eucharist,' 23.

> Upon meeting, the 3 Pillars made their report of the state of things in London. And while the same division of feeling existed there as elsewhere, they all concurred in their report. From that time until the latter end of August their attention was directed to the ascertaining how far these feelings of dissatisfaction & doubts as to rule (I will not say resistance) extended. And then it was that we felt it necessary & [illegible] to visit the angels privately, so as to ascertain beyond all doubt where the evil lay.
>
> The result of this visit was to convince us that it was necessary first of all to lay down the main principles establishing the place & authority of apostles as principles which it was absolutely necessary for <u>all</u> to acknowledge. And after having communicated them to the ministers in Council with us I was authorized to go up to London & to declare those principles to the assembled Council.[13]

In a declaration dated 4 August 1840, referred to by Cardale and delivered by him, the apostles expressed their willingness to serve the churches or to be set aside, but warned that they could only serve on the terms they had set out.[14] The subordination of the prophets was clearly asserted, as was the apostles' freedom to act without waiting for supernatural impulse and their authority as interpreters of prophetic light on Scripture. For the first and only time, the apostles were acting independently of all other ministries.[15]

It was to cost them dearly: Mackenzie, who had been a member of Irving's kirk session, agreed to the drawing up of the declaration, but then felt unable to sign it and withdrew, considering (as Cardale and Drummond had initially done) that he had no right to act as an apostle without the Spirit's direct leading and promised supernatural endowments, i.e., before being sent forth in power. Thus 'it became necessary to transmit the document, not as a perfect and authoritative word of the Apostles, but as an expression of the sentiments of the eleven.'[16] Their actions could never be anything other than provisional thereafter. They briefly suspended activity in the hope of Mackenzie's return, but to no avail.[17]

Another factor in Mackenzie's decision may lie in some pamphlets produced by a minister who was subject to the discipline of the Church. Joseph Amesbury was a surgeon and a priest at Newman Street, who in 1849 issued a *Narrative* of the proceedings against him.[18] He argued that the apostles had (wrongly, in his view) delegated oversight of the seven churches in London, which were not part of any tribe,

---

13. Cardale to Dowglass, 10 May 1852.
14. Woodhouse, *Narrative*, 84; Copinger, 'Annals,' 86. For the text of the declaration to which Cardale referred, see Dodsworth-Drummond papers, MS 4727, 9-16.
15. Woodhouse, *Narrative*, 86-87.
16. Dowglass, *Chronicle*, 28; cf. Anon., 'Changing Uses,' 3.
17. Copinger, 'Annals,' 87.
18. Amesbury, *Narrative*.

to Cardale.[19] They forgot the prophetic word commanding them to act only when they were unanimous, and Amesbury claimed that at least one apostle thought his case 'one of the most disgraceful persecutions that ever came within his knowledge.' Mackenzie, with whom Amesbury appears to have remained in contact, dissented on conscientious grounds (over what is not stated), and the result was division, leading to the suspension of the Council of Zion, the closure of some congregations, and the effective abandonment of others to the care of individual angels.[20] Amesbury was convinced that the apostles had overstepped the mark in suspending the council, and that Mackenzie had seceded because he felt that the other apostles were disregarding his rights and his judgement as an apostle.[21] This may lie behind the story that many years later Woodhouse explained why Mackenzie could not be commemorated at All Saints along with other deceased ministers and members: 'he held and adopted strange views and doctrines, and condemned and discountenanced the doctrines which we held—he held intercourse with persons formerly associated with us, (who had drawn aside), and with others believed by us to be under evil spiritual power.'[22]

The angels accepted the declaration, but the Council of Zion was disbanded on 1 September, and the apostles' ministers, even the pillars (i.e., the heads of the four ministries), were suspended.[23] A later minister asserted that a further reason for the council's dissolution lay in the impossibility of securing sufficient attendance as many ministers had secular jobs; 'the Apostles began to see that it was intended to be a sort of model of the perfection of the saint which had not yet been attained but which they were to work towards.'[24] A ban on prophecy (presumably in the churches) was also imposed, which was not lifted until 1842: ministers were forbidden to act on prophetic words, Woodhouse intimating without any sense of irony that prophecy among the apostles supported this.[25]

In spite of what had been lost, Cardale felt that the overall impact had been positive. 'The effect of that declaration was by God's grace <u>instantaneous</u>, and upon the same being generally communicated, we received from all quarters the expression of adhesion thereto.'[26]

---

19. Amesbury, *Memorial*, 9.

20. Amesbury, *Narrative*, 66 (quotation), 75; Amesbury, *Memorial*, 6–8.

21. Amesbury, *Hope of Zion*, 14, 16.

22. Woodhouse to Carl Rothe, 5 February 1856, in Schröter, *Die Katholisch-apostolischen Gemeinden*, 490 n. 67.

23. Flegg asserts (unfortunately without indicating his source) that some who had travelled abroad to visit the tribes had commented critically on their superiors' lack of success: 'Gathered under Apostles,' 79.

24. LPL, MS 4944, W. R. Stevenson, 'History, Archaeology, Architecture' (April 1905), unpaginated.

25. Woodhouse, *Narrative*, 84–85; Born, 'Lord's Work,' 61; cf. Flegg, 'Gathered under Apostles,' 79.

26. Cardale to Dowglass, 10 May 1852.

## THE INTRODUCTION OF LITURGY AND VESTMENTS

The outcome of the crisis of apostolic authority consolidated Cardale's position as the movement's leader. He now occupied himself in producing a comprehensive liturgy.[27] A lithographed form of consecration for use at the Lord's Supper had been introduced in 1838, but the recall of the apostles to deal with the crisis of 1840 provided an opportunity to make progress toward introducing a full liturgical order, drawing on what they had seen and heard overseas.[28] In 1841, therefore, Cardale drew the apostles' attention to the churches' need for a liturgy, and to the desirability of adopting vestments. Instruction in the principles was given to the churches before the apostles set about producing forms of worship. On 28 July 1842 both liturgy and vestments were introduced at Albury.[29] Subsequently, as Cardale recalled, '[i]n Nov or Decr 1842 I came up to London & then went thro' all the Churches in England, arranging which of the priests were to act in the several ministries.' Neither vestments nor liturgy were enjoined on any church, but apostles approved of them being used as at Albury upon each church's application to do so. In many cases, this took place on Christmas Day 1842.[30] They appear always to have been introduced simultaneously.

Boase and Copinger assert that instruction on these topics was readily received by the flocks, but this glosses over the problems which resulted.[31] Although few members actually withdrew, a number of churches closed temporarily because of the lack of ministers to fulfill the new liturgical requirements. Flocks were directed to the established Church (sometimes being received *en masse*), and full-time ministers were redeployed elsewhere as necessary.[32] For example, the congregation at Lymington was reduced to the status of a 'helpship' under that at Southampton from 15 April 1843, 'being unable to furnish Ministers for the bringing out of the 4 fold ministry'; some ministers were reassigned to Southampton so that the worship could be set up there, where on 18 April the liturgy and vestments were first used.[33] Even Westminster, one of the seven churches in London, was affected, the building being sold in the spring of 1846.[34] As late as 1851 there was a reference to the flock at Eynsham being committed to the care of the local clergyman.[35]

---

27. Ibid.
28. Boase, *Supplementary Narrative*, 832, 834.
29. Anon., Southampton record, 28 July 1842.
30. Boase, *Supplementary Narrative*, 835.
31. Much of the factual information in what follows is drawn from Copinger's 'Annals' for the period, supplemented by sources which have hitherto received little if any scholarly attention.
32. Boase, *Supplementary Narrative*, 836; Rossteuscher, 'Rebuilding,' 588. By contrast, Carlyle ensured that the North German liturgy of 1849 could be performed by a priest alone, or with the assistance of a deacon: Archiv der NAK, Henke, 'Carlyle,' 15.
33. Anon., Southampton record, 15 April 1843.
34. Cardale to Dowglass, 10 May 1852.
35. NC, 17 September 1851.

It has been suggested that the closures were of churches with a nonconformist background or led by ministers who had served under Irving.[36] In the south-west of England, a number of churches were closed after trouble of some kind and their members brought under that at Bath.[37] Since William Keene, who was in charge of an affected congregation at Melksham, had been a Baptist minister, and the area was fertile ground for religious dissent at this period, this may be part of the explanation, especially if one argues that such congregations would be less likely to furnish ministers willing to participate in a liturgical service. On the other hand, the Bishopsgate congregation, whose strong nonconformist roots were evident in its worship as late as the 1950s,[38] remained open.

Certainly the principle of liturgical worship had to be justified by the apostles and accepted by members who had come from non-liturgical backgrounds. In 1843 Drummond produced a *Rationale of the Offices and Liturgy of the Church*, apparently intended to serve as an introduction to the edition of the liturgy published that year, the first for general use. He argued that just as Jewish worship had been minutely prescribed, so Christian worship should keep strictly to the divinely instituted pattern. Vestments were justified as symbolizing God's provision of a covering in which to approach him.[39] In churches under apostles, concluded Drummond, 'all which is most valuable, because most true and catholic, as well in doctrine as in ceremonial, and which hath been observed in Holy Church in all ages, is recovered out of the confusion into which it hath unhappily fallen, and is arranged according to the order and method of God's House, the pattern whereof He showed to Moses on the mount.'[40]

The congregation at Islington seems to have encountered particular problems with the introduction of a liturgy and vestments. As late as 1882 it was reported that it had been formed in difficult circumstances; only now was correction making progress.[41] Was it perhaps a rare example of a 'low' Catholic Apostolic church, with a membership primarily drawn from non-Anglican backgrounds? Mackenzie had been its angel, and his continued insistence on a sense of the moving of the Holy Spirit as essential to apostolic action may reflect an outlook which would have been ill at ease with a less spontaneous and more ordered approach to worship. Moreover, one of the elders, D. G. Foster, published a protest in 1843, which seems from the title to have been actuated by the introduction of a liturgy and vestments and the way the angel (the Revd F. W. H. Layton, an Anglican clergyman) had handled the matter.[42] Foster

36. Manfred Henke to the author, 4 August 2007.
37. Archiv der NAK, Edward Heath to [?H. B. Copinger], 20 December 1912.
38. Anon., 'Touching on Music,' *Newsletter* 4 (April 1953) 7–8.
39. Drummond, *Rationale*, ii, xxii. Boase implied that their introduction was the result of a generally felt desire on the part of ministers and people: *Supplementary Narrative*, 835.
40. Drummond, *Rationale*, xxiv.
41. AR 1882, 10.
42. Foster, *Protest*.

wrote of an 'ecclesiastical revolution in the church at Islington'; ministers had been given just ten days to prepare for the introduction of vestments. He felt 'an abiding sense of darkness' at the prospect, and accused the apostles of making a golden calf (alluding to Exodus 32). Doubtless referring to Mackenzie's defection, Foster asserted that there was evil in a divided apostleship. As vestments bound the body, so liturgy bound the spirit. In an appeal to the apostles, Foster accused the Church of worshipping them now as it had earlier worshipped prophets. He also registered his opposition to the use of the term 'priest' instead of 'minister.' All this is indicative of either a low church or nonconformist outlook.

Even the apostles themselves do not appear to have been of one mind on these matters. On 30 March 1844 they issued what Copinger described as an important document concerning worship to the angels; no copy is accessible, but we may surmise that it included a defence of a liturgical approach to worship. Six of the apostles resumed their search for gold in the tribes of Christendom, but King, Armstrong, Tudor, and Sitwell remained at Albury to care for the churches. Between 1844 and 1847 Cardale largely withdrew from apostolic work, leaving Tudor and King in charge,[43] while he gave himself to liturgical study and the preparation of orders for occasional offices, anthems and 'private occasions.'[44] He did not meet the angels of his tribe between 1842 and 1846.[45]

Late in 1845, the apostles were recalled to Albury because of tensions over liturgical and ceremonial matters; in some churches new rites and ceremonies had been introduced without waiting for apostolic authorization.[46] Perceval (whose charge was Italy) now objected to the use of vestments.[47] The apostolate came from a variety of ecclesiastical backgrounds, and Copinger made a rare admission when he recorded that their meeting on 12 January 1846, which discussed liturgical developments, was marked by 'great divergencies of opinion and want of mutual confidence.'[48] The assembled apostles (apart from Dalton and Mackenzie) resumed their charge of the churches, but the problems remained.[49] Dalton had withdrawn from them for reasons known only to himself, and returned to Anglican ministry. It has to be said that his work in France would have been hindered severely by restrictive legislation, and he had been appointed chaplain to the 3rd duke of Leinster (his wife's cousin) in 1846.[50]

43. Miller, *Miller's Notes*; Copinger, 'Annals,' 79.
44. Boase, *Supplementary Narrative*, 837.
45. Copinger, 'Annals,' opp. 81.
46. Davenport, *Albury Apostles*, 127. There was a concern that opposition to the use of vestments and new liturgical forms could encourage opposition to apostolic authority: Born, 'Lord's Work,' 65.
47. Copinger, 'Annals,' 80. It is said that Perceval was also one of the apostles who never sealed anybody within his charge. His only known visit to Italy was with Drummond in 1838, to deliver the Great Testimony.
48. Ibid., 93–94, quoting the coadjutor Isaac Capadose.
49. Boase, *Supplementary Narrative*, 837.
50. Schröter, *Die Katholisch-apostolischen Gemeinden*, 502 n. 72. For a time he served under the

The Minutes of Conference recorded in 1855: 'In 1846 the Apostles had reassembled; and the unsatisfactory result in the inability of the Apostles at that time to take up matters of moment was in Septr. 1846 communicated to the Angels.'[51] From 29 September Cardale brought the angels of London and England together, and explained to them his understanding of events and of the Church's position at that point, as well as the proposed alterations in the services. In 1844 those apostles remaining at Albury had pledged to devote their attention to devising liturgical orders which could be introduced throughout the churches under apostles, but when the apostles were presented with the results (of what was almost certainly Cardale's work) in January 1846, their approval was lukewarm. Cardale therefore decided to introduce these forms in his tribe on his own account, effectively abandoning the principle of collegiate action (although he anticipated that the apostles would subsequently approve them).[52]

Divergence of opinion is evident in a series of letters from Cardale to Drummond during 1846–47. Things were complicated by the fact that Drummond was effectively landlord of the houses at Albury occupied by the other apostles, a relationship that Cardale alleged had been productive of ill-feeling, even though he himself had always found Drummond very responsive to any requests.[53] Drummond's high-handed attitude matched that shown during the building of the chapter house and church at Albury, but he found that he could not dictate to Cardale (who was his social equal and intellectual superior) in the way that he had been accustomed to do with local builders and tradespeople.

Drummond, who was something of a liturgical *dilettante*, appears to have found fault with Cardale's liturgical work on many occasions, to the point of nit-picking. Indeed, at one point Cardale accused Drummond of bitterly attacking it.[54] 'I don't ask any of you [apostles] to adopt these [Advent] services. I placed them in all your hands & you paid no attention to them nor gave me any help. I have since placed them in the hands of the Angels in London & England & I find them accepted universally with the greatest joy.'[55] Ironically, he had criticized Drummond for introducing certain services in Scotland without consulting the other apostles or seeking comments on draft orders from the angels in his tribe.[56] As for Drummond's complaint that the services had been produced by one man,

> is it my fault that these services now come forth to the churches in England as the production of an individual? Have I not done all in my power to have

---

Tractarian W. F. Hook at Leeds: Copinger, 'Annals,' 80. He appears to have left Leeds early in 1847: Dalton, *Substance of a Farewell Sermon*.

51. MC, 28 February 1855, 8.
52. Cardale to Dowglass, 10 May 1852.
53. DFP: C/11/26, Cardale to Drummond, 20 August 1853.
54. DFP: C/11/9, Cardale to Drummond, 23 February 1847.
55. DFP: C/11/5, Cardale to Drummond, 21 December 1846.
56. DFP: C/11/1, Cardale to Drummond, 29 October 1846.

them revised & considered by, & set forth on the authority of the Apostles of the Lord? Is it not the case that I have ever sought, but have been defeated in my endeavours, to uphold the 12fold unity of the Apostles?[57]

Cardale drew up a list of proposed liturgical innovations, dividing them into two 'schedules,' A and B. Those in Schedule A had been approved by all the apostles and could be introduced without any problem. Those in Schedule B, whilst approved by a majority of the apostles, Cardale was cautious about introducing unless demanded by circumstances. Any which a majority of the apostles had disapproved could not be introduced.[58]

Drummond, whose interests lay more in the direction of missionary work, also withdrew somewhat, expressing his disillusionment in a circular on 'foreign work' (work among Christians of other persuasions). Exasperatedly, he alleged that although he drew this up at the apostles' request, as usual nothing was done with it. He considered the movement's near-total lack of missionary zeal remarkable. Indeed, although he had plenty to say in response to Cardale's development of the movement's ritual,[59] he confessed: 'I am heartily ashamed of the way in which the last ten years of my life have been drivelled away.'[60] Later he would also expose the deficiencies of a Testimony-based approach to mission: 'the formal delivery of a copy of the Testimony to an idiot Emperor and a superannuated Pope, can never be honestly held to be a fair dealing with them.'[61] It is possible that there was a connection between Drummond's divergence of outlook with Cardale, his criticism of the focus on liturgical matters in the circular on foreign work, and his decision to return to parliament in 1847.[62]

## A SENSE OF LASSITUDE

Drummond's frustration was shared by many. Woodhouse records the sense of depression under which the angels were labouring:

> About the year 1847 the Pillar of Apostles ... reported to his brethren that several of the Angels ... had made a complaint to him, or rather had brought up to him their burden, in regard to the flocks under their care. They reported that there was a feeling of deadness, of want of a conscious spiritual life and power observable among the members of their Churches; not indeed among those who were weak and feeble and half-hearted, but more especially among those who had always been distinguished for their zeal and intelligence, and

57. DFP: C/11/7, Cardale to Drummond, 11 February 1847.
58. DFP: C/11/13a, 14, Cardale to Drummond, 29, 31 March 1847.
59. Drummond, *Principles of Ecclesiastical Buildings*.
60. Drummond, *Circular Letter*, quotation at 26; cf. Davenport, *Albury Apostles*, 130–31.
61. Drummond, *Remarks on the Ministry of Instruction*, 24.
62. Ward, 'Death of a Church,' 3.

devotedness and spirituality. They reported that they themselves were conscious of this lethargy in themselves, in their teaching and ministrations; they found nothing to complain of in the conduct of these faithful members of their churches; they could only commend the assiduous labours of the priests and deacons; but with all this, there appeared to be a blight upon the congregations, so that they seemed to make no progress, not even to stand still, but to fall back more and more into coldness and indifference....

The Angels desired to lay this their burden upon the Apostles, as it was more than they could bear; and in doing this they expressed their confidence that the Lord would provide a remedy through the ministry by which the churches had been gathered and built and thus far led forward.[63]

Doubtless the apparent delay of the Second Advent had played a part in producing this state of affairs, but so perhaps had the move from a style of worship and spirituality in which the charismata were prominent to a more liturgical approach.[64] The remedy was intended to hasten the Second Advent and to provide a focus for expectations of the Spirit's working. It had its origins in the words used at Cardale's call as apostle (if not earlier, in Scott's distinction between regeneration and baptism with the Holy Ghost, as well as Baxter's prophecies regarding spiritual ordination), and was thought to have been foreshadowed by prophecy on 1 December 1835 which declared that apostles should lay hands on those reaching the age of twenty.[65] It was the sealing with the Spirit, ministered by apostles, acceptance of which implied acceptance of their authority, thus consolidating their role as the movement's leaders.[66] Those sealed would form part of the 144,000 of Revelation 7, who would escape the Great Tribulation as the first-fruits of the redeemed.[67] According to Drummond, this number was not necessarily to be understood literally, but as representing those in communion with restored apostles; it was 'the number of a Church under Apostles.'[68]

It was in 1847 that Cardale came to believe that the time was right for the introduction of this sacrament.[69] The most cautious of the apostles was dubious but, after beginning a series of discourses in his tribe warning his hearers not to expect it immediately, was convinced as a result of prophecy urging them to be ready.[70] In 1846 the churches had been placed under Cardale's charge until the apostles should reassemble in council, when responsibility would revert to them as a college, and on

---

63. Woodhouse, *Narrative*, 118.

64. Roberts, 'Pattern of Initiation,' 188.

65. Copinger, 'Annals,' 65; Born, 'Lord's Work,' 45; cf. Davenport, *Albury Apostles*, 134.

66. Flegg, 'Gathered under Apostles,' 87; cf. AR July 1853, 4.

67. Miller, *Irvingism*, 1:248–53.

68. NLS, Acc. 4388, Volume of homilies etc, 94 (Drummond, 'Homily at Laying on of Hands (15 September 1856)').

69. The delay was later put down to disobedience: Anon., *Teachings by Priests*, 2.

70. Woodhouse, *Narrative*, 124. One wonders whether this was Woodhouse himself.

2 March 1847 the gatherings of the seven churches in London for worship and teaching were resumed. Their scope was now more limited, since they met as the council of the tribe of Judah rather than of Zion (the seven churches having originally been seen as a demonstration model of the whole perfected Church). The eucharist now formed a part of the proceedings, and Cardale was 'almost invariably Celebrant' until his death.[71] Worship was followed by meetings with their priests and deacons and the angels of the tribe, so that Cardale could prepare them for the introduction of this rite.[72]

According to Cardale's account in the first 'Apostles' Report', his fellow pillars, Taplin, Thompson, and Place, applied to him to be sealed, which he did on 31 May 1847. On 8 June he proceeded to seal the angels of the seven churches in London, along with twenty other angels serving in England; two further services on 9 and 28 June saw 132 priests and over a thousand deacons and laity sealed.[73] His policy of phased introduction of the rite, backed up by careful preparation through teaching, ensured that it met few of the challenges which had been encountered in the introduction of a liturgy. The rite was only to be introduced in a tribe when the faithful were ready to receive it,[74] which may explain why in some tribes it was never administered. What is more, the Church felt itself reinvigorated, turned its gaze outwards, and saw considerable fruit for its labors. The introduction of sealing had a salutary effect on members, reaffirming that the Spirit was indeed given to believers, but liturgically rather than charismatically. This served to enhance the apostles' authority as those through whom this gift was bestowed, rather than eroding it as others claimed to be equally endowed with the Spirit.[75]

It might be wondered whether the rite of sealing as practised by the apostles was in any way dependent on that introduced by Joanna Southcott some decades earlier. My own opinion is that this is unlikely. Southcott charged for it, and the rite was in any case different. Furthermore, Cardale was not the sort of person to have shown credulous interest in her activities. It seems sufficient simply to acknowledge that both movements shared an interest in relevant portions of the book of Revelation.

In spite of the hopeful outlook, it was clear to Cardale that teaching was needed on liturgical matters, not least because of the variety of opinions among his fellow apostles. According to Copinger, he began this late in 1847, although Edward Heath

71. LPL, MS 4937, 'Notes from a lecture on the 7 churches &c. by Mr. Roger Duke, Chelsea, March 6th 1895.' On the assembly, see Rupert M. Heath, *Teaching at Southwark*; Rupert M. Heath, *Lecture on the Assembly of the Seven Churches*.

72. Anon., Southampton record, 2 March 1846; DFP: C/11/25, Cardale to Drummond, 27 February 1851; Bramley-Moore, *Twin-Feasts*, 5; Copinger, 'Annals,' 82. Until Westminster reopened in 1857, there were only six. The council meetings continued until the death of Cardale's coadjutor, John Leslie, in 1897, and the assemblies of the seven churches until 1908.

73. AR July 1853, 1.

74. Davenport, *Albury Apostles*, 134.

75. Roberts, 'Patterns of Initiation,' 188–89.

would later state that it was in 1849 and the two following years that Cardale ministered on this subject at the meetings of the seven churches.[76] Cardale's ministries were published as *Readings upon the Liturgy and other Divine Offices of the Church*, beginning in 1849 with the section on the types of the Law, on which the apostles had received much prophetic light since 1836. Ministry on the eucharist followed in 1851, and on holy days in 1852. Several other sections appeared much later: on baptism (1874), the laying on of hands (1876), and ordination (1878; unfinished). As for the rites themselves, a number were introduced over the next few years: anointing of the sick in 1846, reservation of the sacrament in 1850, and the use of lights and incense in 1852 (earlier in a number of tribes outside England).[77] It would seem, then, that any wariness of liturgical worship had by now disappeared, whether through the impact of the introduction of sealing (as Woodhouse believed) or through the defection of those who disapproved.[78]

In July 1851, the apostles finally approved services prepared by Cardale a number of years earlier, presumably those not approved in 1846, when their meeting had been so disunited. That July they also approved the continuation of the service he had introduced in 1847 for the meeting of the seven churches.[79] These meetings were 'a provision for training for our future work,' so that these churches could fulfill their place 'when brought together as one, and meeting as the Council in Zion.'[80] The teachings given by Cardale and the other three pillars at these assemblies, therefore, are of particular significance. Indeed, the Bradford church gathered them into a bound volume, indicating that congregations elsewhere looked to them as an authoritative source.[81] The importance of these gatherings for fostering a corporate sense of calling and mission meant that 'strangers,' who were attending by the mid-1850s, were not to be invited by members to do so; the rule was that only those known and approved of by the 'Five Pillars' (i.e., the five pillar-evangelists in London) should be admitted. They or their parents had to be sealed, and if coming from a church outside London they had to bring a certificate from their angel.[82]

---

76. Edward Heath, *Paper*, 29 June 1902, 1.

77. Boase, *Supplementary Narrative*, 838–40; Copinger, 'Annals,' 81, 89, 95–96. Reservation of the sacrament was not for adoration, but for communicating the sick and for daily celebrations, as well as 'proposition' before the Lord as an expression of trust in Christ's sacrifice.

78. Woodhouse, *Narrative*, 134.

79. Copinger, 'Annals,' 92, 93.

80. NC, 20 August 1851.

81. WYAS, 53D95/5/3.

82. MC, 1 December 1858, 86–87; cf. 30 January 1878, 80; Rupert M. Heath, *Council of Zion*, 14.

## RENEWED GROWTH

On 3 June 1851 Cardale reported that apostasies were becoming very rare, and that more backsliders were constantly returning. Since 1848 services had begun or been restored in a number of churches.[83] That August he wrote (probably with reference to his own tribe) that numbers of the faithful had pretty much doubled,[84] and in May 1852 he wrote that Sunday attendance had doubled since 1846, that a third of the membership had been added since that date, and that a sixth of the membership was comprised of those who had been restored.[85] We shall see later that these years also saw the establishment of a solid base for future growth in Germany. The retrenchment of the early 1840s was effectively being reversed. In time, of the British congregations in existence by 1843, only Aberystwyth in Wales; Bradford on Avon, Dudley, and Everton (Hampshire) in England, and Irvine and Kirkcudbright in Scotland have no recorded presence at any point after 1847.[86] All the same, reclaiming the ground lost took several decades; the congregation at Aberdeen, for example, was not re-established until the mid-1870s.[87]

A snapshot of the Church's strength is provided by the 1851 Census of Religious Worship. Conducted on 30 March that year, this was the only official attempt ever made to measure the formal religious allegiance of the whole population of Great Britain. Although the returns for individual congregations in Scotland have not survived, those for England have, and we also have the cumulative statistics in the official reports. According to these, there were thirty-two places of worship in England and Wales, with total attendances in the morning of 3,077, in the afternoon 1,607, and in the evening 2,622. In Scotland there were three places of worship, with total attendances of 272, 126, and 190. The largest building in England appears to have been Newman Street, with a seating capacity of 800; Whitechapel could hold 700, and Southwark and Nottingham 400 each. The largest congregations recorded were at Newman Street (500, 400, and 350, doubtless estimated rather than counted), Southwark (250, 300, and 300) and Chatham (234, 271, and 227). A number of the English returns (which were supposed to be completed by the congregation's minister) were signed by him as 'angel or bishop,' and there were frequent protests 'against being classified under any Sectarian name, or among Dissenters from the Church of England.' The statistics were

---

83. AR July 1853, 1.

84. NC, 20 August 1851.

85. Cardale to Dowglass, 10 May 1852; cf. Dowglass, *Chronicle*, 40.

86. Aberystwyth is likely to have been dependent on the leadership of C. M. Carré (1809–54) and to have ceased when he was moved away as an evangelist after 1835. The Irvine congregation appears to have met in the village of Dundonald, towards Ayr, in which town a work was later established. Bradford-on-Avon and Everton were probably connected with nearby congregations at Bath and Southampton, both of which took in outlying members during the early 1840s. That at Dudley was close to both Wolverhampton and Birmingham.

87. AR 1876, 13.

not encouraging, even though the Church was growing at the time. In his pamphlet on the census, Woodhouse was deeply affected by the fact that the Catholic Apostolic Church, for all the richness of its provision as 'the perfect organization, given at the first for the work of the ministry, for the perfecting of the saints, for the edifying of the Body of Christ,' was 'unable to command sufficient attention to get these claims fairly inquired into,' whereas the Brethren, who were characterized by a light estimate of creeds, sacraments and priesthood, and the Mormons, who departed from sound doctrine and (he feared) from Christian morality, were both able to command more adherents.[88] The census must have been a blow to the Church's confidence (as indeed it was to that of the Church of England).

On the other hand, confidence must have been boosted, as was the Church's public profile, by the opening of a splendid new building in Gordon Square in December 1853 as a replacement for that in Newman Street. It became a shop window for Anglicans seeking a more advanced liturgical life than was legally permitted within their own Church. However, whilst the congregation had long wanted to build a new church, it was difficulties with the lease on Newman Street which forced their hand, as the owners would neither renew the lease nor allow the congregation to purchase the property. As originally conceived, the new building was to include a chapel for preaching by the evangelists, as well as an apostles' chapel and council room, residences for ministers, offices, and an institution for the 'poor and friendless.'[89] In the event, not all of these requirements could be incorporated, and the building opened for worship shorn of two bays at the west end and a three-hundred foot spire. The Newman Street congregation was given a quarter's notice, and as there was no seating in the new church they carried the seats through the snow from the old one. Later on a south chapel was added, as well as the English Chapel, where Cardale would celebrate the eucharist for his tribe and confer with his ministers.[90]

## ATTEMPTS TO RECLAIM DALTON AND MACKENZIE

In conference with the angels on 20 August 1851, Cardale on behalf of the apostles outlined what had been done to reclaim the two defectors.[91] They had sought to convince Mackenzie of his error in absenting himself and to induce him to return, but all attempts to do so had been unavailing. As for Dalton,

> It seems that having been led by what appeared to him the guidance of Providence to reside for a time in Yorkshire, he was induced to offer his services to do temporary duty in the Church of England. From this he was led on to

88. Woodhouse, *Census*, 13.
89. Knight, *Building*, 3–4.
90. Rupert M. Heath, 'The Central Church, London,' *Newsletter* 10 (March 1957) 2–3; cf. Anson, *Fashions in Church Furnishings*, 110. For a full account, see Henke, 'Catholic Apostolic Church.'
91. NC, 20 August 1851.

take more permanent duty in the Church of England, and was in this position when we were called together in January 1846. He then wrote to us in answer to the letter requiring his attendance stating that he found it inconsistent with these recently assumed duties to be present in our councils, that he felt he could not ask us to become responsible for his act by giving him any leave of absence, but he avowed the continuance of his faith in the work of the Lord as a whole.... In our answer we expressed the opinion that it was impossible for us to give any leave of absence, that the responsibility of his absence must rest upon himself and that for ourselves we proposed to apply ourselves to our duties towards the churches.[92]

A deputation of two apostles had been sent to each man, but not only did Mackenzie refuse to return, but Dalton now 'absolutely refused, no longer professing to retain his faith unshaken in the work of the Lord as a whole, but expressing not absolute unbelief but serious doubts both as to any proof in Scripture of God's purpose to restore apostles and also as to the Divine character of the work itself.'[93] Dalton's change of mind was recent and the struggle was still ongoing, so the ten apostles simply wrote a letter expressing their pain and surprise and declining to enter into debate, appealing to his former testimony, and warning of the danger if he did not return. They entrusted Mackenzie's case to Woodhouse's care, and appointed William Dow to take charge of the tribe in Sweden. Mackenzie had been suspended earlier, on 8 August 1846. (Woodhouse was with him when he died in 1855, and affirmed that Mackenzie had expressed his belief in the divine origin of the work.)[94] Cardale was aware that some thought that the other apostles could summarily deprive these men of their office and replace them,[95] but he argued that they would need to be sure of the rightness of such a course of action, and could not merely act upon prophetic utterances or notions of expediency. Dalton would return to the apostles' council on one occasion in 1853 before taking up his work again after Perceval's death in 1859, visiting Italy as well as France.[96]

Others among the apostles may also have been less than totally committed. We have noted Perceval's lack of interest in his tribe. Drummond was to remain an active

92. CUL, Hopkinson Papers, Add. MS 7893, Lithographed notes of a conference of the apostles with the angels, 20 August 1851.

93. Ibid.

94. Copinger, 'Annals,' 81, 102.

95. Carlyle appears to have sought such action as a way of restoring the twelvefold unity of the apostolate, but his colleagues evidently disagreed, though the hope of such a restoration remained in North Germany: Henke, 'Apostles' Council 1851,' 4–5. Carlyle's attempt may have been the context for the attempts to reclaim the two defectors.

96. Dalton may have been demotivated, not only with regard to ministry as an apostle, but also with regard to ministry in the Church of England. According to Samuel Rawson Gardiner, he had done very little as curate at Clovelly in Devon: Gardiner letters, Gardiner to Martin Irving, 23 February 1857. Yet his *Four Lectures on the First and Second Advent*, preached in Leeds during Advent 1846, became something of a Catholic Apostolic classic, being reprinted several times.

MP until his death, which must have limited the time available to him for work in the Church, although he travelled frequently to Scotland and elsewhere. Tudor's commitment is also unclear: he and Dalton were the only apostles not to issue reports on their work from 1847 onwards, and the only activity recorded in his charge of Poland before the 1890s was after it had been committed to Carlyle in 1852.[97] That left Armstrong, Cardale, Carlyle, Dow, King-Church (as he was known from 1849), Sitwell, and Woodhouse. The apostles were a long way from being able to act as a college; yet the degree of provisionality which necessarily characterized their activity was often overlooked, not only by members, but also by ministers in their propagation of the movement's distinctive witness and their appeal to others to accept it. The next chapter will show how the first deaths among the apostolate threw the movement into further crisis.

97. Copinger, 'Annals,' 97.

# 5

# Division and Recovery (1855–68)

THE FOURTH CRISIS TO affect the Catholic Apostolic Church concerned the issue of whether gaps in the apostolate should be filled. We have already mentioned that Carlyle was arguing in 1851 that they should, and that Dalton and Mackenzie should therefore be replaced. In a lecture to the newly formed church at Buchwäldchen in North Germany in April 1851, he called on the faithful to pray that the number of apostles would be filled up, as one had proved unfaithful, and that the apostles would be united in all things.[1]

The first deaths among the apostles occurred in 1855 (Carlyle on 26 January and Mackenzie two days later, followed by William Dow on 3 November), stunning the congregations and their surviving colleagues. At a meeting of the seven churches on 30 January, Cardale admitted that he had expected all the apostles who remained faithful to survive until Christ's return.[2] Events had, unusually, taken him by surprise. Some members were expecting that a replacement for Carlyle would be raised up.[3] Christopher Heath, angel at the Central Church until 1876, asked Cardale

> . . . whether any instructions had been given to the Angels by the Apostles that it is the duty of the Church to pray for filling up the number of the Twelve Apostles? such an opinion being prevalent; and there having been public teaching to that effect. The Apostle said that no instruction of the nature alluded to had been given by the Apostles. He had no hesitation in saying that the Apostles have never concurred in, or favoured and such conclusion as

---

1. '[D]ass ihre Zahl voll werde—denn einer der Apostel ist untreu geworden—das sie alle in volle Thätigkeit kommen, dass sie in allen Stücken einig werden': Carlyle, *Die Geschichte*, 16. This was omitted from the English translation, *Short History*. At some point, Carlyle had apparently asserted that the apostles had all believed initially that vacancies should be filled up: Apostelbezirk Hamburg, *100 Jahre*, 85.

2. Quoted by the coadjutor Isaac Capadose in a homily to the angels of the seven churches, 14 July 1899: Newman-Norton, *Hamburg Schism*, v.

3. Henke, 'Carlyle,' 15–16.

that there should be other Apostles called, and separated in order to supply the place of those departed. And in the absence of such conclusion by them such teaching is most improper. For the question must immediately occur[:] what is to be done with our departed brother Mr. Carlyle? If God sees fit to do any such act we may safely leave the matter in His hands. But for us to be speculating on any such matters, before we are taught, and that in the face of such important difficulties is most improper, and very daring.[4]

In 1920 Heath's successor, Henry S. Hume (1840–1928), recalled:

I am old enough to remember the shock occasioned by the first breach in the ranks; and how the faith of some was tried, because it had been too readily assumed that all the Twelve must continue in this life until the Lord's return. I remember also the expression of the alternative hope that other Apostles would be called to fill the vacant places—and I distinctly recollect a ministry by the Pillar of Apostles, Mr. Cardale, at a Meeting of the Seven Churches in London, discouraging such an expectation....[5]

The idea also grew up that the apostles were 'doing a work to comfort the spirits of the departed.'[6] In this way, many thought, the number of the sealed would be filled up.[7] Six of the remaining apostles met at Albury in June 1855, and considered whether replacements should be appointed, but decided that this was not for them to do, and concluded that there was no scriptural warrant for replacing apostles who died.[8] However, the desire for replacements was not thereby quenched: on 17 July 1859, when Charles J. T. Böhm, who had worked alongside Carlyle as an evangelist in North Germany since 1836, was preaching at Albury, Taplin prophesied that Böhm was sent as 'an Apostle of the Lord.' Although this was originally taken to mean that he would replace a dead apostle, the apostles interpreted it as a call to coadjutorship, and Böhm became the first of twelve coadjutors appointed to assist the apostles.[9]

The protagonist in subsequent developments was the first German angel-prophet, Heinrich Geyer (1818–96). As a young schoolmaster, he was a devout believer, evidently influenced by Pietist currents of thought; he held Bible studies and services in his home, and in 1844 founded Bethesda, a rescue institution for neglected children modelled on the famous Rauhes Haus of the Hamburg 'Inner Mission' leader J. H. Wichern (with whom he was in touch). His social activism made him unusual among converts to the Catholic Apostolic Church, which he joined at the end of 1849. Geyer

---

4. NC, 28 February 1855, 21–22.
5. Hume, *Address, 24th November, 1920*, 1.
6. Prophecy at Southampton after Drummond's death, quoted in Ward, 'Death of a Church,' 66.
7. Ibid., 65–66.
8. Copinger, 'Annals,' 102.
9. Miller, *Irvingism*, 1:315–16; cf. Apostelbezirk Hamburg, *100 Jahre*, 38. Woodhouse condemned Miller's statement as 'utterly untrue': Miller, *Miller's Notes*, 2(2). Copinger, 'Annals,' 109, merely states that Böhm was called as a coadjutor.

was made an angel-prophet in 1852, and his combination of oratorical talent, spiritual and pastoral insight, and awareness of the contemporary religious landscape made him greatly valued by the churches as a preacher and counsellor.[10] Although such appointments may not have been made by the Church on a systematic basis until 1863, he functioned as prophet with the apostle for North Germany at a time when there were few prophets of the rank of priest or above in the tribe, and travelled extensively in ministry. Virtually all ministers of the rank of priest and above in that tribe called to office after 1852 were called through his prophetic utterances.[11] Geyer also published the first Catholic Apostolic periodical, *Die Morgenrothe*, from 1860 until his departure from the Church in 1863; this was widely read outside as well as inside the Church.[12] In addition, he was also on the staff of the growing Berlin church, under the former Lutheran pastor Carl Rothe as angel.

Geyer enjoyed a warm and open relationship with the German congregations' most intellectual minister, Heinrich Thiersch, whom we shall meet shortly. He appears also to have got on well with Carlyle, but after Carlyle died and Woodhouse took over responsibility for the tribe, relations were more formal.[13] Woodhouse appears to have been somewhat wary of him, especially after a word through another prophet that Satan was seeking entrance into the tribe. He gave Geyer to understand that he was not to consider himself a minister of the universal Church and therefore not officially the prophet with the apostle; thus Geyer was not invited to Woodhouse's meetings with Böhm and Thiersch as evangelist and pastor with the apostle respectively.[14]

Geyer visited England a number of times, and was one of the twelve angel-prophets invited by the apostles to annual gatherings at Albury from Pentecost 1858. These provided opportunities for the apostles to instruct the prophets, assess their gifts, and read parts of Scripture and also the *Records*, with a view to encouraging the prophets in their ministry. Perhaps it is significant that, of the twelve, only three were from the continent: Geyer from Germany, Petit-Pierre from France, and Faesch from Switzerland.[15] At the 1860 gathering, on Geyer's allocated day to serve as prophet, he called on the apostles to long that the empty places might be filled, and named Böhm

---

10. Apostelbezirk Hamburg, *100 Jahre*, 77–79, drawing on Geyer's unpublished autobiography, 'Aus der Mappe eines alten Schulmeisters von H. Reyeg'; Schröter, *Bilder*, 203–6.

11. Apostelbezirk Hamburg, *100 Jahre*, 76; Schröter, *Die Katholisch-apostolischen Gemeinden*, 264; cf. Archiv der NAK, Work Group History of the New Apostolic Church, 'Split 1862–1863.'

12. Schröter, *Die Katholisch-apostolischen Gemeinden*, 68, 212.

13. It is noteworthy that Woodhouse authored many of the circulars included in the official compilation: Anon., *Sammlung*. All but one postdate Carlyle's death. Clearly Woodhouse had a more formal approach to his role as apostle.

14. Schröter, *Die Katholisch-apostolischen Gemeinden*, 207, 209, 553–54 n. 109.

15. Cardale, *Notes of Lectures* (duplicated), 1 (from a 'Paper to accompany the Words of Prophecy on Ezra and Nehemiah' sent to angels and not in the 1861 edition); Apostelbezirk Hamburg, *100 Jahre*, 79.

and W. R. Caird as apostles (for Germany and France respectively).[16] Proceedings were promptly adjourned for the day, and whilst the prophets present were delighted at this utterance, the following day Geyer was called before Woodhouse, who made it clear that the apostles could not accept any such callings and that the number of apostles remaining would suffice until the Second Coming. Counselled by the angel in Hamburg, F. W. Schwarz, to remain silent and to submit, he continued to be used throughout the tribe, and also in Woodhouse's tribe of South Germany, Roman Catholic Switzerland, and Austria, as well as France, until late in 1862.[17]

However, on a visit with Woodhouse to Königsberg in October 1862, Geyer prophesied that a priest there, Rudolf Rosochacky, was not only called as an apostle but also was to become the first of a new twelve (the New Testament precedent was the call of Paul and Barnabas without reference to the Jerusalem apostles). Expectations had thus shifted from the replacement of apostles who had died. Woodhouse was not present at the time, having retired to bed, and was not told subsequently, but a few weeks later Geyer prophesied in the Berlin church that the Second Coming would not precede the revelation of the Antichrist. This struck at the heart of Catholic Apostolic eschatology because it could not easily be reconciled with the hope that the 144,000 would be translated to heaven before this and the associated Great Tribulation. Geyer also believed that the 144,000 would be drawn from all centuries of Church history and were not restricted to those who had been sealed by the English apostles. Rothe, who played a leading role in the Catholic Apostolic Church in North Germany, judged this to be a false prophecy, but Geyer stood his ground, backing up his case from 2 Thessalonians 2:1–3. Geyer was excommunicated and suspended from office, and Woodhouse confirmed the sentence in Hamburg on 27 January 1863, also excommunicating Schwarz.[18] (Geyer and Rosochacky had visited Schwarz early in January; Schwarz had accepted Rosochacky's call, and Rothe's ministers sent to Hamburg had been refused access to the congregation.) In a circular to the North German angels dated 12 January, Böhm alleged that Geyer had long been conspiring against the apostles, holding private gatherings and calling Rosochacky behind Woodhouse's back.[19]

The apostles' council at Albury in July 1863 discussed Geyer's views but saw no reason to change their position.[20] Woodhouse dissolved the large Hamburg congregation; only a few remained to restart Catholic Apostolic work in the city, apparently in

---

16. That Geyer called a replacement apostle for France indicates that he considered Dalton to have been unfaithful to his charge.

17. Apostelbezirk Hamburg, *100 Jahre*, 81–84; Schröter, *Die Katholisch-apostolischen Gemeinden*, 211–12, quoting Heinrich Geyer, 'Wie ist es gekommen daß zweierlei Apostolische-Gemeinden entstanden sind?' (ms, 1893).

18. Apostelbezirk Hamburg, *100 Jahre*, 85–87, 98–101; Schröter, *Die Katholisch-apostolischen Gemeinden*, 206, 213–16.

19. For the circular, see Apostelbezirk Hamburg, *100 Jahre*, 343–45.

20. Schröter, *Die Katholisch-apostolischen Gemeinden*, 227.

1872.²¹ Rosochacky was fairly soon reconciled to the Church, and the 'Annual Report' for 1885, noting his death, recorded that he had served as coadjutor to the angel at Königsberg.²² No mention was made, however, of his temporary involvement with what became the New Apostolic Church. Indeed there was hardly any mention of that body anywhere in these 'Reports'. There is no reference to these events in Woodhouse's *Narrative of Events* or Boase's *Supplementary Narrative*, the main internal works to cover this period.²³ The Catholic Apostolic Church always found it difficult to acknowledge the existence of the New Apostolic Church,²⁴ and attempts by the new work to achieve reconciliation (or perhaps to win over the old Church to their views) have always been repulsed. In 1886 three apostles of the new Church (F. W. Menkhoff, F. Krebs, and H. F. Niemeyer) wrote to Woodhouse to seek reconciliation, outlining what the two movements agreed on and where they differed, and using the same arguments as the Catholic Apostolic Church had done to justify the appearance of new apostles.²⁵

Division, separation, and competition (notably in Holland, where Schwarz worked as an apostle) all served to harden attitudes, and in 1897 a conference of angels with the coadjutor Edward Heath reported that the most serious issue facing them was 'the activity of the adherents of the Prophet Geyer . . . and of the false apostleship established by him.'²⁶ That autumn Heath circulated a warning to ministers in England:

> the Coadjutor wishes you to be informed that the followers of the prophet Geyer and of the false apostolate set up through him, are showing increased activity in Germany and Switzerland. Their emissaries appear in America and Australia, and have lately been found in Denmark. It is probable that they may visit England and Scotland also.

---

21. Newman-Norton, *Hamburg Schism*, vii–ix; W. H., *Katholisch-apostolische Gemeinden*, 112. Newman-Norton includes the text of Woodhouse's circular of 19 February 1863 reaffirming Catholic Apostolic eschatological teaching in the context of the division, 'On the possible call of New Apostles and the special hope of the Firstfruits, with particular reference to Herr. H. Geyer and his New Apostolic Church' (1863). Woodhouse believed the North German churches to be 'to a certain extent in ignorance as to what the Apostles thought concerning these questions': *Hamburg Schism*, 3. He rejected Geyer's claim that Taplin had been suspended by the apostles for prophesying that replacements should be expected, and justified the refusal to grant formal recognition to Geyer as an exercise of spiritual discernment: ibid., 8, 14.

22. AR 1885, 22.

23. Nor does Miller, *Irvingism*, mention it; if he was heavily reliant on information provided by members, this would not be surprising.

24. A rare exception was L. Langholz, 'Die Neuapostoliske Kirche,' *Ungdomsbladet* 6/3 (February 1958) 6–7.

25. For the letter, see Apostelbezirk Hamburg, *100 Jahre*, 375–84.

26. AR 1897, 25.

> The Angels are therefore warned to be on their guard, and especially to be careful in verifying letters of commendation purporting to come from churches in Germany.[27]

The new movement has never gained much of a foothold in Britain (although it did in several parts of the British Empire); on the other hand, its strength in Germany did not hinder the Catholic Apostolic Church from becoming stronger there than anywhere else. As it matured, the New Apostolic Church moved rapidly away from its roots, ceasing to use vestments and incense, and later banning prophecy in its services. A century later, the main evidence of its origins is the rite of sealing (although this has now been extended to children), the centrality of the eucharist to its worship, and the apostle ministry.

What Schröter calls 'the Geyer affair' posed searching questions concerning the working relationship between apostles and prophets. He argues that Geyer's discontent at the standing of the prophets was a motivating factor behind his call of new apostles.[28] Woodhouse, for his part, felt on one occasion that the prophets at the Albury meetings were failing to show due deference towards the apostles, interrupting the deliberations with utterances on unrelated subjects.[29] Taplin's death in March 1862, followed by events in Germany, led to the temporary suspension of the gatherings, although they resumed from 1864/5 until 1867.[30]

The episode also challenged Catholic Apostolic eschatology, potentially lessening the attractiveness of the offer of a place of refuge from tribulation. Perhaps most importantly, it highlighted the need for the Church to come to terms with the fact that, barring the interposition of the Second Advent, its apostles were going to die. What should happen to it then? How did it begin to prepare for the disappearance of the apostles? These questions will be discussed more fully later, but New Apostolic scholars have argued that Catholic Apostolic expectation did indeed change, with the introduction of the idea that seventy archangels would lead the Church after the removal of the apostles.[31] A crucial aspect of the Church's developing understanding of its place in the divine purposes was that of three stages in the Lord's work. One of the earliest systematic considerations of this appears to have been in 1858, when the apostles and prophets at Albury studied the book of Ezra and Nehemiah 1:1—7:4. They concluded that the raising and translation of the saints were progressive; that the witness would be borne by three successive classes: the first-fruits, the two witnesses, and the great multitude; and that the spiritual captivity into which the Christian Church fell had nevertheless resulted in multitudes coming to Christ.

27. AD, October 1897.
28. Schröter, *Die Katholisch-apostolischen Gemeinden*, 265.
29. Woodhouse, *Teaching on the Prophetic Office*, 8.
30. Schröter, *Die Katholisch-apostolischen Gemeinden*, 210, 560 n. 115.
31. Henke, 'Die Geschichte der Katholisch-apostolische Kirche'; Rothe and Henke, 'Milestone'; cf. Miller, *Irvingism*, 1:316.

The following year they completed Nehemiah and also studied the book of Esther.[32] The May 1860 gathering considered Revelation 1–16, and a manuscript record of the prophecies given that year is extant.[33]

The fruits of these gatherings were mediated to the faithful in Cardale's *Notes of Lectures delivered in the Seven Churches in London in the Months of October, November, and December, 1860* (1861). This work laid the foundation for later thought concerning God's purposes.[34] Three epochs were discerned in Old Testament history after the exile of the Jews, which were taken as a pattern of what God would do in the last days; these epochs were typified by the work of Zerubabbel, Ezra, and Nehemiah respectively.[35] In each epoch God would ensure that a testimony was delivered, warning of judgment and offering refuge.[36] The first stage, initiated by the decree of Cyrus and involving the building of the altar, the restoration of observance of the feasts and sacrifices, and the laying of the foundations of the Temple, was seen as typifying the apostles' gathering and sealing of those who would form the first-fruits of the harvest and their rediscovery of the true principles and order of worship. The second stage, beginning with the decree issued by Darius, involved the building of the Temple and the keeping of the Passover. In its eschatological antitype, the work begun under apostles would be completed, those who had rejected it would be convinced of its truth and sent forth as messengers, the Two Witnesses, who would testify after the first-fruits were gathered; there would be no further gathering during this stage. The third stage began with the decree of Artaxerxes, and included further restoration (as well as a fast in repentance for the mixed marriages contracted) and the building and government of the city under Nehemiah. Its antitype followed an interval of weakness and silence; after the death of the Two Witnesses, sincere Christians who denied the work and the efficacy of sacraments would be brought out of Babylon and a partial and temporary reformation would occur. A final ingathering would take place under the last messengers, in which all who professed the faith of Christ would be brought back to God and saved from the power of Antichrist, although not without enduring the Great Tribulation.[37]

Around this time, anticipation among members was growing: 1865 would mark thirty years since the separation of the apostles, and some expected that as Christ entered on his public ministry at the age of thirty, so this year would see the Second Coming.[38] The following year had been fixed on by Evangelical students of prophecy,

---

32. Cardale, *Notes of Lectures* (duplicated), 1–5.
33. WYAS, 53D95/5/1, 'Words of Prophecy spoken upon the Book of Revelation between 1st and 12th May 1860.'
34. Cardale, *Notes of Lectures* (1861), 2.
35. Ibid., 3–8.
36. Ibid., 16.
37. Ibid., 8–13.
38. Miller, *Irvingism*, 1:290–91, citing Norton, *Restoration*, 188.

and any expectation among members that the Second Advent would occur in 1866 may have owed something to Irving's forecast that the resurrection of the righteous would inaugurate the millennium about 1867/8.[39] W. F. Pitcairn, the angel at Edinburgh, agreed with commentators who fixed the return of the Jews for 1868 and their recognition of Christ as Messiah for 1880, but he explicitly avoided fixing a date for the Second Coming because Scripture stated that its day and hour were known by nobody.[40] Although Miller claimed that there was something of a sceptical reaction after Christ failed to appear, he also noted that on 14 July 1875 (forty years after the separation of the apostles) around a thousand of the faithful gathered at Gordon Square in the expectation of Christ's Second Advent. The coadjutor Isaac Capadose confirmed in 1899 that the translation of the 144,000 had been widely expected to occur on this date.[41] Further date-fixing seems to have been going on during the late 1870s.[42] As late as 1902 another coadjutor, Edward Heath, referred to expectations that Christ would appear first at Albury or among the seven churches, or that the resurrected apostles would appear first at Albury, and warned against over-dogmatism in such matters.[43]

Clearly the movement had not lost its sense of urgency, although it may be questioned how far the more settled 1850s and 1860s offered a hospitable climate for the reception of its apocalyptically charged message. That urgency showed itself in a renewed commitment to outreach. Testimonies had been produced for clergy in Scotland (1842), and for Spain and America (1850). In 1853 a draft was produced for pan-European use.[44] This may be what was referred to by a resolution of the apostles on 19 January 1855 'that a public testimony should proceed from the Angels of Churches to be distributed throughout Europe, the heads of which were provided'; Cardale was to collate suggestions from angels regarding the document's content.[45] In fact, it was drafted by two angels, and unlike the Great Testimony, which was sent from the apostles as heads to the heads of Christendom, this one was seen as emanating from the body of the Church and directed to the body of Christendom; accordingly it was distributed not only among clergy but also (in England at least) by lay members to interested acquaintances.[46] Testimonies were accordingly distributed in Scotland and

---

39. Irving, *Babylon and Infidelity*, 364, 415.

40. Acc. 8837, Two volumes of Ministries, vol. 1, W. F. Pitcairn, 'Copy letter, on the way in which to think of the <u>high</u> Church—& low <u>Church</u> &c.' (February 1867).

41. Miller, *Irvingism*, 1:297, 319; Isaac Capadose, *Homily, 14th July 1899*, 4–5. For a reference from Edinburgh to this expectation, see Acc. 8837, vol. 1, Pitcairn, '15 Sun after Pentecost 1875.'

42. Woodhouse, *Four Addresses*, 1. These were first delivered from 1878–81.

43. Edward Heath, *Paper, 29 June 1902*, 2.

44. NC, 'Heads of Document for circulation throughout Europe,' 1853. For an examination of translations and edited versions of the Great Testimony produced by individual apostles, and differences between them, see Anon., 'Changing Uses.'

45. Copinger, 'Annals,' 103.

46. NC, 26 March 1856, 38–39.

England (both in 1856), North Germany (1856), and North America (1858).[47] Ward suggests that this effort was motivated by renewed expectation of the Second Advent.[48]

We can gain an insight into what was involved in this effort from the letters of Samuel Gardiner and his wife Isabella. In April 1856, his brother Charles was addressing two thousand envelopes for distribution to London clergy and dissenting ministers,[49] and the angel-evangelist Thomas Dowglass, one of the five pillar-evangelists in London, sent a lithographed letter with the Testimony offering a personal interview.[50] That year Dowglass also issued *An Appeal to English Churchmen*. It may be in connection with this that several rooms were registered in London for Catholic Apostolic worship.[51] Gardiner, who was then a deacon-evangelist, offered this Testimony at the close of an evangelist sermon in Newport, Isle of Wight; fifteen hearers took copies at the door on their way out, and more when he preached on it subsequently.[52] By the middle of June, the evangelist Sir George Hewett stated that ten to twelve thousand copies had been distributed, three thousand from the Central Church; no longer was the movement hidden from the public gaze.[53] Yet for all this effort Hewett admitted that none who had responded in writing had regarded the work as divine, and when the annual reports from the apostles were read at the Central Church in July it was acknowledged that results had been meagre.[54]

That autumn we hear of open-air preaching in London once more.[55] In November Cardale was to instruct the evangelists concerning the Testimony at the assembly of the seven churches in London.[56] The following January, Hewett expressed his conviction that evangelists should seek to reach people directly rather than through their ministers (who had proved unresponsive and represented a potential blockage to the message getting through), each individual being responsible for themselves.[57] In this may lie the germ of a change of strategy evident after 1861. Thereafter we find public meetings being arranged for the reading of a Testimony. That year, the 1836 Testimony to the English bishops and clergy was read in various places in England, and an invitation leaflet was produced. This explained that apostles had been shown that the announcement of the restoration of apostleship and prophecy should be made in that

47. Copinger, 'Annals,' 77, 90, 102, 103, 104, 108.
48. Ward, 'Death of a Church,' 64.
49. Gardiner letters, Samuel Gardiner to Martin Irving, 19 April [1856].
50. Isabella Gardiner to Martin Irving, 17–18 May 1856.
51. At Whitecross St, Clerkenwell, and Pentonville: UCL, Tierney papers, Add. MS 384.
52. Isabella Gardiner to Martin Irving, 3 June 1856.
53. Isabella Gardiner to Martin Irving, 18 June 1856.
54. Samuel Gardiner to Martin Irving, 19 July [1856]; Isabella Gardiner to Martin Irving, 20 July 1856.
55. Isabella Gardiner to Martin Irving, 3–4 September 1856.
56. Samuel Gardiner to Martin Irving, 7 October 1856.
57. Isabella Gardiner to Martin Irving, 8 March 1857.

part of Christendom where God's grace had first been shown. Many in various nations had responded to the message and congregations had been formed. But now, events of which the bishops had warned seemed to be coming to fulfillment. Church-state links were weakening; Christ's laws were being cast aside. The Church was in danger of losing its temporalities. Anarchy and confusion were impending, and judgment was hanging over Christendom. God had provided an ark of refuge, to which end the office of apostle had been restored. It was time for God's ministers to warn Christians and show the way of escape; accordingly, the leaflet concluded, the Testimony would be read at notified times and places.[58] The Great Testimony was also read on occasion, possibly in obedience to a prophecy at Albury in May 1860 urging the Apostles to send pairs of ministers with 'the epistle to the One Holy Catholic and Apostolic Church to[?] all her heads in order beginning with Rome.'[59]

Copinger's 'Annals' lists many occasions when a Testimony was delivered, especially after 1870; often an accompanying leaflet was distributed, summing up the Church's message.[60] Alternatively, the address might be printed for publication: an 1867 example from Caird was basically a summary of the Great Testimony, arguing that what it foretold had come to pass.[61] A major outreach was mounted in London during 1866. Four lectures (one specifically for the lower classes) were arranged in public buildings, advertised in newspapers, on railway stations, street corners, and elsewhere. Cards were distributed to attended giving the locations of the seven churches and the times of evangelist sermons. In total, 7–8,000 attended, three-quarters of whom were non-members.[62]

This activity provides the context for Cardale's 1865 statement regarding *The Character of our Present Testimony and Work*. He exhorted ministers to respond to prophecy of coming judgments by engaging in a vigorous work of testimony, forming bands of lay assistants to share in the work. However, he ruled out proselytism of those who received the message, and asserted that forming separate congregations was not the main object of the restoration of apostles.[63] He also acknowledged the movement's failure to carry out its commission hitherto.[64] In spite of the difficulties through which it had passed, the movement was by no means spent; the days of its greatest growth lay ahead.

---

58. Place, *'Twenty-Five Years ago.'*

59. 'Words of Prophecy 1860,' 20; cf. Copinger, 'Annals,' 111.

60. E.g. Anon., *Address* (1867); Anon., *Address* (1894); Anon., *Address for Circulation*. A scrapbook formerly held at Gordon Square and containing invitations to such meetings and to special series of sermons, almost all in England between 1886 and 1901, is in the BOC library.

61. Caird, *Address*.

62. Anon., *Sammlung*, 139–40. For two of the lectures, see Layton, *Address*; Symes, *Address*. The latter went through four editions by the end of the year. A number of similar addresses were published from the mid-1860s onwards. This venture was held up by Böhm early in 1867 as an example to the North German churches: *Sammlung*, 137–39.

63. Cardale, *Character*, 1, 28–39, 41; Miller, *Irvingism*, 1:294–95; Ward, 'Death of a Church,' 66.

64. Cardale, *Character*, 2–3, 45.

# 6

# Expansion I
Survey

It is fortunate that the heyday of the movement, the late nineteenth century, is also the period for which the most official material exists in the public domain. The chief source of information is the 'Apostles' Reports,' issued annually from July 1853.[1] In them each apostle outlined to the college the main developments and challenges in his area of jurisdiction (from 1878, the reports were submitted by the coadjutors). Whereas internal histories of particular congregations or areas were often frustratingly vague and shared the concern evident in Boase's *Supplementary Narrative* and Woodhouse's *Narrative of Events* to present the movement as a divine work at the expense of providing sufficient detail regarding its human agents, these reports contain a great deal of information, enabling us to build up a fairly full picture of the Church's development during the last quarter of the nineteenth century. The first report, although not issued until 1853, included information on the period since 1847.[2] A concluding report covering the months before Woodhouse's death was issued by the coadjutors in August 1901, and a summary of events since then in August 1903.[3] The reports were forwarded to the angels and read at meetings of Catholic Apostolic congregations, and also at the meeting of the seven churches in London, when particular points were highlighted by the apostles.[4] From 1879 the title changed to 'Annual Report' ('Apostle's Record' in 1882) as there was now only one remaining apostle. Much of the information in Copinger's 'Annals' appears to have been derived from these reports.

  1. I was unable to trace copies of those for 1854–73, apart from that for 1870.
  2. AR 1853, 1. It is likely that the introduction of the practice of reporting was connected with the introduction of the rite of sealing and the renewed emphasis on extension work.
  3. AC, August 1901; AC, 7 August 1903.
  4. For references to this practice, see Samuel Gardiner to Martin Irving, 19 July [1856], 18 July [1858], 26 July 1862; CUL, Add. MS 7893, Hopkinson Papers, T. W. Guillod to Lady Dawson, 18 July 1859; AR 1891, 1.

Address books also appeared occasionally, possibly from as early as 1841, before they became an annual publication in 1882.[5] In time they were issued in two parts, one bound in red, covering the English-speaking world, and the other, in German and bound in blue, covering the rest of Christendom.[6] These can be used to chart not only the geographical spread of congregations, but the status of each—whether or not it was independent, whether it had a regular eucharist, and so on. Unfortunately, archive holdings are patchy, especially for pre-World War I editions.

## THE OVERALL PICTURE

The story of the growth of the Catholic Apostolic Church during the later nineteenth century is somewhat different from that of Evangelical nonconformist denominations such as the Baptists, the Brethren, the Congregationalists, and the Wesleyans. A key factor in this is the limitation imposed by the Church's sense of its own mission. This was not primarily to the unbaptized, but directed at the perfecting of the body of the baptized. As the American angel J. S. Davenport stated in 1863, '[o]ur present work is not to convert the world, but to hasten the Parousia.'[7] Having said that, some similar strategies were employed.

There is some evidence, too, that expectations were scaled down somewhat over time. By the mid-1850s Drummond could admit that when restoration began, many thought God would set up such a church in every city of Europe, but:

> Facts of 30 years have silenced these imaginations: In scarcely a single town is there such a Church as God has taught us to know is His perfect form of worship and the true model of the kingdom of heaven. So far from increased numbers being gathered in by Evangelists, the annual additions barely supply the deficiencies created by death and removals. Instead of zeal growing warmer it waxes colder, and it becomes us not to live in a region of delusion and call it piety, but to recognize truth & to guide our steps in its light.[8]

Yet, before we examine each tribe in turn, it is instructive to look at the overall statistical picture. The most important step for those affiliating with the Church was to be sealed. Statistics of numbers sealed were kept meticulously, like all Catholic Apostolic statistics, and they are given by tribe in the *Apostles' Reports*. Numbers of

---

5. MC, 25 January 1882, 136. Previous editions are known to have appeared in 1872, 1878, and 1880, and the *Church Almanac* for 1869 includes a directory of churches. Copinger also refers to lithographed lists of addresses of angels and churches being prepared in 1841 and 1862: Copinger, 'Annals,' 76, 113.

6. The earliest known German address book dates from 1878, and its preface indicates that this was the first edition: I owe this reference to Edwin Diersmann.

7. Davenport, *Edward Irving*, 50.

8. Acc. 4388, Volume of homilies etc, 123–24 (Drummond, Homily, Blessing of Deacon, 21 September 1859).

those sealed for the reporting years 1875–1900 and the final eight months to Woodhouse's death in 1901 total 65,909. This represents an average of almost 2,500 a year, but there was significant year-on-year variation, from 1,403 (1877) to 4,225 (1896). Numbers during the 1890s, however, were above the longer-term average. This was probably the result of a sense of heightened urgency, as Woodhouse was ageing and failing and the movement was engaged in a renewed burst of evangelist work. If we double the total for 1875–1901 to cover the whole period from the introduction of the rite in 1847, we may posit a total of 132,000 sealed members.[9]

North Germany was the area with the greatest number of people sealed from 1875–1901 (30,580). England, by contrast, saw only 13,431. South Germany and Switzerland saw 6,067, and Denmark 4,420. Elsewhere in Europe, there were 2,445 sealings in Russia, 1,368 in Sweden and Norway, 1,313 in Holland, 443 in Austria, 274 in Belgium and France, and just 7 in Italy. No sealings were recorded in Poland, Spain and Portugal, or Greece. Not all the apostles conducted sealings; Miller asserts that two never did so, inaccurately naming King-Church as one.[10] In the rest of the Anglophone world, 2,976 were sealed in Scotland, 1,589 in North America, 826 in Australia and New Zealand, 125 in Ireland, and 45 in India. Clearly, whilst the Church's direction came from England, its center of gravity in terms of membership lay already in the German-speaking world.

Table 6.1: Ratio of Sealings to Ministers

|  |  | Ratio of sealings to Deacons blessed | Sealings to Priests ordained | Sealings to Angels consecrated |
|---|---|---|---|---|
| England | 781D, 400P, 96A | 17.2 | 33.58 | 139.91 |
| Scotland | 169D, 93P, 22A | 17.61 | 32 | 135.27 |
| Australia / NZ | 55D, 54P, 11A | 15.02 | 15.3 | 75.1 |
| N America | 118D, 79P, 29A | 13.47 | 20.11 | 54.79 |
| N Germany | 2,268D, 812P, 208A | 13.48 | 37.66 | 147.02 |
| Denmark | 352D, 153P, 38A | 12.56 | 28.89 | 116.32 |
| S Germany / Switzerland | 354D, 156P, 50A | 17.14 | 38.89 | 121.34 |

For some areas it is also possible to work out the ratio of sealings to ordinations, as shown in Table 6.1, although variations in reporting mean that the figures must be treated as provisional. The low ratio of sealings to ordinations of priests and consecrations

---

9. There were also a large number of members to seal at the start of the period (as is evident from the figures in the 1853 report), which would balance the lower-than-average figures during the late 1870s and early 1880s.

10. Miller, *Irvingism*, 1:252, 294. Copinger records King-Church as conducting sealings in 1852 and 1863: 'Annals,' 97, 114. I think it likely that the two apostles were Perceval and Tudor, and that lack of response rather than lack of willingness forms at least part of the explanation.

of angels in Australasia and North America was probably due to the need to provide ministers for many small and isolated groups of members; by contrast, the high ratio in Germany and Switzerland probably reflected the concentration of members in many areas in larger congregations.

Table 6.2a: Numbers of Congregations, Europe

|  | 1869 | 1900 |
|---|---|---|
| Belgium | 2 | 3 |
| Denmark | 2 | 55 |
| France | 6 | 7 |
| North Germany | 42 | 236 |
| South Germany | 4 | 41 |
| Austria |  | 6 |
| Holland | 1 | 16 |
| Italy | 1 | 1 |
| Norway |  | 10 |
| Russia (incl. Finland, Estonia, and Latvia) | 10 | 13 |
| Switzerland | 5 | 40 |
| Sweden |  | 13 |
| Total | 64 | 441 |

We cannot establish the size of typical congregations, but we can estimate their number. Schröter asserts that this multiplied tenfold worldwide between 1863 and 1901, and that numbers of congregations and members tripled between 1880 and 1901, thanks to a broader evangelist work and natural increase within congregations.[11] The 1862 address list had included details of 111 congregations,[12] and analysis of the lists for 1869 and 1900 (Continental) or 1869 and 1906 (English-speaking world) indicates that the increase in congregations was in the order of eightfold rather than tenfold, but this conceals wide regional variations.

Growth in the Anglophone world was slower, except in the USA, where immigration, especially from Germany but also from Scandinavia, is likely to have been a significant factor, as it was for other Churches.

11. Schröter, *Bilder*, 25.
12. Copinger, 'Annals,' 113.

Table 6.2b: Numbers of Congregations, English-speaking World

|  | 1869 | 1906 |
|---|---|---|
| England | 63 | 299 |
| Scotland | 9 | 29 |
| Ireland | 2 | 5 |
| America (U.S.A.) | 2 | 27 |
| Canada | 3 | 12 |
| Australia | 7 | 14 |
| New Zealand | 2 | 4 |
| India | 1 |  |
| Total | 89 | 390 |

Analysis of my database of known churches, dependent congregations, and other locations where regular meetings were held in Britain, demonstrates when the Church was most evangelistically effective. It is approximate because reasonably precise dates of founding are only available for about half the congregations. The results are tabled below.

Table 6.3: Numbers of Congregations founded in Britain, by Decade

|  | Founded | Refounded |
|---|---|---|
| 1830s | 74 | 1 |
| 1840s | 4 | 7 |
| 1850s | 11 | 4 |
| 1860s | 25 | 4 |
| 1870s | 38 | 1 |
| 1880s | 16 |  |
| 1890s | 14 |  |

As might be expected, in Britain the movement grew most rapidly during its first years: seventy-three congregations had begun meeting by 1836, perhaps as many as half of them in 1834 (some may have owed their origins to Irving's final preaching tour that year). From 1837–61, only sixteen new congregations came into being, and another thirteen were re-founded, having closed during the 1840s. Growth was reasonably rapid from 1865–84, but patchy thereafter, although it is likely that some of the congregations which came into being by 1901 resulted from the evangelistic push of the 1890s.

For comparison, we may take Germany (North and South): address lists supplemented by other information give totals of thirty congregations in 1860, fifty-one in 1869, 214 in 1894, and 347 in 1912. This suggests a reasonably consistent rate of increase during the period to 1894. It is likely that almost all the increase between then and 1912 in fact occurred before 1901, and that there may thus have been a greater than usual rate of growth during the 1890s.

## THE TRIBES

### The Seven Churches in London

Albury was the heart and London the head of the Church, as explained in a teaching by the angel Newdigate Burne in 1878:

> ... Albury is the place where the Twelve are hidden from the world, and the work of intercession which they carry out is one which attracts not the observation of men; whereas London, or the Seven gathered into one, is the place of their manifestation, where their work is displayed unto all who have spiritual eyes to see; where the restored order and worship are seen in full operation under Apostles, Prophets, Evangelists, and Pastors.
>
> The position of the two ... [is] as the head and the heart to the body of a man; Albury being the place whence directions of government proceed, the place of council; London the place where the resolves and determinations of the head are carried out, and flow unto the whole Church.[13]

The seven churches in London thus functioned as a kind of demonstration model of the universal Church. As such they were for some years under the jurisdiction of the whole apostolate, being regarded as not belonging to any one tribe. But in 1846 they were committed to Cardale's charge, this being on a permanent basis from 1851, rather than being renewed at each meeting of the apostles.[14]

In 1853 it was decided that until other arrangements should be made, their angels would function as the seven deacons of the universal Church.[15] This laid upon them the responsibility of handling all funds transmitted to the apostles, keeping all title deeds of Church property, and overseeing the administration of local congregations. It was to be a crucial role, especially as funds for extending the Church's work were not always in liberal supply. After World War II, their successors became the trustees, seven men who continue to administer Church property and funds, and who are in a sense the last remaining office-holders of the Catholic Apostolic Church.

As the population of London migrated outwards from the center with the growth of rail commuting, some of the seven churches followed: Bishopsgate moved to Hackney in 1874, and Southwark to Camberwell in 1876, both keeping their former designation until closure. In 1894 the Paddington congregation moved to a new church, designed by J. L. Pearson. Horn churches were opened at Kentish Town (1864; under

---

13. Burne, *Albury. Feb. 10. 1878*, unpaginated.
14. MC, 28 February 1855, 8; NC, 20 August 1851 respectively.
15. Rawson, *Church in Southwark*, 15.

the Central Church) and Holloway (c.1870, to Wood Green from 1906; under Islington). These too were probably intended for members moving out of the city.

The seven churches were seen as corresponding to those in Revelation 2–3, in order of their foundation. In addition, prophecy through Taplin in 1860 laid the foundation for a further application of the type to seven cities of Christendom which would play a key role in God's future purposes for the catholic Church.[16] A detailed table of the correspondences was provided by a member in India, George Burne, in 1865, which includes the only reference I know to the application of this typology to India (probably this did not meet with apostolic approval). Burne heard the Indian identifications in a prophecy at a eucharist in the Eastern Chapel at Gordon Square (more often known as the English Chapel).[17]

Table 6.4: The Seven Churches

| Ephesus | Central | London | Madras |
| --- | --- | --- | --- |
| Smyrna | Bishopsgate | Berlin | |
| Pergamos | Southwark | Paris | |
| Thyatira | Chelsea | Rome | |
| Sardis | Islington | Vienna | |
| Philadelphia | Paddington | Berne | Loodiana |
| Laodicea | Westminster | 'The North' | |

# England

Early growth was weighted towards London and the south of England, with just a few congregations in the most important metropolitan centres of the Midlands and North. From the 1870s, however, much of the growth appears to have been in the industrial areas of Yorkshire and Lancashire, with virtually no new congregations being founded in southern England. The Church grew in areas which also saw other millenarian movements flourish, such as the Southcottians in Lancashire and the West Country or the Jezreelites in the Medway towns. However, we cannot prove, or even plausibly demonstrate, any direct links between the Church and these movements. Rather, similar factors made each movement attractive, such as the promise of security in times of apocalyptic instability.

One of the problems in attracting people to hear an evangelist was that members themselves seem to have been affected by the prevailing contemporary enthusiasm for sermon-tasting. As an angel-evangelist reported from London, 'our own people do not generally encourage their friends to attend unless the preacher is a man of

16. Born, 'Lord's Work,' 98.
17. Martin family papers, George C. Burne to Martin Irving, November 1865.

some eloquence. They do not encourage them simply in order to hear the word of Testimony.'[18] But in the North of England, there was much more interest. Here, the problem seems to have been the lack of finance which affected the evangelist work throughout the country. It was possible to gather a crowd of three thousand to public lectures, as at Liverpool and Sheffield in 1873/4.[19] Later on, however, the North too would prove unfruitful.[20]

Tribes were to be divided into five angel-evangelist districts, although most did not reach their full complement. In England, these comprised the Eastern, Midland, Southern, Northern, and Western districts. By 1869, most of the angel-evangelists were living in London.[21] Not initially forming part of any tribe, London and the surrounding counties had five more angel-evangelists (sometimes known as pillar-evangelists), which it kept after the churches came under Cardale's jurisdiction.

## Scotland and Protestant Switzerland[22]

Missionaries from the new movement soon reached Switzerland, where Drummond would have had contacts as a result of his involvement in the *Réveil*. However, apart from public theological controversy, no fruit resulted. Only in 1849 did the first congregation came into being, at Basle. This was a branch of that at Edinburgh until 1853, but the following year Drummond could report that it had over five hundred members; in his view, its success was due to the number of people out of whom devils had been cast.[23] After Drummond's death Switzerland was assigned to Woodhouse, alongside Germany.[24] In 1872 there were only seven congregations listed, but by 1901 the total had grown dramatically, to forty-one.[25] There was even one in the socialist-leaning industrial city of Winterthur. Zürich was home to what was the largest Catholic Apostolic building in Europe at the time of consecration of its altar in 1895.[26] The last angel ordained in the Catholic Apostolic Church, on 25 January 1901, was for a thriving congregation in the Reformed village of Gossliwyl, between Solothurn and Biel/Bienne. This had nine branch works, and it was claimed that almost all the village's inhabitants were Catholic Apostolics.[27]

18. AR 1874, 1.
19. Ibid., 2.
20. AR 1891, 5.
21. Anon., *Church Almanac* (1869), 34.
22. For a fuller account of the movement's development in Scotland, see Grass, 'Catholic Apostolic Church in Scotland.' On Switzerland, see (briefly) Th. E. F., 'Switzerland,' *News Letter* 2 (April 1952) 11–13; M. and F. von H., 'Switzerland,' *Newsletter* 10 (March 1957) 10–11.
23. DFP: D/3/33, H. Drummond to his daughter Louisa, 2 September 1854.
24. MC, 18 April 1860, 124.
25. Schröter, *Bilder*, 41.
26. Copinger, 'Annals,' 172, 178. Berlin Wilmsstraße, opened in 1901, was larger.
27. Schröter, *Bilder*, 258.

In Scotland, once the London leaders had sorted out the problems caused by giving free rein to the gift of prophecy, and the disorder which had marked early gatherings had been overcome, the Church experienced some early growth. By 1838 there were ten congregations, with a total estimated congregation of around nine hundred, almost half associated with the Edinburgh church. But by the 1851 Religious Census, this figure had plummeted to three hundred, in just three congregations. It is likely that the introduction of liturgy and vestments had been a major factor in this, but it may also be that the Disruption of 1843, with the formation of the Free Church, had an impact on the religious climate. Drummond ensured that strenuous attempts were made to present the message to the clergy. A Testimony in 1842 addressed the divisions in the Church of Scotland which resulted in the Disruption; it deplored schism but affirmed the insistence of those planning to secede on the true standing of the minister and the evil of lay interference in ministerial appointments.[28] Between 1845 and 1852, nearly all clergy received the Great Testimony, and around 1865 preparations were made for its message to be presented to the public through meetings and lectures.[29] Several Church of Scotland clergymen would be attracted, the best known being John Macleod of Govan (1840–98), who became a leading protagonist of high church thinking within the Kirk.[30]

After Drummond's death the tribe was placed successively under Sitwell, Dalton, and Cardale, each of whom visited their charge.[31] By 1875 the country had been divided into three evangelist districts, and methods used included open-air preaching as well as the more usual public lectures with follow-up meetings for inquirers.[32] New congregations were again coming into being, mostly in the central Lowlands, and whilst Catholic Apostolic outreach often struggled to compete with sensationalist revivalism, response in Glasgow to diligent local outreach was such that in 1891 a horn congregation had to be formed. It was reported in 1882 that many members in Scotland were from the poor and working classes, which had been the case since the beginning.[33] Yet it must be said that the movement did not catch on in urbanized Scotland in the same way that it did in Northern England. Probably the Scottish Episcopal Church, which had a not insignificant following among the working classes and was more advanced than the Church of England in terms of ceremonial and liturgy, met many of the needs which induced middle-class and aspirant English Anglicans to join the Catholic Apostolics.

---

28. Caird, Smith, and Lindsay, *To the Reverend the Ministers*.
29. Anon., *Nearness*.
30. On Macleod, see Mast, *Eucharistic Service*; Murray, 'Macleod,' 27–32.
31. Copinger, 'Annals,' 113, 119, 134.
32. AR 1875, 14–15.
33. AR 1882, 14.

## Belgium, Holland, and Denmark

At various points evangelists had preached in the French-speaking part of Belgium, and King (King-Church from 1849) also visited on his way to or from Holland, but the first congregation in Belgium appears to have been founded at Liège in 1852.[34] A congregation existed in Brussels by 1863, with services alternating between French and Flemish by 1872.[35] Large numbers were apparently gathered subsequently in Liège and also Charleroi: a congregation was functioning in nearby Châtelet by the late 1860s. Most of the men in Belgian congregations were coal miners, and many who had been gathered later fell away, partly because of the obligation to pay tithe; those remaining were seen as very ignorant.[36] The congregations seem to have led a fitful existence, and there was evidently a shortage of ministers. In 1895 Belgium was once more united with Holland rather than France.[37] Clearly the bounds of the tribes proved to be more flexible in practice than the theory of their significance might imply.

King-Church visited Holland a number of times after 1838–39 and 1847 until his death, but initially there was little fruit: a pamphlet by the Evangelical Émile Guers, *Irvingism and Mormonism tested by Scripture* (1854), had a negative impact, and former members of one of the London churches had not helped things by making great predictions regarding the role to be played by a pastor at The Hague, which were being rumoured to have come as from the apostles.[38] By 1856 it could only be reported that a few women had been gathered.[39] However, the German angel-evangelist and future coadjutor Max von Pochhammer (1822–95) worked in the country from 1864–66, in direct competition with the Apostolische Zending under F. W. Schwarz. Von Pochhammer laid most of the groundwork for the Church's later development in the country. A Dutch liturgy was published in 1866, and the following year a congregation was finally set up, at The Hague. After King-Church's death Woodhouse paid two further visits, but by 1894 there were no more than ten congregations, all under the oversight of The Hague. A few others came into being subsequently, giving a total of seventeen by 1901. Many members were drawn from the working classes, and so were unable to support weekday services.[40] But there were a few high-profile accessions, the most notable being from the Capadose family. Abraham Capadose was a Jew who converted to Christianity of a Pietist variety. His son Isaac (1834–1920) joined the

---

34. Copinger, 'Annals,' 95; Schröter, *Bilder*, 43.
35. Copinger, 'Annals,' 114, 130.
36. AR 1875, 27; AR 1876, 32; Copinger, 'Annals,' 121.
37. AD, December 1895, 2.
38. AR 1853, 3. Guers's name is misspelt 'Guorss' in the report.
39. Samuel Gardiner to Martin Irving, 19 July [1856].
40. AR 1882, 19; Copinger, 'Annals,' 120, 122; Schröter, *Bilder*, 43, 338–39; Schröter, *Die Katholisch-apostolischen Gemeinden*, 504 n. 74c; Diersmann, *Notes*, 51 n. 173.

Church and would become a coadjutor.[41] In spite of the initial slowness, the Dutch work was to prove one of the most enduring.[42]

Problems occasioned continued to be occasioned by what became the New Apostolic Church. In Amsterdam, for instance, 'a false apostleship, originating in Hamburg was able to settle thirty years ago, and has ever since been a cause of grief and hindrance, preventing our evangelists from bearing a public witness, which might have provoked open contention.' During the early 1890s work began in the city, but privately, 'so as to prevent any collision or even contact with those who present themselves to the public under the name of "The Apostolic Mission".'[43]

In Denmark, however, the message met with an unexpectedly encouraging degree of response.[44] First contacts were made in the late 1850s, and the first congregation formed in 1861, at Copenhagen. After King-Church died, Cardale took over responsibility in 1865, learning Danish and paying four visits to the country by 1873. King-Church had allowed Hewett to go to Norway because he was insistent that he would willingly go there but not to Denmark, although the apostle was convinced that it was from Denmark that blessing would ensue. All the same, Hewett carried out extensive work in Copenhagen from 1858–61, and was called and chosen as coadjutor in 1865.[45]

By 1875 it was reported that Copenhagen and its dependent congregations numbered over a thousand people. One wonders whether such success was due in part to a depressed national mood in Denmark after it had been defeated by Austrian and Prussian forces in 1864, with the loss of its southern duchies of Schleswig and Holstein. It was thought that the way had been prepared by the influence of the Danish theologian N. F. S. Grundtvig (1783–1872), who had visited Irving in London and whose teaching had resulted in a higher value being placed on the sacraments than was usual in Protestant countries. In no other country, it was reported, had such a high proportion of the population been gathered. By 1901 there were no less than fifty-nine congregations. But as in North Germany, most members were recruited from the working classes and their tithe was not sufficient to support enough ministers, especially in a time of depression. Not until 1892/3, later than many other countries, did a minister from the established Church declare his faith in the Lord's work.[46]

As in the other Lutheran nations of Prussia, Norway, and Sweden, opposition from bishops and clergy made it necessary to appeal to government for recognition as

41. Da Costa et al., *Noble Families*.

42. On the work in Holland, see Tang, *Het Apostolische Werk*.

43. AR 1893, 31.

44. On the work in Denmark to 1877, see Aarsbo, *Komme Dit Rige*, vol. 5/i; Anon., 'Denmark: The Church in Copenhagen,' *Newsletter* 5 (November 1953) 11–13.

45. Schröter, *Bilder*, 43, 45; Schröter, *Die Katholisch-apostolischen Gemeinden*, 498–99 n. 69b; Diersmann, *Notes*, 46.

46. AR 1875, 17; AR 1881, 39–40; AR 1893, 28; W. Kølbel, 'Norway,' *Newsletter* 5 (November 1953) 13–14; Schröter, *Bilder*, 43; Schröter, *Die Katholisch-apostolischen Gemeinden*, 498–99 n. 69b.

a distinct community, but Catholic Apostolic ministers postponed this, explaining to government members that 'any voluntary act of separation from the National Church, or any weakening of its influence, is contrary to our principles, & to our desires, & would be a measure forced upon us by the Church authorities.'[47]

## Italy[48]

It is surprising how much effort was expended on Italy, even though response was minimal; the motivation must have owed much to convictions regarding the importance of Rome in God's purposes. Matthew Fletcher, evangelist with the apostle Perceval for Italy, visited the country from 1841–42. On a later visit he spent almost a year in Florence from 1849–50 and another in Turin from 1851–25; he also made contact with the Waldensians in Piedmont in 1851. However, the climate was too repressive for public work, and such private interest as was shown did not produce much fruit. The ministers involved put their knowledge of Italian to good use on returning to London in the early 1850s, instructing some Italian Roman Catholic priests and helping to provide a weekly Italian sermon in the Central Church. These priests may have been those who accepted the work: F. P. Accolti-Gil, L. P. M. Boccelli, and N. M. Corrado.[49] In 1856, there were hopes that a church would be formed in Turin, but it seems to have come to nothing.[50] A chapel was opened in Florence in 1861, which according to Copinger functioned until 1870. Dalton, who now had responsibility for the tribe, visited Italy in 1860 and 1864, but Copinger comments that Florence was the only place where there was any opening for the message.[51]

No report from Italy was issued between 1872 and 1891. In 1872 Woodhouse and a minister visited Florence and Rome; ten years later a Swiss angel-evangelist had tried in vain to gather the remnants of the congregation in Florence, and Isaac Capadose delivered a public Testimony in a concert hall in Rome. In 1890 or 1891 Capadose again lectured in Rome (as well as Florence and Naples).[52] The renewed efforts may well have owed something to the tribe's transfer to Capadose's coadjutorship in 1890.[53] After he visited Rome in 1894, a deacon there had the liturgy translated and printed.[54] By 1900, it appears that a regular congregation was functioning in Rome, something which the Church had greatly longed for.

---

47. AR 1876, 18.
48. On Italy, see W. H., *Katholisch-apostolische Gemeinden*, 125–26.
49. AR 1853, 3–5; Copinger, 'Annals,' 76, 87, 90, 93; Newman-Norton, 'Biographical Index.'
50. Isabella Gardiner to Martin Irving, 3–4 September 1856.
51. Copinger, 'Annals,' 110, 112, 117.
52. AR 1891, 40–42; Copinger, 'Annals,' 150, 164.
53. AD, June 1890, 1.
54. Copinger, 'Annals,' 169; Anon., *Sermon, Quinquagesima Sunday 1953*, 5.

## Ireland, Greece, and the East

Being Irish, and ordained in the Church of Ireland, it was not surprising that Armstrong should have been designated as apostle to that country; indeed, at his call to apostleship it was said that he was to be a prophet to his own land. But Cardale was the first apostle to visit Dublin, in June 1835, and at the same time another Church of Ireland clergyman, John Hardman, was consecrated angel of the Dublin church. Other ministers were rapidly ordained, particularly evangelists, indicative perhaps of intent to spread the message throughout the country. In the autumn of 1836 Armstrong visited all the Anglican bishops in Ireland with the Testimony, as well as Dublin clergy. Worship was commenced in Cork in 1837, but the only other church to have been set up appears to have been that at Belfast in 1847.[55] Armstrong made a number of visits to Ireland from 1847–53, still seeking to extend the work. Opposition was reported in the early 1870s from the Brethren near Armagh, and Brethren and Wesleyans at nearby Darkley,[56] which indicates that attempts were still being made to spread the message.

Armstrong first visited Greece in 1838, and again in 1839–40, learning Greek and studying the Orthodox Church. A further visit in 1849–50 saw him preaching to expatriate English and Armenians.[57] A copy survives of a letter by him, apparently to some Greek Orthodox inquirers, but that is the only evidence we have.[58] In 1855 he was also given charge of 'the East,' visiting Egypt and the Holy Land from 1855–56.[59] He reported receptive audiences in Egypt (including the patriarch of the Coptic Orthodox Church, which was then quite open to Western influence), Syria, and Athens.[60] A few months later, W. R. Caird met the Serbian patriarch on a train, as a result of which he was invited meet the Serbian Orthodox bishops.[61] It seems possible that Armstrong regarded currents of evangelical renewal within the ancient Churches as offering opportunities to present the Catholic Apostolic message. However, no congregations were ever founded in Greece or anywhere round the Eastern Mediterranean, and Russia was the only Orthodox country in which the Church established a presence. Furthermore, little attention was given to Ethiopian Christianity as part of Christendom, although the Ethiopian Orthodox Tewahedo Church was becoming better known to English Christians through reports from agents of

---

55. Copinger, 'Annals,' 38, 49, 68–69, 84.
56. AR 1875, 20; AR 1876, 17.
57. Copinger, 'Annals,' opp. 72, 88–90; AR 1853, 5. There had been hopes of securing evangelical reform in the Armenian Apostolic Church in Constantinople and elsewhere but those influenced by Western missionaries were forced to secede in 1846.
58. In Hopkinson Papers.
59. Copinger, 'Annals,' 103.
60. Samuel Gardiner to Martin Irving, 19 July [1856].
61. Samuel Gardiner to Martin Irving, 7 January 1857.

the Church Missionary Society.[62] Such dismissal was most probably because contemporary Evangelical missionaries were less open to working with the Ethiopian and Coptic Churches than earlier colleagues had been, but perhaps also because these communions were largely pre-Chalcedonian in their Christology, which would have led Cardale, who was extensively acquainted with Byzantine Orthodox liturgies, to regard these Churches as heretical. The Great Testimony, for instance, had described the Eastern Churches (most of which lay within the Ottoman Empire and hence suffered discrimination and oppression) as 'more devoid of spiritual life, of vital religion, than any other body of Christians.'[63]

One sermon in 1876, probably by W. F. Pitcairn, angel at Edinburgh, argued that Turkey was to be regarded as part of Christendom. In a historical review ranging from the early Church to the contemporary period, Pitcairn sought to show Turkey's key role in maintaining a balance of power in Christendom. Its presence in Christendom was a divine chastisement for the medieval division into East and West; it kept them apart, preventing war between baptized nations.[64] However, Pitcairn's breadth of vision was an exception.

## France and Roman Catholic Switzerland

France was the first country to receive messengers sent by apostles, and work there began very early. Outreach was undertaken by the Guernseyman C. M. Carré (1809-54) and the French Protestant pastor and former Continental Society agent Pierre Méjanel (1785-1856). On 15 July 1835 Carré reported to the Council of Zion on their journey through Eastern France and the Suisse Romande, although the former region proved barren soil for their message and it was to be some years before any churches were planted in the latter. They became acquainted with one Louis Duproix near St Quentin, who was invited to England, returning to France at the end of February 1836. The epicentre of the work was in the Département du Nord, along the Belgian border, a religiously unsettled area where Baptists had established themselves from 1820. The Continental Society, with which Drummond had been intimately involved, had worked here too, and contacts already made were exploited for the new movement, which concentrated on the Protestant community. The first congregations were formed in 1836, in the face of opposition from the Continental Society, and that year Duproix became the first angel on the continent, at the small village of Landouzy-la-Ville. Drummond visited Landouzy in spring 1836, to strengthen those who had received the testimony, and later that year Dalton was also in the area. Curiously, it was the marriage of Duproix in October 1836 which led to a form of service being devised

---

62. The exception was a sympathetic sketch of the nation's history and current position: Heinrich W. J. Thiersch, *Abyssinia*.

63. Anon., *To the Patriarchs, Archbishops, Bishops*, §80.

64. Acc. 8837, Two volumes of ministries, vol. 2, Pitcairn, 'Turkey, Decr 1876.'

and approved by the apostles, before any form had been issued for the eucharist. Dalton and Drummond sought an opening in Paris for some years until 1850, when a congregation was finally formed. A key figure here was the former Roman Catholic abbé Céleste Massiot (1809–97), a gifted preacher who would become evangelist with the apostle for France. The following year Drummond visited Northern France, sealing members in various places; many, both Protestant and Catholic, were drawn through coming to see the worship. However, from the mid-1850s all denominations suffered a decade-long prohibition of evangelistic activity, and from 1858–61 the Paris church was without a building. Furthermore, '[t]he church in Paris was nearly put a stop to by some unguarded speeches about Louis Napoleon.' Once Dalton resumed his apostolic labors in 1860, he visited the country frequently, as did his successors, but the French churches were never strong, and by 1901 there were just seven of them, and the members in Paris in 1900 were still drawn from the less wealthy classes.[65] For Catholic Apostolics, the lack of response was due to the fact that the French nation was seen as embodying the democratic spirit. When the locations of seven churches of Christendom were first shown in prophecy, Paris was declared to be the antitype of Pergamos. 'Satan hath now his seat in Paris,' it was declared in 1860, and this would be made visible after the gathering of the first-fruits: the principle of popular power would 'have its seat in Paris when the institutions of the Lord which form the obstacle to the wicked shall be taken away.'[66]

## Poland

As with some of the other tribes, one wonders why Poland was given independent status rather than being joined with another area, especially as the country as a political entity had been divided up in 1815. The answer may lie in the apostles' perception of the partition as an act of unfaithfulness, part of the dissolution of the old order of things, as well as a 'gross and bare-faced injustice.'[67] If so, such sympathy does not have been shown in practice for many years: Tudor appears never to have sealed any members in Poland, or even to have visited the country. No report from him appeared in 1853, and the previous year responsibility for Poland had been assigned to Carlyle. Indeed, apart from a short-lived congregation in Warsaw (1883–87), almost certainly led by North German ministers, the first mention in the "Reports" of any work in Poland came in 1898, when recent progress in evangelism was noted: many Polish speakers had been sealed, and some Poles were now serving as ministers. Prophecy

---

65. De Caux, *Early Days*; Trimen, *Rise and Progress*, 67; Aarsbo, *Komme Dit Rige*, 4/i:35; Copinger, 'Annals,' 45, 61, 65, 67, 89, 91, 94, 108, 112; R. E. J. and E. G., 'France,' *Newsletter* 4 (April 1953) 12–13; Schröter, *Bilder*, 41, 43, 335–36; Diersmann, 'Die Katholisch-apostolische Gemeinde.' Quotation from Francis Sitwell, annotation to Cardale, *Notes of Lectures* (duplicated), 39.

66. 'Words of Prophecy 1860,' 29–31.

67. Trimen, *Rise and Progress*, 2.

reiterating the Lord's concern for Poland spurred things on, and a redistribution of the districts assigned to evangelists in North Germany resulted in the creation of one for Poland in 1898. The Liturgy was also translated.[68] The congregations which were formed were mostly in the Prussian part of the country, only Warsaw and Łódź being in the Russian part.[69] Given the encouraging signs, one wonders how things might have developed if Woodhouse had not died in 1901.

## North Germany and Prussia

This was by far the most successful field of work, in no small measure because it was led by one of the most active apostles. Carlyle visited the country often from 1836, although he was not involved in presenting the Great Testimony to the Kaiser. Publication of literature in English was slow to get off the ground, but in 1843 the first Catholic Apostolic work in German appeared, *Die Kirche in unserer Zeit*. The content is Carlyle's, but the evangelist assisting him, Böhm, appears to have had some hand in the actual writing of the book.[70] Carlyle's careful observation also enabled him to write *The Moral Phenomena of Germany*, which appeared in English translation in 1845. The book has been described as 'a thoughtfully moderate blend of social and theological conservatism (with a whiff of anti-Semitism) which questioned much of the liberalism that had become fashionable in the years before 1848.'[71] His facility in German enabled him to make contacts at all levels of society, and on 18 February 1847 he addressed a letter to the king of Prussia, Friedrich Wilhelm IV (1840–61), who was keenly interested in religious matters and had been influenced by Pietist thinking. In it he testified to the work by apostles, pointed out the failure of the king's attempts at ecclesiastical reform, and offered him a copy of the Great Testimony.[72] The king had been interested in *The Moral Phenomena of Germany*, and was introduced to its author by Baron von Bunsen, the Prussian ambassador to Great Britain and Christian thinker, who was in frequent contact with Carlyle from 1843.[73]

Apart from Carlyle, evangelists had been actively cultivating personal contacts, and from the mid-1840s it became possible to hold public meetings. The first Catholic Apostolic service of worship in German took place in Frankfurt am Main on 17 October 1847. The congregation which was formed was short-lived, but one of those sealed in what was the first such service conducted outside England was Heinrich

68. AR 1898, 20–21; AR 1900, 22; Schröter, *Die Katholisch-apostolischen Gemeinden*, 545 n. 99; Abel, *Das Werk des Herrn*, 36.

69. W. H., *Katholisch-apostolische Gemeinden*, 186.

70. Manfred Henke to the author, 30 October 2006.

71. Timothy C. F. Stunt, 'Carlyle, Thomas (1803–1855).' In *ODNB*, online edn.

72. LPL, MS 4939, 'Copy of a Letter addressed to His Majesty the King of Prussia by Thomas Carlyle.' The date, just eight days after Drummond's *Circular Letter*, makes me wonder whether the apostles had decided that some kind of special effort was called for.

73. Schröter, *Die Katholisch-apostolischen Gemeinden*, 404–6 n. 26, 453–59 n. 51.

W. J. Thiersch (1817–85), a professor of theology at Marburg who gave up his career when he became an angel in 1849, later serving as pastor with the apostle.[74] The story is told that Böhm became discouraged in his work but was heartened by Carlyle, who told him, echoing Acts 18:10, 'certainly the Lord has a great people in this city.' The first sixty members in Berlin were sealed by Carlyle in a hotel on 19 March 1848, when revolution had closed most of the city's churches. Those sealed included the Lutheran pastor Carl Rothe of St Elisabethkirche: he became the first angel in Berlin, serving until his death in 1876, ultimately as archangel. Rothe was one of those who enabled Carlyle and his colleagues to establish good contacts in Prussian government circles. He played a commanding role in the movement's development in North Germany, not least in the division of 1863. Other early accessions included Hermann Wagener, editor of the *Neue preußische Zeitung*, and Ernst von Gerlach, a politician and jurist involved in the newspaper's founding in 1848; the movement was thus developing an alignment with conservative political opinion. In 1849 congregations were set up outside Berlin, at Marburg, Frankfurt an der Oder, and Stettin. By 1850 there were 500 members in Berlin; whilst some were of high standing, Schröter estimates that about 70 per cent were from the working classes.[75] The movement's success in the city was the more remarkable given Berlin's reputation as godless and its low rates of church attendance.

Early growth seems to have been in the east. Growth in the west came after 1870, only Marburg (1849), Hamburg (1854), and Cassel (1854) being established before that date.[76] The political crisis of 1848 seems to have been the catalyst for growth: when it seemed as if that the end times had already arrived, the offer of sealing and the promise of being numbered with the first-fruits who should escape the coming Great Tribulation proved highly attractive. Another factor in the Church's success was the king's Pietist sympathies, which predisposed him to be sympathetic to Catholic Apostolic concerns, probably because he saw himself as called to unite the Western Churches. However, there was friction between ministers influenced by him and local authorities who were more antagonistic, especially in East Prussia (Ostpreußen), Prussia being subject to political and religious instability during the 1840s and 1850s.[77] As in Berlin, over 70 per cent of early members in Prussia were artisans, domestic servants, or otherwise part of the working classes, and the Church's popularity among them at a time of revolutionary ferment meant that it attracted unwelcome attention and faced stiff opposition from the authorities.[78] Police kept reports on evangelist ad-

74. On Thiersch, see W. H., *Katholisch-apostolische Gemeinden*, 227–32.

75. Bayerische Staatsarchiv, Heinrich W. J. Thiersch, 'Chronik,' 1:3; Copinger, 'Annals,' 84–85; Schwartz, *Chronicle*, 1–2; Schröter, *Die Katholisch-apostolischen Gemeinden*, 30–33, 47; Johanning, 'Prayer.'

76. Schröter, *Die Katholisch-apostolischen Gemeinden*, 177, 182.

77. Ibid., 140, 258–59; Railton, *No North Sea*, 216; Schröter, *Bilder*, 31.

78. Schröter, *Die Katholisch-apostolischen Gemeinden*, 35; Railton, *No North Sea*, 204.

dresses, as at Magdeburg, where those on a series of addresses by Max von Pochhammer run to hundreds of pages.[79] In most states it was necessary for congregations to furnish lists of members; in Prussia these were required in order to receive permission to meet.[80] There was interference from the police, public outreach was hindered or prohibited, church buildings had to be closed, and members were excommunicated from the state Churches.

For example, in Hesse-Cassel the Catholic Apostolic Church was classed as a sect (as elsewhere in Germany) and services were forbidden on 12 February 1852 under the provisions of a state of emergency which had been declared in 1850. Members were also unable to receive communion regularly in the state Churches. Prophecy through Geyer condemning the state Church as reprobate urged the faithful to receive communion, and so the eucharist began to be held in homes. This continued until August 1858, apart from an intermission in 1855. Members who participated in these services were threatened with excommunication from the state Churches, which had taken exception to the Catholic Apostolic assertion that the sacraments of other Churches conveyed only a limited measure of grace.[81]

A German angel (probably Thiersch) informed Samuel Gardiner in 1856 that:

> in his church they are entirely prohibited from meeting for worship, and that the only way he could meet his people was at his own house by having so many of them each Sunday afternoon, and to converse with them, then once a month with the priests & deacons under him celebrate the Holy Eucharist at midnight and afterwards from time to time carry round the Holy Communion to the different houses of the members, gathering two or three at a time so that this way all received the nourishment. He said that notwithstanding this instead of there being any going back apparent amongst his people, he rather saw them growing and receiving strength. Mr. [Rawson] Gardiner mentions in a letter I had from him on Friday that he had seen Mr. Woodhouse who told him of the persecution [of] the people which he says originates with the Roman Catholic priests_ the Civil Governments declare they are their best subjects, that they pay taxes, are obedient to the powers that be & give no trouble, but that they must either crush them or quarrel with the Priests & that them they dare not offend_ In some places, persons, who were employed in towns & with whom their masters are perfectly satisfied, & unwilling to part with them, have been ordered to return to their own villages, and they threatened to flog them as vagrants if they were found out of them. In their villages they can get no work so that it amounts to a sentence of starvation. Both at Berlin & at Basle where they are permitted to assemble for worship the buildings will not hold any

---

79. Manfred Henke to the author, 17 October 2014.
80. Manfred Henke to the author, 30 December 2014, 19 October 2015.
81. Manfred Henke, 'Wo feierten katholisch-apostolische Christen das Abendmahl?'

thing like the numbers gathered & they are too poor to provide anything better. This shows that persecution does not hinder the gathering.[82]

Particular problems arose from the lack of legal toleration. In the kingdom of Hannover, until 1866 the only Churches allowed to function were the Roman Catholics, the Reformed, and the Lutherans.[83] As Carlyle reported:

> Our baptismal register is held to be no evidence of birth or legitimacy, and we cannot avail ourselves of the civil register except by declaring our exit from the National Church. The children cannot enter on life without an attestation of confirmation, and the clergy will not give that unless they have taught the children; and the teaching often is such as no parent should expose his children to....
>
> Many individuals in office hate us heartily; but the Government would be in our favour were it not obliged to treat us ill for consistency's sake, in contending with German Catholics, secret clubs, &c. Many in power rejoice in our certainties, and secretly look to us for ultimate refuge.[84]

A royal edict in 1847 had opened the way for citizens to register religious dissent without losing their civil rights, but Catholic Apostolics were reluctant to take advantage of this because of their desire to avoid being classed as dissenters. Protestant authorities often refused church marriage to Catholic Apostolics in an attempt to force them to register as dissenters in order to take advantage of the provisions for civil marriage.[85] The state churches were not ready at first to allow dual membership, although some had cited the Moravians as a precedent.[86] However, members frequently refused on principle to declare themselves separated from the state Churches, although in Saxony those joining the work were required to separate formally from the state Church first.[87] Small wonder that prophecy at Albury in 1860, when Berlin was declared to be the antitype of Smyrna in Revelation 2, called on the faithful in Germany and especially Berlin to be faithful to death, that they might receive a crown of life.[88] Undoubtedly the sustained opposition and obstruction experienced was a major factor in the German Church's developing and maintaining a more markedly separatist attitude than came to prevail in Britain, and the legacy of this is still evident.

Although there were a few high-profile accessions, such as Rothe and Thiersch, most of those attracted in the first generation were from the lower classes, but the

---

82. Isabella Gardiner to Martin Irving, 2–3 August 1856.
83. W. H., *Katholisch-apostolische Gemeinden*, 113.
84. AR 1853, 6.
85. Manfred Henke to the author, 23 February 2015.
86. Schröter, *Bilder*, 33; Schröter, *Die Katholisch-apostolischen Gemeinden*, 259. Excommunication from the state Churches later gave way to *de facto* toleration which included allowing dual membership.
87. AR 1879, 15.
88. 'Words of Prophecy 1860,' 25–26.

social make-up of the movement appears to have broadened over time as second-generation members went to university and then entered the Catholic Apostolic ministry.[89] This lower-class background meant that congregations were often too poor to pay much tithe, from which ministerial stipends were drawn, and was thus a factor in the shortage of ministers. The Church here was long dependent on support from England.[90]

We have seen already that when Carlyle died, Woodhouse took over responsibility and sought to put ministerial relationships on a more formal footing; apart from differences of temperament between the two, a different approach was becoming necessary with the growth of the work and the impossibility of sustaining it on the basis of personal relationships alone. Woodhouse convened the first council of angels, an event which would be repeated annually until 1933.[91] Although initially unable to visit his tribe, and untaught in German, his attention to language study meant that by 1857 Thiersch could say that Woodhouse spoke and preached in German even better than Carlyle.[92]

As late as 1875, there were a mere fifteen congregations under angels, with a further seventy-four daughter congregations with a regular eucharist. By the 1880s some rural congregations were declining through emigration, whether to the cities or abroad. But by 1897 there were five archangel's seats, thirty-two angel's seats, forty-six dependencies under an angel in immediate charge, and 130 smaller congregations, a total of 213.[93] By this time the Church had become the fifth largest religious community in Germany. At the time of Woodhouse's death in 1901, there were over 230 congregations in the country as a whole, with an estimated 60,000 members.[94] For some years from 1886, the tribe was divided among three coadjutors (the successful church-planter Max von Pochhammer, Friedrich Diestel, and Emil Geering, each of whom also had responsibilities elsewhere), the only country where more than one of these was active.[95]

In appealing to the urban working classes, the movement had to face the fact that they were alienated from existing religious institutions; it was reported that converts often lacked any particular religious background and stood in need of good teaching. Yet charismatic gifts were strongly in evidence, perhaps more so here than anywhere outside England.[96] It is curious, then, that the Church should have been so well received in a city noted for its irreligion, especially as it tended to rely in its outreach

---

89. AR 1874, 10; AR 1875, 26; Schröter, *Bilder*, 31.
90. AR 1880, 24; AR 1892, 17.
91. Schröter, *Die Katholisch-apostolischen Gemeinden*, 56.
92. Isabella Gardiner to Martin Irving, 24 May 1857.
93. AR 1875, 24; AR 1884, 21; AR 1897, 10.
94. W. H., *Katholisch-apostolische Gemeinden*, 169–70.
95. AD, July 1886, 3; Copinger, 'Annals,' 154.
96. AR 1879, 7, 14–15; AR 1880, 4.

on a basic grasp of the Bible and Christian teaching on the part of hearers. We have noted the apocalyptic circumstances of its arrival in Berlin; similarly, the end of the Franco-Prussian war in 1871 (and presumably also the proclamation of a unified German empire) was said to have involved many leaving their homes. This, along with continued successful evangelism after the war, necessitated the division of the Berlin church: 1,500 had already been sealed by 1871, but the church building only seated 600. Accordingly horns were formed in 1873 (North), 1885 (East), 1888 (West), and 1891 (Wedding). By the end of the nineteenth century the mother church was the only one (apart from Hamburg) to have a full complement of four horn congregations, and at one point the Berlin churches accounted for no less than 10,000 members. The North horn had the world's largest Catholic Apostolic congregation, numbering two thousand regular communicants. Well into the twentieth century the other three horns also had well over a thousand members each.[97]

## South Germany and Austria

Woodhouse appears to have been slow to work in South Germany, due to his initial lack of facility in German.[98] Work was therefore pioneered during the early 1840s by W. R. Caird; he was acting evangelist with the apostle for South Germany until 1865, when he became coadjutor for South Germany, Switzerland, and Scotland.[99] We noted earlier that in 1842 Caird made contact with Lutz, who recalled, in an illuminating insight into Catholic Apostolic outreach strategy:

> As soon as I was firmly convinced that the work was the work of the Lord, I should have liked to serve in the churches under the rule of the apostles, but they dissuaded me from it. They said that it was my duty to keep to the place which God had given me in His Church, and there to do the work for which the Lord had set me there. As soon as complaints were brought against me, and I knew that I should not be allowed to remain any longer in the Roman Church, I again thought of escaping from the difficulties which were before me, by seeking a position within the Apostolic Churches; but the apostles considered that I ought to appeal, in the first place, to the archbishop, and then to the pope, so that they, too, might have the testimony borne to them. Thus it happened that both the bishop and the archbishop had a full testimony borne to them in writing.[100]

Eventually, after an ecclesiastical investigation, Lutz was suspended and excommunicated in 1856. About that time, a number of other Catholic priests who refused

---

97. AR 1896, 13; Schwartz, *Chronicle*, 2; Anon., 'Berlin,' *Newsletter* 4 (April 1953) 8–9; Schröter, *Bilder*, 33, 198–99, 201.

98. Henke, 'Carlyle,' 13.

99. Schröter, *Bilder*, 321.

100. Scholler, *Chapter*, 216–17; see also Hamilton, *Short History*.

to recant their belief in the work were excommunicated.[101] Most gravitated to Ulm, and were maintained by Drummond, who had taken oversight of the tribe in 1855 when Woodhouse took responsibility for North Germany. There the first Catholic Apostolic congregation in southern Germany was established that year, composed of those who had left Bavaria on account of their religious beliefs.[102] Caird reported that summer that sixty to seventy Roman Catholics had also joined the church at Basle.[103]

Official permission to found congregations in Bavaria was granted in 1862, almost two decades after work had begun, and the first congregation was set up that year in the village of Hurben bei Krumbach. The 1872 list gave details of fourteen congregations, several of which appear to have been short-lived. The most fruitful area in the tribe was said to be Württemberg, which may have been due to a strong local Pietist tradition. By 1901, there were forty-three congregations in South Germany, with at least 5,000 members.[104]

Legal restrictions undoubtedly hindered the Church's growth in southern Germany. For instance, work began in Nuremberg around 1860, but public delivery of the Testimony was prohibited until 1877, so that a church did not come into existence before 1879. Elsewhere in the tribe, similar restrictions obtained. In Vienna (where the first Austrian church was formed in 1872) and Prague, individuals could hold public lectures, but it was not possible to advertise services, engage in public preaching, or invite strangers to the churches. For about a year around 1880 even worship services were prohibited in Austria, and when they were recommenced, no children of school age were allowed to attend. Even so, by 1901 eight congregations had come into being in Austria, but in Hungary there had only been a short-lived house congregation in Budapest during the mid-1890s.[105]

## Spain and Portugal

Sitwell visited Spain in 1837, 1838, 1840, 1844, 1851–52, and 1853,[106] but it does not appear that any sealings were ever conducted in Spain or Portugal. Religious oppression in Spain for most of the century precluded open outreach, and ministers from Sitwell onwards were restricted to private conversation. The evangelist George Wood-

---

101. Phillipp J. Spindler, Domvikar at Augsburg, J. E. G. Lutz, Johann A. Fischer, Balthasar Fernsemer, Lorenz Egger, and Baron de St Marie Eglisa: Newman-Norton, *Biographical Index*; Schröter, *Bilder*, 37.

102. Scholler, *Chapter*, 195, 202, 212–13; Copinger, 'Annals,' 106.

103. Samuel Gardiner to Martin Irving, 19 September 1856.

104. Samuel Gardiner to Martin Irving, 26 July 1862; AR 1886, 19; Copinger, 'Annals,' 103, 106, 115; Schröter, *Bilder*, 37, 39.

105. AR 1876, 28; AR 1880, 25; AR 1881, 30; Anon., 'Nürnberg, Bavaria,' *Newsletter* 4 (April 1953) 14–15; W. H., *Katholisch-apostolische Gemeinden*, 174–75, 240; Schröter, *Bilder*, 41.

106. Isabella Irving to Mrs Martin, 16 November 1837; Copinger, 'Annals, 72, 75, 94, 99; W. H., *Katholisch-apostolische Gemeinden*, 213.

house was just beginning to see individuals coming to visit him in Granada during 1857 when Sitwell had to withdraw him for health reasons.[107] Those who worked in the country reported a fatal confusion between infidelity, republican politics, and 'Protestantism,' which seemed to amount to a mere negation of Roman Catholic ideas.[108] Although there was a window from 1868–75, thanks to a more liberal political climate following the 'Glorious Revolution,' little advantage appears to have been taken of it, perhaps because ministers could not be found to work in such an unpromising context, although in 1872 the evangelist S. W. Arnald attempted to distribute a Testimony to clergy in Spain. Arnald, who had been angel-evangelist for Spain since 1856, died in 1880, and no minister took charge of it many years. Representations were made to Woodhouse regarding this tribe as being the only one towards which no minister held any charge, and so he entrusted it to Capadose in 1899. As elsewhere, the accession of Capadose, who had described Spain as the only closed tribe, stimulated renewed effort, and another attempt to establish a work was made in 1900, Ludwig Albrecht spending three months in Madrid seeking openings.[109]

### Russia, Finland, and the Baltic States[110]

According to Hermann Thiersch, '[t]he Apostles nowhere experienced so decided a rejection as in Russia.'[111] Yet they put considerable effort into the Russian work. Visits to Russia had begun in 1838, when Dow visited Odessa and other cities. In 1849 the evangelist William Marriott White visited Moscow, and in 1851 he travelled around the Baltic regions and St Petersburg; on seeking to present Tsar Nicholas I a copy of the Great Testimony, he was informed that unless he left the country within eight days he would be deported to Siberia. The following year a German angel, H. W. Hermes, emigrated to the western shore of the Sea of Azov, along with seven of his flock (it is not known whether their motivation was religious or economic).[112] After Dow's death, the work came under Woodhouse's care, before being entrusted to coadjutors.

Some congregations were founded when territory was under Prussian rule, such as that at Memel in 1852. In 1858 members from Estonia and Latvia were sealed in Berlin, but the first real openings for work in the mid-1860s were among Germans,

---

107. Isabella Gardiner to Martin Irving, 11 October 1857.

108. AR 1853, 8–9.

109. Copinger, 'Annals,' 148, 181; Isaac Capadose, *Homily, 14th July 1899*; AD, February 1900, 1–2; AR 1900, 25–26.

110. See W. H., *Katholisch-apostolische Gemeinden*, 201–4; Schröter, *Die Katholisch-apostolischen Gemeinden*, 494–98 n. 69a; Abel, *Das Werk des Herrn*; Ante, 'Eine unbekannte Seite.' Abel's work includes the German original and English translation of Ilsa Rose, 'The Apostolic Congregations in the Tribe of Dan,' transl. Ada Amphlett (1946).

111. Hermann Thiersch, *Our Russian Brethren*, 14.

112. Copinger, 'Annals,' 93, 97; Schröter, *Die Katholisch-apostolischen Gemeinden*, 430 n. 41a, 494 n. 69a.

and the first ministers came from Germany. The authorities therefore viewed the movement as working among the Lutheran community and under Lutheran oversight, although the Lutheran authorities were opposed, even to the extent of excluding a minister in 1865 for propagating Catholic Apostolic teaching (Victor von Dittmann of St Petersburg) and refusing communion and burial to Catholic Apostolics. In Libau (now Liepaja) and Mitau (Jelgava), where services were stopped in the mid-1870s, members were visited by police after signing petitions to the emperor and asked

> ... whether it is still their wish to be reckoned as no more belonging to the Lutheran Communion.... The answer of the members ... has been uniformly to the effect, that they have no desire to withdraw from the Communion of the Lutheran Church, but in as much as the Lutheran Clergy refuse them the Communion, & drive them out, & their only means of obtaining liberty of worship is their consenting to be no more considered as belonging to the Lutheran Communion, they are content that it should be so.

Catholic Apostolic ministers were incorrect in thinking that members all wished to remain on the books of the Lutherans. The Lutheran consistory in Courland was, however, sympathetic, and had a police survey made of 192 signatories to an 1871 permission seeking permission to establish Catholic Apostolic congregations: it found that eighty-eight would be willing if necessary to leave the Lutheran Church, thirty-two wished to have dual membership, and thirty-nine would if necessary withdraw from the Catholic Apostolic Church. Proselytism among the Orthodox was forbidden by both Church and state, and whilst Catholic Apostolic ministers were very ready to admit them to the eucharist, this too was forbidden in 1871. The Orthodox conviction that they alone had preserved the true faith and had never needed a reformation along the lines of what had shaken the sixteenth-century West meant that they were opposed to the suggestion made in Catholic Apostolic apologetic that the Christian Church was in a low condition. Response tended to come, therefore, from Protestants.[113]

Despite the difficulties arising from attempting to minister in a context where there was such a close relation between Church and state, several congregations were planted, mostly among German-speakers in the Baltic region, where Lutheranism introduced a degree of religious plurality. Yet it was reported in 1879 that prophecies in the services were being given in German, Russian, and Lettish, a sure sign that the movement was touching other language-groups.[114] A report in 1893 stated that the Letts had apparently heard of the work and requested help.[115] Parts of the liturgy were translated into Lettish (Latvian; 1880) and Estonian (1890), and published. By the end

---

113. AR 1877, 24 (quotation); AR 1883, 48; AR 1884, 27; AR 1899, 26–27; Abel, *Das Werk des Herrn*, 10, 48; Schröter, *Bilder*, 49; Ante, 'Eine unbekannte Seite.'

114. AR 1879, 24; Abel, *Das Werk des Herrn in Russland*, 14.

115. AR 1893, 38–39.

of the century, it was being reported that a (full?) translation of the liturgy into Lettish had been made, but permission to print it refused.[116]

By 1866 a congregation was worshipping at Mitau and in 1871 one was formed at St Petersburg itself. By 1900 the composition of the St Petersburg congregation was half German and a quarter Estonian, the rest being Letts, English, and Swedes, with a few Russians. Interest in the city was mostly from the higher classes, who were largely non-Russian. Evangelist services tended to be in German or English, and the liturgy in German, Russian not being permitted, although the eucharistic liturgy was translated into Russian.[117] Around the same time, those classes were showing interest in a number of non-Orthodox religious movements, such as the Evangelical Christians (also known as *Radstokisty*). Hence the few Russians who were gathered came from the aristocracy, some of whom made their houses available for worship.[118] Nevertheless, attempts to reach the Russian population continued. Russian evangelization was being carried on at Pskov, Kharkov, and Moscow by 1896. A deacon was ordained about 1892 for work in the Caucasus, and he began in Odessa, a naval port on the shores of the Black Sea. The first eucharist there was held in 1900 and a church was formed with sixty regular communicants. Promising openings were also reported among ethnic Germans in Bessarabia and the Caucasus. A house church was even formed in Moscow in 1900, in which year there were thirteen churches in Russian territory.[119]

The first outreach in Finland was late in 1889. Two congregations were formed, one in Helsinki, but only the Litany appears to have been translated into Finnish (probably Swedish would otherwise have been used). Elsewhere around the Baltic, two more came into being in Estonia.[120]

German and Latvian seem to have been the main languages used in worship. German congregations in Riga and Libau each had a Latvian horn. Indeed, by 1898, Libau had over 800 regular communicants, mostly Letts, and had been divided into two congregations. Riga, however, was said to be the largest in the tribe. By 1901, there were eighteen congregations in the tribe (including Warsaw, then under Russian jurisdiction).[121] Looking back in 1946, one member asserted that most members were in fact Latvian, even in cities such as Odessa, Kiev, and Moscow.[122]

---

116. AR 1899, 28.

117. AR 1875, 28; Copinger, 'Annals,' 129; Schröter, *Bilder*, 47, 49; Schröter, *Die Katholisch-apostolischen Gemeinden*, 496–97; Abel, *Das Werk des Herrn*, 12, 99 (Rose). One source states that Capadose arranged for its publication, as it drew extensively on Orthodox sources: Hermann Thiersch, *Our Russian Brethren*, 14.

118. Abel, *Das Werk des Herrn*, 99 (Rose).

119. AR 1893, 39; AR 1900, 27–28; Schröter, *Bilder*, 49; Abel, *Das Werk des Herrn*, 17, 53–54.

120. AR 1890, 28–29; Abel, *Das Werk des Herrn*, 34.

121. AR 1898, 25; Schröter, *Bilder*, 49; Schröter, *Die Katholisch-apostolischen Gemeinden*, 497 n. 69a.

122. Abel, *Das Werk des Herrn*, 99 (Rose).

### Sweden and Norway[123]

The Testimony was presented by Dalton and Mackenzie to the king of Norway and Sweden in 1838.[124] Scandinavia experienced a measure of Pietist renewal within the state Churches during the mid-nineteenth century, and Böhm reported in glowing terms on one movement within the Lutheran Church ('criers,' or *roparrörelsen*) to the apostles after visiting Sweden in 1844 to investigate how close it might be to the Catholic Apostolic work.[125]

After Mackenzie's defection and the failure of attempts to reclaim him, this tribe came under Dow's care in 1846, passing to Carlyle (1854), King-Church (1855), and finally Cardale (1865). However, the first sustained work was undertaken by the angel-evangelist Sir George J. R. Hewett (1818–76), who was fluent in Norwegian, although the six months he spent in Norway during 1856 were without result and he found more fertile soil in Denmark. The first congregations were not established in Norway until 1872 (Drammen, followed by Christiania—later Oslo—in 1877) and Sweden until 1878 (Stockholm), but by 1901 there were fifteen in Sweden and ten in Norway, although most would not have been fully constituted churches but dependencies of a central church.[126]

Work in Norway was hindered by the legal requirement that those joining a dissenting congregation had first to terminate their membership of the state Church, which meant that they could no longer receive the sacraments in it. It had therefore been decided not to conduct any sealings in Sweden or Norway until it looked likely that the Catholic Apostolic Church would be allowed to celebrate its own sacraments. Once this appeared to be becoming possible, sealings took place, although one at Stockholm in 1874 had to be without the eucharist.[127] A Catholic Apostolic petition in 1876/7 requesting a dispensation from the requirement to withdraw from the Lutheran Church and permission to worship freely was unsuccessful.[128] When it was made clear that no sacraments could be observed unless members of a dissenting congregation declared themselves no longer to be members of the national Church, Catholic Apostolics were reluctantly forced to follow such a course. As the 'Apostles' Report' put it, '[t]he sin of the schismatic act of separation rests upon the Church & Nation, where it is thus enforced upon us. In giving in the Declaration required

---

123. On Norway, see Anon., 'Norway,' Newsletter 5 (November 1953) 13–14; Diersmann, *Notes*; on Sweden, Adell, *De tysta bedjarna*.

124. Copinger, 'Annals,' 73.

125. National Library of Ireland, MS 49,491/2/1463XL, C. J. T. Böhm to unidentified recipient, 24 July 1844; cf. Aarsbo, *Komme Dit Rige*, 5/i:4. It is unclear whether this is to be identified with the lithographed report to the apostles of the same date, but the content is unlikely to differ significantly: Copinger, 'Annals,' 79.

126. Schröter, *Bilder*, 45; Diersmann, *Notes*, 45–46.

127. AR 1875, 18–19.

128. Diersmann, *Notes*, 54–55.

by Law, the believers will accompany it with a protest that they do not voluntarily separate from the National Church.'[129] In 1877 liberty of worship was finally granted to the congregations in Christiania, Drammen, and Stockholm.[130] Thereafter, some individuals were sealed while remaining Lutheran members, as at Bergen in 1880 and 1882 and Aalesund in 1893. A shortage of priests meant that it was impossible to provide regular Catholic Apostolic eucharists, and so Capadose as coadjutor judged it better for such individuals to remain within the state Church so that they could continue to receive communion there.[131] Yet the work did make headway, to the extent that two district evangelists were set apart in 1891.[132] One good consequence of these problems did emerge: a requirement in Sweden and Norway that those considering seceding in order to join the Catholic Apostolic Church should have an interview with their parish minister checked impulsive decisions and meant that those who did join usually proved reliable members.[133]

The national character assigned by the apostles to the Norwegians was that of independency and self-sufficiency. It would not have surprised them, therefore, when congregations were beset by internal problems. In addition, the work in Norway faced opposition from time to time, and was unsettled by political agitation. In 1898 Capadose had to send a minister to sort things out; the following year he came himself, instead of sending a delegation as had been done for several years previously.[134]

The main growth in Sweden came in the 1890s, when membership increased from 600 to 1,380, dropping to 937 by 1907.[135] In Sweden as in Germany, there appears to have been a significant working-class element to the membership: at Uppsala, for example, many worked in the shoe industry (and were former Methodists into the bargain), while in Stockholm the membership was mostly craftsmen. The liturgy was probably translated into Swedish by Dr Björkman, a Lutheran clergyman who became an angel. Its language was described in 1967 as 'the most beautiful ecclesiastical Swedish, much better than all the Church of Sweden efforts during the last hundred years.' The conservative nature of Lutheran reform in Sweden, which meant that the Church retained an apostolic succession, meant that members were allowed to be buried according to Lutheran rites, by contrast with the situation in Denmark, where the apostolic succession had not been retained.[136]

129. AR 1877, 14, 16.
130. AD, January 1878.
131. Diersmann, *Notes*, 65, 114, following AR 1883, 33, and AR 1894, 26.
132. Diersmann, *Notes*, 92, following AR 1891, 35.
133. AR 1898, 28.
134. Diersmann, *Notes*, 80, 103, cf. AR 1884, 38.
135. Adell, *De tysta bedjarna*, 25–26, 93.
136. CRL, H. B. Evans Collection, Box 451, extract from a letter of B. Stolt, 2 September 1967; Adell, *De tysta bedjarna*, 93.

## The 'Suburbs'

Catholic Apostolic belief that Britain had been given a special place in the divine purpose entailed their acceptance of the growing emphasis on the Empire as providentially ordained.[137] However, whereas other Churches took this as laying upon them the work of evangelization amongst the heathen, Catholic Apostolics believed that this could not be done effectively by a divided Church, but was for God to fulfill in a future stage of his purposes, once the Church had been united in acknowledging the ministry of apostles.[138] As the American minister J. S. Davenport stated in 1863: 'Our present work is not to convert the world, but to hasten the Parousia.'[139] They therefore focused their ministry on the baptized expatriate community, and it is likely that many of these found the movement's strong conservatism and opposition to democracy congenial. At no point do we find ministers preaching to the indigenous populations of the imperial dominions.

### Australasia[140]

The Church's first activity towards Australia was when the evangelist Lieut. Alfred Wilkinson was commissioned in 1852 and sent out as apostles' minister to Australia and the East.[141] A few years later, Percy Whitestone was sent out, being given some kind of overall responsibility for the work. Wilkinson, who seems to have been an effective evangelist with the apostles, died in 1896. He was succeeded by Col. A. F. Laughton, who retained existing responsibilities in London and India, indicating that the scope of the work was not such as to occupy him full-time.[142]

The first congregation was formed at Melbourne in the mid-1850s. In New Zealand, the first was at Wellington (c.1865). By 1901 there were fifteen in Australia and five in New Zealand. Work in Australia owed much to Martin Irving (1831–1912), son of Edward. He emigrated in 1855 and became a notable classics professor and school headmaster. In 1890 he was chosen as pastor with the apostles for Australia and New Zealand, returning to England in 1900 to base himself at Albury. Sealings seem to have taken place roughly every three years during the 1880s and 1890s, when a coadjutor or delegation could be sent. Many members lived hundreds of miles from the nearest city, and it was difficult to ensure a regular programme of pastoral visits. In

---

137. The fullest exposition of this theme was Philo-Anglicanus, *Ancient Tyre and Modern England*.
138. Cuming, *Heathen*; Wood, *Report*, 24–26.
139. Davenport, *Edward Irving*, 50.
140. On Australia, see Elliott, 'Nineteenth-Century Australian Charismata,' 26–36.
141. Anon, Southampton record, 14 October 1852. He appears also to have had responsibility for the Cape Colony: Martin, 'Brief Survey,' 4.
142. AD, June 1890, 1; AD, June 1896, 1; AD, July 1897, 3.

at least three cases, at Bukkullah, Dalwood, and Talgai, chapels were built by families on their stations for use by ministers when making pastoral visits.[143]

## North America

The Catholic Apostolic Church's early development in Canada (then British North America) owed much to two well-known clergymen, George Ryerson (1792–1882; Wesleyan) and Adam Hood Burwell (1790–1849; Anglican). Given the tension between Anglicans and dissenters at the time over such matters as the clergy reserves, the fact that the new movement could find room for members from each side must have made an impression.[144]

Ryerson was on a visit to England in 1832 with a Wesleyan petition opposing Anglican claims in connection with the clergy reserves when he heard Edward Irving preach and was converted to his views, attracted by the otherworldly outlook of Irving and his circle. He did not initially regard himself as having left Methodism: stressing the continuities with his earlier beliefs, he argued that Irving had given him what he had previously been seeking. As a minister from a leading Canadian Wesleyan family, he was instrumental in securing the adhesion of many Methodists in Toronto and Kingston, probably helping Caird, who visited Toronto in 1834, to gain access to Methodist pulpits. In the same way, Burwell continued to regard himself as an Anglican missionary, even after his name had been removed from the books of the Society for the Propagation of the Gospel in 1836, and to be well regarded by his former co-religionists.[145]

Caird saw encouraging response to his teaching; indeed, one scholar has judged that the movement saw 'considerable success' in Canada. But they were not the only millennialist group at work: Mormons were active at the same time, and later there would be the Millerites and (from the 1860s) the Brethren. There seems to have been a fair amount of movement between these groups, Mormons included, and it appears that Wesleyanism in particular was vulnerable to Catholic Apostolic and Mormon incursions: the congregation at York began with the expulsion of four Wesleyan class leaders for propagating 'Irvingite' views, and Ryerson joined it on his return from England.[146] Contention and competition between these movements was therefore endemic. An early Mormon elder, Parley P. Pratt, visited Toronto in 1836 and became aware of 'Irvingite' teaching on such topics as the apostasy of the Gentile Church, the need of a divine organization, the restoration of spiritual gifts, Israel, and Christ's

---

143. E. W. T. T., 'New Zealand,' *Newsletter* 4 (April 1953) 11; Martin, 'Brief Survey,' 10–11; Schröter, *Bilder*, 53.

144. On Canada, see Anon., 'Canada,' *Newsletter* 4 (April 1953) 9–11.

145. Sissons, *Egerton Ryerson*, 1:36; Shaw, *Catholic Apostolic Church*, ch. 13; Thomas, *Ryerson*, 63; Dougall, 'Ryerson'; Westfall, *Two Worlds*, 171–73.

146. Shaw, *Catholic Apostolic Church*, 112; Westfall, *Two Worlds*, 167, 176.

Second Coming and millennial reign. He saw the possibilities of making converts among such people, and when Caird returned in 1836 Pratt heard him preach, noted Caird's sudden digression to oppose Mormonism, and arranged meetings to refute his misrepresentations, claiming that Caird withdrew to Scotland as a result.[147]

Work in North America was the responsibility of Woodhouse, who visited the continent eight times between 1836 and 1857. From 1860 it was overseen by Armstrong, and after his death by Edward Heath (who was appointed a coadjutor in 1886), after which sealings happened almost every year, Heath making frequent visits. The first congregations had been formed at Kingston (now in Ontario) in 1836, Toronto (1837), Potsdam in upper New York State (1837), and New York itself (c.1851).[148] But the prevailing religious, social, and economic climate in a newly developing and fast expanding region was not conducive to the message of a movement which was rooted in the milieu of a long-established Christendom. The move of the seat of government to Kingston in 1840, followed by liturgical unsettlement affecting the whole movement, necessitated the closure of the Toronto church from 1844 (a year after Woodhouse visited, presumably seeking to introduce the new liturgy), the flock being entrusted to the local Anglican bishop. Moreover, the rapid growth of Spiritualism from the late 1840s and the adventist expectations fostered by William Miller were liable to confuse adherents and inquirers, as well as offering alternative attractions. Yet there seems to have been less actual confusion with Mormonism here than in Europe. By 1901 there were twenty-nine congregations in the USA and twelve in Canada.[149] However, it had been thought by some that the American laity were 'kept away by the tyranny of public opinion, which was much more efficacious than that of the police in Germany.'[150]

Large-scale immigration brought increasing numbers of foreign-born members in the USA. Some settled thousands of miles from a congregation, which made pastoral work among them extremely difficult.[151] Others were served by German-speaking horn churches established from the 1880s and attached to Anglophone churches in their cities, as at Chicago, New York, and Pittsburgh, or by smaller congregations elsewhere. By 1894, the address book was listing twelve locations in North America where German services were held.

The Church made very little impact among the black community, although one black Episcopal clergyman who had accepted the work asked that if expelled by his congregation he might be sent to his countrymen in Haiti.[152] In the extant reports it

147. Bloxham, Moss, and Porter, eds, *Truth will Prevail*, 24-25, 51.

148. Shaw, *Catholic Apostolic Church*, 130-39; Copinger, 'Annals,' 66, 70; Schröter, *Bilder*, 51.

149. AR 1853, 6; Anon., 'Canada'; Dougall, 'Ryerson,' 797; Shaw, *Catholic Apostolic Church*, 114; Copinger, 'Annals,' 86; Schröter, *Bilder*, 51.

150. Samuel Gardiner to Martin Irving, 18 July [1858].

151. AR 1883, 19.

152. Samuel Gardiner to Martin Irving, 18 July [1858]. This was the Revd J. T. Holly (1829-1911),

was not until 1891/2 that any reference was made to a Catholic Apostolic minister visiting the black community in the southern states.

> A difficulty new to our experience made itself felt in this campaign, namely the determined hostility of the white to the coloured race, which latter constitutes so large a proportion of the population.... It was found necessary at the principal lectures to advertize that a special part of the hall was set apart for the coloured people, in order to obtain the attendance of the whites. Lectures were subsequently given to the coloured people in smaller halls frequented by them. They are emotional and receptive, but require very careful dealing.[153]

Catholic Apostolics also found interest in their message among some of the multitude of small religious groups which sprang up in the country. In the town of Economy, near Pittsburgh, a deacon found an opening among a communal sect of Germans originally from Württemberg.[154] This was the Harmony Society, also known as Harmonists or Rappists, a utopian and celibate group then in a declining state through debt and a lack of new members.[155]

A noticeable feature of the North American work is the high proportion of accessions from clerical ranks: Anglican, Presbyterian, and (in New England) Congregationalist. However, several were then evicted from their charges from 1849 onwards, producing apologias for their views and their attempts to remain in post.[156] Apologias were produced by British ministers who joined the Church, but the publication of defences in ecclesiastical trials is something distinctively American, Irving excepted: British ministers were tried in ecclesiastical courts during the first few years (e.g. A. C. Whalley in 1834 and Henry Dalton in 1835), but none followed Irving's example.

The New England Congregationalist minister William Watson Andrews (1810-97) played a high-profile role as an angel-evangelist. Andrews had learned of the manifestations in England and Scotland fairly soon after they began, and had read some of Irving's works, especially his articles in the *Morning Watch*. In Autumn 1837 he was put in contact with Ryerson and Burwell, the latter being in 1840 the first person he heard prophesy. In 1843 he visited Britain after his health had given way,

---

who was sealed in 1857: Copinger, 'Annals,' 109. Holly, whose background was Roman Catholic and who had only been priested in 1856, advocated black emigration and the creation of a black nationality. He had been ordained with a view to working in Haiti, which he did from 1861 as an Episcopal missionary; in 1874 he became Episcopal bishop of Haiti, the first African American to reach this rank: Anderson, ed., *Biographical Dictionary of Christian Missions*, s.n. 'Holly, James Theodore'; Burkett, 'Reverend Harry Croswell'; Gates and Higginbotham, eds, *African American Lives*, s.n. 'Holly, James Theodore.' Holly's Catholic Apostolic allegiance probably did not last long enough for his bishop to discipline him.

153. AR 1892, 50–51. Two invitations addressed especially to coloured people survive, but neither has a year on it.

154. AR 1898, 30–31.

155. See Clark, 'Heavens on Earth,' 399–400.

156. Copinger, 'Annals,' 91; cf. items in the bibliography by Sterling, Fackler, and Smith.

and attended worship at Newman Street. Apart from being shocked at the use of a liturgy and vestments, he was struck by the fact that there were only a few present. Nevertheless, he was impressed by what he saw, and '[i]f I had not seen the fire and the earthquake, I had heard the still small voice.' In the summer of 1848 he was sealed, and soon after that he resigned his charge in order to serve under apostles, although even after becoming an angel-evangelist in 1857 he would conduct Congregational services in Wethersfield, Connecticut, where he lived.[157] He possessed a marked gift for communicating Catholic Apostolic teaching, and some of his books and pamphlets were frequently reprinted. Andrews deployed a wide range of strategies to communicate his message: he would appeal to ministers, preach where allowed, distribute tracts, hold meetings in public halls, and pen newspaper articles against misrepresentations of the work. Yet even his brother and biographer, Samuel J. Andrews (1817–1906), admitted that little fruit resulted.[158]

*India*[159]

Although technically part of the tribe of Ephraim, India should be treated alongside the other English-speaking 'suburbs.' Its inclusion as part of Christendom was not because of the existence of an ancient Christian Church there which traced its origins to St Thomas himself, and which had fired the imagination of early nineteenth-century Evangelical Anglicans, but because of India's status in the British Empire. This is confirmed by the fact that ministerial labors in India focused almost exclusively on the British expatriate community; no attempt appears to have been made to contact indigenous Christian communities. The Church thus appears to have been unaware of the revival around 1860 associated with the Tamil Christian leader J. C. Arulappen, which included such phenomena as speaking in tongues; normally such events were investigated with keen interest.

Miller stated that Tudor, whose charge it was, visited India, but his health is said to have been seriously affected, and he did not return. However, a note to his own copy of his work denied this.[160] Ministerial visits from English angels began in 1867, but members remained under the pastoral care of the ministers of their home church. Captain H. W. King (son of the apostle and angel for India 1874–88) appears to have visited the country most years, touring isolated members, celebrating eucharists, speaking about the work, and so on. However, although he pressed for a delegation to visit India to seal those gathered, the presence of indigenous Christians among the candidates, who could not be excluded but who could not visit England or in some

---

157. BL, 76415 (uncatalogued), ms letter by William Watson Andrews, 5 January 1853; Samuel J. Andrews, *William Watson Andrews*, 64–68, 188–90.

158. Samuel J. Andrews, *William Watson Andrews*, 100–101.

159. On India, see BOC, Newman-Norton, 'Twelve Tribes I,' Appendix.

160. Miller, *Irvingism*, 1:93; Miller, *Miller's Notes*, 4.

other way make acquaintance with angels of the Church, meant that it was not deemed prudent to send a delegation because there was then no angel or church in India under whose care they could be placed.[161] Nevertheless, by 1887 there were 135 members in India, and by 1891 it was reported that an angel was now resident in Bombay. He acted on behalf of the angels at home, being himself formally responsible only for those committed to pastorship who had no English church membership.[162] As would be the case elsewhere, Anglican clergy in India were said to acknowledge Catholic Apostolics as their most regular attenders and loyal helpers in church work. Catholic Apostolic deacons were given permission in 1898 to offer to assist local Anglican clergy by conducting services or preaching, but enjoined not to abuse the relationship.[163] Clearly the authorities valued the good relations subsisting, probably because this aided the pastoral care of far-flung members.

## Other areas

In the late nineteenth century, a significant segment of the Anglophone community which needed to be reached with the Catholic Apostolic message was made up of missionaries. The most sustained approach to the missionary community which I have discovered was not in any of the fields where large numbers of missionaries were at work, but in Japan. An unnamed Episcopal clergyman there had been sealed in America in 1890. By the mid-1890s a small group there had accepted the work, and the American Episcopal bishop was consulting his colleagues at home regarding what action to take, as a result of which the clergyman was obliged to leave his post.[164] Several other missionaries accepted the work, but it was claimed that they too had had to resign their posts; two Japanese families also became secret Catholic Apostolics, while remaining Anglicans.[165] The angel-evangelist Cuthbert Layton visited the country late

---

161. AR 1884, 13. In 1889 King was looking after members in Gibraltar, Malta, Suez, Aden, and Rangoon: W. H., *Katholisch-apostolische Gemeinden*, 121.

162. AR 1887, 24; AR 1891, 13; MC, 27 August 1890, 56; 18 November 1891, 81–83.

163. AR 1892, 8; AC, Edward Heath, 'Memorandum as to the Employment of Deacons in India, Conference, 30 March 1898,' 4–5.

164. AR 1895, 40; AR 1899, 34.

165. Anon., 'Japan,' *News Letter* 2 (April 1952) 16–19. According to this article, one of the missionaries was Arthur Lloyd (1852–1911), an English missionary who from 1894 served with the Protestant Episcopal Church of the USA: Clement, 'The late Rev. Arthur Lloyd'; Anderson, ed., *Biographical Dictionary of Christian Missions*, s.n. 'Lloyd, Arthur.' Lloyd was an expert on Japanese Buddhism, an influential theologian of mission, and a mediator not only between different Christian traditions but also between Christianity and Buddhism. The *News Letter* claim that Lloyd had to resign his post appears inaccurate, but if he was a Catholic Apostolic member then his exploration of the commonalities between Buddhism and Christianity may be a distinctive application of Catholic Apostolic thinking, which would not have found general approval. It was through Lloyd that the family of the Japanese author of the *News Letter* article (who himself was ordained as an Anglican priest) joined the Church. The author may have been the Revd Peter Hosokai, then ministering in Hirosaki: cf. Peter Hosokai, 'Japan,' *Ungdomsbladet* 5/5–6 (April–June 1957) 2.

in 1899 to assess the situation and assist those who had been suffering on account of their faith in the work, giving lectures to missionaries and to the public. His ministry was aimed not at Japanese but at Europeans, especially missionaries; his judgment was that younger missionaries tended to substitute philosophy for the gospel.[166] No congregation was ever formed in the country.

Other locations visited by ministers included Fiji and South Africa.[167] Work in the latter territory appears to have been a victim of circumstances. In 1899, an evangelist mission was hindered by the outbreak of war.[168] Woodhouse died two years later, after which attempts to gather new members ceased. By the time the angel-evangelist Basil Seton visited those gathered there in 1903, they numbered about 180,[169] but they were under angels in their home countries rather than forming regularly constituted congregations.

No other European power had a Catholic Apostolic presence anywhere in its overseas possessions, apart from Holland: Dutch ministers looked after a small number of members in Java.[170] But there were scattered members elsewhere who were visited by ministers: the angel-evangelist Cuthbert Layton, returning from Japan in 1900, was due to visit scattered members in China and Singapore. Reporting the following year on his trip, he explained that his ministry had been directed primarily to Europeans, and in particular to the missionary community.[171] This was entirely in line with the movement's sense that its calling and message was to Christendom, and not to the world as a whole.

A curious footnote is provided by a group from a Waldensian colony at Rosario in Argentina who corresponded with ministers in Switzerland and France for several years, receiving literature and sending tithe.[172] No church appears to have been formed, and it is not known what became of them.

---

166. AR 1900, 5–7.

167. AR 1899, 6–7.

168. AC, Edward Heath, 'To the Angels in Charge of Churches in London, England, Scotland, Ireland, Canada, Australia and New Zealand,' 14 December 1899; Copinger, 'Annals,' 180.

169. Copinger, 'Annals,' 189.

170. W. H., *Katholisch-apostolische Gemeinden*, 128.

171. AR 1899, 34; AR 1900, 5–7.

172. AR 1887, 304; AR 1890, 17–18.

# 7

# Expansion II
Strategy

### CATHOLIC APOSTOLICS AND THE WIDER CHURCH

THE WORK OF COMMUNICATING the Church's message and seeking to gather new members was spearheaded by the evangelists. To understand what the evangelists were seeking to achieve, we shall first outline how the Church saw itself in relation to other Christian bodies. Briefly, it saw itself as an ark of refuge from the judgments coming upon apostate Christendom, but also as a locus for the reunion of Christians. Christians were urged to accept the mission of the restored apostles in order to be prepared for the return of Christ, but the practical outworking of that was not always the same: sometimes hearers were urged to leave their churches and join congregations gathered under apostles, whilst at other times they were enjoined to remain in their existing churches, often holding dual membership. Sometimes the evangelists denounced existing churches as devoid of the Holy Spirit; at other times they assured their hearers that they sought to build up existing churches. Moreover, the Catholic Apostolic Church upheld the principle of the establishment of religion (although critical of how this had been perverted in the absence of apostles) but never itself enjoyed the status of an established national Church. There was a tension between ecumenism and sectarianism which has never been resolved and this, coupled with the problem of applying the teaching of the apostles in circumstances which they never envisaged, has occasioned continuing internal divergence of opinion and practice, especially regarding attendance at, or membership of, other churches. This became particularly acute during the latter part of the twentieth century, as we shall see.

We have already seen that from the beginning Scottish congregations were referring to themselves as belonging to the 'Holy Catholic Apostolic Church,' and that they were not untypical in this. The apostles were always clear that the name 'Catholic Apostolic Church' was not theirs in any exclusive sense; they took it because they could not take any name which referred to a part of Christendom only, such as Episcopal or Presbyterian. Yet the Church had to justify its separate existence. The task of outreach raised the question of what people were being invited to join, what the congregations gathered under apostles had to offer, and what was wrong with existing churches. The literature could be surprisingly reticent about the movement's distinctive teachings; indeed, like the Brethren, Catholic Apostolics sometimes prided themselves on claiming not to have any, just as they claimed that they needed no other name than that common to all the baptized. An example of this is provided by an undated address for circulation to inquirers.

> It frequently happens that persons, who have been present at a service in this place, ask the doorkeeper as they go out, 'Who are you?' 'What do you call yourselves?' Our answer is, 'We are Christians, and do not call ourselves by any name to distinguish ourselves from other members of the *one* body of Christ.' If a Christian enquire, 'To what Church do you belong?' we answer 'To the same that he does;' and if he add, 'To what portion of it?' we say, 'To no sect, nor portion, nor denomination, but to the Church which is ONE, HOLY, CATHOLIC, APOSTOLIC.'

The address goes on to argue that there is only one body, and that whereas each sect of Christendom glories in its distinctness from all the others, those belonging to the Lord's work repent of the common sin of schism. They have not separated themselves from other Christians as other groups have. Since God has shown how his Church should be rebuilt, and has restored apostles to that end, readers are called to yield to him, that they may join the first-fruits.[1] By the 1890s reports of evangelist work in some continental countries were referring to those who, while unable to go all the way with Catholic Apostolic teaching, still looked on them positively as fellow workers, in the light of the approaching Second Advent. Something of the imperative to join the Church was dissipating. It then became necessary to explain why congregations under apostles continued to worship apart from their Christian brethren, when they professed to be a movement for the whole Church.

Cardale explained in 1865 that the formation of separate congregations was a regrettable necessity, though it might provide a future center for Christian reunion:

> . . . the formation of separate Churches and Congregations, and the ordination over them of Angels and other Ministers, are not the primary end and object of the restoration or mission of Apostles to the Church in these last days. On the contrary, it is to be deplored that the present condition and circumstances of the Visible Church render these acts necessary. Being formed, the Churches under the immediate guidance and government of the Apostles will probably

---

1. Anon., *Address for Circulation*; 1 (quotation).

hereafter furnish a basis or centre on which the divided Churches of Christendom, when they shall receive the Message which they now refuse, may be edified in unity and love: but neither is this the immediate object. The two main objects to which, under present circumstances, the formation of these Churches is directed, are those we have already named,—the spiritual charge of such as cannot otherwise be cared for, and the offering of continual Intercession for the Church and for the World.[2]

Separation from Babylon, he had explained a few years earlier, was to be understood spiritually rather than literally. Indeed, literal separation was often undesirable and inexpedient, as well as being opposed to the spirit of the Great Testimony.[3]

Similarly, in 1877 Henry Hume had explained in his induction address as angel at London's Central Church that those under apostles worshipped apart because: they were forced to by circumstances,; only so could provision be made for those who would otherwise receive no spiritual care, and spiritual gifts be fostered and developed which were not otherwise allowed in any Christian context; those under apostles offered regular intercession for the whole Church; a perfect pattern of Church order had been set up; and these congregations were to form the basis and center of future unity on which the Church could be reformed.[4]

Because of the Catholic Apostolic Church's marked eschatological flavor, a particularly pertinent issue was that of how Roman Catholicism was to be regarded, the more so because ministers and members with an Evangelical background would often have been schooled in interpretations of prophecy which portrayed Rome as Antichrist. Carré offered a modification of this view, referring to the papacy as an Antichrist, 'one form or development of that mystery of iniquity' whose 'final development' would be 'the infidel Antichrist of the last days.'[5] Among the apostles, Drummond had long been, and would always remain, a vocal critic of Roman Catholicism. Yet he showed an ambivalence towards Rome which was particularly marked in his *Discourses on the True Definition of the Church* (1858), in which he could argue that 'if she is a mother, she is doubtless the mother of harlots and of all abominations,' yet also acknowledge that Rome had guarded Christian orthodoxy in the West and might yet make the only real stand against 'neology.'[6] In his 1847 letter on 'foreign work' he had conceded that Catholic Apostolics had more in common with Rome than with any other sect.[7] But between these two publications he had been vocal in his opposition to the restoration of the Catholic hierarchy in England, and put his name to some near-scurrilous pamphlets about the evils of contemporary monasticism.

2. Cardale, *Character*, 39.
3. Cardale, *Notes of Lectures* (1861), 4.
4. Hume, *Address*, 6.
5. Carré, *See of Rome*, 10 n.
6. Drummond, *Discourses*, 12, 14.
7. Drummond, *Circular Letter*, 16.

Catholic Apostolics were strong upholders of the establishment of religion. Disestablishment of the Church of Ireland was seen as disastrous, and Pitcairn offered counsel to his Edinburgh flock on the subject in 1868. He affirmed the value of establishment during the time of the Church's entanglement with the world, to ensure the nation was taught a measure of sound doctrine. Disestablishment destroyed the testimony borne by the nation and undermined the civil constitution based on Christian principles. The Church of Ireland, he contended, was a bulwark 'not only against the political power and progress of a foreign spiritual monarchy, but also against the spread of an infidel liberalism.' His hearers were exhorted to '[f]ollow, then, the apostolic example of reverence, honouring and strengthening what remains of God's ordinances and institutions in the nation. Join not the cry of the multitude to overturn.' Christians were to uphold what remained which was of God, leaving him to overthrow—as in time he would.[8]

But the apostles were not by any means uncritical in their support of establishment. In the controversy of 1850 regarding the restoration of the Roman Catholic hierarchy in England, Armstrong argued that both Churches—Rome and England—were in error: one believed in royal supremacy, the other in papal.[9] As for the Tractarian movement, perhaps the closest apparent parallel to the Catholic Apostolic Church within Anglicanism, it was seen as insubordinate to bishops and insensitive to congregations, as well as failing to understand the significance of particular ceremonies.[10] But the Catholic Apostolic Church sense of having a unique relationship with the Church of England would play out in some surprising ways in the twentieth century, not only in England but also on the continent of Europe. Many of the apostles and indeed much of the British membership had an Anglican background.[11] So it was natural that in 1867 the apostles should comment publicly on the first Lambeth Conference. They even added a prayer for it to the liturgy.[12] Speaking to the seven churches in London, he expressed his delight that the assembled bishops had affirmed their conviction of the nearness of the Second Coming, but balanced it with the argument that the bishops had no right in their resolutions to speak authoritatively in the name of the whole Anglican communion.[13] Moreover, the bishops showed no sense of the shortcomings and sins of their communion, or of the need for preparation before the Lord's return; sadly, the testimony to a restored apostleship given to that end had found no response.[14] Later conferences did not receive the same attention, initially

---

8. Pitcairn, 'Irish Church Question,' 9–13, quotations at 12, 9 respectively.

9. Pinnington and Newman-Norton, *Conciliar and Apostolic Witness*, 9, citing Nicholas Armstrong, *Sermons on Various Subjects*, 1st series, 58–59.

10. Pinnington and Newman-Norton, *Conciliar and Apostolic Witness*, 9.

11. Ibid., 8.

12. Ibid., 11.

13. Cardale, *Remarks on the Lambeth Conference*, 5–6.

14. Ibid., 22–24.

because prophetic light led Woodhouse to concentrate on the inner strengthening of the Catholic Apostolic Church.[15]

Whilst Tractarianism might have looked similar to Catholic Apostolic worship, and the apostles' liturgy attracted many high churchmen who were frustrated by the legal prohibitions affecting attempts to introduce certain rites and ceremonies into the Church of England's worship, the theological roots of many early ministers and members lay not in high church thought but in Evangelicalism. Perhaps by way of reaction, they could be fiercely critical of that movement. In 1853 William Tarbet (whose own background was Evangelical) typically criticized Evangelicals for claiming to know only 'Christ crucified,' arguing that St Paul did not, as they thought, praise such a mindset. They also 'mar not unfrequently their usefulness, by painful narrow-mindedness and harsh judgment of those who adopt not their peculiarities.' One of these 'peculiarities' was to conceive of the Holy Spirit as working in individuals apart from the sacraments, which Tarbet regarded as akin to Quakerism. Evangelical expressions such as 'born again,' 'converted,' and 'faith in Christ' amounted to an implicit denial of the spiritual standing of the baptized. Holding this low view of the sacraments, they made preaching the paramount aspect of worship.[16] Such criticism moderated considerably later on, once the first generation of ministers and members disappeared and to some extent were replaced by those brought up within the movement; moreover, Catholic Apostolics eventually came to recognize Evangelicals as fellow defenders of the authority of Holy Scripture in the face of the challenges to this from some biblical scholarship.

Believing as they did in the rightness of establishment, Catholic Apostolics were often critical of religious dissent. Drummond was particularly forceful in his condemnation—as only an ex-dissenter could be![17] 'Antichrist is the confusion which is the opposite of this organization [i.e., God's order as seen in the universe and human society]—of which Protestant Chapels are the visible exhibition in the Church.'[18] Prophecy in 1860 likened Protestantism to the church at Sardis, confessing Christ as universal bishop in name, but despising his power in practice and so lacking the full grace of the Holy Spirit. Nevertheless, the apostles were to seek to gather such people, 'especially in this land, for they shall be very helpful to you.'[19] This seems to imply an especial concern to gather dissenters, although by contrast with the 1830s very few joined the Church.[20]

15. Pinnington and Newman-Norton, *Conciliar and Apostolic Witness*, 16.

16. Tarbet, *Voice*, 4–5.

17. He had played a leading role in the high Calvinist 'Western Schism' from 1815 onwards: see Carter, *Anglican Evangelicals*, ch. 4, and the sources there cited. For his bizarre condemnation of various forms of dissent, particularly the Baptists, see Drummond, *Stone*.

18. NLS, Acc. 4388, Volume of homilies etc, 94 (Drummond, 'Homily at Laying on of Hands (15 September 1856)').

19. 'Words of Prophecy 1860,' 38, 40.

20. For the stories of two former dissenters who joined the Church, see Simpson, *Reasons for*

Catholic Apostolics were therefore decidedly cool in their attitude towards the '1859 Revival', which affected North America and the British Isles. According to a contemporary ministry, two apostles had had opportunity to witness what was happening. In America the movement seemed to awaken some who had been careless but was now passing away; in Ireland it had attracted the attention of all classes to religion. However, the first thing which was really needed was for the Christian Church to learn its apostasy (and also, presumably, to receive God's ministers), for God's work to begin with the faithful rather than the wicked, who could only see as far as their individual need. The present movement, it was observed, did not tend to unity.[21] We shall note below what British ministers thought of revivalists such as Moody and Sankey, but a major problem with such movements for Catholic Apostolics was that they were disorderly, not only ecclesiastically because of their rejection of ordinances and sacraments but also socially, in despising such principles as women's subjection and children's obedience to parents.

## OUTREACH STRATEGIES

As might be expected from a religious movement led by well educated men, extensive use was made of printed tracts and pamphlets designed to answer questions asked by inquirers, to offer apologetic arguments for the restoration of apostles, and to awaken the careless and perplexed to the imminence of the end and the way of escape offered by God through the Catholic Apostolic Church. Testimonies in various forms were produced, some following the lines of the Great Testimony, and others being more like short tracts. It may have been partly because of the lack of response to the distribution of printed Testimonies and partly in an attempt to adopt a more populist approach at a time of intense revivalist activity that the need seems to have been felt for something more popular, perhaps in the wake of Cardale's assertion in 1865 that the work needed to change in character and pay greater attention to the imminence of the Second Advent. Accordingly, a 'committee of angels' prepared an address for distribution at public lectures.[22]

One popular strategy not employed was the revival meeting, as popularized by Charles Finney and later to reach its apogee in the Moody and Sankey campaigns. This pair of American evangelists visited the UK from 1873 to 1875, creating an immense stir, but in Scotland, one angel-evangelist who kept a watching brief on what was happening concluded that the movement was 'greatly hindering the effect of his testimony.' A couple of years later, the verdict was even more negative: 'The "revivals" of late years have resulted largely, (as was to be feared) in spiritual pride and self sufficient independence, leading to the light estimation & disregard of Ordinances, by

---

*abandoning the Methodist Ministry*; Ridings, *My Testimony* (Brethren).

21. Hopkinson Papers, 'Notes of the Apostle's Ministry, November 29, 1859.'
22. Copinger, 'Annals,' 122.

which many of the Clergy as well as their people have been led away.'²³ In England, it was noted that those reached by these men were not usually the openly wicked or unbelieving; their campaigns were seen as just one more instance of short-lived efforts at religious revival, and it was a pity that the clergy should have welcomed them so eagerly.²⁴ The 'testimony of plain truth finds no entry into ears which desire only sensational addresses, & . . . this tendency has rapidly increased since the visit of Messrs Moody & Sankey.' Likewise, in Canada 'the ears of the people seem mostly closed to the pure truth, while the style of Lectures delivered by men like Messrs Moody & Sankey, are much sought after.'²⁵ Catholic Apostolics do not appear to have attempted to marry revivalism with sacramental Christianity, unlike some high churchmen²⁶ or North American Roman Catholics, although there is some evidence that they did try to widen their appeal. The success or otherwise of outreach was sometimes linked to perceived national characteristics. In 1882, it was reported that 'the Norwegian, with his strong feeling of independence, is not easily brought round to submit to ordinances.' Of the same country it was asserted a few years later: 'Evangelical self-sufficiency & independence suit the national character, much more than the order of the House of God. In consequence, low Church Preachers, Baptists, & the so-called Adventists find much readier audiences than our Evangelists.'²⁷

In the absence of any internal description, Miller provides a useful overview of Catholic Apostolic evangelistic strategy in a new location.

> When operations are commenced in any town, the first measure is to secure the Town-hall or some other important building for the delivery of a course of Lectures. The subject of these Lectures is the immediate coming of the Lord, put forth with all the skill and power at the Evangelist's command. The object appears to be, first to convince, and then to frighten people, so that they may be ready to embrace the safeguard promised against impending tribulation and anguish. When the times [sic] comes, whether at the end of the first course of Lectures, or in the second, or more strongly in a third, the doctrine of the Restored Apostolate is presented, and Sealing is held out as a passport through the great Tribulation, and a title to a place amongst the 144,000. In each succeeding course a smaller room if necessary is taken, according as the attendance and the Lectures are more popular or more select. To these Lectures succeed Classes. Thus the nucleus of a future Church is assembled and established.²⁸

23. AR 1874, 6–7; AR 1877, 9.

24. AR 1875, 4.

25. AR 1878, 6; AR 1877, 26.

26. One such was G. H. Wilkinson, a London vicar who later became bishop of Grahamstown, South Africa; he was said to have received the sealing, but his ministry was exercised within Anglicanism: see Voll, *Catholic Evangelicalism*, esp. Part II.

27. AR 1882, 24; AR 1886, 32.

28. Miller, *Irvingism*, 1:338. The Brethren leader J. N. Darby, probably writing during the 1830s,

Probably in the 1880s, the Yorkshire Brethren teacher A. J. Holiday asserted that distinctively Catholic Apostolic ideas and emphases were introduced only gradually. His account is highly colored, but it is probably typical of the way in which many Evangelicals regarded the Church's activities:

> They will placard a whole town with bills, announcing that an evangelist will give a series of lectures on the coming of the Lord. Sometimes he is announced as 'an evangelist serving under the Lord's restored apostles;' in other cases no hint of his associations is given. If you go to the first of these lectures, you will probably think it all that can be desired, so entirely will it appear in accordance with Scripture. Well, what is that for? To lead you on to have a little confidence in them, and a belief that they are honest and sound in their handling of the Word of God. But as the course proceeds, there comes a gradual unfolding of very strange doctrines indeed. They tell you that they have got a lot of fresh apostles in these latter days; that they have been commissioned to seal the 144,000 spoken of in the Revelation; and that if you want to escape the woes of the great tribulation, you must go to them to be sealed. And what follows after that? Why, most of the doctrines of the Church of Rome over again. Priests in gorgeous vestments, incense burning, baptismal regeneration, and all the rest of it. All this lies behind those simple special meetings about the coming of the Lord, which are made so attractive, in order to lead the unwary into the adoption of their false ideas.[29]

Catholic Apostolic outreach meetings were conducted in a markedly restrained manner. Usually they included hymns (although very few in the English hymnals had a revivalist strain) and liturgical prayers, but they were not intended to form proper services of worship, and majored on a reasoned (or at least argued) presentation of the movement's message. Sometimes addresses were given on pertinent topics: for example, an influenza epidemic in 1890 led evangelists in Switzerland and South Germany to hold meetings addressing the question: 'What is the meaning of the influenza?'[30] Usually, however, evangelists drew on a stock of lectures which they had spent considerable time preparing and which covered 'the many subjects necessary for the full Testimony'; they might give these in several locations.[31] Inquirers would be given opportunity to ask questions, but no pressure was put on hearers to make an immediate or public response. This typical invitation is taken from a handbill: 'The Preacher will be glad to meet with any who may wish to inquire concerning the Lord's special work in these last days in preparation for His own Appearing. Inquiry may be made at the close of any of the Meetings, or questions may be sent in for answers at the Monday

---

claimed that '[t]heir great instrument is terror': 'Letter to a Clergyman,' 32. That said, their focus was on the Great Tribulation, which was limited in time, rather than on hell, which was not.

29. Holiday, *Character*, 61.
30. AR 1890, 17.
31. J. C. H., 'Mr Michael Hall,' *Newsletter* 5 (November 1953) 16–18.

evening Meetings.'[32] Such meetings, which were often arranged as a course of four addresses, were not held during the summer season. If sufficient interest was shown, follow-up series of meetings were arranged, usually in a smaller venue.[33] In North Germany, it became the practice to give a series of three 'witness sermons', inviting interested inquirers to attend Catholic Apostolic worship.[34] The evangelist's name was not normally given.[35] Sometimes, though, it was stated that the lectures would be given by 'an Evangelist serving under the Lord's Restored Apostles' or 'an evangelist of the Catholic Apostolic Church'; this entailed a footnote explaining that 'The name "Catholic Apostolic Church" is not assumed as a title of separation from our Brethren in Christ, but as one testifying to our union with them in that one Church to which all the faithful in Christ profess to belong.'

In preparation for a course of lectures, considerable effort went into publicity, as an instance from 1875 shows: 'In Wolverhampton, the bands of Lay-assistants, previously to the delivery of the public Testimony, were divided into five companies. 15000 bills were distributed, & every house in the town & suburbs, & most of the houses in the adjoining villages were visited, & a special notice directed to every Minister of the Gospel, & official person.'[36] At Huddersfield, for a testimony in 1889 (the sixth since 1873), fifty posters and 12,000 handbills were printed.[37] Invitation cards and handbills were the main means of publicity. However, when one church used women to assist in distributing handbills from house to house, this was deemed unseemly because it was work of a public character.[38] Newspaper advertising was generally rejected as advertisements might appear next to others for profane things, or worse, such as séances.[39] However, the same consideration does not appear to have worried the Church when it came to newspaper reports of meetings, which appeared frequently and often reported the content of addresses in detail.

One experiment was the provision of sermons in French, German, and Italian in London during the Great Exhibition of 1851, in an attempt to reach Europeans.[40] Little response was recorded, but subsequently the Church appointed chaplains to minister to French and Italian speakers in London.[41] It was also proposed to repeat

32. Anon., *Coming Again*.

33. E.g. at the Cory Memorial Hall in Cardiff during the winter of 1898–99: BOC, Scrapbook containing invitations to special services etc, 60.

34. AR 1878, 15.

35. Exceptions were made in the cases of James Heath (whose MA degree was also given) and Col. A. F. Laughton, CB, probably because his decoration was seen as lending authority to the invitation: Scrapbook containing invitations to special services etc, 83, 101.

36. AR 1875, 6.

37. BIA, CAC 4/6, Huddersfield MC, 1 October 1889.

38. MC, 3 November 1880, 122.

39. AC, Edward Heath, 'Remarks on Evangelist Sermons in Churches, 5 January 1898,' 14.

40. NC, 2 April 1851.

41. Miller, *Irvingism*, 1:261, following Dowglass, *Chronicle*, 40.

the effort in 1862, when it was noted that the financial support offered by members in 1851 had largely sufficed to continue work in Italy during the following decade, a contrast with some other evangelist work.[42]

Whilst public halls were frequently used, especially where no Catholic Apostolic congregation had yet been established, on occasion the church building was used. Indeed, it was originally intended that the Gordon Square building should include a chapel specifically for evangelist use.[43] Angels were 'to have an Evangelist sermon preached in their Churches if possible every Sunday in order to shed forth in their own neighbourhood the light of the Gospel to the poor.' In 1877 it was laid down that the subjects of sermons were not supposed to be advertised.[44] However, there is extant a collection of handbills made at Gordon Square which does just this, the earliest items in which come from the mid-1880s, and many of which advertise sermon series at Catholic Apostolic churches.

Interest in biblical prophecy, coupled with a sense of crisis in world affairs, certainly made some receptive to the movement's public testimony. Some angel-evangelists in England noted in 1877 that anxious hearers were attending because they were curious 'to know whether we may not have received some revelation as to coming events. This is no doubt helped on by pamphlets & Lectures, professing to deduce the future fate of Nations from the prophecies of Scripture, as interpreted by those who print or deliver them.'[45] Over time, it was claimed by one former minister, the word 'instant' was dropped from publicity, an implicit acknowledgement that the times were more settled and that an overly apocalyptic message would not secure a response.[46] The adoption of a more popular approach may explain why Miller observed an increased dogmatism in younger evangelists, although he put it down to the fact that as second-generation members they had not had to work out for themselves their answers to the fundamental questions associated with Catholic Apostolic claims.[47]

In 1881, W. W. Wright, angel-evangelist for the Northern district of England from 1871–81, reported that he had spent the year delivering a special Testimony. The last such effort had been seven years before, and seven years before that, in 1866, there had been, as we noted, a large-scale testimony in London and England. As part of Wright's labors, over a million handbills were distributed. He was buoyant about the results, but when an application was made shortly afterwards to engage in such a testimony in London, apparently after John Leslie as coadjutor had requested the opinions of angels regarding the request, Woodhouse dismissed it, considering that the expenditure and

42. MC, 19 February 1862, 145.
43. Miller, *Irvingism*, 1:268; cf. Knight, *Building*, 4.
44. MC, 7 November 1877, 75, 76.
45. AR 1877, 4.
46. Prior, *My Experience*, 44. It reappeared in invitations I have seen from 1900–1901: Scrapbook, 64, 66, 134.
47. Miller, *Irvingism*, 1:298.

effort laid out in 1866 had not been justified by the results.[48] He may also have had in mind the constant struggle to fund evangelist work in London. Woodhouse set out his reasoning in a 'Letter by the Apostle on a proposal for a public testimony by the Evangelists in London.' In his view, what was being proposed amounted to something new, as the Church had not 'lifted up its voice in the streets' before (in fact, open-air preaching had taken place in Irving's day, and from time to time thereafter). The outreach of the mid-1860s 'was not anything which seemed to belong to us as Apostles, & was not undertaken as part of our work; but was quite exceptional.' It might be repeated but not as part of the regular apostolic work. 'I understand the Apostolic work in its present phase to be directed to the gathering of a First fruits, & building them up according to the perfect pattern, as a witness in the midst of Christendom.' The Church's witness was not directed to the godless and infidels but 'to those who profess to be spiritual,' especially their rulers. Churches were its testimony.[49]

Yet by 1888 Woodhouse appears to have modified his thinking in the light of prophecies which not only pointed to a future general testimony but also called for a special one now for England. The fiftieth anniversary of the Great Testimony coincided with the third Lambeth Conference, which brought to London Anglican bishops from all over the British Empire. Accordingly, the angels of the seven churches in London were directed to prepare a short statement of the Lord's work and to deliver it and the Great Testimony to the archbishops and bishops attending the conference.[50] Prophecy had indicated that 'a witness is to be borne in the first instance to England, by the Seven Angels of the Seven Churches in London, for which all things are ready, to be followed by a similar testimony in Germany and other countries. The object of this witness is declared to be to announce the speedy winding up and bringing to an end the work of revival, spoken of in the first Testimony.'[51] It was to be an appeal to Churches through the bishops as heads, a last invitation. The angels sought interviews with the two English archbishops and sent copies of the Great Testimony to all the other bishops, along with a short explanation of why this was being done. Urging the bishops to investigate the work by apostles and not to be misled by appearances into thinking that it had failed, it was explained that God's purpose was not to build up the Church for continued existence, but to prepare those who would heed its message for Christ's return. The apostles welcomed the sacramental revival evident in Anglicanism, as also the revival of the advent hope, but expressed their sorrow that these should have been taken up by two separated parties.[52]

48. AR 1881, 10–12; AR 1882, 4; MC, 22 February, 1882, 142; 22 March 1882, 143; 19 April 1882, 144.
49. MC, 17 May 1882, 149–52.
50. AD, July 1888, 9. For their statement, see Anon., *Word of Testimony*.
51. AR 1888, 3.
52. AR 1888, 4; Copinger, 'Annals,' 157.

In addition, angels were instructed to read the Great Testimony publicly, as the angel at the Central Church (Henry Hume) explained. He planned do so, with comments, on Sundays at 4 p.m. from 28 October for five or six weeks until he had completed it. Members were exhorted to come and hear it: to read it at home was not the same, for it was not a historical document but a living voice. Its focus on rulers meant that it was not intended for all, so the injunction to read it publicly implied the apostle's sense of the seriousness of the time and the nearness of the crisis of which they warned fifty years previously.[53] Elsewhere, the Testimony was widely read to Catholic Apostolic ministers and their flocks in Germany, Switzerland, and Scandinavia. More public testimony took place in London and Berlin, but Paris, which had been intended as a third venue, could not be used as it had no fully organized congregation displaying the fourfold ministry which could be cited as an example. Similarly, Rome, the intended fourth venue, saw no public testimony.[54] The following year, over nine hundred Protestant ministers in North Germany received copies of a Testimony modelled on that delivered in London, along with the Great Testimony and the liturgy.[55]

The early 1890s saw another change in strategy in England, as Leslie reported. In 1893 he submitted to Woodhouse a plan, duly adopted, for a more rapid spread of the message 'in consideration of the serious warnings which we have of approaching judgments.' Hitherto evangelists would stay in one place for many months if there was any likelihood of gathering a congregation, but this meant that they could only cover a small part of the field. The primary objective of evangelist work therefore shifted from gathering to warning. An evangelist would deliver one or two lectures in a place and move on, leaving those interested with a correspondence address and details of nearby Catholic Apostolic congregations. 'Ordinary missions' were thus replaced by 'shorter testimonies'. 'The duty of testifying to coming judgments, & thereby justifying God in the fulfilment of His warnings, as distinct from the duty of gathering His first-fruits' had been urged on the Church in prophecy many years earlier.[56] The result seems to have been a decline in the numbers being committed to pastorship, of about 20 per cent.[57] By 1895, however, Leslie reported that all the towns and larger villages would soon have been covered, after which ordinary missions could be resumed. In two years, 7,064 places in England had been visited and 2,060 lectures delivered. This effort had shown the areas on which the evangelists could now focus their attention.[58]

---

53. Hume, [Letter of thanks].

54. AR 1889, 25–26; AR 1891, 40–41.

55. AR 1890, 10–11; AD, July 1889, 5; Copinger, 'Annals,' 159.

56. AR 1894, 2, 8–9; cf. MC, 20 September 1893, 133–34. In 1873 Cardale justified the relative lack of response to evangelist work in England on the basis that the primary objective was to deliver the Testimony: MC, 12 November 1873, 409.

57. The average for 1887–92 was 355, for 1898–99 it was 282.

58. AR 1895, 4–5, 8.

A highly effective opening into the homes of those living near a church was provided by the requests made for ministers to come and pray for the sick to be healed. We should remember that this was in the West and not in 'mission fields' where medicine acted as a handmaid of the gospel, although even here miraculous healing could have played a high-profile role, as it would in inter-war Britain and North America through Pentecostal evangelistic and healing crusades. In part, such prayer for healing probably represented a counter to scientifically rooted unbelief, and it could have provided encouragement to poorer members who would have struggled to pay doctor's bills. *Angels' Records* detailed cases from several countries of healings occurring through the Church's ministry, sometimes over forty in a single issue. Healing could serve an evangelistic purpose, when the family of an individual who had been healed not only came to render thanks for healing but also accepted the Lord's work and began to receive instruction with a view to joining the Church. Further apologetic value was found in the reactions of doctors treating the sick person, especially if they described recovery as miraculous. Sometimes lapsed members returned to the fold as a result of being healed.[59] Healings of a wide range of diseases were reported, cancers being prominent, as well as cases which could be interpreted as psychosomatic illness. Sometimes planned operations still went ahead, but more often it was reported that they had been deemed unnecessary as the result of divine intervention. There were even accounts of the healing of animals.[60] On occasion the local Anglican clergyman was invited to perform the anointing, joined by a Catholic Apostolic minister.[61] Such accounts might also record whether that minister was a doctor or surgeon. By portraying the observance of due order in such matters as which ministers performed the anointing, they reinforced a commitment to doing everything decently and in order. Expectation grew that in a future phase of the work there would be an even greater manifestation of gifts of healing. Prophecy at Bern in 1896 declared: 'Ye have come to a time when there shall be a great pouring forth of the gifts of healing, in the midst of Christendom.' This would include the discernment of evil spirits.[62] However, no cases of deliverance from evil spirits were reported in the *Record*; since these did occur, certainly in the earlier years, we may infer that it was considered better not to report these. As in Roman Catholic practice, exorcism seems to have been located in the order for baptism, as well as in such forms as that for the benediction of a house. I only found one instance of an illness being rebuked—appendicitis—so we should not jump to a simplistic conclusion about the extent to which Catholic Apostolics regarded physical sickness as the direct result of demonic activity.[63] There were too

---

59. *Record* 6/5 (June 1897) 559–60.

60. E.g., *Record* 3/5 (September 1883) 486–87, where a flock in the Newcastle area was healed of foot and mouth disease.

61. E.g., *Record* 4/2 (July 1886) 288–90.

62. *Record* 6/5 (June 1897) 492.

63. *Record* 10/2 (October 1912) 196. By this time, such an action could have owed something to

many medics among their ministers for such a view to have become official teaching. No cases of healing were reported after 1917 or 1918, which may be due in part to a desire to distance the Church from the growing 'faith-healing' movement.

Building relationships with clergy, especially those of the established Churches, assumed particular importance because of the Catholic Apostolic conception of their mission, as well as their belief in the rightness of establishment. Members in England were enjoined to respect the standing of Anglican clergy. Lay members might give information about the Lord's work if asked by clergy, but it was not their place to engage in direct testimony, this being the task of the angel-evangelist and his ministers. Since it was customary to attend communion in the Church of England without first seeking admission, Catholic Apostolics should do likewise: to make a point of asking the clergy was tantamount to forcing the Lord's work upon them and was in effect a sectarian approach. In any case, it was argued, Anglican clergy could not withhold communion from any baptized communicant member in good standing with their own Church. Attendance without asking was not, therefore, under false pretences, but simply making use of the liberty which existed.[64]

Personal witness had its part to play in outreach. It was often noted in various countries that members were esteemed by those around. 'At Stockholm, the people gathered under the Apostles of the Lord, are so esteemed, that families belonging to the Established Church, often send messages to one of our Ministers, enquiring if they can have any member of our Congregations as maid-servants.'[65] That, incidentally, provides further indirect testimony to the social composition of congregations. However, members had to strike a balance between not trespassing on the angel-evangelist's prerogative and not being backward in giving a reason for their hope: 'it appears that an impression exists that lay-assistants and others when engaged in Evangelist work under the Angel of the Church are not at liberty to speak of the Lord's work under Apostles, nor (unless asked) state from what Church they come. The Coadjutor considers this to be an exaggeration of the principle that lay-assistants do not go out to proselytise nor to blow the trumpet of warning. No one should be debarred from speaking of the Lord's work on legitimate occasion.'[66]

Throughout, the work was conducted in a restrained manner which contrasted with the exuberance of revivalist groups such as the Salvation Army or some of the undenominational evangelists. Not for them the attempt to railroad hearers into making a response. In 1855 W. H. Place as pillar of evangelists had urged a measure of restraint in the approach to be adopted by the ministers under him which contrasted with the sweeping denunciations of the earliest years. They were gathering the first-fruits, but that did not mean that the rest would be destroyed: 'gather whom you gather, full of

---

influences from early Pentecostalism.

64. MC, 11 January 1893, 121–25.

65. AR 1886, 31.

66. MC, 1899/4, 1–2.

hope for the rest; and do not judge the rest to be unworthy; if you do, you let in an element of weakness which will tell upon you more than you are aware of—it comes from not having altogether thrown off the old habit of preaching to baptized men escape from damnation, as all that the gospel means.' Since it was dangerous for hearers to persist to the end in unbelief, evangelists must not force them into a corner so that it was impossible for them to respond later.[67] Such restraint should extend also to speaking about the institutions of fallen Christendom. Place called on the evangelists to remember that God had met people in the divisions of Babylon. It was not their part as ministers to help to destroy it. Those who majored on denouncing Babylon, without pity for those in it whom God had met, lost their sweetness of spirit, which made their message unattractive.[68]

This restraint was to become an important feature of Catholic Apostolic dealings with non-members; even now, it underlies the reserve which they exercise, believing that it is better to withhold information about the work than to provide inquirers with such information as would render them without excuse if they continue in unbelief.

In spite of this restraint, the claims made by Catholic Apostolic ministers were often sufficient to provoke vigorous opposition, which could take curious forms. At Huddersfield, for instance, Christadelphians stood at the doors of the venue being used for evangelistic lectures in 1874, distributing pamphlets giving their views on matters of biblical interpretation. Three years later, when the Catholic Apostolics advertised a series of sermons, so did the Christadelphians—and for the same time, as well as trying to get a hearing in the Catholic Apostolic meetings.[69] The congregation also had to contend with the fact that their first meeting-place had formerly been used by the Mormons, leading to further confusion. Yet they could still assert: 'there is no doubt that our presence has greatly raised the social status of Spring Street.'[70] In Scotland, the Salvation Army once gathered a crowd to sing hymns in front of the hall where a Catholic Apostolic evangelist was speaking; on another evening, the Brethren 'had a grand display of adult Baptism, in one of the public Halls'; and on a third night, a woman ('sister to one of the leading manufacturers in the town') preached a revival sermon to 1,500. By contrast, the evangelist had just forty hearers.[71]

But more often the problem was apathy arising out of a lack of residual Christian belief. In the face of a growing spirit of infidelity, the Church found by the late nineteenth century that evangelist work was becoming less and less fruitful in many countries.[72] It is questionable whether it was able to adapt its presentation from one geared to a religious public to one suitable for an increasingly irreligious public. Cer-

67. Place, *Substance of Teaching*, 10.
68. Ibid., 14–16.
69. BIA, CAC 4/6, Huddersfield Record of Events, 6, 12.
70. Ibid., 11 (May 1876).
71. AR 1881, 21.
72. AR 1881, 3.

tainly its primary appeal, perhaps in keeping with its sense of its mission, was to those who already bore the name 'Christian' rather than to those who had never done so or who had rejected it.

Whilst those who accepted the message were but a tiny fraction of those who heard it, they did exist, and in some numbers. In 1852 Cardale defined the indicators of an enquirer's readiness for being handed over by the evangelist to the pastoral ministry. In a Christian land, he asserted, 'the duty of the Evangelist is not to convert men from Paganism to Christianity, but to recover them from being Christians in name, to be Christians in reality.' The laity had no need of scholastic theology; it was usually enough that they should 'intelligently . . . confess the simple doctrines of the Creed, and that they should have a general understanding of the distinct meaning, object, and effects of the Sacraments of the Christian Church.' A good test of an individual's readiness for membership was willingness to tithe; reluctance implied that he did not really wish to join the Church.[73]

As the century wore on, it was no longer possible for the evangelists in some European countries to assume either that most of their hearers had been baptized, or that those baptisms had always been in the name of the Trinity. In Switzerland, for example, it was stated that an increasingly anti-Christian spirit was observable among clergy and schoolteachers. Clergy were even introducing their own baptismal formulae to replace Trinitarian baptism. As a result, '[t]he Evangelists are obliged to take means to assure themselves that the young people wishing to be committed to Pastorship, have been rightly admitted to Christian Baptism.'[74] And when members were dispersed, the condition of the churches meant that angels could not issue a blanket exhortation urging them to attend their nearest state church congregation, since there was no guarantee of its minister's orthodoxy.[75]

## MEMBERSHIP

According to one observer, 'No Christian community in England of equal size can boast of so many families of rank and wealth, or, we must add, upon the other hand, has made so little progress amongst the poor.'[76] That has been the received view in many quarters regarding the Church's social composition, but the assumption that its appeal was primarily to the upper classes is not borne out by evidence. There were, it is true, some high-profile accessions from the aristocracy during this period, such as the sixth duke of Northumberland (1819–99), who married Drummond's daughter Louisa. Several Catholic Apostolic members of this family would occupy prominent positions in public life. But the primarily working-class nature of the membership,

73. NC, 4 February 1852.
74. AR 1877, 22.
75. AR 1882, 31.
76. Marsden, *History*, 67.

which has already been illustrated by a range of anecdotal and survey evidence, can be demonstrated in England and Scotland from the Church's baptismal registers.

Several early registers are extant, having been surrendered to the government in 1840 along with the great majority of other English nonconformist registers. Some of these included details of the father's occupation, and we can use a scheme of classification to determine the social class to which he belonged. I have used a classification developed by the historian of nonconformity Michael R. Watts, which comprises thirteen categories.[77] Broadly speaking, category I is gentry, III includes higher professionals such as accountants and advocates, VI lower professionals such as ministers and teachers, VIII clerks, X skilled craftsmen, XII the semi-skilled, and XIII laborers. I–VIII could be described as 'bourgeoisie' and IX–XIII as the working classes.

In London, the Chelsea baptismal register has 34 per cent of the entries as coming from categories I–VIII and 66 per cent from categories IX–XIII; the figures for Paddington are approximately 20 per cent and 80 per cent, and for Bishopsgate 26 per cent and 74 per cent. Even more weighted towards the working classes is the register for Cambridge (11 per cent and 89 per cent).[78] In Scotland, the Edinburgh congregation, often thought to be largely middle- and upper-class in composition, turns out to have been much more mixed. Its baptismal register spans the congregation's entire history, shedding light on how its make-up changed over time. Three samples of a hundred entries from the register for the years 1834–43 (17 per cent and 83 per cent), 1870–75 (26 per cent and 74 per cent), and 1905–10 (35 per cent and 65 per cent) show that whilst the congregation (or at least those looking to it for occasional offices) was gradually becoming more middle-class, the working classes remained a clear majority, at least in terms of those baptized at the church (and in the absence of any other registers this is the best evidence-based guess that we can make).[79]

Jane de Gruchy undertook similar research into the early years of the congregation at Bradford, with the advantage of access to a fairly complete set of church registers. This was founded somewhat later than Edinburgh, in the 1870s, but once again 'the general picture is that of a predominantly working-class rather than middle-class congregation.'[80] Occupations listed in the Bradford register included railway servant, tailor, watchmaker, painter, engineer, servant, insurance agent, dressmaker, warehouseman, mill hand, mill manager, joiner, draper, weaver, teacher, dyer, saleswoman, nurse, shoemaker, mason, labourer, engine driver, blacksmith, publisher, engraver, coal dealer, carter, servant, shopkeeper, postman, bookbinder, news vendor, milliner, doctor, surgeon, bank clerk, quarry owner, butter merchant, Venetian blind maker,

---

77. Watts, *Dissenters*, 3:102–4.
78. Kew, TNA, RG4/4294, 4337, 4375, 328 respectively.
79. NAS, RH4/174, Edinburgh baptismal register. It was not possible to analyze addresses in detail to see whether there was any parallel with any gentrification in the immediate locality.
80. De Gruchy, 'Catholic Apostolic Church,' 35.

hairdresser, mill overlooker, solicitor's clerk, music teacher, and horticulturist.[81] However, her investigations into the backgrounds of the ministers show that priests 'were invariably middle-class,' and she postulates that financial constraints would have hindered working-class members from taking office as ministers.[82] Analysis of the ministerial staff of other British congregations would doubtless show a similar picture, and enable comparison with other denominations.

Most of the regular communicants received at nearby Cleckheaton from its formation in 1879 onwards appear to have been skilled working class, as at Bradford. Until 1901, almost all were sealed, and at least half were received from the angel-evangelist (i.e., were new to the work) rather than transferring from another Catholic Apostolic congregation.[83] Even the Central Church, whose popularity with the upper classes is widely known, was finding it appropriate in 1861 to maintain an employment register for members of the flock.[84] The deacons' minutes for the period refer to deaconesses doling out coal tickets and clothing, among other things. Yet we may wonder how integrated the congregation actually was: the letters of Isabella and Samuel Gardiner, who were members for most of the time from their marriage in 1853 until Samuel withdrew at some point after 1866, give a picture of a somewhat close-knit and introverted network of middle-class ministers and their families, of which the poor were not part. One wonders whether this inward-looking tendency meant that congregations were sometimes less welcoming than they needed to be to potential newcomers.

To some extent congregations took on the flavor of the district where they were situated. Bradford was very much a working-class town, for example. The Bishopsgate register is notable for the number of weavers and allied occupations represented among the parents of those being brought for baptism, reflecting its initial location in Spitalfields, just to the east of the City of London; this was an area known for its concentration of weavers. By way of a contrast, Isabella Gardiner recorded in 1857 that the Bath congregation had an unusually high proportion of 'gentlefolk'—again, reflecting the town's social composition as a popular watering-place for the middle classes.[85] We do not find—in Britain, at any rate—predominantly middle-class congregations in working-class areas, or vice versa.

For a variety of reasons, some who accepted the message of the evangelists did not—or could not—commit themselves wholly to a congregation under apostles. On occasion, as reported from Bishopsgate in 1882, evangelist work was explicitly directed towards the strengthening of local clergy and Christians, rather than their gathering into congregations under apostles. At other points, where results were insufficient to

---

81. BIA, CAC 1/2, register 3.
82. De Gruchy, 'Catholic Apostolic Church,' 39.
83. BIA, CAC 2/1, Cleckheaton register.
84. Archiv der NAK, Deaconesses' Minutes, 20 March 1861.
85. Isabella Gardiner to Martin Irving, 23 February [1857].

found a new congregation, contacts might be entrusted to the care of local clergy, especially if they were known to be sympathetic to the work.[86] Supplemental pastorship was also available for those who wanted to help in the work and who accepted the restoration of apostles, but were not free to join the Catholic Apostolic Church because of existing religious commitments, such as serving clergy with duties to their flocks; the same provision was available for laity. In such cases, angels did not put them under care of district elders but looked after them personally.[87] Catholic Apostolic reluctance to be classed as dissenters made this a congenial option, especially since it allowed continued access to the sacraments of the established Church; this was especially important because of their sacramental understanding of the Christian life, and a related pragmatic consideration was that it was not always possible to gather regularly for worship in Catholic Apostolic congregations, especially in Lutheran contexts.

Yet dual membership, whilst widely practised where permitted by ecclesiastical or civil authorities, seems often to have been regarded as something of a second-best, and this must temper our understanding of the Catholic Apostolic Church as an ecumenically minded body. In 1891, an English angel asked whether those committed for supplemental pastorship should be included on the list of absent members prayed for each Easter Monday and their names read in church and placed on the altar. A word of prophecy in response urged prayer for such people as they were still in Babylon, as children of Zion in captivity. The coadjutor (Leslie) thought that their names should be entered on the list and placed on the altar, but that there might be objections to them being read aloud.[88] One wonders whether this was partly out of consideration for some who may have wished to keep their Catholic Apostolic allegiance secret.

Nevertheless, dual membership became fairly common in England, individuals being sealed but remaining in the Church of England. Although in the 1830s a number of clergy had been put out of the Church of England, a generation later it was not uncommon for Anglican clergy to hold dual membership (and if serving under apostles they rarely if ever renounced their Anglican orders but retained their clerical title, a rite of confirmation of orders being observed), although it could give rise to suspicion and controversy. A case in point is that of the Revd W. H. Connor, who was a priest-chaplain in Stratford-upon-Avon during the mid-1870s. When it became known that he held and was disseminating 'Irvingite' views, his vicar, the Revd John Collis, effectively inhibited him from preaching. The bishop was unable to persuade Collis to take a more moderate line, and expressed his continued confidence in Connor, as, it seems, did many parishioners.[89] However, others addressed a requisition to Collis expressing their concern at Connor's continued employment and at the number

---

86. AR 1882, 10; AR 1878, 8.

87. LPL, MS 4937, Edward Heath, 'Notes on Supplemental Pastorship' (1889).

88. MC, 26 July 1891, 130–31.

89. Shakespeare Centre Library and Archive, BRR 13/8/11–17, Records of the Stratford-upon-Avon Corporation, Letters from the bishop of Worcester to Collis.

of 'Irvingites' teaching in the parish's schools. They petitioned the bishop to inform them 'whether, in your opinion, a "sealed" member of the Irvingite Church can be permitted to hold office as a clergyman of the Church of England, and whether we ought to accept, for ourselves and our families, the ministrations of a member of a schismatic community.'[90] Collis's reaction, which was probably typical of clergy in a similar position, was that although he had never had any sympathy with Irvingite tenets, he had until recently considered them harmless. He knew that Connor had long held these views, but had thought that he was keeping them to himself; certainly Connor had never publicly taught anything contrary to Anglican doctrine. However, Collis had discovered that Connor would defend his views if attacked, explain them when questioned, and talk about them and lend material to priests and to converts to the movement. This, Collis feared, might draw others holding such views, so that a parish within a parish grew up as people moved to the town to benefit from Connor's ministry.[91] A leading layman criticized the bishop's failure to act against Connor, arguing that it was not 'a question as to whether the Priest-Chaplain's views permit him to continue to work in the service of the Church of England, for it is one of the most dangerous parts of the Irvingite system that their converts shall continue in their places in other Churches until their "Apostles" call them away. Rather the question is, whether the Church of England can retain in her service one who owes this two-fold allegiance.'[92] Controversy continued: Collis issued a warning against 'Irvingism,' and Connor preached his farewell sermon the following January.[93] He remained a Church of England cleric, later serving at Alnwick, where he would have been sure of the support of successive dukes of Northumberland. The episode would have a wider significance: one local clergyman, Edward Miller, wrote in autumn 1875 to the *Guardian*, a high church newspaper, urging action against what he called the 'unsound and visionary teaching' of the Catholic Apostolic Church.[94] It was Miller who, a few years later, would publish the most influential critique of the movement, *The History and Doctrines of Irvingism*, which begins with the explanation that '[t]he present work arose out of the acceptance of the opinions generally known as Irvingite by Clergymen of the Church of England.'[95]

In the United States, there was perhaps less willingness among Episcopalians to tolerate dual membership. As for Congregationalists, a council of New England Congregational churches in 1880 considered this question, and whilst it affirmed its

90. Shakespeare Centre, DR 724/8/2/13, parishioners to Collis, 29 May 1875; parishioners to the bishop, 29 May 1875.

91. Ibid., Collis to Bernard Rice, 31 May 1875.

92. Ibid., Rice to the bishop, 3 June 1875.

93. Collis, *A Few Plain Words*; Connor, 'Why are ye fearful'?

94. Shakespeare Centre, DR 1067/2, Scrapbook collected by F. C. Morgan, 28, correspondence from the *Church Times*, 8 October 1875, and from Edward Miller, in *The Guardian*, 6 October 1875, repr. in Supplement to *Stratford-upon-Avon Chronicle*, 15 October 1875.

95. Miller, *Irvingism*, 1:vii.

respect for the individuals involved, it concluded that joining the Catholic Apostolic Church was divisive and that a Church was justified in withdrawing care from them after seeking to reclaim them. This provoked an apologia from three Congregational ministers who had taken service under apostles. Among their arguments was an ecclesiological one: whilst dual membership was not possible on Catholic or high Anglican terms, because such people did not recognize the workings of divine grace outside their own communion, Congregationalists did, and therefore 'no one will think it wrong who knows what the unity of the Church is.' Many who were unable to attend Catholic Apostolic services regularly wished to do what they could to strengthen their brethren where they were, and did not reject what they had received in Congregationalism. 'They do not seek to separate themselves by any act of their own from the local church, because they wish to testify to the grace of God that is in it, of which they have been partakers and of which they desire still to partake.'[96]

Scotland saw a few Presbyterian ministers hold dual membership, the best known and most controversial being John Macleod of Govan, whom we noted previously. However, Catholic Apostolic belief that episcopal ordination conferred a fuller degree of grace than that of non-episcopal churches made it less likely that Presbyterians who accepted the work could be content to remain where they were. Macleod himself espoused a much more sacramental ecclesiology than his colleagues, and his views and practice provoked recurring controversy. In Lutheran countries, dual membership was initially forbidden by the state authorities. Catholic Apostolics were thus forced into separation as declared dissenters. We may argue, then, that the practice of dual membership among Protestants varied in popularity according to whether the established Church in a particular tribe was willing to tolerate the practice, but also according to whether its ministers were ordained by bishops in the apostolic succession. As for Roman Catholic priests, Schröter states that eight were known to have remained in that Church (presumably in Germany) after accepting the work by apostles,[97] but we have noticed some who left it to join the Catholic Apostolic Church, although they probably did not number much above a dozen.

## PASTORAL CARE

Clearly if the Church were being restored upon the divine pattern under apostles, its pastoral care could fairly be expected to be such as would promote a high order of personal spirituality. Great attention was therefore paid to this aspect of ministry, and like other aspects its outworking was provided for and prescribed in minute detail. Robert Norton's illustration of how ministerial contact worked in practice offers a good starting-point for considering how the system (for such it undoubtedly was) worked for an individual member:

96. Andrews, Allen, and Thayer, *Duty of Christians*, ii, 17.
97. Schröter, *Die Katholischen-apostolischen Gemeinden*, 551 n. 103.

The working of this divinely organized constitution, as it were out of church and in the private life of individuals, may be illustrated by imagining the case of a poor woman in trouble. She is under the immediate care of a deaconess, who visits her as a sister or mother. If it be exclusively a woman's case, it ends there. If it be a case of difficulty about money matters or other worldly business, the deacon is applied to for assistance or advice; who if necessary takes counsel with his brother deacons, of whom there are seven in a complete church. If it be a matter of conscience or any inward trouble, she is cast upon the pastor for his sympathy, encouragement, and prayers; and, if needed, for absolution. If through ignorance or sin, her views of the Gospel have become clouded, the evangelist teaches her over again what be the first principles of the doctrine of Christ, and what the hope of our calling. If she has had, or imagines she has had, revelations or spiritual experiences of any kind, the prophet helps her to discern their good or evil character, and to cherish or repel them. If it be some hard matter of doctrine or discipline, she is placed under the oversight of the elder; who in dangerous illness would pray over her, anointing her with oil in the name of the Lord. If one and all of these ministries fail to meet her case, the angel of the church is appealed to. He, if at a loss, consults the apostle, and the apostle, if necessary, would confer with his brethren in council. The case would then travel back through the same channels; and even were its result to be the infliction of some ecclesiastical censure, the sisterly deaconess would be at her side to share and soften it.[98]

Whereas the second half of the nineteenth century saw many ministers in the English-speaking world espouse the dictum that 'a home-going parson makes a church-going people,' Catholic Apostolics considered that home visits should only made by certain classes of minister or lay worker and in certain circumstances. Usually this was the task of the deacons, members seeing priests at the church unless there was a particular reason for a priest to make a home visit.[99] Where ministerial numbers were sufficient and the congregation's size required it, each member was allotted to the care of a particular pastor and deacon.[100] Deacon's visits would last up to fifteen minutes once a quarter, and would be concerned primarily with such matters as whether the household was regular in attendance at worship, whether there were any practical needs, and so on.[101] Notice was to be given beforehand so that the whole household could be assembled. 'After the children had received ministry, they would withdraw, and the Deacon would then have opportunity to minister to the head of the family.'[102] Women on their own would normally be visited by a deaconess, as Norton's illustration implies.

98. Norton, *Restoration*, 119–20.
99. MC, 28 February 1855, 14–15.
100. Todd, [Pastoral letter, Advent 1879], 8.
101. BIA, CAC 4/5, Huddersfield MC, 24 June 1896.
102. BIA, CAC 5/4, Halifax MC, 13 July 1893.

Members would also see the priests (other than pastors) once a quarter, at the church.[103] In time, it became the practice for each member to appear at a sitting of 'the Four,' i.e., a priest from each of the four 'borders'—elder, prophet, evangelist, and pastor—in order to discern and provide the most appropriate pastoral ministry to each member, although Miller claimed that such assessments were generally cursory.[104] In 1858, Gardiner recorded that small rural congregations were now to be visited by the four from the mother church.[105] The importance of the fourfold ministry, as we shall see in the next chapter, derived not only from the belief that it was the divinely ordained pattern but also from its perceived correspondence to the make-up of human nature. Effective pastoral ministry, then, was that which ministered to each aspect of the human constitution.

The elders were those priests whose ministry of ruling corresponded to that of the angel and apostle above them. An undated but apparently mid-nineteenth-century teaching copied into a notebook by one of the Bradford ministers outlined how work was to be carried on in the districts of a local church.[106]

> 1. To each district or Division of the Church placed under the charge of an Elder, as many Pastors should be appointed as may be required for the proper care of the people; also at least one Prophet & an Evangelist (ordained to the Priesthood); also one of the Seven Deacons & as many other Deacons as may be needed for Diaconal care & where several are thus used one of them should be Help to the district Seven Deacon_ lastly as many Deaconesses as may be needed.
>
> It is the duty of the Elder to bring under the notice of the Angel any deficiency in the proper number of ministers as above stated.
>
> 2. Every Elder having charge of a District should be instructed to make provision for Elder's or District Meetings, in which he should preside & be accompanied by the Pastor & Deacon & if possible by the Prophet & Evangelist.
>
> The objects of these meetings are not only that the Elder, Prophet, Evangelist, Pastor & Deacon may teach the people, although this has its value & is especially necessary in Districts at a distance from the Mother Church_ but also that the several ministers employed in the District may obtain a more intimate acquaintance with the people. The people on these occasions should be encouraged to ask questions on any subject on which they desire light or instruction & these questions, if of importance, can be reserved to a subsequent meeting. The reservation of such questions will tend to keep alive the interest of the people.
>
> . . .

---

103. Ibid., 6.
104. Miller, *Irvingism*, 1:326–27.
105. Samuel Gardiner to Martin Irving, 18 July [1858].
106. WYAS, 53D95/5/11, Book containing duties of elders, underdeacons etc, 1–6.

3. The Elder sh^d also appoint proper times in wh: accompanied by the P^t Evangelist & Pastor he may see the individual members of his District, & each person if possible once a year or there abouts. Young females sh^d on these occasions be presented by the mother or the Deaconess.

4. The Elder should also arrange with his Prophet & Ev^t & if the Prophet & Ev^t serve also in other Districts, then with the Elders of those Districts also, that they sh^d severally sit in the Church at fixed times in order that the several members of the District may see these ministers from time to time. Notice of these appointed times sh^d be given to each member of the District & the Elders sh^d exhort them to avail themselves of the occasional offices of these two ministers—as well as of the Pastor. But no one sh^d see either of these two ministers with-out [sic] the knowledge and sanction of the Pastor. While it is the duty of the Pastor to encourage those under his care to resort to the other two ministers, he is also the judge as to the frequency of such resort & whether the ministry of one of the two may not be more edifying than that of the other.

5. The Elder sh^d from time to time assemble the other Priests & Deacons of the District, & in the presence of them all sh^d go thro the names on the list of members so that all the ministers may have some knowledge of the circumstances & spiritual condition of each member. By meeting once in two or three weeks for a short time & taking a certain number of names the whole may be passed in review in the course of a year or less.

6. In every large Church where the Districts extend over considerable space each Elder sh^d if possible provide for the holding of one or more prayer meetings in his District.

In smaller Churches & within more confined limits, the Elders sh^d assist the Angel by counsel or otherwise to provide for the same. In these District Prayer Meetings the Elder if not presiding appoints the President who sh^d report to him after each occasion the number present & the persons taking part & any other occurrences of sufficient importance.

Each year members would also be summoned to meet the angel.[107] The Bradford church was probably typical in sending out printed cards to members inviting them to be interviewed by the angel in the church vestry. One such card (a pro forma) survives:[108]

---

107. Anon., 'Persuaded of the common desire,' 4.
108. WYAS, 53D95/5/2, Apostles' Determinations, 1876–1900, inserted in the volume.

**Church in Bradford.**

To_____

You are invited to an interview with

**The Angel** who will sit in the Church Vestry to

see Members of the Flock, on _____

the _____ 190 at _____ p.m.

*If unable to attend please say when convenient.*

Bound up with this intricate system of pastoral provision was the keeping of a variety of church registers, intended to promote effective pastoral care and a disciplined approach to ministry. As laid down by the *Book of Regulations* in 1878, each church in England was expected to maintain a full set of registers (which could be combined in one or more volumes), numbered as follows:[109]

1. Baptisms
2. Marriages
3. Regular lay communicants
4. Occasional communicants (including infants and children)
5. Those sealed with the Holy Ghost
6. Angels, priests and deacons under the pastoral care of the angel but not on the Church's ministerial staff (including ministers of the Universal Church)
7. Lay assistants
8. Candidates for ministry who had formally dedicated themselves in a service of presentation
9. Those called by prophecy to the priesthood
10. Underdeacons
11. Deaconesses
12. Deacons
13. Priests
14. Those departed in the faith
15. The lapsed (i.e., those who persistently declined or rejected the Church's pastoral care; names could only be placed on this register if agreed by the apostle)
16. Those whose addresses had been unknown for at least seven years
17. The unfaithful (i.e., those absenting themselves from communion without good reason for at least a year)
18. Minutes of church councils
19. Record of events in the congregation's history

---

109. Anon., *Book of Regulations*, §611 and Appendix I.

The registers for members whose whereabouts were unknown (16), or who were deemed unfaithful (17), were introduced around 1875, and do not appear in the list of registers in the 1862 *General Rubrics* (neither does register 6). From Germany it was reported that the introduction of these registers had brought to light cases which should have been dealt with before.[110] In England the new rules led to some success in reclaiming members. On the other hand, the numbers of names added to these registers seem to have had a sobering effect on the apostles and their ministers, doubtless bringing home to them the extent of pastoral work required.[111]

Members were encouraged to offer themselves for service in the Church. Registers were kept of such offers, detailing when made, the age of those making them (if not adults), and whether the offers were taken up. Such a register survives for the Eynsham congregation, covering the period 1888 to 1904. Among the tasks which individuals offered to undertake were singing, copying ministries, serving as acolyte or as scribe (tasking down utterances in services), needlework, serving as doorkeeper, underdeacon, or lay assistant, visiting for the deaconess, becoming an evangelist worker, playing the organ, teaching music, cleaning the brass, making communion bread, trimming the sanctuary lamp, maintaining the vestments, and candidating for ministry. Most before 1901 were from young people, although this changed thereafter; and the great majority were accepted.[112]

Finally, a book was to be kept for 'circulars and other letters of instruction' regarding Church government, discipline, and worship; a sample survives for the Bradford congregation.[113]

German churches were to keep the same registers, although 18 and 19 were unnumbered.[114] In Norway, the churches had to use a standard form of register as laid down by the state, which changed in 1892, but they also kept internal registers which followed standard Catholic Apostolic practice.[115]

Not surprisingly, the machinery of pastoral care sometimes creaked. Apart from the perennial problem of personality clashes between ministers and those in their charge, there was on occasion a lack of communication between ministers and people, as Gardiner (himself a deacon) complained in 1857 with reference to the Central Church: 'it is the old story which you used to complain of; the separation between ministers & people seems in full force. Of course I can not do very much in my little sphere here, but I think that I may do something: by really trying to find out what the people to whom I am sent are thinking about & representing it on their behalf, &

---

110. AR 1875, 24; cf. Anon., *General Rubrics*, appendix I.

111. AR 1876, 8; AR 1876, 34.

112. Oxford History Centre, Eynsham CAC records, NX1/A2/1, Register of offers of service 1888–1904.

113. WYAS, 53D95/5/7, Book of papers from Albury and special *Records*, 1901–10.

114. Anon., *Allgemeine Rubriken*.

115. See Diersmann, *Notes*, ch. 4.

by protesting against the uncommunicativeness of both priests & deacons.'[116] Some critics alleged that the rigidity of the system resulted in members being unable to access the guidance they needed, simply because the minister to whose care they were allotted was more concerned with keeping within his border and observing the rules than with the individuals in his care. A former minister, William Grant, asserted that there was much hidden unease in the Church. The cultivation of the inner life had been lost sight of, and an overemphasis on priesthood and rule had led to ministerial officialism, with a clergy who had become narrow and distrustful.[117]

Nevertheless, if the litmus test of any system of pastoral care is the quality of the members it produces, it had much to commend it: from the late nineteenth century Catholic Apostolic Christians were often highly regarded, especially once churches began to close after 1901 and they were forced to make their homes in congregations of other denominations, where the quality of their spiritual life was recognized even if the doctrinal outlook which produced it was not understood.

Table 7.1: Membership Statistics for West Yorkshire Churches

|  | Bradford | Brighouse | Cleckheaton | Halifax | Huddersfield | Keighley |
| --- | --- | --- | --- | --- | --- | --- |
| Baptisms | 601 | 59 | 69 | 24 | 146 | 70 |
| R3 reg. Comms | 472M, 930W; last entry n.d. |  | 75M, 126W | 62M, 174W |  | 64M, 130W |
| R4 occ. Comms | 742 to 1927 |  | 109 | 37M, 43W |  | 49M, 63W |
| R5 sealed | 153M, 368W |  | 33M, 51W | 28M, 82W |  | 21M, 61W |
| R14 departed | 433 to 1936 | 48 | 39 | 26M, 57W | 115 | 53 |
| R15 refuse care | 129 to 1927 |  | 20 | 17 |  | 22 |
| R17 unfaithful | 51 |  | 16 | 4 |  | 3 |

The tabulated statistics from the registers of several West Yorkshire churches provide further evidence regarding the effectiveness or otherwise of the system. Occasional communicants were virtually all children, admitted in line with the regulations. It is clear that whilst many of those baptized would have gone on to be sealed when reaching the age of twenty, a significant proportion of those on the Church's books fell away. This may bear out the complaints sometimes made about lukewarm congregations, a proportion of whom might well have contented themselves with a minimum of religious observance. Pitcairn, as angel at Edinburgh for many years, illustrates

116. Samuel Gardiner to Martin Irving, 30 November 1857.
117. Grant, *Apostolic Lordship*, 9, 11–12, 25.

the concern felt by zealous ministers: many of his pamphlets are studded with comments and warnings about the danger of backsliding. But there is another explanation, not incompatible with that. None of those placed on register 15 at Cleckheaton or Keighley had been sealed; it is possible that the backsliding of such individuals began during teenage years, before the age at which sealing was administered, and that as they began to think for themselves in religious matters they decided not to remain in the faith in which they had been brought up. Miller claimed that many who grew up in the Church left it once they reached adulthood.[118] Whether they found a home in other denominations or whether they ceased to make any active Christian profession would, unfortunately, be virtually impossible to determine.

Those under the care of the angel-evangelist might receive communion occasionally, if they were deemed to have sufficient spiritual apprehension of the work. Individuals visiting members might also receive communion. However, Cardale seems to have been somewhat ambivalent about this: whilst it was impossible to refuse communion to baptized visitors, they were to be warned that if they communicated apart from faith in the mission of the restored apostles, it was at their own peril.[119] Later practice, however, seems to have been to adopt a more inclusive approach, not unlike that of some Brethren.

Inevitably some joined a Catholic Apostolic church who lived at a distance from it and could not attend worship there regularly; often they were the fruit of evangelist work in a district which had not led to the formation of a viable congregation. Others had to move because of army postings or employment changes, but it was deemed unnecessary, inappropriate, or impossible to move their membership to another congregation. One leaflet, apparently designed as a pro-forma for use by any congregation, offered general exhortations regarding the maintenance of a witness, with a special word for soldiers and emigrants.[120] Ministers kept in touch regularly with 'absent members' by post and occasional visits. To members of the congregations in Ottawa and Potsdam, their angel wrote: 'any communicants who reside at a distance from the Restored Altar should keep up a regular correspondence with their Pastor, in order that he may acquaint them with the substance of the teaching delivered in the Church, by sending copies of ministries and homilies, and by suitable words of counsel and encouragement.'[121] In India, one minister was sending homilies and sermons to members which are 'calculated to keep alive in them the knowledge & faith of what God has taught us.'[122] Such a strategy would come into its own in the twentieth century. Sermons were also circulated round congregations in manuscript form. Some from Albury survive with lists of names and addresses attached so that

---

118. Miller, *Irvingism*, 1:305–6.
119. MC, 1 March 1876, 44–45.
120. Anon., *To such members of this flock*; the copy in LPL is endorsed 'Address. Paddington 1863.'
121. Todd, [Pastoral letter, Advent 1879], 8.
122. AR 1876, 9.

members could read them and then pass them on to the next recipients.[123] The lists ensured that the whole congregation could be covered in a typically orderly manner.

## THE CARE OF CHILDREN

Given that many of the members in established congregations would have been brought up in the Church from infancy, it is worth looking at how it cared for its children. It should be noted that, unlike some Evangelical denominations and congregations, children were not seen as sinners needing a decisive experience of conversion. W. W. Andrews may have been reacting against his New England Congregationalist background, as well as perhaps drawing on his erstwhile co-religionist Horace Bushnell's *Christian Nurture* (1847), but his own posthumously published sermon of the same title enjoyed a fair measure of influence in Catholic Apostolic circles.[124] Andrews argued, as Bushnell had done (controversially, in the Congregationalist context of the time, which was strongly coloured by revivalistic conversionism), that children should be brought up as already Christian.

The pastoral care and spiritual nurture of children were, then, particular concerns of the apostles. There survives a pro-forma first communion certificate, stating that the children '[m]ay be brought up by . . . parents to receive Holy Communion on the next convenient occasion. . . . This certificate is to be presented to the deacon.'[125] Children were communicated once at the age of two. At the age of eight they were then admitted to occasional communion on the great festivals (Christmas, Easter, Pentecost, and All Saints), but if sufficiently instructed and showing evidence of spiritual progress, they could be bought to communion once a month. Corresponding to Anglican confirmation, children were instructed in preparation for receiving the angel's benediction, which followed upon their declaration of their faith. On receiving this they were admitted as regular communicants, usually around the age of fourteen. As they grew older, they were to be treated increasingly as independent agents, and parents were to be warned against trying to hothouse them, religiously speaking. However, until the age of twenty, which the Church saw as that of maturity and which was recognized by the rite of sealing, they were only committed to pastorship in their own right in exceptional circumstances, normally being regarded as under parental headship. During this period they were under the care of the fourfold priestly ministry, and after sealing young men were eligible for ordination.[126]

123. E.g. those attached to DFP: DNM/H/2/103, 104: Mr Vowles, 'Sermon. First Sunday after Circumcision [1884]. Apostles' Chapel. Albury'; Vowles, 'Sermon. Second Sunday after Circumcision [13 January 1884]. The Apostles' Chapel.'

124. W. W. Andrews, *Christian Nurture*. This was reprinted in 1914 and 1938.

125. BIA, Inserted CAC 4/1, Huddersfield Register of Baptisms.

126. Anon., *Book of Regulations*, §§533–38; MC, 31 July 1889, 7–12; Rupert M. Heath, *Lecture: The Lord's Pattern*, 9–10; this lecture offers a valuable concise summary of the topic. See also Davenport, *Albury Apostles*, 240.

As well as encouraging attendance at worship, churches gave attention to catechizing children. At Gordon Square in 1861, this was taking place during the 4 p.m. preaching on Sundays.[127] But the Catholic Apostolic Church seems to have vacillated regarding Sunday Schools. In 1873 Cardale warned the churches in London not to allow children to attend Sunday Schools or services in other places of worship when their own was in reach. 'The Lord long ago warned us of this sin. It is the abomination of causing your children to pass through the fire to Moloch.' And the result had been the loss of hundreds of children as they encountered teachers and companions who, however kind, were antagonistic towards Catholic Apostolic faith.[128] Some kind of gathering for children was often held in Catholic Apostolic congregations; the Bridgnorth church's summary of activities, under the heading 'Sunday School,' urged parents to bring their children for instruction on Sundays at 3 p.m., special catechizing being undertaken in the weeks preceding the four great feasts.[129] Where such meetings existed, the problem became one of the relative responsibility of the ministers and the parents for the religious instruction of children. In 1888 a prophecy stressed the responsibility of parents to bring up their children in God's ways. It seems to have had a wide impact: for instance, a special meeting was held in the New York church to hear it read from the *Record*.[130] The irregular meetings for children at Huddersfield, which had been monthly since the summer of 1887, became weekly from September 1889.[131] A syllabus survives from the Leeds church for the children's services during the year 1888–89; subjects to be covered were:

October: Spiritual beings
November: Saints of God
December: Types of the Saviour
January: Covenants of God
February: Worship
March: The fourfold ministry
April: Resurrection
May: Symbols in worship
June: Harvest work

Each month concluded with an address and catechizing on the theme. It was stressed that instruction by teachers and ministers did not release parents from their duty; they were encouraged to acquaint them with each week's subject, and to see they repeated the catechism correctly and learned the hymn. Parents were also invited to attend the

127. Deaconesses' Minutes, 1861.
128. Cardale, *Address at the Close of the Visitation*, 10–11.
129. Anon., 'Persuaded of the common desire,' 4.
130. Anon., 'A short time ago.'
131. Huddersfield Record, 37.

sessions, each Sunday at 4 p.m.[132] A traditional feature of English Sunday Schools, the annual outing and treat, also became a fixture in some congregations.[133]

However, a few years later such gatherings were ordered to cease in the light of the conviction that the primary responsibility for teaching the children lay with their parents, as an Edinburgh deacon explained:

> It has been pressed upon us by the Apostles' coadjutor at the late visitation that it is not in accordance with God's perfect way that young children should be instructed in these matters at Sunday Schools by Priests, Deacons, or Lay Assistants, but that the proper ordinance for imparting such instruction is the father and mother, and the sponsors of the child. You are aware that some time ago there were classes on Sundays for the children of the flock, and that means were taken with a view to getting as many children as possible to attend them. For several years past we have been taught that we should regard these classes as subordinate, and only helpful to the parents' teaching; but there being naturally a desire on the part of those engaged in the work of teaching the children to see it prosper in their hands, and thus to have a good attendance at their classes, the Apostles' Coadjutor, from an apprehension that the parents' teaching will, in the growth and prosperity of the classes, be made little of, has more recently directed that the classes shall be given up, and that means shall be taken for bringing the proper ordinance to bear upon the children.

Confronting the risk that parents might fail to take up the task, the deacon reminded them that it was a duty. If they felt themselves inadequately instructed, they could seek help from priests or deacons; in teaching others, they would be blessed themselves.[134]

Children were also encouraged to attend midweek services. To the church at Edinburgh, the coadjutor in his visitation in 1876 had made the point that if they could be trusted to go out on their own to play, they could be trusted to attend at least one weekday service each week.[135]

Increasing attention was given from the early 1870s to the pastoral care of young people.[136] The movement was now old enough for a second generation of members to have appeared, who would not have had to make the same sacrifices or grapple with the same challenges to their religious views as their parents had done. They therefore needed to be firmly grounded in the faith. In 1873 the apostles issued a paper 'On

132. Anon., *Catholic Apostolic Church, Leeds*.

133. BIA, CAC 1/9, Bradford Register of Services, 20 August 1881; Huddersfield Record, opp. 40 (26 May 1890). One wonders whether Sunday School work developed more in the industrial North of England, where it was particularly important in local culture.

134. Dickson, *Diaconal Teaching*, quotation at 3–4.

135. Acc. 8837, Two volumes of ministries, vol. 2, 'Exhortation Oct 8, 1876. After visitation Sept 27 to Oct 2d.'

136. Cardale et al., *Fourfold Ministry*, 29; AR 1874, 3; cf. *Record* 5/1 (July 1889) 111, one of several prophecies around this time regarding the importance of pastoral care of the young of the flock.

the Instruction of the young & newly gathered, by the Angel and Ministers of the Churches,' which advocated the practice of catechizing by ministers, but also the use of young men who had themselves been recently catechized to instruct the boys in the flock: this would not only fix the truth in their minds but also aid in retaining them in the congregation.[137]

This development, of course, occurred at the same time as the introduction of compulsory primary education in Britain following the 1870 Education Act. Many nonconformist churches had set up day schools before this, in order to shield their young from what was regarded as Anglican indoctrination; this motive was lacking in Catholic Apostolic thinking, since in England at least they were by now happy to see themselves as in some sense members of the established Church. This is one reason why, in contrast with almost all other denominations, very few Catholic Apostolic day schools came into existence in Britain. But in 1853 the Central Church deaconesses expressed their conviction that 'the secular instruction of the children of the poor in the flock' needed to be provided for, so that parents did not seek it in schools which would be hostile to the Church. A school eventually opened on 15 October 1855, with twenty-five girls from church families.[138] In 1857, Cardale reported that a recent visitation in London had shown a general need to provide education for younger children of poor members. 'In many instances these children are educated in neighbouring schools, induced to attend other Churches, and ultimately led away from our Churches.' Young persons, he thought, could serve as lay assistants for this purpose.[139] By 1871 the Central Church also had a school for boys.[140] However, by 1873 the establishment, which appears to have metamorphosed into a choir school, was coming under fire after a member had refused to send his son there because of its bad reputation; it was alleged that choir boys were taught things which would be of no use to them in commercial life, as if they were the sons of gentlemen. That they were not may be inferred from their 'addiction' to breaking the schoolroom windows. A few years later the deacons discussed 'the outrageous character of some of the boys both in the Church before the Altar & outside in the playground throwing stones & getting over the wall adjoining the University Hall; [and] their disorderly conduct on Sunday afternoons during the teaching by the ladies of their several classes.'[141]

In Germany the problem with state education was rather different: there ministers reported that it was rationalistic in character, and parents were urged to take seriously their own responsibilities.[142] Danish ministers likewise reported their con-

---

137. AD, August 1873, 8–14.

138. Deaconesses' Minutes, 22 June 1853, 19 December 1855.

139. MC, 22 April 1857, 62.

140. Henke, 'Catholic Apostolic Church,' 10.

141. Gordon Square Deacons' Minute Book 2, 19 December 1873, 11 October 1872, 24 March 1876.

142. AR 1875, 25.

cern to defend their young against 'infidelity, socialism & worldliness,' and regarding marriages with non-members.[143]

## WITHDRAWAL OF THE APOSTLES

The death of the last apostle in 1901 is usually represented as the point at which the Catholic Apostolic Church turned inwards and its life-support systems began to shut down. Whilst many internal writers have indeed presented such a picture, and borne witness to the profound shock and disorientation to which this event gave rise, we shall see later how ministers stressed that this event had not come unheralded. The first step was the apostles' cessation from travelling in the course of their work and their retreat (if it can be so called) to Albury. This began as early as 1855, when Cardale moved out of London to Albury, although he arranged to come up to the capital one day a week.[144] From 1875, the remaining apostles ceased to visit the areas under their charge, giving priority to maintaining services at Albury and overseeing the work.[145]

The second step in this process was precipitated by Cardale's sudden death in 1877. An account of his departure was given by Pitcairn to his Edinburgh flock. As usual, members had gathered at the Central Church to celebrate the Separation of the Apostles on 14 July, but this year there was a particular sense of expectation, prophecy having spoken of it as filling up a measure of time (it was forty-two years since the separation, i.e., 12 x 3½ years). Cardale came up to London the night before, apparently in good health. Soon after midnight, he began to feel unwell; as the service approached, he felt unable to celebrate and Woodhouse took his place, Cardale being present as an unofficiating minister. Around the time of the homily, Cardale tottered out of the sanctuary; 'the Apostle retired as one who had done his work, finished his course, and kept the faith.' Some had seen him separated, now they saw him removed. 'The Church would not have Apostleship, and lo! the Pillar of that ministry is removed.' Prophecy in the service announced 'that the Lord had accomplished a full measure of time in this stage of His work.' Cardale returned to Albury that afternoon, and was anointed on the 17th, dying the following morning. This was, Pitcairn concluded, both a time of trial and the gateway to blessing.[146]

Another angel, George Bousfield at Nottingham, testified that Cardale was

> ... known to so many not only as one of the Apostles of the Lord, but as a father and a friend, a man who had a kindly word for every one: a loving word for each who had to draw out the love: and a word of guidance and sympathy for all who looked to him to lead and pity. ...

---

143. AR 1883, 30.
144. MC, 28 February 1855.
145. AR 1876, 33; Schröter, *Bilder*, 25.
146. Pitcairn, *Address on occasion of Cardale's Removal*, 3–7, quotation at 4.

> We who have known him in his ministry have the same testimony to bear. No one in the churches has had anything like the work which has fallen to his lot, and few men at his time of life have laboured so long or done so much as he. . . . He experienced in himself that which he had to rule and guide in others, and if he had not been an Apostle, he might have been a Prophet. From the beginning of the manifestation of gifts he had been used in prophecy: and the last word of which I have heard through him was the earnest warning of the Spirit that God had done for His Church all that He could do.

It had not been part of Cardale's 'personal faith and expectation' that apostles had died, for he was looking for the day when they would be caught up to be with the Lord. But his death had not come as a total surprise to some. On 14 July 1876, prophecy told the faithful to count fifty-two weeks, for at end of the 12 x 3½ years 'the Lord would mark the time, and fulfil His work in His Apostles (or some such words).' They had been long warned of a 'time of excessive trials,' and words had been addressed to Cardale intimating that he would be removed. As for the apostles as a body, 'Even if none remained, we still should bear our witness that they <u>had been</u>.'[147] His death was not the loss of the Lord's work alone; 'while we lament the removal of a father and a friend, Christendom loses an intercessor, and the Catholic Church a guide.'[148]

Woodhouse now gave a series of teachings lasting several years to the seven churches in London, helping ministers adjust to the changes which this entailed and preparing them to face the future, when there might indeed be no apostles remaining. It is not without significance that many of these teachings continued to be made available in duplicated form, even into the 1970s. The refusal to provide for the work's continuance proved difficult for some ministers to accept, but, speaking after Armstrong's death in 1879, Woodhouse explained his position:

> A question was asked, or rather a suggestion was made by one of the ministers, perhaps by more than one, at our late meetings, whether the Apostles would not see it good, in contemplation of the possibility of their being taken away, to leave directions, written or oral, how the Coadjutors should act in such a case. The answer then given was to the effect that, if we could contemplate, as being according to the mind and purpose of God, the taking away of the Apostles, and the leaving of the Coadjutors and the Churches who had followed the faith of the Apostles behind, it might be a duty on the part of the Apostles to make the best provision they could for such a state of things, but inasmuch as we had always from the first believed that the Apostles and those sealed by them formed one band of firstfruits, to be led forward and translated together, and to be made partakers together, whether dying or living, of the same dignity and glory in being gathered to the Lord as a First-fruits, they

---

147. Bousfield, *Sermon after the Death of Cardale*, 1.
148. Ibid., 2.

could not, they dare not take any steps in providing for a state of things the very thought of which they shrank from, as from the voice of the tempter.[149]

As he had earlier stated, 'The Apostles have always felt the impossibility of attempting to take steps or introduce any order for meeting the event of their being taken away. An entirely new dispensation will then commence, the nature of which we cannot now apprehend.'[150]

And in 1885 Woodhouse expressed the view that the apostolic work was finished, as far as it involved gathering and sealing the first-fruits, setting up churches, and ordering worship. Their (or rather his) remaining work was to take a different shape, focusing on intercession for the whole of Christendom. No provision was to be made for the work's continuance after apostles were removed: it was the Lord's work and those who remained were content to leave it in his hands.[151] This was a time of overlapping between the period when restored apostles were active and that following their removal.

Shortly after Cardale's death, it had been resolved at the apostles' council that the duty of visiting the tribes should fall to the coadjutors (and apostolic delegations), 'not as acting under an individual Apostle, but as acting under the Apostleship.'[152] The coadjutors were now to hold their charges permanently. Woodhouse gave them a fresh commission, formally divesting himself of immediate responsibility for action.[153] In an address to the seven churches in London in August 1877, he argued that Cardale had been taken away because the work of apostles was now done.[154] Accordingly, the coadjutors oversaw and directed work in each tribe, although at first they were reluctant to take decisions without consulting Woodhouse; in 1881 he had to reaffirm in council their responsibility to act.[155] In turn, their ability to travel became progressively limited as they grew older and their numbers shrank, and as Woodhouse's increasing age required the intercession (regarded as the highest work of apostles) to be offered at Albury by coadjutors.[156]

Once apostolic visitations therefore became all but impossible, conferences of coadjutors with the angels in a tribe assumed increasing importance, those from Scandinavia meeting with Dr Capadose at Copenhagen, and those from Switzerland and South Germany meeting Edward Heath in Zürich, both in 1896.[157] However, by

149. Woodhouse, *Four Addresses*, 8.
150. Woodhouse, *Teaching, 9th October, 1877*, 9.
151. Woodhouse, *Narrative*, 142.
152. AR 1878, 1.
153. AC, 'Report of the Statement made by the Coadjutor Mr E. Heath at a Conference of Angels in London, England & Scotland, held at Gordon Square on the 27th March 1901,' 2.
154. Woodhouse, *Address, 14th August 1877*, 12.
155. 'Report, 27th March 1901,' 2–3.
156. Woodhouse, *Homily, 24 June 1886*, 2.
157. AR 1897, 7–8, 24.

that year there were only four coadjutors still alive, and since their primary work was now to maintain the intercession at Albury, they were not able to visit their charges so frequently as before.[158] Delegations were therefore extensively used during the later 1880s and 1890s, as we shall see in the next chapter.

---

158. Anon., *New York, Pastoral Instruction 187*, 65.

# 8

# Catholic Apostolic Polity

FOR A BODY WHICH placed such stress on the charismata, and whose origin owed so much to them, it is remarkable how strongly Catholic Apostolic ministers insisted upon the proper functioning of each minister in his place. Indeed, on occasion the Church was even compared to a machine, whose smooth action depended on 'the fulfilment by each part of its allotted function.'[1] But, as with most complicated machines, development and construction took some time, and the Church itself acknowledged that the true value of some ministries was only 'brought out' much later than that of others. The fullest development of Church organization was evident only in England, under Cardale's jurisdiction, which explains the Anglo-centric approach of this chapter. No other tribe, for example, had a council corresponding to the Council of Zion, although it was hoped that they would do so eventually.[2] What follows relates for the most part to the period from the late 1860s until the death of Woodhouse in 1901, and we should not assume that the same understanding was evident or worked out during the earlier years of the movement—or that it could always be followed in detail once the structure had begun to be dismantled, when an increasing measure of flexibility had perforce to be allowed.

## WHAT MADE A CHURCH A CHURCH?

It is not easy to determine what secured the recognition of a local gathering of those accepting the restored apostles as a church, and as independent of any other congregation to which it owed its founding. However, perhaps the crucial issue was the ministerial staff which any local congregation possessed. About 1839, the apostles determined that this consisted of an angel (and his help), an ordained prophet (if

---

1. 53D95/5/11, Book containing duties of elders, underdeacons etc, 45, J. Peck (pillar of pastors), 'On Elders' (at the Assembly of the Seven Churches in London, 1 February 1876).
2. Miller, *Irvingism*, 1:174.

possible), an elder (and help), and a deacon.³ The eucharist could be celebrated in any congregation where there was a priest.⁴ However, it was necessary to have an angel in order to qualify as an independent congregation not subject to the jurisdiction of a mother church.

The earliest exposition of the ministry needed in a local congregation comes in the 'Mystery of the Golden Candlestick,' which as we saw earlier had been dictated by Cardale in 1832. As fully developed, the ministry of a local congregation looked like this:

**Diagram 8.1: The Local Congregation**[5]

| Clergy | | | | |
|---|---|---|---|---|
| *Bishops* | Angel (+ help) | | | |
| *Priests* | 6 Ruling Elders | 6 Prophets | 6 Evangelists | 6 Pastors |
| | (+ 6 helps) | (+ 6 helps) | (+ 6 helps) | (+ 6 helps) |
| *Deacons* | 7 Deacons (& 7 Helps); Supernumerary Deacons | | | |
| Laity | Acolyte, Choir member, Deaconess, Doorkeeper, Lay Assistant, Subdeacon / Underdeacon | | | |

Each elder would preside over up to five hundred adult communicants. However, very few if any congregations ever reached complete development in this respect.⁶ For instance, by 1901, only about sixty churches worldwide had an angel and at least one priest of each of the four borders.⁷ And the more incomplete a local congregation's complement of ministers was, the more it became necessary to allow some flexibility regarding who did what, or (if ministers stuck strictly to their borders) the more unbalanced its ministry to each member became. There must therefore have been pressure, both on men to offer themselves as candidates for ministry and on prophets to call men for particular ministries. Congregations of any size were divided into districts, each under an elder, with as many pastors as needed and at least one prophet, priest-evangelist, and seven deacon, plus other deacons as required and deaconesses.⁸

Horn churches were almost independent, being led by an angel in immediate charge with priests of the four characters, and might offer the full range of services.⁹ However, the coadjutors admitted in 1908 that they did 'not feel competent to define

---

3. Woodhouse, *Narrative*, 36; C. E. Lewis Heath, *Lecture*, 3.
4. Flegg, 'Gathered under Apostles,' 114.
5. Woodhouse, *Narrative*, 31–32.
6. In 1878 Miller could assert that it had 'never been realized': *Irvingism*, 2:53.
7. Born, 'Lord's Work,' 77.
8. BOC, Cardale, 'Observations,' §§I.1–2.
9. Anon., *General Rubrics*, I.XI.1.

precisely the spiritual relation of horn congregations to the angel's seat.'[10] According to regulations issued (presumably in Germany) in 1895, a metropolitan church might have up to four horns, 'adjacent churches integral with the mother church and necessary to its full development.'[11] Berlin was the only place where this was fully realized, but about thirty congregations, mostly in Germany, had one or more horn congregations.[12] In Britain, only Glasgow and the Central Church and Islington in London had horns. Horns might also be set up to cater for different language groups; thus English-speaking churches in Chicago and New York had German-language horns, and the German church at Riga had a Lettish (Latvian) horn. Helpships were local congregations entirely under the rule of the mother church and led by a priest or deacon. They could not have services which required the fourfold ministry.[13] Dependencies also existed; indeed, in England they seem to have become more common than helpships, although the first mention of them I found was not until 1876. But apart from their being under the rule of a mother church, from which ministers might be sent to conduct services, it is not clear what their status was, nor how they were distinct from helpships as dependent congregations.

## THE CHURCH'S MINISTRY

### Orders and Characters

Like the Orthodox, Roman Catholic, and Anglican communions, the Catholic Apostolic Church believed in the threefold order of ministry of angels (bishops), priests, and deacons.[14] Its distinctive contribution was expressed in what it called the 'fourfold ministry' (see the table below), the division of these three orders into four 'borders' or 'characters' of apostle / elder, prophet, evangelist, and pastor. These were seen as typified by the four cherubim of Ezekiel 1, as reflecting the fourfold nature of Christ's work as presented in the Gospels, and as answering to the fourfold human constitution.[15]

---

10. AC, 10 July 1908, 5.

11. Copinger, 'Annals,' 172.

12. For lists, see W. H., *Katholisch-apostolische Gemeinden*, 119; Schröter, *Die Katholisch-apostolischen Gemeinden*, 507 n. 76.

13. Anon., *General Rubrics*, I.XI.3; Miller, *Irvingism*, 2:54.

14. One source adds a fourth, that of underdescon: Davson, *Sermon, Leeds, 21st September 1958*, 7.

15. For a fuller exposition of Catholic Apostolic thinking regarding the fourfold ministry, see Flegg, *'Gathered under Apostles,'* 152–78.

Table 8.1 The Fourfold Ministry

| Cherub | Minister | Faculty |
| --- | --- | --- |
| Lion | Apostle / Elder | Will |
| Eagle | Prophet | Imagination |
| Man | Evangelist | Reason |
| Ox | Pastor | Affections |

A man might be a priest-prophet, for example, holding the rank of priest but with a specifically prophetic ministry, or an angel-evangelist, holding the rank of angel but used particularly in evangelistic work towards outsiders rather than as the head of a particular congregation. From a sociological angle, Gretason describes orders as the institutional and successional aspect of Catholic Apostolic ministry, and borders or characters as the charismatic aspect.[16]

The idea of the fourfold ministry can be traced back very early. Certainly the concept of borders of ministry was around by late 1834: when terminally ill in Glasgow, Irving refused the proffered ministrations of two elders who had come from Greenock to anoint him with oil and pray for his healing (cf. James 5:16) on the ground that they would be acting outside their border (as the prophetess had been who commanded them to make the visit).[17] But its outworking was only developed gradually during the following decade. A later Catholic Apostolic writer commented that the evangelists had no work to do at first, and the ministry of pastor was the last of the four to be brought out, with its work being initially undertaken by helps to the elders.[18]

However, once the concept of the fourfold ministry was clearly understood by the apostles, the Church seems to have hastened to put it into practice. Arguably they saw the realization of the perfect structure almost as an end in itself, and it seems that in England at least, the early days saw a superfluity of ministers ordained in relation to the size of the membership. From 1841 Cardale therefore sought to balance things.[19] Yet only two years later liturgical developments created a need for many more ministers, which a number of local congregations could not meet, hence the round of closures in Britain at this point.

Initially, ordination was directly to one of the four borders of ministry, but after the apostles' travels gathering gold, ordination as a priest admitted the candidate into the ministerial hierarchy. After ordination, a man's border was left undefined for a trial period, so that that angel in consultation with the apostle could decide which suited him best.[20] Care was thus taken to ensure that a minister served in the best

---

16. Gretason, 'Authority, Provisionality and Process,' 156.
17. DFP: C/9/46, Woodhouse to Drummmond, 20 November 1834.
18. C. E. Lewis Heath, *Lecture*, 4.
19. NC, 1 February 1854.
20. Stevenson, 'Catholic Apostolic Church: History and Eucharist,' 42 n., following Anon., *Book of Regulations*, §76; Anon., '"Perfecting the Ordinances",' 5.

place for the exercise of his gifts. The system must have worked sufficiently well, since I have not come across any instance of ministers being transferred from one border to another—although it is noteworthy that several of the apostles were deemed to have not only gifts of rule, but also gifts in such areas as prophecy, indicating a certain flexibility in application of the concept of borders. One result of this structure was that the ministries of prophet and evangelist were tied in tightly to the Church's polity, thus minimizing the risk of 'loose cannons' in either ministry saying or doing things which would be unacceptable to the leadership locally or universally, and lessening the likelihood that such ministries would compete with those of elder and pastor for the loyalty of members.

The manner in which a particular character of ministry was exercised would differ according to a minister's rank; thus a priest-evangelist's ministry would not be quite the same as that of a deacon-evangelist, some aspects of evangelist ministry being deemed inappropriate for a deacon to exercise, e.g., because they treated issues relating to the constitution of the Church, on which a deacon did not have the authority to teach. However, the elaborateness of the structure (complicated further by the need for each minister to have his 'help' or deputy) continued to divert ministers into a preoccupation with its maintenance and perfection as an end in itself. In addition, some became fearful of transgressing their border of ministry, with the result that, as the Minutes of Conference recorded in 1855 with unusual frankness, 'for 20 years men have been occupied in keeping borders. Just so at Balaklava, every body is at this work, and so all starve. This routine system must be broken down.' It had 'destroyed the four-fold ministry.'[21] The careful delineation of ministry according to borders could also have a stultifying effect. In 1900 Heath expressed the wish that angels and churches would not leave evangelism to the evangelists, and that 'fervent preaching of the gospel were more customary in our churches.'[22] If this was at all typical, it bespeaks a continuing preoccupation with ritual and structure.

The overall structure of the Church came to look something like the diagram below (ministers in the universal Church were drawn from the rank of angel).

In practice, the pastor with the apostle was the link between the apostles and local congregations, playing a key role.[23] The Church was fortunate to be served by some outstanding men in this position, such as Heinrich W. J. Thiersch in North Germany and Martin Irving in Scotland. The role of such men in securing a remarkable degree of unity within the movement and ensuring that grass-roots views were heard at Albury would bear further investigation.

---

21. MC, 28 February 1855, 19–20.
22. AR 1900, 2.
23. Davenport, *Albury Apostles*, 233.

**Diagram 8.2 The Universal Church**

CHRIST, the Angel of the Universal Church, represented on earth by:

12 apostles (each over a tribe, with the right to appoint 1 coadjutor and as many apostolic delegates as necessary)

Each ministry (apostle, prophet, evangelist, pastor) headed by a pillar (*primus inter pares*)

In each tribe:

– A prophet / evangelist / pastor with the apostle, heading the ministry in that tribe

– 5 district evangelists (each over a district in which worked 12 evangelists)[24]

There were also ministers set apart for duties in the Universal Church, such as financial oversight

## Orders

Each of the four characters or borders was headed up by a pillar, who served as the link between that kind of minister and the apostles, speaking as its mouthpiece in councils and relaying their directives. Cardale noted a useful working definition in the margin of his New Testament: 'The relation of Peter to the rest has been opened to us by the Holy Ghost under the name of Pillar, who ought to be the sustainer & counsellor of his brethren & equals . . . but not their Ruler.'[25] However, when the pillars died, only acting replacements were appointed; indeed, after the death of Dr John Thompson (pillar of pastors) in 1872, arrangements were made for angels in a tribe to receive care from the pastor with the apostle.[26] Already the provisional nature of the Church's structures was becoming evident; doubtless, too, there was no obvious candidate to succeed Thompson.

### Apostles

Apostles were unique in that they alone were directly called by Christ; their calling was neither from man nor through man. Their ultimate responsibility was to present the Christian Church before Christ at his appearing as his spotless bride.[27] Certain acts

---

24. The only tribes in which the full complement of district evangelists were appointed were England, North Germany, and Holland and Denmark: W. H., *Katholisch-apostolische Gemeinden*, 45. There could, however, be more than this number of angel-evangelists, as in North Germany, where in 1901 there were five district evangelists and twelve other angel-evangelists: ibid., 78.
25. Cardale archive, Cardale, New Testament, annotation to Luke 21:31–34.
26. Copinger, 'Annals,' 130.
27. Dalton, *Apostleship*, 9.

were reserved for apostles (or their coadjutors or delegates), most notably ordination and sealing, both of which required the imposition of hands, but they gave a lead in all areas of Catholic Apostolic ministry, as Dalton showed:

> ... they appoint and ordain to the ministry of the Lord Prophets, Evangelists, and Pastors; and hence the fourfold ministry of Christ, given in the gift of the Holy Ghost, is eliminated [sic] and established 'for the perfecting of the saints.' They baptize in the name of the Father, Son, and Holy Ghost. They impart the Holy Ghost by the laying on of hands, whereby the faithful are 'sealed unto the day of redemption;' and the Body of Christ, the Church, is formed and endowed with the manifold gifts of the Holy Ghost. They declare and enforce the doctrine of the Lord. They teach the observance of those things He commanded them. They rule in the exercise of Prophecy and of all other spiritual gifts. They establish holy worship such as had never been given before. They form that fellowship, celebrate that breaking of bread, and give those prayers in all which believers continue. Deacons are appointed; Bishops and Priests are set over the flocks.[28]

Much later, W. M. Davson, who was to be the last remaining Catholic Apostolic priest, summed up the work of apostles as being to deliver the Testimony and gather congregations of first-fruits; to set churches in order, sealing, ordaining, and visiting; and to offer the intercession for the whole Christian Church. Increasingly, the apostles came to focus on the third of these aspects, the first being delegated after 1838 and the second after 1875.[29] Irving had expected apostles who would work miracles, but Cardale's idea appears to have been closer to Anglican bishops.[30]

Woodhouse summed up the crucial role played by apostles: 'Through the Apostles alone the authority of the Lord in His Church finds its legitimate exercise, through them the Church is admitted into the fellowship of the Father and of the Son, through them the Holy Ghost is ministered, through them the gifts are given, through them all officers of authority are constituted, by the laying on of their hands; and to them all the other ministers are subordinate.'[31] Though apostles alone could the divided Church be unified and prepared to meet Christ at his return. At the heart of this was the idea of rule: in Woodhouse's words, 'The Apostles rule over Churches, and the Elders minister and rule in Churches.'[32] This did not replace but rather enabled the proper exercise of other ministries, as Tarbet explained: 'As the will directs and regulates the heart, the understanding, and the imagination, each according to its nature; so the apostle is the executive of the Lord's mind and will, and directs and regulates all the

---

28. Ibid., 7.
29. Davson, *1850 to 1950*, 16.
30. Manfred Henke to the author, 4 February 2016.
31. Woodhouse, *Narrative*, 68.
32. Woodhouse, *Substance of a Ministry*, 36.

other ministries.'³³ Initially their jurisdiction was seen as including the whole Christian Church, which goes some way to account for the boldness of the Great Testimony. In time, however, perhaps as a measure of realism set in, this was postponed to the eschatological future and their ministry confined to the congregations under them.

Apostles' ministers were those appointed to assist them in certain aspects of their work. An apostles' minister might be sent into a particular congregation, either as an interim leader until an angel should be called and consecrated,³⁴ or as a kind of trouble-shooter. Spencer Perceval seems to have fulfilled such a role at Oxford in 1833,³⁵ and W. F. Pitcairn may have done so when he was transferred to Edinburgh in 1841. An apostles' minister might also exercise interim leadership within a tribe, as when Adolf Fleischer was consecrated angel by King-Church and put in charge of work in Denmark in 1862.³⁶ In time, the term came to be used of the prophets, evangelists, and pastors with the apostles. As early as 1836 each apostle had been directed to choose a prophet, an evangelist, and a pastor to head up those ministries within his tribe.³⁷ When an apostle visited his tribe, they were to accompany him. But it is not clear how far the posts were actually filled: by 1873 only five or six ministers of each border had been chosen, and by 1901 they numbered eight prophets, ten evangelists, and nine pastors for the twelve tribes.³⁸ Many were based at Albury; this would have helped to minimize the risk of any of them acting independently (as Geyer had done), but it would also have hindered the development of indigenous ministry within the tribes.

These ministers met in council with the apostles at Albury twice a year. The winter gathering would have dealt with administrative matters such as the arrangement of a rota for services at Albury, Albury being the focus of the worship and intercession to be offered by the universal Church; visits to the tribes had to be fitted round this charge. The summer meetings dealt with more substantive issues. Also part of the apostles' councils were the coadjutors and the archangels of the universal Church (on whom see below).

To assist the apostles there were coadjutors and delegates, as well as apostles' ministers. 'Both delegation and Coadjutorship were brought to the notice of the Apostles in prophetic openings of Scripture at the very earliest times of the work. Each only waited till opportunity should arise for its development.'³⁹

---

33. Tarbet, *Shadows*, 2:31.
34. Cf. Copinger, 'Annals,' 123.
35. Rossteuscher, 'Rebuilding,' 464.
36. Copinger, 'Annals,' 114.
37. Boase, *Supplementary Narrative*, 825.
38. Copinger, 'Annals,' 134, 184.
39. MC, undated paper [1893], 9.

## Coadjutors

Each class of ministers was to have its helps, and those for the apostles were the co-adjutors.[40] According to Cardale, the need for coadjutors had been revealed as early as 1838.[41] In 1852 the apostles had laid down rules empowering one of their number to make such an appointment with the approval of his colleagues. Prophecy in 1864 promised that God would give one for each apostle (including those who had died), but this was not a provision for the withdrawal or death of apostles.[42] The first (Böhm) had been chosen in 1859, under rules set down in 1852, but in 1865 the matter was 'pressed upon their attention by the present circumstances of the church' and the surviving apostles decided that it was time to make further appointments.[43] This was not only, or even primarily, a response to the death of apostles, but to the growth of the work, since it enabled apostles to be in more than one place at a time.

Unlike the apostleship, the coadjutorship included men from continental Europe. Seven were British, three German (von Pochhammer, Diestel, and Geering), one Danish (Böhm), and one Dutch (Capadose).[44] Another minister had been called (Hewett senior), but died in 1862 before being chosen by an apostle.[45] All had served as angel-evangelists before being called by prophecy and chosen by apostles.[46] Whilst coadjutors could perform all apostolic acts, they could not do so in their own right; apostles alone had been sent immediately by God, whereas coadjutors had been sent by apostles. That being so, their commission to perform apostolic acts lapsed with Woodhouse's death, although they continued to exercise *de facto* leadership of congregations gathered under apostles.

In 1870, Cardale set out more fully the Church's understanding of the office of coadjutor. The apostles as a college were Christ's one coadjutor. It was by apostles that the Holy Spirit was to be ministered, but most had now died and too few remained to visit the tribes. Nevertheless, God had brought 'helpship' into exercise on their behalf, as he had done earlier with other ministries, in the form of coadjutors. They were not part of the fellowship of the college of apostles, and did not share their supreme authority, but by them apostles could dispense the fullness of the Spirit to people they could not personally visit.

---

40. Cardale, *Notes of a Ministry*, 7–8.
41. Cardale, *Homily, June 21, 1876*, unpaginated.
42. Cardale, *Notes of a Ministry*, 8–13.
43. Ibid., 3; cf. Copinger, 'Annals,' 118.
44. For details, see the Appendix. Capadose became a British citizen in 1891: *London Gazette*, 1 January 1892, 6.
45. Schröter, *Die Katholisch-apostolischen Gemeinden*, 547 n. 101, following Born, *Das Werk des Herrn*, 72.
46. Lively, 'Catholic Apostolic Church,' 132.

> The fulness of Apostolic grace is dispensed through the Coadjutor: one with the Apostle in the spirit, distinct from him in person; the same grace, through a different man, and with equal authority though through a subordinate minister; apostolic benediction through one who is not an Apostle, but by the absent Apostle through his Coadjutor present; all the grace and power, both towards ministers and people, which the Apostle, if present, could convey to them; for He, the Holy Ghost, effects it, who is the bond by which the whole Church, including the Apostleship, is one, as the Father and the Son are one. He makes the Apostle, absent in body, to be present with the coadjutor in spirit. And thus the prerogative of the Apostolic office,—of Jesus, the Apostle,—is preserved inviolate, while the full discharge of all its functions is provided for.

That few apostles remained indicated that the time before Christ's return must be short; the faithful were therefore urged to pray that through coadjutors the altar would be rebuilt in every land and the full number of first-fruits gathered.[47]

Whilst a coadjutor was chosen to serve alongside a particular apostle, they could be deployed wherever their services were called for. Coadjutors who died could also be replaced by another of the twelve.[48] Until 1877 they were given specific authorization by their principal each time they were to visit a tribe to perform apostolic acts, but we noted that in the wake of Cardale's death their commissions were made permanent.[49]

## Apostolic Delegations

In time even the coadjutor ministry could no longer suffice, especially during the surge of outreach which occurred in the 1890s. The first apostolic delegation was sent to Denmark in 1865 (which included Böhm, who was already a coadjutor).[50] They became particularly useful after 1879, once there was only one remaining apostle and the coadjutors took up the burden of maintaining the intercession at Albury. In 1893 a paper from the coadjutor, Edward Heath, to the angels in England rooted the development of apostolic delegations in a prophecy of 25 September 1836 expounding the idea of 'covered wagons' as found in Numbers 7, which he quoted: 'Ah, covered wagons, they are covered, delegations of Apostolic ministry by the consent of two Apostles, under their hand, by the hand of two Ministers to perfect the pattern of their churches in other cities. Oh but the altar, and the table and the candlestick may not be moved, they may not be borne by delegation, nor the ark of the holiest touched. Ah! Ye must plant them yourselves.'[51] Apostolic delegates were drawn from the senior angels, and

---

47. Cardale, *Homily, January 11th, 1870*, quotation at 9.
48. Schröter, *Die Katholisch-apostolischen Gemeinden*, 547–48 n. 101.
49. Copinger, 'Annals,' 142.
50. Ibid., 118.
51. MC, undated paper [1893], 2.

could perform all the functions of apostles except consecrate angels,[52] but required express permission for their tasks rather than holding a permanent commission.[53]

## Angels

As early as 1834 Carlyle asserted (perhaps following and developing Irving's thinking) that during the earliest centuries an angel probably acted as superintendent of the church in a town or city, which met in separate groups in homes under elders.[54] This is what other writers have understood as the pattern advocated by Ignatius of Antioch soon after AD 100. An angel's duties included leadership of the particular congregation and any horns, helpships, or dependencies under it; presiding at the eucharist; offering the intercession; discerning spirits and evaluating prophetic words; screening those offering themselves for ministry; and blessing minor offices and lay workers.[55]

There were, however, different types of angels. An inducted angel required the presence in a church of the fourfold priestly ministry, and the unanimous vote of its members in favor of his induction, which was usually for life. Such congregations could offer the full great intercession morning and evening. By 1901, just sixty congregations worldwide had inducted angels.[56] An angel in charge was responsible for an independent congregation. If the fourfold priestly ministry was present, it could offer a simpler form of the great intercession. An angel in immediate charge looked after a branch of a church which had an angel inducted or in charge. An angel's help was a consecrated angel who represented and assisted the angel of a congregation. An angel of the horn occupied a similar position to an angel in immediate charge, but with the fourfold ministry present could offer the full great intercession and the complete form of the Sunday eucharist.[57] Inducted angels and angels in charge could find their areas of jurisdiction extended far beyond the one town or city, even before 1901 and the gradual decline in numbers of remaining ministers. In 1895 it was reported that W. A. Copinger (1847–1910), angel at Manchester, had no less than nineteen congregations under his care.[58] Evidently success in the north-west of England had outstripped the Church's capacity to set up, and find ministers for, fully functioning local congregations.

Whilst they wielded considerable power, angels were also accountable. Extensive reporting was expected from them each quarter, covering such matters as the numbers

---

52. AR 1891, 33.

53. Stevenson, 'Catholic Apostolic Church: History and Eucharist,' 26.

54. Carlyle, *Church of Christ*, 196; cf. Grass, *Lord's Watchman*, 118–19.

55. Flegg, 'Gathered under Apostles,' 133–34.

56. Schröter, *Bilder*, 17, 19. For a list of those congregations, see W. H., *Katholisch-apostolische Gemeinden*, 77.

57. Schröter, *Bilder*, 19, 21.

58. AR 1895, 10.

exercising spiritual gifts, words of prophecy for transmission to the apostles, evangelist work undertaken, and the occurrence of remarkable events such as healings.[59] Indeed, prophecies were later requested to be sent every month.[60] Printed forms were supplied for all this, although none have been traced. An angel might take counsel of his elders and deacons, and pastoral wisdom dictated the appropriateness of doing so regularly, but he was the one who decided which issues merited such a course, and he alone was responsible for deciding how far to act on the counsel received.[61] An angel was in some senses the guardian of the church: Edward Heath asserted that 'no teaching of any sort should come into any Church except through its Angel.'[62] He was responsible, in addition, for detecting and countering any working of the enemy within the congregation, just as the angel-evangelist sought to counter this in society at large.[63]

A newly consecrated angel would expect to be used in accordance with his border, which his apostle would have determined before his consecration to the episcopate, while he was yet a priest. 'Angel-prophets, of whom there were few, would be employed in a large congregation, serving under the Angel of the Church or after experience of their ministry might be selected to be the prophet with the Apostle for the Tribe.' Angel-evangelists we shall meet shortly. Angel-pastors (which most angels probably were) would serve as priests under other angels until they were needed to take charge in a church.[64]

## Archangels

Gradually Catholic Apostolic writers formulated the concept of a class within the episcopate known as archangels. Prophecy had indicated the future establishment of the archangel ministry.[65] Taplin is recorded as having prophesied to the apostles on 23 February 1836: 'Unto you is given help. Oh! ye have a blessing of the Lord yet in store. Ye shall have delegates. Ye shall have the archangels of God flying through the midst of heaven. Oh! seek ye for them! Long ye for them! But commit not yourselves.'[66] On 7 December 1838, the office of archangel was considered, presumably by the apostles, who passed a resolution the following year authorizing any one of their number to bring up an angel for presentation for calling as an archangel; on 11 February 1839

---

59. MC contains references to these from 1851 onwards.
60. MC, 19 October 1892, 106.
61. Book containing duties of elders, underdeacons etc, 46–54, J. Peck, 'Angel's Councils' (to the assembly of the seven churches in London, 29 February 1876).
62. MC, 7 March 1894, 141.
63. MC, 28 August 1889, 27.
64. Rupert M. Heath, *Lecture: Office of Angel*, 12.
65. Woodhouse, *Teaching, 29 January, 1878*, 7–8.
66. Anon., 'History and Doctrines of Irvingism,' quotation at 56; cf. Copinger, 'Annals,' 60.

A. F. Bayford and A. C. Barclay were 'set as Archangels by the laying on of hands,' and a week later the angels of the seven churches in London were named as archangels.[67] Such a decision hints at an early belief that this office had to do with the working of the universal Church, of which those churches were to be a demonstration model. George Ryerson was called in prophecy as an archangel on 4 July 1839, and W. F. Pitcairn on 11 August 1847, but no other early calls are known apart from that of G. C. Gambier at an unspecified point.[68] At that stage it is not clear what understanding of the archangel's office obtained.

In 1873 the apostles in their determinations reported a prophecy spoken while Pitcairn's call was under consideration as part of a review of the status of the principal church in a tribe; they admitted that it had caused quite a stir because it intimated the removal of apostles.

> It is a preparation by the Head of the Church for that which shortly cometh to pass. He prepareth to remove His Twelve & the Seventy shall go forth, & at the head of the Seventy shall be the Coadjutors who are left, & the Prophets, & Evangelists, & Pastors of the Twelve who are left, & there shall be added to them those whom ye shall name according to the mind of Jesus, as Archangels. Berlin, Basle, Edinburgh, Dublin, Birmingham, & the Lord hath yet more to name in season, Copenhagen, & they shall be joined (to/with) their brethren, & they shall go forth & they shall head up the witness, O the witness for Jesus against the Beast that cometh up out of the sea, & by their witness one of his heads shall be wounded unto the death, & yet when he shall live & when he becometh the Beast from the abyss & the witness is perfected then shall he slay them. Jesus will have the faithful men chosen by you O ye Twelve who shall go forth, who shall stand at the head of their people with their lives in their hands. <u>Ye are preparing</u> (3) for the witness that shall follow your testimony.[69]

Things had become much clearer by 1880, when a memorandum was directed to be entered in the apostles' minute book concerning the standing and use of archangels. There were several classes of these: (1) apostles' ministers (i.e., the prophet, evangelist, and pastor with the apostle); (2) the five pillars in London and all (angel-) evangelists chosen to be of the sixty to the nations (five per tribe); (3) angels of the seven churches in London; (4) angels of churches designated as archangels' seats, known as metropolitan congregations (six per tribe); and (5) those personally called by prophecy and recognized as archangels by apostles.[70] This last group constituted 'a body of Ministers always ready & at the disposition of the Apostles, in order to help

---

67. AD, July 1894, 5–7; Copinger, 'Annals,' 73, 74.

68. Copinger, 'Annals,' 74; AD, January 1873, 2; W. H., *Katholisch-apostolische Gemeinden*, 81. Pitcairn was called a second time at the opening of the new church in Edinburgh on 5 April 1876, so could not have been set as an archangel before then: Copinger, 'Annals,' 139.

69. AD, January 1873, 2.

70. AD, January 1880, 4–8.

them in visiting the Churches, and in carrying out under their direction, the duty of setting the order of the Lord, in the congregations gathered.' This class (again, six per tribe, but known as the 'seventy') was to be appointed with a view to the time after the apostles had been removed, to sustain those remaining after the first-fruits had been taken.[71] Personally called archangels could work anywhere they were required, unlike *ex officio* archangels. Archangels could perform all apostolic acts except the consecration of an angel, and one of the two ministers in an apostolic delegation was always to be an archangel.[72] Whilst their main ministry would be exercised after the first-fruits had been translated to heaven, it was also partly applicable now; they could visit distant congregations now just as the seventy would one day visit the whole of Christendom.[73] Andrews explained in 1891 that the seventy would gather in the great harvest from the seventy families of the earth in a stage of the work subsequent to the gathering of the 144,000 first-fruits.[74]

Shortly before Woodhouse died, the coadjutors conferred with the apostles' ministers and others. Taking into account prophecies being given, they decided to hold a service at Albury for presentation of candidates to the office of personally called archangel, or (as they now preferred to term it, to distinguish this class from the others) archangel in the universal Church. This took place at Albury on 14 June 1900 and six men were called.[75] However, the full complement of archangels was never set in office, and whilst they played an important role in the years immediately following 1901 by visiting and strengthening churches, their ministry declined in importance as their ranks were reduced by death and the need to adapt to the loss of ministers became increasingly pressing.[76] After the archangels had gone, angels and then priests in turn took on wider responsibilities, although no formal recognition of this could be given.

*Priests*

The Catholic Apostolic understanding of priestly ministry does not appear to have differed too much from that of the contemporary Church of England. They were to assist the angel, presiding at the eucharist if there was no angel to do so, baptizing, offering absolution, blessing marriages, and visiting the sick to offer communion and anointing with oil, among other duties.[77] Priests ordained in other Churches by bishops in the apostolic succession had their orders confirmed by the apostle with the laying on of hands; this was deemed essential if they were to administer the sacraments

---

71. Woodhouse, *Teaching,* 29 January, 1878, 19–20.
72. Schröter, *Bilder,* 23.
73. Woodhouse, *Teaching,* 29 January 1878, 2; cf. *Record* 3/1 (October 1879) 11.
74. W. W. Andrews, *Review of God's Mode of Working,* 4.
75. AD, June 1900, 1–3; AD, July 1900, 2–3.
76. Manfred Henke to the author, 6 October 2005.
77. Flegg, 'Gathered under Apostles,' 140–41.

in the Catholic Apostolic Church.[78] Out of respect for their standing, they kept the title 'Rev.,' which was not otherwise used by Catholic Apostolic ministers.

## Deacons

In Catholic Apostolic practice the diaconate was seen as a permanent office rather than a stepping-stone to priesthood, although it was not uncommon for serving deacons to be called and ordained as priests. Deacons, and especially the seven deacons, were seen as the representatives of the flock in worship, through whom offerings of service as well as money were transmitted. In a fully staffed local church there were to be seven of them, but if required a church might have further, supernumerary deacons. Their duties involved baptizing in the absence of a priest, undertaking home visits, offering practical help and advice, preaching, providing religious instruction, undertaking the initial reception of converts, and presiding at prayer meetings. The seven deacons also had financial and administrative responsibility for congregational affairs.[79]

The Great Testimony asserted that whereas elders (pastors) and evangelists were called by prophecy 'the Deaconship are waiting for the time when the Apostles, being sent forth in the fullness of the blessing of the Gospel of Christ, may lay their hands on all the people, bestowing the gift of the Holy Ghost; when also the people may bring up their Deacons, filled with the Holy Ghost, and set them before the Apostles, as in the beginning.'[80] Once members of the churches had begun to receive the sealing, therefore, the choice of the seven deacons was entrusted to them, unsealed members not being allowed to participate. Successive rounds of voting eliminated candidates until one remained. Once their choice had been made, and its unanimity made clear to the apostle, the candidate was elected by the congregation, his election was confirmed by the apostle, and he was received at a eucharist. Either then or subsequently, he received the apostle's blessing for his ministry. Additional deacons were chosen with the concurrence of the members rather than by them.[81]

Yet the diaconal ministry seems to have been undervalued, both by potential candidates and by the membership at large. According to W. H. Place, the deaconship was 'lacking to the Church in the way of active operation,' certainly in the seven churches in London. In a forthright statement, he alleged that whilst deacons who were not pulling their weight claimed that the cause was their duties in the world, they could easily remedy this by resigning some of their worldly responsibilities. The real cause, in his view, was a 'lack of apprehension in us all of the important character

78. Ibid., 143.
79. Ibid., 144–46.
80. Anon., *To the Patriarchs, Archbishops, Bishops*, §112.
81. Anon., *Book of Regulations*, §§683–95; Herbert Heath, *Sermon on Seven Deaconship*, 4–5; Hume, *Election*; Hamilton, *Memoranda*.

of the office itself.' It was, he insisted, a vital ministry; 'without Deaconship, priesthood is but priestcraft—a machinery for acquiring power over the bodies and souls of men.'[82] It seems likely, too, that some in the churches were tempted to look down on the ministry of deacons as inferior to that of priests. Prophecy at Bishopsgate during 1888 warned:

> They who despise the work of Deacons, despise the Living God, & they will be in danger of losing their reward, for there are those who will burst through the bounds which the Lord God setteth round about His holy Mount, & instead of the glory of God being their glory & their salvation, it will be their death. The Lord warneth, He warneth the whole of His Congregation, that they despise not the work & ministry of the Deacons. And the Lord warneth His Deacons also, that they despise not the honour that is put upon them, for their work is great indeed, even in the days of weakness, but it shall be greater still in the day of the revelation of His power and His glory.[83]

## Characters

### Elders

In the Church of Scotland, the eldership had been a lay office, but soon after Irving's ordination as angel in 1833 six were ordained to assist him in a ministry which was now seen in priestly terms. Catholic Apostolic writers continued to regard assisting the angel as the essential role of an elder, just as in the primitive Church elders were priests who assisted the bishop.[84] Elders did this primarily by ensuring that members were able to access the particular ministries they needed, as Cardale explained:

> It is the office of the Elder, in the district committed to his charge, by all means in his power to bring to those under his charge the several ministries of the House of God. He commits the individual souls to the care of the Pastor, for the Pastor has the immediate care of souls. He makes provision that each member, with the knowledge of his pastor, shall have access to the Prophet and the Evangelist. He sees that those under his charge receive sufficient diaconal visitation, either by the seven Deacons, or through means of those assisting them; or, as regards the female portion of his charge, through the Deaconess. He institutes district meetings for teaching and instruction, and prayer-meetings; and he appoints occasions when the four priests should sit together, or singly, in order to receive the flock.[85]

---

82. Place, *Notes of a Ministry*, 3–5.
83. *Record* 4/4 (July 1888) 515.
84. Davenport, *Albury Apostles*, 85–86.
85. Cardale, *Address at the Close of the Visitation*, 8–9.

## Prophets

A definitive exposition of this ministry came from Cardale, in his *Short Discourse on Prophesying and the Ministry of the Prophet in the Christian Church* (1868). He stressed the difference between the gift of prophecy and the ministry of the prophet, and the need for the latter to observe the appropriate borders. What a priest-prophet might do was not appropriate for a prophet of diaconal rank, or for a lay person exercising the gift of prophecy. The words of the Holy Ghost were not to be privately interpreted, but were 'spoken into the ear of the Ruler', whether the angel in the local church or the apostle in the universal Church. God led the Church into all truth, not through prophetically gifted individuals but through the twelve angel-prophets who served with the apostles. Doubtless with Geyer's case in mind, Cardale warned that even true prophets might exercise their gift wrongly and then be forsaken by God (and hence left to the machinations of Satan).[86] Coming soon after Dalton's *An Address delivered to the Prophets assembled at Albury, on Whit Monday, 1865*, and Woodhouse's *Teaching on the Prophetic Office, delivered at Albury on Whit Monday, 1867*, it shows that the Church was trying to set down some clear guidelines for how this ministry should be exercised, perhaps still responding to events in Germany as well as to the excessive credulity shown by some members towards predictions that the Second Advent was just around the corner. It was alleged that Cardale's discourse on prophesying had had a sensational impact because it sought to limit the action of the prophets in the local context.[87]

## Evangelists

The fundamental difference between evangelist work as understood by Catholic Apostolics and the approach adopted by most other Churches was that they understood the primary mission of the evangelist as being to those who were already baptized, seeking to bring them into the reality of their standing in order to prepare them for Christ's return.[88] Gretason argues that only in the 1870s do we see much effort being expended on reaching the unbaptized,[89] although the Edinburgh baptismal register indicates that something of this nature was going on in that congregation during the mid-1850s. It may be that, both in Edinburgh and later more generally, the Church was more influenced by the prevailing revivalist climate than it acknowledged.[90] Another difference from evangelism as often understood was the remarkably rational approach deemed appropriate: evangelists were to address their hearers by means of arguments

---

86. Cardale, *Short Discourse*, 7–8, 10.
87. Grant, *Apostolic Lordship*, 51.
88. Davenport, *Albury Apostles*, 104; Anon., '"Perfecting the Ordinances"', 2–3.
89. Gretason, 'Authority, Provisionality and Process,' 205.
90. Grass, 'Catholic Apostolic Church in Scotland.'

appealing to reason and common sense.[91] If one looks at the approach adopted by evangelistic addresses, one sees how this was done. It should not be confused with the influential approach of the American revivalist Charles Finney, which appealed to the will, nor with the more emotionalist approaches adopted by other evangelists of the time. This stress on appealing to the rational faculty in the evangelist's hearers demonstrates too that the characterization of the Catholic Apostolic Church as a movement flourishing in the soil of romanticism, which stressed the limitations of reason, needs to be nuanced.

There had been some false starts with this ministry: the street preaching which had gained Irving and his followers such notoriety (and a number of court appearances) in 1832–33 was directed to cease while the outpouring of the Spirit was awaited, and early in 1834 Irving and Taplin were rebuked for having appointed sixty evangelists in the absence of the apostles. From the time of the separation of the apostles, this was regarded as an ordained ministry: in 1836 sixty evangelists were appointed in London and divided into five bands, each under an angel-evangelist.[92] This, like so much else about Catholic Apostolic polity, was seen as patterned on the structure of the tabernacle, and it became the ideal for each tribe to be divided into five districts under angel-evangelists. Drummond argued that similar bands should provide a place for every man in the churches under apostles to share in evangelist work.[93] However, like others of Drummond's ideals, this was never realized to any great extent, although some churches did organize willing members into such bands, Glasgow being a notable example.[94] Indeed, far from involving all men in the Church, it seems that this ministry was not always valued as highly as those in authority thought it should have been; certainly around 1877 Hume claimed that the Gordon Square congregation knew little of it.[95] On the broader scene, sixty evangelists to the nations were also called for in 1836, to precede the apostles in their travels. However, few were appointed, little more was heard of them, and by 1860 this group was regarded as belonging to the future.[96]

In the local setting, the book referred to in the previous chapter also included teaching regarding the work of the evangelist in the local church.[97]

> It is impossible that the work of our Testimony can be carried on by the sole labour of the Evangelists of the Universal Church, however active they may be

---

91. Anon., *Description*.
92. Boase, *Supplementary Narrative*, 825.
93. Drummond, *Discourses*, 80.
94. Grass, 'Catholic Apostolic Church in Scotland.'
95. Hume, *Address* (1877), 16. For a description of the work of one evangelist, see J. C. H., 'Mr Michael Hall,' *Newsletter* 5 (November 1953) 16–18.
96. Copinger, 'Annals,' 62–63; Anon., '"Perfecting the Ordinances"', 4, 9.
97. Book containing duties of elders, underdeacons etc, 6–10.

there is a large residuum of work to be done by the Ministers of the particular church & the members properly organized under the ministers.

The public ministry of the word of Testimony by Lectures, Evangelist services & Sermons is carried on by the Angel Evangelists & those acting under them & ought not to be undertaken by the Particular Church except with the knowledge & concurrence of the A.E when the services of himself & his ministers are required elsewhere.

But beside Public Ministry there is the whole field of labour in cottage or small room meetings visiting the Poor sick rooms & Hospitals & conversation in our intercourse with others either in the business of the world or in society. This work if it is to be done efficiently must be organized. It should if possible be given into the hands of an Elder or in a full Ch: of the two Elders who are given to the Angel for this purpose. If there be no such Elder, a P E$^t$ sh$^d$ be selected & in any case under the Elder one or more P$^t$ Ev$^{ts}$ sh$^d$ be placed—& in the hands of the P$^t$ Ev$^{ts}$ as many D.Ev$^{ts}$ as are available; and to each Deacon a band of lay Assts: should be assigned. . . .

All subordinate agents sh$^d$ be instructed to give in frequent reports to their immediate principals—lay Assts to Deacons, Deacons to Priests, P$^t$ Ev$^{ts}$ to the Elder, or if no Elder in charge of the work, to the Angel & whoever has charge under the Angel sh$^d$ give to the Angel a full summary of all the Reports at the end of each Quarter, wh: Quarterly reports the Angel forwards to the Apostle thro' the proper channel with the Q$^y$ reports of the Church.

With regard to the dealings of the minister of the P$^r$ Ch with individuals whether these individuals are met with in private meetings or in society or otherwise we may assign these two limitations_

1st If any Clergyman or minister of religion is led to enquire, he should be referred as soon as maybe to the Angel E$^t$.

2nd If anyone being a layman professes his belief in the truth of the work of the Lord he should be referred immediately to the Angel Ev$^t$ or other nearest Ev$^t$ serving under him.

In 1898 Edward Heath set out the character which he believed evangelistic preaching should possess. He began by pointing out that the different orders of evangelists had distinctive ministries; all ministers shared in preaching the gospel, but the angel-evangelist was to warn men that God's judgment was imminent, and to reprove the sins which were provoking it. He was to testify to God's present work of mercy and grace, and to invite his hearers to receive it; to recall them to the forgotten hope of Christ's kingdom; and to announce that the coming of the Lord was near. His proclamation was to be like a trumpet, contrasting with the illuminating nature of the gospel preaching of the angel.[98] We might borrow George Herbert's contrast, and suggest that the angel was to inform and the angel-evangelist to inflame. Another part of the angel-evangelist's ministry was that of 'preparing those already gathered by the preaching

---

98. AC, Edward Heath, 'Remarks on Evangelist Sermons in Churches, 5 January 1898,' 2–3.

of the Gospel to be admitted to the full communion of the Church, in its worship & sacraments.'[99] This was 'typified by the five pillars of the holy place. This is a ministry of cleansing and instruction in order to prepare those who believe and are baptized to take part with spiritual intelligence in sacramental and liturgical rites.'[100] Not surprisingly, Heath rejected the idea that members of other denominations should not be invited to hear sermons by angel-evangelists; whilst the movement's separate existence was sad, it was necessary, and there could be nothing schismatic about inviting others to see and hear what God had done.[101] Clarifying things a few months later, Heath explained that the angel-evangelist's ministry was 'directed towards those who are already baptized and walking in righteousness, and . . . intended to prepare them for the spiritual rites or functions which are proper to our heavenly standing.'[102]

The angel-evangelist William Anderson offered detailed guidance to ministers employed in evangelism under him. The provision of such guidance may have been one reason for the success of the Northern district in England, which he headed up from 1864 until his death in 1871.[103] He laid down that a priest-evangelist should require reports from the deacons under him at least fortnightly; these were to be forwarded with his own reports, using printed forms supplied, to the angel-evangelist; 'being regularly filed, they constitute an official register.' Evangelist sermons should be 'of moderate length, not exceeding forty or fifty minutes, except under very unusual circumstances.' Priests should make work for themselves and their deacons: visiting the sick, holding house-meetings, taking schoolrooms for public addresses, assigning districts for tract distribution, and engaging in outdoor preaching.[104] Anderson saw a chain of command operating: Christ—the apostles—the pillar of evangelists—angel-evangelists—priest-evangelists—deacon-evangelists, the last of whom formed the key link with the people. 'In the Deacon's hands lies to a large extent the making or marring of the Lord's work in any particular place.'[105] The deacon-evangelist received all candidates for his teaching from the priest-evangelist, and was to begin by checking that they were of good local report, baptized, and had not contracted a marriage within the prohibited degrees. His teaching should cover the basic truths of redemption, regeneration, the eucharist, the Second Advent, the restoration of apostles, the practice of righteousness and holiness in daily life, and family worship. More Church-related matters, such as the right constitution of the Church, spiritual symbolism,

99. MC, 10 October 1877, 70.

100. Heath, 'Evangelist Sermons,' 1–2.

101. Ibid., 14–15.

102. AC, Edward Heath, 'Remarks by the Coadjutor, 27 April 1898, on the Ministry of Angel-Evangelists towards Particular Churches,' 3.

103. Newman-Norton, 'Biographical Index,' 2.

104. Anderson, *Northern Evangelist District*, 2, 5, 7.

105. Book containing duties of elders, underdeacons etc, 16–17, William Anderson, 'Evangelist Work (Deacons employed under the Angel Evangelist in the Universal Church).' This is a ms version of the printed work cited above.

sacraments, priesthood, sealing, and tithe were to be left to the priest-evangelist.[106] Anderson's guidance struck a balance between the various facets of an evangelist's activity: reporting, preaching, and personal contact. Sadly, not all evangelists seem to have achieved this balance.

### Pastors

As with the priests, there was probably little distinctive about the Catholic Apostolic understanding of pastors. But as with more sacramentally orientated communions, pastors were to hear the confessions of the faithful and pronounce absolution.[107]

### Lay Ministries

#### Underdeacons

The role of underdeacon was one which many Catholic Apostolic men would have filled, but many congregations could have done with more of them. A church with a full complement of ministers was to have forty-eight of them, corresponding to the containing boards of the tabernacle. However, even at the Central Church in London, in 1877 the largest Catholic Apostolic congregation, there were only about half this number.[108] A paper 'On the Office of Underdeacons,' apparently from a meeting of the seven churches in London, explained that such men were to be heads of houses, and of good repute. Their chief duty was in church. They were assigned particular seats (in the Dundee church, plaques marking the underdeacons' seats can still be seen), so that they could observe whether people were attending regularly, joining in decorously, and generally fulfilling their part, and inquire into any apparent neglect or deficiency; often an informal inquiry of this nature would be enough to sort things out.[109] Edward Heath gave a paper on the duties of underdeacons based on the *Book of Regulations* and the *General Rubrics* in which he stressed as often neglected their duty of assisting a deacon in overseeing the walk and conversation of those in his charge, which involved regular home visits.[110]

The office of underdeacon came into full play after 1901, but is treated here because it was an integral part of the Church's ministerial structures. In 1926 Hume, still angel at the Central Church after almost half a century, gave a teaching which

---

106. Ibid., 19–21.
107. Flegg, 'Gathered under Apostles,' 171.
108. Hume, *Address* (1877), 8.
109. Book containing duties of elders, underdeacons etc, 12–13; cf. Cardale, 'Observations,' part III.
110. MC, 13 January 1892, 91–97.

showed how Catholic Apostolic hermeneutics derived patterns of ministry from Tabernacle typology.

> The Underdeacons in a particular church have a relation to the Elders and the Priests associated with them in the pastorship of the flock, who are typified by the containing boards of the Tabernacle. These boards were 48 in number. The Tabernacle had a cubic or solid measurement of 3,000 cubits: and the weight of the golden candlestick was 3,000 shekels. The number of the converts on the Day of Pentecost was 3,000 souls: and the strength of a complete church is 3,000 communicants. In such a church the full complement of elders and of Deacons would be seen, and the full number of Underdeacons, 48, *i.e.*, one Underdeacon to about every 60 communicants.[111]

Hume feared that the office was looked down on as menial and fitting only for those in humbler walks of life, and was sure this was one reason why it was hard to find candidates. The result, he claimed, was evident in the empty places at Sunday worship. 'When we find that all the exhortations of Angel, Priests and Deacons have failed to secure anything approaching an adequate attendance at the 10 o'clock service on Sundays, we are led to reflect whether this may not be a proof to us that we have neglected to use the proper ordinance to effect the end so much desired.'[112]

By contrast, we shall see that from the mid-twentieth century an active underdiaconate played a vital role in maintaining the worshipping life and spiritual cohesion of congregations bereft of higher ministers.

*Deaconesses*

It is entirely likely that the apostles were stimulated to thought by contemporary developments in the area of deaconess ministry, such as the Deaconess Institution founded by Theodore Fliedner at Kaiserswerth in Germany in 1836 and the Anglican sisterhood established by the Revd T. T. Carter in 1852, both of which owed much to Roman Catholic practice. Drummond went so far as to draw up a basis for a body of what he called 'Sisters of Charity,' which would minister to the poor and would welcome non-members as associates. In his scheme, every angel's seat should have a group of sisters of charity to provide nursing, clothes, food, fuel, and medicine to the poor. Their membership would not be restricted to Catholic Apostolics: 'The society should consist of all the lone women under the Angel: but should admit into their community, any other person without respect to sect, as associates with them.' The angel should appoint a directress, and a deacon as general. All members of the order should wear some distinguishing badge or cross.[113] It was a remarkable proposal,

---

111. Hume, *Office of Underdeacon*, 1.
112. Ibid., 3–5, quotation at 4–5.
113. LPL, MS 4942, W. R. Stevenson, Notebook, 235–37, 'Sisters of Charity, as defined by Henry

especially from one who was so vociferously opposed to Roman Catholic religious orders, but we do not know what the other apostles thought of it, and it does not appear to have been realized to any great extent anywhere.

Nevertheless, a ministry of deaconess had been formally recognized, with a particular focus on providing pastoral care for women where it was inappropriate for a male minister to do so. As early as 1835 we find them being set apart as the apostles set the churches in order,[114] and it is likely that they were recognized at Newman Street before that. They did not exist as a distinct order of ministry but were 'to assist the priest and the deacon in their several ministrations towards the women of the flock.'[115] Apart from offering general encouragement to women in fulfilling their duties in the Church, the family, and the world, deaconesses could have a more specifically pastoral role:

> Deaconesses have no commission to teach, that is, to teach with authority, but as elder sisters fully instructed in the ways of God, a great deal of their work will necessarily partake of the nature of teaching. They will have to deal with & remove difficulties arising out of an imperfect understanding of the ritual & teaching of the Church. They will have to minister comfort to the wounded spirit or distressed conscience, or to point out the right way for the attainment of that comfort. They will have to help the weak to resist the power of the enemy & accuser, to console and pray with the sick & afflicted.[116]

### Lay Assistants

Those who did not wish to offer (or could not offer) as candidates for ministerial office nevertheless had plenty of scope for service as lay assistants. A sermon at Albury in 1898 reinforced an invitation to the flock to offer for service as lay assistants, i.e., 'to fulfil such duties under the ministers, including also the Deaconesses, as may be done by those not actually ordained to the ministry, & to aid the ministers generally in the subordinate duties & service of the Church of God.' Even children should not be held back from serving as appropriate.[117] Men were to serve under the deacons, and women under the deaconesses; their work was described by the *Book of Regulations* as 'charitable and pious services.'[118] A register of those offering for service (which

---

Drummond for the Tribe in Scotland & Switzerland.'

114. Copinger, 'Annals,' 55.

115. Anon., *Book of Regulations*, §664. For the practical outworking of this ministry, see Henke, 'Catholic Apostolic Church,' 7–9.

116. Book containing duties of elders, underdeacons etc, 57–58, 'Deaconesses, a few hints for the guidance of.'

117. DFP: DNM/H/2/106, 'Sermon. Albury. Sunday March 24th 1898.'

118. Anon., *Book of Regulations*, §595.

included those offering to serve as underdeacons, deaconesses, deacons, or priests) was to be kept.

Even a local congregation could have a large ministerial staff, and its organization could be correspondingly complex. The Bradford registers, because of their relative completeness from 1872 until the end of 1927, enable us to gain a fuller picture of the ministry of a large congregation. There are listed thirty priests (register 13), forty deacons (register 12), thirty-four deaconesses (register 11), thirty-nine underdeacons (register 10), and no less than 308 lay assistants (register 7). When we set this against the fact that 521 persons had been sealed by 1901 (register 5), it is clear that a high proportion of members were active in the work. Yet in several tribes there were recurrent shortages of ministers, especially at the higher levels, and in 1858 special prayers (the so-called 'Three Seasons Prayers') were introduced for use during the week preceding each of the three great feasts, in which congregations besought God that ministers would be raised up.[119]

## Recognition

In a Church so carefully structured, it is not surprising that great care was taken to set down the process by which ministerial gifts were recognized and ministers set in office.

Ordination as a priest and consecration as an angel both required that a man be called by a word of prophecy. This usually occurred in the context of a service of presentation of those who had offered themselves as candidates for ministry. The holding of such a service had to be sanctioned by the apostle, and once held, it was the apostle's interpretation of the words spoken which determined whether a particular candidate had in fact received a call thereby.[120] But prophecy alone was not enough; for ordination to the priesthood, the apostles had also to be convinced of a candidate's fitness and availability for the work; the angel bore primary responsibility for ascertaining this, and had also to confirm that the man's services were needed and that there was sufficient funding available to support him, whether from his own income or from Church funds. Once these requirements had been met, a man might be ordained by the laying on of apostle's hands.[121] As for consecration as an angel, a priest could only offer himself if his apostle had signified that he might do so, usually on the basis of the local angel's assessment of his gifts and potential.[122] The system did not always work smoothly: by the late nineteenth century it was not uncommon for a man to be called as a priest or angel many years before he was ordained, if indeed he ever was.

---

119. Samuel Gardiner to Martin Irving, 21 February–11 March 1858; Copinger, 'Annals,' 108.
120. Anon., *Book of Regulations*, §§602–10.
121. Ibid., §§696–702; Woodhouse, *Narrative*, 36; cf. NC, 5 February 1851.
122. Anon., *Book of Regulations*, §§708–12; cf. NC, 5 February 1851.

Recognition of ministry was for the most part a matter for the universal Church and not merely for a local congregation. Accordingly, central records were probably kept in most tribes, and several certificates of letters survive for men ordained as priests or angels. These used pro formas, such as this one used in England during the 1870s for priests:

> No. \_\_\_. in Apost. Reg:
>
> These Letters are to certify unto all the faithful in Christ that _____ having been called by the Holy Ghost through prophecy to the holy Order of the Priesthood was on the _____ day of _____ in the year of our Lord one thousand eight hundred and _____ presented before the Apostle of the Lord in the _____ Church in _____ by the Angel _____ of the _____ in _____ for ordination unto the said Order of Priesthood and for ministry _____
>
> And the said Angel _____ of the _____ in _____ having certified the said _____ to be fit and worthy of the same, the said _____ was thereupon ordained by the said Apostle with imposition of hands to be a Priest in the One Holy Catholic and Apostolic Church in the presence of divers witnesses.
>
> In testimony whereof by the direction of the Apostle in charge of the _____ we have also subscribed our Names to these Letters.
>
> _____ [signed]
>
> _____ with the Apostle.
>
> _____
>
> _____ with the Apostle.[123]

From the numbers on extant certificates, mostly for the Bradford church, it appears that a central register was maintained listing ordinations to the priesthood in the tribe, with another for consecrations to the episcopate. When one priest was ordained on 16 February 1865, his certificate was numbered 417;[124] by March 1899, the list had reached 968 names. We may infer, then, that around a thousand priests were ordained for service in England. The register of those consecrated as angels stood at 315 in September 1874, but only ninety-six consecrations were recorded in the 'Annual Reports' from 1875 until 1901; evidently the pre-1874 rate of consecrations was not maintained. It could be that greater caution was now being exercised, but a more significant factor was probably economic. Edward Heath commented in 1893 on the great lack of men who were suitable, qualified, and free to give themselves to the work of an angel; some churches also needed more priests. He suggested that it might be worth ordaining some who could not be full-time in the work,[125] but there was little opportunity before 1901 for practice to change as a result. The apparent slowdown in the rate of ordinations means that by the 1880s references began to appear to the

---

123. WYAS, 53D95/2/1, certificate for Joseph Dearman James, issued 25 July 1872.
124. Prior, *My Experience*, 41, which gives the text of the certificate in full.
125. MC, 15 November 1893, 136.

ageing staff of ministers. By contrast with the early days, reported Leslie from England, very few young men were showing a willingness to give themselves to the work.[126]

Once ordained or otherwise set in office, ministers were expected to function as part of a tight-knit structure. At the congregational level, there were frequent meetings of ministers, often presided over by the angel. Such 'councils' were the occasion for reading the apostles' determinations, minutes of conference, and other circulars sent out from Albury. As well as disseminating instructions, councils dealt with local matters, such as building work, service arrangements, and committals to pastorship.[127]

## Training

With customary pungency, Drummond asserted that '[a]n ignorant evangelist is an incompetent evangelist'; evangelists should study to fit themselves for their ministry just as assiduously as they would for their worldly trades or professions.[128] Elsewhere he asserted that evangelists needed a good grasp of divinity (recommended authors included Paley, Pearson, Butler, and above all Hooker), as well as of composition and grammar.[129] Many angels seem to have been well educated, but I suspect that this was true of a smaller proportion of priests, and so on down the line.[130] There appears to have been a barrier to how high those of lesser education could rise, which was due in part to the Church's failure to establish a robust and thorough system of training for ministry, at a time when most denominations were making great efforts in this respect.

Dr Thompson, the pillar of pastors, was well placed to see the need, and developed a scheme of training intended not only for candidates for ordination, but also for those already in holy orders who had never received any training. The social background of these men further challenges the notion that the Church failed to achieve much penetration among the working classes. Speaking at the inauguration of his institution in London in 1850, Thompson explained:

> ... the petition before me, which is the occasion of our present meeting, originated with a certain number of ministers, chiefly of the Central Church. It reports that certain of the brethren, being desirous of cultivating their natural gifts, met together for instruction. Poor, and few in number, they could not afford to pay regularly appointed lecturers set apart for this work. . . . Before applying to others for help, the brethren to whom I have alluded, supplied from their own resources the necessities under which they laboured, by

---

126. AR 1887, 10.

127. The Bradford minutes of councils are probably complete: WYAS, 53D95/3/6 (1880–99); BIA, CAC 1/7 (1899–1913), CAC 1/8 (1913–38).

128. Drummond, *Discourses*, 135.

129. Drummond, *Remarks on the Ministry of Instruction*, 8–9.

130. Cf. Jane de Gruchy's findings: 'Catholic Apostolic Church,' 29–41.

having recourse to mutual instruction; thus teaching and being taught in the best way they could.[131]

Eventually their meetings had to end and they resolved to seek help. Delay ensued, due to the novelty of their petition and the petitioners' 'lying within the precincts of the Seven Churches' and so, at that point, under the college of apostles as a whole. But Thompson undertook to begin something on his own account, hoping it might grow into a regularly endowed college 'for the education of candidates for Holy Orders throughout the Catholic Church.'[132] He was aware that not all would approve of such training, any more than was the case in other denominations, but he argued for the pressing need, insisting that this had been recognized by those for whom the institution was intended. Other arguments which he rejected (and which he presumably thought some might hold) were those based on the failure of other such institutions, and the idea that training negated divine grace. The first disciples spent three-and-a-half years with Christ; Paul, the first apostle to the Gentiles, was also theologically trained. Ministers needed to know and speak the theological language of Christendom in order to reunite it: that would not happen miraculously, contrary to the expectations of some.[133] Lectures were promised on Dogmatics; Ecclesiastical History; the Scriptures; Pronunciation (Elocution); Grammar, Logic and Composition; Ethics or Morals, especially with reference to 'the deportment of Priests in the house of God'; Natural Philosophy; Jurisprudence and Law (further evidence of the Church's strong legal ethos); Classics; Languages; and Music, for those who had to chant in the services. He announced that a room had been taken at 52 Great Marlborough Street, and the first lecture was to be given on 27 May, on Jurisprudence, open to all ministers.[134]

Nothing more was heard of this effort from official sources, and it seems to have died a death. Prior wrote in 1880 that the classes had soon moved to Newman Street but were discontinued after a year or two due to poor attendance, presumably before the move to Gordon Square at the end of 1853.[135] Thereafter training at the local level in England seems to have been left largely to the angels, and I know of no systematic efforts to provide training in any other tribe. It is noteworthy that the Church's brightest intellectual star, the historian Samuel Rawson Gardiner (1829–1902), was not invited to assist in providing instruction, perhaps because by around 1860 his coolness towards the Church in which he had been brought up was becoming evident.[136]

A more focused (and international) form of training probably got under way from 1865, as angels from overseas were invited to Albury to spend a fortnight with the

131. Thompson, *Inaugural Address*, 3–5.
132. Ibid., 5–6.
133. Ibid., 8, 14–16, 19, 22.
134. Ibid., 23–24.
135. Prior, *My Experience*, 21; Copinger, 'Annals,' 89.
136. On Gardiner, see Grass, '"Telling lies",' 398–412.

apostles and other ministers of the universal Church, sharing in the round of worship and receiving instruction. Weston Dene, a house in the middle of the village, became a guest house for these visiting ministers.[137] Later, such help would become vital in maintaining the weekly schedule of services at Albury.

Those offering for ministry were supposed to give time under the direction of their angel to being prepared and instructed.[138] But lack of knowledge was a recurrent problem in Catholic Apostolic ministers, as Gardiner was all too aware. Evidently it was still felt that more could be done, which may explain why in 1887 Edward Heath was due to give a course of exegetical lectures on the book of Acts at the Central Church, intended for ministers and candidates for the ministry.[139] A letter from the coadjutors to the pastor for the angels in 1898 dealt with the need for training at the local level. The recent ordination of large numbers to the priesthood had highlighted the need for the newly ordained to be instructed; angels had not always been sufficiently alert to this aspect of their duties, and had tended to forget that what was familiar to them regarding such matters as how to take part in services might not be so to new ministers, who were being left to fend for themselves. Yet such training was almost the most important aspect of the angel's work. A cause for concern at higher levels was the defective biblical knowledge of some candidates for the priesthood. The coadjutors wondered how angels could have satisfied themselves that these individuals were learned in Scripture. Public teaching, too, needed to be treated more seriously. 'This branch of the Priest's duty presents special difficulty to those of our Ministers who have either had but little school training in their youth or little occasion to practise literary composition.' In this connection, the coadjutors pointed out the different scope and character of homilies, teachings by the four, pastoral teachings in shorter services, and sermons.[140]

Reporting formed a major element of the work of ministers, enabling those over them to keep track of what was happening and to see where instruction might be required on particular matters. Thompson summarized the content of a paper by Cardale in 1848 which dealt with the organization of the service of lay members. Cardale had urged that each minister or lay person involved should keep a diary of the services they had performed, especially angels in charge of churches, and district evangelists, who would need to produce such a record as required. Angel-evangelists were to report to the pillar of evangelists their activity and that of the ministers under them; angels were to report quarterly to the pillar of pastors. Reports should include healings, notable happenings in services (especially in meetings for the exercise of prophetic gifts) or reported by priests, 'wanderers reclaimed,' numbers admitted to full communion, baptisms, candidates for ministry, those called to ministry, deacons

---

137. Burne, *Albury*, 1; Copinger, 'Annals,' 118; Schröter, *Bilder*, 15.
138. Anon., *Book of Regulations*, §602.
139. MC, 11 May 1887, 232–33.
140. MC, 27 August 1898, 1–6, quotation at 5.

chosen or admitted, priests ordained, sealings and other occurrences connected with the visits of apostles or other ministers, and the work of priest- and deacon-evangelists.[141] It was possibly from such reports that what amounted to publicity brochures for evangelist work in Scotland were compiled, such as David Ker, *Leaves from Report Books of Visitors of the Poor* (1865), and Anon., *A Summary of Reports given at a General Meeting held on the 27th of March, 1879, in connection with the Evangelist Work of the Church in Glasgow*.

## Writing and Publication

Although plenty of works by critics of the Church appeared during the 1830s, Catholic Apostolics were themselves slow to engage in publication. Apart from the Testimonies and the *Record*, only a handful of works appeared up to 1840, and several of those were by Drummond, who had always been a prolific pamphleteer on subjects political and ecclesiastical. A few apologetic and expository works appeared during the early 1840s, but even as the flow began to gather pace it is worth noting that most of the apostles had not yet gone into print. It is possible that there was a feeling that the living stream of revelation by the Holy Spirit through prophecy could not adequately be captured in print: such an attitude was evident in the early aversion to recording words of prophecy.

However, on 27 January 1846 the apostles issued a minute setting out the parameters for publication by the Church's ministers. The Minutes of Conference for 6 November 1878 incorporated the minute of 1846 as a benchmark, and were called forth by the fact that over the previous three years, publications had appeared under the names of apostles or ministers of the universal Church, or known to be by them (publications were supposed to appear anonymously). As a result, certain points, on which the apostles as a group had not come to a decision, had come to be regarded as dogmatically affirmed or as sanctioned by particular apostles. But it was stressed that the only authoritative works were those which, one way or another, had the sanction of the apostles collectively. Non-official publications, even if authored by high-ranking ministers, were purely the expression of private opinions.[142] A note concerning a book published that year indicates why such sanction was required:

> A Book has lately been published with the Title of 'Primary Truths of Christianity for the Hour of Temptation.'
> 
> Lest this book should be taken by the Ministers to be of authority Mr Woodhouse wishes it to be understood that the author alone is responsible for the doctrinal statements, some of which are questionable.[143]

141. Book containing duties of elders, underdeacons etc, 111–12, J. Thompson, 'On the Office of Deaconess.'

142. MC, 6 November 1878, 96–98.

143. WYAS, 53D95/5/2, undated note to ministers.

The author was Robert Norton, who had written widely on doctrinal themes. The publisher was Thomas Bosworth, who at that point (1878) was issuing many of the Church's official publications.[144]

From time to time, the apostles would continue to find it necessary to remind ministers that they were not to publish without formal sanction, and that only works which had received this could be regarded as in any way authoritative or as acceptable presentations of the Church's teaching. This was not so much about control as about the conviction that the distinctive Catholic Apostolic witness was its proper organization as a body through which God could act, and the belief that the truths committed to it were not private property.[145] By 1893, there was an official bookseller in London (probably George J. W. Pitman at 140 Gower Street), but even he was pulled up for publishing a book which did not have the requisite sanction.[146] And in 1905 the Bradford council minutes record the reading of a letter from the archdeacon for the tribe 'respecting the publications sold by Messrs Hobbs & Co & said that all official forms & books should be obtained from the Seven Deacons or Archdeacon as the case may be.'[147] A few months earlier the angel at Huddersfield 'read a circular from the Coadjutor referring to the reissue by Hobbs & Co of Glasgow of unauthorised books, pamphlets & tracts.'[148] These would have been works written by ministers, perhaps even apostles, but not formally sanctioned. Even so, in 1911 the angel at Huddersfield had to read memoranda from the coadjutor regarding 'ministers writing & publishing anonymously books on religious subjects.'[149] The great majority of works by ministers appeared through a few recognized publishers; yet it is in this area of publication that ministers seem to have shown the greatest degree of independence. In fact, as a later sermon explained, 'only two writings were ever issued by the College of Apostles (apart from the writings of individual Apostles). They are the Apostles' Testimony and the Apostles' Liturgy.'[150]

By the mid-twentieth century no more new printed works were appearing, but remaining stocks of older works, as well as second-hand works, remained on sale. During the 1930s, the Bedford Bookshop at 10 Tavistock Place, London, published Catholic Apostolic works, but from 1939 its proprietor, H. B. Copinger (1880–1951), moved his business to his home in Wembley. His *A Bibliography (begun Easter 1908)* became available for sale in 1955 after a Catholic Apostolic bibliophile in Zürich had

---

144. Bosworth entered business in 1848, and was in partnership with a Mr Harrison from 1856 to 1864. In 1888 he retired, becoming librarian to the duke of Northumberland: Tyacke, 'Unnoticed Work,' 245. Earlier publishers included George Barclay and then John Strangeways, later Strangeways & Walden, both in London.

145. MC, 29 July 1891, 73–74.

146. MC, 13 December 1893, 139.

147. BIA, CAC 1/7, Bradford MC, 3 May 1905.

148. BIA, CAC 4/5, Huddersfield MC, 22 February 1905.

149. Ibid., 31 May 1911.

150. Anon., *Sermon, Quinquagesima Sunday 1953*, 5.

copies made of the original typescript.[151] It is a standard, if incomplete and occasionally inaccurate, reference work for Catholic Apostolic material. Copinger's successors, David Priddle and his son Norman, continued the service which he had provided and also duplicated typescript copies of many out of print items in response to demand from members. However, with Norman Priddle's death in 1978, the trustees tightened things up so that non-members were no longer normally able to obtain material through such channels.

We turn now to consider the genres of published Catholic Apostolic material. Sermons, pastoral letters, and other such items were used extensively to keep in touch with the faithful, especially those living at a distance. Easter was a favorite time for issuing these, as absent members were commemorated at a eucharist on Easter Monday. In the English-speaking world, these were usually published as individual pamphlets by particular churches or groups of churches, sometimes as a regular numbered publication. For example, in Australia and New Zealand, where there had always been a high proportion of isolated members, the *Pastoral Instruction* continued to appear until no. 696 in 1972.[152] In German and other Northern European languages, such material appeared in periodicals issued centrally. One long-running periodical was the German *Pastorale Mitteilungen* (*Pastoral Communications*). This included homilies, sermons, and pastoral instructions, but for some years at least it gave no indication of author, date, or place of origin. Its first editor was Carl Rothe, and the need to counter the influence of Geyer was probably a major factor precipitating its appearance in April 1863. The death in 1931 of Ludwig Albrecht, the last archangel of the universal Church, may have been why it ceased publication that year, being replaced by *Hirtenbriefe* (1932–41), and from 1948 by *Smyrna-Stimmen* (*Smyrna Light*; initially *Stimmen in der Smyrnazeit*, now largely reprints of articles from *Pastorale Mitteilungen*).[153] In Danish there was *Pastorale Meddelelser* (*Pastoral Communications*; 1866–1958), and in Swedish *Pastorale Meddelanden* (1893–1945), which from 1935 was published from Copenhagen and is said to have been a translation of the Danish title.[154] In Dutch there was *Herderlijke onderwijzingen* (*Pastoral Teachings*; 1872–1999 or later). No French-language periodical is known. It is noticeable that the Danish, Dutch, and Swedish publications each appeared within a few years of the first congregations in those countries being set up. We may surmise that the Church had learned from Geyer's *Morgenrothe* the value of a periodical in strengthening a sense of Catholic Apostolic identity and keeping local teaching on sound lines.

151. *Newsletter* 8 (August 1955) 1.

152. Martin, 'Brief Survey,' 14–15. In that year the last Catholic Apostolic deacon died, in Sydney; the two events may have been connected, since the need was usually felt of ministerial approval for such publications.

153. W. H., *Katholisch-apostolische Gemeinden*, 76, 181; Schröter, *Bilder*, 192. For a short period at some point, *Pastoralblatt* also appeared for the South German churches.

154. Adell, *De tysta bedjarna*, 26.

The main channel for dissemination of official teaching and policy, however, was the flow of circulars of several types issued from Albury. These included:

- Apostles' Determinations (1859–1900). These were issued about twice a year, containing decisions arrived at by the apostles in council with their ministers and notices of appointments in the universal Church, as well as occasional papers on particular ministry issues and words of prophecy not published in the *Record* (see below) with a bearing on the issue determined.

- Circulars issued from Albury (from 1851 if not earlier, until the 1920s). A German collection of these appeared as *Sammlung kirchlicher Circulare* (3rd ed., 1895, containing fifty-eight circulars issued 1855–84; first published 1867). Incidentally, the apostles were concerned to ensure that only officially approved versions of the Church's teaching were disseminated, even informally. In 1856 Cardale instructed that the practice of note-taking at the assemblies of the Seven Churches in London and the circulation of those notes and keeping records of what was taught must cease.[155] Whether it ever ceased completely is doubtful, given the existence in the public domain of notes taken after this prohibition.[156]

- Notes (later Minutes) of Conferences of the apostle for England with his ministers, and more rarely with the English angels also (1850–1912). In German there was *Mitteilungen aus den Apostelkonzilen 1855–1900* (1901).

- 'Apostles' Reports' (later 'Annual Reports'), summarizing the work undertaken and the progress achieved in different parts of the world (1853–1901)

Such circulars were intended to be kept. In 1868 Cardale advised that 'all circulars and other letters of instructions relating to the government, discipline or conducting of worship in the Churches generally, or in the particular Church, should be filed as Church documents, or preferably should be copied into a Church Book to be kept for that purpose.'[157]

A periodical whose circulation was restricted, and which constituted an official circular, was the *Angels' Record*. In some form, this appears to have been issued from the beginning,[158] for around 1835 '[t]he Angels were directed to keep the "Record" of words of prophecy, but while it was to be sent to all the churches, it was not to be looked

---

155. Deaconesses' Minutes, 19 September 1856.

156. E.g. BOC, 'Notes taken nearly verbatim.'

157. MC, 21 October 1868, 281.

158. Holdings at Bradford comprise a virtually complete run from 1876 of the new series, which ran from 1869 to 1928: WYAS, 53D95/1/1–28. Visiting Albury in the early 1990s, I noticed that the bound volumes of the *Record* kept in the apostles' council chamber began at 1869; since one would have expected a complete set to be kept there for reference purposes, it may be inferred that before then they were circulated in a different format. The library in this room was said to have included much of what was spoken, written or published between 1837 and 1901: Anon., *Albury: Extract*, 2.

upon as the Scriptures, but when read to be destroyed or locked away carefully.'[159] In 1836 a critic wrote: 'You must be sure to be at Church on Monday evenings, to hear the new book read, namely, THE RECORD, if you cannot get in time to hear the Bible read, and you must obey it in all things.'[160] German translations also survive from 1853 and 1862–67, from which we find that the publication had reached issue 90 by 1853, and 104 by 1867.

In 1861 the apostles directed that at head of each issue should appear this restriction:

> The Records sent to Angels are sent to them for use in their Churches. Every Angel is at liberty in his discretion to give the perusal of them to Priests or Deacons under his charge. Such Priests or Deacons are bound to reserve them for their own reading exclusively and are to return them to the Angel without taking copies or making extracts.[161]

Discretion was to be exercised in using content of the *Record*; Woodhouse referred on one occasion to words of prophecy sent from the apostles having been communicated indiscriminately to congregations, with much harm resulting.[162] Despite this, copies sometimes circulated more widely. One New Zealand minister quoted the local Anglican bishop, who had evidently read some of them, as saying that volumes could be 'obtained from members.'[163]

Each issue followed a set pattern: prophecies were given first, followed by cases of healing. Both were selected for wider circulation because of their significance. This was the prerogative of the apostles or (after 1897) the coadjutors. Within each category, the order was dependent on the place or context of origin: Albury—assemblies of the seven churches in London—apostolic visitations—and then the tribes. For each prophecy, the details given included place, date (from 1897 onwards), service in which uttered (and sometimes also the point in the service), and any Scripture passage taken up by the utterance.

Many sermons and teachings drew their inspiration from words of prophecy recorded therein, and prophecy thus exercised a vital formative influence on Catholic Apostolic self-understanding. This must be balanced, however, by the fact that prophecies delivered in local congregations were sent up to Albury for consideration by the apostles; only those so validated and approved could be circulated. Publication appears to have ceased as a result of the death of the last coadjutor in 1929, there being nobody else with the authority to make a selection from the words sent to

---

159. St Andrews Special Collections, MS 38594, Anon., 'History of the Lord's Work,' 75–76.

160. Linney, *Narrative*, 12.

161. MC, 10 July 1861, 140. Gretason states that deacons needed special permission to read these records: 'Authority, Provisionality and Process,' 278.

162. AD, December 1895, 11.

163. 'Minister of the Gospel,' *God's Work*, 10.

Albury, although individual prophecies were occasionally quoted or referred to in sermons for some years after that.

Apart from what was published, close supervision was exercised over all that was preached or taught. Ministries appear to have been written out in full and kept in the church vestry, partly for record and partly for reading. For the Edinburgh church, two bound volumes of ministries by its angel, Pitcairn, are extant in the National Library of Scotland, most dated between 1871 and 1884. Each bears a library bookplate with the words 'Not to be taken out of the Church,' and the second is entitled 'Sermons. Angel of Edinburgh. Vol. X.' Manuscript ministries were often circulated among other ministers in the congregation. One at Pentecost 1876 was annotated: 'The attention of the Ministers is recalled to the Substance of this Teaching, in order that the instruction whether doctrinal or practical, to the flock here, and at the Dependencies, may point in the same direction until further notice, according to each Ministers [sic] gift, and place.' A third volume, 'Ministries. July /69,' comprises short ministries of about two hundred words each from the years 1869–71; these would probably have been given at the weekday services. There is also a volume of ministries by visiting apostles and others, covering the period 1853–59.

## FINANCIAL ARRANGEMENTS

From 1853, the angels of the seven churches in London (which were intended to be a kind of demonstration model of what the universal Church was to look like) were appointed as seven deacons of the universal Church, responsible for the management of Church property on behalf of the apostles.

At the heart of the Church's financial set-up was the practice of tithing. As early as November 1834 this had been declared to be a duty, and six months later prophecy indicated that a tithe of the tithes should be set aside for the work of the apostles and the ministers with them.[164] Tithe was to be paid on net income after income tax had been deducted.[165] The expectation that those who joined the Church would tithe was clearly laid down in basic teaching. In 1870, Cardale determined that nobody should be committed to pastorship who did not understand and intend to pay tithe; this was not a term of communion, but the special blessings available through apostles and their ministers could not be received by those who defrauded God of tithe. However, tithing, whilst clearly taught, remained between the individual and God. Ministers were strictly enjoined to avoid anything like spying in this matter.[166] According to Isaac Capadose, backsliding almost always began with an individual's withholding tithe, 'that touch stone of true consecration to God.'[167] In some tribes, the low income

---

164. Dowglass, *Chronicle*, 15; Boase, *Supplementary Narrative*, 813; Miller, *Irvingism*, 1:50.
165. MC, 8 November 1854, 4.
166. MC, 9 February 1870, 319–20.
167. AR 1888, 23.

of most members meant that little tithe income was available for the support of ministers. In Scandinavia, for instance, almost all ministers had to work, with the result that they had little time for the solid Bible study required in order to feed their members.[168]

Although the poor were mentioned in 1875 as being exempt from this requirement,[169] Cardale does appear to have expected the working poor to pay tithe. In a communication sent on his behalf in 1873, in reply to the question of whether working men whose wages were insufficient to maintain them should pay tithes, it was clearly laid down as a duty commanded in the Bible, since tithes belonged to the Lord himself. Whether they earned enough was not the question. Apostles could not exempt from tithe, so they could not delegate that prerogative to angels. Neither was the fact that such poor members received some maintenance from church offerings any excuse for not paying tithe. Financially speaking, the tithes of all churches were insufficient to cover the maintenance of ministers, and the offerings on the three great feasts were therefore used primarily to help poorer churches fulfill their duty to support their ministers. Debtors should pay tithe too, as it was the best way of getting out of debt, through the consequent divine blessing. Conversely, lack of blessing was believed to result from refusal to tithe: evangelists in Europe had been told by some of their hearers that it was all very well for rich English members to pay tithe, but they were poor and could not do so. In the country where this objection was raised, the work had made no progress.[170]

Tithe was even seen on occasion as the great point at issue between those gathered under apostles and other Christians. A prophecy given at Birmingham declared that tithe was a practice 'which the Lord declared that He would send through Christendom as a wedge, and it should separate unto Him those who acknowledge Him as Lord, from those who acknowledge Him not.'[171] Detailed discussions occurred at various levels as to whether particular categories of income were subject to tithe, the Gordon Square deacons' minutes recording in 1857: 'Agreed that a wife does not pay tithe on her pin-money, but she may make offerings.'[172]

Members were also expected to give what were known as first-fruits. These were the first year's income on property coming to a person from a source on which they had no legal claim, such as a gift or a bequest from one to whom the individual was not a legal heir.[173]

Over and above all this were offerings of various types.[174] Standard instructions regarding these, often reprinted by local congregations, appeared in the 1869 *Church*

168. AR 1889, 19.
169. MC, 8 December 1875, 37–39.
170. Anon., *Two Letters*.
171. *Record* 7/3 (July 1901) 301.
172. Archiv der NAK, Deacons' Minute Book 2, 18 March 1857.
173. MC, 1 March 1876, 44.
174. For fuller details, see Flegg, *'Gathered under Apostles,'* 179–86.

*Almanac*. General offerings were for the expenses associated with the conduct of worship. Special offerings were taken on three feasts: for the poor (Good Friday), for travel costs of apostles and other ministers of the universal Church (14 July), and for widows and orphans of ministers (All Saints). On the days when the seven churches in London met, offerings were received for the travel expenses of those. Offerings for the poor included clothes, usually administered by the church doorkeeper, so that they could attend worship fitly attired. Offerings for the universal Church were received on the three great feasts, and applied for the benefit of poor ministers and churches by the seven deacons of the universal Church. There were also offerings for evangelist work, offerings by candidates for the sealing, thank-offerings for particular blessings and mercies received, other offerings for the poor, offerings at apostolic visitations (for travel expenses), and offerings for building and repairing churches.[175] Local churches might also receive quarterly offerings for particular needs.[176]

The common perception of the Catholic Apostolic Church is that it was, and is, a wealthy body. However, it would be a serious error to read the present state of affairs back into the nineteenth century. Indeed, in 1892 the archdeacon for England reported: 'the bulk of all our congregations are poor people—many very poor. In Churches reputed to be richer, the additional Tithe may be supposed (in fact, is known) to come from a few individuals. Of late years the gathering by the Evangelists has been almost exclusively from the poorer classes.'[177] He went on to express the suspicion that not all members were paying tithe as faithfully as they might, and called on poorer churches to cut their suit according to their cloth, financially speaking.[178]

It appears to have been a constant source of anxiety to secure sufficient funds for such purposes as evangelist work and the support of ministers.[179] When special appeals were made, it proved easier to obtain funds for church buildings than for evangelist work, a source of recurrent complaints by the apostles and their ministers. In 1872, it was laid down that mission work in England would only receive the apostle's sanction if sufficient funds were in hand or if the offerings were estimated to be likely to be sufficient. Angel-evangelists were to arrange annually with the evangelist with the apostle the work for their districts in the coming year, providing estimates of expense of each mission proposed. He then would report to the archdeacon for the tribe on their relative urgency and ascertain whether the available funds justified them.[180] During the late 1880s and early 1890s evangelist work in England seems to have been largely dependent on the liberal giving of one congregation (we do not know which).[181] Indeed,

---

175. Anon., *Church Almanac* (1869), 31–33.
176. Anon., *'Persuaded of the common desire,'* 6.
177. MC, 19 October 1892, 109.
178. Ibid., 110, 113.
179. AR 1900, 31.
180. AC, August 1872, 1.
181. MC, 27 August 1890, 57–58.

Leslie reported in 1893 that mission had been dependent on liberal support from one individual.[182] In 1899 it was reported that the deficiency of funds for evangelist work was now almost as much in London (which was treated as a separate entity) as it was for England. Unless offerings increased, work probably could not continue on the scale contemplated by the angel-evangelists.[183]

On occasion, lack of funds seems to have precluded the establishment of an independent congregation, as at Aalesund in Norway, of which Capadose reported in 1894 that 'unless a congregation can be established there, numerous enough to maintain by their tithes a resident Priest, it seems wiser to let them abide in the established church,' because once a Catholic Apostolic altar had been set up members would not be allowed to take communion in the established Church, and it would only rarely be possible to send a priest under apostles.[184]

By no means all ministers were expected to give themselves full-time to the work, however. Many were what would nowadays be called non-stipendiary. Moreover, they came from a range of occupations; in Norway there were priests who were joiners, bakers, and chemists. In the Bradford congregation, they included a schoolmaster, a butter factor, a grocer, a clerk, and a carpenter.[185] In 1854 Cardale expressed the opinion that evangelists did not need to be full-time; for prophets it was better if they could have time to study and meditate; and pastors usually needed to be free of the cares of business. Therefore elders, since they superintended pastors and evangelists, should not be in secular work.[186]

Those ministers who did receive tithe had no legal right to it, and it was paid to God, not as a means of supporting the clergy.[187] As with the Old Testament Levites, a fixed portion was to be given only to those devoting their whole time to the work, but others could receive on occasion as they had need.[188] A circular issued in 1879 set out the official understanding regarding ministerial stipends. These were given out of love, not for reward or as part of a bargain, and were to be applied as apostles directed. Payments to ministers were 'not to be received as a payment for services rendered or to be rendered, but simply as a gift from God.' They were paid quarterly in advance, but with the proviso that they were always liable to cease. The fact that a minister had received a 'benefice' conferred no legal right or claim, and he was just as obligated whether or not he was beneficed. At the bottom of the circular, a pro-forma declaration was printed for ministers to sign: 'I ___ of ___ at present serving under the Apostles as ___ in the Church in ___ hereby testify my entire assent to the above

---

182. AR 1894, 8.
183. MC, 1899/1, unpaginated.
184. AR 1894, 26.
185. De Gruchy, 'Catholic Apostolic Church,' 36.
186. NC, 1 February 1854.
187. MC, 10 October 1855, 33.
188. Ibid., 35.

Principles, and my willingness to be bound thereby.'[189] A widely reported court case in the mid-1880s, Whitestone *v.* Woodhouse, put the status of these payments to the test; the verdict was that such money was received as a gratuity, and that ministers had no legal claim to it.[190]

189. AC, 'General principles relating to the Benefices of Ministers and to the Appropriation and Distribution of Tithe,' printed circular (endorsed January 1879).

190. For newspaper cuttings of a number of reports, see BL, 764n19, Newspaper cuttings, 184–87.

# 9

# Catholic Apostolic Liturgical Development

## THE HISTORICAL DEVELOPMENT OF THE LITURGY

ACCORDING TO THE LITURGICAL scholar Horton Davies, the apostles 'made the most comprehensive attempt to return to the teaching and practices of the Primitive Church during the whole of the nineteenth century, for they conceived that it must be charismatic and institutional, prophetic and priestly in its ministries, and this is what accounts for its interest and for its impact on worship.'[1] In a work on Catholic Apostolic history, it is appropriate for us to adopt a historical perspective, outlining briefly the main stages in the development of the liturgy. Other works discuss the theological aspects, and the development of particular services, in fuller detail than is possible here.[2] The English version of the liturgy has been regarded as the normative one, not least because it was usually the direct or indirect basis for translations, although some local variations did occur.

Weekly celebration of communion had been the rule at Albury from 19 July 1835, but was only introduced in the churches a year later, on 24 June 1836.[3] Drummond sent out a letter detailing the order to be observed for a weekly communion service (at 10 a.m. and 2 p.m. on Sundays), introduced on 7 August. A lectionary was also introduced, which was said to have been drawn up by Tudor, Carlyle, and Woodhouse. Prophecy at Wells on 31 July (when the congregation was being set in order)

---

1. Davies, *Worship and Theology*, 4:153.

2. See Christopher B. Heath, *Development*, based on C. E. Lewis Heath, *Lecture*; Copinger, 'Annals'; and among secondary sources, Shaw, *Catholic Apostolic Church*; Tripp, 'Liturgy'; Stevenson, 'Catholic Apostolic Eucharist'; Stevenson, 'Catholic Apostolic Church: History and Eucharist'; Stevenson, 'Liturgical Year'; Roberts, 'Pattern of Initiation'; Flegg, *'Gathered under Apostles'*; Mast, *Eucharistic Service*.

3. Boase, *Supplementary Narrative*, 822; Rossteuscher, 'Rebuilding,' 574; Shaw, *Catholic Apostolic Church*, 104.

had commanded the churches to begin reading the Bible in order that day, with the apostles being instructed to make provision for this to be done in all the churches. A lithographed letter was accordingly sent out.[4] Oddly enough, the next form of service to be introduced (in France) was one for marriage, occasioned that October by the wish of an angel there to marry.[5]

Before the apostles began to issue forms of prayer, many angels had begun doing so, which Woodhouse interpreted as evidence of a general desire for them.[6] In May 1837 the apostles 'issued instructions on the Order of Baptism', although this has not been traced.[7] A manuscript order for the Lord's Supper from that year has, however, survived.[8] There is also extant an undated manuscript volume containing orders for morning and evening services and for parts of the eucharist; Stevenson dates this to 1838–42, considering it to be perhaps a draft for the 1842 liturgy.[9]

Orders for baptism and communion (following much Reformed and dissenting practice, it was still called the Lord's Supper at this stage) were lithographed and issued on 17 February 1838. If anything, it was Presbyterian practice which was being followed, extempore prayer within a general structure being the norm, as with the *Directory of Public Worship* (1645), and the congregation receiving in their seats (albeit kneeling), being served by the deacons. In his covering letter, Thompson emphasized that the orders were to be regarded as provisional, subject to improvement as further light was received and only to reach perfection once all the tribes had been gathered, which explains why a succession of editions appeared over the years.[10] That being so, angels were not to regard them as offering a prescription to be followed exactly, but as providing direction and assistance in their conduct of the services.[11] Both the stress on provisionality and the apparent encouragement of flexibility were to fade gradually from Catholic Apostolic liturgical thought.

Copinger's bibliography also lists instructions issued in 1839 for the conduct of the forenoon service which preceded the Sunday eucharist; these may equate to the manuscript item above.[12] By now, altars rather than communion tables were being installed in many churches, and the space around them demarcated as sacred. By

---

4. Perceval papers, 115; Copinger, 'Annals,' 64.

5. Copinger, 'Annals,' 67.

6. Woodhouse, *Narrative*, 97 n.

7. Copinger, 'Annals,' 70.

8. BL, 764n14, Miscellaneous articles, tracts, etc.

9. Archiv der NAK, 'Manuscript Book,' dated by a later hand to c.1838/9; Stevenson, 'Lord's Supper,' 727.

10. Given the differences of opinion among the apostles regarding liturgical matters, it is possible that some innovations could not occur until certain apostles had died.

11. Dowglass, *Chronicle*, 31; Boase, *Supplementary Narrative*, 822; orders reproduced in Shaw, *Catholic Apostolic Church*, 104–8.

12. Copinger, *Bibliography*, 81.

1841, it had become the norm for people to come forward and receive communion kneeling.[13]

In 1842 another liturgy was produced for use at Albury, the first of eight English editions to be published.[14] Once again, Albury served as a model for other congregations, but use of the order was permitted to churches who applied to do so. Accordingly, the liturgy—and vestments—were first used in London and elsewhere on Christmas Day. Included were orders for the forenoon and evening services, regarded as corresponding to the morning and evening sacrifices under the Mosaic Law.[15] As yet there was no special provision for Christmas, Easter, or Pentecost, although a service was provided for All Saints' Day. With the movement's maturity, there was an increasing consciousness of the need for occasional offices, but the only ones in this edition were for baptism and the churching of women. According to Stevenson, the main shape of the eucharist was already evident in this edition.[16] The liturgy was largely Cardale's work, drawing on what the apostles had brought back from their travels; he now emerged as the Church's chief liturgical expert.[17] The aim was not only to combine the best practice of all the Christian communions whose worship had been observed, but to do so in a way which reflected Catholic Apostolic belief that there was one divinely revealed pattern for Christian worship, prefigured in the Tabernacle (ironically, just as the idea that there was one divinely sanctioned original was beginning to be questioned by liturgical scholars such as the Anglican William Palmer), and brought out by prophecy.[18]

Published in 1843 by general request for wider use, this edition also included a psalter arranged for chanting (previously published separately in 1840). The Church's broadening outlook was evident in the choice of Gregorian psalm tones rather than Anglican chant; we have come a very long way from the metrical psalms used in Irving's days at Newman Street. This edition also included Drummond's *Rationale of Liturgies and of Public Worship*.[19] Drummond was evidently trying to position himself as a liturgical expert, but we have seen that his views often diverged from Cardale's, and the latter was usually on firmer ground in his arguments. Stevenson reminds us that Drummond's *Rationale* used Tabernacle typology rather than catholic tradition

13. Miller, *Irvingism*, 1:223.

14. *Order for the Daily Services at Albury*. Subsequent editions appeared in 1847, 1851, 1853 (first used in 1854: Copinger, 'Annals,' 100), 1856, 1863, 1869, and 1880.

15. W. W. Andrews, *Catholic Apostolic Church*, 39; Copinger, 'Annals,' 77.

16. LPL, H6565.S8, Papers of Kenneth Stevenson, chart A/II, 'Eucharist: Evolution of Component Parts.'

17. Another possible source was the Jewish Christian and oriental traveller Joseph Wolff, who had been a friend of Irving and Drummond; while in England between 1838 and 1843 he published a digest of oriental liturgies: Mast, *Eucharistic Service*, 159.

18. Ibid., 24–25. For an exposition of Catholic Apostolic thinking, see Carlyle, *Mosaic Tabernacle*.

19. The use of metrical psalms continued in Edinburgh for seven years after the church was set up in March 1834: Pitcairn, *To the Members*, unpaginated.

as the yardstick for evaluating liturgical innovations.[20] Given the journeys which the apostles had undertaken to gather material for use in the Church's services, this might be seen as somewhat surprising, but demonstrates the continuing significance of duly approved prophetic light for determining the Church's course.

Vestments for ministers were introduced at the same time as this edition.[21] A full explanation of these would be too detailed for this book, but the basic principle follows from that governing the pattern of worship: just as under the Mosaic Law the priests were prescribed particular vestments which symbolized spiritual truths, so too ministers under the new covenant were to wear vestments which expressed the truth that human beings could only approach God in the covering he provided.[22]

A second edition of the liturgy appeared in 1847, the year when the Church's life assumed renewed vigor. The eucharist was still not placed at the beginning of the book, indicating that the apostles had not yet come to regard it as the ground of all other acts of corporate worship. But provision was now made for the great feasts of the Christian year, and a rite was introduced for the laying on of apostles' hands.

The eucharist was moved to the beginning of the book in the 1851 edition; forms were also added for the eucharist at the assembly of the seven churches in London, and for ordinations. Another inclusion was the reservation and proposition of the sacrament, introduced the previous year at a time of heightened anti-Roman sentiment in Britain. Cardale took care to distance Catholic Apostolic thinking regarding these rites from that of Roman Catholicism: reservation was for the purpose of communicating the sick and not for adoration or benediction, and proposition (at morning and evening prayer) was intended to express entire trust in the sufficient sacrifice of Christ once offered.[23] Given that Drummond was hitting the ecclesiastical headlines at this time on account of his declared anti-Romanism, no perceptive observer would have been likely to confuse the two approaches.[24] In 1851 Cardale also sought the counsel of the angels in his tribe regarding the conducting of marriage ceremonies. Applying his legal mind to the options, he concluded that the only way forward, in spite of the objections he had hitherto felt, was to have Catholic Apostolic buildings registered for this purpose.[25] It was not long before the first registrations took place, for Southwark and Paddington, followed by the Central Church.[26]

---

20. Stevenson, 'Catholic Apostolic Eucharist,' 9.
21. See especially Anon., *General Rubrics*, Appendix III; Rupert M. Heath, *Vestments*.
22. Drummond, *Rationale*, 24–25.
23. Davenport, *Albury Apostles*, 240–41; Standring, *Albury*, 73; Mast, *Eucharistic Service*, 29.
24. See, e.g., his *Remarks on Dr. Wiseman's Sermon on the Gorham Case* (London, 1850); *Speech of H. D. in the House of Commons on Thursday, March 20th, 1851, on the second reading of the Ecclesiastical Titles Bill* (London, 1851).
25. NC, 5 February 1851.
26. NC, 2 April 1851.

In 1852 lights and incense were introduced to worship generally, a lithographed service being provided for use from Pentecost onwards; Cardale stated on 6 January that they had been used for several years in some churches in Switzerland, Scotland, and France—Drummond's sphere of influence—and since the beginning of the year also in Germany. Having taught about lights and incense in worship in response to a request from the angels of the seven churches in London, Cardale had expressed his willingness at a conference of angels to sanction their general introduction if requested, but it was left to them; they reported that ministers generally were in favor, and the laity did not object.[27] He was sensitive to the need to 'hasten slowly,' and we should not see liturgical innovations as imposed by him. This year also saw the first celebration of the Separation of the Apostles, on 14 July; the observance took place at Albury until 1868, and thereafter at the Central Church (and throughout the Catholic Apostolic Church). Another edition of the liturgy was accordingly issued in 1853. This now included the shorter morning and evening services, and introduced the observance of All Angels (29 September). Copinger states that it included forms prepared by Cardale, Drummond, and Carlyle, but does not say who was responsible for what.[28]

The increasing complexity of the Church's round of liturgical worship required definitive guidance as to the manner of its observance, and 1852 also saw the first edition of *General Rubrics*; before this, such rubrics as existed formed part of the service books.[29]

The next introduction was the use of holy water, in 1868. The long gap may have been to allow congregations to become familiar with the innovations, for as Isabella Gardiner had informed her brother in 1858, 'there are many to whom they do not give satisfaction.'[30] Cardale recalled that in 1853 the apostles had expressed their willingness for any tribe to introduce holy water, although no request had been made. The apostles had never intended that it should become compulsory; it was merely something which they had found widespread when they were gathering gold. He therefore would not sanction it until strong party feelings had been overcome, demonstrating again his sense of caution in liturgical matters. At the next meeting, however, he stated that prophecies had been given when the apostles were assembled at Albury, with the result that they had decided to adopt it in their chapel.[31] It was then taken up throughout the rest of the Church. No dissent appears to have been voiced, perhaps because Cardale followed his usual practice of preparing the way by teaching about it.[32] (Miller stated that its general introduction followed a request by a convert from

---

27. NC, 7 January 1852; Boase, *Supplementary Narrative*, 840.

28. Copinger, 'Annals,' 98.

29. Stevenson, 'Catholic Apostolic Eucharist,' 56. A further English edition appeared in 1878, and a Scottish edition in 1900.

30. Isabella Gardiner to Martin Irving, 8 December 1858.

31. MC, 3 June 1868, 271–74; 29 July 1868, 275.

32. Cardale, *Discourse on Holy Water*.

Roman Catholicism, although it had previously been used on an occasional basis.³³) The 1869 edition of the liturgy therefore included a form for the blessing of holy water, and also a form for the removal of the sacrament on the Lord's day. Before this, it had been removed in silence, and prophecy indicated that the time would come when this would again be the practice (it was so from 1901).

An edition of 1863 saw the Athanasian Creed moved to a point in the book which implied its use at all the great feasts, not simply All Saints (the Catholic Apostolic Church did not observe Trinity Sunday, believing that a feast was not intended to commemorate a doctrine but the saving acts of God).

From 1870 other forms continued to be added, two being for the assembly of the seven churches in London and for the presentation and dedication of candidates for the ministry. The apostles' final labors to do with the Church's outward organization included revision of the *Rubrics* and the provision of a *Book of Regulations* for England, which appeared in 1878 and was an extensive enlargement of *Regulations as to the Building and Repairing of Churches*, a small pamphlet issued in 1863. Work on the *Book of Regulations* had been one of Cardale's last tasks before he died, although Stevenson suggests that it was probably the work of (or completed by) Cardale's coadjutor from 1865, John Leslie, who had also completed the *General Rubrics*.³⁴

The final edition of the liturgy appeared in 1880. Woodhouse was now the only surviving apostle, and all additions to the liturgy after Cardale's death (notably the Prayer for Resurrection and Change) were issued on separate sheets, even if intended to be permanent.³⁵ Woodhouse considered that he had no authority to make any additions on his own, since these required approval by the apostolic college.³⁶

For all the stress on correct liturgical practice, however, it remained 'open to any minister, when moved by the Holy Ghost to do so, to vary the prayers, and to offer extempore prayers.'³⁷ We may see in this a recognition that the present liturgy, whilst greatly in advance of anything else in use in Christendom, was not yet perfect. But the relative perfection which was nevertheless deemed to inhere in the liturgy was now being advanced as an apologetic argument for accepting the Lord's Work.

The Church's distinctive views came to the fore in debate about whether to provide a rite of burial. Its hope was that the Lord would return and the faithful would be translated without seeing death, but of course it was not long before members and ministers began to die. In 1852, therefore, Cardale urged ministers to apply to the Church of England; he was very reluctant to supply a burial service, and prophecy

---

33. Miller, *Irvingism*, 1:301. He appears to claim support from Cardale's discourse for this statement, but Cardale made no reference to any such request.

34. Todd, [Pastoral letter, Advent 1879], 5; Stevenson, 'Catholic Apostolic Eucharist,' 59; Lancaster, 'Cardale,' 7, citing Stevenson to the author, 4 March 1977.

35. Flegg, 'Gathered under Apostles,' 243.

36. Anon., *Church in Bishopsgate. Sermon, October 14th, 1934*, 3.

37. Sitwell, *Purpose of God*, 224; cf. Carlyle, *Concerning the Right Order*, 44.

was 'very strong against it' (he might also have noted the problems faced by dissenters seeking burial in Anglican graveyards and the consequent need in many cases to provide their own burial grounds). But if Anglican clergy refused, as the Roman Catholic Church did in France, he would provide a service.[38] In fact, it was only in 1902, after all the apostles had died, that an order for the burial of the dead was published in England, although Drummond had issued an order for Scotland which was almost identical to the Church of England rite.[39]

Elsewhere, an edition of the liturgy for use in Canada first appeared in 1850, and the first for the USA in 1851. Drummond issued an edition for Scotland in 1849/50, and another in 1854 which followed the 1853 English liturgy but included collects for each week of the liturgical year; a further edition followed in 1862. One wonders whether the existence of a separate Scottish edition for so long owed something to Drummond's liturgical disagreements with Cardale. After Drummond's death, the English liturgy was adopted from Advent 1870 at the request of the Scottish angels.[40]

Editions in other languages tended to follow the latest English edition. German was the language in which the most translations and editions of the liturgy appeared. In 1849 an edition was published for North Germany, translated by the newly sealed Ernst Rossteuscher.[41] Among other features, it included a preface 'Ueber die rechte Weise des Gottesdienstes in der christlichen Kirche' (later published separately in English as *Concerning the Right Order of Worship in the Christian Church*), and metrical settings of the creed and liturgical hymns. Carlyle reported to the apostles that his 'first object' had been 'to introduce into the churches under my care the Liturgy in so far as it has been agreed upon by the Apostles at Albury.' That said, some material was included from Drummond's Scottish edition, including the placing of the eucharistic liturgy at the beginning of the book. Carlyle also introduced a few things of his own, including a collect for the division of the apostles (16 July). Another innovation which he introduced was the commemoration on 15 January of the appointment of the apostles to their fields of service, which he stated was following a medieval tradition of marking the dispersal of the first apostles.[42] An edition in 1850 added the psalter and a lectionary.

Apart from the liturgy itself, the only counterpart to the *General Rubrics* which I have traced was that compiled by Rossteuscher for use in North Germany: *Allgemeine Rubriken zu der Liturgie etc oder Regeln über die Vollziehung der Gottesdienste und der anderen kirchlichen Handlungen* (1864). A new book of rubrics and regulations

38. NC, 3 March 1852.

39. Christopher B. Heath, *Development*, 14.

40. Copinger, 'Annals,' 91, 128; Stevenson, 'Evolution'; cf. Priddle, 'List "E".'

41. Copinger, 'Annals,' 88, states that the 1849 edition was produced for South Germany, but it was published in Berlin.

42. DFP: C/11/19b, Carlyle, memorandum to the apostles, 21 March 1849; Copinger, 'Annals,' 91; Manfred Henke to the author, 6 June 2016.

modelled on those for England, *Allgemeine Rubriken oder Anweisungen zur Ausführung der Liturgie und andern Gottesdienste der Kirche*, was introduced at Pentecost 1880.[43] This was revised in 1895, when a third edition also appeared of the equivalent of the *Book of Regulations*: *Vorschriften für den Kirchendienst und die kirchliche Verwaltung*.

The liturgy was also translated into French (1850,[44] Swiss French 1851), Flemish (1851),[45] Danish (1861 from German, 1908 directly from English),[46] Dutch (1866), Italian (1894, after a visit by Capadose to Italy),[47] Swedish (1893/5), and Wendish and Polish (1902). In French, German, Dutch, and Danish, several editions appeared. Partial translations lacking most of the occasional offices appeared in Lettish or Latvian (1880) and Estonian (1890). Parts were also translated into Russian in 1901; although Russian-speakers would mostly have been Orthodox and hence legally forbidden to convert, there were a few in the country's congregations. Never was any part of the liturgy published in Spanish, probably because it was not until 1900 that any significant openings appeared. In general, once work in a particular country had begun to show promise, at least part of the liturgy was translated and published as soon as possible.

It is surely significant that the primary exposition of Catholic Apostolic theology was a work of learned liturgical theology, Cardale's *Readings upon the Liturgy*. This reflects the status of the liturgy, which came increasingly to be seen as one of the chief legacies of the restored apostles. After the problems of the early 1840s, Cardale saw the need to provide clear teaching on the liturgy so that ministers could grasp the rationale behind each part and so be enabled to offer it with understanding and conviction.[48] We have already seen that such careful preparation by teaching was his practice with successive liturgical and ceremonial innovations. Much of *Readings upon the Liturgy* was based upon courses of lectures given at the Central Church between 1847 and 1852 and published in parts from 1849, the sections on baptism, sealing, and ordination (left unfinished at Cardale's death) appearing from 1874.[49] Cardale worked his way through the eucharist (and other services in later parts), providing a commentary which is detailed but not complex, making it suitable for untrained but not unintelligent ministers who would have heard the original lectures on which the work was based. His approach, both in producing liturgical orders and in writing liturgical commentary, combined scholarship with prophetic light.[50] He argued that

43. AR 1880, 24.
44. Apparently translated by Dalton: Ackery, *Paper*, 15.
45. Copinger, 'Annals,' 92.
46. Stevenson, 'Catholic Apostolic Eucharist,' Chart D.
47. Copinger, 'Annals,' 169.
48. Miller, *Irvingism*, 1:244–45.
49. Copinger, 'Annals,' 84, 86, opp. 87, 91, 92, opp. 95; Lancaster, 'Cardale,' 89 (although Lancaster states that the lectures began in 1849). Section III of Lancaster's work offers an overview of key theological themes in *Readings upon the Liturgy*.
50. Mast, *Eucharistic Service*, 34.

he used existing liturgical material where possible, but since this had been compiled when the Christian Church was in an apostate condition, it was impossible to avoid modifying them or producing new forms.[51] So he combined the quest for a primitive liturgical order, from which all others derived, with the application of prophetic light concerning the divinely ordained pattern of worship, and the attempt (in obedience to prophecy) to collate the 'best practice' of various branches of contemporary Christendom. He was thus primitivist, prophetic, and ecumenical. We should note that in this respect Cardale and his fellow apostles appear to have restricted themselves to the older established portions of Christendom—I have found no evidence that they drew on British dissenting or continental Pietist traditions, such as the Moravians, and it is noteworthy that *Readings upon the Liturgy* engaged with Roman Catholic, Orthodox, Anglican, and medieval Jewish thinking, but almost never with Protestant thought or practice. According to Cardale, much of the prophetic light on which he drew came over a period of time from 'one Prophet distinguished by the gift of God bestowed on him'—almost certainly Taplin.[52] However, none of Taplin's published writings appear to relate to this, and there are no accessible copies of the *Record* from the period, so we cannot explore how this process worked.

Prophecy was a primary source for the fundamental principle governing the structure and content of Catholic Apostolic worship, which was that the Christian Church was the antitype of the Mosaic Tabernacle. 'The Spirit of Christ speaking through prophets in these last days has shown in divers ways, and at many times, that the forms of worship prescribed of old to the Jews, present the true method in which God must ever be approached by His fallen and redeemed creatures.'[53] As the correspondence between the two was worked out in the light of prophecy, the apostles came to understand the extent of Christendom's departure from God's ways; the restoration of a right order of worship in the churches under them was intended as a pattern for all others.[54] The appeal to the Levitical pattern has been seen more recently as evidence of a lack of appreciation of the element of development in Scripture,[55] but in this the Church would have been no different from the pre-critical approach of most other contemporary clergy and writers. One feature of the liturgy which reflected the Levitical ordinances—perhaps unintentionally—was its complexity: Prior as a deposed former minister may have been jaundiced in describing it as 'a greater puzzle than Bradshaw's time table,' but he explained that often he had to find the right place in the service for his colleagues.[56]

---

51. DFP: C/11/7, Cardale to Drummond, 11 February 1847.
52. Cardale, *Readings*, 1:548.
53. Drummond, *Rationale*, 5.
54. Sitwell, *Purpose of God*, 203.
55. Tripp, 'Liturgy,' 452.
56. Prior, *My Experience*, 20 (quotation), 21. Bradshaw was by this point the main railway timetable for Britain and Ireland.

Whilst the apostles sought to use as much existing material as they could, there were some services for which this was not possible, usually because the Catholic Apostolic understanding went beyond that of existing Churches, or because the service had no parallel in existing liturgies. For instance, Christopher B. Heath later wrote, with reference to the order for All Saints' Day (most of which was newly composed): 'It is not surprising that so little was found that could be used, since the Exhortation and Confession refer to Catholic sins which no Christian body outside Apostles' fellowship has so far found grace to acknowledge; and the prayers for the fulfilment of God's promises of salvation to all men cover too wide a field to come within the range of any ministry less than apostolic.'[57] The baptismal order, too, was largely new. By contrast, the litany and the marriage service were very largely as found in the Book of Common Prayer.[58] Heath reckoned that three-quarters of the liturgy was new,[59] but Stevenson's researches demonstrate that this was a serious overestimate. Stevenson's verdict is judicious: the liturgy was 'Roman in its overall shape and structure; Anglican in its language and comprehensiveness; Oriental in certain defined themes; Biblical in a great deal of new and old but adapted material; and liturgically erudite in its original features.'[60] Liturgy, then, was another area of tension between the Catholic Apostolic Church's desire to be seen as a focus for Christian reunion and its sense of mission to gather gold from all quarters of Christendom, and its enforced separate existence and worship.

Critics might ask why the apostles gave so much attention to the preparation of a liturgy when they were expecting the Second Coming of Christ.[61] The answer would be that the restoration of the right order of worship was integral to the preparation of the Church for presentation to Christ as his bride, and in a sense therefore could be said to hasten the Lord's return.

## THE PATTERN OF WORSHIP

The weekly pattern of services as finally developed was as follows. On Sundays there was a morning service at 6 a.m, forenoon service and eucharist at 10 a.m., afternoon service at 2 p.m. (when communion was given to those unable to attend in the morning), 5 p.m. evening service, and an evening sermon, often followed, or replaced by, an evangelist sermon. At times, as we saw, there was also a teaching session for the children during the afternoon.

On weekdays in larger churches there were morning and evening services at 6 a.m. and 5 p.m. (said to be the first and last hours of the day according to Jewish

---

57. Christopher B. Heath, *Development*, 13.
58. Ibid., 11, 13.
59. Ibid., 15.
60. Stevenson, 'Catholic Apostolic Eucharist,' 304.
61. Tripp, 'Liturgy,' 451.

reckoning),⁶² and prayers at 9 a.m. and 3 p.m. where there were sufficient ministers, as well as the litany each Wednesday and Friday, and a daily eucharist where there were sufficient clergy.⁶³ There were also meetings, often on Wednesday evenings, for such purposes as teaching, the exercise and training of spiritual gifts, reading the *Record* (which might well stimulate further prophetic utterance), and district meetings for elders to meet the portion of the flock under their care.⁶⁴ So tightly organized was the Church's worship that the 1869 *Church Almanac* even included 'Forms of Notices' to be given out on specific dates during the year and covering every observance.⁶⁵ The three great feasts observed were those of Christmas, Easter, and Pentecost. Good Friday was kept as a day of humiliation, and All Angels and All Saints as days of thanksgiving.⁶⁶ Special observances were also appointed from time to time. In 1892 a day of humiliation was observed on account of an influenza epidemic, and another the following year on account of apprehended famine. The cessation of the epidemic was marked by a day of thanksgiving.⁶⁷

With such a full round of worship, Woodhouse showed himself reluctant to introduce extra-liturgical gatherings such as prayer meetings. In 1883, he laid down that if a full complement of services could be held, the place of such meetings was unclear. Moreover, it was impracticable to hold them during the daytime and wrong to bring the flock together in the evening to pray for things already prayed for during the day's services. Evening prayer meetings were therefore to be exceptional, and for a specific object. Another argument against them was that the time from 6 a.m. to 6 p.m. was for work, and the hours after that for rest; this rhythm was not to be interfered with unnecessarily. A final argument was more pragmatic: 'The gathering of young people together in the evenings in the Churches of the land, & the bringing of them in this way together, is believed in many cases to lead to very painful consequences, & it has been spoken of among us as a very serious evil.' But he admitted that such meetings could have a purpose where there was not a full complement of services.⁶⁸

In practice, prayer meetings could have more of a place in Catholic Apostolic life than Woodhouse allowed. They were introduced because extempore prayer had been virtually extinguished by liturgical forms, to enable laymen to pray from the heart under the impulse of the Holy Spirit; they also provided an opportunity for gift in young men to be developed by practice and observed by ministers. They may also have expressed the same impulse which had led to the introduction in 1858 of

---

62. These appear to have been observed generally since the earliest days; cf. Isabella Irving to her parents, 2 January 1835.

63. Cf. Sitwell, *Purpose of God*, 225; Miller, *Irvingism*, 2:58.

64. E.g. at the Central Church in London: Rupert M. Heath, *Lecture: The Lord's Pattern*, 6–7.

65. Anon., *Church Almanac* (1869), 26–30.

66. Sitwell, *Purpose of God*, 225.

67. BIA, CAC 1/2, 12 February, 20 April 1892, 4 July 1893.

68. AD, June 1883, 89–92, quotation at 92.

the 'Three Seasons Prayers', calling on God to raise up men for ministry, and may have reflected the popularity of prayer meetings in Evangelical circles influenced by the revival outbreak of 1858–62. It is perhaps significant that the first of the topics suggested for prayer in the *Book of Regulations* is the outpouring of the Holy Spirit. In 1861 Cardale expressed his concern to the angels in his tribe that in some churches they were declining. Three years later, in a ministry given in London, he urged the support not only of the liturgical intercession but also of prayer meetings. Doubtless some members, especially if they were reacting against an upbringing in which such gatherings were popular, were tempted to despise them.[69]

Extant registers of services, similar in conception to those still kept in the Church of England, detail how this pattern of worship worked out in practice. One for Bradford, covering the years 1880–85, has columns for date, type of service, officiating ministers, attendance (broken down under angels, priests, deacons, male and female lay members, and non-communicants), the presiding ministers, baptisms or churchings, the homilist or preacher, and 'Subjects of ministries, &c., and Remarks,' which could include comment on such matters as the weather and its effect on attendance.[70] On Sundays, there was a full round of services. During the week there were daily services at 6 a.m. and 5 p.m., a 10 a.m. eucharist on Tuesdays, and a 9 a.m. forenoon service on Wednesdays, along with a eucharist and a meeting for the flock at 7.30 p.m. However, the services for Monday and Saturday mornings were usually omitted; indeed, weekday services were very poorly attended, sometimes by nobody apart from the ministers. (In some congregations, the 1870s saw the formation of guilds of lay members who organized themselves in relays to attend the weekday services.[71]) Lay attendance generally was over two-thirds women, but that was compensated for by the number of male ministers. Most months, the Wednesday evening meetings included one for the exercise of spiritual gifts and another for reading the *Records*. There were monthly teachings by deacons, and also by priests. Less frequently there were elders' meetings, special meetings, congregational meetings, and committals to pastorship (equivalent to reception into membership in nonconformist churches), as well as the reading of the 'Annual Reports' or of ministry by the apostle. Evangelist sermons became a weekly feature. There were also district meetings in various parts of the city and in local towns.

Among the more unusual items recorded in the Bradford council minutes is the decision in 1902 to commence weekday services at six minutes past the hour, only

---

69. MC, 10 July 1861, 137; *Book of Regulations*, §§520–29; AC, 26 June 1912, 5; the coadjutors cited as their sources a German circular from Woodhouse dated October 1860 and Cardale's comments in MC, 30 November 1859, 10 July 1861. The German circular (with another on the same topic from 1883) appears in Anon., *Sammlung*, 103–8. See also Copinger, 'Annals,' 117.

70. BIA, CAC 1/9, Bradford Register of Services.

71. Miller, *Irvingism*, 1:324.

special services commencing on the hour (at 'town time').[72] The roots of this lay in the injunction that the times of the hours of morning and evening prayer were to be determined by the sun, not by Greenwich mean time (which had become the legal time in Great Britain in 1880). In this way there would be a chain of churches encircling the world and offering prayer.[73] Similarly, one Edinburgh deacon explained in 1908 that services there began a quarter of an hour later than appointed by the apostles (as a divine command) because the city lay thirteen minutes west of Greenwich.[74]

There are occasional references in the literature to other types of gathering apart from those already mentioned, but these would have been permitted rather than prescribed. For example, the young men at the Central Church formed 'The Gordon Square Literary and Scientific Society.'[75] Some items connected with young people's meetings were published.[76] After 1901 such meetings would become increasingly important in maintaining a sense of group identity.

Regrettably, space precludes consideration of the architecture and internal layout of Catholic Apostolic church buildings as expressing the apostles' convictions regarding worship.[77] We may note, however, that the first purpose-built church opened in 1834, in Islington, and the first on the continent at Bublitz in Germany in 1851.[78] Buildings were always to be open, and ministers available to speak with any wishing spiritual counsel.[79] This was certainly the case at Gordon Square, for a late nineteenth-century invitation card giving service times and church opening hours noted: 'A Minister is always in attendance to answer any enquiries concerning the faith and hope of the Church, particularly as to the Lord's present work by His restored Apostleship.'[80]

## Music

Another move away from Irving's Presbyterianism came with the introduction of hymns. The 1842 liturgy had only three: *Adeste fideles*, 'Hark the glad sound,' and *Veni Creator*. However, the flourishing of English hymnody around the middle of the century led to a felt need for a Catholic Apostolic hymnal.[81] A number of Catholic Apostolic writers had issued collections of verse in hymn form intended for private

---

72. BIA, CAC 1/7, Bradford MC, 14 May 1902.
73. Rupert M. Heath, *Lecture: The Lord's Pattern*, 4.
74. Laing, *Diaconal Teaching*, 5–6.
75. Samuel Gardiner to Martin Irving, 16–19 October 1862.
76. Anon., *The Apostles' Testimony 1838*; Wood, *Reports*.
77. For more detail, see Grass, 'Architecture.'
78. Copinger, 'Annals,' 44; Schröter, *Bilder*, 159, 216.
79. Drummond, *Rationale*, 15.
80. BOC, Scrapbook containing invitations to special services etc., 15.
81. Hughes, 'The Hymn Book,' in idem, *Readings*, 369–79, at 372.

devotional use, although the only apostle who would write any hymns was Woodhouse.[82] The first Catholic Apostolic hymnal to appear was not in English but the German *Hymnologium* (1859), which included no hymns by Catholic Apostolic writers or expressing the movement's distinctive ideas among its 145 items.[83] A second edition, edited by Rossteuscher, appeared in 1866, and by the fifth (1877), the book had grown to 344 hymns.[84]

Cardale, who was perhaps proceeding cautiously, stated in 1862 that he saw no objection to compiling a hymnal for each tribe, which would cover the main feast days as well as possibly including a range of hymns for subordinate and evangelist services.[85] Accordingly the first English edition, *Hymns for the Use of the Churches*, appeared in 1864, containing 205 hymns, and the second, definitive edition in 1871, containing 320 hymns (arranged in sections corresponding to the major divisions of the liturgy, and including some which reflected distinctive Catholic Apostolic beliefs and practices) and a section of doxologies. It was edited by E. W. Eddis (1825–1905), who also contributed around sixty hymns to the revision, almost all written after 1860 and possibly produced in response to perceived needs. Some hymns from other traditions were amended to make them conformable to Catholic Apostolic doctrine.[86] This was an era in which the ancient hymns of the Christian Church were enjoying a renaissance under the aegis of the Oxford Movement and kindred groupings, but rather than using well-known renditions of Greek and Latin texts, these were often re-translated for the volume, doubtless for copyright reasons, although no Catholic Apostolic translations have achieved wider currency. As with the liturgy, much existing material was used; even so, ninety-three hymns were by Catholic Apostolic authors, including those by Eddis.[87] Six were said to have begun as prophetic utterances, and Hughes argued that hymns developed that part of human nature which was addressed by prophecy.[88]

In 1908 a Danish edition appeared which was modelled on the English book but which, whilst including a few hymns by Catholic Apostolic writers, gave far more space to hymns by the Danish theologian N. F. S. Grundtvig (1783–1872).[89] His thought had affinities with Lutheran Pietism, and its influence in Denmark undoubtedly helped to prepare the way for the Church's success in that country.[90] A Swedish hymnal appeared in 1886, and hymnals are also known to have been produced in French, Norwegian

---

82. Woodhouse, *Poems*.
83. *Hymnologium*.
84. Kohler, *Het Irvingisme*, 427; Rossteuscher, ed., *Hymnologium*.
85. MC, 19 March 1862, 147.
86. J. E. G., 'Touching on Music,' *News Letter* 2 (April 1952) 20–22, at 21.
87. Hughes, 'Hymn Book,' 372–73.
88. Ibid., 375, 378.
89. *Kirkelig sangbog*; K. N. and H. H., 'Kirkemusik,' *Ungdomsbladet* 5/4 (February 1957) 3–5.
90. Cf. AR 1881, 39–40.

and Polish.⁹¹ Hymnody, then, was one way in which Catholic Apostolics could relate a form of spirituality which was regarded as transcending national distinctions to varying local religious contexts.

A number of tunes were written for the English book by Dr Edmund Hart Turpin (1835–1907), who served as organist and choirmaster at Gordon Square from 1860 until his death. Although his connection with the Church was 'purely professional,' the musical side of its worship bore his stamp as clearly as the liturgical side did that of Cardale.⁹² His compilation of *Hymn Tunes* (1872) was intended to accompany the revision of the hymnal. It came to be treated as the main, or even the only, source of tunes, although one writer in the 1950s ventured to criticize this monopoly, claiming that some congregations had been prohibited by the authorities from using any other collection.⁹³ Given the amount of new tunes which had achieved widespread use in various denominations since Turpin's collection appeared, which members migrating to those denominations would have encountered, one can understand that some might have felt that Catholic Apostolic worship had become stuck in a hymnological time warp. Other musicians—not known to be Catholic Apostolic members—also wrote for the Church, such as Paul Della Torre and Peter Dickson in Edinburgh.⁹⁴ Among members, the angel Walter A. Copinger, a man of many parts, produced a collection of thirty-five hymn tunes in 1883, enlarged to seventy-five two years later.⁹⁵ However, no tunes written for Catholic Apostolic worship became widely known outside the Church, certainly not in Britain.

In spite of Turpin's dominance, there may have been some regional variation in matters connected with music. For instance, the nonconformist background of the Bishopsgate congregation in London was still evident as late as the 1950s in its preference for hymn tunes which allowed for hearty congregational singing (something which would have rendered some Catholic Apostolic writers on music distinctly uneasy) and the use of Anglican rather than Gregorian chants.⁹⁶

Smaller booklets of hymns also appeared in England from 1870 onwards, some were designed for evangelist services, and others for use with children; the evangelist service booklets were basically selections from the main hymnal. In 1890 there appeared Newdigate Burne's *Hymns, with Tunes, for the Use of Children and Young Persons*, probably intended for Sunday School and home use, but also used by some

---

91. *Hymnologium*.

92. Pearce, *Biographical Sketch*, 17, quoting Henry S. Hume in the *Musical Herald*, 1 December 1907.

93. J. E. G., 'Touching on Music,' 20.

94. Works by both are included on a CD recorded by the choir of St Mary's Episcopal Cathedral, *Music of the Catholic Apostolic Church* (2004).

95. Copinger, *Contributions*.

96. W., 'The Church in Bishopsgate,' *Newsletter* 4 (April 1953) 8; cf. Peck, *Church Music*. For general principles, see Anon., *Book of Regulations*, §§530–32.

Catholic Apostolic day schools.[97] Whilst many of the hymns were by Catholic Apostolic authors (such as Eddis, Jane E. Leeson, A. E. Maxwell, George Morris, and Esther Wiglesworth), surprisingly little reference was made to distinctive Catholic Apostolic teachings, especially when we remember that hymnody often served as an important means of inculcating religious teaching in children.

## Preaching

Given the importance of preaching as a mode of edifying and instructing the faithful and presenting the Church's message to outsiders, it is worth outlining Catholic Apostolic thinking regarding the nature and function of preaching. A primary consideration to bear in mind is the distinction between the homily form, used in the eucharist and intended primarily to draw out the hearts of the hearers toward God in worship, and the sermon proper, which might be addressed to members as an exposition of 'the things most surely believed' among them, or to outsiders. Within the sermon form, preaching and teaching could be distinguished. Paying tribute to the New England puritan preachers, Samuel J. Andrews, at the opening of a new Catholic Apostolic place of worship in 1876, asserted: '[p]reaching is for those without; teaching is for those within.'[98] Many years earlier, Cardale had also distinguished between preaching and teaching, but slightly differently: the former was not necessarily to insiders; it aimed to persuade and to win the heart, and deployed rhetoric. Evangelists and pastors had distinctive approaches, but each gift partook to some extent of the other. Where a church required preaching, angels should use whichever ministers were gifted.[99] Lay preaching, however, was not approved of, which put the Church at odds with late nineteenth-century revivalist movements, in which lay agency was extensively used. Lay assistants might not preach or expound in public; if they were fit to preach, then they could be ordained as deacons. Preaching and teaching, in Cardale's view, needed 'the grace of orders.'[100]

But ordination was evidently not enough; frequent criticism was made, especially during the late nineteenth century, of the poor quality of much preaching within the movement. This may be put down in part to the lack of formal training. As with the Brethren, a likely problem was a lingering belief that what mattered most was the inspiration of the Holy Ghost. Occasionally a short practical course of lectures was

---

97. Burne, ed., *Hymns*; J. E. G., 'Touching on Music,' 22.

98. Samuel J. Andrews, *Sermon on entering*, 13. His comment anticipated a key thesis of Dodd, *Apostolic Preaching*, which was that in the New Testament there was a distinction between *kerygma*, preaching addressed to those outside the Church which presented the foundational truths of the gospel and called for commitment, and *didache*, teaching addressed to Christians which dealt with doctrinal and ethical themes.

99. NC, 4 February 1852.

100. MC, 13 February 1866, 228. This is why services today, which are conducted by underdeacons or lay assistants, include the reading of an old sermon rather than the preaching of a new one.

given, Bayford lecturing on sermon composition in London during 1862, for example.[101] A few short works also offered advice. In 1889 James Heath, angel at Birmingham, issued a three-page lithographed memorandum which posed four questions to homilists.

- Who are you speaking to? God's people, who have just confessed their sins and been absolved, so 'they are to be addressed as being perfect in Christ, as being already what they should be.' No blame is therefore to be assigned for any shortcomings.
- Who are you speaking for? The Lord, 'but immediately for the Celebrant.'
- Why are you speaking? A homily is to be an enforcement of the gospel which prepares the hearers to offer their sacrifice of thanksgiving.
- What are you speaking about? The homily should be based on the Gospel reading, not the epistle, although other readings will help the homilist determine the keynote for the day.

Heath pointed up a common failing in homilies: 'it is most wearisome to be told for the five hundredth time that we have now arrived at such and such a period of the Church's year, that we have been celebrating this, that and the other, and we are now going to celebrate something else. All this is mere packing, mere paper and string; why should you not open your parcel beforehand, and show us at once what you have got inside?' This was all the more necessary because the homily should last only ten minutes at the outside. To affect the hearers, it should have only one idea, and its great aim was 'to show the people their oneness with the Lord Jesus Christ . . . and calling [them] to join Him in offering the sacrifice of thanksgiving.'

Delivery was another issue which Heath felt it necessary to address: 'how is it that with scarcely an exception homilies are read and not spoken, even by ministers who on other occasions speak without manuscript?' If keeping to time was the issue, in the Birmingham church there was a clock in front of the preacher! And as the object was to move the heart rather than the head, the homilist who read could not be totally successful.[102] But another reason for the prevalence of reading homilies, not mentioned by Heath, must have been the fact that texts were supposed to be retained by the church for future reference.

William H. B. Proby (1832–1915), an Anglican priest whose orders were confirmed in 1874, gave a series of lectures to a Catholic Apostolic congregation on preaching, published in 1901.[103] He distinguished preaching from prophecy very clearly: 'In prophecy, the Holy Ghost speaks by the man. In preaching, the man speaks by the grace of the Holy Ghost: and in thus speaking, the man uses his own natu-

---

101. Samuel Gardiner to Martin Irving, 19 January 1862.
102. James Heath, *Memorandum*.
103. 'Old Preacher,' *Letters*.

ral faculties.'[104] That being so, preachers were to make every effort to develop those faculties, and to acquire the necessary range of learning, including the biblical languages. Proby wanted to see an intelligent, thoughtful approach to the task, rather than dogmatic restatement of familiar themes. His work is most notable, however, because he ventured to criticize the preaching of the apostles, especially Armstrong and Cardale: 'neither Mr. Armstrong nor Mr. Cardale is to be considered as forming a good model for sermon-composition. And I have no doubt that the heaviness of which I seem to have to complain so often when listening to discourses from apostolic ministers is owing in large measure to the fact of Mr. Cardale and Mr. Armstrong being studied amongst us so much.'[105]

At the local level, considerable concern was shown about the length of homilies and other pulpit utterances. According to the Huddersfield council minutes in 1892, teachings after the shorter evening service were not to exceed twenty minutes; evangelists when preaching to the flock were not to exceed forty-five minutes, and the elder was asked to report any minister from Manchester (the parent church) who went on too long![106] The following year, a new angel laid down maximum lengths as: homilies ten minutes, sermons twenty minutes, teachings with shorter evening service an hour, and teachings by the four ten minutes each.[107]

## WHAT HAD HAPPENED TO THE CHARISMATA?

For a definition of the nature and function of prophecy as it came to be understood by the apostles, we turn to Cardale's 1868 discourse. He defined prophecy as speech by inspiration of another spirit; true prophecy was under the gifted individual's control, and used their voice and modes of thinking and expression.[108] We noted earlier his stress on prophesying appropriately and keeping within one's border. At all times the ruler was the discerner and judge of prophecy, whether the angel in the local church or the apostle in the universal Church.[109] The stress on observing boundaries was also evident in a paper given by Edward Heath in 1891: women were not to prophesy as independent or as having authority, laymen were not to prophesy as ministers, deacons were not to prophesy as priests, and ministers in a local church were not to prophesy as ministers of the universal Church.[110] The detailed instructions regarding

---

104. Ibid., 4.
105. Ibid., 65.
106. BIA, CAC 4/5, Huddersfield MC, 20 April 1892.
107. Ibid., 12 July 1893.
108. Cardale, *Short Discourse*, 3–5; cf. Flegg, *Nature, Character and Place of Prophecy*, 10: 'the light and the words are of the Holy Ghost, but the construction of the sentences, and the general form of the word, are such as are peculiar to the man who is being used.'
109. Cardale, *Short Discourse*, 8–9.
110. Edward Heath, *Paper on Prophecy*, 8–9.

prophecy imply that it was not viewed *tout court* as the word of God, since it could be prophecy and yet not to the point, out of place, and so on. As was explained to a conference of angels in England in 1889, the individual was responsible for what was human in the exercise of the gift: the time, place, occasion, manner, mode, words, and acts. In addition, a prophetic gift could be practised in meetings for spiritual gifts, implying that it was capable of human development.[111]

The charismatic gifts, especially those of tongues and interpretation, prophecy, discernment of spirits, and healing, remained significant in Catholic Apostolic spirituality. In a rare account of what it felt like to experience 'the power,' one minister made the point that '[w]hat is history to other Christians is present experience to us. The miracles & other wonders of the Bible are no difficulties to us because we experience the same power in which they were done.'[112] Certainly prophecy was meant to be experienced: indeed, an impulse to speak was the sign that words were being given.[113]

Enthusiasm in the exercise of spiritual gifts was not approved of. In a sermon preached after Taplin's death in 1862, Cardale summed up his contribution to the Church, and commended his manner of speaking as sober rather than excitable, unlike many who engaged in prophetic utterance.[114] Similarly, when the acting pillar of prophets, James F. Prentice, died in 1881, Woodhouse paid tribute to his quiet and calm manner of speaking in power without excessive wordiness or excitement, which inspired confidence in the purity of his utterances.[115] A paper from Woodhouse in 1890 called on angels to ensure that prophets avoided excessive loudness and extravagant gesture.[116]

Any member might speak in prophecy at meetings for spiritual gifts.[117] But recognition as a prophet required ordination, and hence approval by one's superiors. 'Except by special permission, lay persons were not allowed to speak in prophecy in the services of the church.'[118] Woodhouse summed up what was required in a prophet, showing incidentally the way in which the charismata were now firmly subordinated to apostolic rule and also exercised within an ongoing tradition, thus lessening (though by no means eliminating) the risk of what might be called 'loose cannon' utterances.

> For the due fulfilment of the prophetic office it is necessary that the Prophets should have an intimate knowledge of, and acquaintance with Holy Scripture;

111. MC, 31 July 1889, 14, 18; cf. Heath, *Paper on Prophecy*, 9.

112. Hopkinson Papers, Algernon Willis to Mrs [M.] Parnell, Good Friday [25 March] 1910.

113. Flegg, *Nature, Character and Place of Prophecy*, 12.

114. Cardale, *Sermon on the Death of Taplin*, 4; cf. Woodhouse, 'Ueber das prophetische Amt,' in Anon., *Sammlung*, 69–82, at 78–81. Compare Cardale's comments with the description in ch. 2 above.

115. AR 1881, 1.

116. MC, paper following 7 May 1890.

117. Flegg, *Nature, Character and Place of Prophecy*, 14.

118. Rupert M. Heath, *Lecture: The Lord's Pattern*, 7.

soundness of doctrine, not a doctrine derived from supposed prophetic light or revelation, not a doctrine that he learns from his own spirit, but that derived from the teaching of the Apostles and the ministers under them; an acquaintance with the light of prophecy already given, and accepted by the Apostles as true and suited to the present time; a knowledge of his true place and standing as one of a fourfold ministry, all equally inspired by the Holy Ghost according to the character and duties of their respective offices; a clear recognition of the Apostolic office, whether in the Apostles themselves or in those appointed by them to places of rule, as that to which he is subordinated and by which he is upheld and preserved; and a cheerful and ready submission to their discernment regarding the words spoken by him, and regarding the way on which they should be acted upon, or, for the present passed by; and a perfect consciousness of the border of the individual prophet and of the suitableness of his word to the place he is for the time occupying.[119]

Prior presented another side to Catholic Apostolic practice regarding spiritual gifts, however, claiming that any suggestion by a prophet that the apostles' views were wrong would lead to being suspected of having an evil spirit. 'A difficulty of this kind, in one instance, led to the closing of a church for some years, and the congregation being told to go to their parish church.' A falling off in prophecy led to the introduction of meetings for spiritual gifts, which Prior called 'a school for the manufacture of prophets.' Finally, there was a temptation for gifted men to seek distinction by means of prophetic utterances: 'I have seen more than one case of a poor man of scanty education being put into a position as a minister and a gentleman, because he prophesied although he could not preach.'[120]

Angels were responsible for gifted persons, and should preside at meetings for the exercise of spiritual gifts.[121] In at least one instance (at Drammen in Norway) a minister was raised to the episcopate specifically in order to provide the necessary instruction and oversight.[122] As part of this oversight, they might take exception to words of prophecy which went beyond Scripture or contradicted it, overstepped the prophet's place or border, had the character of teaching or laid down doctrine, were obscure or unintelligible, too long or rambling, mixed the agent's own words with it, were not in place, or were not in harmony with the service.[123] The relationship between prophecy and ministry (we might say, between charisma and authority) was stated in the minutes of council during 1889:

> Difficulty in properly ordering this matter, had arisen from the exaggerated and almost superstitious estimate of the gift of Prophecy, placing the word of

---

119. Woodhouse, *Teaching on the Prophetic Office*, 6.
120. Prior, *My Experience*, 34–36.
121. On the conduct of such meetings, see Anon., *General Rubrics*, §§I.XII.2, 10.
122. Diersmann, *Notes*, 73–74, following AR 1887, 50.
123. MC, 30 November 1881, 129–31.

Prophecy above the word of ministry, which prevailed in the first days of the Lord's work, and was then the source of much trouble and confusion.

We must remember that the word of ministry for which the Minister is responsible, is, if legitimate ministry, the word of the Lord Jesus Christ, as much as the word of Prophecy for which the prophetic person is answerable, is the word of the Spirit of the Lord Jesus Christ, and that the word of ministry is the word of authority, which the word of prophecy is not.[124]

But how was prophecy to be disseminated once spoken? In 1832 Irving wrote regarding the utterances: 'Unless the Spirit says, Write, it is more than questionable whether any thing ought to be written.'[125] In Scotland, the Macdonalds ceased to record utterances as they were not sure that it was right to do so.[126] Prophecy in both England and Scotland repeatedly forbade the writing down or verbatim reporting of prophetic utterances.[127] Yet very soon scribes were appointed to take them down, Baxter's case having shown that prophets were often less able than others to recall their own words.[128] In the mature movement, prophecy was taken down by a scribe at the time of utterance. These transcriptions were kept locally for a year, but also forwarded to the apostles at Albury.[129] 'The consideration of words of prophecy and the use to be made of them was a duty to which the Apostles devoted a large part of their time and the greatest attention and care.'[130] Their revision before submission entailed considerable work, and angels were asked to be selective in what they sent.[131]

We noted above that the Church did not regard prophecy as possessing an authority equal to that of Scripture. In this connection, it is significant that none of the words in the *Record* were cast in the first person, as if God were speaking them directly: this would have given them a tone of authority which was inappropriate, and it would have made it harder for ministers to evaluate or 'weigh' them before sending them on. These words often reflected on aspects of the passages read during a particular service, and, as Cardale explained, Scripture was God's word for all times, committed to the Church's perpetual custody, whereas prophecy was given for particular times and places. 'The Records were never intended to be a perpetual Commentary on the Scriptures. If they were they would necessarily be of equal authority. And therefore when the Records were first sent to the Angels they were bidden to burn them as soon as used.'[132] But, as we have seen, they were kept, and published in permanent form.

---

124. MC, 31 July 1889, 13.

125. Lacy, *General Delusion*, 150 n.

126. Norton, *Memoirs*, 159–60.

127. Baxter, *Narrative*, 126.

128. Rossteuscher, 'Rebuilding,' 362.

129. Stevenson, 'Liturgical Year,' 134 n.

130. MC, 16 March 1864, 193.

131. Cf. MC, 17 July 1878, 89.

132. MC, 21 May 1856, 43; cf. MC, 4 November 1857, 73. This may be one reason why none are

Ministers referred to reading them over, and meetings were convened for doing so. By 1873, therefore, Cardale had to issue a clarification:

> The rule enjoining the destruction of words of Prophecy did not apply to words of Prophecy contained in the Records sent to the Angels, & still less to those accompanying the Determinations of the Apostles in Council. All such documents were intended to be preserved, & to form part of the Records of the particular Church. Copies ought not to be left in the hands of individuals. It is to such copies that the direction to destroy Records applies; extra copies, therefore, ought to be destroyed.[133]

There was, then, a sense in which words of prophecy, even if published, were not to be hoarded. Just after Cardale's death, Woodhouse found it necessary to remind the seven churches in London that:

> The words of prophecy sent round in the Records were referred to many years ago, and compared to the manna by which the children of Israel were fed in the wilderness.
> We were told to use them as subjects of meditation from day to day; they were not to be laid up; they were like manna, and as the manna would breed worms and stink when laid up, so of the words of prophecy . . .[134]

It is not surprising that, given the prominence of women in prophecy in Irving's day, when a typical defence of their public speaking had been that it was the Holy Ghost speaking through them,[135] the question of whether women could prophesy received careful consideration from Cardale in some directions issued in 1866. Working through the Pauline passages taken by some as silencing women, he concluded that 1 Corinthians 14:34-35 could not be an absolute prohibition on women speaking in assemblies for religious purposes, but on speaking which was indicative of non-subjection, and '[w]hether prophesying comes under this head depends upon the character of the prophesying.' As for where women might prophesy, the injunctions regarding women's head covering in 1 Corinthians 11:1-12 could not refer to domestic life, since Paul would not prescribe head coverings for home, or encourage prophesying at home. Indeed, 'I am quite clear that prophesying in the private or domestic circle—prophesying except in the presence of the Angel, or other person duly authorised to rule in the Church—is ordinarily, and otherwise than exceptionally, an abuse and disorderly exercise of the gift. We have full experience of the great danger of this practice, both to the persons gifted, and to those in habitual intercourse with them.' Here he doubtless had in mind the work's early history. That being so, the only sphere left was that of the congregation, and especially (but not

---

extant from the earliest years.

133. MC, 15 October 1873, 405.
134. Woodhouse, *Teaching,* Sep. 11, 1877, 2.
135. Bayford, 'Prove all things,' 8–9.

exclusively) meetings for spiritual gifts. In prophesying, just as laypeople and ministers were to take care not to go beyond what was appropriate to their position, so too women should not go beyond what was appropriate to them. 'It is not the mind of the Lord ordinarily to teach through women, or to reveal mysteries, or to give light upon Holy Scripture, or to give light to the ruler of the church.' Taking 1 Corinthians 14:6 as referring to three types of prophecy—edification, exhortation, and comfort—he saw the last as particularly appropriate for women.[136]

In the Apostles' Determinations, it is noticeable how often, when a matter was discussed and a minute formulated, prophecy was spoken confirming the rightness of what had been done. Care was taken that prophets spoke as befitted their rank and border as well as the context, thus making prophecy more than usually pertinent, and much less of an explosive risk. Even so, words could be spoken—and acknowledged as genuine—which presented problems because once in circulation they were widely misinterpreted. In this way expectations regarding future developments could take root which the apostles or their coadjutors later found it necessary to deal with. After Cardale's death, for example, there were a number of prophecies, forwarded by apostles to the angels and hence deemed suitable for wider circulation, which could be (and sometimes were) interpreted as predicting that particular events would come to pass on certain dates. However, angels were warned against taking their interpretation into their own hands; this was a matter for the apostles, who were divinely guided in this just as the prophets were in speaking. Congregations were warned against date-fixing, but also against spiritualizing away these words.[137]

As for the relationship between prophecy and tongues, Woodhouse explained that either prophecy rendered the tongue in English, or the tongue called attention to a following prophecy. A member given an interpretation of a message in tongues should inform the angel at the time.[138] In 1891 Edward Heath, in a private paper to the angels, expressed the view that 1 Corinthians 14 was not directly applicable in the current situation, which seems a somewhat more sophisticated approach than that of Cardale, perhaps because Heath was much younger and of a generation which was more likely to have been influenced by new thinking in the area of biblical studies. For one thing, it was no longer possible to determine the exact nature of the gatherings there described. Heath was conscious of the relative poverty of the Church's experience of spiritual gifts and consequently reluctant to offer systematic teaching which might come across as more dogmatic than that experience warranted.[139] The conference at which this paper appears to have been given also heard how, at a visi-

---

136. Cardale, *Directions*, 1–2. The authorities at Gordon Square kept this work circulating until at least 1970, long after prophecy had been effectively prohibited in worship. Prophecy has continued to occur among Catholic Apostolics and to be taken down and circulated.

137. Pitcairn, *Notes*.

138. MC, 17 May 1882, 154–55.

139. MC, 16 December 1891, 83–85.

tation of the Nottingham church, Cardale had once instructed a prophet with the apostle that unless he had reason to expect a word of prophecy would follow (which would make that an interpretation of the tongue), he should not speak in a tongue. Heath went on to distinguish different types of tongues and explain their relation to the English word which followed them, with input from angels at Bishopsgate, the Central Church, and Islington. No firm conclusions were drawn, and the minutes have a tentative feel, marked by expectation of further light from experience. Accordingly, angels were invited to send up their experience of these things.[140] In spite of these loose ends, prophecy would assume renewed significance after Woodhouse's death in 1901, as the Church felt its way forward in a situation which many had never expected would come about.

---

140. Paper accompanying MC, 16 December 1891, 1–2, 12.

# PART III

## 1901 Onwards: The Church after Apostles

# 10

# The Church under Coadjutors (1901–29)

On 3 February 1901, the last of the twelve apostles, Francis Valentine Woodhouse, died at the age of ninety-five. Four Catholic Apostolic deacons were the bearers at his funeral, which took place in the parish church at Albury, and he was buried in the churchyard.[1]

In a pastoral letter written a few days later, Henry Hume of the Central Church wrote:

> This is an event of great moment, not only for us, who have been in the more immediate fellowship of the Apostles in these days, but for the whole church throughout the world. Its significance is emphasized by its occurrence within a few days of the death of the Sovereign of this realm, Queen Victoria, during whose long and blessed reign, and under whose protection, the work of the Lord by His Apostles has been carried on in peace and without hindrance.
> 
> These two actings of God constitute a very striking sign to the Church and to the world; and we may expect that they will be followed by great and unmistakable evidences of their importance.[2]

The force of this combination of events derived from the fact that the Catholic Apostolic Church owed a great deal to the Victorian soil in which it took root, as Walter Copinger acknowledged the following Sunday.

> While the nation mourns in courtly grief the loss of the greatest Sovereign . . . the Church experiences the loss of one of her mighty princes—the last survivor of her highest ministry on earth. Stranger still that the heavenly work in which this last master builder was engaged, was undoubtedly fostered and

---

1. Anon., 'Death of Woodhouse,' 5.
2. Hume, *Pastoral Letter*, 1.

> helped in development by the liberal and happy institutions of the country, whereof our beloved Queen was the representative and head.[3]

Ironically, when she came to the throne in 1837, Drummond had prognosticated that

> The death of the King, and the throwing of the government into the hands of a young girl will cause the feebleness of the hand that holds the reins to be felt throughout the whole; thus giving encouragement to the violent to bully and intimidate, while she will never have strength to bear up against the torrent of the age; it is said she expects her elevation is only a step to the scaffold, and such indeed seems the probable end of all the Sovereigns of Europe.[4]

As with the British Empire, things were never to be the same again for the Catholic Apostolic Church. Since the conferring of apostolic grace and commission was an essential part of ordination, no ordinations could take place after the apostles died; gradually the Church's structures and ministry were to be dismantled by death.

Although Hume exhorted his hearers to remain quietly at their posts, ready to endure mockery from outsiders, he acknowledged that the removal of the apostles was 'not that for which we once hoped' and that no provision had been made for such an eventuality. It appeared that the movement had come to the time prefigured in Revelation by the half-hour's silence following the opening of the seventh seal, a time of waiting to hear what God would speak.[5] Yet, although no provision for the future had been made, Hume could point to the fact that members had been forewarned, and could urge them to put their confidence in God whose work it was.[6] This period was not to be interpreted as the end of the Lord's work, but as the prelude to another stage (the second in the work by restored apostles). For the first time, the faithful were on the eve of God's act in raising the dead.[7] This sense of imminent expectation has remained strong over the decades and can still be picked up from remaining members.

How did those gathered under apostles in Britain carry out Hume's injunctions, what fulfillment of the vision did they recognize, and how were they affected by this turn of events? Part III of this book attempts to answer these questions. In what follows, little is said about their expectations regarding future events, partly because these were what members were specifically commanded to be silent about and I wish to respect that, and partly because they have not always been realized. Such expectations are therefore discussed only where they have influenced what happened.

---

3. Copinger, *Present Position*, 2.
4. Ward, 'Death of a Church,' 52–53, quoting Drummond, letter book, 131.
5. Hume, *Pastoral Letter*, 2–3.
6. Hume, *Address, 10 February 1901*, quoted by Newman-Norton, *Time of Silence*, 2.
7. Hume, *Address, 10 February 1901*, 7; quoted by Newman-Norton, *Time of Silence*, 5.

## PROPHETIC FOREWARNING OF WHAT WOULD HAPPEN

After 1901, the fact that the coadjutors and the churches did remain behind was often interpreted as evidence of the movement's failure to fulfill the will of God for it. This struck deep into the hearts of many: by one angel, the removal of apostles was seen 'both in the beginning and in the end of this dispensation, [as] the result of their rejection, through the sin and unfaithfulness of the Church.'[8] Yet although sermons frequently referred to the fact that this was not what many had expected and would test their faith, Woodhouse's death did not take the movement completely by surprise; leaders consistently emphasized that prophecy had forewarned that the work would enter another stage. Indeed, the loss of apostles could be seen not only as a chastening for unfaithfulness but also as a step forward in the divine purpose. At a conference of angels in London, Edward Heath agreed that it was right for the faithful to humble themselves, for they had hindered the work, but regarded the removal of apostles not as a punishment for sin but as 'a mighty step forward' in God's purpose; 'the very changes in our circumstances which are necessarily trying, are nevertheless tokens that we are nearer to the goal.'[9] This was in line with what the remaining apostles had written to the angels in 1875: 'This apparent withdrawal of the Apostles from your midst, to which many references have been made in words of prophecy is the *greatest advance* that has yet been made towards the bringing in of that day of the Lord, for which we have waited during the forty years which come to a close at the late Anniversary of their Separation.'[10]

However, Heath warned members against falling into the same error as other Christians, that of making schemes laying out what would happen in connection with the Second Coming; such prognostications represented a distraction from the need to watch for an event which would occur suddenly. The faithful were not to postpone their expectation simply because past predictions had proved false, but should realize that there were no events which must necessarily take place before the Second Coming and prepare themselves accordingly.[11]

The death of the last apostle could have led to a rash of prophetically-inspired speculation and date-fixing: within a few weeks Heath noticed 'sometimes a certain wildness in the words sent up' and there was a danger that members would view prophecy as a short-cut to obtaining divine guidance, as in the Old Testament dispensation.[12] He therefore enjoined great caution upon members in a paper on the subject the following year. He considered that statements concerning the Second Advent

---

8. Anon., *Ministries issued from Manchester*, 10.

9. AC, 'The following remarks were made by the Coadjutor Mr E. Heath at a conference held in London on the 22nd May 1901,' 2–3.

10. Copinger, 'Annals,' opp. 137.

11. Edward Heath, *Homily, November 5th, 1905*.

12. 'Report, 27th March 1901,' 26.

had too often been treated as dogmatic, whereas such matters, while objects of hope and prayer, were not defined, neither did they form part of the corpus of definitive apostolic teaching.[13] He continued to voice concern, presumably because there was a recurrent tendency among the rank and file to read into words of prophecy more than he considered justified: particular danger could arise from the prolongation of the time of silence and a consequent longing for light as to the movement's future direction.[14] In September 1923 he wrote:

> In sending out another number of the Record I desire to remind my brethren the Angels, and through them the Churches generally, that while the word of prophecy is indeed a light that shineth in a dark place, yet the right use of prophecy is not to enable us to determine times and seasons or to fix dates, but rather it is to quicken in our hearts the love of the Lord's appearing, and to help us to purify ourselves as He is pure.[15]

It is important, then, to note the extent to which post-1901 developments were interpreted as fulfilling previous prophetic words couched in quite specific terms, as well as more generally along the lines of Cardale's three-stage model, itself the fruit of prophecy inspired by study of Scripture. However, Catholic Apostolics sometimes commented on the overlap between successive stages of the Lord's work. Capadose provides a sample of their approach:

> The act of God in removing the last apostle from our midst, has suddenly altered not our hope, but our present condition here on earth. We cannot but thankfully acknowledge, that our Lord had forewarned us. For almost thirty years words of prophecy have pointed with always growing clearness to a possible removal of the apostleship. At the same time the churches were always more weaned from direct contact with apostles. In 1875[,] the fortieth year since their separation, the apostles determined to withdraw from personal visitation of the churches, committing this part of their work to their coadjutors.[16]

The gradual nature of the transition between stages meant that they were not totally unprepared for Woodhouse's death. Prophecy in 1868 had implied that the liturgical form introduced that year for the removal of the consecrated elements from the sanctuary was a sign of God's purpose to remove apostles, the sign of his presence, once again,[17] and in January 1873 it indicated (to the astonishment of many) that

---

13. Edward Heath, *Paper,* 29 June 1902, 1.
14. AC, 17 June 1910, 8.
15. *Record* 12/1 (1 September 1923) 1.
16. AC, Isaac Capadose in a statement on behalf of both coadjutors, 'Record of the Assembly of the Seven Churches in London held on the 26th February 1901,' 2.
17. Copinger, 'Annals,' 126, opp. 185.

all the apostles would eventually die and their work be taken up by coadjutors and archangels.[18]

In consequence, in spite of the fact that the situation came to pass for which the apostles had refused to provide, the work proceeded in an orderly manner, appealing to earlier prophecies and directives. Woodhouse's death entailed changes in many aspects of Catholic Apostolic belief and practice, and the two remaining coadjutors, Capadose and Heath, admitted that they were in a situation analogous to that of the movement's first years, when leaders had to feel their way without any precedents to guide them; it was, Heath believed, a salutary experience for those who, like him, had been brought up in the work.[19] Nevertheless, if an apostle did not consider that he had any right to leave instructions as to how the work should be ordered after his departure, much less did any coadjutor, angel, priest, deacon, or underdeacon see it right to do so, nor would the present trustees see it as their prerogative. As the legal successors of the seven deacons of the universal Church, the trustees appoint replacements to fill up their number, but refuse to go beyond implementing policies laid down by previous generations.

## THE WORK OF THE COADJUTORS

Prophecy in the apostles' council after Cardale's death had warned the coadjutors to be ready instantly to assume the burden of caring for the churches, although it seems fairly clear that many did not expect that the death of the last apostle would be what precipitated this.[20] Indeed, Capadose in 1899 asserted that it had been fulfilled when Woodhouse devolved to the coadjutors the celebration of the eucharist at Albury and at the assemblies of the seven churches in London.[21] After 1901 the last two coadjutors, through their conferences and circulars to the angels and angel-evangelists, provided light for the movement and direction which kept it together.

Given their crucial role, it is worth introducing these two men. The Dutchman Isaac Capadose (1834–1920) came from an influential family (his father Abraham had been a noted convert to Christianity from Judaism in 1822) and had given up a promising diplomatic career (he refused the offer of the governorship of Surinam) to become a minister. How he came to join the Catholic Apostolic Church is not known, and he was capable of taking an independent line on some matters. For one thing, he was politically liberal, something highly unusual among Catholic Apostolics, and at one time was said to have viewed Marx's ideas favorably.[22] He had been appointed to

---

18. Ibid., 132.

19. 'Record, 26th February 1901,' 14.

20. Capadose, in 'Record, 26th February 1901,' 2; 'Report, 27th March 1901,' 7; Copinger, 'Annals,' opp. 184.

21. Isaac Capadose, *Homily, 14th July 1899*, 6.

22. Bertram Brewster, 'Some Account of the Capadose Family,' in Da Costa et al., *Noble Families*,

the work in Holland and Denmark in 1876; although seriously ill in 1905–7 and again in 1910, as a result of which he was confined to a wheelchair and so unable to minister at the altar, he remained active in supervising Church affairs.[23]

Edward Heath (1845–1929) came from a family which supplied more leaders than any other to the Church. His father was Christopher Heath, angel at the Central Church from 1835–76; three brothers were angels (James and then Charles at Birmingham, and Herbert at Bishopsgate); two sons were elders (James at Glasgow and Christopher at Southwark); and a nephew was one of the last prophets (C. E. Lewis Heath, at Melbourne and Paddington). In 1886 he was chosen as a coadjutor and commissioned to visit Australia and New Zealand.

With the passing of the other coadjutors, by 1901 Capadose was responsible for North Germany, Scandinavia, the Low Countries, France, Spain, Italy, Russia, and Poland; Heath had oversight of the work in the English-speaking world, South Germany, Switzerland, and Austria.[24]

Although their right to perform apostolic acts such as ordination had ceased, the two were clearly the obvious people to turn to as the faithful sought counsel and leadership, and they alone had the right to transfer ministers between churches. Prophecy in their councils with the angels of the seven churches in London and the ministers of the universal Church indicated that their ministry, though a high one, was inferior to that of the apostles and concerned only the gathered congregations.[25] This restriction of their ministry would have facilitated the development of an inward-looking mentality. They led the Church as those who had companied with the apostles, just as Joshua had companied with Moses. Joshua was seen as the type of coadjutorship, as Moses was the type of apostleship: immediately after Woodhouse's death this parallel was a prominent topic in the words reported in the *Record*. However, they were not now acting as coadjutors to apostles, but simply as heads of the people; they, along with all other ministers, retained their God-given office but could only function 'in a modified & limited manner.'[26] Nevertheless, prophecy indicated that, like the apostles, the coadjutors enjoyed a relationship with God which was not mediated through any human agency, and the faithful should therefore remain submissive to them.[27]

Their duties were outlined as resumption of the intercession in its lesser form, completion of the building of the Lord's house, and preparation of the congregations

163–88, at 177, 181–86.

23. Newman-Norton, *Time of Silence*, 11; cf. Davenport, *Albury Apostles*, 178.

24. Newman-Norton, *Time of Silence*, 12–13; AD, January 1880, 7–8; July 1886, 2–3; 'Report, 27th March 1901,' 3. For more details, see James Heath, *Descendants*.

25. 'Report, 27th March 1901,' 16; Newman-Norton, *Time of Silence*, 2. Flegg, 'Gathered under Apostles,' 459, argues that prophetic direction should not have been accepted in the absence of apostolic validation, but I suspect that this requirement was replaced by an expectation that prophecy would be in line with earlier apostolic teaching.

26. Capadose, in 'Record, 26th February 1901,' 4–5.

27. AC, 19 January 1918, 8.

for entering a time of humiliation.[28] Accordingly, they took over responsibility for the meetings of apostles' ministers and archangels of the universal Church at Albury which had formerly been chaired by the apostles; such meetings were now known as conferences rather than councils.[29] During 1901 they also visited the tribes to confer with the angels.[30]

One of the most important aspects of the work of the apostles had been the sealing of members attaining the age of twenty. The coadjutors had been allowed to seal as delegated by the apostles, and there was some initial uncertainty as to whether they could do so now that there were no apostles left alive.[31] It was concluded that they could not, and in June 1903 a dedication (later known as commendation) of those who would have been sealed took place instead. The names of those who would otherwise have received the sealing were to be read and placed on the altar on the Monday after Pentecost; in preparation for this, they were to undergo the usual instruction.[32] Such a ceremony was not repeated in 1904, but from 1905 angels were encouraged to remember such people annually on a convenient day and provide suitable instruction.[33] The Central Church, for one, was very careful to do so, and a number of sermons and instructions addressed to those being commended still survive. A somewhat more flexible approach came to apply after a few years, perhaps as congregations got over the shock of no longer being able to receive the sealing: by 1910 the coadjutors were advising angels not to attach exaggerated importance to these services, intervals between them depending on the size of the congregation and the number to be so commemorated. As for instruction beforehand, 'the object of it should be to arouse or strengthen in each individual a personal conviction of the great truths of the Christian faith, a personal allegiance to the Lord Jesus Christ, an apprehension of His purpose in the Catholic church, and a sincere expectation of His coming.' It was deemed desirable for the angel to see or write to each one, 'and endeavour to elicit some response of faith in the Lord's work by His apostles and hope for His appearing.'[34]

On 16 April 1914 the last coadjutors' conference took place at Albury.[35] The outbreak of war meant that no more took place. Prophecy in 1915 indicated that the

---

28. Davson, *Sermons*, 12–13. The weekday offering of intercession could not continue in its full form because it grew out of the Sunday eucharist. As offered by angels, this was itself rooted in the eucharist offered in the Apostles' Chapel at Albury: AC, 'Record of the Service fulfilled in the Apostles' Chapel at Albury in the Forenoon of 3rd March 1901, being the 2nd Sunday in Quadragesima,' 2.

29. Ward, 'Death of a Church,' 95; cf. Copinger, 'Annals,' 184, 185.

30. 'Summary of Events,' 7 August 1903, 3–4.

31. 'Report, 27th March 1901,' 23.

32. AC, 'To the Angels (Results of Conference held at Albury by the Coadjutors with the Apostles' Ministers resident in Albury and a few from abroad; with words of prophecy),' January 1903, 5–6; Copinger, 'Annals,' 189.

33. AC, July 1905, 3.

34. AC, 17 June 1910, 1–2.

35. Copinger, 'Annals,' 200.

coadjutors would shortly be removed, and Capadose's death in 1920 left the tribes for which he had been responsible without any leadership, since Heath was not empowered to exercise any authority towards them.[36] In March 1920 Heath met the English and Scottish angels and urged them to prepare for the covering of the altar and the offering of a confession of sin on behalf of the whole Christian Church, two things which it had earlier been thought would be preceded by the Second Advent.[37] Prophecy in Berlin in 1923 warned that the time was coming when the eucharist would be celebrated for the last time in apostolic churches and the altar would be veiled; deep silence in the sanctuary would follow, and many would fail in the ensuing time of trial.[38]

The 1920s show Heath as feeling his increasing age, hesitating to issue the *Record* on his own account 'lest I should unconsciously be exceeding my jurisdiction';[39] the gaps between issues became longer, and the issues themselves shorter. Apologizing for the delay in issuing what was to be the final issue, he had a request to make of the angels:

> . . . some of the Angels unwittingly add to the burden by sending up far too many words. I will ask them to exercise their discretion rather more freely, and to send only such words as they may deem suitable for the Record, or which they may think it right to send me, either for explanation or correction. I again express the hope that this number of the Record may be the last; but this only because I hope and pray that we may speedily stand in the presence of the Lord.[40]

With the loss of nearly all the ministers of the universal Church, the movement was about to enter another phase, typified by the church at Laodicea (which represented the last epoch of Church history before the Lord's return); members were urged not to fall prey to lukewarmness. 'The time of collective dealing has passed. It may be that the dealing with His church as a body by His ordinances is already passing away. No longer are His ministries in active exercise to deal with the whole congregation as they were in the past. It is Christ who must deal now with each one individually and separately.' The letter to Laodicea was the only one addressed to individuals rather than to the whole congregation in the person of its angel.[41]

Paradoxically, it was at this time that the ministry of archangels experienced a significant measure of development, although this effectively ceased with the outbreak

---

36. Davson, *1850 to 1950*, 13–14; Newman-Norton, *Time of Silence*, 19.
37. Grundy, *Teaching*; Copinger, 'Annals,' 206.
38. *Record* 12/1 (1 September 1923) 34.
39. *Record* 11/6 (25 July 1922) 337.
40. *Record* 12/4 (23 February 1928) 167.
41. Herbert Heath, *Church in Bishopsgate: Sermon, 1st January, 1928*, 2; exegetically, he was on shaky ground in this claim. Of the seven churches in London, Laodicea was seen as corresponding to Paddington, the last to continue Sunday worship.

of war. The archangels came to be seen as a foreshadowing of the ministry of the seventy, to be sent forth in the future.[42] According to W. W. Andrews, God intended to gather not only the twelve tribes of Christendom under the twelve restored apostles (who would form the 144,000 of Revelation 7) but also the seventy families of the earth under seventy archangels (the great multitude).[43] The seventy would only be sent forth, however, after the first fruits had been taken away.[44] The idea of their sending forth was taken from the writings of the English mystic Jane Lead (1623–1704), founder of the Philadelphian Society, although it is not known who among the apostles and their ministers had studied her writings.[45]

Even before Woodhouse died, a conference of coadjutors and archangels in June 1900 had proposed the systematic visitation of the churches by pairs of archangels and their use on apostolic delegations. This was not readily accepted, although it was undertaken.[46] Following his death, it was decided in August 1901 that they would visit the churches to prepare them to undertake the services of humiliation appointed for July 1902.[47] This seems to have met with a large response. At Eynsham, for example, attendance at their addresses on Sunday, 15 December 1901, was 158, whereas teachings on Sunday evenings normally drew around twenty.[48] A coadjutors' conference in 1903 commissioned the personally called archangels to visit the metropolitan churches to prepare them for their future role as 'storehouses'.[49] (Judah was the only tribe in which the full quota of six such churches was designated—Birmingham, Manchester, Newcastle, Leeds, Bristol, and Southampton.[50]) Accordingly, pairs of archangels of the universal Church visited the angels of such seats, seeking to rouse them and their flocks to a fuller consciousness of their calling as patterns and centres of blessing and light to apostolic congregations and in the future to all the baptized.[51] Coadjutors could also send personally called archangels in pairs, as their eyes and ears, to visit and set in order local churches, although they were restricted to giving advice; they could not compel churches to act in accordance with the coadjutors' wishes.[52] On such visits

42. Newman-Norton, *Time of Silence*, 6, 10, following Davson, *1850 to 1950*, 27–29.

43. Andrews, *Review of God's Mode of Working*, 4.

44. LPL, MS 4937, 'Cath. Apos. Church, Mansfield Pl, Edinburgh: Notes of Teaching by Mr. Heath, 25th June 1893.'

45. Albrecht, *Work*, 4.

46. AC, 24 June 1903, 7; Copinger, 'Annals,' 182.

47. AC, August 1901, 4.

48. Oxford History Centre, Eynsham CAC records, NX1/A1/1, Register of attendance 1901–6.

49. AC, 24 June 1903, 6; Copinger, 'Annals,' 189. The allusion is to Gen. 41:56.

50. Anon., *Pastoral Instruction, 15th November 1953*, 7.

51. AC, 18 January 1904, 4–5.

52. Visitations might also be ordered of particular churches by the coadjutor, as at Wigan in 1915, when concern at the congregation's spiritual condition led to the sending of an angel-evangelist: Wigan Church Council minutes, 30 May 1915. He gave sermons and addresses on fundamental themes of the gospel and Christian spirituality.

they conferred with the angel in private before meeting with all the ministers and then with the whole flock. Attendance figures demonstrate that such services drew a much larger than average attendance, indicating that congregations took these visits very seriously. This system of visitations was not intended as permanent, but would enable the faithful to prepare for whatever step God wanted them to take.

A conference in 1904 agreed to give archangels a measure of oversight of local angels, in order to strengthen and help them, and to experiment by giving some metropolitans a sphere of office which would include the seats of other angels in order to provide some measure of spiritual relationship for them.[53] In England at least, this was meant to fill the gap left by the death of the pastor with the apostle.[54] The address books show how this was worked out. For example, all congregations in Holland were placed under the care of the archangel at The Hague; many North German congregations were placed under that at Hannover; and in north-western England many congregations came under the wing of Manchester. In the event, the main utility of such an arrangement was when a congregation's own angel died, rather than for angels feeling the need of counsel.

## THE CESSATION OF ORDINATIONS

Ordinations had previously been carried out by apostles or those personally empowered by them, so this was a pressing issue. Around the time of Woodhouse's death and shortly afterwards, there were a number of words of prophecy about the vital role played by deacons in protecting and cleansing the flock, which may have resulted in inquiries to the coadjutors about whether deacons could still be ordained. Heath was initially unclear as to whether he could still ordain deacons, but quite certain that an angel could not do so,[55] and in August 1901 the coadjutors stated that they did not feel free to ordain deacons themselves or to delegate this commission to others.[56]

We can only guess what it must have been like for younger men not to be able to receive ordination. Whilst the coadjutors could express their joy at seeing the committed service of many younger members,[57] their ministers were all ageing and no newcomers were being added, yet the same round of services continued. At a service of commendation, Hume stated the problem: 'They are at an age when it is natural and right to desire activity and development: and we can offer them no opening for spiritual development, no scope for their energies: we cannot present them for ordination

---

53. AC, 10 June 1904, 4–5; Copinger, 'Annals,' 190.
54. Grundy, *Pastoral Letter*, 6.
55. 'Report, 27th March 1901,' 24–25.
56. AC, 'Results arrived at in the Conference recently held at Albury by the Coadjutors with the Apostles' Ministers and the Archangels in the Universal Church: Together with certain Words of Prophecy spoken during the Conference,' August 1901, 2; Copinger, 'Annals,' 185.
57. AC, 23 June 1913, 4.

to the priesthood, nor even to the deaconship; there is no work of testimony in which they can be employed. The offering of the Holy Intercession is stayed, and the mouths of the Evangelists are closed.'[58]

Hume assured them that they would not miss out by not being sealed. Many had died, including Irving, before sealing was introduced, but surely these would be numbered among the sealed.[59] Yet his audience could have been forgiven for wondering what the point was. Some younger members did move to other Churches, even seeking Anglican ordination. Mar Georgius (Hugh George de Willmott Newman, 1905–79) of what became the Orthodox Church of the British Isles (now the British Orthodox Church) was brought up in the congregations at Southwark and Wood Green, serving in the latter as a scribe; from the age of sixteen he had a clear sense of calling to the Christian ministry. The ministers advised him to wait patiently for God's guidance, and he recalled that as Catholic Apostolic ordination had ceased it was seen as acceptable for lay members to enter the Anglican ministry because the Church was seen as comprising all the baptized; indeed, Philip Peck, the angel at Paddington, had advised him to follow what he believed to be God's will. However, his sense of mission to perpetuate the Lord's work within the historic Churches was probably not shared by others who sought ordination elsewhere.[60] On the other hand, in 1924 a preacher at Southwark advised listless younger members who felt that their gifts might be better used in the 'sects' not to jump ship but to wait for God's call and to develop themselves for future service.[61] From the Anglican side, Archbishop Davidson ruled in 1916 that those continuing to hold Irvingite views should not be ordained.[62]

Some were looking a long way ahead in connection with the worsening shortage of ministers; as early as September 1905 a paper from the coadjutors to the angels expressed their growing burden regarding the future importance of the deacons' ministry when nothing else remained. Prophecy had indicated that future ministry of the word would be diaconal in character, brotherly advice rather than authoritative proclamation; all ministers, not just deacons, were to serve in this spirit. With the manpower shortage beginning to worsen, prayer was requested for the deacons, who were shouldering an increasing burden of the work with inevitable effects on their family life. But there was no remedy for the worsening lack of ministers apart from the Second Advent.[63]

58. Hume, *Substance of an Address*, 6.

59. Ibid., 9.

60. Mar Georgius I, *Personal Statement*, 3–7; LPL, Anson papers, MS 4234, 323, Mar Georgius to ?P. F. Anson, 16 March 1964.

61. Anon., *Sermon, March 23rd, 1924*, 25–26.

62. LPL, BM 6:148, 27–28 January 1916.

63. AC, 'Some Thoughts on two Matters brought to the Coadjutors' Notice; and Words of Prophecy,' 14 January 1905, 4–5; cf. Isaac Capadose, *Sermon, 20th November 1904*, 9; AC, 17 January 1906, 5–6.

PART III—1901 ONWARDS: THE CHURCH AFTER APOSTLES

## A TIME OF SILENCE

It was the silence of members regarding the work of which they have been a part, rather than the nature of its claims, which earned the movement most criticism during the twentieth century. Such silence was seen as enjoined by divine action, and was compounded by the death of those writers who were well-known or read outside the Catholic Apostolic Church, such as the Anglican priest W. J. Bramley-Moore, the Astronomer Royal E. W. Maunder, and the Professor of Law Walter Copinger.

The coadjutors came to the conclusion that the whole Church, and not merely their own movement, was now in a 'time of silence.' Woodhouse's death was seen by the apostles' ministers as one fulfillment thereof, and an increase in the number of prophetic words about the time of silence was evident just before it.[64] This silence, foreshadowed by the half-hour's silence of Revelation 8:1, had been the subject of prophecy since 1865; it was 'when the voice of the [apostolic] intercession shall not be heard and the voice of the evangelist shall not be heard & the golden spoon full of incense shall not be offered.'[65]

No longer did the apostles engage in their ministry of intercession at Albury; no longer could the evangelists engage in the work of public testimony.[66] In Heath's mind, this was not the time for testimony to what God had done or might yet do through the movement. However, the widespread decline of belief in the fundamental Christian truths had given rise to a clear need for their forthright proclamation, and he encouraged members to invite friends to hear such sermons from Catholic Apostolic pulpits. Ministers were reminded that 'the successful handling of these foundation truths requires greater ability and spiritual power in the preacher than more advanced truths.... What is wanted is not a theological essay, nor even an elder's teaching, but the bringing home of these truths to men's hearts and consciences.'[67] It was probably in response to such a call that Henry Hume preached three sermons before Easter 1903 on *Fundamental Truths* at the Central Church. The truths he covered, by means of sermons on crucial passages from Romans 5–6, were human sin, Christ as the Lamb of God, and the possibility of new life.[68]

This silence was to be a time of spiritual preparation; the first disciples, it was pointed out, were commanded to observe a time of silence between the Ascension and Pentecost.[69] An anonymous and undated sermon, 'Keeping the Lord's Secret,' pointed to the deeper significance of this time. 'We are all only too prone to suppose that we honour God by making known that which he speaks and does. But, in so doing, we

---

64. *Record* 7/2 (June 1900); Capadose, in 'Record, 26th February 1901,' 7.
65. *Record* 1 (1874) 389, quoted in 'Record, 26th February 1901,' 7; cf. Copinger, 'Annals,' opp. 184. For the 1865 prophecy, see AC, 'Two Papers by the Coadjutors to the Angels,' 12 March 1901, 7.
66. Cf. Valentin, *Present Time*, 4.
67. MC, 1903/1, 5.
68. Hume, *Fundamental Truths*.
69. Albrecht and Heath, *Visit of two Ministers*, 3; cf. *Record* 3/1 (October 1879) 89.

hinder the steps which he has to take.'[70] Carelessness in spreading the testimony to the Lord's work had provoked resentment instead of repentance as members had put themselves on a higher plane than their brethren. Members had been wrong to assert that only those sealed by apostles would escape the judgment coming upon Christendom. It was a time for a chastened and quiet spirit, for awe at what God was doing. His ways, mysterious as they were, were too holy to be the subject of careless talk, and so members were to keep silent until God should bid them speak.[71] One circular emphasized the risk of misunderstanding which resulted when members spoke too freely to outsiders: a recently published pamphlet had asserted that Catholic Apostolics expected their movement to continue, on the basis of an informant's comments regarding the expectation of the appointment of the seventy.[72] Even ministers needed such warnings, a prophetic word in 1923 suggesting that there were some among them who wished to break the silence.[73]

The Catholic Apostolic Church's attitude was not intended to imply the rejection of other Christians; after all, it was asserted that the apostles had set up separate congregations so that blessing might accrue to all Churches through the work of intercession. But in its full sense this had perforce ceased as a result of the death of the last apostle (although in a lesser sense it was to continue until the death of the last priest in 1971), and their responsibility henceforward was thus to focus on God's purposes for them in removing Woodhouse; it was for God to provide for other Christians. Whilst those wishing to join the work might well receive better pastoral care in it than they could elsewhere, that was beside the point; God (it was asserted) had not led them to join, because he had other priorities for the movement.[74]

The conviction that the movement had entered a time of silence had profound implications, then, for its mission to those outside. The initial guidance offered by the coadjutors was that evangelist work should be modified, and should use churches rather than public halls for lectures where possible. Lectures could still be advertised, but in a quieter way. The four main themes of the message remained unchanged: 'the warning of approaching judgments, the testimony to God's present grace, the gospel of the Kingdom, the tidings of the coming of the Lord.' But evangelists should avoid rash statements about first two, such as the claim that the day of grace was now past. As for the congregations under apostles, 'preachers should quietly state the fact of the withdrawal of the apostleship, and say plainly that we do not know as yet how the Lord will carry on His work of mercy and grace, but we know He will be faithful to them who turn to Him, and therefore we call on men to repent.'[75] In practice, though, 'the

---

70. Anon., *Keeping the Lord's Secret*, 2.
71. Ibid., 1, 3.
72. AC, 26 June 1912, 17.
73. *Record* 12/1 (1 September 1923) 30.
74. AC, 22 January 1902, 7–8.
75. AC, 12 March 1901, 1–2.

voice of witness could not continue as before. Lectures & addresses in public halls, a few particular cases excepted, were stopped at once.' The scrapbook of invitations referred to previously contains three for February and March 1901, and an isolated one for June; all were in the London area, and all used public buildings.[76] Members might testify as individuals but there could be no more gathering, 'whether for ever, we do not know.' Those who recognized the Lord's work could not be sealed or share in the intercession, so it was better for them to stay where they were 'in the established churches, which as we confidently expect are soon to be visited by our Lord's messengers.' Committal to pastorship was thus now restricted to close relatives. Evangelists were to focus on 'uplifting the churches, strengthening the lukewarm, following after the strayed, and ministering to the lapsed.'[77]

Edward Heath admitted that his views on receiving new members had changed. In an address on 27 March 1901, he treated the matter as one of expediency, depending on the differing religious contexts in the tribes. He reminded ministers that Catholic Apostolic congregations had come into being for the benefit of the whole Church, and committal to pastorship was in order to share in a work on behalf of the whole of Christendom; but now that the apostolic intercession had been suspended, what reason could there be for individuals to leave existing churches if they could there receive a measure of sacramental ministry and pastoral care? It was not clear that there remained any higher spiritual work in which they could take part. But where there was no established Church (and therefore people were without pastorship and sacramental rites), it was still acceptable to move.[78] By 1903, however, he had come to view the matter as one of principle. He

> ... then thought the Angel Evangelists at liberty to commit to pastorship unless cause were shown to the contrary; I now think the case reversed, and that they are not at liberty to commit to pastorship unless special reason and justification can be shown. I then recommended the Angel Evangelists to be a little slower in counselling people in the Church of England to leave their present places; I now think that the Angel Evangelists should urge people to remain in their places, in the Church of England or elsewhere, unless and until God by His providential dealing intimates very clearly His will that they should make a change.[79]

Whilst there was a reluctance to admit new members, it was recognized that relatives might wish to receive communion occasionally, including spouses, and there was no reason why they should not do so; 'if a person got so far as the altar rails, that

---

76. 'Summary of Events,' 8; BOC, Scrapbook containing invitations to special services etc., 134–35.
77. 'Summary of Events,' 8–9.
78. 'Report 27th March 1901,' 22–23.
79. MC, 1903/1, 2.

person was not to be turned back, unless [the ministers] knew of some special reason why they should not come to communion.'[80]

In 1910, Heath elaborated his thinking. Ministers should not encourage interested individuals to forsake their own church: 'We may thus be removing from the midst of our brethren around us the very means by which God would prepare for another stage of work.' Nor were they to be admitted to meetings for spiritual gifts, for they could not use such gifts because they were not under the angel's covering, or be present to hear the *Record* read, for they were not trained to receive it. Occasional admission to communion (three or four times a year) remained allowable, however, and angels should not insist that such folk should leave nonconformity for the Church of England as a condition of continuing to minister to them.[81]

Some were slow to accept the changed situation. In North Germany, work continued almost as before except without lectures in hired halls, although in August 1901 Capadose explained to the angels that '[t]he work of gathering cannot now be prosecuted as a general rule.' There could be no more sealing at present. Evangelists could answer those who initiated inquiries, but no more.[82] The following year, the coadjutors reiterated the need for restraint in committing people to pastorship; in some countries the numbers being received indicated that restrictions were not being followed.[83] One preacher in 1918 surely caught the feelings of many members old enough to look back on the Church's heyday:

> When we look out upon the activity of our Christian brethren, do we ever chafe under the restrictions imposed upon us? Do those of us who are old enough, remember the glorious days when we offered our full Intercession, watching the ascending cloud of Incense with the feeling that the High Priest in Heaven was covering the Mercy Seat with that cloud? Do we remember our enthusiastic support of the Evangelists when they delivered the testimony to God's coming judgments and the nearness of the second coming of the Lord? How we listened spellbound to their eloquence, with hearts ablaze at the gracious words they uttered in power! No such preachers nowadays, we are inclined to say, no such glorious services nowadays as we used to have. The times are certainly changed with us, and we cannot complain that we have not received plenty of warning of a time of trial. I do not refer to the trials which the affairs of the world bring upon us, but to the more subtle trials of our faith, our love, our constancy and our submission.[84]

---

80. Wigan Church Council minutes, 10 November 1902.

81. MC, 1910/4, 98–102, quotation at 98.

82. AC, 'Translation of some Remarks which have been sent by Dr Capadose to the Angels in North Germany, as a Supplement to the Circular Containing the results of the recent Conferences at Albury,' August 1901, 1–2.

83. Ibid., 7.

84. Anon., *Sermon: Teaching Delivered in Manchester*, 5–6.

Members might desire to proclaim to their brethren that which the Lord had revealed through apostles and prophets, but that would be to run before the Lord. Quiet obedience was better than unbridled zeal exercised without authority.

Not only were no efforts to be made to gather new members; inquirers were to be positively discouraged because of the possibility that they might prove self-willed or sectarian in spirit, because they might jeopardize the condition of those already gathered by lowering the spiritual temperature of congregations, and because such additions could hinder the recognition by the faithful of their unworthiness as intercessors. However, new members could be received if they had close relations within the work or if they 'cleave like Ruth to Naomi', refusing to be put off. An underlying fear was that new members would create a new category of Christian: unsealed, not partaking in the work of intercession entrusted to the movement, and not definitely numbered with the 144,000 (the first-fruits).[85]

Mission was turned inwards, therefore, as the coadjutors sought to deepen and purify the worship and spiritual vitality of the congregations.[86] Preaching was to play a major part in this. It was noted in 1904 that congregations gathered under apostles had suffered from a mediocre and powerless ministry arising from an erroneous belief that all ministers could preach:

> ... in many churches the ministry of the word is often without any power or efficacy; redundance of words but lack of thoughts; monotonous, not to say sectarian, ebullitions concerning the prominence of the sealed above all other Christians. There have been not a few instances of members who have been disgusted and driven away.
>
> The complaint is often heard that the attendance of the flock at sermons is far less than at the services. The cause may be found not so much in laxity on the side of the flock, as in the unpreparedness of the preacher. This is evident from the fact that as soon as a minister is preaching who has something to give, the church is crowded.

The flocks were hungry, and were tempted to stay at home or to go to hear favorite preachers of other denominations.[87] Once again, then, the need for homiletical training, which angel-evangelists might be freer to offer than local angels, pressed upon the Church.[88] These men had been under-employed since 1901, and the remaining part of their work was a dispiriting one—dealing with the lapsed. It would be an encouragement to them to be invited to preach on fundamental themes, as they

---

85. AC, 'Results arrived at in the Conference recently held at Albury by Coadjutors, with the Apostles' Ministers resident in England . . . together with some of the Archangels in the Universal Church,' 22 January 1902, 8.

86. Cf. Thonger, *Pastoral Letter*, 3; 'Two Papers,' 3.

87. AC, 18 January 1904, 8–9.

88. Ibid., 12. Such criticisms were in line with Proby's *Letters on the Art of Christian Preaching*, which we examined in ch. 9.

were uniquely fitted to do: 'sin, atonement, the expiatory death of the Incarnate Son of God, His resurrection, the work of the Holy Spirit.'[89]

The need for instruction was seen as paramount; the complaint was made that some members only knew the distinctive aspects of the Catholic Apostolic principles and position and were ignorant of fundamental Christian verities. Ministers were therefore exhorted to provide instruction in basic truths, if necessary calling in suitable preachers from elsewhere.[90] The urgency arose in part because it was proving difficult to hold on to young people; they had little recollection of the full eucharistic service and the fourfold ministry in services which arose from it. They could be deployed in local evangelist work, but there was also a need to familiarize them (and indeed all members) with the full liturgy and explain the significance of all its parts.[91] This explains why, even into the 1950s when the full eucharist would have been remembered by only an elderly minority, such lectures were still being given, explaining the symbolism, vestments, and typology of the liturgy.

An idea of the content of Catholic Apostolic teaching during this period may be gained from an analysis of the sermons, teachings, and addresses sent to members by the Central Church about six to twelve times a year. From 1906 these printed ministries bore a serial number, and it seems that a record of printed ministries issued had been kept for many years previously, perhaps reaching as far back as the church's founding.[92] Catholic Apostolic distinctives and developments were the most frequent category of subject, not surprisingly since part of the aim was to strengthen 'absent members' living at a distance and often worshipping in their local parish churches. Another (considerably smaller) group of sermons dealt with fundamental Christian teaching. Those on social and ethical topics tended to stick to the traditional themes of marriage and family life, the role of women, tithing, and Sunday observance. Current errors were also addressed on occasion, spiritualism, freemasonry, and the theory of evolution all being covered. Another group addressed topics of national interest—voting, the accession of a new monarch, industrial unrest, and wartime issues. There were ministries on developments in the ecclesiastical sphere, such as the emergent ecumenical movement. Only a few sermons focused on expounding or introducing passages or books of Scripture, however.

The family, too, was to be a place of instruction. This, claimed Heath, was the best way to counter prevailing social trends such as unbelief and sabbath desecration. Religion should not be the one thing never spoken of at home. This had practical

---

89. AC, 18 January 1904, 11. Some were redeployed as angels of churches: W. H., *Katholisch-apostolische Gemeinden*, 18.

90. AC, January 1903, 4–5, 7.

91. AC, 17 January 1907, 3.

92. That year's sermons began with no. 911. A new series of sermons commenced after the death of the church's last priest in 1954, possibly because these could no longer be issued on the authority of a priest.

ramifications: he confessed himself shocked by the failure of some parents to ascertain whether a child's prospective marriage partner was baptized or a Christian. Furthermore, he had 'painful evidence that parents need to warn their children on the subject of my confidential circular of May 23rd'—probably contraception, which would form the subject of another letter to angels the following autumn.[93] Noting that there were over 1,500 couples in London and England alone in which the wife was a member but not the husband, Heath admitted that he had modified his former view that such husbands should not be received, because of the importance of family unity in spiritual things; they should be received if they initiated an approach. The family was seen as a great safeguard against spiritual decline, and parents were urged to converse with their children on spiritual matters and issues of conduct.[94] Such an outlook has helped to ensure the survival of the movement on the continent: it has been asserted that marriage to non-members 'has emptied the CAC churches' in Britain, whereas in Holland and Germany endogamy has helped to conserve its strength.

Although evangelist work was virtually at a standstill, members were urged not to assume that local evangelist work among the poor, needy, and ignorant was also to cease. Young people were to be encouraged to undertake such work, even offering to assist clergy of other denominations so long as this did not call into question their own peculiar standing and duties as those gathered under apostles. A shift in perspective was evident: 'In former days there was a perpetual tendency to confuse this work with that work of testimony which was the special function of the Angel Evangelists, and there was a tendency also to prefer the latter work to the former. The idea of making converts was too much in all our minds, and the idea of giving a cup of cold water because men belong to Christ, too little. We wanted a sectarian return for our outlay.'[95] How far such words were heeded is not known; we have much less evidence for such activity during the twentieth century than for the nineteenth.

Silence was seen as extending to written as well as oral ministry, even when books were published anonymously. A minute of conference in 1911 dealt with two cases of ministers writing books against error anonymously and setting forth the truth as the movement had received it, although without explicit reference to the Lord's work. Apart from the fact that a minister was supposed to consult his superior on such matters, it was a time of silence. 'How then can it be right to do anonymously and as private persons, that which God has forbidden us to do officially and with His authority?'[96] At least one book intended for the wider Church, however, was not

---

93. AC, 17 January 1907, 8–9; cf. AC, 7 October 1907, later reissued in duplicated form under the title *Confidential Letter on Sexual Matters*. Its general and continued availability indicates that the church's leadership felt the need for such teaching among new generations of members. For contemporary Anglican opposition to contraception, see Davidson, ed., *Five Lambeth Conferences*, 327.

94. AC, 17 January 1907, 7–8, 10.

95. Ibid., 6–7.

96. MC, 1911/1, 109–11, quotation at 111.

anonymous and did include a clear witness to the Lord's work and an invitation to accept the hope of translation, Bramley-Moore's *The Church's forgotten Hope* (1902); this was not the only occasion when its publisher, David Hobbs, issued works which strayed from official directives regarding publication.

Nonetheless, there are indications that the period of silence was not intended to be absolute. The angel Samuel Mee Hollick (1869–1949) of Manchester argued in 1935 that 'this time, which we have rightly learned to speak of as a time of silence, should not be a time of inactivity, but of earnest and diligent service.' The silence was of two voices: 'first, the voice of the Church, headed up by apostles, in the great work of intercession; and second, the voice of testimony, through the lips of evangelists, giving warning of coming judgments and proclaiming God's work of mercy and grace whereby all who hear might find a way of escape.' But there was still a (lesser) work of intercession to undertake, and a witness to bear. Being in a time of silence did not free members from the obligation to be ready to give a reason for their hope as Christians when asked (1 Peter 3:15). 'We can hold godly converse upon spiritual things, with Christian brethren in private circles, without any breaking of the silence.' They should certainly be silent, even when talking to one another, on things revealed in prophecy concerning 'the future steps which the Lord will take in the accomplishment of His purpose (such as the sending forth of the seventy, the sounding of the trumpets of testimony, the offering of much incense, and the disclosing of the mystery of resurrection life).' On such topics, they could only say 'that we are looking for the appearing of the Lord, and waiting for His guidance.' But if earnest Christians inquired about the past work, 'you should feel free to bear your witness without in any way pressing it beyond their desire to hear it.... There can be no secret about that which the Lord has already done by His apostles before the eyes of men.'[97] The principle that a witness might indeed be borne to the past dimension of the Lord's work has not generally been upheld by the trustees (although in my experience members have spoken readily of the work), but if followed could allow a measure of opening up of the Church's archives to non-members, as well as enabling the public to visit the church at Albury. Such measures would diminish the mystique which tends to surround the Catholic Apostolic Church in the eyes of outsiders and facilitate serious and scholarly consideration of it.

## A TIME OF HUMILIATION

We noted that reaction to Woodhouse's death marked a step forward in the divine purpose on the one hand, but that on the other it was interpreted as resulting from human failure. The time of silence and inner mission was therefore to be marked above all by a deep sense of humiliation. Prophecy soon indicated that but for the unfaithfulness of many of those gathered under apostles and called to be first-fruits,

---

97. Hollick, *Our Present Work and Witness*, 1–3.

the Lord would already have returned.[98] Out of Catholic Apostolic reflection upon their failure emerged a new dimension to their understanding of their particular ministry: just as the movement had been intended as a pattern of God's perfect order for the rest of the Church, so it was now to lead the whole of Christendom in repentance and humiliation for its failure and sin.[99] The movement had been a symbol of what the Church should be; now it had become a symbol of what the Church actually was.[100]

This humiliation found particular expression in the weeks following Woodhouse's death, during which the faithful observed a eucharistic fast. The coadjutors were bidden by prophecy to assemble the congregations for services of humiliation. First of all the coadjutors and the ministers of the universal Church met at Albury for a week to offer a service based on that appointed in the liturgy for the Eve of Pentecost. In the second week, the congregations shared in similar services, culminating in a meeting of the seven churches in London on 26 February 1901, after which the eucharist was resumed.[101] During this time even the weekday services drew much larger congregations than usual, with lapsed and backsliders returning to the Church.[102]

But the following year Capadose expressed the belief that the faithful were still not ready to be translated to heaven because of their pride.[103] In the light of prophecy, it was felt that before local congregations held services of humiliation, the seven angels and five evangelists in London, headed up by the coadjutors, should offer their confession, and that this should be repeated at the close of the period appointed for services of humiliation, thus summing up the confession offered by local churches.[104] A two-week eucharistic fast was observed, and daily services of humiliation were held in which confession was made on behalf of the whole Church, climaxing with the assembly of the seven churches in London on 14 July 1902.[105] No absolution was given as no earthly minister was deemed competent to pronounce it.[106] However, the apparent lack of a divine word appears to have unsettled at least some members: prophecy at Stettin in Germany on 28 December enjoined the people not to pressurize angels, nor angels the coadjutors, but wait and trust patiently.[107]

The time of humiliation was expected to culminate in the offering of a confession on behalf of the whole of Christendom and the reception of absolution from heaven, but a warning was sounded against rushing to introduce a service of catholic

---

98. Davy, *Teaching*, 5.
99. Albrecht, *Work*, 43.
100. Davson, *Sermons*, 117.
101. Ibid., 15–16; Newman-Norton, *Time of Silence*, 3.
102. 'Record, 26th February 1901,' 10.
103. Capadose, 'Shut thy doors,' 6–7.
104. AC, 7 July 1902, 1.
105. Valentin, *Present Time of Silence*, 10.
106. Copinger, 'Annals,' 187; Davson, *Sermons*, 42–43.
107. *Record* 8/1 (February 1903) 114–15.

confession in an attempt to obey prophetic light; while it was right to pray for the whole Church, the body was not to act as its mouthpiece without divine authority. Crucial to this would be a deeper sense of humiliation on the part of the movement's ministers. Before the whole movement offered confession on behalf of the wider Church, ministers should be meeting to do this.[108]

These years were particularly difficult for the membership; there was evidence that continual preaching on the need for penitence, and the prolongation of this time of trial, could produce a sense of weariness and resignation, with a cooling of the advent hope and a lessening sense of humiliation—the opposite of what was sought. As the coadjutors observed in 1913, in 1901 hardly any thought the time of silence would last so long: 'year after year has passed in alternate hope and perplexity.' Not surprisingly, a certain impatience may have led some to ask what should be done to hasten God's purpose, but the answer, hard as it was to accept, was 'nothing.'[109] Penitential eucharists for those whose faith was failing or who were wandering away were authorized by the coadjutors seven times between 1903 and 1917.[110]

Another aspect of the humiliation came from the fact that outsiders were pointing to the visible evidence of the movement's decline:

> Already this work of the Lord in which we have been engaged is exhibiting the appearance of weakness and failure. In many of the smaller congregations the services have had to be reduced or discontinued altogether. Even in the larger ones it is becoming difficult to keep them up, and none of us can say that it may not be the mind of the Lord to permit what would appear to the eyes of men to be a complete collapse of His work. Many of the words spoken in our midst seem to indicate that this is possible. If this should prove to be the case it would, in this respect, bear some likeness to our Lord's own work. Men rejected Him—the Sent-one of God—and *His* work was suffered to end in what appeared outwardly to be total failure. His work by apostles in these days has also been almost entirely rejected; why should we expect it to be brought to a close after a different manner? . . . Men may point the finger of scorn at the Lord's work in these days, and say, 'What has become of your hope? If this were really the work of God, which you profess it to be, why is it dying out?'[111]

If members would face such reproaches in humility and faith, going outside the camp to bear Christ's reproach (Hebrews 13:13), they would be cleansed from boasting, superiority, and fleshly enthusiasm, resulting in increased fruitfulness—a cleansing which could continue until they should see Christ face to face.[112]

---

108. AC, 3 February 1910, 6–7; 10 February 1911, 7; 22 January 1912, 1, 4.

109. AC, 25 June 1909, 5; 21 January 1913, 2–3.

110. Gordon Square MS 864, 'Remarkable Incidents,' quoted in Pinnington and Newman-Norton, *Conciliar and Apostolic Witness*, 30.

111. Anon., *Ministry to the Flock in Manchester*, 8.

112. Ibid., 9–10.

But the severest trial of faith, according to one prophecy, would result precisely from the hearing and answering of their prayers that God would bring back apostles and complete his work: the first news that Christ had reappeared in the churches with his apostles would come from those who were not part of the Catholic Apostolic community.[113] The coadjutors wondered whether members were afraid that others would supersede them in some supposed place of prominence, but God's work was not to be exclusively identified with the body known as the Catholic Apostolic Church. Members had to learn the same lesson as John the Baptist's disciples: for all his greatness, he was but a forerunner.[114]

## LITURGICAL CHANGE

Humiliation was not the only factor dictating changes in Catholic Apostolic worship. As Gretason points out, liturgy marked out Catholic Apostolics as distinct and yet part of the wider Church, so it is not surprising that it occupied much of the coadjutors' deliberations from 1901 almost until 1914, as they reconsidered the nature of this relationship.[115] Each alteration to the liturgy, or the cessation of another special service, represented another step into deeper silence. We saw that the coadjutors' response to Woodhouse's death was to suspend celebration of the eucharist while they waited for clearer light. During this period a liturgy based upon the service of humiliation appointed for the Eve of Pentecost was used instead.[116] Prophecy then directed them to restore the eucharist, but in a shorter form as previously used on weekdays or in dependent congregations. It was also altered to reflect the absence of apostles from the Church on earth; the angels ceased to offer the solemn intercession accompanied by incense, the commemoration of the living was replaced by the litany, and that of the departed reduced to one prayer. The worship thus took a more austere form; no longer could the fourfold ministry find expression therein, although fourfold teaching was still given (addressed to the heart, will, intellect, and emotions) since human nature remained unchanged.[117] These changes were significant because the eucharist had hitherto been seen as an offering of the universal Church: angels celebrated it as authorized by apostles, whose eucharist at Albury was 'the heading up of the worship of the whole Catholic Church.' This explains the initial doubt as to whether the eucharist could continue in the absence of apostles.[118] It was now offered in local churches as 'separate families' rather than as microcosms of the universal Church.

---

113. AC, 'Words of Prophecy referred to in the Coadjutors' Circular of 18 May 1914,' 4; cf. *Record* 9/4 (September 1909) 471.

114. AC, 7 January 1915, 4, 6–7.

115. Gretason, 'Authority, Provisionality and Process,' 181.

116. Davenport, *Albury Apostles*, 174.

117. Davson, *Sermons*, 16; Newman-Norton, *Time of Silence*, 4.

118. Davenport, *Albury Apostles*, 173–74; Edward Heath, in 'Record, 3rd March 1901,' 2.

On 24 November 1908, the final assembly of the seven churches in London took place. The death of one of their angels, J. W. Ackery of Southwark, a few days later was seen as breaking the sevenfold unity of these churches, because the coadjutors were not 'competent, jointly or severally, to set an Angel in permanent charge, or to effect between an Angel and a congregation, the relationship which was formerly established by the apostolic act of induction'; the replacement of Ackery could only be provisional in character.[119] Responding to Ackery's loss, the coadjutors followed the apostolic example of never taking 'any weighty determination without gathering their full council,' conferring with ministers of the universal Church residing at Albury and the five evangelists and six remaining angels in London. It was deemed inappropriate to continue the assemblies, and in explanation the coadjutors set down an understanding of God's purposes which would become central to twentieth-century Catholic Apostolic self-understanding. They asserted that the death of the last apostle had initiated the process of covering the ecclesiastical structure typified by the Tabernacle. Firstly the ark (the apostleship) had been covered, then the golden altar (the intercession) and the candlestick (the assembly of the seven churches in London); prophecy indicated that a time would come when the eucharist would no longer be celebrated in churches under apostles, a time typified by the covering of the table of shewbread. Only the outer court with the brazen altar would be left.[120] However, a time would come when absolution would be pronounced from heaven and these things again be uncovered. In the meantime, God would not desert his people; prophecy declared that 'His presence shall remain upon the altar during the time when thou art not allowed to draw nigh to eat and to drink.'[121]

From 16 February 1909 the observance of every fourth Tuesday by local churches therefore replaced the assemblies in London. The coadjutors saw this as a provisional measure adopted for pastoral reasons, to moderate the impact of the assembly's cessation,[122] and a circular in 1916 ordered that this in turn should be discontinued as looking back instead of forward to what the assembly had symbolized. A previous attempt in 1914 to get local churches to do so had failed, even though the incongruity of celebrating the separation of the apostles thirteen times a year (when none remained) and the incarnation only once was pointed out.[123]

With the death of the last apostle, the litany came into its own as the Church clarified its sense of calling to prepare to offer 'the catholic confession' on behalf of the whole Christian Church. One teaching at Albury expressed the view that before 1901 members had probably not entered into the spirit of the litany, not least because apart from special occasions such as Good Friday and the Eve of Pentecost

---

119. Hume, *Observations*, 1.
120. AC, 30 January 1909, 1–2, 5, 7.
121. AC, 'Words of Prophecy to accompany the Coadjutors' Circular of 30th January 1909,' 7.
122. AC, 18 May 1914, 6; Hume, *Observations*, 6.
123. AC, 15 June 1916, 1; Copinger, 'Annals,' 200, 202.

it was usually offered in the Forenoon Service, at which few were present (in spite of repeated appeals).[124] Now, however, the litany proved well suited to the condition of the body, and it has been offered ever since, at gatherings in homes as well as in churches.

The coadjutors also continued the practice of issuing special forms of prayer or appointing special services. This formed the typical response to any national crisis. To give two rather different examples, special prayers were appointed to be offered on 20 December 1905 in view of the political situation in England, in October 1908 for employers and employed, in November 1908 for the unemployed, and in September 1911 on account of labor unrest.[125] When floods occurred in September 1912, a special eucharist was appointed, to include confession of the spoliation of the Church and the desecration of the Lord's Day. Copinger noted that the weather improved and that thanks were duly returned.[126] Whether such prayers were issued for other tribes is not known, however.

As gaps began to appear in ministerial ranks, Heath encouraged churches to be flexible in their approach to ministry. 'I would suggest that in times of stress and pressure we must not cling too tenaciously to modes of action which are suitable for a full complement of workers. The point of most importance is the pastoral care of individual souls.' So if pastors or evangelists were lacking, for example, elders might have to supply the deficiency, even at if that meant going outside their own border. And ministers should not try to do more than was realistically possible: 'Ministers must not be fanatical in endeavouring to achieve more than God allows.'[127] Yet in spite of the increasing age of ministers and gradual decline in frequency of services, relatively few churches were closed during this period, and the regular pattern of worship continued; it has been suggested that members would have been slow to realize the significance of events, although the cessation of the sealing and the full intercession would surely have affected all.[128]

As loss of ministers led to difficulty in maintaining services in dependent congregations, the faithful were advised that where local churches of other denominations could provide a measure of food, it would be sectarian and self-centered to continue worshipping apart. Obstinacy should not be mistaken for fidelity, and they should not try to do what God had not given them the resources to do. However, if those churches neglected or denied fundamental truths, the mother church should be prepared to sacrifice some of its own ministers in order to maintain services in its dependencies.[129] Evidently some members were reluctant to go elsewhere, objecting that there was a

124. Anon., *Congregation in Albury, August 1st, 1915*.
125. Copinger, 'Annals,' 191, 194, 197.
126. Ibid., 198.
127. AC, 17 January 1907, 2.
128. Newman-Norton, *Time of Silence*, 13–16.
129. AC, 10 February 1911, 1–3.

contradiction between the teaching that the services of those gathered under apostles conveyed special spiritual blessing and the injunction to attend other churches.[130] This tension is still present within what remains of the movement.

As churches became unable to provide the full complement of services, prayer meetings were increasingly encouraged.[131] They were regarded as a blessing at the beginning and now at the end of the work; 'let them be as they were, not hedged in by rubrical restrictions nor by officialism, which too often stifles the spirit of prayer.'[132] Topics for prayer could include the raising up of powerful preachers and teachers to equip Christians to withstand the adversary, the manifestation of the seven candlesticks in Christendom (i.e., the seven centres of God's work in a future stage, as previously identified by prophecy), and the establishment of a witness in Rome, something which exercised Catholic Apostolics increasingly.[133] At Wigan, the angel encouraged the holding of small meetings for prayer, not at set times but spontaneously: 'in the vestry, a prayer meeting may be had at any time when desired, & members of the congregation could be present.' They were not to be arranged in homes unless a minister was to be present, but that did not stop two or three in a house from having one spontaneously.[134]

A problem arising from the increasing proportion of regular communicants who were unsealed related to prophecy within the services. The apostles had determined in 1865 that such people should only prophesy in 'meetings for the exercise of spiritual gifts', although Cardale in communicating this to English angels had restricted its application to members under twenty. It was now felt that the preponderance of unsealed members in many congregations could necessitate the cessation of all prophecy in services if the rule were to be rigidly applied. The main point for angels to consider was whether their gift served to edify. Exceptional cases (such as children or those newly committed to pastorship) were left to angels to decide, as they were responsible for fostering and regulating the development of spiritual gifts in their flocks; even if such members were to be allowed to prophesy, they still needed the angel's permission and training. Those who did prophesy without being sealed were warned against thinking themselves superior to sealed members who did not prophesy.[135] Some concluded that prophecy should be discouraged, but the angel at Wigan expressed surprise that 'anyone should think that prophecy is declining, or should decline at this stage of the Lord's work, saying that it is chiefly by this means that the Lord is comforting His people in this time of silence.'[136]

130. AC, 7 January 1915, 2, 4, 6.
131. 'Report, 27th March 1901,' 25.
132. AC, 18 January 1904, 13.
133. BIA, CAC 1/7, Bradford MC, 2 March 1904, cf. 27 July 1910.
134. Wigan Church Council minutes, 8 March 1903.
135. AC, 17 June 1910, 4–6.
136. Wigan Church Council minutes, 22 October 1905.

Inevitably, certain types of service began to die out as the ministers to supervise them died. Meetings for the exercise of spiritual gifts, or for reading of the *Records*, were among them. Prophecy had instructed the coadjutors to give time to searching out from the *Records* the light stored up there for the present time, and the value of such meetings was acknowledged.[137] At Eynsham in 1901, for example, these meetings were being held each month. *Records* could be read by a priest but meetings for gifts required the presidency of the angel and so these became confined by 1903 to the angel's visits. By 1906 he was always at the meetings for reading the *Records* as well, and by 1916 the two meetings had been combined. They were still taking place in 1927, but would have ceased when the church no longer had an angel.[138]

## CATHOLIC APOSTOLICS AND THE WIDER CHURCH

A significant proportion of Catholic Apostolics saw their separate existence as a regrettable necessity, preferring to regard themselves as a movement for the revitalization of the whole Church. One angel saw the story of Joseph and his brothers as a type of what God would do for other Churches; like Joseph, the faithful were called to endure a time of humiliation, and as in his case the dreams of primacy which they had entertained were offending others. Yet there was hope for the future: those gathered under apostles were 'not without signs that our brethren are coming towards us.'[139] There was some evidence for such claims: for instance, during the early twentieth century several Church of Scotland ministers would attend services at the Dundee church.[140] It is also noticeable that the flow of anti-Irvingite publications slowed down considerably, doubtless because the Church's most controversial feature, the apostolate, no longer existed.

Attitudes towards the modern ecumenical movement varied, however. When a call to prayer for unity was issued for Pentecost 1906, it received a warm welcome from ministers; Hume approved of its recognition of the need for humiliation and further divine light, and revealed that the coadjutors had sent a letter to the angels, urging them to join in.[141] But in 1909 prophecy in Germany warned that while the coming movement for unity was borne out of a sense of confusion and helplessness and to that extent based on truth, it was not of God and the results would prove the failure of human wisdom to bring about God's purpose. Members were not to join in, but should nevertheless include the whole Church in their prayers.[142] The idea

---

137. AC, March 1901 [Special record of prophecy], 18–19.

138. Oxford History Centre, Eynsham CAC records, NX1/A1/1, Register of attendance 1901–6; NX1/A1/4, Register of attendance 1916–28.

139. McMichael, *Joseph*, 2.

140. Gretason, 'Idea of the Church,' 211.

141. Hume, *Prayer for Unity*, 3.

142. AC, 'Additional Supplement to Circular of 25 June 1909,' 4.

that ecumenism was a human expedient appeared in a sermon on Ezekiel 37:3–10, which asserted that the 1929 union of the Church of Scotland and the United Free Church 'may be a step in the right direction; but is it effectual? It is the effort of two pieces of the stick to join *themselves* together,' forgetting that Christians were already part of one body and not letting the Holy Spirit work.[143] Just as members were wary of trying to perpetuate the Lord's work by human means, so too they did not support what they saw as human attempts to overcome the Church's disunity, although this gave rise to a measure of frustration, as a 1939 sermon admitted: 'The sections agree that the Church should be one; but as to the way of *attaining* unity they are hopelessly divided. *We know the right way;* but we are bidden to be silent. It is when the brethren themselves cry out unto the Lord to effect the reunion in His own way, and to save them from all the unhappy conditions which have beset the great mystic Babylon—it is then that the Lord will hear and answer their supplication and ours.'[144]

The formation of the World Council of Churches in 1948 was seen as a symbol of secularism invading the Church, since there was no expectation or desire for the Lord's return.[145] An article on the World Council of Churches assembly at Evanston, Illinois, in 1954 in the *Newsletter* commended the keynote emphasis on unity. However, the writer also noted the assembly's inability to agree concerning the hope of the Lord's return, its confusion, and its ignorance of the prophetic Scriptures, a fruit of the wider Church's rejection of the Lord's work during the nineteenth century.[146]

On occasion, though, a more positive estimate could be expressed. Thus, an early twentieth-century compilation of teaching on Revelation included this assessment:

> What we hear now about the reunion of divided Christendom, the effort and schemes and yearnings of those who love the Lord Jesus to draw nearer to one another from the various severed portions of Christendom, these were not known a hundred years ago. However mistaken many of the schemes proposed may be, they are surely results of an awakening of the Philadelphia spirit throughout the sundered parts of Christendom.
>
> Every movement that has had the effect of awakening the spiritual life of Christendom, or of developing a true catholicity of spirit, disposing Christians to common confession and common intercession, and to a more definite expectation and desire for the coming of the Christ in His glory, may surely be regarded in like manner as expressing a call from the Lord Himself to make ready for His appearing.[147]

---

143. Anon., *Sermon, 23 November 1930*, 9.

144. Parker?, *Two Sermons*, 9.

145. Anon., *Sermon: Seeing Jesus*, Manchester, December 1948, 2–3, quoted by Pinnington and Newman-Norton, *Conciliar and Apostolic Witness*, 70.

146. R. G. B., 'The Evanston Conference,' *Newsletter* 7 (December 1954) 10–14.

147. Von Dittmann, *Revelation*, 14.

Similarly, a sermon from Manchester in 1910 welcomed the awakening consciousness of the need of spiritual power to stem the tide of worldliness and materialism, as seen in high Anglican devotion and zeal, Roman opposition to secularism, nonconformist concern for the deepening of spiritual life, and the effort being expended on finding a basis for reunion. Imperfect though these developments appeared to those brought up under apostles, the Holy Spirit was creating a faith which looked to God and not to men.[148]

A development of particular interest to Catholic Apostolics was the growing interest in divine healing, sometimes misleadingly called 'faith healing'; during the early twentieth century many Churches showed considerable interest in it. Heath issued a note on it in response to the activity of James Moore Hickson (1868–1933), an Australian Anglican layman who travelled the world seeking to encourage his communion to rediscover the healing ministry and holding meetings at which the sick were prayed for. Catholic Apostolics believed that there were two modes of healing ministry, the first being through outward sacramental ordinances and the second through charismatic gifts. In the first the initiative lay with the individual of the minister involved and in the second with God who impelled a gifted individual to exercise their gift. In their eyes, whilst Hickson would be within the bounds of order to arrange prayer meetings among friends to pray for the sick, he was out of order in arranging public meetings without engaging in any act of ministry thereat.[149] Catholic Apostolics numbered several doctors among their ministers, and were careful not to reject medicine. As Ackery had explained in 1890, the error of the Peculiar People, a sect with Wesleyan roots who had a congregation near him in Camberwell, was that they saw divine healing as superseding natural remedies.[150]

When news broke of the Welsh revival in 1904, concern was expressed lest it be diverted from the correct course because of a lack of rule and oversight. A sermon asserted that 'there is no doubt that the power of the Holy Ghost is working, but at the uttermost danger of being quenched by the flesh, or even by the Devil—the utmost danger because of the entire absence of order, rule, and oversight.' Members were to pray that God's purpose through it would be fulfilled, that many might be awakened.[151] Its emphasis on the Church was welcomed, but a warning was sounded against expecting this movement to succeed where previous mission had failed.[152] But one prophetic word made an implicit contrast between contemporary movements and the work of God: 'The Lord bringeth to pass the true revival, the revival which is

---

148. Anon., *Sermon delivered July 1910*, 11–12.

149. Edward Heath, *Note on Spiritual Healing*. Lambeth 1908 had neither sanctioned nor prohibited the practice of anointing with oil: Resolution 36, in Davidson, ed., *Lambeth Conferences*, 326.

150. Ackery, *Teaching*, 2–3.

151. Wagener, *Sermon*, 7.

152. Pinnington and Newman-Norton, *Conciliar and Apostolic Witness*, 31.

spiritual, and not according unto the ways of men.' This would come about when the Lord comes with 'His holy servants and His sleeping ones.'[153]

A related movement, in which Catholic Apostolics might be expected to take a keen interest, was Pentecostalism. In June 1907 a report was brought to the coadjutors' conference from the evangelist with the apostles for Sweden and Norway. He had attended meetings in which spiritual gifts were being exercised, and reported a true work of the Holy Spirit going on, albeit marred by ignorance and in need of discernment and guidance. Similar manifestations were reported from America. 'Probably such movements, irregular and spasmodic as they may be, are symptoms of the working of the Spirit of life and power in the one body.'[154] The next year, further information reached the coadjutors concerning spiritual gifts appearing in England, Norway, Germany, and America; once again, it was felt that lack of oversight could endanger that work.[155] In view of the problems which dogged the Lord's work in its earliest days, ministers were doubtless very sensitive to the need for order and regulation, which had long been a major emphasis in Catholic Apostolic teaching regarding the charismata. Lest members should be led astray, they were warned in 1910 against thinking that possession of spiritual gifts could be counted as equal with apostolic sealing. These manifestations were exceptional, and did not represent God's normal way of dealing with his people, which required the ministry of living apostles.[156] Yet prophecy in the 1920s apparently rebuked members for not believing that God could work among the 'most despised,' the Pentecostals.[157] Copinger noted the Pentecostal manifestations in his chronicle, adding only the wry comment that, by contrast with those of 1830, these were almost welcomed by the Churches.[158]

As for Evangelicalism, which has become arguably the strongest current in Anglophone Christianity during the twentieth century, it is noteworthy that it attracted little comment from Catholic Apostolics, whose focus tended rather to be on what we might call 'mainline' Christianity. This may be in part because Evangelicalism's rise to prominence in Britain came after 1945, by which time there were relatively few ministers remaining to offer comment and guidance. However, there was an exception when the American evangelist Billy Graham conducted a mission in London in 1954 which received wide media coverage. A priest in London commented that 'it has been a striking experience in this city, fairly recently, how when a missioner has come amongst us, declaring the first principles of the gospel, the populace has flocked to hear him.' It was true that most such preaching focused on Christ crucified at the expense of Christ risen and ascended and Christ returning, but without missionaries

---

153. *Record* 9/1 (August 1906) 44–45.
154. AC, 24 June 1907, 3–4.
155. AC, 9 January 1908, 5.
156. AC, 17 June 1910, 10.
157. Christenson, 'Pentecostalism's Forgotten Forerunner,' 33.
158. Copinger, 'Annals,' opp. 192.

preaching a partial gospel England would never have received Christianity, and it was better than nothing. On that ground, members in the Church of England were therefore advised not to withhold support from foreign missions. One day, though, the gospel would again be preached in its fullness, by the seventy.[159]

Most prominent in Catholic Apostolic comment about the twentieth-century Christian world, however, was Roman Catholicism. We saw earlier that as early as 1837 Henry Drummond had expressed his approval of Roman Catholic worship.[160] In 1840 he wrote: 'I feel persuaded that the regeneration of the Church can never come out of Protestantism and that it can only come out of popery.'[161] Yet he also published a number of anti-Catholic works in the wake of the restoration of the Roman hierarchy in England in 1850. Cardale manifested something of the same ambivalence: 'In no portion of the Church, in its most degraded state in time past, hath there been, and in no portion of the Church, in time to come, shall there be, such examples of grace, and such extremes of abominable wickedness in God's sight, as in Rome and the Roman Church.' The Church from which would emerge the mightiest testimony against the Antichrist would become the handmaid of the beast.[162]

Despite this ambivalence, there is evidence of a growing burden for Rome and an expectation that God would work in her in the future. In 1880, Woodhouse reported:

> In the Protestant countries generally, the work goes forward satisfactorily. The Roman Catholic & Greek communities are generally speaking untouched by our ministry. As far as we can judge from past experience, a very different form of testimony than that which we now bear, will be needed to open the hearts that are now closed to our witness, & to deliver those who are entangled & fast bound in the meshes of human systems. To convince them of the fact that Babylon is about to be judged, & her walls and bulwarks thrown down, only by such a testimony can her children be delivered.[163]

In January 1905 the coadjutors confessed themselves struck by the fact that Rome was the only one of the seven designated cities of Christendom in which a metropolitan congregation had not yet been established; prayer for this was essential to the progress of God's purposes. Rome might have been the centre of God's acting on earth, but (like Esau, its type) it had thrown away its birthright and been replaced; coming from a Protestant background, members of the Lord's work might not realize what they owed to Rome and needed to understand that Rome might have something against them.[164] A sermon preached in Edinburgh on 14 May commended the witness

---

159. Anon., *Sermon by a Priest*, quotation at 6.
160. Anon., 'History and Doctrines of Irvingism,' 63.
161. Ward, 'Death of a Church,' 57.
162. Cardale, *Notes of Lectures* (1861), 30–31.
163. AR 1880, 4.
164. AC, 14 January 1905, 2–4.

given by Rome to the unity of the Church and to the need for an office above that of bishop, comparing the pope and the cardinals to the ministers of the universal Church. According to prophecy, God had an important purpose for Rome as the middle branch of the seven-branched candlestick representing the seven churches of Christendom; it would be led by its own archangel,[165] although it had 'only a priest in charge of a small congregation,' and that since Woodhouse's death.[166]

Constantly members were enjoined to pray for Rome. Prophecy reminded them that 'the Lord loveth the glorious city of Rome: and there is much in her wherein the Lord looks down with pleasure,' and so they were to pray that 'the bright light of the gospel may soon shine.'[167] Rome had continued to maintain the faith against unbelief, and accordingly it was to be prayed for.[168] The coadjutors' conference in January 1912 therefore recommended more earnest private prayer for Rome.[169] Hitherto the greatest hindrance to the restoration of unity, it would become the most effective instrument for it.[170] Not only was Rome to be commended and prayed for; one catches a sense that it was to be loved, because the Lord loved it:

> O the Lord looketh into the heart of His Church in Rome, and He knoweth His servants there, and their love and devotion, and how they would gladly give their lives for the gospel's sake. And He knoweth how they tied and bound by the system that has risen up. But the Lord looketh upon them in love, He looketh not upon their sins and upon their errors. He looketh into the hearts that love Him . . . . [B]y the love of the Lord Jesus in the hearts of His servants in Rome He will break the bonds.[171]

Such a note was never sounded so clearly with reference to Anglicanism, as we shall see.

---

165. Wagener, *Sermon*, 8; cf. *Record* 9/1 (August 1906) 72; 11/1 (September 1916) 5.
166. Perry and Heath, *Four Sermons*, 12; cf. Perry and Heath, *Notes of Sermons*, 28.
167. *Record* 8/2 (October 1903) 213.
168. *Record* 9/5 (August 1910) 517.
169. Copinger, 'Annals,' 198.
170. Prophecy in Vienna during 1911, quoted in AC, 22 January 1912, 18–19.
171. *Record* 11/4 (September 1919) 237.

# 11

# The Church under Angels (1929–60)

EDWARD HEATH'S DEATH ON 29 August 1929 meant that the remaining angels and their congregations were now bereft of any earthly leader; the movement was thus transformed into a network of independent churches.[1] No longer would it be in a position to act in any concerted manner; no longer was there any institutional means of ensuring that all churches followed the same policy. From now on there was to be an increasing risk of disunity.

## THE 'COVERING OF THE ALTAR'

During these decades, the truth began to sink in for many members that they would shortly cease to be able to celebrate their eucharistic liturgy. Awareness of the death of ministers and the closure of increasing numbers of churches played a part in this, but another significant factor was the constant reiteration of this theme in prophetic words. An elder at Newcastle-upon-Tyne quoted one such word:

> Behold, the day comes suddenly when ye shall for the last time celebrate the holy supper of love after this manner: for the Lord is about to cause the passover to cease and to veil the Altar. Oh, then shall it become quiet in the sanctuary of the Lord: quite quiet, yea, deep silence. Then shall the singers no longer go before, for the ministry of song must be silent in the Lord's House, because there is no worship; for the passover has ceased . . . .[2]

An important sermon from the angel Karl Schrey of Siegen in Westphalia interpreted the covering of the altar not as the cessation of the eucharist, but as the cessation of it in that form given by apostles, in which intercession was made on behalf

---

1. Rawson, *Teaching*, 1.
2. Parker, *Covering*, 2. The prophecy first appeared in *Record* 12/1 (September 1923) 34. That it was being quoted sixteen years later indicates that it was seen as significant.

of the universal Church.³ After this, judgment could not long delay. When judgment came upon Christendom, there would indeed be a covering of the altar, and he thought it possible that this was being seen first in Catholic Apostolic congregations as a warning for the whole Church. Such silence and cessation of the services, though foretold as far back as 1874, would nonetheless prove a severe trial to members; 'that would be the signal for any faithless ones amongst us either to rebel, and remonstrate with those in authority, and demand a resumption of the services, or to go out from us altogether, saying that all was over and done with; or that a huge mistake had been made.'⁴ Remarkably, few voices have been heard to this effect, and surviving members are known for their steadfast adherence to the directions they believe God has given the movement. Encouragement was rarely given to those who offered to celebrate the liturgy for them,⁵ although they were (and are) happy for ministers of other Churches to draw upon the liturgy for use in their own congregations. The reasoning behind this appears to have been that a commission was seen as a prerequisite for ministry to a Catholic Apostolic congregation, and in the absence of apostles there was nobody to give it.⁶

The expectation was voiced in 1945 that members would eventually have nothing else to draw upon for spiritual nourishment but the Scriptures, an interesting parallel with the approach adopted by the Exclusive Brethren, who believed that the Christian Church had been irreparably ruined and could not be restored. In Hollick's words:

> The time to which we have come is a solemn one. The work of the Lord as we have known it has almost passed away. The restored altars are being rapidly covered up, as the Lord has warned us. The ministers who still exercise pastoral care in the gathered congregations are now but few and aged. The time may come of which the Holy Spirit has given warning, when nothing shall remain but the Written Word, that living Word of the living God, to which everyone must then hold fast.
>
> Such thoughts as these should cause us no dismay. The closing of one phase of the work of the Lord is, to the faithful, an assurance that He is about to carry His work forward by a new step.⁷

The preacher went on, as so often, to exhort his hearers to look forward all the more earnestly for the Second Advent.

In another sermon, Hollick pointed out that members were increasingly cast back on their own resources in private study as opportunities for teaching became fewer. They had a responsibility to know and preserve the truth—especially the foundation

---

3. Schrey, *Ark*.
4. Ibid., 3-4.
5. Newman-Norton, *Time of Silence*, 28.
6. LPL, J. A. Douglas papers, MS 1468, 257-58, Edward Heath to E. H. Osmund Cooper, 18 September 1916.
7. Hollick, *Three Sermons*, 15.

truths which they had received. He concluded his exposition of their position and duty with this exhortation:

> The Lord is seeking to prepare you for the day of His appearing. He would find you pleading for your brethren, that in this time of trouble, their hearts may be turned to Him in penitence. He would have you praying for His Coming and the bringing back of His Apostles and all who sleep in Him. And He would have you to be vessels of His grace, filled with love and with the knowledge of His truth, that He may be able to use you as instruments of blessing to your brethren.[8]

Not surprisingly, some sermons from this period exhibit a defensive tone. For example, one on 2 Peter 1:16–18 entitled 'Not cunningly devised Fables' asserted that although the movement's 'notions' concerning the Second Advent and its claims to spiritual gifts and the restored fourfold ministry were treated as delusions and fables, the time would come when critics would have to eat their words.[9]

The Church's position was summarized by Ward in 1935 as one of 'chaotic hopelessness' resulting from the concentration of power in the hands of the apostles, and in particular Cardale.[10] He wrote of members expecting Christ to return in the flesh to the church at Albury, and alleged that they haunted the part of the parish churchyard there where many of the movement's leaders lay buried, especially at Whitsun. He implied that even Lord Eustace Percy (of whom more below) expected to see the dead rising from the graves there.[11] A Dutch member recorded that the locals gave this spot the name 'Resurrection Corner,'[12] so perhaps their outlook was not as hopeless as Ward implied. Further evidence for the strength of Catholic Apostolic convictions comes from their rejection in 1938 of another attempt by the New Apostolic Church to close the breach which had existed since 1863.[13]

---

8. Hollick, *Address*, 1–3.

9. Levesley, *Sermon*, 1–2.

10. Ward, 'Death of a Church,' 95. He later described the movement as 'authoritarian to the last degree, imbued with the reactionary, Tory spirit of Cardale which has led to a sheep-like docility on the part of all its lay members and to a [*sic*] utter unwillingness on the part of its ministers to take any responsibility without the guidance of an "Apostle"': LPL, Fisher papers 25:37, Ward to the bishop of Guildford, [February 1947].

11. Ward, 'Death of a Church,' 98. It may be that they were simply doing what many visitors to graveyards do, trying to decipher the names on lichen-encrusted tombstones. Evidence of interest in the graveyard's inhabitants is provided by the issue from Gordon Square of a guide: Anon., *Apostles and Other Ministers*.

12. Anon., *Albury: Extract*, 3.

13. Davenport, *Albury Apostles*, 159.

## THE CESSATION OF PROPHECY

It might be thought that the loss of ministers would result in an increased dependence upon charismatic gifts such as tongues and prophecy, and that the wheel would turn full circle as the Church returned to its origins. These gifts had certainly continued to be manifest in the services. A Church of Scotland minister who had been brought up in the Edinburgh church, Harry Whitley (1913–93), recalled how on one occasion during his childhood:

> After the Celebration and before the Communion Anthem, I became aware of a voice proclaiming loudly from one of the benches occupied by the officiating clergy. An under-deacon had hurried forward armed with notebook and pencil ready to take down in shorthand the message which was being uttered. I could make nothing of what was being said, nor could I understand anything of the language which was being spoken. I remember still something of the awe and apprehension which came upon me. This may have accounted for the fact that I did not dare to ask of my parents what it meant. I had, as I learned later, been listening to one 'speaking with tongues'.[14]

However, it was stressed that as the mind of the Lord had formerly been made known through apostles, now it was through the remaining ministers, and not through prophetic words.[15] The loss of ministers (in particular, of angels) to regulate the exercise of these gifts made inevitable their cessation in the services; an address by the priest A. E. Capadose at the Central Church on 24 February 1946 reiterated the angel's crucial role in watching over the exercise of the prophetic gift. Outlining how prophetic words used to be taken down by scribes, handed to the angel for a judgment and a selection sent to the apostles, Capadose recalled that Basil Seton (the last angel of the church, who had just died) had told him how a priest in one church decided after the death of his angel that prophecy should no longer be allowed. Accordingly, when Seton died, Capadose forbade the exercise of the gift of prophecy during services.[16]

## CLOSURE OF CHURCHES AND DISPOSAL OF BUILDINGS

A vivid, if perhaps one-sided, picture of Catholic Apostolic worship at this period has been supplied by Eustace Percy's nephew, the writer and naturalist Gavin Maxwell (1914–69), who recalled

> ... sitting wearily through the age-long sermons and services held by tottering old men who had no power to ordain successors. . . . Hope there must

---

14. Whitley, *Blinded Eagle*, 75.
15. Anon., *Address*, 1954, 2.
16. A. E. Capadose, *Address*, 2–3. Prophecy must still have been allowed in smaller meetings such as meetings for the exercise of spiritual gifts, over which a priest could preside, since there are references to it occurring in the mid-1960s: cf. Davson, *Sermons*, 3.

> have been, to hold those dogged congregations together even after, many years later, almost all of the ministers had died and the churches stood for the most part empty, but hope was not in those days evident to a child; the tired trembling old voices—voices belonging, each one, to personalities of patently unusual saintliness—that read the prayers seemed to be reciting dirges of dreary defeat, and the adult choirs sang at a tempo so slow that all music seemed to be lament. The churches of our faith were to me from the beginning places of infinite depression and sadness . . . .[17]

One of the churches he had in mind was that at Albury. In 1901 it was estimated that most of the 150–200 members of the congregation lived locally,[18] and Maxwell himself referred to a 'colony' of members, 'mostly spinsters,' in the village.[19] However, over time the ministers of the universal Church living there died. The last Sunday eucharist had been in 1929, before Edward Heath's death, after which H. G. Rees, the pastor, celebrated it midweek until he became ill in 1944. After the angel died in 1930 there were some in the Church who wished to see the eucharist cease. Seton apparently condemned Rees for opposing the closure of the Apostles' Chapel at that juncture, but Rees, whose concern was for his flock, intended that it should only close when he died, which was in 1953.[20] Such a difference of approach would become more serious in the 1960s, and result in internal criticism of official church policy.

The story from now on is one of continuing decline, marked by the deaths of the last of successive orders of clergy. Members also ceased to be blessed for lay ministries such as acolyte or chorister. The clergy statistics for 1948 explain why Hollick could foresee a movement entirely bereft of ministers; in England there remained just two angels, two dozen priests, and about fifty deacons; in Scotland, four priests and a few deacons; in Ireland just one deacon. The USA had an angel, a priest, and a few deacons, Canada two priests and a few deacons, and Australia four priests and a few deacons.[21] From this point, Copinger's 'Annals' and then the *Newsletter* become very much a record of deaths of ministers and closures of churches. Of the locations listed in the *Church Address Book* for 1948 where services were held, many were occasional rather than regular, most remaining churches being responsible for members in a number of other locations. Bishopsgate, for example, had responsibility for the churches at Romford, Ipswich, and Norwich, as well as providing occasional teaching or pastoral visits to ten other locations throughout East Anglia, while Newcastle had charge of an area stretching from Hull to Hexham; other examples could be given of the astounding efforts made by ageing ministers to ensure continuing provision for the spiritual

17. Maxwell, *House of Elrig*, 23.
18. Anon., 'Death of Woodhouse,' 5.
19. Maxwell, *House of Elrig*, 166.
20. Ward, 'Death of a Church,' 104–5; Newman-Norton, *Time of Silence*, 30; W. H., *Katholisch-apostolische Gemeinden*, 13.
21. Copinger, 'Annals,' 237.

needs of the flocks. The two surviving angels, Charles W. Thonger (1867–1956) in Birmingham (great-grandson of the first minister there, the former Baptist Thomas Thonger, whose congregation provided the nucleus of the Birmingham church) and Hollick in Manchester each had oversight of a number of other churches. Since 1923 Thonger's responsibilities had included oversight of the church at Belfast with its dependent people in Dublin.[22]

Yet large congregations could still gather; in 1947 there were a thousand names on the registers at Gordon Square (including those who had moved away), and 469 attended the Easter eucharist in 1951.[23] Registers for Eynsham and Bradford show that attendance increased dramatically on Sundays when there was to be a celebration of the eucharist; most members would have attended their local parish church at other times. Elsewhere, coaches might be hired to take members to a neighboring congregation for a celebration of the eucharist, especially on the great festivals of the Christian year.[24] But another side to the story is provided by the complaint of one minister that younger members, whose attendance was needed as elderly ones became less able to get out to services, were rarely seen and had become preoccupied with the affairs of this world.[25]

In 1950, after Hollick's death the previous year, Thonger issued a pastoral letter on the 'Present Condition of Churches under Apostles.' There was now no central headship of the Church, no universal Church minister, and no angel-evangelist. Only three angels remained worldwide; Britain could muster only twenty priests and thirty deacons. Yet Thonger's church in Birmingham was restored after war damage and renovated that summer; if he was a realist, he was certainly not a defeatist.[26] Similarly, the damaged Southwark church was rebuilt in 1953, although on a smaller scale as the licence necessary did not permit a full reconstruction. But by 1955 the ranks of the clergy in England and Scotland were reduced to one angel, six priests, and twenty acting deacons.[27] In many cases, therefore, it was lack of ministers rather than lack of members which led to the closure of churches. For example, Dundee still had five hundred members when the death of its last remaining minister necessitated its closure in 1948.[28] The church at Manchester lost its last minister (a deacon) on 18 January 1955; a sermon in Bradford the following Sunday (23 January) referred to its immediate

---

22. Ibid., 209; Newman-Norton, *Time of Silence*, 25. One of his nineteenth-century predecessors had responsibility for churches in an area stretching from Stoke-on-Trent to Barrow in Furness, and across to Hull: Anon., *Address to the Flock*, 7.

23. Fisher papers 25:41, Memorandum, 27 February 1947; E. V. Hayes, 'Easter Sunday at the Central Church,' *News Letter* 1 (October 1951) 6.

24. L. H. Halliwell, 'Bolton,' *News Letter* 1 (October 1951) 3; D. W., 'Kiel (Germany),' *Newsletter* 4 (April 1953) 16–17.

25. Middleton, *Pastoral Letter*.

26. Copinger, 'Annals,' 240.

27. F. D., 'Southwark,' *Newsletter* 4 (April 1953) 5–6; Albrecht, *Work*, 44.

28. Copinger, 'Annals,' 237; Gretason, 'Authority, Provisionality and Process,' 63.

closure as a result.[29] The underdeacons' address to the congregation explained what this meant in practical terms. The church 'must now be regarded as having been closed, but we can, for the present, use this building for meetings,' which would take place monthly on Wednesday evenings in the council room, the underdeacons presiding.

> At the meetings we are permitted to offer the Litany, hold a Congregational Prayer Meeting, read the Bible and any ministry sent to us from another church, and to sing psalms and hymns. These meetings will help to keep alive in our hearts the fullness of our precious faith and hope, and to remind us of the pure gold of Apostles' doctrine, while we give our full support to the services in our Parish Churches, waiting patiently and watchfully for the coming of the Lord and our gathering together unto Him.
> 
> ... [I]t was the hope and belief of those over us, that this church would still be used for divine worship, and it has been decorated and repaired with that object in view. The building will be disposed of by the Trustees in the Universal church, but we have reason to hope that it will be possible for accommodation to be reserved for our monthly meetings....[30]

The congregation would now be ministered to by underdeacons, deaconesses, and lay assistants; pastoral visits would continue, as would the issuing of printed ministries. Tithe was to be rendered in parish churches, although members could still make general and poor offerings in their own church. Senior ministers had urged members to communicate regularly in the Church of England and to benefit from its pastoral care, so strengthening what remained. A final request, which conjures up a vivid mental image for anyone who has ever visited a recently closed church, was that members would remove their books and private property.[31] Similar processes of closure occurred at Edinburgh and Birmingham, among others. At the latter, the church retained three vestries for storing records, using as an office, and holding monthly prayer meetings.[32]

A sense of bereavement was evident in the report by a deacon of the closure of the Norwich church on the death of its pastor: '[t]o me, the sole survivor of those who have fulfilled their duty and await their reward, falls the somewhat melancholy task of taking down and removing much that for a century has contributed to the worship and service of God.'[33] This approach to closures could sometimes cause a measure

---

29. BIA, CAC 1/10, Bradford Service Book, 23 January 1955. In fact, the last service appears to have taken place on 13 February: Copinger, 'Annals,' ed. Newman-Norton, 233. Closure came on the instructions of the acting archdeacon for the tribe: R. B. M., 'The Former Church in Manchester,' *Newsletter* 9 (April 1956) 7–8.

30. Anon., *Church in Manchester*, 3, 4; cf. A. F. R., 'Manchester,' *Newsletter* 8 (August 1955) 7–8. At Thonger's instruction, the Dublin church had also been cleaned and decorated in 1938, the year that it was closed: Anon., 'The Church in Dublin,' *Newsletter* 7 (December 1954) 4.

31. Anon., *Church in Manchester*, 5–6.

32. A. B. O., 'Birmingham,' *Newsletter* 12 (May 1959) 4–5.

33. T. W. I., 'Norwich,' *Newsletter* 5 (November 1953) 4–5.

of distress to members who wished to continue holding such services as they could, and was one of the points on which Davson would differ from the trustees during the 1960s.

A difference of approach between England and Germany now became increasingly evident. The death of the last angel in England came in 1956, while the last of all the angels to die was Schrey, on 2 November 1960.[34] In Germany, Schrey presciently ensured continuing pastoral provision for members by issuing pastoral guidelines for the conduct by underdeacons of services comprised of the litany and intercessions, and by blessing a large number of young underdeacons, the last at New York in August 1957.[35] When the last priest in Copenhagen consulted Schrey because members were reluctant to take communion in the state Church, which ordained women, he advised that the Danish churches be kept open and promised to visit when he could.[36] Schrey's actions were criticized because he went well beyond his area of jurisdiction, but such men provided a measure of stability on the continent which was lacking in English-speaking countries, with results which were soon to become apparent. The Germans never found their state Churches as congenial as the English found the Church of England, partly because, as we have seen, there had been intense opposition to the movement during the 1840s and 1850s. Although they resorted to them for baptisms, confirmations, marriages, and funerals, they would have been more open to the possibility of a continuing separate existence. Similarly, in Holland the last priest at The Hague, Johannes Landsman, nominated a council of underdeacons to take over responsibility for the Dutch work when he died.[37]

Even in Britain, however, there were some who saw a limited measure of worship as possible for churches which had only underdeacons.

> In those churches where there is no priest or deacon, and there are many of them now, no services can be held in the lower choir—that is, none at all can be held in the chancel of the church. But there still remain in many cases members of the congregation with underdeacons at their head, and these can and do fulfil acts of prayer and confession and listen to a word of ministry supplied to them....
>
> If there were no underdeacons left there would still seem to be no reason why members of a congregation should not meet together and offer prayers of confession and supplication.[38]

During this period a divergence was thus developing between those who saw continued existence under underdeacons as spiritually desirable and pastorally

---

34. Davson, *Sermons*, 3.

35. Copinger, 'Annals,' ed. Newman-Norton, 234; Anon., *Neue Apostelgeschichte*, 131, following Born, *Das Werk des Herrn*.

36. Davson, *Church in Paddington 80*, 5.

37. Anon., 'Holland,' *Newsletter* 12 (May 1959) 19–21, at 20.

38. Anon., *Three Pastoral Instructions*, 3, 4.

helpful, and those who considered that the loss of priests and deacons necessitated closure.

The church at Eynsham provides us with a window onto the process of decline. In 1901, attendance at the eucharist ranged between fifty and ninety, and services were held on several days each week. By 1918, attendance at the eucharist had dropped to between twenty-five and forty-five. By 1932, services were only being held on Sundays, and that every two or three weeks. In 1953, there were services three or four times a year, though still with a congregation of thirty to fifty, which confirms that shortage of ministers rather than shrinkage of congregations was the problem. Records then peter out, although the church did not close until 1982, when the last underdeacon died.[39]

The loss of ministers led to withdrawal into deeper silence. It became rarer for anyone to join the Church. Congregational records were often destroyed as churches closed (although records for congregations in Britain were supposed to be transferred to Gordon Square), and there was increasing emphasis on the need for secrecy regarding circulars and other publications meant for members.[40] One angel put at the beginning of a printed homily: 'I am anxious that those who receive them should reserve them for their own perusal, and would remind them of the rule that printed ministries which they receive should not pass out of their hands. When they have finished with them they may be destroyed.'[41]

Since 1853 the angels of the seven churches in London had served as deacons of the universal Church, being responsible for temporal matters such as the distribution of tithes and offerings and the upkeep of church premises until other arrangements should be made. The last (and the last archangel) to die was Philip Peck of Paddington in 1940.[42] Upon Peck's death, the solicitor who was treasurer of the Seven Churches' Fund instructed the executors to appoint seven new trustees.[43] Accordingly, in 1946 a group of seven trustees was set up as successors of the angels of the seven churches in London.[44] This avoided the need for the Charity Commission to step in and dispose of Church property. The trustees, who are drawn from all parts of Britain, remain responsible for property and financial matters; they do not give any kind of spiritual lead, since this is not part of their office. According to the most recent financial accounts, trustees are not necessarily members of the Church, but must be in sympathy

---

39. Oxford History Centre, Eynsham CAC records, NX1/A1/1–5, Registers of attendance 1880–1953; 'Eynsham: Protestant Nonconformity,' in A. Crossley and C. R. Elrington, eds, *A History of the County of Oxford*, 12: *Wootton Hundred (South) Including Woodstock* (London, 1990), 154.

40. Newman-Norton, *Time of Silence*, 25.

41. Hollick, *Homily, 25th December 1929*, 1.

42. Copinger, 'Annals,' 227.

43. Ward, 'Death of a Church,' 129.

44. In 1854 these angels had executed a declaration of trust, as a result of which they were empowered to hold church property and to manage it for the Apostles: Copinger, 'Annals,' 100–101. One source states that the trustees took over responsibility for financial affairs in England on 9 February 1948: Schröter, *Bilder*, 29.

with its beliefs and practices. Nonetheless, they had authority to instruct congregations to cease meeting.[45] The equivalent body in North Germany is the Vermögensverwaltung der Katholisch-Apostolischen Kirche—Stammeskasse Norddeutschland, based in Frankfurt am Main. This holds the deeds to almost all Church property and its funds have enabled large-scale renovation, as at Berlin-Süd.[46] Elsewhere, there appears to have been some kind of committee based in Zürich. During World War II, continental churches were overseen by it, and after the war it was sent a report on the starving condition of members in Leipzig. More recently, the temporal affairs of the Paris church were said to be under its jurisdiction. Francophone churches now have an 'Association des chapelles catholiques et apostoliques,' but little is known of this body apart from a controversy surrounding recent attempts to dispose of the Paris building (which neither the association nor its tenants, a Gallican Catholic parish) could afford to maintain.[47] This is, incidentally, the only instance I have encountered of any controversy in connection with the disposal of Catholic Apostolic buildings; the norm has been appreciation for the condition in which they have been maintained and for the Church's generosity in handing them over to other users.

The maintenance of buildings had a theological rationale. When that at Bradford was renovated and the organ overhauled in 1951, a deacon explained that it had been dedicated to God's service and therefore was to be maintained in hope of the Second Coming. The same year it was reported that a new stained glass window, designed by a member of the Paddington congregation, had been installed in the English Chapel of the Central Church, depicting Christ ruling among the four living creatures—a portrayal of the fourfold ministry. Further windows were installed there in 1955.[48]

As with provision for ministry post-1901, the lack of formal guidelines for disposal of property did not spring from neglect or indolence on the part of the trustees, nor even from refusal to face the facts, but rather from conviction. Archbishop Fisher recalled being told (possibly when he met two priests from the Central Church, H. F. Laughton and A. E. Capadose), that they were very willing for their property to pass into Anglican hands, but could make no advance arrangements to this effect as that would amount to a denial of their expectation of the Lord's immediate return.[49] A number of buildings were indeed taken over by the Anglicans, while some (such as Nottingham) were used by the Roman Catholics,[50] as Westminster had been in the 1920s. Various other denominations also acquired former Catholic Ap-

---

45. As happened at Hull: S. C. G., 'The former Church in Hull,' *Newsletter* 9 (April 1956) 11.

46. Fischer, 'Katholische-apostolische Gemeinden.'

47. E. S., 'Paris,' *Newsletter* 12 (May 1959) 13–14; S., 'Leipzig,' ibid., 16–17; Diersmann, 'Die Katholisch-apostolische Gemeinde in Paris'; Anon., 'Une mystérieuse petite église.'

48. E. V. Hayes?, 'Bradford,' *News Letter* 1 (October 1951) 5; eadem, 'Easter Sunday,' 6; H. P., 'Central Church, London,' *Newsletter* 8 (August 1955) 3–5, at 4.

49. Fisher papers 80:180, Fisher to J. W. C. Wand (bishop of London), 3 October 1951.

50. Ibid., 175, C. L. Berry to Fisher, 20 September 1951.

ostolic buildings. West Bromwich, Newcastle, Birkenhead, and Huddersfield went to the Elim Pentecostal Church. Camberwell, Kentish Town, Wood Green, Bishopsgate, Bristol, and Birmingham passed ultimately to the Greek Orthodox Church. When the Stoke-on-Trent church closed in 1951, it was leased to Brethren,[51] who also took over the Buxton and Romford buildings; they also used the church at Chelmsford, the chancel area being walled off. Plymouth was given to the Baptists after the war,[52] while Coventry went to the Welsh Presbyterians.[53] The fine building at Mansfield Place, Edinburgh, which from the 1990s was the subject of a successful campaign to save it and the Phoebe Traquair murals inside, had been taken over by a Reformed Baptist church in 1971. Some German buildings likewise passed to other denominations, among them Görlitz (to the Adventists in the 1970s) and Liegnitz / Legnica (to the Baptists after 1945). Around 1980 Hurben bei Krumbach and Cottbus were both being used jointly by Catholic Apostolics and the Evangelische Kirche in Deutschland. Bromberg (after 1945 Bydgoszcz in Poland) passed to a free church congregation. Elsewhere, in Melbourne the building was taken over by the Anglicans but with the Romanian Orthodox also retaining the right to use it. Launceston, Tasmania, passed to the Church of Christ.[54] Winterthur in Switzerland went to the Old Catholics, and Lausanne to a renewal movement among Reformed clergy in the canton of Vaud.[55] In North America, Anglicans took over San Francisco and Vancouver.[56]

Furniture, vessels and vestments were treated as devoted to sacred use, which meant that when a church closed, they were to be destroyed rather than used for secular purposes.[57] Similarly, the altar might be destroyed before the building was given to another denomination, as with the New York horn church in 1948.[58] Consecrated items and things of value were, like buildings, under the control of the seven deacons of the universal Church and their successors the trustees.[59] However, it was not uncommon for furniture and vestments and even communion plate to be given to the Anglicans (sometimes anonymously).

In disposing of buildings, the trustees have not been making money, nor have they acted for financial reasons; indeed, on one occasion they returned the sale price once the new congregation was settled, on the grounds that both were part of the one Church and the money was not needed. In the same way, they have consistently and

51. Copinger, 'Annals,' 241.

52. Ibid., 235.

53. Jones, 'Catholic Apostolic Church,' 154–55.

54. W. H., *Katholisch-apostolische Gemeinden*, 51, 63, 120; Schröter, *Bilder*, 221, 231, 245, 268, 301, 303.

55. Th. E. F., 'Switzerland,' *Newsletter* 12 (May 1959) 22–24, at 23.

56. J. Z., 'The Church in San Francisco,' *Newsletter* 5 (November 1953) 11; J. H. T. et al., 'The Church in Vancouver, British Columbia,' *Newsletter* 8 (August 1955) 9–12.

57. Anon., *Book of Regulations*, §§754–55.

58. Copinger, 'Annals,' 237.

59. Anon., *Book of Regulations*, §757.

generously supported Anglican ministerial training, although in recent decades they have done so in such a way as to ensure that this support was directed to male ordinands.[60] More recently, they have also made regular donations towards the support of some Orthodox parishes.[61]

With the decline in numbers of active or retired ministers and dependants needing financial support, there was less financial need. Yet tithe income continued to flow in. Catholic Apostolics were commanded not to pay tithes to their local parish church, even if they lived at a distance from the nearest Catholic Apostolic congregation and could not regularly attend it.[62] They were members of the Catholic Apostolic Church as a 'body within a body' and thus should pay tithes as the movement's ministers directed.[63] Tithes were meant for the upkeep of the ministry, not of buildings, and were to be paid to the work under apostles; offerings could be given at the church where members worshipped.[64] Of course, the fact that members continued to tithe even after most of the ministers supported by their tithes had died meant that a surplus began to accumulate. However, a circular on the subject of tithing issued in 1949 marks a change of position, probably a result of the appointment of the trustees: members were encouraged to continue tithing, but since the tithes were intended for the maintenance of the ministry, and there were few Catholic Apostolic ministers left, they were now permitted to pay them to their local parish church, in an envelope suitably marked.

> ... the Tithe presented in a particular church was used primarily for the support of the ministers in that church, and such amount as was not required for that particular church was sent up to the Seven Deacons of the Universal Church and was used by them for the help of poorer churches. Since the death of the last of the Seven Deacons the administration of the Universal Church funds has devolved upon others who have recently pointed out that owing to the greatly reduced numbers of ministers serving under apostles there is no longer the necessity to make the same provision as formerly. In view of this they have considered the question as to whether the time has not now come when Tithe could be better employed in the service of the Anglican or other branch of the Church.[65]

---

60. Flegg, 'Gathered under Apostles,' 186. On occasion, they requested that the source of their donation be not divulged: Fisher papers 82:114, Christopher B. Heath to Archbishop Fisher, 6 June 1951.

61. This has also happened in Sweden: Anon., speech, 7 September 2011.

62. Burne, Letter, 4.

63. Rawson, Copy of Ministry, 6–7.

64. Geere, Deacon's Ministry, 2.

65. Anon., To gathered Members; cf. Anon., Position of Absent Members, 4; Flegg, 'Gathered under Apostles,' 185–86.

Some members sent tithe money to their diocesan bishop for his discretionary fund, asking that it be used for the support of male priests and their dependants. However, I am given to understand that tithe money from the congregation at Paddington, and from those in Germany, has simply accumulated.[66]

But the Central Church continued to struggle to make ends meet, as was explained to the congregation in 1948. General offerings were used for bread and wine, maintaining buildings, and providing necessities for worship, but:

> ... for a long period of time the amount of the offerings have never been equal to the call on that fund. The deficit has been made up partly by a grant from the Archdeacon out of tribal funds. This grant has been made because the Apostle recognised that this building was specially large to accommodate worshippers at the Meetings of the Seven Churches, and too large for the congregation of a particular church. Consequently the expense of upkeep was more than the congregation could be asked to provide unaided. The balance of the deficit has been made up out of legacies, but we ought to look to the living not to the dead to provide what is needed. The legacies are steadily being used up, which is right; the Apostles never approved of a church becoming endowed, it is the certain way to destroy love-gifts.[67]

Perhaps the fullest explanation of the Catholic Apostolic Church's financial mechanisms and current state was provided by the Central Church deacon Malcolm Lickfold in a sermon of 1949. Explaining his unusual choice of topic, he 'proposed to give some information about the properties and funds of the Church. You are entitled to know about these matters.' (This could have been in response to media comment, or simply concern on the part of the trustees at the Church's financial state.) Peck had 'left written instructions to his executors to take the necessary steps as soon as possible to appoint new trustees of the properties, and he named six ministers of whom not less than three should be appointed.' As one died, the survivors elected a replacement, but '[t]he day may come when the burden of this trust may devolve on Underdeacons, and indeed on layman [sic].' He admitted that nobody had contemplated the need to make such arrangements, but the Church had had to put its affairs in order. After explaining how tithe was applied, he stated that the Church until recently had operated a Superannuation Fund for aged or infirm ministers. This was no longer needed, because '[a]ll our ministers seem to carry on in their ministry to the end.'[68]

Once the last priest died and the eucharist ceased to be celebrated, remaining ministers at Gordon Square and elsewhere were forced to modify previous instructions regarding tithes and offerings. A pastoral instruction from 1954 commented that offerings were expected to decrease when the eucharist ceased to be celebrated

---

66. This appears to be borne out by the 2014 Paddington church accounts.
67. Anon., *Sermon on Tithes*, 9.
68. Lickfold, *Sermon*.

there after the death of the last priest, but the reduction was such that it might not be possible to continue the expense of the limited services now held, and payments to poor members might also have to be cut. Members also appeared to be giving much more of their tithe than they should in the churches where they were worshipping; 'we can only be sure that the tithe is duly presented and dedicated according to God's commandments and properly used and applied in honour of His name when presented at a restored altar. Our brethren know neither the law nor the practice relating to God's tithe.'[69] Clearly it would be simplistic to assume that the financial history of the Catholic Apostolic Church during this period is solely a matter of accumulated tithe. Local congregations could be affected in ways which ran counter to general trends.

## MAINTAINING A SENSE OF IDENTITY

As churches closed in the English-speaking world, the production and distribution of sermons for absent members became increasingly important in maintaining their sense of belonging. Smaller churches might often reprint sermons from elsewhere, as would larger churches when a particular sermon was deemed worthy of wider circulation. When a church ceased to issue such sermons, usually once it had closed, members were added to the distribution list of sermons issued from elsewhere. By the 1970s, such sermons were being issued, presumably from London, for members of churches in many locations throughout the British Isles. The exception was Paddington, which has continued to issue its own sermons, which only began to be numbered in 1948.

We noted earlier that periodicals for German and Scandinavian Catholic Apostolics have continued to be issued. These were supplemented by *Rundschreiben* (1946–51), edited by the priest Carl Lehmann of Flensburg and sent to members dispersed across Germany after the war; from 1951 there was the duplicated Danish *Almindelige kirkelige efterretninger* (*General Church Intelligence*).[70] There was no official periodical in English, but as the movement's decline gathered pace some felt the need for a link between scattered members. From 1951 there appeared thirteen issues of the *News Letter* (from no. 3 *Newsletter*), an unofficial publication designed to keep members in touch with one another. It was the initiative of a priest at Bolton concerned for the congregations in his care.[71] Initially intended for churches in north-west England, it soon achieved global circulation. Explicitly disclaiming any official status, it welcomed contributions from readers, and offered news of remaining congregations, accounts of members' experiences testifying to fundamental Christian truths in the churches

---

69. Anon., *Pastoral Instruction*, 11 July 1954, 3–5.

70. Anon., 'Tidens tegn,' *Ungdomsbladet* 3/5 (April 1955) 6; cf. a stray reference in 1952 to 'an information paper about the situation of the churches in Germany' edited by one of the priests: *News Letter* 2 (April 1952) 13.

71. 'Foreword,' *News Letter* 1 (October 1951) 1.

of other denominations where they had settled, and photographs of ministers and church buildings. The *Newsletter* ceased to appear in 1961 because its continuance was deemed inappropriate, possibly as a result of the death of the last priest in England apart from Davson (Christopher B. Heath at Southwark) and the consequent lack of anyone to keep an eye on the publication's soundness and discretion. A similar publication in Danish (which exchanged articles with the *Newsletter* and may have been inspired by it) was *Ungdomsbladet for Katolsk-Apostoliske Menighedslemmer* (*Catholic Apostolic Youth Magazine*; 1952–60); this seems to have been an initiative from the Aarhus church.

A further means by which a measure of cohesion was maintained (and marriage within the movement encouraged) was the facilitating of contact by letter and visit between members in various countries. After the war ended, Hollick encouraged correspondence between British and European young people, and the *News Letter* carried an appeal for German penfriends.[72] It often reported visits overseas by British members, always including information about the state of the congregations visited. Advertisements were also carried for Catholic Apostolic books and pamphlets available from the authorized bookseller at Gordon Square, which would ensure that dispersed members could continue to benefit from sound teaching. When stock of a title ran out, a typescript was made and duplicated copies were produced for sale.[73] In this way, hundreds of works from the earliest days of the movement, as well as those from later generations, were kept in circulation. Such an operation continues, though greatly scaled down and intended for members only.

A particular concern in all this was to ensure that those born into Catholic Apostolic families grew up well taught. In Manchester, the felt need of teaching resulted in an underdeacon giving a series of addresses on the history of the work, as well as monthly young men's meetings at which papers on biblical and theological topics were discussed and passages from Scripture and the Great Testimony studied. In Rotterdam, an association was formed for young people, the 'Katholiek Apostolische Jongeleiden Vereiniging.' In Melbourne, monthly socials were organized. And the importance of private reading was stressed, with guidance given on helpful Catholic Apostolic writings.[74] In Copenhagen and elsewhere in Denmark, reading groups were even formed, comprised of four or five families and meeting in homes.[75] But the training and teaching provided in the home was fundamental, and it became all the more important as the opportunities to share in Catholic Apostolic worship diminished.[76]

72. Ibid.
73. E.g. *Newsletter* 13 (April 1961) 5; cf. occasional advertisements in *Smyrna-Stimmen* and *Ungdomsbladet*.
74. P. Harrison, 'Manchester,' *News Letter* 1 (October 1951) 2; J. M. and Prudence N. Pattie, 'Visit to Holland, 1948,' ibid. 15–16; I. McKinney, 'Australia,' ibid., 17; J. G., 'Books,' *Newsletter* 4 (April 1953) 17–20.
75. C. N., 'Læsekredse i hjemmene,' *Ungdomsbladet* 5/4 (February 1957) 9.
76. Anon., *Our Duty to our Children*; Anon., *Churches in Manchester and Bolton*.

# 12

# Catholic Apostolics and Anglicans after 1901

RELATIONSHIPS WITH THE CHURCH of England and its sister Churches form a thread that runs throughout Catholic Apostolic history. Its significance lies not only in the historical movement of individuals between the two communions, but in the light shed on the still-evolving Catholic Apostolic sense of who they were. We have already noted the increasing burden during the early twentieth century to pray for Rome, and the surprisingly positive estimate of that communion being expressed. Among English-speaking congregations, Anglicanism was regarded less idealistically than Rome, doubtless because ministers and members had more first-hand experience of it. Yet in spite of their awareness of what they saw as its shortcomings, many of them gravitated towards Anglican worship.

Catholic Apostolics were keen if critical observers of developments in the wider Anglican communion. They cautiously welcomed the 1908 Lambeth Conference, Hume feeling that it could be used to open eyes to the Church's need and God's way ahead. He approved of its call for penitence, but felt that it was mixed up with a potentially dangerous desire for the Church's enlargement; noting the absence of reference to the Second Coming coupled with concern for the extension of the kingdom, he saw this as implying that human effort could achieve such extension. In addition, he detected an assumption that the Church of Christ was in some way connected with the British Empire.[1] Lambeth 1920 was similarly criticized for its lack of reference to the Second Coming and the hope of resurrection. This, coupled with its inadequate apprehension of the Church's calling as an election, had doubtless given rise to a perceived confusion of Christian *koinonia* with a sense of common humanity. It was the Holy Spirit who must bring Anglicans to a true understanding of the nature of the Church, the sin implicit in schism, and a sense of helplessness; otherwise all schemes

---

1. Henry S. Hume, *Observations on the Lambeth Conference*, 2–4, quoted in Pinnington and Newman-Norton, *Conciliar and Apostolic Witness*, 32–33.

for union were doomed to failure.² Such criticisms highlight key aspects of Catholic Apostolic ecclesiology as it had developed. The Christian Socialist movement, which influenced some Anglicans during the earlier twentieth century, received a surprisingly sympathetic assessment from one writer, although the main burden of his criticism was that it, like Catholic Modernism, represented an outgrowth of a wider movement of critical thought which would lead to spiritual danger and pave the way for Antichrist. It misinterpreted the Sermon on the Mount and confused the Church and the kingdom of God.³

For their part, some Anglican bishops felt themselves on the back foot when dealing with Catholic Apostolics, notably in New Zealand. Samuel Tarratt Nevill, bishop of Dunedin, wrote to the archbishop of Canterbury, Frederick Temple, in 1897, regarding the agenda for the forthcoming Lambeth Conference. 'I find that not a few of the bishops would like to have the assistance of their brethren upon the question of the position of Irvingites and how to deal with them?'⁴ In a pastoral letter that year, Nevill warned his flock against Catholic Apostolic ministers whom he had heard were visiting the islands; his verdict was that 'this novel organisation is in some respects another gospel.'⁵ Nevill's request does not appear to have borne fruit, but two years later, William Garden Cowie, bishop of Auckland, wrote requesting advice: 'In this Province members of the so called Catholic Apostolic Church have of late been taking aggressive action; and our Bishops are in doubt how to deal with them.'⁶ So the context for this chapter is one of critical interest on one side and episcopal caution on the other.

## DEVELOPING CONTACTS IN BRITAIN

Shortly after Woodhouse died, one clergyman wrote to the archbishop of Canterbury, Frederick Temple, suggesting that the time could be right for an approach to the Catholic Apostolic Church: since it was in accord with the Church of England in most of its beliefs and practices, it should be possible to find a 'modus' for union.⁷ That autumn, the bishop of Wakefield suggested that a message be sent 'assuring them of our brotherly sympathy + regard in their time of expectation, and offering to receive their Communicants at our Altars, or to administer Sacraments for them in urgent cases—that is, provided that the report is true that ministerial acts are suspended just

---

2. Samuel M. Hollick, *Sermon, September 1920, On the Unity of the Church*, and C. E. W. Stuart, *Central Church, Sermon, October 1920*, Central Church no. 1057 (London, 1920), quoted ibid., 46.
3. Orr, *Lecture on Socialism*.
4. LPL, Lambeth Conference committee papers, LC 58:113, letter of 6 July 1897.
5. Nevill, *Pastoral*, 4.
6. LC 75:423, letter of 22 September 1899.
7. LPL, Temple papers 43:331–32, C. E. Medhurst to Temple, 28 February 1901.

now?'⁸ Temple put the matter on the agenda for the next two bishops' meetings, but it does not appear to have been discussed.⁹

His successor from 1903, Randall Davidson, was more sympathetic. In reply to a letter from the bishop of Oxford concerning the need for 'Irvingites' to be confirmed in order to receive communion in the Church of England, Davidson acknowledged that this was logically defensible, but sought to place discussion on a different footing, referring to his having had contact with them since boyhood. He confessed that his approach was 'neither logical nor regular,' but since they themselves were exceptional in their approach to ecclesiastical questions, it was impossible to deal with them according to normal rules; they were in a class of their own, 'eccentric rather than heretical.' He would allow Irvingites to be confirmed and communicate without insisting that they cease to communicate as Irvingites.¹⁰ This policy paralleled that of Lambeth 1908, which resolved that members of Orthodox jurisdictions who were eligible for communion in their own churches might be admitted to communion when cut off from their own ministrations.¹¹

From the Catholic Apostolic side, where there was an altar at which to communicate, members were discouraged from communicating in the Church of England as well.¹² But not all were able to attend a Catholic Apostolic church, so the coadjutors issued a paper in 1912 offering guidance regarding members seeking confirmation and communion in the Church of England. Those who lived at a distance from the nearest Catholic Apostolic church could do so, recognizing the real measure of blessing conveyed in the confirmation rite. However, some bishops had apparently instructed their clergy to receive them to communion without insisting on confirmation as a prerequisite; since confirmation was no substitute for apostolic sealing, it amounted to presumption or unbelief to seek it unless required to do so.¹³ Of course, there were limits to approval of the Church of England; members were not to be encouraged to go to the Church of England if it was openly unbelieving, but rather to find a church of another denomination which at least preached the gospel.¹⁴

It was not long before conversations with the authorities at Gordon Square began to be advocated in Anglican circles. A figure who emerges as a major participant and a thorn in the side of a sometimes reluctant episcopate is Samuel Royle Shore (1856–1946), a Birmingham solicitor and musicologist who had become interested in the Catholic Apostolics through studying their revival of the diaconate as a permanent

---

8. Ibid., 335–36, Bishop of Wakefield to Temple, 21 March 1901.
9. LPL, BM 4, 26 June, 12 November 1901.
10. LPL, Davidson papers, 144:356, Davidson to the bishop of Oxford, 17 June 1908.
11. Davidson, ed., *Five Lambeth Conferences*, 332 (Resolution 62).
12. Wigan Church Council minutes, 11 June 1903.
13. MC, 1912/1, 117–19.
14. AC, 10 July 1908, 2.

order of ministry. Davidson responded cautiously to Shore's urgings, waiting to see whether Catholic Apostolics were seriously interested in taking things further:

> At present, although I have not felt that it would be desirable for me to make a definite approach to the authorities of the body with a view to inviting conference, which I greatly doubt whether they would desire, I am not failing to take such opportunities as are mine of keeping touch with some of its leading men and allowing it to be known that I am quite ready to be approached more formally by them if they should deem such a step desirable.[15]

It appears that they did not, and nothing further on this subject was heard from Davidson until 1927. A memorandum recorded a conversation that year between him and Eustace Percy. Percy (1887–1958) was then Conservative MP for Hastings, president of the Board of Education, a Privy Councillor, and a leading Anglican layman. Davidson asked whether the body was 'decadent' (i.e., declining) and whether members felt that the loss of apostles was forcing them to reconsider their position, since he 'had been informed by leading Irvingites that it had become apparent to them that they must have misunderstood the original revelation made, as that revelation had indicated that the Second Advent would take place while the "Apostles" were still on earth.' Percy indicated that they felt no need to reconsider their situation as a separate body; while aware of the difficulties presented by the lack of ordinations to the priesthood, he was not aware of any significant numerical decline. As for the situation in twenty-five years' time (when ministers would be still fewer and more elderly), he acknowledged that the body's witness might indeed turn out to have failed. Davidson recorded his belief that the community was declining and his surprise that Percy was not more disquieted.[16]

After the death of the coadjutors, there was no leader with authority to speak for the movement as a whole, with whom Anglicans could seek to enter into negotiations. There would also emerge a serious divergence of opinion over the desirability of closer links with Anglicanism: the deepening of the silence was closely linked to increasing isolationism and introversion. The Anglican hierarchy, for their part, were slower to show interest. As yet there was no clear policy governing relations with the Catholic Apostolic Church, as evidenced by continuing requests from Anglican bishops for guidance from Lambeth concerning Catholic Apostolics wishing to take communion in the Church of England. The opinion of Archbishop Lang, who succeeded Davidson in 1928, was that no standing rules had been laid down by the bishops in conference, but that Catholic Apostolics could be admitted without being confirmed.[17] However, while he was therefore prepared to allow 'Irvingites' to communicate in the parish

---

15. Davidson papers 186:67, Davidson to Shore, 10 May 1913.

16. Ibid., 201:128, Memorandum of conversation held 16 July 1927.

17. LPL, Lang papers 100:76, A. C. Don (archbishop's chaplain) to the archbishop of York (William Temple), 12 December 1930.

church at Albury, he condemned as irregular the reciprocal suggestion that Anglicans might communicate in a Catholic Apostolic church.[18] As a general rule, 'it has been not uncommon in England for members of the Catholic Apostolic Church to be allowed to make their communion at our Altars.'[19] But this, it was later reiterated, was for reasons of pastoral economy, there being so few of their ministers remaining, and did not imply recognition of the Catholic Apostolic Church as such.[20]

Shore continued to promote negotiations for reunion, and thought these might actually benefit from the passing of the coadjutors.[21] Now, he argued, it might be necessary to appeal directly to the laity, rather than to work through official channels.[22] He therefore arranged to meet Basil Seton, who was serving provisionally as angel at the Central Church, on 4 November 1929. Shore envisioned the regularizing of Catholic Apostolic ministerial orders, and urged Seton to consider the contribution the movement could make to the cause of Christian unity: the wider Church could learn from the Irvingite operation of the diaconate, its expectation of the Second Coming, its practice of tithing, and its liturgy, among other things. Seton, however, refused to allow that remaining ministers might submit to anything which amounted to reordination. In response to Shore's suggestion that the resolutions of Lambeth 1920 offered a way forward, Seton stood the discussion on its head by calling attention to the provision in the liturgy for confirmation of other episcopal Churches' orders. For him, it was the Anglicans whose orders were in need of supplementing. However, the meeting was not completely fruitless; Seton was evidently struck by the idea that the Catholic Apostolic Church might have a contribution to make to the wider Church (the novelty of the suggestion to his mind was itself a demonstration of the movement's increasing isolationism).[23]

Shore was fundamentally out of sympathy with the refusal to make any provision for the continuance of the work after the death of the apostles. He felt that it was hard for churchmen to enter into discussion knowing that the fundamental principle of 'Irvingism,' belief in the restoration of apostles, had to his mind broken down and been rejected or ignored by all other Churches. Accordingly, he considered their policy 'hardly more than one of despair—it may be a pure[ly] selfish one—on the part of the higher ministers to avoid anything like a recognition of the utter failure of the dreams of the founders and themselves, and to "save their face".'[24] Furthermore,

18. Ibid., 109:303, Don to Edmund R. Morgan, 19 March 1932.

19. DEA, folder 'Episcopi Vagantes: Catholic Apostolic Church (Irvingites),' A. C. Don for Lang to the archbishop of Dublin, 31 December 1937.

20. Ibid., M. V. W.? to the bishop of Fulham, 18 August 1950.

21. J. A. Douglas papers, 235, S. Royle Shore, 'The "Irvingite" Communion. Notes of an Interview with the Bishop of London at Fulham Palace, on Saturday, Nov. 9, 1929.'

22. Ibid., 227–33, S. Royle Shore, 'The "Irvingite" Communion. An Interview at the Gordon Square Church on Monday Novr 4th, 1929,' at 232.

23. Ibid., 227, 230.

24. Ibid., 232.

with hindsight he could say that he had long considered it hopeless to approach the ministers, although he still hoped that something could be done to secure the buildings for the continuing use of the laity.[25] On the other hand, he also believed there to be considerable Catholic Apostolic goodwill towards the Church of England. As he commented to Lang in a 1930 report: 'They are increasingly unconscious of being separated from the Church, and in effect seem to regard themselves as members of a guild, with special forms of worship, in association with the Church.'[26] Some certainly felt this way, but others, even in England, followed a much more separatist line.

Among the recommendations in Shore's report to Lang were that where a Catholic Apostolic church was to close, the local incumbent could be consulted about providing ministrations using Catholic Apostolic forms. The 1908 Lambeth resolution concerning the Moravians offered a precedent for recognizing the Catholic Apostolic Church as a guild within Anglicanism or as a uniate Church (i.e., one retaining its own liturgy and customs).[27] Finally, since union or intercommunion required recognition of each others' orders, the bishops' offer at the 1920 Lambeth Conference to accept a form of commission and recognition from other religious bodies might allow Anglican clergy to submit to Catholic Apostolic confirmation of orders.[28] Shore's interest in the Catholic Apostolic Church was, however, subservient to another agenda, in which Catholic Apostolics would play a role in securing acceptance of Anglican orders by Rome.[29]

Lambeth 1930 adopted a resolution which proved a useful guideline for Anglicans in relations with Catholic Apostolics. Resolution 42 dealt with the intercommunion: laying down the general principle that Anglicans should only receive communion from ministers of their own Church, it recognized the need for flexibility in certain situations, such as when Anglican ministrations were not readily available. The same principle was interpreted as allowing members of other communions to communicate in Anglican congregations when their own ministrations were unavailable, or in other special or temporary circumstances.[30]

There seemed no way forward, however, towards any more formal understanding, and in 1931 Shore set down his conclusions in a final report to Lang:

---

25. Ibid., 260, Shore to E. H. Osmund Cooper, 2 October 1931.

26. Lang Papers 100:44–48, S. Royle Shore, 'Catholic Apostolic Churches under a Restored Apostolate: The Present Position at Home and Abroad,' 7 July 1930, at 44.

27. Resolution 70 allowed Anglican bishops to participate in consecrating bishops of the *Unitas Fratrum* (Moravians), provided that, *inter alia*, (i) the latter could give assurance of doctrinal agreement with Anglicanism in all essentials; (ii) the rite was judged sufficient by Anglican standards; and (iii) the *Unitas Fratrum* were willing to explain their position as that of a religious community or missionary body in close alliance with the Anglican communion: Davidson, ed., *Five Lambeth Conferences*, 334–35.

28. Shore, 'Catholic Apostolic Churches,' 45–46.

29. J. A. Douglas papers, 226, Shore to T. Norman Skene (rector of Albury), 13 July 1921.

30. Anon., *Lambeth Conference 1930*, 52–53.

- There was no hope of regularizing Catholic Apostolic relations with the Church of England.

- There was now no corporate entity with which to negotiate or establish regular relations.

- It was ministerial policy not to prevent the Catholic Apostolic Church from dying out.

- Schism among them was unlikely in the United Kingdom, and their ministers probably would not listen to any independent overtures.

- If important churches fell derelict, former members could ask the Charity Commissioners to appoint trustees to sell them and put the proceeds to appropriate use; Shore expected that the body's links with Anglicanism would be taken into account in the application of such income.

- Even though negotiations looked impossible, Anglicans should nonetheless be prepared for them.

No time should be lost in developing contacts with individual ministers and congregations, the most important being Seton; Shore believed other ministers would follow his lead.[31] However, Lang's response (through his chaplain) was merely to regret that 'it confirms his impression that at present it is quite futile to make any even quasi-official approach to the few remaining authorities of the Catholic Apostolic Church' and to express the hope that personal friendly relations with them might be maintained.[32] Shore complained in 1932 of the 'unanimous ineptitude of the Episcopate' in the whole business, alleging that words were not matched by action. He also expressed frustration that whilst individual Catholic Apostolic ministers seemed cooperative, as soon as they conferred with their colleagues they withdrew.

Lang (and later Fisher) brought a more cautious and analytical, and yet also respectful, judgment to bear on Anglican relations with Catholic Apostolics. There was a shift from Davidson's somewhat *ad hoc* approach to a more consistent and principled one. For example, in 1941 the bishop of Guildford drew attention to the condition of the Catholic Apostolic Church and the loss of many of its ministers. Noting that the pastor at Albury was no longer able to celebrate the eucharist on a Sunday, he commented that the previous archbishop had encouraged the rector of Albury to offer the Catholic Apostolics eucharistic hospitality. Lang allowed this within the framework provided by Lambeth 1930 Resolution 42: baptized but unconfirmed communicants of other Churches could be admitted to communion when cut off from their own ministrations.[33] Lang's caution may have been due in part to his

---

31. Lang papers 105:115–28, S. Royle Shore, 'The Irvingite or Catholic Apostolic Churches,' 4 November 1931, at 122–26.

32. Ibid., 207, Don to Shore, 17 November 1931.

33. LPL, BM 9:115–17, 20–21 January 1941.

awareness that approaches by the Church of England could be misconstrued: as he wrote in 1940 to his brother of Guildford, 'Remember, Macmillan, that we are both Scotchmen and that the Irvingites might think we are after the dibs.'[34]

It was not only in England that Anglicans were making contact with Catholic Apostolics; in 1930 the primus of the Scottish Episcopal Church asked bishops under his jurisdiction to make contact with ministers of Catholic Apostolic congregations in their areas and to report back. James Heath, one of the ministers of the large and influential Glasgow church, apparently told the bishop of Glasgow that, rather than his flock being left without ministers, they might look to the bishop to shepherd them.[35] However, the primus reported that nothing came of these approaches, partly, it was thought, because Heath possibly considered the Episcopalians unorthodox on some points and faithless in their view of the Second Advent.[36] Shore soon became involved; in 1931 he wrote to Heath inquiring whether a Scottish Episcopal bishop would be able to confirm according to the 'Irvingite' rite, and whether ordination would be possible for qualified and called members of the movement.[37] In his reply, Heath expressed a readiness to receive the bishop's pastoral ministry, and if necessary to submit to confirmation in order to receive communion, but rejected the possibility of further ordinations for service in the Catholic Apostolic Church. He also expressed disinterest in outsiders' plans for the work: 'While we appreciate the interest the clergy of the land take in us, we do not want them to make any move or take any step on our behalf: the Lord will look after us. But we do want them to take all the steps they can on their own behalf, and to use the Liturgy and any of our teaching that they appreciate, for the benefit of their own people—or rather that of the whole Church.'[38] Shore responded by accusing the movement's leaders of fatalism, condemning the laity to deprivation and (what was probably worse in his mind) Presbyterianism, and short-sightedness, failing to see the help that they could give the wider Church.[39] Heath, by now probably driven to courteous exasperation, posed him a question: if the work was a delusion, why perpetuate it? if not, why not accept it?[40]

Shore's next step might be considered breathtaking impertinence, given the responses he had been receiving; he wrote to Heath inquiring how Catholic Apostolic churches held their property, and alleging that their adoption of the principle of uniting with the established Church meant that, depending on the country, they could become Roman Catholic, Anglican, or Presbyterian. Worst of all, he charged the movement with isolationism and secretiveness, failing to let its light shine so

---

34. Lang to the bishop of Guildford, 1940, quoted in Ward, 'Death of a Church,' 133.
35. J. A. Douglas papers, 248, Shore to J. A. Douglas, 1 September 1930.
36. Lang papers 100:60, The primus to the bishop of Glasgow and Galloway, 10 September 1930.
37. J. A. Douglas papers, 267, Shore to James S. Heath, 22 July 1931.
38. Ibid., 268, Heath to Shore, 5 August 1931.
39. Ibid., 270, Shore to Heath, 30 August 1931.
40. Ibid., 273, Heath to Shore, 19 September 1931.

that others could see and hear of their example.[41] In his final reply, Heath concluded that the best thing that his fellow members could do for the Church was to pray, and refused to be drawn on the question of Catholic Apostolic properties or endowments.[42]

Nobody else would pursue the matter of Anglican-Catholic Apostolic relationships with Shore's tenacity.[43] His persistence is partially explained by his conviction that time was running out, and that there was a real danger of the potential Catholic Apostolic contribution to the cause of Christian unity being lost through their becoming extinct.[44] The failure of his approach was, however, inevitable, given the consistent emphasis on both sides upon the observance of due order and the differing views of the two Churches as to the means by which that order was legitimated. It is highly unlikely that any substantial agreement could ever have been reached. Anglicans were slow to recognize this, but Catholic Apostolics (whom Shore described, following Bishop Gore, as 'very good, but very impracticable') saw it clearly; they could not give up their belief in the restored apostles in order to gain their own bishop.[45] Furthermore, there were now almost no remaining universal Church ministers to take the lead: 1931 brought the death of the last apostles' minister, the archangel Ludwig Albrecht.[46] Most importantly, the concentration on matters of order completely overlooked what made Catholic Apostolics 'tick': the expectation of the Lord's return. There was no eschatological dimension to Shore's thinking, nor to that of most other Anglicans seeking to develop links with the Catholic Apostolics at that time.

Not all Catholic Apostolics wanted closer relations with the Church of England anyway. The divergence of attitude towards Anglicanism was increasingly evident after 1930, many seeing themselves as already members of the Church of England; as Seton explained, they had never broken away from it and they prayed each Sunday for the primate.[47] Lang himself admitted: '[m]any of them have regarded themselves as members of the Church of England[,] regarding their membership in the Catholic Apostolic Church as, so to say, giving an additional spiritual security not inconsistent with that belonging to the National Church.'[48] Not all would have held such views, however. Unexpectedly, the Albury congregation sought permission to worship at the

---

41. Ibid., 278, Shore to Heath, 26 September 1931.

42. Ibid., 280, Heath to Shore, 2 October 1931.

43. Although Fr Desmond Morse-Boycott had studied the movement for many years and was keen to place his knowledge at Lang's disposal in order to save a body which 'might, at this stage, yield to careful negotiation' (Lang papers 100:53, Morse-Boycott to Lang, 22 October 1930), little appears to have been done to take up his offer either. His recollections of the movement are found in his book, *They Shine like Stars*.

44. Lang papers 100:45, 'Catholic Apostolic Churches.'

45. Ibid., 50, Shore to Lang, 1 August 1930; Gretason, 'Authority, Provisionality and Process,' 285–86.

46. Copinger, 'Annals,' 218.

47. Anon., 'Church Peril of Extinction.'

48. Lang papers 100:52, Lang to the bishop of Gloucester, 16 October 1930.

parish church while their own was repaired during August 1931,[49] but as the rector of Albury, Philip Gray, told an official at Lambeth: 'They have no desire to become a sort of Guild within the Church of England and they will never come over to the Church as a body. They will simply go on as they are whatever happens awaiting the coming of the Lord. . . . [I]t would not be wise to approach any of their leaders at present. It would be misunderstood and they are still very ardent in their expectation.'[50] He had good reason for thinking this: Rees told him that he would give the congregation at the Apostles' Chapel no direction, as they came from a variety of places outside Albury and he did not want to break them up; indeed, Rees thought that it could be God's will to deprive them of the eucharist.[51]

And not all Anglicans were sympathetic towards Catholic Apostolics: in 1935 there appeared a study of the Catholic Apostolic Church and its current situation by the Anglican spiritual director Reginald Somerset Ward. Although Ward saw the differences between the two Churches as lying in the area of orders rather than that of faith, he criticized Catholic Apostolics as latter-day Montanists, setting up their claims to the gift of prophecy over against the rest of the Church.[52] He alleged that they took the neglected doctrine of the Second Advent and over-emphasized it,[53] and he did not accept that the apostles had been called by divinely inspired prophecy. However, he acknowledged that the movement had a real contribution to make to Anglicanism; noting the moderation of their statements regarding the real presence and the practice of reservation of the sacrament, he commended their eucharistic rite as 'unusually clear and well developed.'[54] Furthermore, their provision for a range of minor orders served to allow zealous laity a means of service in the Church. Even their expectation of Christ's return could, he felt, enrich the Church of England.[55] But their reserve he saw as 'the shielding of spiritual nerves which are raw with inward doubt and cannot bear in addition outward scepticism.'[56] If left to themselves, they would do nothing, so it was the Church of England's responsibility to save them. As with a dying individual, they should be treated with more sympathy than would be appropriate if the movement were alive and well. In Ward's view, the celebration of the eucharist was something which would attract Catholic Apostolics to the Church of England: the weak and the young stood in special need of such provision.[57] However, like others,

---

49. Ibid., 105:109, Gray to Lang, 27 June 1931; Ward, 'Death of a Church,' 103.

50. Ibid. 100:107, C. C., 'Catholic and Apostolic Church,' memorandum of a meeting with Gray, 22 July 1931.

51. Ward, 'Death of a Church,' 102, 104–5.

52. Ibid., 108–9, 119.

53. Ibid., 72.

54. Ibid., 92.

55. Ibid., 115, 125.

56. Ibid., 100.

57. Ibid., 97, 116–18, 120, 125–27.

Ward appears not to have understood what made Catholic Apostolics tick. He urged that no mention of apostles be made in negotiation, since it would be impossible to reach an accommodation if they stuck to their views. It is inconceivable, however, that any member would have failed to raise the issue. It did not help that he urged the hierarchy to act partly on the grounds that thousands of members and upwards of £2 million worth of Church property would thus come into Anglican hands.[58]

Archbishop Fisher, who took office in 1945, also sought to apply established guidelines in relations with the Catholic Apostolics. In a letter to the bishop of Norwich, he pointed out that the Catholic Apostolic Church was not in communion as a body with the Church of England, although its communicant members could receive communion at Anglican altars when out of reach of their own ministrations; regular Catholic Apostolic attenders at Anglican churches ought therefore to be confirmed.[59] To another correspondent he stated that children, who were admitted to communion for the major feasts of the Catholic Apostolic calendar, should not be admitted to communion in the Church of England until confirmed.[60] With the loss of the movement's ministers, the care of its children and young people became an increasingly significant factor in the migration of Catholic Apostolics to the Church of England; even at Albury, parents were bringing their children for Anglican confirmation.[61] Indeed, Hollick as acting archdeacon in England reminded members in congregations left without any ministers apart from underdeacons that the coadjutor had advised them to go to the local Anglican church, to give their offerings (but not usually their tithes) there, and to seek pastoral care there.[62]

An appendix to Ward's work details further official contacts during the 1940s. Eustace Percy was regarded as 'the only man whom they would follow as a body' and his friendship with the archbishop was noted, but Fisher thought Percy would be difficult to approach, and considered that there was a need for greater clarity about what offer the bishops should make to Albury and other surviving congregations.[63] The idea was mooted of approaching Percy through Lord Halifax, but several years elapsed before this suggestion was followed up; when it was, Halifax was somewhat reluctant as a layman to comply, feeling that Percy would not welcome it: he preferred

---

58. Ibid., 119–21. This figure first appeared in the *Daily Express* during October 1930, as a conservative estimate of the body's wealth: cutting in Lang papers 100:54. The premature nature of Ward's suggestion is evident from the fact that, as late as 1935, Catholic Apostolics had still not ruled out the completion of the Gordon Square church: Lickfold, *Catholic Apostolic Church*, 40.

59. LPL, Fisher papers 25:18, Fisher to the bishop of Norwich, 8 March 1944. This policy was reaffirmed on other occasions.

60. Ibid., 21, Fisher to A. E. O. Anderson, 7 September 1945.

61. Ibid., 25, 29, Bishop of Guildford to Fisher, 18 December 1946; Fisher to Lord Halifax, 18 January 1947.

62. Hollick, *Memorandum*, 1.

63. Ward, 'Death of a Church,' 131.

Fisher to make the necessary moves.[64] Fisher agreed, although like his predecessor he was apprehensive lest he be suspected of 'angling to receive their reversionary rights' to the Catholic Apostolic Church's property and wealth, and sought reassurance from the bishop of Guildford.[65]

Fisher then wrote to Laughton, seeking a meeting.[66] Laughton and Capadose met him a few days later, and Fisher's recollections are preserved in a memorandum. It was, apparently, generally known among Catholic Apostolics that they should seek a home in the Church of England, and the need for confirmation presented no obstacle. But when Fisher suggested that one of their ministers might be consecrated as a bishop in order to restore their power of ordination, he was failing to understand Catholic Apostolics on their own terms, and the idea was inevitably rejected. Anglicans had orders and a concept of ministry which was valid for them, but Catholic Apostolics, whilst recognizing these, could not accept them for themselves, since their own theology of orders and ministry made ordination dependent upon apostolic action. Fisher realized that Catholic Apostolics could accept nothing from Anglicans except their hospitality; there was nothing which could be done for them as a body now as a network of independent congregations. He and Capadose were alike aware of a tension between theory and practice in the Anglican offer to Catholic Apostolics of eucharistic hospitality: '[Capadose] detected that on our principles we ought not to admit them to our altars. . . . We, as denying their theory of their Apostolate, ought strictly to say that they are heretics and ought therefore to exclude them. In fact they are right to come and we are wrong to admit them, but they appreciate the hospitality we give.'[67]

Concerned to uphold his own Church's position regarding intercommunion, Fisher was perhaps better able to appreciate the stand taken by other bodies. Some years later, Fisher's recollection was that he 'fully understood and sympathised with the position that they took.'[68] This was a considerable advance on the approach of earlier archbishops, and is borne out by the generally positive tone of his letters on the subject. But one factor which he did not take into account—perhaps unsurprisingly—concerns the function of prophecy within the Catholic Apostolic Church. At all important junctures in the movement's history, prophetic light had intimated or confirmed the course of action to be taken. With the loss of ministers authorized to speak to the movement as a whole, and the entering of the 'Time of Silence,' there could be no prophetic light to provide authoritative direction concerning negotiations

---

64. Ibid., 134; cf. Fisher papers 25:22, Bishop of Guildford to ? Cheshire, n.d.; ibid., 31, Halifax to Fisher, 24 January 1947.

65. Ibid., 25:32–33, Fisher to Halifax, 29 January 1947; Fisher to the bishop of Guildford, 29 January 1947.

66. Ibid., 34, Fisher to Herbert F. Laughton, 10 February 1947.

67. Ibid., 41, Memorandum, 27 February 1947.

68. Ibid., 80:170, Fisher to Charles W. Thonger, 22 November 1951.

with the Church of England.[69] Capadose died in 1952, and Laughton's death in 1954 put paid to any further such conversations.

It must be said that whilst much Anglican effort was expended on working out how to bring Catholic Apostolics back to the Church of England, the movement had never been anything like totally Anglican in terms of the denominational background of its members or ministers. Moreover, its membership was international, and an Anglocentric approach could not but create significant problems, although the Church's own ministers often saw themselves as having particularly close ties with Anglicanism, as did many congregations, even abroad. Indeed, we shall show now how their attachment to Anglican worship would cause ecumenical problems.

## CATHOLIC APOSTOLICS AND ANGLICAN CHAPLAINCIES ABROAD

After the end of World War II, Catholic Apostolics in some European countries began to seek out Anglican congregations originally founded for expatriates or tourists.[70] Outside southern Europe, congregations attached to the Church of England formed part of the diocese of London's Jurisdiction of North and Central Europe, overseen by the suffragan bishop of Fulham (an area of London) until its merger with the diocese of Gibraltar in 1980 to form the diocese in Europe. The Church of England's staff in Europe had a policy of not interfering with the internal affairs of continental Protestant Churches, and of not proselytizing; chaplains saw their ministry as being to British subjects and their families, but during the late 1950s a number of Catholic Apostolics expressed a desire to join the Church of England. Such accessions had the potential to embarrass the Anglican Communion in its ecumenical relations. In particular, tensions arose between the Anglican Communion and the Old Catholic Church. especially in Holland. The Old Catholic Church saw itself as the most appropriate adoptive home for former Catholic Apostolics, since Anglicans and Old Catholics were in full communion with each other following the Bonn agreement of 1931.[71]

Part of the reason why Anglicanism attracted many Catholic Apostolics was the perceived downgrading of the sacraments in Protestant churches, as in Holland: 'The preaching there was philosophic and political to a large extent, the Sacraments were thought nothing of, and the congregations there felt that they could not let their young people go and hear such sermons and come into contact with such indifference to the Holy Sacraments.'[72] What follows will pay particular attention to Anglican efforts to provide sacramental ministrations.

---

69. Gretason, 'Authority, Provisionality and Process,' 327 n. 24.
70. Newman-Norton, *Time of Silence*, 28.
71. Fisher papers 200:247, Fisher to J. Malcolm Lickfold, 27 March 1958.
72. Davson, *Church in Paddington 29*, 5.

Catholic Apostolics came to Anglican worship with fairly set expectations regarding the celebration of the eucharist and occasional offices on their behalf, but one chaplain, Paul Collins of Brussels, expressed his scruples about conforming to these. In 1956 he explained to Bishop Stopford (bishop of Fulham 1955–57) that after his installation in 1954 he had been reluctant to minister to them as his predecessor had done, celebrating the Catholic Apostolic liturgy once a month in French, but Bishops Ingle (bishop of Fulham 1949–55) and Wand (bishop of London) had wished it continued. Johannes Landsman of The Hague, the last Catholic Apostolic priest in Holland and Belgium, had decided to cease celebrating their liturgy in Brussels. To fill the gap, therefore, Collins ministered as required, performing occasional offices and sick communions at the Catholic Apostolic churches in Brussels, Châtelet, and Montigny, using Catholic Apostolic rites. The sticking point had come when he was informed that he might be asked to perform a baptism in Paris; the Catholic Apostolic argument was that he, unlike the Church of England clergy there, had been 'commissioned' by Landsman. Collins felt that he was being treated as an extension of Landsman, ministering when the latter could not, with no connection to the Anglican Communion. 'I am expected to do things in his own manner, and each occasion is accompanied by the reading of a Pastoral Letter from him.' What purpose, he asked, were Anglican ministrations to these people serving, except that of indefinitely perpetuating a sect? Catholic Apostolics appeared to regard such Anglican ministry as implying acceptance of their movement's divine origin, while Belgian Roman Catholic clergy viewed it as cooperating with schism or heresy among their flocks.[73]

Stopford's response was that the Catholic Apostolic Church could not last long, and the Church of England was 'in a sense, its residuary legatee. It is our policy to be as helpful as we can in these last stages.' Stopford had told Landsman that no commissioning was needed for local chaplains to minister to Catholic Apostolic people, and the two had agreed that the Catholic Apostolic liturgy was not to be used. Catholic Apostolics were in Anglican charge because they were unhappy with any other Church. 'In necessity, therefore, we admit them to our Sacraments and are willing, for their sakes, to depart from our normal rule that we use only English in our services.' Stopford reasoned that this approach was not perpetuating a sect; when Landsman died, the Catholic Apostolic Church in the Low Countries would probably come to an end.[74] Events would prove him wrong.

The catalyst for wider problems appears to have been Landsman's death on 12 January 1958.[75] On 6 February Fisher indicated that he was setting up a committee

---

73. LMA, CLC/320/F/004/MS32521, Jurisdiction of North and Central Europe, Correspondence concerning the Catholic Apostolic Church in Belgium and the Netherlands, 1950–60, P. D. Collins to the bishop [Stopford], 20 April 1956; Anon., 'Holland: The Hague,' *News Letter* 1 (October 1951) 8.

74. CLC/320/F/004/MS32521, [Stopford] to Collins, 13 May 1956.

75. Landsman's father Jacobus had been the church's first angel: Tang, *Het Apostolische Werk*, 243. One wonders whether it was due in any measure to Catholic Apostolic influence that this chaplaincy later became involved in the charismatic renewal movement: cf. Lewis, *Something Happened at The*

to consider the issue of non-English Christians wishing to join continental Anglican congregations. A particular concern for Fisher was the position of Catholic Apostolics.

> Here in this country the Catholic Apostolic people, though out of loyalty refusing to surrender their expectation of Our Lord's return within a short while, do rely upon us, and we do everything we can for them.
>
> What can we do for these continental Catholic Apostolics? Should it be along the following lines?
>
> (a) Discussion with the leaders of the Catholic Apostolic Church in England to get their good will?
>
> (b) Discussion with the Old Catholics to get their interest and co-operation?
>
> (c) Church supported both by ourselves and by the Catholic Apostolic Church in this country until such time as they wish to throw in their lot totally with some other Church?[76]

The 'Continental Church Questions' committee met on 12 March,[77] and a memorandum produced for it by Roderick Coote, Stopford's successor as bishop of Fulham, outlined the problem presented by members of the Catholic Apostolic Church:

> . . . our Anglican clergy minister to the members of the Catholic Apostolic Church in the Netherlands, in Belgium, France, Germany and elsewhere, whose clergy are dying out one by one with no possibility of the ordination of others to take their place. These ministrations are offered in the language of the country in one or two cases where the chaplain is capable of so doing. Should the eventual dying out of that Church mean the absorption of their membership into the Anglican Church, the Anglican Church would be faced with the problem of ministering to a large group of persons unable to speak English. In the Netherlands alone the Catholic Apostolic Church is, I am told, numerically greater than the Anglican Church and possesses many Church buildings.[78]

Language appears to have been the primary issue for Coote: services could only be provided on any consistent basis by nationals, who would need to be trained (in English) and ordained. It was most acute in the case of the Catholic Apostolics:

---

*Hague*. The Anglicans had used the Catholic Apostolic building for several years while their own was rebuilt after the war: Anon., 'Holland: The Hague,' 8.

76. LPL, CFR AC 5, 'Council on Foreign Relations, Anglican Chaplaincies abroad: Function in Europe,' 19, Fisher to J. R. Satterthwaite (secretary of the Church of England Council on Inter-Church Relations), 6 February 1958.

77. Ibid., 22, agenda.

78. Ibid., 28–39, R. N. Coote, 'Memorandum on the Function of the Anglican Church in North and Central Europe,' at 33.

> ... there being in that Church a number of very fine men who are deacons or underdeacons, once it becomes clear through the death of their last priest ... that their expectation of Our Lord's immediate return has failed, it is quite likely that the Catholic Apostolic Church may provide the Anglican Church not only with a number of Church buildings and a large flock, but also with the Dutch men who would be willing and able to be ordained priests to minister to those persons requiring such ministrations in the Dutch language. Again, there is now quite a considerable body of Dutch membership in the Anglican Church from which future ordinands might be drawn if they were to be sought out and encouraged.[79]

In his view, the Church of England had already become Dutch, and given that the Old Catholics were not well regarded in that country, he felt it was time to institute a more open policy, welcoming all who came for spiritual help and ordaining nationals; in any case, most Dutch chaplaincies were staffed through the Evangelical Commonwealth and Continental Church Society, whose ministers would hardly be likely to sympathize with Old Catholic high churchmanship.[80]

Coote's suggestion was not well received by Herbert Waddams, general secretary of the Church of England's Council for Foreign Relations. Waddams was concerned that its apparent endorsement of proselytism could have serious implications for relations with the Orthodox Churches; it would be impossible, he contended, to do anything for the Catholic Apostolics without the full agreement of the Old Catholics.[81] At the committee on 12 March, he suggested a conference with the Old Catholics to discuss the question of Catholic Apostolics and Dutch Reformed who wished to join the Church of England.[82] Coote therefore wrote to Archbishop Andreas Rinkel of Utrecht on 21 March, suggesting a meeting to discuss the situation.[83] This took place on 24 April, and Waddams was asked to formulate some propositions and practical suggestions to submit to Canterbury and Utrecht.[84] These stipulated that the Catholic Apostolic Church could not be recognized as a Church because it possessed no valid *officium* in Old Catholic eyes, and therefore it was impossible to provide communion for them as a group, but members could be received as individuals if they accepted the Niceno-Constantinopolitan Creed and affirmed their belief in the real presence of Christ in the eucharist. They would be encouraged to be confirmed and become Old Catholic or Anglican, and expected to submit to the discipline of their new Church

---

79. Ibid., 35.
80. Ibid., 38–39.
81. Ibid., 40–42, H. M. Waddams, comments on Coote's memorandum, 30 January 1958, 41.
82. Ibid., 52, committee minutes, 12 March 1958.
83. Fisher papers 200:245, Coote to Rinkel, 21 March 1958.
84. CFR AC 5, 54–57, H. M. Waddams, 'Utrecht Meeting between Old Catholics and Anglicans: An unofficial Account by HMW,' 57.

(which would prohibit them from receiving communion among Catholic Apostolics or Protestants).[85]

It was not going to be easy to achieve this: on 3 March Collins had written to Coote, informing him that since Landsman's death, the Catholic Apostolics wanted regular celebrations of communion in their Brussels church, a request which indicated their determination to continue a separate existence.[86] From the Catholic Apostolic side, Lickfold explained to Fisher why they were so reluctant to join the Old Catholics. A prominent member in Holland had asserted that the Old Catholics had made no move to welcome them, their services were formal and few communicated, the mode of doing so—receiving bread dipped in wine—was unfamiliar, and they seemed spiritually dead. Catholic Apostolics preferred Anglican worship, and there were members willing to translate the services into Dutch if necessary.[87] In the face of such determination, Fisher acknowledged to Lickfold that the final outcome was likely to be that Catholic Apostolics would be allowed to go wherever they wished.[88] The solution proposed by a subcommittee reporting to the Lambeth Conference that year was that Old Catholic priests be invited to celebrate the Anglican eucharist in Dutch for Catholic Apostolics, if Coote and Rinkel would permit this; Anglican priests might be granted similar permission to celebrate according to the Old Catholic rite and in Old Catholic churches in English.[89]

The numbers involved gave the issue a high profile: in 1959 it was reported that there were about nine hundred Catholic Apostolics in Holland and a further hundred in Belgium, with eleven churches in use in Holland and three in Belgium.[90] When a new Anglican chaplain was installed in Brussels and Catholic Apostolic ministers had a visible presence at his installation, the English Anglican newspaper *The Church Times* apparently thought it 'amazing that it is only now, when the sect is practically extinct, that it comes out into the open like this.'[91] Conversely, at Landsman's com-

---

85. Fisher papers, 200:249, draft memorandum, 30 April 1958; ibid., 237:81, 'Catholic Apostolic People in Holland,' memorandum no. CFR 666, 16 December 1958. In November, Waddams's draft had been approved with minor amendments by the Old Catholics: CFR AC 5, 70–72, 'Rules for Pastoral Practice in respect of the "Catholic-Apostolics",' 11 November 1958, in Dutch and English versions.

86. CLC/320/F/004/MS32521, Collins to Coote, 3 March 1958.

87. Fisher papers, 200:250–51, Lickfold to Fisher, 26 April 1958. By 1962 members in Holland and Belgium had produced translations which were sufficiently acceptable for Coote to express the desire for their authorization for Anglican, as well as Catholic Apostolic, use: CFR CFC 45, 'Old Catholics: Netherlands: The Catholic Apostolics, 1958–70,' 47, Coote to Satterthwaite, 13 February 1962. It is still asserted that Old Catholics in Germany have never offered eucharistic hospitality to Catholic Apostolics: Fischer, 'Katholische-apostolische Gemeinden: einst und jetzt.'

88. Fisher papers, 200:252, Fisher to Lickfold, 13 May 1958.

89. CFR CFC 45, 2, L.C.1958/Committee II/10, report by the bishop of Willesden (chairman of the Continental Church Questions committee), concerning Anglican ministrations in Holland, with special reference to the Catholic Apostolics.

90. Ibid., 8, E. F. Alderwereld to J. R. Satterthwaite, 18 June 1959.

91. Ibid., 10, C. L. Berry to H. M. Waddams, 24 June 1959, note.

memoration ministers had been present from the Protestant, Roman Catholic, and Old Catholic traditions, and an Anglican priest assisted Davson with the administration of communion, indicative of how Catholic Apostolics were now part of the web of ecumenical relationships in Holland and Belgium.[92] In a sense, their profile was perhaps higher than it had ever been.

In 1960 Coote outlined to Fisher how things had developed and asking what he should do. After Landsman's death, Catholic Apostolics had decided to attend Anglican eucharists once a month *en masse*, which meant over two hundred extra communicants at The Hague. Coote explained that on the first occasion the chaplain had accepted an underdeacon's offer to assist with the administration of the chalice, the latter assuring him that Stopford and Wand had permitted this, but Rinkel found out and complained that this implied recognition of the Catholic Apostolic Church as a Church rather than a heretical sect. Such perceived rigidity on his part ensured that they continued to prefer Anglican ministrations. The underdeacon was, in Coote's eyes, a fine man, and a potential Anglican ordinand, who was trying to bring his flock into the Church of England without betraying their convictions. It was not clear to Coote, however, what the best course of action was.[93]

The response of the Department of Ecumenical Affairs at Lambeth was firm: Catholic Apostolics preferred Anglican ministrations not because there was less rigidity and formalism, but because it was easier for them to retain their distinct identity, thanks to the language difference. The Old Catholics were alleging that the Anglicans were not keeping to the agreement between the two Churches, and that the latter were admitting the Catholic Apostolics for financial benefit; it was not acceptable to them for the Anglicans to use the underdeacon, and in Lambeth's opinion there was no way that he could be admitted and licensed as a reader. The bishop was therefore to license an Anglican as a reader in order to administer the chalice.[94] In the last analysis, Fisher instructed, the agreement with the Old Catholics had to be observed, and the Catholic Apostolics had to accept that.[95]

They did so readily.[96] By 1961 several Catholic Apostolic congregations were benefiting from a monthly Anglican service, sometimes in Dutch, conducted by the local chaplain or Old Catholic priest.[97] In Belgium, there was a monthly special celebration in Brussels, members being joined four times a year by those from Châtelet, and members in Antwerp attended services at the Anglican chaplaincy there each

---

92. Davson, *Church in Paddington 88*, 7–8, calling the occasion 'truly catholic'; Anon., 'Holland,' *Newsletter* 12 (May 1959) 19–21, at 19.

93. Fisher Papers, 237:77–79, Coote to Fisher, 1 April 1960.

94. Ibid., 80, Satterthwaite to F. Temple, 14 April 1960; ibid., 82, Fisher to Coote, 5 May 1960.

95. Ibid., 85, Fisher to Coote, 13 May 1960.

96. CFR CFC 45, 30, J. van Engelen and T. A. Leenman (Catholic Apostolic Church, The Hague) to Coote, 21 September 1960.

97. Ibid., 32, E. F. Alderwereld to Satterthwaite, 20 July 1961.

month.[98] The Anglican chaplain at The Hague explained the strategy which he and his colleagues followed. 'The general policy of the Church of England in the Netherlands is to show such hospitality and friendship with the Catholic Apostolics that when they reach the crisis and have to decide which way to turn for help, they may feel they are already largely Anglican in almost their entire outlook and would be happier to be absorbed with us than any other body.'[99] He baptized Catholic Apostolic children, with the participation of an underdeacon, and conducted marriages for Catholic Apostolic couples. These services used the Book of Common Prayer, partly in Dutch. Catholic Apostolics also held their own services, including catechetical groups and weekly Bible classes. Old Catholics would not have approved of his expressed intent to see these people become Anglicans, and a staff member at Lambeth considered that the chaplain was letting his heart run away with him by admitting Catholic Apostolic children to communion, but no action appears to have been taken.[100]

Admission of children to communion had been a problem for another chaplain, Philip Boulton in Utrecht. He wrote to Coote in 1957 requesting a ruling concerning the custom of bringing a child for communion on the feast day nearest its second birthday, and continuing to do so each year until the age for confirmation was reached. Coote's response was that

> ... having accepted the anomalous position of ministering to Catholic Apostolic church members at all, we should not have scruples about administering the sacrament in their accustomed manner, provided we use our own Anglican liturgy.
>
> I do not, therefore, feel it necessary to refuse to give the sacrament to their children just because we do not do things in that way in the Anglican church.[101]

We do not know how things worked out in any detail; certainly there does not appear to be any material in the archbishops' papers at Lambeth which have been released for public consultation, but it is likely that Catholic Apostolics simply continued to attend Anglican eucharists while also continuing to meet apart. Remaining French members occasionally joined those in Brussels or The Hague for an Anglican eucharist.[102]

More recently, I am informed that in 2000 the Catholic Apostolic congregation at Amersfoort in Holland was attending Anglican communion in Utrecht each month, the service having been translated into Dutch by a chaplain there. That chaplaincy

---

98. Ibid., 37, 'Harold' to Satterthwaite, 19 July 1961.

99. Ibid., 33–34, V. B. Wynburne to Satterthwaite, 22 July 1961.

100. Ibid., 45–46, M. A. Halliwell, memorandum regarding visit to the Netherlands, December 1961.

101. CLC/320/F/004/MS32521, P. D. Boulton to Coote, 1 June 1957; Coote to Boulton, 20 June 1957.

102. W. H., *Katholisch-apostolische Gemeinden*, 93.

also hosted Catholic Apostolic services twice a month.[103] At the Hague, by the late 1990s a Dutch non-stipendiary Anglican minister conducted a monthly service for the Catholic Apostolics at the Anglican chaplaincy.[104] This service was still continuing in 2012, but an increasing number of Catholic Apostolics were becoming fully involved in the life of the Anglican congregation.[105] The Rotterdam chaplaincy continues to host a 'Catholic Apostolic Sung Eucharist' one Sunday a month.[106] Similarly, Holy Trinity pro-cathedral in Brussels was welcoming Catholic Apostolics to their eucharist in 2015.[107] The Utrecht Anglican chaplaincy has experienced substantial growth in recent years and in 2014 issued a paper outlining 'A Vision for a Church Plant in Amersfoort,' identifying Catholic Apostolics as one of the three main groups for which worship provision needed to be made in the plant, which was set up in 2015. A number had been attending services in Utrecht, some once a month on Sundays when a traditional Anglican eucharist was offered in Dutch, but others making the chaplaincy their home church and attending regularly. Many of these were young families, with some exploring the possibility of Anglican ordination. The paper's perception of them is worth quoting: 'The CA's form a close knit community, combining evangelical faith with a love for liturgical worship and the Eucharist. Almost all will be traditionalist on ethical subjects as same sex marriage and women's ordination. But it is difficult to tie them to typical Anglican churchmanships such as evangelical, Anglo-Catholic, liberal catholic etc. Some like more free worship with bands, others a catholic liturgy with Gregorian chant.' However, the paper recognized 'a risk that further development within the Church of England on ethical issues would estrange part of the CAs.'[108] This indeed could be what will halt the migration of Catholic Apostolics to the Church of England.

It is worth asking why so many Catholic Apostolics have migrated to the Church of England in Holland (and Belgium), but apparently not in countries such as Germany and Switzerland where the Church of England also has a number of chaplaincies. As a general rule, Catholic Apostolics have settled in the state Church (or what was perceived as the main traditional expression of Christianity in a particular country), if it possessed an episcopally ordained ministry. This, and not merely a Church's status as established, was a key consideration. The apostles had affirmed the validity of such orders, and acknowledged that those thus ordained were truly priests and could thus offer the eucharistic sacrifice, whereas such an affirmation could not be made regarding the ministers of other Churches. Even those who had been

---

103. Underwood, *Faith and New Frontiers*, 92.
104. Ibid., 94.
105. Anon., 'Profile of St John and St Philip,' 4.
106. Anon., *Anglican Sphere*, 2.
107. Anon., 'Holy Trinity Brussels Newsletter.'
108. Anon., 'Holy Trinity, Utrecht.'

converted in nonconformist settings should therefore attend an Anglican church.[109] Thus, in England they joined the Church of England, in Sweden the Lutheran Church, and in Austria the Roman Catholic Church.[110] Where the established Church did not possess an episcopally ordained ministry, things were more fluid, because the two main considerations—establishment and the possession of a priestly ministry—pointed in different directions: some might settle in the state Church, others in a non-established episcopal communion. Thus in Scotland members were advised to attend the Church of Scotland or the Scottish Episcopal Church.[111] In Switzerland, some appear to have migrated to the Reformed Church, although they found it to lack sanctuary or altar as they understood them.[112] Others appear to have settled among the Old Catholics. But I am not aware that significant numbers settled in Anglican chaplaincies. In Germany, most resorted to the state Churches for occasional offices and some found a home there, but many continued their separate existence, as probably also happened in Denmark. By contrast, Dutch and Belgian Catholic Apostolics found it almost natural to turn to the Church of England, even though other options existed which were also present in Germany and Switzerland—the Old Catholics or the Dutch Reformed Church in Holland, and the Roman Catholics in Belgium. That they did not take those options may be because the Old Catholics and Roman Catholics in those countries had both expressed negative opinions regarding the ecclesial status of Catholic Apostolics in a way which they had not done in Switzerland or Austria respectively, while the Reformed Church was probably insufficiently sacramental in ethos. The Church of England, by contrast, was accessible, welcoming, and already providing a home for many of their English co-religionists. Moreover, it has been suggested that Dutch members were happy to follow English practice. The presence of members of the influential Capadose family in leadership in both countries would also have aided this process: as well as Isaac and his son Antonius in England, another son, Abraham, was archangel at The Hague from 1903–29.[113] In addition, there may have been some variation in ethos between tribes, and in this case it may be that the Pietist background of the Capadose family had left its mark on the Dutch congregations, leading them to prefer a warmer service, spiritually speaking, than they felt the Old Catholics offered.

---

109. Gandy, *Pastoral Letter*. See also Woodhouse, 'Ueber die Stellung der nicht von Bischöfen ordinirten Geistlichen,' in Anon., *Sammlung*, 149–50. Not all Catholic Apostolic ministers would have given such advice, as noted above.

110. W. H., *Katholisch-apostolische Gemeinden*, 33.

111. James S. Heath, *Pastoral Letter, June 1957*. However, members were not to take communion in the Church of Scotland if unfermented wine was used.

112. M. and F. von H., 'Switzerland (Berne),' *Newsletter* 7 (December 1954) 9.

113. W. H., *Katholisch-apostolische Gemeinden*, 21, 111.

## PERPLEXITY IN THE PARISH

Whatever their criticisms of the Church of England, many Catholic Apostolics in England felt obliged to support it once their own ministries had been taken away.[114] Many recognized that unlike some of their continental brethren they could have recourse to a Church in which the eucharist had its central place, although there were the problems associated with its status as an established Church, the prominence of social activities, and the failure to understand the calling of the Church and the coming of God's kingdom.[115] At the end of life it was deemed 'far better for the ministers of the Church of England to officiate at funerals.'[116] However, in 1946 a deacon at the Central Church acknowledged that whilst thankful for hospitality at points when services could not be held there during the war, members had missed much—'the richer food, the better order, the sound doctrine, the more perfect form of worship.' Absent brethren endured this permanently, and their faith and hope might weaken as a result; in the past ministers had been able to visit them occasionally and hold small meetings, but this was rarely possible now.[117] They were encouraged to bear witness to their unity with their brethren and to join the Church of England, of which they were already members by virtue of its position as the national Church. Their position was hard to explain, but they need say nothing about it to their fellow Anglicans; such a course was not dishonest since Catholic Apostolic beliefs did not contradict those of Anglicanism. Yet the Catholic Apostolic altar would always have first place in members' hearts, and the word of life could not be received in its fulness within Anglicanism, which was one reason why, since the late nineteenth century, sermons had been issued to absent members.[118] As one sermon put it, the Church of England had the truth and nothing but the truth, but it did not have the whole truth; members would prefer to worship where prophecy could be heard and their hope of the Lord's return thus invigorated.[119] Such pastoral care as they could receive within the Church of England was regarded as supplementary, since, as we might put it, once a Catholic Apostolic, always a Catholic Apostolic.[120]

Some bishops treated Catholic Apostolics joining the Church of England with considerable courtesy, one example being the bishop of Birmingham, who in 1957 conducted a private confirmation ceremony in his chapel for about forty people after the closure of the church in the city in order to spare them the embarrassment of

---

114. Pinnington and Newman-Norton, *Conciliar and Apostolic Witness*, 78.
115. Anon., *Position of Absent Members*, 6–7.
116. Wigan Church Council minutes, 12 March 1908.
117. Anon., *Deacon's Teaching: Absent Members*, 3–5.
118. Anon., *Position of Absent Members*, 1–3.
119. Anon., *Homily, 4th April, 1943*, 3, 5.
120. Anon., *Sermon: The Lord's Tenth*, 6–7.

having to attend confirmation classes with candidates who were considerably younger (and doubtless less well taught).[121]

However, members did not always find their new homes congenial. The reluctance of some to settle in the Church of England received short shrift from Hollick:

> ... my heart has been made sad by finding that on the part of some of our members there has been a reluctance, even an unwillingness, to attend services in the Parish Churches when they could not attend services at the restored altar. These complain that they do not feel at home in the Church of England, and that they cannot enjoy the services. To such I feel bound to use great plainness of speech. I can of course understand that the Ministry of the Word which you hear from the pulpit falls far short of the fullness of what you have been accustomed to hear from those who have received the teaching of Apostles. I can also understand that you miss the richness of the worship to which you have been long accustomed at the restored altar, and especially the fact that Christ's coming again, which is the one hope of the Church, is so rarely the subject either of the prayers or preaching. But that these things should ever be made a ground for not attending the services in the Established Church is most deplorable. God has called us to be a strength to our brethren. ... If you abide faithful, may you not be as live coals which may help to kindle a flame in a smouldering fire? Your fellow-worshippers in the Parish Churches are of your brethren in Christ for whom you have been taught to pray in the services you have been accustomed to offer at the restored altar. If your love goes out to them, surely you should feel at home among them. To fail to join with them in worship can amount to nothing less than bearing a false witness to the true character of the Work of the Lord by Apostles in these days.[122]

An American correspondent reported in 1954 that he felt he had achieved nothing in his attempts to broaden the vision of his rector, although he had begun a small Bible study and prayer group.[123] In reply, a Sheffield member recorded how his mention of the Second Coming in a parish Bible study had precipitated an explosive reaction, and the curate afterwards admitted that he had never heard this doctrine before, commenting: 'I wish I could place you; in one breath you appear to be an ardent Roman Catholic and in the next you are the staunchest Protestant. You are neither High nor Low church yet you are both, and your logic is so sound. You puzzle me. I wish I could place you but would not know where to put you.'[124] Reflecting on the encounter, the writer advocated remaining silent about one's Catholic Apostolic allegiance, so as to avoid provoking a rejection of the Lord's work, while still bearing witness to the

---

121. A. B. O., 'The Church in Birmingham,' *Newsletter* 10 (March 1957) 3–5, at 5.

122. Hollick, *Ministries*, 9–10.

123. Anon., 'When Brethren are dependent on other Denominations,' *Newsletter* 6 (June 1954) 17–18.

124. G. D. A., 'Reply to a Reader in America,' *Newsletter* 8 (August 1955) 24–26.

apostles' doctrine. This approach appears to have been followed frequently: an article on 'Witnessing in the Parish Church' recounted how the writer was able to point out prophetic truth from the Scriptures in study groups connected with a parish mission, without breaking silence concerning the Lord's work.[125] And even the act of attendance was seen as bringing a blessing: James S. Heath in Glasgow wrote that members could 'expect that a blessing comes to you from acknowledging God's ordinance in His ministers.'[126]

But how should Catholic Apostolics respond to practices and teachings which they regarded as positively unscriptural? In 1936 one angel advised absent members, to whom he hoped to send 'teachings received from the Lord through His Apostles,' to show a right attitude towards the clergy and not to attempt to set them right. 'Regard the Clergy who minister to you, with all reverence, as God's servants. Uphold them by your regular attendance and loyalty. Never attempt to argue with them: that would be unbecoming and improper. Even if you think they need teaching, it certainly is not according to God's order for you to give it.' Private prayer was to be their recourse in such a situation.[127] Two decades later, another angel advised members to testify to what they knew and thought seemly, in this case regarding such issues as the position and ministry of women.[128] By now the issues where disagreement could be expected were changing, and since that time their number has increased.

Other members who had joined the Church of England felt a desire for an Anglican fellowship which would express Catholic Apostolic eschatological hopes and beliefs. The Guild of Prayer for the Return of Our Lord was founded in 1920 by Canon W. H. Connor, whom we encountered earlier. Its publications have set forth Catholic Apostolic eschatological and social teaching.[129] Subsequently, however, it ceased to be exclusively Anglican in composition or to be so aware of its roots. More recently, individual church members have become involved with such groups as Intercessors for Britain and Prayer for Israel, although the anti-Catholic views of some of these groups must have presented a problem. Such commitments represent a continuation in some form of the Catholic Apostolic practice of dual allegiance.

---

125. H. D., 'Witnessing in the Parish Church,' *Newsletter* 10 (March 1957) 16.

126. James S. Heath, *Pastoral Letter, June 1958*, 1.

127. Rawson, *Absent Members*, 2.

128. Anon., *Bishopsgate Church Teaching*, no. 290, July 1957, quoted in Pinnington and Newman-Norton, *Conciliar and Apostolic Witness*, 79.

129. Flegg, 'Gathered under Apostles,' 439.

# 13

# The Church under Priests (1960–71)

IN 1961 THERE REMAINED just two active priests and twenty-two deacons worldwide.[1] That year, Christopher B. Heath of Southwark died, leaving the priest-prophet Dr Wilfred Davson (1875–1971) as the last active representative of the priesthood.[2] He had been sealed in 1897 and ordained priest in December 1900, a few months before Woodhouse died.[3] Since 1949 he had been the sole priest at Paddington, and from his writings it is evident that he felt a keen sense of responsibility as he sought to guide his own congregation, and latterly congregations abroad. As the last remaining Catholic Apostolic priest in the world, his celebrations of the eucharist at Paddington drew members from many countries, especially at Easter.[4] Such mobility for purposes of pilgrimage was a function of the movement's decline, but could not have happened before the growth in popularity of air travel; moreover, in earlier days members were not supposed to visit other churches without a letter of commendation from their own, and had no need to do so when their own churches were still functioning. In some ways, Davson was 'a prophet without honour' in his own country, due to his principled separatism, being far more respected abroad than in Britain, where some questioned his authority to guide any other congregation than his own. The differing attitudes to Davson reflect divergent views about the future of the Lord's work.

His views found expression in two published series of sermons. The first series were preached at Paddington in 1949–50, and published under the title *1850 to 1950 in the Lord's Work*; the second series, *Sermons and Homilies on the Third Stage of the*

---

1. CRL, H. B. Evans Collection, Box 449, Seraphim Newman-Norton, continuation of Copinger, 'Annals,' 236.

2. W. H., *Katholisch-apostolische Gemeinden*, 188. There was another priest, H. B. L. Carter in Sydney, but he was unable to minister, and died in 1970: Newman-Norton, continuation, 237.

3. Davson, *Sermons*, 26. This was translated into German as *Das dritte Stadium im Werke des Herrn. Siebenunddreißig Predigten von einem Priester* (Siegen, 1970).

4. Newman-Norton, *Time of Silence*, 32–33.

*Lord's Work*, were preached between 1961 and 1965, mostly in Paddington, but some in churches on the continent (especially Siegen), which Davson visited a number of times. His activity there was occasioned by Schrey's death. In both works he drew on extensive study from 1940 of the coadjutors' official circulars to angels and the minutes of councils and conferences, as well as the record of prophecy preserved in the angel's vestry at Paddington, of which he saw himself as the custodian. A particular concern was to see what they said about the third stage of the Lord's work, so that he could prepare his flock to enter it.[5]

There is a risk of paying too much attention to the thinking of one minister, but his influence may be inferred from the fact that his services in Germany appear to have been very well attended: on one occasion at Siegen, administration of the communion took two hours, including three breaks to sing a hymn.[6] In addition, his second book in particular had a wide circulation, as well as being translated into German, although it was controversial and lacked official authority, and aspects of it have been questioned by members of a different outlook.

Davson's approach to ministry was marked by flexibility in the face of changing circumstances. The objective was to ensure the continuing provision of the guidance needed by the faithful, and as justification for flexibility he instanced the placing of Dutch congregations under The Hague before 1929 and the enlargement of the scope of the ministry of remaining underdeacons and others.[7] In the same way, when the last deacon at Manchester died, the angel arranged for his work to be covered by underdeacons, deaconesses, and lay assistants.[8]

Crucial to Davson's thinking was the belief that after 1901 there had been a shift in the centre of spiritual gravity of the Lord's work from England to Germany. Prophecy had already warned England that, like Ephesus in Revelation 2, it was in danger of losing its first love, and that its candlestick would be removed; it must humble itself and repent of its self-sufficiency.[9] Davson pulled no punches in his treatment of the English congregations' shortcomings but his exposition of biblical prophecy and typology is, to say the least, complex, and space precludes full consideration here.

*1850 to 1950* was cast as a typological interpretation of the visions in Revelation. Davson saw the restoration of apostles and prophets as forming a part of the opening of the sixth seal, and the bringing out of the ministries of coadjutor and archangel as part of the seventh (which itself comprised the sounding of the seven trumpets).[10] The next event would be the gathering of the whole Church; the model furnished by the Catholic Apostolic Church was therefore being taken down to be replaced by the

---

5. Davson, *Sermons*, 3; cf. Davson, *Church in Paddington* 29, 4.
6. *Newsletter* 13 (April 1961) 13.
7. Davson, *Church in Paddington* 88, 7.
8. Bryan, *Pastoral Letter*, 1.
9. *Record* 7/2 (1900) 167; cf. 11/6 (1922) 339; AD, July 1891, 3.
10. Davson, *1850 to 1950*, 4, 16.

reality. The time of silence in that model, which corresponded to that in heaven, was now past. Davson elaborated on the three-stage model first expounded by Cardale, regarding the rebuilding of the Temple as 'the antitype of the Lord's permanent work of gathering His Church into the Heavens through its Translation.' Related to this was his exposition of the work by apostles as itself being carried out in three stages:

- The delivery of the Testimony and the gathering of congregations of first-fruits.
- The setting in order of the churches, sealing of their members, ordering of the subordinate ministries, and visitation of the tribes.
- The offering of the intercession (which came to be undertaken by angels in local churches in the same way that angel-evangelists took up the apostles' work of delivering the Testimony).

The first aspect of the work was delegated after 1838 to the angel-evangelists, and the second to the coadjutors, leaving the apostles free to concentrate on the intercession.[11]

*Sermons and Homilies* was occasioned by Schrey's death, which in Davson's understanding brought the body into the third stage of the Lord's work. He saw the real significance of the movement's history as hidden: 'All that we are about to say is not to be received as a record of outward things. The true history of the Lord's Work in its three stages is the record of the Lord Jesus Christ speaking to His Church from Heaven by the Holy Ghost and through Christ's restored Ordinances.'[12] In the first stage, they were under apostles, who spoke to the whole Church. In the second, they were under coadjutors and then archangels, who spoke to the congregations under apostles, which were now partially separated from the rest of the Church. The third stage would end with the Lord's return and their translation to Mount Zion before the gathering of the whole Church. He recognized that in this stage congregations were unsealed and had not had the instruction which his generation had enjoyed, but those who were now being commended could make up for this lack of instruction by reading and by contact with sealed parents and older members.[13] Davson believed that the congregations rather than the ministries now assumed a primary position in what God was doing.[14] Davson had also begun to read to his congregation the 'Record of Words of Prophecy' (probably the *Record*) which had been spoken between 1901 and the mid-1920s. The abundance of prophecy was not inconsistent with its being a time of silence, for it represented God's secret dealing with those gathered under apostles, whereas the silence had reference to their message for the Church in general.[15]

11. Ibid., 16, 23 (quotation), 28–29, 32.
12. Davson, *Sermons*, 27.
13. Ibid., 3, 16, 26, 92.
14. Schröter, *Bilder*, 55.
15. Davson, *Sermons*, 37, 230.

Davson sought to guard against the problems resulting from the loss of a sense of distinctive identity which could occur as the Church's visible structure disappeared, a danger which is reflected in scholarly comments on the movement's lack of a clear focus for members' commitment.[16] In September 1961 he issued a paper on the subject of *Confirmation in the Church of England and Admission to Regular Communion among the Churches under Apostles*. Facing the question of whether younger members should be confirmed in the Church of England (as earlier ministers had often advocated where it was deemed necessary by the Anglican authorities), he pointed out the differences between confirmation and sealing. One was that confirmation focused on the individual, whereas sealing fitted that individual to serve within the body in preparation for the Lord's return; hence the third part of the Catholic Apostolic catechism, which has no Prayer Book counterpart, deals with such matters as the fourfold ministry and the Second Advent.[17] Moreover, confirmation was administered at an earlier age than sealing, which marked the passage to active spiritual maturity; parents of children being confirmed needed to realize that their children still had much to learn and more to receive which could only be found in the Catholic Apostolic Church. Sealing could no longer be administered, but candidates could be commended in a special service, although he was unclear exactly what the grace was which was conveyed in it. However, few members would have been in a position to attend such a service, since he was now the only priest left.

In his view, the movement should continue its separate existence as long as possible: 'everything for our purification is being provided in the midst of the Congregations gathered under apostles, and nowhere else at present, as a sign and symbol to the whole Church when, in their turn for offering their Day of Atonement, all things will be provided for them.'[18] This separate existence he described as 'going outside the camp' (Hebrews 13:13). He reminded his hearers that the removal of the last apostle had been typified by the covering of the ark and the altar of the Tabernacle, and the removal of the last angel by the covering of the candlestick. The altar represented the apostolic intercession, and the table of shewbread the eucharist. Prophecy had warned that God intended to cover the table, although Davson emphasized that this had not yet come to pass.[19]

Disapproving strongly of the turning out of congregations into the liberalism of the Church of England,[20] he insisted that the right course of action would be to strengthen what was still alive.

16. See, for example, Jones, 'Catholic Apostolic Church.'

17. Davson, *Confirmation*; Pinnington and Newman-Norton, *Conciliar and Apostolic Witness*, 105 n.

18. Davson, *Sermons*, 105.

19. Ibid., 138.

20. Davson's disillusionment with Anglicanism may have been the result of closer contact during and after World War II, as Catholic Apostolics whose churches had been bombed or had closed were forced to worship with Anglicans: Pinnington and Newman-Norton, *Conciliar and Apostolic*

Brethren, those words of 'strengthening the things that remain and are ready to die' are not such as can be passed over lightly as referring to some vague principle; they mean life and death to those concerned, because the things referred to are <u>living ministers</u> and <u>congregations</u>. We have first of all to remember that they pass on from the Coadjutors to every lower ministry in turn, because it is the time of taking down and removing; and consequently such ministry, be he angel or underdeacon, has to decide first of all whether his congregation is alive or dead before he treats it as dead by depriving it of its building and assembly; and, having decided that it is not dead, has to ensure that it is receiving the means for its strengthening; and a congregation is alive when it has within it the hope of the Lord's Coming and the desire to be purified to meet Him.[21]

The coadjutors had seen to it that living congregations had deacons and underdeacons who knew how to offer the litany and other services and were fed from the table of a neighboring church.[22] There was a danger that ignorance could lead to underdeacons doing more or less than they ought; deacons and underdeacons were not to teach the word themselves, but could impart the teaching which they had received in years past.[23] The ordinances had been removed but the obligation to assemble remained, and it could only be fulfilled under deacons or underdeacons. Those going outside the camp were commanded to meet together (Hebrews 10:19–25); houses were not sufficient for this, thus there was a continuing need for church buildings, which had been given by the Lord for the worship of those who had been separated from the rest of the Church.[24] His own congregation has therefore continued to function since his death without any deacons or underdeacons.

A temporary Tabernacle had been set up outside the camp because God's voice was not allowed to be heard in the Churches. Twice the apostles had invited bishops and clergy to come and see; twice the invitation had been declined.[25] Davson could therefore contemplate with equanimity the prospect of the movement's imminent extinction: Christ was taking them outside the Tabernacle, where only the lowest of ministries remained, before he took it down and the gathered congregation set off on the final journey to the promised land.[26]

---

*Witness*, 69.

21. Davson, *Sermons*, 232–33.

22. Ibid., 233.

23. Ibid., 125; Newman-Norton, *Time of Silence*, 31.

24. Davson, *Sermons*, 206; Anon., *Neue Apostelgeschichte*, 142.

25. Davson, *Sermons*, 250–51. The concept of meeting 'outside the camp' of Christendom was also central to the thinking of some Brethren, especially those who had followed Darby after the division of the 1840s: cf. Trotter, *Origin*, 5. This text has long been ingrained upon the consciousness of separatist Evangelicalism.

26. Davson, *Sermons*, 113.

While the first stage of the work had been centered on England, the stage shifted for the second to Germany, Holland, and Denmark. Carlyle as apostle to North Germany had been given a special work of preparation for the second stage of the Lord's work, which represented the antitype of the Mosaic Day of Atonement ritual.[27] The last English angel, Charles Thonger, had told Davson just before he died in 1956 that the Lord was doing a great work in the German congregations, and when Davson travelled in Germany he was impressed by the evidence of growth through marriage and additions to families. Visiting Hamburg to commemorate its last deacon, he discovered that it had seven hundred members, and the congregation included babies being brought for him to give them their first communion. Individuals were confirmed in the state Church in order to receive the eucharist there, but parents and underdeacons were still instructing children regarding the Lord's work. In some churches, deacons baptized and married the faithful,[28] but in others the state Church was used for these rites. By contrast, England was asleep, hardly aware of what God had done in other tribes; pride meant that English members were not interested.[29] German congregations had recognized that Zion (the Catholic Apostolic Church) must be purified before Jerusalem (the whole Church) could be built up, but the churches in England had not seen this, and thus had entered the wilderness, the place of absolution not received, by joining the Church of England and announcing the building up of Jerusalem before the time. In any case, prophecy had indicated that its building up would begin with Roman Catholicism rather than with Anglicanism.[30] Even today, there are members who never take communion in the Church of England.

Sources differ as to whether Davson was never invited to be a Catholic Apostolic trustee or whether he resigned from such a position.[31] Either way, he protested vehemently when in 1963 the trustees leased the Central Church to the Anglican Chaplaincy of the University of London for five years. Oral history confirms that the outlook of the chaplaincy was indeed very different from that of its Catholic Apostolic hosts; in the words of one member, 'a whole book could be written on this era.'

Such a use for the Gordon Square building had first been mooted in the 1920s.[32] When the post-war expansion of University College, London, was under way, it was suggested that it become the university church and be completed according to the

---

27. Ibid., 115–16.

28. I am informed that in some German congregations underdeacons now read the marriage service in church after the civil ceremony in the town hall.

29. Davson, *Sermons*, 92–93; Newman-Norton, *Time of Silence*, 32.

30. Davson, *Sermons*, 125; Newman-Norton, *Time of Silence*, 32. He reiterated the description of Rome as 'the Lord's Central shaft of His future Golden candlestick': Davson, *Sermons*, 69.

31. For the former opinion, see Newman-Norton, *Time of Silence*, 30; for the latter, see Born, 'Lord's Work,' 250.

32. J. A. Douglas papers, 221, J. A. Douglas, 'Note on the Documents re the Irvingites appended' (n.d.).

original Catholic Apostolic plans as a war memorial to former students.[33] William Wand, bishop of London, informed archbishop Fisher that he was hoping to be made residuary legatee of the building.[34] Davson's ability to recognize legitimate differences of opinion (as in Germany regarding recourse to the state Church for baptisms and marriages) means that we should take his protest all the more seriously. He saw the trustees' action as nothing less than the setting up of the synagogue of Satan, the home of the False Prophet, in imitation of the Christian Church.[35]

> ... he has leased to him one of the Lord's own church buildings, in which all the holy arrangements are set forth outwardly and ready to hand, and a congregation as well, ready to be welded into the ones which the buddings of Antichrist and the false prophet will bring with them. How terribly blind and foolish have our Trustees been. One great mercy has been shown us by God. The lease is but for five years, and taking a year for a month, it is the time which the locusts let loose from the bottomless pit are allowed to do their evil work.[36]

Those of the Lord's congregation in it would, he hoped, flee from its blasphemies and rejoin others of the body.[37] His opposition to Anglicanism was partly based on what he saw as doctrinal apostasy (the bishop of Woolwich, John Robinson, sparked off an epochal theological debate in the public arena with his *Honest to God* in 1963) and the encouragement by clergy of insubordination to the lawful authorities, exemplified by their involvement in anti-government marches (here he would have had in mind the high-profile activities of the Campaign for Nuclear Disarmament).[38] Congregations were turned out of Catholic Apostolic churches to attend the Church of England, but its theological liberalism made it difficult for most to find a home there.[39] Never again would he refer to the Church of England by name; in his sermons he made veiled references to it as 'Babylon.'[40]

Those returning to Babylon did so because they were half-hearted, and thought that the Lord's work had ended.[41] Members were not to wander from church to church, nor from Zion to Jerusalem (i.e., ceasing to worship in Catholic Apostolic congrega-

---

33. 'Episcopi Vagantes: Catholic Apostolic Church (Irvingites),' letter from A. H. Henderson-Livesey, 31 May 1946.

34. Ibid., Wand to Fisher, 1 March 1950.

35. Davson, *Sermons*, 157–58.

36. Ibid., 158.

37. Ibid.; Newman-Norton, *Time of Silence*, 30.

38. Davson, *Sermons*, 160. Ironically, the land on which the Paddington church building stands was owned by the (Anglican) Church Commissioners, from whom the church purchased the freehold in 1986.

39. Newman-Norton, *Time of Silence*, 30.

40. Pinnington and Newman-Norton, *Conciliar and Apostolic Witness*, 91–92.

41. Davson, *Sermons*, 206, 207–8.

tions) 'as some are doing who, in their pride think that they can teach the rest of the Church about what the Lord is about to do there.'[42] 'We must solemnly warn any of us who are alive and remain, who choose to go elsewhere for their worship, that they do so at the risk of entering into that tribulation on the threshold of which all Christendom stands.'[43] Others, however, admitted that they were returning to Babylon; indeed, one lay writer saw it as their lot to do so.[44] And Davson himself recognized that in certain circumstances it was right for absent members to worship in other churches.[45]

An interesting sidelight on tensions within the movement is provided by the fact that the Central Church congregation had preferred to be restricted to services conducted by their own deacons (and thus not to have celebrations of the eucharist) rather than use the priestly services of Davson or Christopher Heath of Southwark. It was evident to at least one Anglican observer that those in charge there did not see eye to eye with Davson.[46] This tension is, of course, rooted in that between two aspects of historic Catholic Apostolic teaching: the burden for the renewal of the whole Church, and the pessimistic judgment that Christendom was apostate and therefore the faithful must separate from it.

Davson grew increasingly frail during the early 1960s; in 1964 he had decided henceforth to celebrate the eucharist only monthly.[47] As he grew weaker, the services took longer, the last celebration taking place on Christmas Day 1970.[48] On 16 February 1971 he died. His death marked the end of an era, as the eucharist ceased to be offered in Catholic Apostolic churches. The death of the last deacon, C. W. Leacock of Sydney, aged ninety-five, followed in 1972.[49] Pilgrimage to receive the eucharist was now ended; what remained was pilgrimage to the building at Albury. But before looking at how the Catholic Apostolic community has maintained itself since then, we shall survey developments in the various tribes since 1901.

---

42. Ibid., 254.

43. Ibid., 240.

44. Dougharty, *Last Days*, 2.

45. Davson, *Church in Paddington 94*, 2.

46. 'Episcopi Vagantes: Catholic Apostolic Church (Irvingites),' C. L. Berry to J. R. Satterthwaite, 22 July 1961.

47. Davson, *Sermons*, 222.

48. Newman-Norton, *Time of Silence*, 33.

49. Flegg, 'Gathered under Apostles,' 94.

# 14

# The Church Contracts

## THE OVERALL PICTURE

AFTER 1901, ONE MINISTRY to those outside (that of apostle) had been removed by death; the other (that of evangelist) was to be virtually silenced through prophecy. Yet numbers continued to increase. Estimates of the movement's strength vary widely: Tierney, following Newman-Norton, estimated the total Catholic Apostolic membership in the world in 1900 as about 30,000, while Born stated that in 1901 there were 938 congregations, including 315 in England, twenty-eight in Scotland, and six in Ireland; he estimated the total of members worldwide as 200,000, of whom 60,000 were in northern Germany.[1] In terms of numbers of congregations and members, this area was the Catholic Apostolic heartland from the late nineteenth century, and it has remained so, although members would still look to England as the Church's 'mother country'.

It is impossible to arrive at accurate figures for the number of functioning congregations because of the difficulty of determining when a congregation ceased to function as such: was it when the eucharist ceased to be offered? Or when services of teaching and prayer ceased to be held? And should one differentiate between the treatment of congregations shown as possessing their own registers (indicating their autonomous status; something which the continental address books did not do) and those which were not? The following tables, however, are based on Edwin Diersmann's calculations and include small groups only holding occasional meetings, perhaps when a minister could visit. They indicate that growth continued after 1901 in mainland Europe, and evidence offered below will support this.

---

1. Born, 'Lord's Work,' 159; Tierney, 'Catholic Apostolic Church,' 304. Dependent outstations and those without the fourfold ministry were not included in Born's figures.

Table 14.1a: Numbers of Congregations, Europe[2]

|  | 1900 | 1912 | 1933 | 1962 | 1990 | 2014 |
|---|---|---|---|---|---|---|
| Belgium | 3 | 3 | 3 | 3 | 3 | 2 |
| Holland | 16 | 16 | 12 | 8 | 7 | 5 |
| Denmark | 55 | 59 | 46 | 29 | 8 | 1 |
| Italy | 1 | 1 | 1 |  |  |  |
| France | 7 | 7 | 5 | 3 |  |  |
| Switzerland | 40 | 41 | 34 | 16 | 11 | 2 |
| Poland |  | 2 | 7 |  |  |  |
| North Germany (incl. Freistaat Danzig and Memelland) | 236 | 305 | 240 | 150 | 86 | 35 |
| South Germany | 41 | 43 | 29 | 18 | 14 |  |
| Austria | 6 | 8 | 3 | 1 | 1 |  |
| Czechoslovakia |  |  | 2 |  |  |  |
| Russia (incl. Latvia and Estonia) | 13 | 16 | 17 |  |  |  |
| Finland |  |  | 2 | 1 | 1 |  |
| Norway | 10 | 10 | 8 | 4 |  |  |
| Sweden | 13 | 15 | 9 | 3 |  |  |
| Total | 441 | 526 | 418 | 236 | 131 | 45 |

Table 14.1b: Numbers of Congregations, English-speaking World[3]

|  | 1906 | 1912 | 1933 | 1962 | 2014 |
|---|---|---|---|---|---|
| England | 299 | 314 | 272 | 20 | 1 |
| Scotland | 29 | 23 | 18 | 2 |  |
| Ireland | 5 | 5 | 4 | 1 |  |
| America (U.S.A.) | 27 | 27 | 19 | 2 |  |
| Canada | 12 | 10 | 12 |  |  |
| Australia | 14 | 14 | 12 | 2 |  |
| New Zealand | 4 | 4 | 4 | 2 |  |
| India |  |  |  |  |  |
| **Total** | 390 | 397 | 341 | 29 | 1 |

2. Diersmann, *Notes*, 5–7, amended.

3. Sources: ibid., supplemented by *Church Address Book* 1933. It has not been possible to trace English address books for 1900 or 1990, or a German address book for 1906, to enable more exact comparison.

During the twentieth century the balance shifted away from the English-speaking world: this had provided about three-fifths of the congregations in 1869, but only one-ninth by 1962. As noted earlier, growth during the last three decades of the nineteenth century was slower among English-speaking communities; decline during the mid-twentieth was faster, perhaps in part because Anglicanism offered a home for members of such congregations, and also because underdeacons were not generally allowed to continue conducting services after the death of all the ministers of a particular church and so closure ensued.

As part of the continuing growth during the early twentieth century, some congregations also reached their peak. For example, it was reported in 1910 that numbers in Vancouver had increased to the extent that a place of worship had been built, which was now to have a weekly eucharist, and that registers were now being kept.[4] In this case, growth was probably due to immigration, but there were congregations in Germany and Norway which were also growing, and there the explanation was probably natural increase. When a congregation still had ministers, growth could occur through baptisms of children born into Catholic Apostolic families. New buildings also continued to be opened, and existing ones extended, improved, or decorated. As one church council's minutes recorded, 'many Churches under Apostles are now being beautified.'[5] However, we also see the beginning of an inexorable succession of church closures and the dismantling of the movement's ministry. Ultimately, this was expected to end in the complete disappearance of the Lord's work as an organized body; all that was left would be the Word of God, as prophecy indicated in 1921: 'It shall be His word which shall go out into the world as a trumpet, when sacraments and all ordinances cease.'[6]

In 1971 the sociologist R. K. Jones estimated the total number of members worldwide as between four and five thousand.[7] This was very probably an underestimate: New Apostolic sources suggested that in 1978 there were still about ten thousand Catholic Apostolics in West Germany alone, an estimate which is likely to be more accurate if based on access to such official sources as census statistics.[8] The Church's current strength can be seen from Table 14.1a. It is clear that the Catholic Apostolic community is more strongly German than it has ever been; Karl Schrey was undoubtedly the main architect of this, even if it was seen as fulfilling prophecy.

---

4. MC, 1910/5, 105.
5. Wigan Church Council minutes, 22 October 1905.
6. *Record* 11/6 (25 July 1922) 369.
7. Jones, 'Catholic Apostolic Church,' 158.
8. Anon., *Neue Apostelgeschichte*, 148.

## CATHOLIC APOSTOLIC INTERNATIONALISM AND TWO WORLD WARS

From one perspective, the greatest test of the Catholic Apostolic Church's claim to be a movement to reunite the whole of Christendom was presented not by doctrinal or liturgical divergence but by war and the surge of national feeling associated with it on both sides, just as war offered such a challenging test to the development of the modern ecumenical movement. It has to be said that the Church was remarkably successful in remaining united, even while consistently upholding the duty of Christians to bear arms if called to serve in their country's armed forces.

### The Impact of World War I

The First World War could have been a shattering experience for the Church, since its two main tribes, England and Germany, found themselves the two main antagonists.[9] The day after permission was given for the use of the order for the eucharist in times of war, the angel at London's Central Church told his congregation that it was a good thing if a nation could wage war knowing that it had sought to avoid it and had not provoked it, because then God's blessing on the nation's cause could be sought with confidence—which he believed Britain could do.[10] However, the coadjutors' circular of 10 July 1915 reported that they were still in communication with all congregations apart from Montigny (which would have been in the thick of the fighting on the Western Front) and Libau (now Liepaja, on the coast of Latvia, and occupied by the Germans from May 1915). They expressed satisfaction that there was no evidence of international hatred in the Church, something against which angels were exhorted to guard their flocks.[11] Prophecies continued to be received from Germany throughout the war, possibly being sent to Albury via neutral Holland or Switzerland. And in conferring with the angels in 1916 about the discontinuance of the observance of fourth Tuesdays (which had formerly marked the assemblies of the Seven Churches in London), Capadose received letters from almost all angels in Germany, Scandinavia, Holland, and France.[12]

Later, communication became more difficult. Capadose later recalled that correspondence had ceased almost completely as a result of the war.[13] In January 1918 the coadjutors apologized that the issue of the *Record* planned for August 1917 had been delayed, 'firstly by the difficulty experienced in providing the necessary paper and labour, next by the stringency of the censorship'; the international nature of the

---

9. Newman-Norton, *Time of Silence*, 18.
10. Hume, 'In Times of War'; cf. Charles Heath, *Pastoral Letter*.
11. AC, 10 July 1915, 10.
12. AC, 15 June 1916, 1.
13. Copinger, 'Annals,' opp. 206.

work must also have laid the publication open to some suspicion. They had also been greatly hindered in communicating with the angels, letters often taking three months to reach their destination. Even so, it had been possible to maintain services in all congregations, even in Russia and France, and they rejoiced at the absence of national animosity or bitterness in the prophetic words sent up to them.[14] These words made clear God's care for all. At Rostock on 3 October 1915, after the names had been read of members who were wounded, held prisoner, or missing, words of comfort were uttered, assuring the faithful that God knew each one.[15] Prophecy in Kiel during 1916 stated that God would break off the war suddenly and called on members to remain silent, unlike those around them, regarding their opinions on war and peace.[16] But however valuable the comfort provided by prophetic words, the coadjutors warned against jumping to apply biblical prophecy to the events of the war; in their opinion, some of the utterances forwarded to them appeared to have been prompted by the newspaper or patriotic feeling, and, in any case, '[t]o apply the visions of the Apocalypse to particular historical events on earth is a very hazardous endeavour.'[17] Such reserve contrasted with the excitement evident in parts of the English-speaking Evangelical world, especially after the Balfour Declaration (2 November 1917) indicating Britain's support for the establishment of a homeland for the Jewish people in Palestine.

This transnational outlook was tested by war in surprising ways. The pastor with the apostles for North Germany, A. O. T. Friebe, who had resided at Albury since 1907, handling the Church's German-language correspondence, was caught by the outbreak of war while on holiday in his native Germany. A suspended priest from Leipzig then denounced him to the authorities, as a result of which he was accused of spying for England. Leading ministers of that congregation were duly interrogated by the military police, but the accusation turned out to be groundless. However, Friebe was unable to return to England until 1922.[18]

The Church's success in maintaining its international spirit was undoubtedly due to the fact that the hopes of members were set on something higher than national prosperity. In Germany, a pastoral letter reprinted in *Pastorale Mitteilungen* referred to those fighting for king and fatherland, but did not appear to assume the rightness of the German cause.[19] An article on patriotism acknowledged the rightness of a love of one's country, but balanced this with the recognition that the fatherland was an

---

14. AC, 19 January 1918, 1–2.

15. *Record* 11/1 (September 1916) 80–81.

16. Ibid., 70.

17. AC, 7 January 1915, 9–10.

18. W. H., *Katholisch-apostolische Gemeinden*, 94; Schröter, *Die Katholisch-apostolischen Gemeinden*, 192; cf. Born, *Das Werk des Herrn*, 105.

19. Anon., 'Aus einem Hirtenbrief an Gemeindeglieder in der Zerstreuung in der Kriegszeit,' *PM* 1915/4, 60–63.

earthly and temporary entity, whilst the Church was heavenly and eternal. God would bring to pass his purposes for both sides in answering the prayers of each.[20]

In England, this higher aim was evident in the Church's response to appeals from the archbishops of Canterbury and York for united Christian prayer. The archbishops proposed that a pastoral letter from them should be read in all English churches on 6 June 1915, and shortly before this the coadjutors issued a circular to help angels to exhort their flocks in accordance with the spirit of this letter. They approved of its clear distinction between the standing and duties of Christians in this world as subjects of a particular realm and their standing as members of the body of Christ and citizens of heaven. At home or in prayer meetings, prayer could beseech God to show mercy to the nation, as well as confessing individual sins and those of the nation. In church, however, prayer was to transcend national aspirations for victory, majoring on the themes of repentance and longing for the Lord's return. Enemies were to be prayed for, and it was emphasized that ultimately deliverance could only come through Christ's return.[21] Congregations abroad probably participated in similar observances; thus there is a reference to a prayer meeting being held at Rostock in northern Germany to mark a day of national humiliation on 28 November 1914.[22]

There were limits to the extent to which Catholic Apostolics could co-operate with other Christians in such ventures. In 1916, the National Mission of Repentance and Hope was supported by most of the main Churches in England. Members needed guidance as to what part they should play, in view of the involvement of many in their local parish church and the likely pressure to join in. Heath urged ministers to welcome the archbishops' call for national acts of humiliation and confession (whilst noting that the call focused on national sins to the exclusion of those of the Church) but reminded them that God's kingdom could not be brought in by human effort; thus it would not be right for the Church to join in as such, the more so since it had entered the time of silence: the coadjutors had no authority without a direct divine command to issue any kind of testimony to the archbishops and bishops, as had been mooted. However, once the programme was settled, larger congregations might hold services in connection with the mission, as had happened in January 1915 and January 1916, and members attending Anglican churches were permitted to take part in services held in those. Another circular followed, in which Heath encouraged angels to offer the eucharist beforehand to ask God's blessing on it.[23]

As the conflict dragged on, congregations were affected in new ways. In 1917, a deacon at the Central Church in London painted a picture of the impact there. Over

20. Anon., 'Patriotismus,' *PM* 1917/7, 107–8.

21. AC, 31 May 1915.

22. AC, 10 July 1915, 7; see also 'Homilie am Kriegsbußtag,' *PM* 1915/6, 81–83.

23. AC, Edward Heath, 'Notes on Matters dealt with by the Coadjutor in Conference of March 28th and 29th. 1916 no. 1,' 155–58; cf. AC, Edward Heath, '1916 no. 3. Paper by the Coadjutor on the National Mission,' 25 September 1916, 166–67; Hume, *National Mission*.

the past year, the obligation to pay tithe had been faithfully met; 'twice recently I have received from the battle-front of France, tithe sent from the small pay of the private soldier, looking to the altar to which he is attached, and rendering faithfully his obligation to God.' But circumstances had affected general offerings, which showed a deficiency of around £80, caused partly by the need to take out insurance against the new threat of aircraft damage. More seriously, there was a deficiency on the Poor Fund of about £170; even though those administering it had tried to curtail payments, heavy calls were being made on it. Many members had suffered economically, and some had been taxed more heavily and were unable to give as much; indeed, some even needed to be restrained from giving because they had not the means to do so. Liberal special offerings had been made for the sick and wounded, Red Cross Funds, and hospitals (this in itself was a new departure, since Catholic Apostolics had not usually responded corporately to such appeals from the wider religious and philanthropic community), which had possibly affected offerings for the congregation's poor. The special funds on which the angel and deacons could draw were shrinking, so a special appeal was now being made.[24]

Once the war ended, Catholic Apostolics were in no mood to entertain unrealistic hopes of peace. In a sermon on the armistice, one minister interpreted the number eleven, so significant in its timing, as symbolic of disorder; concluding that peace would not result from it, he also condemned the League of Nations as godless and republican in spirit.[25] But while the coadjutors offered the eucharist at Albury, the intercession in which the apostles had engaged was not entirely withdrawn;[26] judgment was being held back. Immediately following the cessation of hostilities Edward Heath made some 'Remarks on the Project of a League of Nations,' addressed to ministers. He acknowledged its noble aims, but criticized the lack of any reference to Christ's Second Advent and kingship, as well as the assumption that all government was to be democratic. Such a venture could, he felt, pave the way for Antichrist. Yet he would 'not advise that [the angels] should discuss the project of a league of nations from the pulpit, much less that they should publicly denounce it.' Rather, they should instruct their flocks concerning the personal reign of Christ and the stages by which this would come to pass, so that they would not be deceived.[27]

## The Impact of World War II

The approach of war in 1939 forced many Christians to consider their views concerning military service. Unlike most other denominations, the Catholic Apostolic

24. Anon., *Deacon's Teaching*, May 1917.
25. Anon., *Armistice and Peace*, 1, 3.
26. Ibid., 4.
27. LPL, MS 4941, J. Miller, Teachings and sermons, 239–43, Edward Heath, 'Remarks on the Project of a League of Nations,' 14 November 1918, quotation at 243.

Church does not appear to have had any pacifists in its membership or ministerial ranks. Indeed, a sermon preached at the Central Church in 1936 ruled out pacifism as a legitimate option, at a time when clergy in all denominations were advocating it. The preacher argued that the apostles had deemed war legitimate, as did Article 37 of the Church of England, and that Anglican pacifist clergy were therefore guilty of violating their ordination vows to uphold the teaching of the Thirty-Nine Articles.[28]

Once again, as in other denominations, Catholic Apostolics reflected on the national sins for which war represented divine judgment. They did not come up with anything distinctive in this regard, but one preacher did assert that quite apart from the rightness of the British cause, the nation could perhaps have averted or abbreviated the conflict if it had repented.[29]

A practical consequence of war was the requisitioning of some buildings by the military. Thus the schoolroom of the newly closed church at Bridgnorth became a forces' rest room.[30] At Walsall in 1945, the church was being used by Toc H as a dormitory for servicemen on leave.[31] Many more were damaged or destroyed in air raids, forcing temporary or permanent move to another venue or dispersal of the congregation. In Germany, about forty churches were destroyed and others damaged, and many ministers and members lost their lives. So, for instance, in a raid on Hamburg in July 1943, the city's last two priests and about a hundred members were killed, and services ceased abruptly.[32] The destruction of three important churches, at Hamburg, Hannover, and Frankfurt am Main, was interpreted by the Vienna angel Anton Valentin as a sign that the altar was about to be covered and the eucharist no longer celebrated because the intercession was ending.[33] Valentin was already alert to such a possibility, having preached five years earlier that when Christ ceased his intercession in heaven (with which the offering of the eucharist was sacramentally connected), it would be time for Catholic Apostolics to do so on earth.[34] This understanding helps us to see why some Catholic Apostolics were not necessarily anxious about keeping open or reopening their churches: they saw a possibility that the cessation of services might be the will of God for them. Others, though, confessed that '[n]obody expected this sudden covering of the altar in such a manner.'[35] Some English congregations whose churches had been rendered unusable through war damage were advised to

---

28. Anon., *Sermon, Third Sunday after Pentecost*, 8–9.

29. Anon., *Churches in Southwark, Bristol and Bath*, 2–3.

30. B. M. S., 'Bridgnorth (now closed),' *News Letter* 2 (April 1952) 12.

31. Copinger, 'Annals,' 234.

32. *Newsletter* 11 (February 1958) 13; Schröter, *Die Katholisch-apostolischen Gemeinden*, 195, following Born, *Das Werk des Herrn*, 118.

33. Valentin, *Sermon*, 8.

34. Valentin, *Sacrament*, 6.

35. Anon., 'Continental Awakening to the Blessed Hope,' *Newsletter* 6 (June 1954) 8–10, at 9.

attend their local parish churches;[36] one wonders how many were thus lost to the movement. Conversely, at Kiel the damaged church, once repaired, was the only one in that part of the city available for use, and hospitality was accordingly extended to the Roman Catholics; it was also used to train young organists from elsewhere.[37]

An article in the Danish periodical *Ungdomsbladet* offered some personal recollections of one member's involvement in the Hitler Youth as a young person during the war,[38] but otherwise I have not traced any discussion of this subject. Under the Third Reich the Church's legal position as a registered association remained unchanged, and it experienced few difficulties until late in the war, doubtless because of its strong conviction that obedience was the proper attitude to adopt towards the civil power. Such difficulties as arose were due to the prohibition of religious services during working hours.[39] It was allowed to continue its existence so long as it did not engage in any comment or activity which could be deemed politically controversial, but members would have been privately sceptical regarding Hitler's claim to be instituting a thousand-year Reich in the light of their expectation of the coming and reign of Christ. Once again, their hopes were set on higher things.

As in World War I, there is anecdotal evidence that the Church's internationalist outlook persisted, although now in the absence of ministers of the universal Church to maintain contact with the tribes. On 1 October 1939, a day set aside for prayer by the archbishops of Canterbury and York, the preacher at the Central Church, while acknowledging the rightness of the Allied cause, commented regarding the German congregations with which good fellowship had been enjoyed: 'Their trial must be greater than ours. . . . Twice in twenty-five years Satan has prevailed to put enmity between us and our brethren in Germany.'[40] The story is told of a German officer who walked into a Dutch Catholic Apostolic church during the occupation of Holland; when challenged as to the reason for his presence, he explained that he was a Catholic Apostolic member who had come to pray, whereupon he was welcomed and taken home for lunch after the service, to the disapproval of neighbors. The host's defence was that 'I am first an Apostolic, then a Dutchman.'[41] When the war ended, a further sermon at the Central Church reminded members that whilst the victory was God's doing, their enemies were also part of the one Church.[42] In March 1945, almost at the end of the war in Europe, a priest in Cologne asserted that England

---

36. Copinger, 'Annals,' 227. The minister in charge at Bishopsgate saw such a circumstance as an act of God depriving his flock of the privilege of participating in Catholic Apostolic services: Ward, 'Death of a Church,' 129.

37. D. W., 'Kiel (Germany),' *Newsletter* 4 (April 1953) 16–17, at 16.

38. L. Langholz, 'Hitlerjugend og Kirken,' *Ungdomsbladet* 6/4 (April 1958) 5, 7.

39. Schröter, *Die Katholisch-apostolischen Gemeinden*, 194.

40. Anon., *Sermon, 31 October 1939*, 4–5.

41. L. H. Halliwell, 'Foreword,' *Newsletter* 13 (April 1961) 2–3.

42. Anon., *Homily, Day of National Thanksgiving*, 48.

and Germany, as the two countries where there had been the greatest response to the Catholic Apostolic message, should recognize that they were brothers.[43] And a few years later, another German correspondent thought it 'remarkable that a German Catholic Apostolic congregation has been under the protection of that country where a sheltering Cherub has covered the work of the Lord in former times, and all the German congregations have had their spiritual foundations from England.'[44] An English visitor to Düsseldorf commented that she had encountered no bitterness.[45] This spirit found practical expression as a number of congregations began to send aid parcels to fellow members in greater need, and were still doing so during the early 1950s. English-speaking congregations sent parcels to German ones, while West German congregations sent assistance to their brethren in the Russian Zone.[46]

With the end of the war, refugee movements and the redrawing of political boundaries had a dramatic effect on some continental congregations. Certain congregations experienced significant growth as the result of a refugee influx, such as Düsseldorf, Flensburg, and Neuwied in West Germany.[47] In certain North American congregations, this was probably just the latest in a succession of waves of migration: at Chicago, for instance, recent Latvian refugees became part of a congregation which was mostly European in origin.[48] On occasion, this movement of people even restored priestly ministry to a congregation: Hamburg had been without priests since 1943, but from 1950 a priest from Riga was celebrating the eucharist there.[49] Other congregations were wiped out as members moved westwards, as when the Polish boundary was redrawn in 1945. And even within a country, the war served to accelerate a process of outmigration from city centres, as at Bishopsgate.[50]

## THE TRIBES

### The Seven Churches in London

The first of the seven churches in London to close was Westminster in 1922; closure had been mooted by its angel in 1919 but only commended itself to all after his death.[51] The Kentish Town horn closed in 1938, although the Central Church, its

---

43. F. Hutz, 'A short History of the Church in Cologne,' *News Letter* 1 (October 1951) 10.
44. Herr Ritscher, 'Kleve,' ibid., 9.
45. Miss Dennison, 'Düsseldorf,' ibid., 13.
46. P. Harrison, 'Manchester,' ibid., 2; L. H. Halliwell, 'Bolton,' ibid., 3; Dennison, 'Düsseldorf,' 13; J. Z., 'The Church in Chicago,' *Newsletter* 5 (November 1953) 10–11.
47. Dennison, 'Düsseldorf,' 13; D. W., 'Kiel'; Anon., 'A Holiday in Germany, 1954,' *Newsletter* 7 (December 1954) 18–21, at 19.
48. J. Z., 'Church in Chicago.'
49. Anon., 'Continental Awakening,' 9.
50. W., 'The Church in Bishopsgate,' *Newsletter* 4 (April 1953) 7–8.
51. Edward Heath, *Address, 3rd May, 1922*, 1; Albrecht, *Work*, 42.

parent congregation, used the building temporarily after being damaged during the war. Chelsea closed after being bombed in 1941. Bishopsgate, Islington, and Southwark all lasted until the 1960s, as did the Wood Green horn. The Central Church, which was deprived of the eucharist after the last priest died in 1954, continued to hold services (latterly a monthly litany) until the death of the last underdeacon in 1989; members still meet several times a year for prayer in the adjoining offices, the Cloisters. In 2001, such meetings were being held in various parts of the English-speaking world, including Bristol, New York, Chicago, Vancouver, Melbourne, Adelaide, and Sydney. The church itself was vacated by the university chaplaincy in 1994, since when the English Chapel has been used by 'Forward in Faith,' a traditionalist Anglo-Catholic body whose outlook would be far more acceptable to most Catholic Apostolics (the trustees were opposed to its use by a Church which sanctions the ordination of women); the sanctuary has been used for special services, and I understand that it has also been used occasionally by Ethiopian Christians. In 2015, the trustees offered the use of the church to an Anglican church-plant from St Helen's, Bishopsgate, Euston Church, who now meet there on Sundays.[52]

Now only Paddington remains. As in other surviving congregations, the services used are those of the Litany and the Forenoon service, which may be conducted by laymen. Some in the movement, however, believe that services should have ceased and that only prayer meetings should be held, since no underdeacons remain.[53] The congregation when I visited it a couple of times in the late 1990s numbered between forty and sixty (a contrast with that of 1,200 before 1914), some of whom travelled up from Albury.[54] It gathered at the back of the nave, giving symbolic expression to its sense of deprivation of priestly and sacramental ministrations.[55] As on the continent, it included a number of children and young people, born and brought up within what remains of the movement. I was told that most of the congregation would observe a eucharistic fast. A sermon by one of the movement's ministers was re-read; prayers were offered; and hymns were sung, accompanied by a fine pipe-organ.[56]

---

52. Anon., 'Euston Church: Story.' St Helen's would be aligned with the Reform wing of Evangelical Anglicanism, which does not generally accept the ministry of ordained women.

53. Flegg, 'Gathered under Apostles,' 94.

54. A similarity of outlook between the two congregations appears to have existed for a long time: Eustace Percy, who in spite of his Anglican involvement advocated continuing to worship apart, worshipped at both churches (Lang papers 100:64, cutting from *Evening Standard*, 22 October 1930), and H. G. Rees had served at Paddington before moving to Albury.

55. Gretason, 'Authority, Provisionality and Process,' 277–78.

56. For a sympathetic illustrated article on the Paddington building, see Powell, 'Uncompromised by Change,' 192–93.

## England

Closures did not really begin to bite until World War I, after which they continued fairly steadily until the early 1960s. By 1981, the only churches remaining open outside London were Eynsham and Liverpool, both closing soon afterwards. We have noted elsewhere that buildings passed to a range of denominations, Protestant, Catholic, and Orthodox. The only buildings now in church ownership are Paddington, the Central Church, Albury, and Wolverhampton (used by a Pentecostal church). That at Albury is kept in excellent order but no services are held and no visitors apart from members are now allowed: that policy has caused misunderstanding and disappointment locally because it has precluded the church's use for appropriate functions or occasional visits by the public.

## Scotland

Closures really hit hard from the 1930s onwards, the last remaining congregations being at Edinburgh and Glasgow, both closing in the late 1950s. The Edinburgh building suffered many vicissitudes before finally being restored during the early years of the new millennium as an events venue. Varying fates have befallen other buildings, but that at Dundee was fortunate to become the home of a Scottish Episcopal congregation who have retained much of the previous furniture and layout, even down to the plaques marking the underdeacons' seats. As in England, the Church's legacy has been in its impact on the liturgical and sacramental thinking of certain clergy in the national Church. In both cases, however, this appears to have been divorced to a great extent from the eschatological perspective of Catholic Apostolic worship.

## Belgium, Holland, and Denmark

The churches in this tribe proved remarkably resilient. In Denmark, the fifty-nine congregations of 1901 had declined only slowly by 1922, to fifty-five.[57] On 31 October 1936, however, the Danish king convened a meeting with 150 invited guests and all the Church leaders present in the country to mark the four hundredth anniversary of the Reformation in the country, to whom he read parts of the Great Testimony. According to one Catholic Apostolic member, those present wished the Testimony had been accepted when first given.[58] Following this, therefore, a group was formed within the state Church to confess the sin of rejecting apostles and to pray for them to be sent once again; it was still meeting in 1945.[59] As late as 1955 the central church in

---

57. Schröter, *Bilder*, 45.
58. Anon., *'The following is a translation'*; Newman-Norton, *Time of Silence*, 23.
59. Anon., *Pastoral Instruction no. 773*; J. C. H., 'Extracts referring to Spiritual Events on the Continent,' *Newsletter* 8 (August 1955) 18–23.

Copenhagen was described as 'overcrowded,' with a congregation drawn from all age groups.[60] This may have been due in part to what one member described as a move to centralize the services there because it was an archangel's seat.[61] The last priest in Denmark died in 1958 and the last deacon in 1964, but there were still five congregations meeting for prayer in 1990.[62] Three churches were said to remain open in 2006.

By 1996 seven or eight congregations remained in Holland, where closure had come relatively late in most cases. In 2010, at the time of the last underdeacon's death, a total of seven hundred members were still meeting in congregations at The Hague, Rotterdam, Utrecht, Amersfoort, and Scheemda. At Amersfoort, so I was informed in 2006, numbers had increased to the extent that extra chairs were being put out in the side aisles. By contrast, the church at Groningen, which the Anglicans had been using, was sold to the Old Catholics in 2011.[63] Holland was the only tribe apart from England to assign the care of colonial members to a particular minister, the 1922 address book listing a deacon in Java with oversight of members in the Dutch East Indies.

In 1990 the three Belgian congregations (which had been under the care of The Hague since 1922 if not earlier) still remained at Brussels, Antwerp, and Châtelet,[64] and two still function to some extent.

## Italy

Despite the growing concern for Rome evident in the *Records*, no further work could be attempted in this tribe. The church in Rome was still listed in 1922, but disappeared soon afterwards; surviving members were cared for from Switzerland.

## Ireland, Greece, and the East

In 1923, the churches at Dublin and Belfast were placed under the care of Thonger at Birmingham. Dublin closed in 1938, and after being used by the Church of Ireland it is now home to a Lutheran congregation.[65] Belfast lasted until the early 1950s. Nothing is known of any further work or contacts in Greece or 'the East.'

## France and Switzerland

After the death of William de Caux in 1929, who combined oversight of the Paris congregation with that of the Central Church in London, the French churches came

60. CRL, H. B. Evans Collection, Box 451, extract from a letter of Bengt Stolt, 2 September 1967.
61. 'Anon., 'Denmark: The Churches in Copenhagen,' *Newsletter* 5 (November 1953) 11–13.
62. Schröter, *Die Katholisch-apostolischen Gemeinden*, 45, 498 n. 69b.
63. Anon., 'Old Catholic Church is Growing!'; Anon., 'Home Pages of Anglican Churches.'
64. Schröter, *Bilder*, 43.
65. Copinger, 'Annals,' 209, 225.

under the care of Abraham Capadose at The Hague, and then Ludwig Albrecht.[66] This illustrates the expedients which the Church was forced to adopt as the ranks of ministers were depleted by death, to the extent of taking responsibility in more than one tribe. The church in Paris was also rebuilt after World War II, with the altar being brought forward off the east wall and the front made less cluttered—both arguably owing something to the thinking of the liturgical movement then affecting Roman Catholic and liturgical Protestant churches and stressing the eucharist as the offering of the whole people of God. Given the movement's weakness in France, it is remarkable that three congregations survived until 1980, at Paris, Montigny, and Strasbourg.[67] None, however, remain.

Numbers of congregations in Switzerland were slow to decline until the mid-1930s. In 1990 there were still ten Swiss congregations. However, many members now attend Old Catholic churches, which are relatively strong in Switzerland.[68]

## Poland

According to the coadjutors (who appear not to have taken into account the brief existence of a congregation during the 1880s), the first eucharist in Poland took place at Warsaw in December 1902 (in German).[69] A Polish liturgy was finally published the same year, but the work never saw the success which had looked likely before Woodhouse's death halted outreach. One source states that at the time of World War I remaining members were incorporated into the same tribe as Russia.[70] The 1922 address book lists seven congregations in Poland, all except Warsaw formerly in German territory and overseen by the church at Hannover, but by 1928 all except Starogard were being looked after by a district evangelist from the Baltic republics. All were still functioning in 1939, but further redrawing of boundaries in 1945 forced many ethnic German members to leave Poland and resulted in church closures at Jelenia Góra (formerly Hirschberg) and Legnica (formerly Liegnitz). Yet as late as 1968 there was an underdeacon, implying the existence of a network of members and possibly even a degree of corporate presence.[71]

---

66. Ibid., 215.

67. Schröter, *Bilder*, 43.

68. W. H., *Katholisch-apostolische Gemeinden*, 33; Schröter, *Bilder*, 41.

69. AC, Isaac Capadose and Edward Heath, 'Albury, 7 August 1903: Summary of Events which have transpired since the Decease of Mr Woodhouse,' 11.

70. Abel, *Das Werk des Herrn*, 36.

71. Anon., 'Poland,' *Newsletter* 12 (May 1959) 21–22; W. H., *Katholisch-apostolische Gemeinden*, 65; Schröter, *Bilder*, 37; Schröter, *Die Katholisch-apostolischen Gemeinden*, 546 n. 99.

## North and South Germany, Austria, and Hungary

As noted above, redrawing of boundary lines and resettlement of ethnic Germans meant that congregations east of the Oder-Neisse line ceased to exist.[72] This, of course, was not the first time German congregations had been affected by boundary moves and consequent migration, since congregations on the eastern shore of the Baltic Sea had been affected after 1918. And the division of Germany resulted in the division of the Berlin-Nord congregation into two parts.[73]

About two dozen German churches were rebuilt after the war, often in a modern style which contrasted with traditional Catholic Apostolic architecture. Essen (1954) was described as having 'an air of newness uncommon among our churches today.'[74] Bremen (1955) included a kitchen and sitting-room for visitors from other congregations.[75] The most recent new building is that at Magdeburg (1998).[76] This building programme owed much to Schrey's order as acting archdeacon from 1949 that all church buildings be put into excellent condition, and his diligent labor to ensure that congregations had fitting settings in which to worship.[77] It was not just a matter of what some might regard as sentiment: the buildings were needed. When Davson visited Germany in 1962, he noticed how many of the congregations there were experiencing biological growth, one building even having to be enlarged.[78] When the last priest for the three Leipzig congregations died in 1952, there were still 900 in the flock.[79] Likewise, about 1,500 people remained in the central Berlin church when the last priest and deacon in the city both died in January 1956.[80] Natural increase not only slowed decline in membership but in at least one congregation (Potsdam, near Berlin), it resulted in the recommencement of services during the 1960s due to rapid growth.[81] The contrast is indicative of the differing convictions regarding continued separate existence, but perhaps also of the strength of the relationship subsisting between members and the Church. Just as younger members were committed to the Church, so the Church was committed to them: a number in Berlin had no home,

72. Schröter, *Die Katholisch-apostolischen Gemeinden*, 195.

73. W. H., *Katholisch-apostolische Gemeinden*, 42

74. A Young Member of the Church in Liverpool, 'A Holiday in Germany, 1954,' *Newsletter* 7 (December 1954) 18–21, at 20.

75. Anon., 'Bremen,' *Newsletter* 11 (February 1958) 7. For an earlier example from Ipswich (1907), see Wolfe, 'Ipswich Congregation,' 21–22.

76. Schröter, *Bilder*, 235.

77. Anon., 'Hamburg,' *Newsletter* 12 (May 1959) 17–18; Davson, *Church in Paddington* 97, 6; W. H., *Katholisch-apostolische Gemeinden*, 33.

78. Davson, *Sermons*, 92–93.

79. CRL, H. B. Evans Collection, Box 449, Newman-Norton, continuation of Copinger, 'Annals,' 231.

80. Ibid., 233; cf. Box 449, H. B. Evans, ms notes on continental churches.

81. Schröter, *Die Katholisch-apostolischen Gemeinden*, 88, 196–97.

family, or work after the war, and it was natural for them to turn for help to a deacon or underdeacon.[82] Thus the new church at Wuppertal-Barmen (1948) included flats for homeless members.[83] In 1980, 103 congregations remained, and 86 a decade later, although membership was by then below 3,000.[84] An internet list included fifty-six registered local associations as at 30 March 2013, although if the registration of places of worship in England and Wales is anything to go by, not all will still be functioning or holding regular services.[85] Diersmann's figure of thirty-five is likely to be much closer.

We have already noted in various tribes that as ministers died, their charges might be added to the responsibilities of ministers from other tribes. The German context illustrates the general principle which was at work in such cases. At the last German angels' conference in 1933, it had been decided that on the death of an angel his area of jurisdiction should be taken over by his neighbor. Later on, the same policy was applied in connection with the remaining priests.[86] This explains why Schrey in Germany and Davson in England were happy to exercise their ministry beyond the bounds of the jurisdiction assigned to them by the apostles. Especially after 1945, remaining priests (and Schrey as angel) travelled considerable distances in order to celebrate the eucharist, and members travelled to participate, resulting in large congregations. Once the last priest in the world was in England, members would cross the Channel to participate in a Catholic Apostolic eucharist, especially at major festivals. The last priest in Berlin died in 1956; accordingly, the last remaining priest in what was then the German Democratic Republic would often celebrate the eucharist in Berlin, with up to 2,500 communicants. The lack of ministers, however, did not inhibit the members of the Berlin-Ost congregation from erecting a new building in 1988, and in 1993 the seven Berlin area churches still counted 1,200 members.[87]

In addition to the factors noted above, the Church's continued strength in Berlin and elsewhere in Germany owes much to the reluctance of many members to return to the state Churches. Whilst they are obliged to do so in order to have their children baptized, they are divided as to whether to take communion in these Churches. The separate existence of these worshipping congregations has been possible because Schrey blessed many young men to serve as underdeacons, but now that they are all elderly the Church's future is unclear. Whatever is done to ensure that the doors stay open will have to be something which lacks precedent, and this would go against the grain. Lay assistants will play an increasing role, but how can they be recognized? Once

---

82. Anon., 'Visits to Berlin in 1951 and 1954,' *Newsletter* 8 (August 1955 ) 13–14.

83. H. and L. B., 'The Church in Wuppertal-Barmen, North Germany,' *Newsletter* 3 (October 1952) 8–10, at 9.

84. Schröter, *Bilder*, 35.

85. Netzwerk apostolische Geschichte, 'Katholisch-apostolische Gemeinden.'

86. Schröter, *Bilder*, 55.

87. Schröter, *Die Katholisch-apostolischen Gemeinden*, 72.

again, the Catholic Apostolic Church is back where it started, without any earthly heads. Members are 'caught in the tension between seclusion and open-mindedness,' between being the first-fruits set apart from Christendom and the calling to be the grain of wheat falling into the ground and dying.[88]

## Spain and Portugal

Remarkably, an attempt was made to follow up Pastor Albrecht's visit to Spain. No gathering could be undertaken now, but 'it seemed permissible and desirable to follow up the slight openings found in 1900.' Albrecht paid three more short visits to Madrid, 'if possible to prepare the way for any future witness, which the Lord may send unto that stronghold of Edom. He has also published a few tracts in Spanish, which have been not unfavourably commented upon in one or two of the religious reviews, and which have opened unto him an opportunity of entering into correspondence with some even amongst the clergy.'[89] Here, as perhaps in Rome, Catholic Apostolic work was being undertaken with a longer-term perspective, in preparation for a further stage of the Lord's work after the removal of the first-fruits.

## Russia and Finland

Unrest which broke out in Russia during 1905 was keenly observed. The coadjutors were thankful to report that the congregations there had been preserved, with services maintained and crowded. The true character of this unrest was, they believed, seen most fully in France, where opposition to religion was evident. The disturbances betokened the approach of the final flood of infidelity, as foretold in the Great Testimony. Because there was no existing form for the eucharist to pray about a danger which was not localized but threatened all Christendom, they inserted a prayer for the restraint of anarchy and ungodliness, to be used until 7 April.[90]

During World War I, most German members left Riga for White Russia; three churches there came to be composed mainly of Latvians: Mogilev, Grudinowka, and Petrowitschi (Smolensk). At the outbreak of revolution in 1917, there were eight churches in Latvia, two in Estonia, and seven in Russia. But as revolution took hold all came under increasing restrictions and were forced to close; members were exiled or died in prison. St Petersburg closed fairly soon after 1917: most Russian members had been drawn from the nobility and were therefore banished to Siberia and elsewhere. Reval was closed because, in the minds of the civil authorities, people who were expecting the Second Coming could not possibly be good citizens. In 1929 it was reported that some members had been transported to Siberia for continuing to meet

88. Schröter, *Bilder*, 57.
89. Capadose and Heath, 'Summary, 7 August 1903,' 12.
90. AC, 17 January 1906.

for worship. In Latvia and the other Baltic republics, however, there was somewhat more freedom, and the congregation at Riga effectively cared for several in Russia, even sending relief parcels to members in exile, although Lutheran opposition continued and in 1935 Lutheran authorities attempted to close down Catholic Apostolic services. World War II brought the cessation of most work in Latvia, as buildings were destroyed and German members fled or were repatriated, but German occupation from 1941 brought not only relief from persecution but a temporary influx of members in Riga. After fleeing at the end of the war, some continued to meet in refugee camps in Germany and Austria. In two neighbouring camps in Bavaria Latvian and Estonian members were ministered to by the youngest priest in the Church, an Estonian then aged sixty-six. By 1985, however, small congregations remained at Riga, Jelgava, Liepaja, and Tallinn, all in the Baltic republics.[91]

Events in Russia must have affected the Finnish members, who had been overseen from St Petersburg. In 1920 oversight was transferred to Norrköping in Sweden, then to Stockholm, Riga (during World War II), and finally Copenhagen.[92] In 1951 it was reported that the first Catholic Apostolic eucharist in the country since 1937 had taken place; optimistically, two people were admitted to regular communion.[93]

## Sweden and Norway

Christiania (now Oslo) may have reached its largest number of members as late as 1930.[94] But very few of the accessions would have been spouses joining the Church: in Norway, of twenty-seven mixed marriages recorded after 1901, this occurred in just three cases.[95] This was probably typical of what happened elsewhere, given the coadjutors' expressed reluctance to receive such individuals.

A council of Scandinavian ministers was held in Copenhagen in 1930, and Sweden was placed under Danish oversight in 1933.[96] Doubtless the same thing happened to Norway, since for temporal and financial matters the whole of Scandinavia came to be assigned to Copenhagen. By 1980 the only Scandinavian congregation was that at Oslo, the last one in Sweden having closed in the 1970s, and that at Bergen after 1978.[97] Again, buildings sometimes passed to other denominations. That in Stockholm was

---

91. Abel, *Das Werk des Herrn*, 17, 37–38, 51, 53; Ilsa Rose, 'The Apostolic Congregations in the Tribe of Dan,' transl. A. Amphlett, ibid., 98–113; Copinger, 'Annals,' opp. 206, 209, 216, 226; Schröter, *Bilder*, 49, 51.

92. Copinger, 'Annals,' opp. 206; Anon., 'Finland,' *News Letter* 2 (April 1952) 14–15.

93. Newman-Norton, continuation of Copinger, 'Annals,' 231.

94. Diersmann, *Notes*, 22, though elsewhere he suggests that the peak occurred between 1901 and 1908: ibid., 139.

95. Ibid., 119.

96. Copinger, 'Annals,' 217; Adell, *De tysta bedjarna*, 93.

97. Schröter, *Bilder*, 45, 47, 285; Diersmann, *Notes*, 132.

used by the Greek Orthodox after it closed in 1970. Similarly, Oslo, which had stood unused for twenty years, was used by the Greek Orthodox from 1987.[98]

During World War II and the German occupation of Norway, a Norwegian priest's widow (aged ninety) was on a list of prominent anti-Nazis in the Bergen area.[99] This is the only instance I have encountered of a member of the Church being known as a political opponent at any period.

## The 'suburbs'

The Australian cattle station congregations proved remarkably long-lived, Bukkullah and Pokolbin surviving until at least 1938, but by the end of World War II the only congregations left were those in the cities of Brisbane, Melbourne, and Sydney (the last to close, in the late 1970s). Several church buildings passed to Anglicans or Orthodox, e.g. Perth, which was given to the Anglicans in 1940.[100] There had never been many congregations in New Zealand, but Wellington remained functioning until around 1960, and Auckland until the 1970s.

As in Australia, members in Canada were widely scattered; most of the Canadian congregations seem to have faded out of existence during the 1930s and 1940s, the last churches to close being Toronto and Vancouver in 1954. In the USA, some small groups seem to have disappeared before World War I, but most churches seem to have lasted until the 1930s. The last to close were New York and Philadelphia, which were certainly open in the early 1960s and may have survived into the 1980s.[101] As for the German congregations, of which the seven in 1922 had decreased to two by 1928, the Chicago angel S. T. Pearl was constrained to advise German ministers that many members emigrating to America had been disappointed. He had no priests able to speak enough German to minister to them, and asked angels to forewarn emigrating members. The great distances between congregations could mean that members would only be able to attend a Catholic Apostolic service every year or two—hardly an ideal situation.[102] As in Britain, where possible buildings were given to other denominations. The New York horn building went to a black congregation in 1948, and is now used by the Church for all Nations, a congregation affiliated to the Lutheran Church Missouri Synod.

Meetings were listed in 1906 as taking place in South Africa at Johannesburg, Cape Town, and (Pieter)maritzburg, and a deacon was living at Durban, but any corporate presence here seems to have disappeared fairly quickly. In 1909 it was reported that Colonel Laughton's health now made it unlikely that he would be able to visit

---

98. Adell, *De tysta bedjarna*, 10; Diersmann, *Notes*, 134.
99. Ibid., 131.
100. Copinger, 'Annals,' 229.
101. Schröter, *Bilder*, 51.
102. S. T. Pearl, in *Kirkliches Adreßbuch* 1929, 35.

members in India, and other arrangements were to be made.[103] Subsequent address books, however, merely included the statement that there was currently no minister serving members in India.

103. BIA, CAC 1/7, Bradford MC, 30 June 1909.

# 15

# Vestiges of a Church (1971 onwards)

## THE CATHOLIC APOSTOLIC CHURCH TODAY

IT IS TIME TO assess what remains of the church, now that its ministry has been all but completely dismantled and most of its churches closed. Few underdeacons now remain, and so remaining congregations tend to be led by laymen. The need for makeshift and unauthorized arrangements to provide for the spiritual nourishment of remaining members has proved a recurrent problem, especially as it runs contrary to the belief that services should only be conducted by those divinely authorized to do so. Like Davson, some feel that the trustees should not have closed down churches so quickly, since this has resulted in many abandoning Catholic Apostolic views as they settled in Anglican and other congregations. The argument is that the lack of ministers should not prevent a church from continuing to meet if there is a viable congregation, since the church is the whole congregation. The difference of opinion which became evident with Davson's protest is thus still present. The two streams, which are also present in Germany, have been classed as 'introverts', those who feel that members should continue to meet separately, and 'extroverts', those who (in England) make their home in exile with the Church of England or occasionally with nonconformist congregations which they see as faithful to the Scriptures, although they may also continue to meet with other Catholic Apostolics for prayer. Some have become Anglican readers, and there have been clergy and even bishops with a Catholic Apostolic background. Since the movement regards all the baptized as members of one Church, lay members wishing to enter the Anglican ministry have been free to do so.

In a sense, though, all members are introverted, in that the movement's enforced inactivity has produced a different type of spirituality; no longer ministering or evangelizing, it has turned inward to focus on intercession and the cultivation of the advent hope.[1] Yet they are well informed concerning contemporary religious trends. Many are in favor of the principle of spiritual gifting emphasized by the Charismatic movement. In a piece of writing unique for its assessment of contemporary church life, one lay member, Walter Dougharty, offered the opinion that the Pentecostal movement, 'in spite of much disorder, is bearing a strong and increasing witness to the presence of Spiritual Gifts in the Church.'[2] This is balanced by widespread disapproval of its perceived tendency to anarchy and lack of structure, and wariness of novelties such as (during the mid-1990s) the Toronto Blessing and the Kansas City prophets; the Catholic Apostolic Church had regulated the exercise of spiritual gifts, providing spaces within the liturgy, special meetings under the angel's presidency, and clearly defined positions and expectations for those with the gift of prophecy. However, there is some evidence of Catholic Apostolics gravitating towards independent charismatic teachers, and of sympathy for the conspiracy theories put forward by some such leaders. One wonders whether their tradition of reliance upon ministerial judgment in discerning and regulating prophetic gift has left them ill-equipped now that they are without ministers.

As for ecumenism, the desire for unity is seen as 'undoubtedly inspired by the Holy Spirit, although the same cannot be said without qualification of some of the schemes put forward for achieving it.'[3] Such things are seen as signs of the last days, and the faithful should look up, for their redemption is drawing near. Other events interpreted as signs of the last days have included the restoration of apostles and the apparent failure of their work (on the lines of God's dealings with humanity in each previous dispensation, which have always ended in human failure), the return of the Jews to Israel, and the enlargement of the European (Economic) Community.

We should beware of assuming that 'extroverts' are happy with all that goes on in their new spiritual home. Dougharty enjoined members to remain faithful under trial until the Lord should come for them. Unlike those who advocated continuing to worship apart, members with more outgoing views believed that, now that the churches under apostles were closing, it was God's will that they return to Babylon and worship in other churches. There was no longer any room for a pharisaical attitude which looked down on other Christians since members were now forced by circumstances to worship with them, sharing in responsibility for what took place in the Churches even though they personally disapproved. This, Dougharty asserted, was the first time in Church history that a group had been put in such a position; yet readers could draw comfort from the fact that this was the position of Christ, who took our sins upon

---

1. Anon., *Neue Apostelgeschichte*, 132, quoting a German Protestant periodical, *Materialdienst*.

2. Dougharty, *Last Days*, 1. Whilst Dougharty's essay was without authority and written by a layman, its dissemination in print indicates that its content was deemed helpful and in line with the apostles' teaching. Given that it is unique, extended discussion of its content is, I believe, justified.

3. Ibid.

himself and confessed them as his own.[4] The faithful were to take comfort from the letter to the Hebrews, written to those who had been cast out for their faith in Christ. The last message from the priesthood under apostles, in the person of Davson, was that the faithful should go outside the camp. Christ's return could not be long delayed; there was little doubt that this present age would end around the turn of the millennium.[5] Meanwhile, they would find that their views on such matters as the inspiration of Scripture, disorder in the eucharistic liturgy, misuse of church buildings for secular purposes, the lack of biblical teaching regarding present evils, and the idolizing of democracy in the Church would be misunderstood by their brethren. Such humiliation had often been foretold in prophecy. Yet they were to say nothing in reply, since this would be to oppose the Lord's anointed ministers, although if women priests were introduced they might be forced to worship elsewhere.

According to Flegg, members were instructed not to remain at a service in which a woman was to preach or officiate, and to make no secret of the reason for departing or absenting themselves. He noted members turning off the television if a woman read a lesson or prayed in a broadcast service.[6] On the other hand, as one member commented to me around 2001, 'If we withdrew from churches where women read lessons, we wouldn't have attended anywhere for about twenty-five years.'

How, then, given the closure of church buildings and the gradual cessation of Catholic Apostolic worship, does the movement maintain any degree of cohesion? Jones asserts that the movement was not conversionist, and that in Britain it emphasized its close ties with the Church of England and opposed exclusivism and separatism; thus commitment to it would inevitably become diffused once the central focus (the apostles) was lost.[7] However, this model is less applicable to other countries, in which relationships with the established Churches have been less positive. Even in Britain many remaining members maintain close contact with others, and count it a real privilege to have been brought up in the Catholic Apostolic Church. This is not said out of any sense of pride; rather, they are all too aware that the revelation given to them, and the body of teaching which they have received regarding the fundamentals of the Christian faith, has made them all the more responsible for what they do with what they have received. From this conviction is derived the movement's sense of having failed to live up to its calling. Furthermore, there is a sense in which their particular understanding of biblical typology and its outworking in their Church binds members together as the movement becomes progressively more inward-looking.[8]

4. Ibid., 2.
5. Ibid., 4–5.
6. Flegg, 'Gathered under Apostles,' 150.
7. Jones, 'Catholic Apostolic Church,' 151; cf. Lively, 'Catholic Apostolic Church,' 287.
8. This has been compared with the use of secret codes by other groups: Flegg, 'Gathered under Apostles,' 207–8.

Hopes for the future, in which the Second Coming will inaugurate a new phase of the Lord's work, find tangible expression in the maintenance of their remaining buildings. The church at Albury had electricity installed as recently as 1991; with a new roof and a new heating system, and maintained to a standard that puts most regularly used church buildings to shame, it is ready for use when the Lord returns, should he have need of it.[9] Soon after 2000, Paddington, too, was painstakingly restored with the help of young people from overseas, thanks to the initiative and talent of the then-caretaker; the same was being done at Gordon Square during the late 1990s. Yet in spite of the care lavished on these buildings, one member expressed to me the conviction that God would work in the open air and did not really need buildings (which could well prove too small in any case); as examples of men fired by the Spirit, he instanced (in the same breath) Billy Graham and Edward Irving. Both, it may be noted, were accustomed to preaching outdoors. We are, perhaps, back where we began.

Since Davson's death, many of the more separatist Catholic Apostolics have practised eucharistic fasting; this is based on the belief that those in the Lord's work may be called to special self-denial following the removal of apostles. In view of the importance which members have always attached to the sacraments as channels for divine blessing and nourishment, such fasting does indeed represent considerable self-denial. However, it is an area on which members are not agreed; for example, I am given to understand that some in Germany fast whereas others attend Lutheran or other Protestant eucharists; similarly, those in Holland do not practice eucharistic fasting. German members are also said now to have problems in obtaining confirmation and admission to communion in the former state Churches or *Landeskirchen* comprising the Evangelische Kirche in Deutschland (EKD), something which was the case when the movement first took root there.

Apart from the legacy of rejection by the state churches and the belief that these were part of Babylon, one reason for eucharistic fasting was the belief, based on an apostles' circular of 1868, that whilst priests in Anglican, Roman Catholic, and Orthodox Churches were properly ordained, ministers of the Lutheran, Reformed, and United Churches of the German *Länder* were not. Against that, however, could be cited an 1895 circular in which Woodhouse refused to say that the communion of non-episcopal Churches was not communion, or that their ministers were not servants of Christ. A more open approach was evident during the 1960s in the writings and practice of the under-deacon Hermann Leitz of Freiburg im Breisgau, who held the Litany in the afternoon so that members could attend other churches in the morning. According to Schröter, not a few members think the same way, and some are active in the EKD, even in its leadership and synods; some pastors also have Catholic Apostolic roots. Moreover,

---

9. Anon., 'Albury Chapel is preserved.' In 1931 Philip Gray asked the congregation why they were repairing the building when their future was so uncertain; the response was that even if there was no new revelation of the Holy Spirit and the building was no longer required for Catholic Apostolic use, at least it would be in good condition for others to find: Lang papers 105:109, Gray to Lang, 27 June 1931.

some young Catholic Apostolics had been involved in charismatic renewal in the German Democratic Republic during the 1970s.[10]

Even in the English-speaking world where few congregations remain and members usually worship in other churches, there is a strong network which ensures that members and former members retain their sense of a distinctive identity. International contacts and friendships provide mutual support and result in not a few marriages. The wheel has turned full circle; as in the earliest days, members meet in homes for private prayer meetings and the offering of the Litany. Other means of maintaining cohesion include annual international youth camps. These began as the initiative of a Dutch family[11] and drew most of their attenders (who around 2000 numbered up to 120) from Catholic Apostolic homes; Switzerland, the United Kingdom, Denmark, and Holland took turns to host them. In the German Democratic Republic, several youth gatherings were arranged each year to provide teaching regarding Catholic Apostolic history and doctrine.[12] Such events not only provided teaching but have helped to maintain the commitment of the movement's young people in the face of pressure from the world and from liberal churches, and (in the East German context) competition from the state sponsored youth organizations.

One might have thought that Davson's death would signal the end of the time of silence,[13] but as yet this has not been the case. The last librarian at Gordon Square to make material available to outsiders was Norman C. Priddle (1905-78), who used to issue lists of second-hand items and typescript reprints for sale. In 1969 he wrote to members regarding the continuing demand for Catholic Apostolic material, which was becoming very difficult to obtain. He asked to be informed if members had any for disposal, reminding them that it was undesirable for 'our books' to come onto the open market and that adequate arrangements needed to be made before members died.[14]

On the other hand, he was prepared to assist serious researchers. Among significant sales which he made was that of a large quantity of Catholic Apostolic literature to the Bodleian Library in 1972, including many sermons and other internal circulars from the early twentieth century.[15] He also made important items available during the 1960s to the Archiv der Neuapostolische Kirche Norddeutschland in Hamburg, which given the antipathy between the two churches constitutes remarkable testimony to his openness. It was probably also during this period that (so I was told) he invited

10. Schröter, *Die Katholisch-apostolischen Gemeinden*, 198–200.

11. In the late 1960s, German singing weeks and Dutch youth camps were also being held.

12. Schröter, *Die Katholisch-apostolischen Gemeinden*, 201.

13. Pinnington and Newman-Norton, *Conciliar and Apostolic Witness*, 102.

14. N. C. Priddle, Letter from Gordon Square about surplus literature, January 1969; for the same request in Germany, see *Smyrna-Stimmen* 1952/8, back page [unpaginated].

15. Geoffrey Groom (assistant librarian) to me, 30 March 1993. A large collection of such material in the library of Yale Divinity School was acquired from the Bodleian Library in 1973, and is presumed to represent duplicates from that collection: Anon., 'Guide to the Papers.'

several booksellers to Gordon Square to bid for a stock of second-hand material; the winner took away an estate car full. Virtually all of it was sold within a few months. Priddle's business was run separately from the Church, and his openness represented a continuation of the approach of his father David and before him H. B. Copinger. Just before his death he wrote: 'For my own part, I think I can say that I have gone further than any of my predecessors in making Apostolic literature available to Christians outside the Apostles' communion. This has earned me some criticism from the Trustees, as you may well imagine.'[16]

Perhaps unsurprisingly, in 1975 the trustees decided to ban the sale of literature to outsiders. This decision may have been in part a reaction to Priddle's openness, but it is also likely to have been motivated by the conviction that as a work of God it was inappropriate to allow the movement to be subjected to academic dissection. We cannot exclude, either, the possible existence of an element of more or less conscious fear of being misunderstood. Since the 1970s, this policy has been applied with increasing strictness: whereas in the early 1990s I was able to purchase a few second-hand items from the then secretary to the trustees, I and other inquirers have more recently met with categorical refusal to do this. The consequence (which is unwelcome to the trustees but inevitable) has been that second-hand Catholic Apostolic works command high prices, as demand far outstrips supply, although a number of nineteenth-century works have now appeared in digitized form on the internet or have been issued by small special-interest publishers, and some are appearing as e-books.

A memorandum from the internet age underlines the call for silence as essential to avoid hindering the Lord's action, and stipulating that 'these writings should not be made available indiscriminately or disposed of in such a manner that they become generally available.' Those without descendants to whom to will their Catholic Apostolic writings are encouraged to leave instructions for their disposal to the libraries at Gordon Square or Paddington. A footnote cautions against transmitting writings by e-mail or putting them on web pages.[17] This is locking the stable door after the horse has bolted, since others—not, so far as I can tell, members—have made such writings available on the web.[18] It is to be hoped, therefore, that the trustees will see their way clear to a more restricted interpretation of the time of silence. This, coupled with readiness to answer legitimate scholarly inquiries on the basis of the archive material they preserve, would be of undoubted public benefit.

Apart from Gordon Square, the only official Catholic Apostolic publisher now is Verlag Hermann Meier in Germany, formerly based in Siegen, then in Berlin, and

---

16. Priddle to Seraphim Newman-Norton, November 1977, *Glastonbury Bulletin* 51 (October 1978) 20–21.

17. Anon., *Safekeeping*.

18. See, for example, the collection uploaded by the late Peter Sgotzai and now maintained by the Netzwerk apostolische Geschichte, online at: <http://www.apostolische-dokumente.de/>.

now in Bochum. Almost all its output consists of reprints of older works, and these are not available through booksellers.[19]

## REDISCOVERY OF THE CATHOLIC APOSTOLIC CHURCH

As noted in the introduction, other writers have discussed the influence of the Catholic Apostolic liturgy on the thought and practice of other Churches, so we shall not consider this here. Neither is there much to say regarding the extent to which Pentecostalism and the Charismatic movement drew on this precedent, since more often they distanced themselves from it. Christopher B. Heath estimated that only 1/2000 of the Christian Church had accepted the Lord's work by apostles.[20] So it might seem that the Church's witness had been largely in vain.

Some movements, however, have sought to reappropriate aspects of Catholic Apostolic structure and teaching. One example in Britain is the British Orthodox Church, a small denomination which was for some years in communion with the Coptic Orthodox Patriarchate of Alexandria. In November 1969 its general assembly passed a resolution affirming its acceptance of the restored apostles and of the work of the seventy 'now commencing in our midst in succession thereto,' a move which it saw as significant because this was the first time that a part of the historic Church had given corporate recognition to the Lord's work.[21] In Germany, Holland, and Austria, a movement formed in 1932 seeks to replicate Catholic Apostolic structures and liturgy; needless to say, this has caused some trouble and is disapproved of.

But at an individual level, the Church's witness appears to have been somewhat more widely noticed. Many members admit that while they are bound to keep silence regarding the future, others are not. As one member put it to me, 'we can neither prohibit their reading "our" literature (which was meant for the Church Universal) on the grounds that they are not members and have no right to it, nor request them to stop sharing their finds, since they are not bound to keep silent as we are.' The migration of most English-speaking members to Anglicanism, especially from the 1950s, helped to create a wider awareness of the movement and of its central tenets.[22] As part of this migration, the practice of dual membership in the Catholic Apostolic Church and the Church of England or another mainline denomination, which had always been evident in the movement's history (as it had in that of the Pietists and the Moravians), became increasingly widespread.[23] There is no evidence that this has led to any kind of spiritual schizophrenia, although more recent generations have not infrequently lost contact or fallen away from the faith, especially if marrying outsiders.

19. Schröter, *Die Katholisch-apostolischen Gemeinden*, 201.
20. Christopher B. Heath, *Sermon, 10 August 1941*, 1.
21. *Glastonbury Bulletin* 10 (November 1971) 32–33.
22. Pinnington and Newman-Norton, *Conciliar and Apostolic Witness*, 79.
23. Flegg, 'Gathered under Apostles,' 196.

In various countries, a few individuals are quietly embracing Catholic Apostolic teaching, sometimes as the result of marrying a member (there appears to have been something of a change in attitude towards mixed marriages during the last century). Members hope that others in the wider Church will rediscover the truth in the Catholic Apostolic work, although one wonders how this squares with their refusal to make literature available to interested inquirers. Of course, the absence of any ministers to present an authoritative opinion on matters of doctrine means that any explanations by lay members are to be treated as personal opinions and nothing more. Even so, as Schaff put it back in 1877, 'The Irvingite movement has directed the attention of many serious minds to a deeper study of the supernatural order and outfit of the Catholic Apostolic Church, the division and reunion of Christendom, and the eschatological questions connected with the second advent.'[24]

Scholars, too, have rediscovered the Church, although their assessment has not always been positive. Horton Davies alleged that it 'hugged itself to death' though its lack of concern for the outside world.[25] Even Christenson, who sought in the Church a precedent and exemplar for the Charismatic movement, accused surviving members of remaining 'in the clutch of a stultifying exclusivism.'[26] Tierney described the movement as a 'self-liquidating sect.'[27] Jones claimed, somewhat inaccurately, that '[t]he gradual demise of the movement was due to its belief in the imminence of the Second Advent and not to its inability to adapt to existing institutions.'[28] More moderately, Schaff's assessment remains as pertinent now as when it was written: 'It is one of the unsolved enigmas of church history: it combines a high order of piety and humility of individual members with astounding assumptions, which, if well founded, would require the submission of all Christendom to the authority of its inspired apostles.'[29] This, to my mind, comes closest to the truth; most other verdicts fall into the trap of attempting to assess the Lord's work according to criteria which its members would reject, and thus failing to 'get inside' its thinking.

## CONCLUSION

Throughout this account a tension has been evident to a greater or lesser extent, both aspects of which must be heeded by those who would enter into the mindset of those who were a part of the Lord's work. The Catholic Apostolic movement claimed to be a pattern of God's purpose to restore his Church, yet it finally exhorted members to accept that this would not happen until the Second Coming. This tension is explained

24. Schaff, *History*, 1:910–11.
25. Davies, *Worship and Theology*, 4:162.
26. Christenson, 'Pentecostalism's forgotten Forerunner,' 33.
27. Tierney, 'Catholic Apostolic Church,' 290.
28. Jones, 'Catholic Apostolic Church,' 154.
29. Schaff, *History*, 1:908.

firstly by the belief (not unique to them by any means, for it is fundamental to dispensationalist Evangelicalism) that every human dispensation ends in failure and is the occasion for a new and better one being brought in, and secondly by the consistent opposition to the idea that human effort could ever achieve God's purpose, whether in mission or church-building. The problems posed for members by the movement's apparent lack of success are thus rather different from those faced by modern, usually postmillennial, restorationist groups coming to terms with the failure of their hope that in their movement God would at last restore the Church. Gretason points out that while it is true that the changes made during the twentieth century can be understood as a sticking to principle, it must also be borne in mind that references in sermons and circulars to a sense of disappointment indicate that many in the congregations understood their mission in a less provisional way than they should have done.[30] They must therefore have found the changes difficult to accept, even when these represented the application to changing circumstances of unchanging fundamental principles.

So we return to a question posed earlier. How have those gathered under apostles carried out Hume's injunction in 1901 to remain quietly in their places and faithful in their duties? We can but marvel at the consistency with which many do so, even when the place allotted to them has turned out to be in an environment which is increasingly uncongenial and the duties admit of no retirement because of the lack of others to shoulder them.

What fulfillment of the vision do they recognize? 'They regard the failure of their labours to gather the Churches of Christendom into their communion as being after the analogy of the failures at the close of all preceding dispensations, and as furnishing no argument against the reality of their divine mission.' Whilst the first-fruits might be few, a great multitude would be saved out of tribulation at the time of the Antichrist.[31] Although it must be a sore disappointment for them that their Church was to be progressively dismantled until nothing remained, most have remained convinced that God is still working, and that the vision of a restored Church, perfect and waiting to meet her returning Lord, which has fired their own movement is one which will nevertheless be fulfilled on a larger scale in God's time. And in one way the work has not been a failure at all: one Catholic Apostolic preacher (at the closing service of the Glasgow horn congregation) used the image of temporary buildings erected to serve the construction of an industrial estate, which are cleared away when the project is completed.[32]

Catholic Apostolic spirituality in the movement's current phase may be summed up as one of continual repentance. The feeling is still that the movement has not confessed as it should have done, and that it has become sectarian rather than identifying itself with the sin of Christendom. But that is not the whole story: their work is seen as

---

30. Gretason, 'Authority, Provisionality and Process,' 255.
31. W. W. Andrews, in Schaff, *History*, 1:915.
32. Anon., *Sermon preached at the South Side (Horn) Church*, 5.

but one phase of God's plan, and those who remain expect another and greater work of God before the return of Christ. In the words of Pinnington and Newman-Norton:

> Its Apostles are indeed 'no more,' its model of the Church <u>has</u> been taken down and its altar 'covered,' and its members have indeed declared repeatedly that <u>their</u> work is at an end—that is to say the specific work with which they were entrusted. But it is implicit in the whole conception of the Lord's work and explicit in many of the writings of the Restored Apostles and their Ministers that this particular work is but one stage of a larger one.[33]

There is a remarkable consistency about their interpretation of events in their movement's history, and in their submission to the loss of all their ministers. As a measure of the genuineness of this attitude, one may point out that there has been no breakaway movement in Britain.

Though cast down, they do not despair; though convicted of their own failure, they are not (at their best) negative towards other Christians; though shaken at the turn which events have taken, many continue to base their lives on the things most surely believed among them. In Davson's words, 'our true answer to those who ask, "Who are you?" is: We are those who followed the Lord's Restored Apostles, being led to do so by the Holy Ghost.'[34] But their hope is not based ultimately on the apostles themselves. In its essentials, it remains unchanged from the days immediately after Woodhouse's death, when, as Bramley-Moore wrote: 'Apostles have again been removed; but, since our trust is NOT IN THEM, but in the living God, who raiseth the dead, we are looking and waiting for the resurrection; for, as we believe that none but apostles can do apostles' work, so do we look forward to the apostles being raised from the dead to finish their work, and to present the Church as a chaste virgin to Christ, and therefore, earnest and daily prayer is made for the first resurrection.'[35]

Prayer meetings usually include the concluding prayer before communion from the Liturgy, 'Hasten, O God, the time when Thou shalt send from Thy right hand Him whom Thou wilt send; at whose appearing the saints departed shall be raised, and we which are alive shall be caught up to meet Him, and so shall ever be with Him,' or the 'Prayer for Resurrection and Change,' introduced in 1878:[36]

> O Lord Jesu Christ, Who art the Resurrection and the Life, we acknowledge Thy goodness in restoring the ministry of Thine apostles, in gathering and sealing Thy first fruits, and in warning us through Thy prophets of the nearness of the day of Thine appearing.

---

33. Pinnington and Newman-Norton, *Conciliar and Apostolic Witness*, i–ii.
34. Davson, *Sermons*, 169.
35. Bramley-Moore, *Church's forgotten Hope*, 267–68.
36. C. E. Lewis Heath, *Lecture*, 8.

Hasten that day, that we may see Thee as Thou art, and be changed into Thy likeness. Bring back (Thine apostles and)[37] those our brethren who have rejoiced with us in Thy returning grace unto Thy Church and have fallen asleep, and all who sleep in Thee. Restore to them their bodies raised in glory and immortality; and vouchsafe to us who are alive and remain to be sanctified wholly; and may our whole spirit and soul and body be preserved blameless unto Thy coming.

We pray that the time may speedily come when we, and all Thy saints in all generations who have been elected to this glory, may stand with the Lamb upon Mount Zion, a holy first-fruits redeemed from among men, without fault before the throne of God: and unto Thee, with the Father and the Holy Ghost, be all honour and glory, now and for ever.

Those who find themselves unable to accept the movement's claim to a restored apostleship may nevertheless concur with one Anglican writer who, considering them to be 'as near, or nearer, to perfection, as any Church in the world,' concluded:

> We should approach these people not only with sympathy, but with humility. For what they have to show us looks much more of God rather than of man. . . . Wherever they appear they bring with them a conception of loyal and faithful Churchmanship that puts many of us to shame. It is to be hoped that [their witness] will be remembered and treasured by the whole Church of Christ . . . .[38]

---

37. This phrase was not part of the prayer as originally composed, but is regularly inserted.
38. Clark, 'Commonly called "Irvingites"'.

# Appendix

## Leading Ministers in the Church

SOURCES: ANON., APOSTLES AND other Ministers; Anon., The Lord's Restored Apostles; Newman-Norton, 'Biographical Index'; Anon., Neue Apostelgeschichte, 414; Flegg, 'Gathered under Apostles', 65–66, 71; Schröter, Die Katholisch-apostolischen Gemeinden, 547 n. 101.

### Apostles

| Name | Denomination | Occupation | Date first called | Tribe (jurisdiction) |
|---|---|---|---|---|
| John Bate Cardale (1802–77) | Anglican | Solicitor | 31 Oct. 1832 | Judah (England) |
| Henry Drummond (1786–1860) | Anglican | Banker and former MP | Dec. 1832 | Reuben (Scotland, Protestant Switzerland) to Dalton 1865, then Cardale 1870 |
| Henry King (1787–1865; later changed his name to King-Church) | Anglican | Clerk in the Tower | 3 Apr. 1833 | Gad (Denmark, Holland, Belgium) Denmark to Cardale 1865; Holland to Woodhouse 1865; Belgium to Dalton 1865, then Woodhouse 1870 |
| Spencer Perceval (1795–1859) | Anglican | Former MP | 14 Dec. 1833 | Asher (Italy) to Armstrong 1865 |
| Nicholas Armstrong (1801–79) | Anglican | Clergyman (rector, St Dunstan in the West; Protestant Reformation Society) | 18 Jan. 1834 | Naphtali (Ireland, Greece, and the East from 1855) |

# Appendix

| Name | Denomination | Occupation | Date first called | Tribe (jurisdiction) |
|---|---|---|---|---|
| Francis V. Woodhouse (1805–1901) | Anglican | Barrister | 13 Aug. 1834 | Manasseh (Austria, S. Germany; also N. America as 'suburb')<br>S. Germany and Austria temp. to Drummond 1855 |
| Henry Dalton (1805–69) | Anglican | Clergyman (curate, St Leonard's, Bridgnorth) | ?Jan. 1835 | Simeon (France, RC Switzerland)<br>to Woodhouse 1869 |
| John O. Tudor (1784–1861) | Anglican | Artist | 18 Feb. 1835 | Levi (Poland; also India, Australia as 'suburbs') |
| Thomas Carlyle (1803–55) | Presbyterian | Advocate | 1 May 1835 | Issachar (N. Germany)<br>to Woodhouse 1855 |
| Frank Sitwell (1797–1864) | Anglican | Gentleman | 20 May 1835 | Zebulun (Spain, Portugal)<br>to Armstrong 1865 |
| William Dow (1800–55) | Presbyterian | Clergyman (Tongland) | 3 June 1835 | Joseph aka Dan (Russia) |
| David Dow (1798–1878) | Presbyterian | Clergyman (Irongray) | early July 1835 | – |
| Duncan Mackenzie (1785–1855) | Presbyterian | Wholesale chemist | 14 July 1835 | Benjamin (Norway, Sweden)<br>to Dow 1846, Carlyle 1854, King-Church 1855, Cardale 1865 |

## Pillars

Apostles: J. B. Cardale to 1877

Prophets: E. O. Taplin to 1862; J. F. Prentice (acting) to 1881; G. Vowles (acting) to 1890; C. Hammond (acting) fl. 1901

Evangelists: W. H. Place to 1866; A. F. Bayford; E. L. Hooper; W. W. Wright (acting) to 1911

Pastors: H. Drummond to 1836; J. Thompson to 1872; thereafter the pastor with the apostles for each tribe

## Coadjutors

| | |
|---|---|
| England | J. Leslie 1866–97; E. Heath 1897–1929 |
| Australia | J. Leslie 1866–97; E. Heath 1886–1929 |
| India | J. Leslie 1877–97 |
| Ireland | C. J. T. Böhm 1865–80 (J. Leslie temp. 1875); E. L. Hooper 1881–88; J. Leslie 1888–97 |
| North America | J. Leslie 1866–75; W. R. Caird 1875–fl.1880; E. L. Hooper 1881–88; E. Heath 1888–1929 |

## Leading Ministers in the Church

| | |
|---|---|
| North Germany | C. J. T. Böhm 1859–80; M. von Pochhammer 1880–95 (supported by F. B. A. Diestel 1886–99, E. L. Geering 1886–94); I. Capadose 1895–1920 |
| Switzerland | W. R. Caird 1865–75; E. L. Geering 1875–94; E. Heath 1895/6–1929 |
| France & Belgium | L. R. Symes 1870–75; W. R. Caird 1875–fl.1880 I. Capadose 1899–1920 |
| Denmark & Holland | Sir G. Hewett 1865–76; I. Capadose 1875–1920 |
| Norway & Sweden | Sir G. Hewett 1865–76; I. Capadose 1876–1920 |
| Scotland | W. R. Caird 1865–75; J. Leslie temp. 1875; E. L. Geering temp. 1875–80; E. L. Hooper 1881–88; E. Heath 1888–1929 |
| Italy | W. Flewker 1870–76; I. Capadose 1890–1920 |
| Spain & Portugal | W. Flewker 1870–76; I. Capadose 1899–1920 |
| Poland | I. Capadose 1899–1920 |
| South Germany | W. R. Caird 1865–75; M. von Pochhammer 1875–95 (supported by E. L. Geering 1886–94); E. Heath 1895/6–1929 |
| Austria | M. von Pochhammer 1873–95; E. Heath 1895/6–1929 |
| Russia | C. J. T. Böhm 1870–77; M. von Pochhammer 1877–79; F. B. A. Diestel 1879–99; I. Capadose 1899–1920 |
| Japan | E. Heath 1891–1929 |

NB: the dates are often approximate, and there was a greater measure of fluidity regarding areas of jurisdiction than was the case with the apostles themselves. Also, there were apparently two lists of tribes, which explains why some sources may give a somewhat different list: Davson, *Church in Paddington 80*, 2.

# Select Bibliography

## UNPUBLISHED AND MANUSCRIPT SOURCES

### Alnwick, Archives of the Duke of Northumberland at Alnwick Castle

Drummond Family Papers, Correspondence, homilies, sermons, and other papers (much of this is on microfilm at Oxford, Bodleian Library, Department of Western Manuscripts, MSS Film 1606–9).

### Birmingham, University of Birmingham, Cadbury Research Library

MS Boxes 449–55, H. B. Evans collection of material relating to the Catholic Apostolic Church.

### Bradford, West Yorkshire Archives Service

53D95, Registers, correspondence etc., from the church in Bradford.

### Cambridge, Cambridge University Library

Add. MS 7893, Hopkinson Papers.

### Edinburgh, Banner of Truth Trust

Letters to, by, and relating to Robert Baxter.

### Edinburgh, National Archive of Scotland

RH4/174, Edinburgh Catholic Apostolic Church, Baptismal register, 1833–1958.

# Select Bibliography

## Edinburgh, National Library of Scotland

Acc. 4388, Volume of homilies etc, mostly preached at Edinburgh Catholic Apostolic Church, 1853–59.
Acc. 8813(i), W. R. Caird and G. Ryerson. 'Journal of a Voyage to New York; and several places in Canada made by W. R. C. and G. R. of London commencing 1st Feby 1834'
Acc. 8813(ii), 'Ministries. July /69'.
Acc. 8837, Two volumes of ministries from Edinburgh Catholic Apostolic Church, 1848–84, many by W. F. Pitcairn.
Acc. 12489, Journals and papers of James G. and Jane Simpson.

## Edinburgh, New College Library

Chalmers Collection, Correspondence.

## Hamburg, Archiv der Neuapostolische Kirche Nord- und Ostdeutschland

Albury Circulars, 1851–1914.
Central Church, London, minutes and papers.
Notes and Minutes of Conference, 1850–1912.
Anon. 'Manuscript Book found at Albury apparently of a very early Date and containing Drafts made for Forms of Morning and Evening Services and Part of the Communion Service.' c.1838/9.
———. 'The Tribes 1838.' Notebook.
Copinger, H. B. 'Annals: The Lord's Work in the Nineteenth and Twentieth Centuries.' Typescript, n.d.
Henke, Manfred. 'Thomas Carlyle, Apostel für Norddeutschland. Festschrift zum 170. Jahrestag seiner prophetischen Rufung am 1. Mai 1835.' Typescript, 2005.
Work Group History of the New Apostolic Church. 'The Split between the Catholic Apostolic Church (CAC) and what was to become the New Apostolic Church 1862–1863.' Typescript, 2004.

## Kew, The National Archives

RG4, Baptismal registers: /328 Cambridge, /2424 Ware, /3194 Bridgnorth, /4143 Chelsea, /4170 Westminster, /4249 Newman St, /4294 Chelsea, /4201 Southwark, /4337 Paddington, /4375 Bishopsgate, /4531 Islington, /4533 Newman St.

## London, British Library

Add. MSS 49192, Spencer Perceval papers.
MSS Eur F206/105, 106 (Oriental and India Office Collection), letters from John MacLeod Campbell to Jane Mary Macnabb, 1830–34.
76415 (uncatalogued), ms letter by W. W. Andrews, 5 January 1853.

764n13, Ernst A. Rossteuscher. 'The Rebuilding of the Church of Christ upon the Original Foundations. An Historical Narrative of its Commencement. A free Translation' [by Miss L. A. Hewett], ms, n.d. German original: *Der Aufbau der Kirche Christi auf den ursprünglichen Grundlagen. Eine geschichtliche Darstellung seiner Anfänge* (Basel, 1871; 2nd ed. 1886).

764n14, Articles, pamphlets, etc., relating to the Catholic Apostolic Church, 1833–92.

764n19, Newspaper cuttings relating to Edward Irving and the Catholic Apostolic Church, 1835–1905.

X203/482, Seraphim Newman-Norton. 'A Biographical Index of those associated with the Lord's Work.' Typescript, 1972.

## London, British Orthodox Church

Born, Karl. 'The Lord's Work under Apostles', translated by Hywel B. Evans. Typescript, n.d.

Cardale, J. B. 'Observations made upon the Visitation of the Seven Churches in London 1869.' March 1869.

Copinger, H. B. 'Annals: The Lord's Work in the Nineteenth and Twentieth Centuries', transcribed, edited and updated by S. Newman-Norton. Typescript, n.d.

Hamilton, R. M. 'Notes taken nearly verbatim at the Meetings of the VII Churches, also a few other ministries.' 1875–81.

Newman-Norton, Seraphim. 'The Twelve Tribes of Christendom: Volume I. Congregations in the Tribe of Judah.' Typescript, 2007.

Scrapbook containing invitations to special services etc.

## London, Lambeth Palace Library

BM 3, 4, 6–9, 11, Bishops' Meetings minutes.

CFR AC 5, 'Council on Foreign Relations, Anglican Chaplaincies abroad: Function in Europe'

CFR CFC 45, 'Old Catholics: Netherlands: The Catholic Apostolics, 1958–70'.

H6565.S8, Papers of Kenneth Stevenson.

H6572.34.11, F. V. Woodhouse, 'Apostle's Teaching on the Tabernacle. Mr Woodhouse 1887'

LC 58, 75, Lambeth Conference committee papers.

MS 1468, J. A. Douglas papers.

MS 2689, Reginald Somerset Ward. 'The Death of a Church and the Problems arising therefrom: An Account of that Body which called itself "THE CATHOLIC APOSTOLIC CHURCH" and was sometimes called by its Opponents "THE IRVINGITES".' Typescript, 1935.

MSS 4234, 4237, Peter F. Anson papers.

MS 4727, Dodsworth-Drummond papers.

MS 4937–47, Miscellaneous ms volumes relating to the Catholic Apostolic Church, 1835–1957.

Frederick Temple papers, vol. 40.

Davidson papers, vols 144, 163, 186, 201.

Lang papers, vols 100, 105, 109, 132, 175, 181.

Fisher papers, vols 25, 80, 82, 95, 136, 193, 200, 237.

Uncatalogued papers formerly at the Department of Ecumenical Affairs, 'Episcopi Vagantes: Catholic Apostolic Church (Irvingites)'.

## London, London Metropolitan Archive

CLC/320/F/004/MS32521, Jurisdiction of North and Central Europe, Correspondence concerning the Catholic Apostolic Church in Belgium and the Netherlands, 1950–60.

## London, University College London, Special Collections

Add. MS 384, papers of David Tierney.

## Munich, Bayerische Staatsarchiv

Thiersch, Heinrich W. J. 'Chronik der apostolischen Gemeinde in Marburg und der Umgegend, von ihre Stiftung im Jahre 1847', 3 parts. Typescript transcription, n.d.

## Oxford, Oxford History Centre

NX1/A1/1–5, NX1/A2/1, NX1/F1/1, Eynsham Catholic Apostolic Church records.

## Oxford, Pusey House

H., M. 'Narrative [of the Early History of Irvingism].' c.1850.

## St Andrews, University Library, Special Collections

MS 38594, Flegg Collection of material relating to the Catholic Apostolic Church.

## Stratford-upon-Avon, Shakespeare Centre Library and Archive

BRR 13/8/11–17, DR 153/229, DR 724/8/2/13, Records of the Stratford-upon-Avon Corporation, papers and correspondence concerning the Revd William Connor.
DR 1067/2, Scrapbook collected by F. C. Morgan.

## Wigan, Wigan Archives Service

D/NCa Ap/1, 'Wigan. Special Minute Book for Church Councils'.

## Woking, Surrey History Centre

Zg/16, A. Browne. 'Albury Park and Village: Notebook relating to History.' n.d.

## York, Borthwick Institute for Archives

Records relating to Catholic Apostolic congregations at Bradford (CAC 1), Cleckheaton (CAC 2), Keighley (CAC 3), Huddersfield (CAC 4), Halifax (CAC 5), and Brighouse (CAC 6).

## In private hands

Anon, Record of events in connection with the Southampton church, 1833–62.
Cardale family papers, Correspondence, handbills, homilies, prophecies, sermons, teachings, an annotated New Testament, drafts of publications.
Letters and papers relating to the Irving, Gardiner, and Martin families.
Martin, John S. 'A Brief Survey of the Lord's Work in Australia.' Typescript, 1992.
Priddle, Norman C. Letter from Gordon Square dated January 1969 about surplus literature.

## THESES

Flegg, Columba Graham. 'The Catholic Apostolic Church: Its History, Ecclesiology, Liturgy, and Eschatology.' PhD thesis, Open University, 1990.
Grass, Timothy George. 'The Church's Ruin and Restoration: The Development of Ecclesiology in the Plymouth Brethren and the Catholic Apostolic Church, c.1825—c.1866.' PhD thesis, King's College London, 1997.
Gretason, Mark Nicholas. 'The Idea of the Church in Catholic Apostolic Theology.' MPhil thesis, King's College London, 1992.
Gretason, Mark Nicholas. 'Authority, Provisionality and Process in the Catholic Apostolic Church.' PhD thesis, University of Brighton, 1995.
Lancaster, John. 'John Bate Cardale, Pillar of Apostles: A Quest for Catholicity.' BPhil diss., University of St Andrews, 1978.
Lively, Robert L., Jr. 'The Catholic Apostolic Church and the Church of Jesus Christ of Latter-Day Saints: A Comparative Study of two minority Millenarian Groups in Nineteenth-Century England.' DPhil thesis, University of Oxford, 1977.
Newell, J. Philip. 'A. J. Scott and His Circle.' PhD thesis, New College, Edinburgh, 1981.
Roberts, Paul J. 'The Pattern of Initiation: Sacrament and Experience in the Catholic Apostolic Church and Its Implications for Modern Liturgical and Theological Debate.' PhD thesis, Manchester University, 1990.
Shaw, Plato E. O. 'The Catholic Apostolic Church (sometimes called "Irvingite"): A Historical Study.' PhD thesis, University of Edinburgh, 1935.
Stevenson, Kenneth W. 'The Catholic Apostolic Eucharist.' PhD thesis, Southampton University, 1975.
Weber, Albrecht. 'Die Katholisch-apostolischen Gemeinden. Ein Beitrag zur Erforschung ihrer charismatischen Erfahrung und Theologie.' Doctoral diss., Phillipps-Universität, Marburg an der Lahn, 1977.

# Select Bibliography

## PUBLISHED SOURCES

Almost all the items described below as duplicated are versions of previously published works produced by successive Catholic Apostolic librarians and booksellers at Gordon Square between c.1945 and 1975. These were intended for private circulation among members. Because of the extreme difficulty in determining which items were 'published' in a formal sense, and the existence of many works in both printed and duplicated versions, all circulated items have been treated here as published material.

A placename and reference number after a title indicate that it was issued as an official publication of that congregation. The British Orthodox Church library holds lengthy runs of such material for certain important congregations.

Author attributions, where not shown on title pages, have virtually all been taken from the bibliography by H. B. Copinger, the catalogues by Clement Boase, or lists of items for sale issued by Norman Priddle.


Aarsbo, J. *Komme Dit Rige: Vidnesbyrd og Livsbilleder fra Herrens Værk I Kirken 1830–1880*, 5 vols in 6. Copenhagen: Katolsk-Apostolisk Kirkes Bogdepot, 1930–43.

Abel, Jorg M. *Das Werk des Herrn in Russland und im Baltikum unter Aposteln und Propheten*, 3rd edn, 2012. http://www.apostolische-geschichte.de/docs/a-dokumente/a-0631.pdf, accessed 20 October 2015.

Ackery, J. W. *Paper on the Anointing of the Sick*. London: lithographed for private circulation, 1890.

———. *A Teaching by the Angel of the Church on the Sacramental Rite of Anointing the Sick*. London: printed for private circulation, 1890.

Adell, Bo. *De tysta bedjarna. Redogörelse för den katolsk apostoliska Kyrkans verksamhet i Sverige från omkring 1860*. Västerås: the author, 2000.

Albrecht, Ludwig. *The Work by Apostles at the end of the Dispensation*. Rev. ed. Dundee: Paul & Mathew, 1955.

———. and James Heath, *Visit of two Ministers of the Universal Church, Islington, 30th October, 1904*. London: duplicated for private circulation, n.d.

Amesbury, Joseph. *The Hope of Zion: A Letter to Henry Drummond, Esq*. London: Vinton, 1854.

———. *Memorial to the Ministers and other Brethren of the Churches in Zion*. London: Vinton, 1853.

———. *A Narrative of the proceedings of Mr C. Heath, Angel of the Church in Newman Street, against Mr J. Amesbury, Officiating Evangelist and formerly Helping Elder in that Church in consequence of his Refusal to withdraw or suppress his Pamphlet, entitled 'The Immediate and Glorious Advent of Our Lord Jesus Christ.' Addressed to the Apostles, Elders, and Brethren of the Gathered Churches*. London: Houlston & Stoneman, 1849.

Anderson, Gerald. H., ed. *Biographical Dictionary of Christian Missions*. Grand Rapids: Eerdmans, 1998.

Anderson, W. *Northern Evangelist District, Evangelist Work: Priests Employed under the Angel-Evangelist, in the Universal Church*. n.pl.: printed for private circulation, 1869.

Andrews, Samuel J. *Sermon on Entering a New Place of Worship: Preached in the Catholic Apostolic Church, Enfield, Conn., October 6, 1878*. Hartford, CT: Case, Lockwood & Brainard, 1878.

———. *William Watson Andrews: A religious Biography, with Extracts from his Letters and other Writings*. New York: G. P. Putnam's Sons, 1900.

———, S. H. Allen, and David H. Thayer. *The Duty of Christians to the Lord and to His Church: A Letter to the Members of an Ecclesiastical Council Held at Windsor Locks, Conn., March 17, 1880*. Hartford, CT: Case, Lockwood & Brainard, 1880.

Andrews, William Watson. *The Catholic Apostolic Church: Its History, Organization, Doctrine, and Worship, together with its Relation to the Churches: Reprinted from Bibliotheca Sacra for January and April 1866*. 5th ed., London: H. J. Glaisher, 1928.

———. *Christian Nurture: A Sermon*. Waterbury, CT: Waterbury Blank Book Mfg. Co, 1905.

———. *Edward Irving: A Review*. 2nd ed. Glasgow: David Hobbs, 1900 (first publ. 1864).

———. *Reasons for Withdrawing from the Congregational Ministry: With a Sermon, preached in Kent, Conn., May 20, 1849*. Hartford, CT: J. H. Bardwell, 1849.

———. *A Review of God's Mode of Working among His People by '12' and '70', 1891*. London: duplicated for private circulation, n.d.

Anon. '245205—Catholic Apostolic Church (Paddington) General Purposes Fund'; '245250—Catholic Apostolic Church—Trust Property held in connection therewith.' http://www.charitycommission.gov.uk, accessed 3 August 2016 (annual accounts).

———. *An Address*. London: West Middlesex Advertiser, 1867.

———. *An Address*. London: n.p., 1894.

———. *Address, 1954*, Central Church 2nd series 4. London: printed for private circulation, 1954.

———. *An Address for Circulation amongst Enquirers as to the Lord's present Work*. N.pl.: n.p., n.d.

———. *Address to the Flock on the Death of the late Angel in Manchester, delivered October 14th, 1894, and taken down in shorthand*. Manchester: Thiel, 1894.

———. 'Albury Chapel is Preserved for Second Coming.' *Surrey Advertiser*, 31 August 1990, 7.

———. *Albury: Extract from 'De Kapel der Apostelen te Albury en de Zeven Gemeenten te Londen.'* London: duplicated for private circulation, n.d.

———. *Allgemeine Rubriken*. http://www.katholisch-apostolische-gemeinde.de, accessed 23 February 2010 (based on the 1895 ed.).

———. *Anglican Sphere*, April 2016, 2. http://stmarys.nl/wp-content/uploads/2014/09/AS-2016-April-w.pdf, accessed 7 June 2016.

———. *Apostles and Other Ministers of the Catholic Apostolic Church Buried in Albury Parish Churchyard, Surrey (from the Parish Registers)*. London: duplicated for private circulation, n.d.

———. *The Apostles' Testimony 1838: An Analysis of the Contents. Young Men's Meeting, Session 1903–4*. Edinburgh: printed for private circulation, 1903.

———. *The Armistice and Peace (the Number Eleven): A Sermon*. London: duplicated for private circulation, n.d.

———. *Book of Regulations: England*. London: John Strangeways, 1878.

———. *British Museum. Catalogue of Printed Books. Accessions: Boase Collection*. London: British Museum, 1913.

# Select Bibliography

———. *Catholic Apostolic Church, Leeds, and Dependencies: Instruction of the Children, Year 1888–9*. Leeds: printed for private circulation, 1888.

———. 'Changing Uses Made of the Great Testimony in the Catholic Apostolic Church', 2006. http://www.nak.org/fileadmin/download/pdf/Testimony_ChangingUseCAC.pdf, accessed 22 July 2016.

———. *Church Almanac*. London: Strangeways & Walden, 1869.

———. *Church in Bishopsgate. Sermon, Sunday, October 14th, 1934: 'Resurrection Prayer'*, Bishopsgate 136. London: printed for private circulation, 1934.

———. *Church in Manchester. Address prepared by the Underdeacons and delivered 13th February, 1955*. Manchester: printed for private circulation, 1955.

———. 'Church Peril of Extinction: "We are not alarmed," says London Minister.' *Evening Standard*, 22 October 1930, 15.

———. *Churches in Manchester and Bolton. The Instruction of Children*. Manchester: printed for private circulation, 1953

———. *Churches in Southwark, Bristol and Bath: Peace Celebrations*, Southwark 1945/4. London: printed for private circulation, 1945.

———. *The Coming Again of the Lord: The First Principles of Christian Truth*. Dumfries: n.p., 1888.

———. *The Congregation in Albury: Teaching, August 1st, 1915*. N.pl.: printed for private circulation, 1915.

———. *Conversation between Two Disciples of Mr Irving and a Clergyman of the Established Church*. Dublin: Richard Moore Tims, 1836.

———. *A Deacon's Teaching: Absent Members, 5th May, 1946. Pastoral Instruction, 24th March 1946*, Central Church 1225. London: printed for private circulation, 1946.

———. *Deacon's Teaching, May 1917*, Central Church 1035. London: printed for private circulation, 1917.

———. 'Death of Mr F. V. Woodhouse: The "Last Apostle" and the Father of the English Bar.' *Surrey Advertiser*, 9 February 1901, 5.

———. *Description of the Mural Paintings on the Great Chancel Arch, &c., at the Catholic Apostolic Church, London St., Edinburgh*. Edinburgh: the church, n.d.

———. *Our Duty to our Children (A Sermon preached in March, 1944)*. N.pl.: duplicated for private circulation, 1944.

———. 'Euston Church: Story.' http://www.eustonchurch.com/about/, accessed 7 June 2016.

———. *'The following is a translation of a letter by a Danish member of this flock . . .'* London: duplicated for private circulation, n.d.

———. *To the gathered Members under Apostles now worshipping habitually in the Church of England or other branch of the Church*. N.pl.: printed for private circulation, 1949.

———. *General Rubrics; or, Rules for the Celebration of the Divine Offices, etc. England*. London: George Barclay, 1852.

———. *General Rubrics or Rules for the Celebration of the Divine Office etc. Scotland*. Edinburgh: Turnbull & Spears, 1900.

———. '"The Great Testimony": A Crucial Document of the Catholic Apostolic Church' (Part 1). http://www.nak.org/fileadmin/download/pdf/GreatTestimony1_engl_01.pdf , accessed 22 July 2016.

———. 'Guide to the Papers of the Catholic Apostolic Church (Record Group No. 55).' http://drs.library.yale.edu/HLTransformer/HLTransServlet?stylename=yul.ead2002.xhtml.xsl&pid=divinity:055&clear-stylesheet-cache=yes., accessed 8 June 2016.

———. 'The History and Doctrines of Irvingism.' *Church Quarterly Review* 7 (1878–9) 34–65.

———. 'Holy Trinity Anglican Church, Utrecht: Amersfoort.' http://www.holytrinityutrecht.nl/amersfoort/, accessed 7 June 2016.

———. 'Holy Trinity Brussels Newsletter', 28 June 2015. http://holytrinity.be/sites/default/files/newsletter/2015-06-28_weekly_newsletter.pdf, accessed 7 June 2016.

———. 'Home Pages of Anglican Churches in the Netherlands, Belgium, & Luxembourg.' http://www.hull.ac.uk/php/abspjl/Angl/Benekerk.html, accessed 7 June 2016.

———. *Homily, Day of National Thanksgiving, Sunday after Ascension, 1945; Sermon*, Central Church 1220. London: printed for private circulation, 1945.

———. *Homily, Fourth Sunday in Quadragesima (4th April, 1943); Sermon*, Central Church 1206. London: printed for private circulation, 1943.

———. *Keeping the Lord's Secret*. London: duplicated for private circulation, n.d.

———. *The Lambeth Conference 1930: Encyclical Letter from the Bishops with Resolutions and Reports*. London: SPCK, n.d.

———. *The Lord's Restored Apostles: Arranged in the Order of their Call, together with Details of their allotted Tribes (original and spiritual), Foundation Stones and their Spiritual Meaning (Rev. VII, 5–8; 19–20); corresponding Zodiacal Signs, with their Meaning, and a few Details of personal History*. London: duplicated for private circulation, n.d.

———. *To such Members of this Flock as are separated from us by Distance, and so prevented from attending the Services of Worship and Instruction which the Lord has set in order by His Apostles*. London: Fieldson & Jary, 1863.

———. *Ministries delivered in Newcastle-upon-Tyne. Homily, Pentecost 1918. The Anniversary of the Separation of the Apostles, 14th July 1918*. N.pl.: printed for private circulation, 1973.

———. *Ministries issued from Manchester in 1926 and 1928; Homily, 20th Sunday after Pentecost 1928, delivered in Manchester*. N.pl.: printed for private circulation, 1986.

———. *Ministry to the Flock in Manchester November 1922: The Purging of the Fruitful Branches of the Vine*. N.pl.: printed for private circulation, 1994.

———. *Mitteilungen aus den Apostelkonzilen 1855–1900*. Rendsburg: H. Müller, 1901.

———. 'Une mystérieuse petite église, en plein cour du XVème arrondissement . . .' *Paris historique, revue de presse*, 16-05-Q1 (2016) 8–9. http://www.paris-historique.org/images/document/presse/revuedepressemai2016-1.pdf, accessed 15 June 2016.

———. *The Nearness of the Coming of the Lord, and the Preparation Needful for the Same*. n.pl.: n.p., [c.1865].

———. *Neue Apostelgeschichte / New Acts of the Apostles*. Rev. ed. Frankfurt am Main: Friedrich Bischoff, 1985.

———. *New York, Pastoral Instruction no. 187, May, 1896*. New York: printed for private circulation, 1896.

———. 'Old Catholic Church is Growing!' 22 April 2011. http://oldcatholicnews.blogspot.com/2011_04_01_archive.html, accessed 7 June 2016.

———. *Pastoral Instruction, 11 July 1954*, Central Church 2nd series 6. London: printed for private circulation, 1954.

———. *Pastoral Instruction no. 773, New York, July and August, 1946*. New York: printed for private circulation, 1946.

———. *To the Patriarchs, Archbishops, Bishops, and Others in Places of Chief Rule over the Church of Christ throughout the Earth, and to the Emperors, Kings, Sovereign Princes, and*

## Select Bibliography

*Chief Governors over the Nations of the Baptized*. London: Moyes & Barclay, 1837 (the Great Testimony).

———. '"Perfecting the Ordinances"—Historical Observations on the Ministry of Evangelist in the Catholic Apostolic Church', 2007. http://www.nak.org/fileadmin/download/pdf/EvangelistamtArtikel_engl_200707.pdf, accessed 1 August 2016.

———. *'Persuaded of the common desire and purpose to observe all the commandments and ordinances of the Lord, the deacons of the church present the following directions for the instruction and guidance of their brethren . . .'* Bridgnorth, UK: printed for private circulation, n.d.

———. *The Position of Absent Members*, Southwark & Bristol 1955/2. N.pl.: printed for private circulation, 1955.

———. *Regulations as to the Building and Repairing of Churches*. London: Strangeways & Walden, 1863.

———. *Regulations for the Distribution of Tithe*. N.pl.: printed for private circulation, 1858.

———. *Safekeeping of 'Catholic Apostolic' Books, Ministries and Writings*. London: duplicated for private circulation, n.d.

———. *Sammlung kirchlicher Circulare pastoralen und anderen Inhalts*. 3rd ed. Berlin: J. Hoffmann, 1895

———. *Sermon, 31 October 1939*, Central Church 1179. London: printed for private circulation, 1939.

———. *Sermon by a Priest from a London Church, 27 February 1955*, Central Church 2nd series 13. London: printed for private circulation, 1955.

———. *Sermon delivered in Manchester, July 1910, Ye are our epistle,—known and read of all men*. N.pl.: printed for private circulation, 1990.

———. *Sermon: The Lord's Tenth*. Newcastle-on-Tyne: printed for private circulation, 1931.

———. *Sermon preached at the South Side (Horn) Church, Glasgow, on the Occasion of the Last Service to be held there, Pentecost 1949*, Glasgow 460. N.pl.: printed for private circulation, 1975.

———. *Sermon, Quinquagesima Sunday 1953*, Central Church 1273. London: printed for private circulation, 1953.

———. *Sermon: Teaching delivered in Manchester by a Deacon of the Seven 1918. Sunday within the Octave of the Feast of the Presentation of our Lord in the Temple*. N.pl.: printed for private circulation, 1973.

———. *Sermon, Third Sunday after Pentecost*. Central Church 1154. London: printed for private circulation, 1936.

———. *Sermon on Tithes and Offerings, 31st October 1948. Pastoral Instruction, 22nd August 1948*, Central Church 1239. London: printed for private circulation, 1948.

———. *Sermon (3rd Sunday in Quadragesima) March 23rd, 1924*, Southwark 1924/2. London: printed for private circulation, 1924.

———. *'A short time ago the Angel's vicar read to us . . .'* New York: printed for private circulation, 1888.

———. *Special Form of Confession for use on Sunday Morning, March 31st, 1901*. N.pl.: printed for private circulation, 1901.

———. *Special Services for Congregational use, July, 1902*. N.pl.: printed for private circulation, 1902.

———. Speech given at a lunch in honour of the Catholic Apostolic trustees, Thyateira House, London, 7 September 2011. http://www.thyateira.org.uk, accessed 10 December 2012.

———. *A Summary of Reports given at a General Meeting held on the 27th of March, 1879, in connection with the Evangelist Work of the Church in Glasgow.* Glasgow: printed for private circulation, 1879.

———. *Table of the Council of Zion, London 1835.* London: duplicated for private circulation, n.d.

———. *Teachings by Priests, 5 May 1926,* Central Church 1088. London: printed for private circulation, 1926.

———. *Testimoniet til kirkens biskopper og kristenhedens statsoverhoveder.* Copenhagen: Spuhrs Bogtrykkeri, 1938 (Danish translation of the Great Testimony).

———. *Three Pastoral Instructions (from Another Church),* March 1959, Glasgow 518. Glasgow: printed for private circulation, 1959.

———. *A Word of Testimony Respectfully Addressed to the Archbishops and Bishops of the Church of England.* London: n.p., 1888.

———. *Ein Wort des Zeugnisses ehrerbietigst uberreicht den hochwurdigen General-Superintendenten, Superintendenten und anderen hoheren Geistlichen der evangelischen Kirchen Nord-Deutschlands.* Berlin: n.p., 1889.

Anson, Peter F. *Fashions in Church Furnishings, 1840–1940.* 2nd ed. London: Studio Vista, 1965.

Ante, Kristine. 'Eine unbekannte Seite der baltischen Geschichte. Die religiöse Bewegung der Irvingianer im späten 19. Jahrhundert.' *Forschungen zur Baltischen Geschichte* 6 (2011) 84–100.

Apostelbezirk Hamburg [Karl Weinmann]. *100 Jahre Neuapostolische Kirche 1863–1963.* Frankfurt am Main: Friedrich Bischoff, 1963.

Arnot, William. *Life of James Hamilton, D.D., F.L.S.* London: James Nisbet, 1870.

Baxter, Robert. *Irvingism, in Its Rise, Progress, and Present State.* London: James Nisbet, 1836.

———. *Narrative of Facts, Characterizing the Supernatural Manifestations, in Members of Mr Irving's Congregation, and Other Individuals, in England and Scotland, and formerly in the Writer himself.* London: James Nisbet, 1833.

Bayford, A. F. *'Prove all things: hold fast that which is good.'* London: duplicated for private circulation, n.d. (first publ. 1833).

Bellett, George. *Reasons for Refusing a Message lately sent to the Ministers of the Church of England, on the authority of some who call themselves 'Prophets of our Lord Jesus Christ': Two Sermons, preached in St Leonard's Church, Bridgnorth.* Bridgnorth, UK: Gitton & Smith, 1836.

Bloxham, V. Ben, et al., eds. *Truth will Prevail: The Rise of the Church of Jesus Christ of Latter-day Saints in the British Isles 1837–1987.* Solihull, UK: Church of Jesus Christ of Latter-day Saints, 1987.

Boase, Clement. *Catalogue of Books, Pamphlets, and Writings by certain of those in the Fellowship of the Apostles since their Restoration in 1835: With an Appendix of the Publications contra 'Irvingism' in the Library of Clement Boase.* Edinburgh: privately printed, 1st ed. of catalogue and appendix, 1885; 2nd ed. of appendix, 1887.

Boase, Charles W. *Supplementary Narrative to The Elijah Ministry in the Christian Church.* Edinburgh: R. Grant, 1868.

# SELECT BIBLIOGRAPHY

Böhm, Charles J. T. Letter to unidentified recipient, 24 July 1844. Dublin, National Library of Ireland, MS 49,491/2/1463XL. http://catalogue.nli.ie/Record/vtls000547985#page/1/mode/1up, accessed 4 July 2016.

Born, Karl. *Das Werk des Herrn unter Aposteln: wie es sich im 19./20. Jahrhundert in den Katholisch-apostolischen Gemeinden vollzogen hat, seine Entstehung, ein Fortgang und sein Abschluss, Darstellung in der Form einer Zeittafel*. Bremen: the author, 1974.

Bousfield, George B. R. *Sermon on the Sunday after the Death of the Apostle Cardale, Wednesday, July 18th, 1877, Nottingham, 22 July 1877*. London: duplicated for private circulation, n.d.

Bramley-Moore, W. J. *The Church's forgotten Hope; or, Thoughts on the Translation of the Saints*. 3rd ed. Glasgow: David Hobbs, 1905.

———. *Twin-Feasts: A Sermon on the Synchronism or Conjunction of the Feasts of the Separation of the Apostles and the Meeting of the Seven Churches in London, July 14th, 1903*. London: George J. W. Pitman, 1903.

Bryan, G. T. *Pastoral Letter, Manchester and Bolton, Easter 1953*. Manchester: printed for private circulation, 1953.

Burkett, Randall K. 'The Reverend Harry Croswell and Black Episcopalians in New Haven, 1820–1860.' *The North Star* 7/1 (Fall 2003). https://www.princeton.edu/~jweisenf/northstar/volume7/burkett2.html, accessed 13 May 2016.

Burne, Newdigate H. K. *Albury. Feb. 10. 1878*. N.pl.: duplicated for private circulation, n.d.

———. *Albury and the Apostles' Chapel: An Address, Dundee, 18 August 1895*. London: duplicated for private circulation, n.d.

———. *Letter addressed to Members of the Congregation in Albury*. Albury: printed for private circulation, 1894.

Caird, W. R. *An Address on the Instant Coming of the Lord, and the Preparation of the Church for His Coming, delivered in the City Hall, Glasgow on Tuesday, January 8, 1867*. London: Thomas Bosworth, 1867.

———. *A Letter to the Rev. R. H. Story, Rosneath, respecting certain Misstatements contained in his Memoir of the late Rev. R. Story*. Edinburgh: Thomas Laurie, 1863.

———, Micaiah Smith, and Martin Lindsay. *To the Reverend the ministers of the Established Church; the right Reverend the bishops and their Clergy; and the Rev. the Clergy of all other Christian Congregations in Scotland*. N.pl.: n.p., 1842.

Campbell, Donald, ed. *Memorials of John McLeod Campbell, D.D.: Being Selections from His Correspondence*. 2 vols. London: Macmillan, 1877.

Capadose, Anton E. *An Address delivered at the Central Church in London on Sunday, 24th February, 1946*, Central Church 1223a. London: printed for private circulation, 1946.

Capadose, Isaac. *Homily delivered in the Assembly of the Seven Churches in London, 14th July 1899*. London: printed for private circulation, 1899.

———. *Sermon delivered in the Apostles' Chapel at Albury, 20th November 1904: 'The Laver.'* London: Crerar & Smith, 1905.

———. *'Shut thy doors': Sermon preached at Albury on Sunday, 1st June 1902*. London: Crerar & Smith, 1902.

Cardale, J. B. *An Address to the Churches in London: Delivered at the Close of the Visitation, Tuesday, 4th March, 1873*. London: John Strangeways, 1873.

———. *The Character of Our Present Testimony and Work*. London: Strangeways & Walden, 1865.

———. *Directions on the Subject of Women Prophesying in Church, February 1866.* London: duplicated for private circulation, n.d.

———. *A Discourse on Holy Water and on the Removal of the Sacrament on the Lord's Day.* London: Strangeways & Walden, 1868.

———. *A Discourse upon the Obligation of Tithe, delivered in the Catholic and Apostolic Church, Gordon Square, on Tuesday, October 5, 1858.* London: Bosworth & Harrison, 1858.

———. *The Duty of a Christian in the Disposal of His Income: A Supplement to 'A Discourse on the Obligation of Tithe.'* London: Bosworth & Harrison, 1863.

———. 'On the Extraordinary Manifestations at Port Glasgow.' *MW* 2 (1830) 869–73.

———. *Homily, 7 Churches, June 21, 1876, on the Presentation for Coadjutors.* N.pl.: duplicated for private circulation, n.d.

———. *Homily delivered in the Assembly of the Seven Churches, on Tuesday, January 11th, 1870, being the Day before the Presentation of Candidates for the Office of Coadjutor to the Apostles.* London: Strangeways & Walden, 1870.

———. *A Manual or Summary of the Special Objects of Faith and Hope in the Present Times: For the Use of the Catholic Churches in England.* London: Moyes and Barclay, 1843.

———. *Notes of a Ministry on the Office of Coadjutor, and particularly on the Office of Coadjutor to an Apostle, delivered on . . . August 1, 1865.* London: Strangeways & Walden, 1865.

———. *Notes of Lectures delivered in the Seven Churches in London in the Months of October, November, and December, 1860.* London: Strangeways & Walden, 1861.

———. *Notes of Lectures delivered in the Seven Churches in London in the Months of October, November and December 1860.* London: duplicated for private circulation, n.d.

———. *Readings upon the Liturgy and Other Divine Offices of the Church.* 2 vols. London: Thomas Bosworth, 1878–79.

———. *Remarks on the Proceedings in the Lambeth Conference (held September 1867): Addressed to the Ministers of the Churches in London.* London: Strangeways & Walden, 1868.

———. *Sermon on the death of Mr Edward Oliver Taplin, Pillar of Prophets, 1862.* London: duplicated for private circulation, n.d.

———. *A Short Discourse on Prophesying and the Ministry of the Prophet in the Christian Church.* London: Strangeways & Walden, 1868.

———. *Two Letters on Tithes, 4 June 1873.* N.pl.: printed for private circulation, n.d.

———, et al. *The Fourfold Ministry: Delivered in the Assembly of the Seven Churches in London, 7th March, 1871.* London: Strangeways & Walden, 1871.

Carlyle, Thomas. *The Church of Christ, in Her Offices, Gifts, and Privileges, taken solely from the Word of God.* Edinburgh: William Oliphant, 1834.

———. *Concerning the Right Order of Worship in the Christian Church.* London: Crerar & Smith, 1905.

———. *Die Geschichte des apostolisches Werkes in kurzer Uebersicht.* Berlin: C. G. Brandis, 1851.

———. *The Moral Phenomena of Germany.* London: W. E. Painter, 1845.

———. *The Mosaic Tabernacle, in Its Arrangement and Worship, as the Symbol of the Christian Church.* New York: John Moffet, 1857.

———. *A Short History of the Apostolic Work.* London: G. Barclay, 1851.

## SELECT BIBLIOGRAPHY

Carré, C. M. *The See of Rome: Its Claims to Supremacy examined*. London: Thomas Bosworth, 1852.

Carter, Grayson. *Anglican Evangelicals: Protestant Secessions from the Via Media, c.1800–1850*. Oxford: Oxford University Press, 2001.

De Caux, William. *Early Days of the Lord's Work in France*. London: duplicated for private circulation, n.d. (first publ. 1899).

Christenson, Larry. *A Message to the Charismatic Movement*. Minneapolis, MN: Bethany Fellowship, 1972.

———. 'Pentecostalism's Forgotten Forerunner.' In *Aspects of Pentecostal-Charismatic Origins*, edited by Vinson Synan, 15–38. Plainfield, NJ: Logos, 1975.

Clark, Cecil. 'Commonly called "Irvingites".' *The Guardian*, 17 May 1946.

Clark, Christopher. 'Heavens on Earth: Christian Utopias in Nineteenth- and Twentieth-Century America.' In *God's Bounty? The Churches and the Natural World*, edited by Peter Clarke and Tony Claydon, 396–418. Studies in Church History 46. Woodbridge, UK: Boydell, 2010.

Clement, E. W. 'The late Rev. Arthur Lloyd.' http://opensiuc.lib.siu.edu/cgi/viewcontent.cgi?article=2647&context=ocj, accessed 10 May 2016.

Collis, John Day. *A Few Plain Words to My Parishioners on Irvingism*. Stratford-upon-Avon, UK: n.p., 1875.

Connor, William H. *'Why are ye fearful'? A farewell Sermon preached in the Church of the Holy Trinity, Stratford-upon-Avon . . . 30th January, 1876 . . .* Stratford-upon-Avon, UK: Alfred Palmer, 1876.

Copinger, Harold B. *A Bibliography (begun Easter 1908)*. London: duplicated for private circulation, 1955.

Copinger, Walter A. *Contributions to the Hymnody of the Church*. Manchester: Guardian Printing Works, 1883; 2nd ed. Manchester: Forsyth Bros, 1885.

———. *Our Present Position: An Address, delivered February, 1901*. London: printed for private circulation, 1901.

Crossley, A., and C. R. Elrington, eds. *A History of the County of Oxford*, 12: *Wootton Hundred (South) including Woodstock*. London: Oxford University Press, 1990.

Da Costa, Isaac, et al. *Noble Families among the Sephardic Jews*. London: Oxford University Press, 1936.

Cuming, Robert S. *The Heathen in Their Relation to Christendom: A Sermon*. 3rd ed. London: G. J. W. Pitman, 1900.

Dalton, Henry. *An Address delivered to the Prophets assembled at Albury, on Whit Monday, 1865*. London: duplicated for private circulation, n.d.

———. *Apostleship: A Sermon*. London: Bosworth & Harrison, 1864.

———. *Four Lectures on the First and Second Advent of our Lord and Saviour Jesus Christ, delivered in the Parish Church of Leeds*. London: W. J. Cleaver, 1846.

———. *The Substance of a Farewell Sermon preached at St. Mary's Middleton, on Sunday, the 14th of February, 1847*. Leeds: T. Harrison, 1847.

Darby, J. N. 'A Letter to a Clergyman on the Claims and Doctrines of Newman Street', *Collected Writings* 15: 16–33. Kingston-on-Thames, UK: Stow Hill Bible and Tract Depot, n.d.

Davenport, John S. *Edward Irving and the Catholic Apostolic Church*. New York: John Moffet, 1863.

Davenport, Rowland A. *Albury Apostles: The Story of the Body known as the Catholic Apostolic Church (sometimes called 'the Irvingites')*. 2nd ed. London: Free Society, 1973.

Davidson, Randall T., ed. *The Five Lambeth Conferences 1867–1908*. London: SPCK, 1920.
Davies, Horton. *Worship and Theology in England, 4: From Newman to Martineau, 1850 to 1900*. Princeton, NJ: Princeton University Press, 1961.
Davson, W. M. *1850 to 1950 in the Lord's Work, being eight Sermons preached in the Church in Paddington between July, 1949 and June, 1950*. Loughborough: Echo, n.d.
———. *Church in Paddington 29: Address delivered at the Evening Service, 10 June 1951*. London: printed for private circulation, 1951.
———. *Church in Paddington 80: The Visit to Holland, May, 1957*. London: printed for private circulation, 1957.
———. *Church in Paddington 88, Homily delivered in the Church in Leeds, September 21st, 1958 (17th Sunday after Pentecost). Sermon, Leeds, 21st September 1958, December 1958*. London: printed for private circulation, 1958.
———. *Church in Paddington 94, Sermon, 4th Sunday after Circumcision, 24 January 1960*. London: printed for private circulation, 1960.
———. *Church in Paddington 97, Address to the Absent Members, 24 January 1961*. London: printed for private circulation, 1961.
———. *Confirmation in the Church of England and Admission to Regular Communion among the Churches under Apostles*. London: printed for private circulation, 1961.
———. *Sermons and Homilies on the Third Stage of the Lord's Work, by a Priest*. Loughborough: printed for private circulation, 1966.
Davy, J. T. *Teaching on our Present Position, by a Deacon, Bedford, 1902*. London: duplicated for private circulation, n.d.
Dickson, Thomas Goldie. *Diaconal Teaching in the Catholic Apostolic Church, Mansfield Place, Edinburgh on January 27, 1895*. Edinburgh: St Giles' Printing Co., 1895.
Diersmann, Edwin. 'Die Katholisch-apostolische Gemeinde in Paris. Eine lange und wechselvolle Geschichte', *Rundbrief*, Fruhjahr 2015, 10–21. http://www.apostolische-geschichte.de/download/Rundbrief_Fruehjahr_2015-CAC_Paris.pdf, accessed 20 October 2015.
———. *Notes on the History and Ministers of the Katolsk-Apostoliske Menighet (Catholic Apostolic Church) in Norway*. Bielefeld: Punctum Saliens, 2014.
Von Dittmann, Victor. *Book of the Revelation*. London: duplicated for private circulation, n.d.
Dodd, C. H. *The Apostolic Preaching and its Developments*. London: Hodder & Stoughton, 1936.
Dougall, C. 'Ryerson, George.' *Dictionary of Canadian Biography*, 11: *1881 to 1890*, 795–98. Toronto, ON: University of Toronto Press, 1982.
Dougharty, Walter. *The Last Days*. London: duplicated for private circulation, c.1971.
Dowglass, Thomas. *An Appeal to English Churchmen*. London: Bosworth & Harrison, 1856.
———. *A Chronicle of certain Events which have taken place in the Church of Christ, principally in England, between the Years 1826 and 1852*. London: Charles Goodall, 1852.
Drummond, Henry. *A Brief Account of the Commencement of the Lord's Work to Restore His Church*. London: C. Whittingham, 1851.
———. *Circular Letter on 'Foreign work.'* London: G. Barclay, 1847.
———. *Discourses on the True Definition of the Church, One, Holy, Catholic, and Apostolic, and Kindred Subjects*. London: Bosworth & Harrison, 1858.
———. *Narrative of the Circumstances which led to the Setting up of the Church of Christ at Albury*. London: duplicated for private circulation, n.d. (first publ. 1834).

———. *No. I: The Church of Christ, A.D. 1834*. London: duplicated for private circulation, n.d.

———. *Principles of Ecclesiastical Buildings and Ornaments*. London: Thomas Bosworth, 1851.

———. *Rationale of the Offices and Liturgy of the Church*. London: Moyes and Barclay, 1843.

———. *Remarks on the Ministry of Instruction in the Church*. London: G. Barclay, 1854.

———. *Remarks on Dr. Wiseman's Sermon on the Gorham Case*. London: Thomas Bosworth, 1850.

———. *Speech of H. D. in the House of Commons on Thursday, March 20th, 1851, on the second reading of the Ecclesiastical Titles Bill*. London: Thomas Bosworth, 1851.

———. *The Stone cut out of the Mountain; the Woman with the Man Child of the Apocalypse: or the last ruling spiritual Church of Christ; the Bride of the Lamb: the CXLIVM, preparing by the sent holy spiritual Elias, the prophetic 'Testimony of Jesus', for the Coming of the Lord . . .* London: duplicated for private circulation, n.d. (first publ. 1857).

Edel, Rainer-Friedemann. *Heinrich Thiersch als oekumenische Gestalt*. Marburg an der Lahn: the author, 1962.

Elliott, Peter. *Edward Irving: Romantic Theology in Crisis*. Milton Keynes, UK: Paternoster, 2013.

Fackler, David Morris. *A Letter from David Morris Fackler, Presbyter of the Protestant Episcopal Church in the United States, to the Right Rev. G. W. Doane, Bishop of . . . New Jersey; vindicating the Catholicity of his Priesthood*. New York: John Moffet, 1852.

Fischer, Alfons. 'Katholische-apostolische Gemeinden: einst und jetzt', *Mitteilungen aus der Union von Scranton*, January–March 2014. http://www.christ-katholisch.de/mitteilungen1–14.html, accessed 8 June 2016.

Flegg, Columba Graham. *'Gathered under Apostles': A Study of the Catholic Apostolic Church*. Oxford: Clarendon, 1992.

Flegg, Robert G. *The Nature, Character and Place of Prophecy in the Christian Church. A Sermon delivered in the Central Church in London: 15th January 1888*. London: C. Goodwin Norton, 1888.

Foster, David G. *The Protest of an Elder of the Church in Islington in October, 1842, against the Introduction of a Liturgy and Vestments, with subsequent Appeal to the Apostles against the Angel's Refusal to countenance any Communication to the Flock; with Notes on both*. London: printed for private circulation, 1843.

Gandy, Charles. *Pastoral Letter, Newcastle-on-Tyne, Easter 1902*. Newcastle-on-Tyne: printed for private circulation, 1902.

Gates, H. L., Jr and E. B. Higginbotham, eds. *African American Lives*. New York: Oxford University Press, 2004.

Geere, H. G. *Deacon's Ministry: Tithe, How and Where to be Rendered. Southwark 1945/7*. London: printed for private circulation, 1945.

Georgius I, Mar. *A Personal Statement . . . concerning his Mission*. London: Metropolitical, 1971.

Grant, William. *Apostolic Lordship and the Interior Life: A Narrative of Five Years 'Communion with Catholic Apostolic Angels.'* London: J. T. Hayes, 1873.

Grass, Tim. 'Architecture and the Catholic Apostolic Church.' *Chapels Society Newsletter* 59 (May 2015) 5–9.

———. 'The Catholic Apostolic Church in Scotland.' *Records of the Scottish Church History Society* 46 (forthcoming).

———. John Bate Cardale, Bloomsbury Apostle', 2011. http://www.ucl.ac.uk/bloomsbury-project/articles/events/conference2011/grass.pdf, accessed 14 June 2016.

———. *The Lord's Watchman: A Life of Edward Irving*. Milton Keynes, UK: Paternoster, 2011.

———. 'The Restoration of a Congregation of Baptists: Baptists and Irvingism in Oxfordshire.' *Baptist Quarterly* 37/6 (April 1998) 283–97.

———. 'The Taming of the Prophets: Bringing Prophecy under Control in the Catholic Apostolic Church.' *Journal of the European Pentecostal Theological Association* 16 (1996) 58–70.

———. '"Telling lies on behalf of the Bible": S. R. Gardiner's Doubts about Catholic Apostolic Teaching.' In *Doubting Christianity: The Church and Doubt*, edited by Frances Andrews, Charlotte Methuen, and Andrew Spicer, 398–412. Studies in Church History 52. Cambridge: Cambridge University Press, 2016.

———. '"Walking together in unity and peace and the fear of God": The Challenge of Maintaining Ecumenical Ideals, 1780–c.1860.' In *A Protestant Catholic Church of Christ: Essays on the History and Life of New Road Baptist Church, Oxford*, edited by Rosie Chadwick, 147–70. Oxford: the church, 2003.

Greville, C. C. Fulke. *The Greville Memoirs*. Edited by H. Reeve. Vol. 3, London: Longmans, Green & Co., 1899.

De Gruchy, Jane W. 'The Catholic Apostolic Church in Bradford, 1872–1882.' *Local Historian* 36/1 (February 2006) 29–41.

Grundy, James. *Pastoral Letter, Liverpool, Easter 1910*. Liverpool: printed for private circulation, 1910.

Guers, Émile. *Irvingism and Mormonism Tested by Scripture (with Prefatory Notice by James Bridges, Esq.)*. London: James Nisbet, 1854.

H., W. *Katholisch-apostolische Gemeinden. Lexikalische Sammlung von Daten und Begriffen*. Berlin: printed for private circulation, 1979–84.

Hamilton, R. M. *Memoranda upon the Proposed Election of a Deacon of the Seven, in January, 1890*. London: printed for private circulation, 1889.

———. *Short History of Some Remarkable Spiritual Occurrences in 1827–8, among Peasants in Bavaria, and the Sequel in 1842, 1870*. London: A. W. Godwin, [1881].

Hanna, William, ed. *Letters of Thomas Erskine*. 2nd ed. Edinburgh: David Douglas, 1878.

Harding, W. *The Trial of the Rev. Edward Irving, M.A. before the London Presbytery; containing the whole of the Evidence; exact Copies of the Documents; verbatim Report of the Speeches and Opinions of the Presbyters, etc.* London: W. Harding, 1832.

———. *The Trial of the Rev. Edward Irving, A.M. before the Presbytery of Annan, on Wednesday March 13, 1833: Also, Mr Irving's letter to his Congregation. Taken in Shorthand*. Dumfries: W. Harding, 1833.

Heath, Charles. *Pastoral Letter, Birmingham, Easter Monday, 1915*. Birmingham: printed for private circulation, 1915.

Heath, Christopher B. *The Development of the Liturgy and the Origin of its Prayers: Two Discourses delivered recently in the Southwark Church, January 1950*. London: printed for private circulation, 1950.

———. *Sermon, 10 August 1941*, Central Church 1192. N.pl.: printed for private circulation, 1976.

Heath, C. E. Lewis. *Lecture to the Young Men of the Central Church on the Evolution of the Apostles' Liturgy, 23 November 1898*. London: duplicated for private circulation, n.d.

Heath, Edward. *Address delivered at a Conference held in the English Chapel, Gordon Square, 3rd May, 1922*. London: duplicated for private circulation, n.d.

———. *Confidential Letter on Sexual Matters: Paper for Angels*. London: duplicated for private circulation, n.d.

———. *Extract from a Sermon on 'The Chapel of the Great King.'* London: duplicated for private circulation, n.d.

———. *Homily delivered at Albury, on the Sunday within the Octave of All Saints, November 5th, 1905*. London: Crerar & Smith, 1905.

———. *Note on Spiritual Healing, Albury, 1925*. London: duplicated for private circulation, n.d.

———. *Paper on the Danger of Regarding as Definite Dogmatic Statements Things concerning the Coming of the Lord, which God Has Revealed in Part by Prophecy, Albury, 29 June 1902*. London: duplicated for private circulation, n.d.

———. *Paper on the Gift of Prophecy and the Duty of Angels with regard to Prophetic Persons, Albury, April 1891*. N.pl.: printed for private circulation, 1891.

Heath, Herbert. *Church in Bishopsgate: A Sermon preached by the Angel on Sunday the 1st January, 1928*, Bishopsgate 64. London: printed for private circulation, 1928.

———. *The Ministry of Archangels: Sermon at Bristol, 5 February 1905*. London: duplicated for private circulation, n.d.

———. *Sermon on Seven Deaconship*. London: printed for private circulation, 1884.

Heath, James. *Descendants of Jacob Heath of Birmingham*. Birmingham: n.p., 1912.

———. *Memorandum for Homilists*. Birmingham: lithographed for private circulation, 1889.

Heath, James S. *Pastoral Letters to the Members of the Church in Glasgow*. Glasgow: printed for private circulation, 1957–60.

Heath, Rupert M. *The Council of Zion (Lecture by an Underdeacon), November 1956*, Central Church 2nd series 29. London: printed for private circulation, 1956.

———. *Lecture on the Ceremonial and Symbolism of the Service for the Assembly of the Seven Churches in London, Brighton, 1946*. London: duplicated for private circulation, n.d.

———. *Lecture by an Underdeacon: The Events of 14th July 1835, 9 November 1954*, Central Church 2nd series 12. London: printed for private circulation, 1954.

———. *Lecture (by an Underdeacon): The Lord's Pattern—The Organisation and Administration of a Particular Church and Its Significance*, Central Church 2nd series 2. London: printed for private circulation, 1954.

———. *Lecture by an Underdeacon: The Office of Angel, 6 April 1954*, Central Church 2nd series 9. London: printed for private circulation, 1954.

———. *Teaching at Southwark on the History and Meaning of the Monthly Assembly of the Seven Churches in London, 4 October 1936*. London: duplicated for private circulation, n.d.

———. *The Twelve Tribes of Israel, Literal and Spiritual (Lecture by an Underdeacon), February 1956*, Central Church 2nd series 23. London: printed for private circulation, 1956.

———. *Vestments as Ordered by Apostles: A Lecture delivered 1 Oct. 1942*. London: duplicated for private circulation, n.d.

Henke, Manfred. '175 Years ago: The Call of John Bate Cardale and the Contemporary Idea of Apostleship', 2010. http://www.nak.org/fileadmin/download/pdf/Call_of_Cardale-2010.pdf, accessed 20 July 2016.

———. 'Apostles' Council 1851: No Agreement on Measures to restore the Twelvefold Unity of Apostles', 2007. http://www.nak.org/en/news/publications/article/15103/, accessed 5 July 2016.

———. 'The Catholic Apostolic Church and its Gordon Square Cathedral', 2011. http://www.ucl.ac.uk/bloomsbury-project/articles/articles/CAC-Gordon_Square.pdf, accessed 22 July 2016.

———. 'Die Geschichte der Katholisch-apostolische Kirche in kurzer Übersicht.' *Unsere Familie*, 20 September 2007, 37–39.

———. 'Wo feierten katholisch-apostolische Christen das Abendmahl?' *Unsere Familie*, 20 October 2005, 34–37.

Hewett, Louisa A. *The Story of the Lord's Work: A Book for the Young. By a Lady*. Glasgow: D. Hobbs, 1899.

Holiday, A. J. *The Character of the Last Days*. Glasgow: Pickering & Inglis, n.d.

Hollick, Samuel Mee. *Address. Delivered by the Angel-in-charge of the Church in Manchester. 26th July, 1942: 'Our Present Position and Duty.'* Stoke-on-Trent: printed for private circulation, n.d.

———. *Church in Liverpool and Dependencies: Three Sermons by the Angel in Charge. The Value of the Holy Scriptures, Witnessed to by I. The Lord Himself; II. Apostles at the Beginning; III. Apostles in the Latter Days, August 1945*. Liverpool: printed for private circulation, 1945. Reprinted as *Three Sermons delivered in Manchester 1945: 'The Value of the Holy Scriptures.'* N.pl.: printed for private circulation, 1985.

———. *Church in Manchester and Dependencies. Address delivered by the Angel in Charge. Our Present Work and Witness, October 1935*. N.pl.: printed for private circulation, 1965.

———. *Homily, Church in Manchester, 25th December 1929*. London: duplicated for private circulation, n.d.

———. *Memorandum with Reference to the Position of a Congregation or Gathering of Members which includes Under-deacons but is left without the Headship of any Angel, Priest, or Deacon, and is therefore without Pastoral Care, January 1947*. N.pl.: printed for private circulation, 1947.

———. *Ministries delivered in Manchester. Homily: 3rd Sunday after Circumcision, 19th January 1930. Pastoral Letter before Easter 1945 by the Angel-in-Charge*. N.pl.: CAC, 1975.

———. *Three Sermons delivered in Manchester 1945: 'The Value of the Holy Scriptures.'* N.pl.: printed for private circulation, 1985.

Horrocks, Don. *Laws of the Spiritual Order: Innovation and Reconstruction in the Soteriology of Thomas Erskine of Linlathen*. Carlisle, UK: Paternoster, 2004.

Hughes, Richard. *Readings for the Sundays and Holy Days of the Church's Year: Second Series*. London: Thomas Bosworth, 1881.

Hume, Henry S. *An Address*. London: printed for private circulation, 1877.

———. *An Address delivered by the Angel of the Central Church, London, on Wednesday Evening, 24th November, 1920, Central Church 1050*. London: printed for private circulation, 1920.

———. *'Address delivered by the Angel of the Church on the Death of Mr Woodhouse', Central Church, 10 February 1901*. London: printed for private circulation, 1901.

———. *On the Election of One of the Seven Deacons*. London: lithographed for private circulation, 1887.

# Select Bibliography

———. *Fundamental Truths: Three Sermons delivered in the Catholic Apostolic Church, Gordon Square, London, in March–April, 1903*. London: George J. W. Pitman, 1903.

———. [Letter of thanks to angels respecting their testimony and the redistribution of the Great Testimony]. London: lithographed for private circulation, 1888.

———. *The National Mission of Repentance and Hope, July 1916*, Central Church 1031. London: printed for private circulation, 1916.

———. *Observations on the Cessation of the Monthly Assemblies of the Seven Churches in London, 1909*, Central Church 951. London: printed for private circulation, 1909.

———. *On the Office of Underdeacon: Teaching by the Angel*. London: printed for private circulation, 1926.

———. *Pastoral Letter on the Death of Mr Woodhouse, 6 February 1901*. London: printed for private circulation, 1901.

———. *Prayer for Unity of Christians, Central Church, 1906*. London: duplicated for private circulation, n.d.

———. *Substance of an Address to those who, having attained to the Age for the laying on of Apostles' Hands, cannot now receive that Rite, delivered on Sunday, 12th October, and a Homily delivered at the Service of Commendation of those desiring the Sealing, on Wednesday, 15th October, 1919*. London: printed for private circulation, 1919.

———. *'In Times of War', Central Church, London, 7th August 1914*. London: printed for private circulation, 1914.

Innes, Henry. *The Catholic and Apostolic Sect, and its Pretensions of Apostleship*. London: Macintosh, 1873.

Irving, Edward. *Babylon and Infidelity Foredoomed of God: A Discourse on the Prophecies of Daniel and the Apocalypse, which relate to these Latter Times, and until the Second Advent*. Glasgow: Chalmers and Collins, 1828.

———. *The Discipline of the Church, by the Rev. E. Irving; with two Addresses in the Open Air, by Missionaries*. London: W. Harding, 1832.

———. *Exposition and Sermon, delivered at the Church in Newman-Street, on Wednesday Evening, October 24, 1832*. London: W. Harding, 1832.

———. *Exposition and Sermon, delivered at the opening of the New Chapel, Newman Street, Oxford Street, Sunday Afternoon, October 21, 1832*. London: W. Harding, 1832.

———. 'Facts connected with Recent Manifestations of Spiritual Gifts.' *Fraser's Magazine* 4 (1831–2) 754–61; 5 (1832) 198–205, 316–20.

———. *A Judgment, as to what Course the Ministers and the People of the Church of Scotland should take in Consequence of the Decisions of the Last General Assembly*. Greenock: R. B. Lusk, 1832 (extracted from *MW* 5 [1832] 84–115).

———. *The Rev. Edward Irving's Preliminary Discourse to the Work of Ben Ezra: entitled The Coming of Messiah in Glory and Majesty: To which is added, an Ordination Charge, delivered by Mr Irving in 1827; and also his Introductory Essay to Bishop Horne's Commentary on the Psalms*. London: Bosworth & Harrison, 1859.

———. *Scripture Reading and Exposition by the Late Rev. Edward Irving, A.M. at the Church in Newman Street, on Sunday Afternoon, 12th January 1834*. London: W. Harding, 1834.

———. *To the Church of God in London, with the Elders and Deacons*. Edited by J. B. Cardale. London: Mills, Jowett and Mills, 1834.

———, and Nicholas Armstrong. *Expositions and Sermons by the Rev. E. Irving and the Rev. N. Armstrong*. London: W. Harding, 1832.

Jennings, Ruth. 'Archibald Campbell Barclay and the Catholic Apostolic Church.' *Camden History Review* 33 (2009) 13–18.

Johanning, Peter. 'A Prayer at the Grave of English Apostles.' http://www.nac.today/en/157547/132997, accessed 24 March 2016.

Jones, R. K. 'The Catholic Apostolic Church: A Study in Diffused Commitment.' In *Sociological Yearbook of Religion* 5, edited by Michael Hill, 137–60. London: SCM, 1972.

Ker, David. *Leaves from Report Books of Visitors of the Poor*. Edinburgh: Thomas Laurie, 1865.

Knight, J. P. *On Building a Church for Divine Worship: By One of the Deacons of the Central Church*. London: Goodall, 1850.

Kohler, J. N. *Het Irvingisme. Eene historische-critische Proeve*. The Hague: Mensing en Visser, 1876.

Lacy, John. *The General Delusion of Christians, touching the Ways of God's revealing himself to and by the Prophets, evinced from Scripture and Primitive Antiquity; and many Principles of Scoffers, Atheists, Sadducees, and Wild Enthusiasts, refuted*. Edited by Edward Irving. London: R. B. Seeley and W. Burnside, 1832.

Laing, John G. *Diaconal Teaching given in the Catholic Apostolic Church, Mansfield Place, Edinburgh, on March 29th, 1908, on 'The Importance of being Present at the Beginning of Services of Worship.'* Edinburgh: printed for private circulation, 1908.

Layton, Frederick W. H. *An Address on the Instant Coming of the Lord, and the Preparation of the Church for his Coming, delivered at the Hanover Square Room, on Thursday, June 28th, 1866*. London: J. Paul, 1866.

Levesley, W. C. *Sermon: Not cunningly devised Fables, Sheffield, 26 June 1932*. London: duplicated for private circulation, n.d.

Lewis, John. *Something Happened at The Hague*. London: Hodder & Stoughton, 1974.

Lickfold, J. Malcolm. *The Catholic Apostolic Church, Gordon Square, London: Notes on the Architectural Features and the Furniture*. London: Bedford Bookshop, 1935.

———. *Sermon, 31st July 1949*, Central Church 1244. London: printed for private circulation, 1949.

Linney, John. *A Narrative of Facts, relating to the Congregation who meet in Southampton-Street, Southampton, known by the Name of Irvingites*. Edited by James Crabb. Southampton: J. Coupland, 1836.

Lutz, Johann E. G. *Gottes Werke in unserer Zeit, dargelegt vor dem hochwürdigsten Domkapitel des Bisthums Augsburg in der Untersuchungsfache des Johann Evangelist Georg Lutz*. Ulm: H. Müller, 1857.

McMichael, A. J. W. *Joseph and His Brethren: Sermon . . . , 27 November 1910*, Toronto 261. London: duplicated for private circulation, n.d.

M'Neile, Hugh. *A Letter to a Friend in the Country on reading Mr Baxter's Narrative of Facts*. London: James Nisbet, 1833.

Marks, Henry J. *Narrative of Henry John Marks, a Jew; now a Follower of the Lord Jesus Christ*. 3rd ed. London: the author, 1842.

Marsden, J. B. *History of Christian Churches and Sects from the Earliest Ages of Christianity*. London: R. Bentley, 1856.

Mast, Gregg A. *The Eucharistic Service of the Catholic Apostolic Church and Its Influence on Reformed Liturgical Renewals of the Nineteenth Century*. Lanham, MD: Scarecrow, 1999.

Matthew, H. Colin G., ed. *Oxford Dictionary of National Biography*. Oxford: Oxford University Press, 2004. http://www.oxforddnb.com.

Maxwell, Gavin. *The House of Elrig*. London: Longmans, 1965.

## Select Bibliography

Middleton, Harry. *Pastoral Letter, to the Members of the Church in Leeds and Dependencies, January 1947*. Leeds, UK: printed for private circulation, 1947.

Miller, Edward. *The History and Doctrines of Irvingism*. 2 vols. London: C. Kegan Paul, 1878.

———. *Miller's Notes to his Own Work*. London: duplicated for private circulation, n.d.

'A Minister of the Gospel' (J. Moore Ritchie). *God's Work by Restored Apostles: Also an Answer to Bishop Wallis, Diocese (Anglican) of Wellington*. Glasgow: D. Hobbs, 1902.

Morgan, Edmund R. *Reginald Somerset Ward 1881–1962: His Life and Letters*. London: A. R. Mowbray, 1963.

Morse-Boycott, Desmond. *They Shine like Stars*. London: Skeffington, 1947.

Murray, Douglas M. 'John Macleod of Govan: A Distinctive High Churchman.' *Liturgical Review*, November 1978, 27–32.

Netzwerk Apostolische Geschichte. 'Katholisch-apostolische Gemeinden.' http://www.apostolische-geschichte.de/wiki/index.php?title=Katholisch-apostolisch#Literatur, accessed 8 June 2016.

Nevill, Samuel Tarratt. *The Claims of the 'Holy Catholic Apostolic Church' Examined*. Dunedin, NZ: J. Braithwaite, 1901.

———. *A Pastoral upon Irvingism: Now Called the Holy Catholic and Apostolic Church*. Dunedin, NZ: J. Wilkie, n.d.

Newman-Norton, Seraphim. *The Time of Silence: A History of the Catholic Apostolic Church 1901–1971*. 3rd ed. Leicester, UK: Albury Society, 1975.

———. *The Hamburg Schism and the Apostle Woodhouse's Teaching on the Possible Call of New Apostles*. Leicester, UK: Albury Society, 1974.

Norton, Robert. *Memoirs of James and George Macdonald, of Port-Glasgow*. London: J. Shaw, 1840.

———. *Neglected and Controverted Scripture Truths, with an Historical Review of Miraculous Manifestations in the Church of Christ, and an Account of their late Revival in the West of Scotland*. London: J. F. Shaw, 1839.

———. *The Restoration of Apostles and Prophets in the Catholic Apostolic Church*. London: Bosworth & Harrison, 1861.

'An Old Preacher' (W. H. B. Proby). *Letters on the Art of Christian Preaching: Addressed to a Minister of the Catholic Apostolic Church*. Glasgow: David Hobbs, 1901.

Oliphant, Mrs. M. O. W. *The Life of Edward Irving, Minister of the National Scotch Church, London*. 2 vols. London: Hurst & Blackett, 1862.

Oliver, W. H. *Prophets and Millennialists: The Uses of Biblical Prophecy in England from the 1790s to the 1840s*. [Auckland]: Auckland University Press, 1978.

Orr, Frederick L. *Lecture on Socialism*. N.pl.: n.p., 1908.

Ouwerkerk, J. H. 'Fragmenten uit het reis-dagboek van een Engels geestelijke.' *Gens Nostra* 17/1 (January 1962) 12–13, 28.

Parker, T. H. *The Covering of the Holy Table, Newcastle-upon-Tyne, 26 March 1939*. London: duplicated for private circulation, n.d.

———? *Two Sermons delivered in Newcastle-on-Tyne in October, 1939, 2: Elijah*. N.pl.: printed for private circulation, 1988.

Pearce, C. W. *A Biographical Sketch of Edmund Hart Turpin, Hon. Secretary of the Royal College of Organists, 1875–1907*. London: Vincent Music, 1911.

Peck, Kendrick. *Church Music*. London: Strangeways, 1894.

Perry, C. L., and James Heath. *Four Sermons preached in the Catholic Apostolic Church, Melbourne, during February 1903*. Melbourne: Walker, May & Co., 1903.

———. *Notes of Sermons delivered in Sydney and Pokolbin, November and December, 1902*. Sydney: Ross, May & Co., 1902.

Philo-Anglicanus (W. J. Bramley-Moore). *Ancient Tyre and Modern England; or, the Historical Type of Ancient Tyre in Its Prophetic Application to Modern England*. London: Elliot Stock, 1906.

Pilkington, George. *The Unknown Tongues discovered to be English, Spanish, and Latin; and the Rev. Edw. Irving proved to be erroneous in attributing their Utterance to the Influence of the Holy Spirit*. 2nd ed. London: Field & Bull, 1831.

Pinnington, Judith E., and Seraphim Newman-Norton. *Conciliar and Apostolic Witness: The Catholic Apostolic Church and the Lambeth Conferences, 1867–1968*. London: Albury Society, 1978.

Pitcairn, William F. *Pastoral letters, 7 August 1860—Easter 1874*. Edinburgh: printed for private circulation, 1860–74.

———. *Address by the Angel to the Flock at Edinburgh, on the Occasion of Mr Cardale's Removal, and of the Celebration of the '14th July 1877', 22 July 1877*. Edinburgh: lithographed for private circulation, 1877.

———. *'Irish Church Question': Pastoral Counsel in the Present Crisis*. Edinburgh: Thomas Laurie, 1868.

———. *Notes of Instruction on the Place and Use of Words of Prophecy forwarded by Apostles*. Edinburgh: lithographed for private circulation, 1877.

———. *To the Members of the Congregation of the Catholic Apostolic Church, Mansfield Place, Edinburgh, 21 March 1884*. Edinburgh: lithographed for private circulation, 1884.

Place, W. H. *Notes of a Ministry to the Deacons of the Churches, 29th May, 1854*. London: George Barclay, 1854.

———. *The Substance of Teaching addressed to the Evangelists, assembled at Birmingham, the 17th & 18th of May, 1853*. London: C. Goodall, 1853.

———. *'Twenty-five years ago . . .'* London: Strangeways & Walden, 1861.

Powell, K. 'Uncompromised by Change.' *Country Life* 181/36 (3 September 1987) 192–93.

Priddle, Norman C. *List 'E': Secondhand Liturgies, Psalters, Hymn Books, Tune Books, and Epistles and Gospels*. London: duplicated for private circulation, n.d.

Prior, Henry M. *My Experience of the Catholic Apostolic Church*. Stratford, UK: Wilson & Whitworth, 1880.

Railton, Nicholas M. *No North Sea: The Anglo-German Evangelical Network in the Middle of the Nineteenth Century*. Studies in Christian Mission 24. Leiden: Brill, 2000.

Rawson, T. E. *To the Absent Members of the Churches in Southwark, Bristol, Bath and the Dependencies, Lent 1936*, Southwark 1936/2. London: printed for private circulation, 1936.

———. *The Church in Southwark: A Slight Sketch of Its early History, as Illustrating the Progress of the Lord's Work of Restoration in his Universal Church*. London: printed for private circulation, 1926.

———. *Copy of Ministry on Tithe*, Southwark 1941/5a. London: printed for private circulation, 1941.

———. *Teaching on the Removal of the last Apostle and the last Coadjutor, Southwark, 13 October 1929*. London: duplicated for private circulation, n.d.

Ridings, Philip S. *My Testimony, containing my Reasons for accepting the Doctrines and Practices set forth by the Lord's restored Apostleship*. Oldham: n.p., 1891.

Røstvig, Kristian. 'En døende kirke: Edward Irving og Irvingianismen.' *Tidsskrift for teologi og kirke* 16 (1945) 128–52.

Rothe, Andreas, and Manfred Henke. 'A Milestone in Church History.' www.nac.today/en/157547/265701, accessed 24 March 2016.

Schaff, Philip. *A History of the Creeds of Christendom*. 3 vols. London: Hodder and Stoughton, 1877.

Scholler, Ludwig W. *A Chapter of Church History from South Germany, being Passages from the Life of Johan Evangelist Georg Lutz*. Translated by W. Wallis. London: Longmans, Green, & Co., 1894.

Schrey, Karl. *The Ark of God in Prison*. London: duplicated for private circulation, n.d.

Schröter, Johann Albrecht. *Bilder zur Geschichte der Katholisch-apostolischen Gemeinden / Images of the History of the Catholic Apostolic Church*. Jena: Glaux, 2001.

———. *Die Katholisch-apostolischen Gemeinden in Deutschland und der 'Fall Geyer.'* 2nd ed. Marburg: Tectum, 1998.

Schwartz, G. C. *The Chronicle of the Setting up of the Church in Berlin, 18 February 1951*. London: duplicated for private circulation, n.d.

Scott, A. J. 'Answer to the Question, What was the Reformation?' *MW* 1 (1829) 628–40.

Sgotzai, Peter. *Verzeichnis von Personen die der KAG angehörten oder der KAG nahestanden*, 2001. http://www.apostolische-dokumente.de/a-dokumente/a-0636.pdf, accessed 20 July 2016.

Shaw, Plato E. *The Catholic Apostolic Church, sometimes called Irvingite*. Morningside Heights, NY: Kings Crown, 1946.

Shaw, T.? Letter of 21 April 1835, LDS Church History Library, MS 22503. http://josephsmithpapers.org/paperSummary/letter-from-thomas-shaw-21-april-1835#!/paperSummary/letter-from-thomas-shaw-21-april-1835&p=2, accessed 20 November 2015.

Simpson, John. *Reasons for Abandoning the Methodist Ministry, and for Embracing the Work of God under the Restored Apostleship*. Leeds, UK: John Parrott, 1871.

Sissons, C. B. *Egerton Ryerson, His Life and Letters*. 2 vols. Toronto, ON: Clark, Irwin & Co., 1937.

Sitwell, Francis. *Copy of a Letter from Mr Francis Sitwell to his Sister, Mary (probable date 1834)*. London: duplicated for private circulation, n.d.

———. *The Purpose of God in Creation and Redemption: And the Successive Steps for Manifesting the Same in and by the Church*. 8th ed. Edinburgh: Robert Grant, 1899 (first publ. 1865).

Smith, Elijah B. *Appeal of the Rev. E. B. Smith to the General Assembly of the Presbyterian Church (United States) May 1875*. Hartford, CT: Case, Lockwood & Brainard Co., [1875].

Spindler, Philipp J. *Aktenmässige Darstellung der offiziellen Verhandlungen über die Glaubensansichten betr. des sogennantes Irvingianismus und die deswegen erfolgte Privation und Exkommunikation des Verfassers*. Kaufbeuren: Reichel, 1857.

Standring, G. Lancelot. *Albury and the Catholic Apostolic Church: A Guide to the Personalities, Beliefs and Practices of the Community of Christians commonly called the Catholic Apostolic Church*. Albury, UK: the author, 1985.

Sterling, John Canfield. *Defence of John Canfield Sterling, Presbyter, on His Trial upon Presentment for Alleged Schismatical Conduct, in the Protestant Episcopal Church of the United States of America*. 2nd ed. New York: John Moffet, 1852.

Stevenson, Peter K. *God in our Nature: The Incarnational Theology of John McLeod Campbell.* SEHT. Carlisle, UK: Paternoster, 2004.

Stevenson, Kenneth W. 'The Catholic Apostolic Church: Its History and its Eucharist.' *Studia Liturgica* 13 (1979) 21–45.

———. 'The Liturgical Year in the Catholic Apostolic Church.' *Studia Liturgica* 14 (1982) 128–34.

———. 'The Lord's Supper according to the Order of the Catholic Apostolic Church.' In *Coena Domini II. Die Abendmahlsliturgie der Reformationskirchen vom 18. bis zum frühen 20. Jahrhundert*, edited by Irmgard Pahl, 726–48. Fribourg: Academic, 2005.

Stewart, Hugh. *Sermon: The Ministry of Archangels.* London: duplicated for private circulation, n.d.

Strachan, C. Gordon. 'Carlyle, Irving, and the "Hysterical Women".' *Carlyle Annual* 12 (1991) 17–32.

———. *The Pentecostal Theology of Edward Irving.* London: Darton, Longman & Todd, 1973.

Stunt, Timothy C. F. *The Elusive Quest of the Spiritual Malcontent: Some Early Nineteenth-Century Spiritual Mavericks.* Eugene, OR: Wipf & Stock, 2015.

———. '"Trying the Spirits": The Case of the Gloucestershire Clergyman (1831).' *Journal of Ecclesiastical History* 39 (1988) 95–105.

———. 'Trying the Spirits: Irvingite Signs and the Test of Doctrine.' In *Signs, Wonders, Miracles: Representations of Divine Power in the Life of the Church*, edited by Kate Cooper and Jeremy Gregory, 400–409. Studies in Church History 41. Woodbridge, UK: Boydell, 2005.

Surman, Charles E. 'Surman Index of Congregational Ministers.' http://www.qmulreligionandliterature.co.uk/research/surman-index-online/.

Symes, John. *An Address on the Instant Coming of the Lord and the Preparation of the Church for His Coming, delivered at St James's Hall on Thursday, June 21st 1866.* London: J. Paul, 1866.

Tang, Marinus J. *Het Apostolische Werk in Nederland.* The Hague: Boekencentrum, 1982.

Taplin, Edward O. *On the Distinction between the Gift of Prophecy and the prophetic Ministry, and its Relation to the other Three Ministries.* London: duplicated for private circulation, n.d.

———. *Prophetic Light concerning the Twelve Tribes, received while reading the 49th Chapter of Genesis in connection with the 33rd Chapter of Deuteronomy (From Letters addressed to Mr Drummond at Paris, 1840).* London: duplicated for private circulation, n.d.

Tarbet, William. *The Shadows of the Law; the Realities of the Body of Christ.* 5 parts, Glasgow: D. Hobbs, 1892 (first publ. 1855).

———. *A Voice, through 'Christmas,' to his 'Evangelical Brethren,' by One of the Baptized.* Liverpool: Joshua Walmsley, 1853.

Thiersch, Hermann. *Our Russian Brethren.* Translated by Lady Margaret Percy. London: duplicated for private circulation, 1933.

Thiersch, Heinrich W. J. *Abyssinia.* Translated by Sarah M. S. Perreira. London: James Nisbet, 1885.

Thomas, Clara. *Ryerson of Upper Canada.* Toronto, ON: Ryerson, 1969.

Thompson, John. *A Brief Account of a Visit to some of the Brethren in the West of Scotland; with Remarks on certain Doctrines contained in 'The Truth as it is in Jesus.'* London: J. Nisbet, 1831.

## Select Bibliography

———. *Inaugural Address . . . on laying the Foundation of an Institution or College for General Instruction, 22d April, 1850.* London: Sevey, Robson, 1850.

Thonger, James. *Pastoral Letter, Leeds, April 1901.* Leeds, UK: printed for private circulation, 1901.

Tierney, David. 'The Catholic Apostolic Church: A Study in Tory Millenarianism.' *Historical Research* 63 (1990) 289–315.

Todd, Alphaeus. [Pastoral letter to the congregations at Ottawa and Potsdam, Advent 1879]. N.pl.: printed for private circulation, 1879.

Torrens, W. M. *Memoirs of the Right Honourable William, Second Viscount Melbourne.* 2 vols. London: Macmillan, 1878.

Trimen, Edward. *The Rise and Progress of the Work of the Lord: Thirteen Lectures.* London: duplicated for private circulation, n.d.

Tripp, David. 'The Liturgy of the Catholic Apostolic Church: A Minor Chapter in Ecumenical History.' *Scottish Journal of Theology* 22 (1969) 437–54.

Trotter, William. *The Origin of (so called) Open Brethrenism.* Lancing: Kingston Bible Trust, 1987 (first publ. 1848).

Turpin, Edmund H. *Hymn Tunes.* London: Weekes, 1872.

Tyacke, Nicholas. 'An Unnoticed Work by Samuel Rawson Gardiner.' *Bulletin of the Institute for Historical Research* 47 (1974) 244–45.

Underwood, Brian. *Faith and New Frontiers: A Story of planting and nurturing Churches, 1823–2003.* Warwick, UK: Intercontinental Church Society, 2004.

Valentin, Anton. *The Present Time of Silence: A Retrospect.* London: duplicated for private circulation, n.d. (first publ. in German, 1938).

———. *The Sacrament of the Eucharist and Its Solemn Removal from the Altar.* London: duplicated for private circulation, n.d.

———. *Sermon on Isaiah vi.1–8.* London: duplicated for private circulation, n.d.

Vero Catholicus (George Ryerson). *Address to the Female Members of the Church of Christ in Toronto.* Toronto: n.p., 1837.

Voll, Dieter. *Catholic Evangelicalism.* London: Faith, 1963.

Wagener, Carl L. W. *Sermon delivered in the Catholic Apostolic Church, Mansfield Place, Edinburgh, on 14th May 1905.* Edinburgh: printed for private circulation, 1905.

Watts, Michael R. *The Dissenters, 3: The Crisis and Conscience of Nonconformity.* Oxford: Oxford University Press, 2015.

Way, Lewis. *The Flight out of Babylon: A Sermon preached before the Continental Society, for Promoting Religious Knowledge on the Continent; on Tuesday, April 7, 1822, at the Church of St. Ann, Blackfriars.* London: Continental Society, 1822.

Westfall, William. *Two Worlds: The Protestant Culture of Nineteenth-Century Ontario.* McGill-Queens's Studies in the History of Religion. Kingston, ON: McGill-Queens University Press, 1989.

Whitley, Harry C. *Blinded Eagle: An Introduction to the Life and Teaching of Edward Irving.* London: SCM, 1955.

Wolfe, Roger. 'The Ipswich Congregation of the Catholic Apostolic Church ('Irvingite').' *Suffolk Review* 32 (Spring 1999) 20–26.

Wolffe, John. *The Protestant Crusade in Great Britain 1829–1860.* Oxford: Clarendon, 1991.

Wood, Hugh Myddelton. *Reports of the Meetings of a Class of Young People: Ottawa, 1906–1907.* Ottawa, ON: printed for private circulation, 1907.

Woodhouse, F. V. *Address to the Seven Churches in London, 14th August 1877*. London: lithographed for private circulation, 1877. Reprinted as *Address to the Seven Churches in London: On the Death of Mr Cardale, 14 August 1877*. London: duplicated for private circulation, n.d.

———. *The Census and the Catholic Apostolic Church*. London: Thomas Bosworth, 1854.

———. *Four Addresses... delivered at the Assembly of the Seven Churches in London*. London: duplicated for private circulation, n.d.

———. *Homily, Service of Presentation of an Angel for Coadjutorship, in the Assembly of the Seven Churches in London, 24 June 1886*. London: lithographed for private circulation, 1886.

———. *A Narrative of Events Affecting the Position and Prospects of the Whole Christian Church: Part I. Second Edition, with a Second Part, containing a Continuation to the Present Time*. London: Bedford Bookshop, 1938 (first publ. 1847, 2nd part 1885).

———. *Poems, Fugitive Pieces and Hymns*. London: Norman, 1884.

———. *The Substance of a Ministry on the Office of Apostle in the Gentile Church*. London: Thomas Bosworth, 1882 (first publ. 1835).

———. *Teaching delivered by the Apostle (Mr Woodhouse) in the Seven Churches in London, 9th October, 1877*. London: duplicated for private circulation, n.d.

———. *Teaching delivered by the Apostle [Mr Woodhouse] in the Seven Churches in London, 29 January, 1878*. London: duplicated for private circulation, n.d.

———. *Teaching on the Prophetic Office, delivered at Albury on Whit Monday, 1867*. London: duplicated for private circulation, n.d.

———. *Teaching in the Seven Churches, Sep. 11, 1877*. London: duplicated for private circulation, n.d.

## LITURGIES AND HYMNALS

*The Order for the Daily Services of the Church and for Administration of Sacraments, as the same are to be conducted at Albury*. London: Moyes & Barclay, 1842.

*The Liturgy and other Divine Offices of the Church*. London: H. J. Glaisher, 1922 (1880 ed.).

(Estonian) *Liturgia ja Ristikoguduse teised Jumala teenistused. Esimene jagu*. Riga: M. Jakobsoni juures, 1890.

(Flemish) *De Viering der heilige Eucharistie en de uitdeeling der Communie*. N.pl.: n.p., 1861.

(French) *Liturgie et autres divins offices de l'Église. (Le livre des Psaumes)*. Paris: Georges Chamerot, 1882.

(German) *Die Liturgie sowie den anderen Gottesdienste der Kirche*. Neue Ausgabe, Berlin: L. Hoffmann, 1877.

(Italian) *Liturgia ed altri divini uffizi della Chiesa. (Libro dei Salmi)*. 2 vols. Florence: G. Barbèra, 1894–95.

(Lettish) *Liturjija, ka arri basnizas zittas deewkalposchanas*. Jelgawâ [Mitau]: J. W. Steffenhagena, 1880.

(Polish) *Liturgia i inne nabozestwa koscioa*. Charlottenburg: J. Załachowskiego, 1902.

(Swedish) *Liturgien och Kyrkans öfriga gudstjensthandlingar*. Stockholm: Nye Tryckeri-Aktiebolaget, 1895.

Burne, Newdigate H. K., ed. *Hymns, with Tunes, for the Use of Children and Young Persons*. London: Crerar & Smith, 1890.

(Danish) *Kirkelig sangbog*. Copenhagen: Carl C. Werner, 1908.

(German) *Hymnologium. Eine Sammlung der besten Lieder und Lobgesänge aus allen Jahrhunderten der Kirche, mit beigefügten Melodieen.* Berlin: Ferdinand Schneider, 1859.
(German) Ernst A. Rossteuscher, ed. *Hymnologium. Eine Auswahl geistlicher Gesänge zum kirchlichen und häuslichen Gebrauch.* 5th ed. Berlin: L. Hoffmann, 1877.
(Norwegian) *Tillæg til Kirkelig sangbog.* Christiania: Carl C. Werner, 1908.
(Polish) *Hymnologium: wybór pieśni duchownych do użytku kościelnego i domowego.* Charlottenburg: J. Załachowskiego, 1902.

## PERIODICALS AND DIRECTORIES

*Angels' Record*
Apostles' Reports / Annual Reports
*Church Address Book*
*Glastonbury Bulletin*
*Kirchliches Adressenbuch*
*News Letter / Newsletter*
*Pastorale Mitteilungen*
*Smyrna-Stimmen*
*Ungdomsbladet for Katolsk-Apostoliske Menighedsmedlemmer*

# Index

144,000, 66, 76, 80, 123, 124, 166, 225, 232

Aarsbo, J., 7
Aberdeen, 69
Aberystwyth, 69
Absolution, 27, 138, 166, 173, 207, 236, 239, 292
Ackery, J. W., 239, 244
Adventism, 112, 123, 258
Albrecht, L., 49, 105, 183, 271, 308, 311
Albury, 2, 25, 80, 88, 110, 166, 179–80, 184, 185, 217, 250, 298, 299
   Apostles at, 43–45, 47, 52, 54, 58, 63, 64, 74, 88, 149, 197, 211
   Conferences of ministers at, 6, 75, 76, 78, 160, 223, 236, 239
   Conferences on prophecy at, 13, 15, 29
   Congregation at, 21–22, 35, 44, 46, 61, 144, 191, 193, 195, 221, 238, 252, 267, 269, 271–72, 273, 305
   Intercession at, 151, 152, 160, 162, 228, 301
All Angels, feast of, 195, 201
All Saints, feast of, 60, 145, 188, 193, 196, 200, 201
Amersfoort, 281–82, 307
Amesbury, J., 59–60
Andrews, S. J., 114, 206
Andrews. W. W., 8, 113–14, 145, 166, 225
Angels, 5, 25, 27, 33, 35, 36, 38, 44, 49, 58, 59, 60, 63, 64, 65–66, 67, 68, 69, 70, 77–78, 80, 83, 86, 90, 96, 102, 114–15, 128, 135, 138, 139, 140–41, 145, 151, 154, 155, 157, 158, 162–64, 166, 169, 176, 177, 178, 179–80, 185, 189, 206, 208, 209, 210, 211–12, 213, 223, 224, 226, 231, 233, 236, 238, 241, 242, 248, 251, 255, 289, 290, 310, 316
   Of the seven churches in London, 34, 37, 67, 88, 127, 165, 186, 195, 222, 236, 239, 256
   Angel-evangelists, 90, 130, 134, 144, 156, 158, 164, 165, 169, 171, 172, 180, 188, 225, 230, 232, 234, 289

Angel-prophets, 75, 164, 169
*Angels' Record*, 37, 75, 129, 146, 181, 184–85, 199, 201, 202, 211–12, 220, 222, 224, 231, 242, 289, 298, 307
Anglican Communion, 120, 155, 263, 268, 275
Annual Reports / Apostles' Reports, 67, 72, 77, 83, 84, 85, 94, 97, 112, 177, 184, 202
Anointing, 68, 129, 166
Anonymity, 8, 181, 182
Antichrist, 13, 49, 76, 79, 119, 121, 264, 301, 323
Apostasy (of the church), 13, 21, 22, 25, 111, 117, 122, 199, 294
Apostles, 2, 3, 15–17, 24–25, 26–28, 29, 31–35, 37–40, 43–50, 56–65, 66–68, 71, 75, 76, 78, 79, 80, 97, 120, 127, 128, 137, 138, 139, 142, 145, 147, 151, 155, 156, 157, 158–60, 161–62, 164, 167, 169, 171, 176, 181, 184, 185, 187, 188, 191–92, 195, 196, 197, 199–200, 208, 211, 213, 223, 235, 237, 238, 245, 250, 282, 289, 317, 324, 327–28
   Apostles, call of, 17, 20, 22, 24, 31, 32, 35, 272
   Apostles, conferences with ministers, 6, 160, 223
   Apostles, areas of jurisdiction and journeys of, 36, 44–45, 47, 50–55, 57, 63, 85, 194
   Apostles, removal of, 3, 73–74, 78, 149–52, 165–66, 217–21, 229, 238–39, 249, 266, 267, 290, 318, 324
   Apostles, restoration of, 1, 2, 17, 30–31, 45, 82, 117, 118, 120, 122, 198, 225, 267, 271, 288, 316, 321
   Apostles, separation of, 32, 34, 43, 79, 80, 195
Apostles' Chapel (Albury), 54, 223, 235, 252, 272, 294, 306, 318
Apostles' Determinations, 36, 153, 165, 178, 184, 213, 241
Apostles' ministers, 60, 110, 160, 228, 271
Apostles' Reports. *See* Annual Reports

# Index

Apostolic College, 66, 72, 83, 161, 179, 182, 196
Apostolic delegations, 109, 110, 114–15, 151, 152, 160, 162–63, 166, 225
Archangels, 33, 78, 102, 160, 164–66, 221, 224–26, 256, 288–89
Archbishops of Canterbury, 264, 300, 303
    Davidson, 227, 265–66, 269
    Fisher, 257, 259, 269, 273–77, 279–80, 293
    Lang, 266, 268–71
    Temple, F., 264–65
Archdeacons, 182, 188
Argentina, 116
Armstrong, N., 21, 22, 28, 32, 33, 34, 45, 51, 63, 72, 95, 112, 120, 208, 327–28
Australia, 5, 45, 85, 87, 110–11, 183, 222, 252, 296, 313, 328
Austria, 5, 76, 85, 86, 103–4, 222, 273, 296, 309–11, 312, 321, 328, 329

Babylon, 20, 21, 22, 25, 57, 79, 119, 131, 135, 243, 246, 293–94, 316, 318
Baltic republics, 5, 105–7, 309, 312
Baptism, 46, 124, 129, 132, 192, 193, 198, 200, 255, 276, 293, 297
Baptism with the Holy Ghost, 66
Baptismal registers, 53, 101, 133, 141, 169
Baptists, 19, 62, 84, 96, 121, 123, 258
Basle, 90, 100, 104, 165
Bath, 29, 62, 69, 134
Bavaria, 31, 104, 312
Baxter, R., 16–17, 18, 23, 26, 27, 30, 32, 34, 45, 66, 211
Bayford, A. F., 165, 207, 328
Belfast, 95, 253, 307
Belgium, 5, 85, 86, 92–93, 276, 277, 279, 280, 282, 283, 296, 307, 327, 329
Berlin, 5, 75, 76, 89, 90, 99, 100, 101, 103, 105, 128, 155, 165, 224, 257, 309, 310
Berne, 89
Bible, 103, 187, 192, 209, 281, 285
Birmingham, 29, 32, 33, 185, 207, 222, 225, 253, 254, 258, 284, 307
Bishops, 47, 48, 120, 127, 137, 154, 155, 159, 166, 264, 265, 266, 268, 284
Bishopsgate, 6, 28, 29, 62, 88, 89, 133, 134, 205, 222, 252, 258, 304, 305
Boase, C., 8, 336
Boase, C. W., 77, 83
Böhm, C. J. T., 74, 75, 76, 82, 98, 99, 108, 161, 162, 328–29
*Book of Regulations*, 24, 101, 175, 196, 202
Booksellers, 7, 182–83, 262, 319–20, 321, 336
Borders of ministry, 28, 139, 143, 154–57, 158, 164, 169, 210, 213, 240

Bradford, 6, 68, 133–34, 140–41, 142–43, 176, 178, 189, 202, 253–54, 257
Bradford on Avon, 69
Brethren, 34, 70, 84, 95, 111, 118, 131, 144, 206, 249, 258
Bridgnorth, 29, 33, 44, 47, 53, 146, 302
Brighton, 29, 32, 46
Bristol, 29, 225, 258, 305
Brussels, 92, 276, 279–82, 307
Buildings, 29, 53, 188, 194, 203, 251, 257–58, 268, 277–78, 291, 293, 297, 302, 306, 309–10, 312, 313, 318
Burwell, A. H., 111, 113

Caird, Mary, 18, 20
Caird, W. R., 17, 30, 31, 76, 82, 95, 103, 111–12, 328–29
Cambridge, 29, 133
Canada, 29, 51, 87, 111–12, 123, 197, 252, 296, 313
Candlestick, mystery of the, 25, 154
Capadose family, 80, 283
Capadose, Antonius E., 252, 257, 274–75
Capadose, I., 80, 92–93, 94, 105, 107, 109, 151, 161, 186, 198, 220, 221–22, 224, 231, 236, 298, 329
Cardale, Emily, 15, 17, 18, 19, 20, 43
Cardale, J. B., 4–5, 8, 15, 18, 19, 22–28, 31, 32, 33, 36, 37, 43, 45–48, 50, 52, 54, 56, 58–60, 61, 63, 64–65, 66–68, 70–72, 73–74, 79, 80, 81, 82, 88, 91, 93, 95, 96, 108, 118, 122, 132, 144, 146, 148, 149–51, 153, 154, 156, 158, 159, 161, 168, 169, 180, 184, 186–87, 189, 193–97, 202, 204, 206, 208, 211, 212–14, 220, 241, 246, 250, 327–28
    *Readings upon the Liturgy*, 198–99
Cardale, Mrs, 15, 17, 43
Carlyle, T., 18, 32, 44, 46, 51, 61, 71, 72, 73, 75, 97, 98–102, 108, 163, 191, 195, 197, 292, 328
Carré, C. M., 69, 96, 119
Catechism, 146, 148, 290
Catholic Apostolic Church (name), 53–54, 117–18
Census of religious worship (1851), 53, 69–70, 91
Central Church, 6, 35, 81, 94, 134, 142, 148, 155, 173, 178, 194, 195, 198, 203, 223, 233, 260, 292, 294, 300–301, 304–5, 306. *See also* Gordon Square
    English Chapel at, 70, 89, 257, 305
Charismata. *See* Gifts of the Spirit
Charismatic movement, 10, 316, 321, 322
Châtelet, 92, 276, 280, 307

## INDEX

Chelmsford, 29, 258
Chelsea, 28, 29, 53, 89, 133, 305
Chepstow, 29, 46
Cherubim, 54, 155
Chicago, 112, 155, 304, 305
Children, 101, 122, 138, 141, 143, 145–49, 175, 200, 205–6, 234, 241, 273, 281, 290, 292, 297, 310
Christ, 14, 15, 19, 48, 49, 121, 155, 172, 179, 194, 200, 223, 224, 228, 238, 245, 257, 289, 291, 302, 316–17, 324
  As angel, 54, 158
Christendom, 2, 4, 22, 25, 32, 35, 44, 45, 47, 48, 50–51, 57, 63, 80, 82, 89, 96, 112, 114, 116, 117, 118–19, 127, 131, 151, 166, 179, 187, 199, 200, 229, 230, 236, 243, 249, 291, 294, 298, 311, 323
  Seven churches of, 97, 241, 246, 247
  Twelve tribes of, 225
Christenson, L., 10, 322
Christiania, 108, 109, 312
Christmas, 145, 193, 201
Church as bride, 158, 200
Church, nature of, 48, 249
Church records, 5, 212, 256
Church of England, 1, 10, 13, 21, 46, 70, 120, 121, 130, 135–36, 166, 196–97, 246, 254, 255, 263–86, 290, 292, 293, 315, 317, 321
Church of Scotland, 14–16, 25, 27, 91, 168, 243, 283
Circulars to ministers, 6, 75, 142, 178, 184, 221, 288, 319, 323
Clergy (of other denominations), 33, 129, 130, 134–37, 166, 171, 234, 268, 282, 286, 315
Closure of churches, 60–62, 87, 100, 112, 156, 240, 248, 251–58, 261, 290, 297, 306, 307, 315, 317
Coadjutors, 74, 83, 150–52, 158, 160, 161–62, 165, 185, 213, 217–47, 266, 288–89, 291, 300, 301, 328–29
Commendation of those of an age to be sealed, 223
Communion, 100, 109, 130, 141, 144, 145, 166, 172, 180, 186, 189, 191–93, 200, 230–31, 255, 265–70, 273, 276, 279–81, 283, 292, 310, 318
Conference, Notes / Minutes of, 6, 178, 184
Confession of sin, 173, 200, 224, 236–37, 239, 243, 255, 300
Confirmation, 145, 255, 265, 270, 273–74, 281, 290, 318
Confirmation of orders, 135, 166, 267, 268
Congregationalism, 30, 84, 113, 136–37, 145
Connor, W. H., 135–36, 286
Conversion, 23, 145, 317

Copenhagen, 5, 93, 151, 165, 183, 255, 262, 307, 312
Copinger, H. B., 7, 8, 61, 63, 82, 83, 182, 192, 195, 252, 336
Copinger, W. A., 163, 205, 217, 228
Council of Zion, 35–38, 43, 57, 60, 153

Dalton, H., 32, 33, 44, 47, 51, 63, 70–72, 73, 91, 94, 96, 97, 108, 113, 327–28
Davenport, J. S., 8, 84, 110
Davenport, R. A., 8–9
Davson, W. M., 159, 255, 280, 287–94, 309, 310, 317
Deacons, 35, 36, 61, 67, 134, 138, 139–40, 141, 145, 154, 155, 157, 159, 164, 167–68, 171, 175, 176, 180, 183, 185, 192, 202, 206, 208, 226–27, 291, 292, 294
  Deacon-evangelists, 81, 157, 172, 181
Deaconesses, 134, 138, 140, 141, 142, 148, 154, 174–75, 176
Democracy, 49, 97, 110, 301, 317
Denmark, 2, 7, 85, 86, 93, 108, 109, 158, 160, 162, 204, 222, 262, 283, 292, 296, 306–7, 319, 327, 329
Diersmann, E., xi, 3, 84, 295, 310
Discernment of spirits, 20, 77, 129, 209
Dissent, 21, 29, 62, 69, 101, 108, 111, 121, 135, 137, 192, 197, 199
Dow, D., 25, 32, 34, 328
Dow, W., 32, 71, 72, 73, 105, 108, 328
Dowglass, T., 15, 81
Drummond, H., 5, 10, 13, 20, 21–22, 24, 26, 29, 31, 35, 36, 37, 43–46, 49–50, 51–52, 53, 59, 62, 63, 64–65, 66, 71–72, 84, 90, 91, 96–97, 104, 119, 121, 132, 170, 174, 178, 181, 191, 193, 194, 195, 197, 218, 246, 327–28
Dual membership, 53, 101, 106, 117, 135–37, 321
Dublin, 29, 95, 165, 253, 254, 307
Dudley, 33, 69
Dundee, 173, 242, 253, 306

Easter, 145, 183, 193, 201, 287
Easter Monday, 135, 183
Eastern Churches, 9–10, 95–96, 106–7, 155, 198, 199, 227, 258, 259, 265, 278, 306, 313, 318, 321
Ecumenism, 54, 117, 135, 199, 233, 242–43, 280, 298, 316
Edinburgh, xi, 6, 28, 29, 32, 90, 91, 133, 160, 165, 169, 186, 193, 203, 205, 251, 254, 258, 306
Eddis, E. W., 204, 206

# Index

Elders, 27, 35, 37, 135, 138, 139-40, 153, 154, 155-56, 157, 159, 163, 164, 168, 171, 174, 189, 201, 202, 240

England, 1, 3, 5, 32, 44, 45, 51, 61, 69, 80-81, 85, 87, 89-90, 120, 126-28, 130, 135, 141-42, 148, 153, 155, 156, 158, 177, 179, 188-89, 196, 211, 226, 234, 245, 246, 252, 253, 255, 256, 268, 283, 284, 288, 292, 295, 296, 298, 300, 306, 315, 327, 328

Ephesus, 89, 288

Episcopate, 164, 177

Eschatology, 4, 7, 14, 56, 76-79, 119, 160, 286, 306

Estonia, 86, 105, 106, 107, 198, 296, 311, 312

Eucharist, 8, 44, 48, 67, 68, 70, 78, 84, 154, 163, 166, 167, 172, 192-94, 197, 200-2, 206, 223, 224, 233, 238, 239, 248, 253, 272, 276, 282, 284, 290, 292, 294, 302, 308, 310, 317

    Eucharistic fasting, 236, 305, 318

Evangelicalism, 13, 51-2,79, 84, 96, 114, 119, 121, 123, 145, 202, 245, 291, 299, 305, 323

Evangelische Kirche in Deutschland, 258, 318

Evangelists, 16, 17, 20, 23-4, 26, 27, 31, 36, 37, 48, 52, 53, 54, 81, 84, 88, 95, 126, 138, 139, 154, 155, 156, 157, 158, 159, 167, 169-70, 178, 189, 205, 227, 230, 231, 235, 295

    District evangelists, 109, 158, 180, 308

Evangelist services / sermons, 81, 82, 99-100, 107, 125, 126, 171, 172, 200, 202, 204, 205, 208

Evangelist work, 45, 85, 86, 87, 90, 91, 98, 110, 117-18, 122-32, 134, 144, 157, 164, 169-73, 181, 188-89, 228, 229, 233, 234

Exodus, 44, 63

Exorcism, 129

Eynsham, 33, 61, 142, 225, 242, 253, 256, 306

Ezra, 78-79

Family, 138, 227, 233-34

Finland, 86, 105, 107, 296, 312

First-fruits, 44, 66, 78-79, 97, 99, 118, 128, 130, 150, 151, 159,162, 166, 232, 235, 289, 311, 323, 325

    As an offering, 187

Flegg, C. G., 4, 8, 9-10, 60, 155, 317

Forenoon service, 192, 200, 202, 240, 305

Foster, D. G., 62-63

Fourfold ministry, 37, 54, 139, 145, 155-56, 233, 238, 257

France, 5, 44, 51, 63, 71, 76, 85, 86, 96-97, 192, 195, 222, 296, 298, 299, 307-8, 311, 328, 329

Frankfurt am Main, 98, 257, 302

Gardiner, S. R., 6, 81, 134, 142, 179, 180

Geering, E. L., 102, 161, 329

*General Rubrics*, 24, 142, 195, 196, 197

Germany, 2, 3, 5, 9, 44, 50, 54, 69, 71, 73-78, 81, 85, 86, 87, 90, 98-104, 124, 125, 127-28, 137,55 142, 148, 151, 155, 158, 169, 174, 195, 197, 222, 226, 231,234, 245, 255, 257, 258, 260, 261, 277, 279, 282-83, 288, 292-93, 295, 296, 297, 298-300, 302-4, 308-11, 312, 315, 318-19, 321, 328, 329

    German Democratic Republic, 310, 319

    German horn churches, 107, 112, 155, 258, 313

Geyer, H., 74-87, 100, 160, 169, 183

Gifted persons, 17-21, 26, 39, 40, 210

Gifts of the Spirit, 14-16, 20, 21, 24, 28, 30, 40, 47, 57, 102, 111, 119, 159, 164, 209, 210, 213, 241, 244, 245, 250, 251, 316

    Meetings for exercise of, 180, 201, 202, 209, 210, 213, 231, 241, 242, 251

Glasgow, 14, 27, 33, 91, 155, 170, 181, 222, 270, 306, 323

Gordon Square, 2, 5, 6, 7, 8, 9, 70, 80, 89, 126, 146, 170, 179, 203, 205, 213, 250, 253, 256, 260, 262, 265, 273, 293-94, 318, 319-20, 336. *See also* Central Church

Greece, 45, 85, 95, 307, 327

Greenock, 14-15, 29, 39-40, 156

Gretason, M. N., 6, 9, 156, 169, 238, 323

Hague, The, 92, 226, 255, 276-77, 280-82, 283, 288, 307, 308

Hall, Miss, 18-19

Hamburg, 74, 76, 93, 99, 103, 292, 302, 304

Hannover, 226, 302, 308

Heads of church and state, 2, 45, 80, 82, 127

Healing, 14, 129-30, 156, 164, 180, 185, 209, 244

Heath, Christopher, 73, 222

Heath, C. B., 200, 222, 262, 287, 294, 321

Heath, E., 77, 80, 112, 151, 157, 162, 164, 171-72, 173, 177, 180, 208, 213-14, 219, 221, 222, 224, 226, 228, 230-31, 233-34, 240, 244, 248, 300, 301, 328-29

Heath, H., 222, 224

Heath, J. B., 125, 207

Heath, J. S., 222, 270-71

Heathen, 110

Henke, M., xi, 3

Hewett, Sir George H., 81, 161

Hewett, Sir George J. R., 93, 108, 329

Hewitt / Huott, 29-31

Holland, 2, 5, 51, 77, 85, 86, 92–93, 116, 158, 222, 226, 255, 275–83, 288, 292, 296, 298, 303, 307, 318, 319, 321, 327, 329
Hollick, S. M., 235, 249, 252, 253, 262, 273, 285
Holly, J. T., 112–13
Holy Spirit, 5, 13, 14, 16, 18, 21, 24, 47, 62, 66, 121, 158, 159, 161, 162, 167, 169, 177, 181, 196, 202, 206, 207, 208, 210, 212, 243, 244, 245, 249, 263, 289, 316, 318, 324
Homily, 144, 180,183, 206–8
Horn church, 88–89, 91, 93, 107, 154–55, 163, 304–5. *See also* German horn churches
Huddersfield, 125, 131, 143, 146, 182, 208, 258
Hull, 252, 253, 257
Human nature, 14, 139, 155, 204, 238
Hume, H. S., 74, 119, 128, 170, 173–74, 217–18, 226–27, 228, 242, 263
Hungary, 104
Hurben bei Krumbach, 104, 258
Hymns, 124, 146, 197, 203–6, 254

Idolatry, 21, 40, 317
Imagination, 156, 159
Incense, 68, 124, 195, 228, 231, 235, 238
India, 29, 44, 45, 51, 85, 87, 89, 110, 114–15, 144, 296, 314, 328
Infidelity, 105, 119, 120, 127, 131, 149, 311
Intercession, 88, 119, 151–52, 159, 160, 163, 202, 222, 223, 227–32, 235, 238–40, 243, 248, 255, 289–90, 301, 302, 315
Ipswich, 252, 309
Ireland, 5, 29, 45, 51, 85, 87, 95, 122, 295, 296, 307, 327, 328
Irving, E., 8, 10, 13–20, 22–29, 31, 35, 37, 40, 45, 59, 62, 80, 87, 93, 111, 113, 156, 159, 163, 168, 170, 193, 211–12, 227, 318
Irving, M. H., 110, 157
Islington, 28, 29, 34, 62–63, 89, 155, 203, 305
Italy, 45, 51, 63, 71, 85, 86, 94, 126, 198, 222, 296, 307, 327, 329

Japan, 115–16, 329
Java, 116, 307
Jerusalem, 292–93
Jews, 62, 79, 80, 199, 200, 299, 316
Judgment, 2, 3, 4, 45, 50, 79, 82, 117, 128, 171, 229, 235, 249, 301, 302

Kentish Town horn, 88, 258, 304
King-Church, H., 43, 51, 63, 72, 85, 92, 93, 108, 160, 327–28
Kingston, ON, 30, 111–12
Kirkcudbright, 29, 69

Lambeth Conferences, 120, 127, 244, 263, 264, 265, 267, 268, 269, 279
Lancaster, J., 8, 198
Landsman, J., 255, 276, 279
Laodicea, 89, 224
Lapsed, 129, 141, 230, 232, 236
Law of Moses, 25, 44, 68, 193, 194
Lay assistants, 3, 82, 125, 130, 141, 142, 147, 148, 154, 175–76, 206, 288, 310
Laying on of apostles' hands, 24, 68, 159, 165, 166, 176, 194. *See also* Sealing
Leacock, C. W., 294
Leeds, 64, 71, 146, 225
Leslie, J., 67, 126, 135, 196, 328–29
Liberalism, 98, 120, 221, 290, 293
Lickfold, J. M., 260, 273, 279
Litany, 200, 201, 238–40, 254, 255, 291, 305, 318, 319
Liturgical worship and thought, 9, 24, 50, 52, 61–68, 70, 91, 112, 124, 156, 172, 238–42, 248, 282, 306, 317
Liturgy, Catholic Apostolic, xi, 1, 39, 61, 121, 128, 182, 191–200, 233, 249, 267, 270, 276, 316, 321
 Special prayers, 120, 176, 240
 Translations of, 92, 94, 98, 106–7, 109, 197, 198, 308
Liverpool, 6, 29, 90, 306
London, 15, 22–26, 28, 29, 32, 39–40, 58–59, 64, 68, 81, 82, 88, 89, 90, 125, 126–28, 148, 165, 178, 189, 193, 234, 245, 261. *See also* Seven churches in London
Lord's Work, 4, 7, 10, 78, 93, 118, 127, 129–30, 150, 151, 172, 196, 211, 218, 220, 223, 227, 229, 230, 234–35, 237, 241, 243, 245, 246, 286, 287–88, 292–93, 297, 311, 318, 321, 322, 324
Lutheranism, 31, 93, 101, 106, 108–9, 135, 137, 204, 283, 312, 318
Lutz, J. E. G., 31, 103
Lymington, 29, 61

Macdonald family, 15, 20, 39–40, 211
Mackenzie, D., 34, 43, 59–60, 62–63, 70–71, 73, 108, 328
Manchester, 6, 163, 208, 225, 226, 253–54, 262, 288
Maunder, E. W., 228
Maxwell, G., 251–52
Melbourne, 110, 258, 262, 305, 313
Melksham, 29, 32, 62
Methodism, 109, 111, 121–22
Miller, E., 4–5, 43, 48, 50, 77, 77, 85, 114, 123, 126, 136, 139, 144, 195–96
Miller, J. L., 28, 32

Montigny, 276, 298, 308
Moore, W. J. Bramley, 228, 235, 324
Moravians, 101, 199, 268, 321
Mormons, 30–31, 46, 70, 92, 111–12, 131
*Morning Watch*, 15, 113
Music, 179, 203–6, 252

Nehemiah, 75, 78–79
New Apostolic Church, 39, 77–78, 93, 250, 297, 319
New England, 113, 136, 145, 206
New York, 112, 146, 155, 255, 258, 305, 313
New Zealand, 5, 85, 87, 110, 183, 185, 222, 264, 296, 313
Newcastle upon Tyne, 225, 252, 258
Newman Street, 22, 28, 29, 30, 34, 35, 36, 53, 59, 69, 70, 114, 175, 179, 193
Newman-Norton, S., xi, 7, 9, 77, 295
Newport (isle of Wight), 29, 81
*Newsletter*, 115, 252, 261–62
North America, 5, 8, 29–31, 44, 45, 50, 80, 81, 85, 86, 87, 111–14, 115, 122, 245, 258, 296, 304, 313, 328
Northumberland, dukes of, xi, 5, 10, 132, 136, 182
Norton, R., 39, 54, 182
Norway, 85, 86, 93, 108–9, 123, 142, 189, 245, 296, 297, 312–13, 328, 329
Norwich, 29, 252, 254
Nottingham, 32, 38, 69, 214, 257

Old Catholic Church, 258, 275, 277–81, 283, 307, 308
Ordination, 3, 15, 17, 22, 23, 25, 26, 28, 29, 33, 34, 35, 39, 66, 68, 90, 95, 118, 137, 145, 156, 159, 166–68, 176–78, 180, 194, 198, 206, 209, 218, 222, 226–27, 251, 266–67, 270, 274, 277–78, 282, 318
Orthodoxy. *See* Eastern Churches
Oxford, 19, 29, 32, 33, 38, 160

Paddington, 6, 29, 53, 88, 89, 133, 194, 222, 224, 260, 261, 287–88, 293–305, 306, 318, 320
Papacy, 51, 119
Paris, 50, 89, 97, 128, 257, 276, 308
Particular Churches, 34, 58, 171, 174, 183, 184, 212, 225, 259, 297
Pastoral letters / teachings, 6, 180, 183
*Pastorale Mitteilungen*, 183
Pastors, 16, 24, 27, 31, 37, 48, 51, 54, 57, 88, 138, 139, 144, 154–58, 159, 160, 165, 167, 168, 173, 178, 189, 206, 240
Pastorship, committal to, 115, 128, 132, 145, 186, 202, 230–31, 241

Pastorship, supplemental, 132, 135
Pentecost, 145, 174, 193, 201
  Eve of, 236, 238, 239
  Monday after, 223
Pentecostalism, 129–30, 245, 258, 306, 316, 321
Perceval, S., 18, 32, 34, 46, 47, 49, 54, 63, 71, 85, 94, 160, 327
Percy, E., 250, 251, 266, 273, 305
Periodicals, 183, 261–62
Pillars, 59, 60, 67, 68, 158
  of apostles, 58, 65, 74, 149, 328
  of evangelists, 130, 172, 180, 328
  of pastors, 38, 44, 153, 158, 178, 180, 328
  of prophets, 209, 328
  pillar-evangelists, 37, 68, 81, 90, 165, 172
Pitcairn, W. F., 80, 96, 120, 143–44, 149, 160, 165, 186
Place, W. H., 67, 130–31, 167, 328
Plymouth, 29, 258
Pochhammer, M. von, 92, 100, 102, 161, 329
Poland, 5, 51, 72, 85, 97–98, 222, 296, 304, 308, 328, 329
Port Glasgow, 39–40
Potsdam (Germany), 309
Potsdam, NY, 112, 144
Prayer meetings, 15, 16, 18, 21, 140, 167, 168, 201–2, 241, 244, 254, 300, 305, 319, 324
Preaching, 21, 115, 121, 131, 157, 167, 171, 173, 206–8, 228, 229, 232–33, 237, 245–46. *See also* Homily, Sermon
  Open-air, 23–24, 81, 91, 127, 170, 172, 318
  Training for, 232
Presbyterianism, 24, 113, 118, 137, 192, 203, 270
Priddle, N. C., 6, 183, 319–20, 336
Priests, 36, 61, 63, 67, 124, 134, 138–41, 145, 147, 154, 155–56, 163, 164, 166–67, 168, 171, 176–81, 185, 189, 202, 229, 242, 251, 287, 310, 317
  Priest-evangelists, 154, 157, 172–73, 181
  Priest-prophets, 156, 169, 287
  Roman Catholic, 94, 100, 103, 137
Proby, W. H. B., 207–8, 232
Prophecy, biblical, 13, 28, 79, 119, 126, 286, 299
  Cessation of, 251
  False, 29, 76
  Gift of, 14, 15, 17, 20, 56, 57, 60, 91, 157, 169, 180, 207–14, 241, 316
  Interpretation of Scripture (Light), 54, 59, 68, 121, 160, 193, 194, 198–99, 274
  Testing, 19–20, 38, 57, 163, 208, 210
  and tongues, 213–14
  by women, 212–13

Word(s) of, 2, 7, 10, 16, 20, 22–26, 28–38, 39–40, 43, 44, 46, 47, 51, 54, 57–58, 60, 66, 71, 74, 75, 76, 79, 82, 89, 97, 100, 101, 121, 127, 128, 129, 135, 146, 147, 149, 150, 161, 162, 164–68, 176–77, 181, 184–86, 187, 191, 194, 196, 201, 204, 210–13, 219–21, 222, 223–24, 226–29, 235–38, 239, 241, 242, 244–45, 247, 248, 288–90, 292, 297, 298–99, 317

Prophets, 16, 24, 26–27, 30, 32, 33–34, 35, 37–38, 39–40, 48, 56, 57, 59, 78, 88, 95, 138–40, 153–59, 165, 168, 169, 189, 209–10, 211. *See also* Angel-prophets; Priest-prophets

With the apostle, 51, 75, 160, 164, 165

Seven, 37, 43

Protestantism, 21, 45, 49, 121, 137, 246, 275

Prussia, 51, 93, 98, 99–100, 105

Publication by ministers, 8, 181–82, 235

Publishers, 182, 320–21

Records of events, 17, 34, 36, 37, 142

Records of prophecy, 38, 79, 288

Reformed Churches, 192, 283, 318

Registers, 5, 53, 101, 133–34, 141–42, 143–44, 169, 172, 175, 176, 177, 202, 253, 295, 297

Reports by ministers, 5, 140, 163–64, 171, 172–73, 180–81

Reserve, 4, 9, 131, 272

Resurrection of the dead, 80, 263, 324

Revelation, Book of, 44–45, 66, 67, 79, 89, 101, 124, 218, 225, 228, 243, 288

Revival(ism), 31, 91, 114, 122–23, 127, 130, 145, 169, 202, 206, 244

Riga, 107, 155, 304, 311–12

Roman Catholicism, 1, 31, 49, 119, 120, 124, 194, 246–47, 270, 276, 283, 292, 318

Rome, 82, 89, 94, 119, 128, 241, 246–47, 263, 307

Romford, 252, 258

Rosochacky, R., 76–77

Rossteuscher, E. A., 7, 32, 38, 44, 51, 197, 204

Rothe, C., 75–76, 99, 101, 183

Rotterdam, 262, 282, 307

Russia, 5, 45, 51, 85, 86, 95, 105–7, 198, 222, 296, 299, 304, 308, 311–12, 328, 329

Ryerson, G., 30, 111, 113, 165

Sacraments, 22, 25, 48, 48–49, 70, 79, 100, 108, 121, 122, 132, 135, 166, 264, 275, 276, 297

Salvation Army, 3, 130, 131

Scandinavia, 5, 86, 108, 128, 151, 187, 222, 261, 298, 312

Schrey, K., 248, 255, 288, 297, 309–10

Schröter, J. A., 9, 86

Schwarz, F. W., 76, 77, 92

Scotland, 3, 5, 14, 26, 27, 29, 31, 32, 33, 50, 53, 56, 64, 69, 80, 85, 87, 91, 103, 133, 137, 181, 195, 197, 211, 283, 295, 296, 306, 327, 329

Scottish Episcopal Church, 91, 270, 283

Scripture. *See* Bible

Sealing, 29, 56, 63, 66–68, 74, 76, 79, 83, 84–85, 97, 99, 103, 104, 108, 109, 110, 112, 123–24, 134–35, 141, 143–44, 145, 150, 151, 159, 167, 176, 181, 188, 198, 223, 227, 229–32, 241, 245, 265, 289, 290,

Second Advent / Coming, 1, 2, 13, 15, 49, 57, 66, 76, 79–81, 112, 118, 120, 122, 169, 172, 200, 219, 224, 227, 250, 257, 263, 266, 267, 270, 272, 285, 290, 301, 311, 318, 322

Sectarianism, 1, 51, 53, 69, 117, 130, 232, 234, 240, 323

Sermons, 6, 16, 89, 126, 144, 180, 183, 185–86, 200, 206–8, 228, 232–33, 250, 251, 261, 284, 319, 323. *See also* Evangelist services / sermons

Seven churches of Christendom, 89, 97, 247

Seven churches in London, 36, 43, 44, 46, 47, 54, 57, 59, 61, 67, 80, 82, 88–89, 146, 150, 167, 179, 224, 304–5. *See also* Angels of the seven churches in London

Assembly / meeting of, 36, 49, 67, 68, 81, 83, 184, 185, 188, 194, 196, 221, 236, 239, 260, 298

Seven deacons of the universal church, 88, 182, 186, 188, 221, 256, 258, 259

Seventy, 78, 165–66, 225, 229, 235, 246, 321

Shaw, P. E., 9

Shore, S. Royle, 265–71

Simpson, James and Jane, 16, 19–20

Sitwell, F., 29, 43, 44, 51, 63, 72, 91, 104–5, 328

Sixty to the nations, 36, 165, 170

Smyrna, 89, 101

Social class, 2–3, 33–34, 43, 57, 91, 92, 93, 99, 102, 109, 130–34, 178

Socialism, 149, 264

South Africa, 116, 123, 313

Southampton, 5, 29, 61, 69, 225

Southwark, 28, 29, 69, 88, 89, 194, 239, 253, 305

Spain (and Portugal), 44, 51, 80, 85, 104–5, 222, 311, 328, 329

Stevenson, K. W., 1, 8, 192, 193, 196, 200

Stockholm, 108–9, 130, 312

Stoke-on-Trent, 258

Suburbs, 45, 110, 114, 313–14, 328

Sunday schools, 146–47, 205

Sweden, 71, 85, 86, 108–9, 245, 259, 283, 296, 312, 328, 329
Switzerland, 5, 45, 51–52, 76, 85, 86, 90, 96, 103, 124, 128, 132, 151, 195, 222, 282, 283, 296, 307–8, 319, 327–28, 329
Sydney, 183, 287, 294, 305, 313
Symbolism, 172, 233

Tabernacle, 25, 36, 37, 44, 57, 170, 173, 174, 193, 199, 239, 290–91
Taplin, E. O., 17, 18, 20, 24–27, 30, 31, 33, 43, 44, 45, 58, 67, 74, 77, 78, 89, 164, 170, 199, 209, 328
Tarbet, W., 121, 159, 284, 286
Teachings, 68, 150, 180, 185, 202, 208, 233, 286
Temple, 79, 289
Testimonies, 7, 37, 45–50, 65, 79, 80–82, 91, 94, 95, 104, 105, 122, 124, 125–28, 181
  Testimony, Great / Catholic, 47–50, 51, 53, 57, 63, 80, 82, 91, 96, 98, 105, 108, 119, 127–28, 159, 160, 167, 182, 262, 289, 306, 311
Thiersch, H. W. J., 75, 99, 101, 102, 157
Thompson, J., 34, 67, 158, 178–79, 180, 192, 328
Time of Silence, 79, 218, 220, 228–35, 237, 238, 241, 248, 249, 256, 289, 300, 319–21
Tithing, 49, 92, 93, 102, 116, 132, 186–90, 254, 256, 259–61, 267, 273, 301
Tongues, gift of, 14, 16–18, 20, 114, 209, 213–14, 251,
Toronto, 111–12, 313
Translation, hope of, 34, 78, 80, 235, 289
Tracts, 7, 122, 182
Training for ministers, 68, 178–80, 206, 232
Tribes, 29, 32, 44–45, 51, 63,67, 90, 92, 151, 160, 161, 176, 177, 186, 192, 224, 225, 283, 289, 303, 310, 329
Tribulation, Great, 2, 34, 66, 76, 78, 79, 99, 123, 124, 294, 323
Trimen, E., 15, 34, 37
Trustees, 7, 88, 183, 221, 235, 254–60, 269, 292–93, 305, 315, 320
Tudor, J. O., 32, 33, 34, 36, 44, 45, 48, 51, 63, 72, 85, 97, 114, 191, 328
Turkey, 96

Turpin, E. H., 205
Typology, 54, 89, 174, 193, 233, 288, 317

Underdeacons, 3, 141, 142, 154, 173–74, 176, 206, 254, 255, 260, 273, 288, 291, 292, 297, 305, 306, 310, 315
*Ungdomsbladet*, 77, 262, 303
United States, 136, 313. *See also* North America
Universal Church, 36, 54, 58, 88, 158, 160, 165, 169, 177, 186, 188, 208, 238, 249
  Ministers of, 54, 141, 157, 158, 180, 181, 184, 188, 208, 222, 224, 236, 239, 247, 252, 253, 271, 303
Utrecht, 281–82, 307

Vancouver, 258, 297, 305, 313
Vestments, 39, 51, 61–63, 78, 91, 114, 124, 193–94, 233, 258
Vienna, 89, 104
Visitations, 151, 185, 188, 220, 225, 226, 289

Ward, R. S., 10, 31, 81, 250, 272–73
Wellington, 110, 313
Wells, 29, 32
Westminster, 29, 53, 61, 67, 89, 257, 304
Whitley, H. C., 4, 251
Wigan, 225, 241
Will, 35, 156, 170
William IV, 45, 46
Winterthur, 90, 258
Wolverhampton, 29, 33, 125, 306
Women, ministry / ordination of, 35, 40, 125, 174, 213, 255, 282, 286, 305, 317
Women, social roles, 122, 175, 233
Women, speaking in church, 18, 208, 212
Wood Green horn, 89, 227, 258, 305
Woodhouse, F. V., 7, 18, 28, 32, 34, 36, 37, 44, 45, 46, 49, 50, 51, 54, 60, 66, 68, 70, 71–72, 74–78, 83,85, 90, 92, 94, 100, 102–5, 112, 121, 126–27, 128, 149, 150–51, 181, 190, 191, 192, 196, 201, 204, 209, 217, 221, 318, 327–28

Zürich, 90, 151, 257

www.ingramcontent.com/pod-product-compliance
Lightning Source LLC
Chambersburg PA
CBHW080406300426
44113CB00015B/2421